The Domestic Sources of American Foreign Policy

The Domestic Sources of American Foreign Policy

Insights and Evidence

Sixth Edition

Edited by
James M. McCormick

ROWMAN & LITTLEFIELD PUBLISHERS, INC.
Lanham • Boulder • New York • Toronto • Plymouth, UK

Published by Rowman & Littlefield Publishers, Inc.
A wholly owned subsidiary of The Rowman & Littlefield Publishing Group, Inc.
4501 Forbes Boulevard, Suite 200, Lanham, Maryland 20706
www.rowman.com

10 Thornbury Road, Plymouth PL6 7PP, United Kingdom

British Library Cataloguing in Publication Information Available

Library of Congress Cataloging-in-Publication Data

The domestic sources of American foreign policy : insights and evidence / [edited
  by] James M. McCormick. — 6th ed.
    p. cm.
  Includes bibliographical references and index.
  ISBN 978-1-4422-0960-2 (cloth : alk. paper) — ISBN 978-1-4422-0961-9
(pbk. : alk. paper) — ISBN 978-1-4422-0962-6 (electronic)
  1. United States—Foreign relations—1945–1989. 2. United States—Foreign
relations—1989– 3. United States—Foreign relations—Decision making.
  4. United States—Foreign relations administration. I. McCormick, James M.
  E840.D63 2012
  327.73—dc23   2012010219

∞™ The paper used in this publication meets the minimum requirements of
American National Standard for Information Sciences—Permanence of Paper
for Printed Library Materials, ANSI/NISO Z39.48-1992.

Printed in the United States of America

To the students in my American foreign policy courses,
whose insights and questions have taught me a great deal

Contents

Acknowledgments

"The Future of American Power: Dominance and Decline in Perspective" by Joseph S. Nye Jr., from "The Future of American Power," *Foreign Affairs*, vol. 89, no. 6 (November/December 2010): 2–12.

"Think Again: American Decline" by Gideon Rachman. From "Think Again: American Decline," *Foreign Policy*, no. 184 (January/February 2011): 59–63.

"The Tea Party, Populism, and the Domestic Culture of U.S. Foreign Policy" by Walter Russell Mead. Abridged from "The Tea Party and American Foreign Policy," *Foreign Affairs*, vol. 90, no. 2 (March/April 2011): 28–44.

"Ethnic Interest Groups in American Foreign Policy" by James M. McCormick. Abridged from "Ethnic Interest Groups and American Foreign Policy: A Growing Influence?" in Allan J. Cigler and Burdett A. Loomis, eds., *Interest Group Politics*, 8th ed. (Washington, DC: CQ Press, 2012), 317–44.

"The Israel Lobby" by John Mearsheimer and Stephen Walt. Abridged from "The Israel Lobby," *London Review of Books*, vol. 28, no. 6 (March 23, 2006): 3–12.

"American Veterans in Government and the Use of Force" by Peter D. Feaver and Christopher Gelpi. Excerpt from "The Impact of Elite Veterans on American Decisions to Use Force," in Peter D. Feaver and Christopher Gelpi, *Choosing Your Battles: American Civil-Military Relations and the Use of Force* (Princeton, NJ: Princeton University Press, 2004), 64–94. The references were taken from pages 215, 219–20, and 222–24.

"Events, Elites, and American Public Support for Military Conflict" by
Adam J. Berinsky. Abridged and edited from "Assuming the Costs of
War: Events, Elites, and American Public Support for Military Con-
flict," *Journal of Politics*, vol. 69, no. 4 (November 2007): 975–97.
"Person and Office: Presidents, the Presidency, and Foreign Policy" by
Michael Nelson. An extensively revised and expanded version of "U.S.
Presidency," in Joel Krieger, ed., *The Oxford Companion to the Politics of
the World*, 2nd ed. (New York: Oxford University Press, 2001), 690–92.
"Leading through Civilian Power" by Hillary Rodham Clinton. Slightly
abridged from "Leading through Civilian Power," *Foreign Affairs*, vol.
89, no. 6 (November/December 2010): 13–24.
"A Leaner and Meaner Defense" by Gordon Adams and Matthew Leather-
man. Slightly edited from "A Leaner and Meaner Defense," *Foreign Af-
fairs*, vol. 90, no. 1 (January/February 2011): 139–52.
"Why Intelligence and Policymakers Clash" by Robert Jervis. Slightly
abridged from "Why Intelligence and Policymakers Clash," *Political
Science Quarterly*, vol. 125, no. 2 (Summer 2010): 185–204.
"Policy Preferences and Bureaucratic Position: The Case of the American
Hostage Rescue Mission" by Steve Smith. Abridged and reprinted with
permission from "Policy Preferences and Bureaucratic Position: The
Case of the American Hostage Rescue Mission," *International Affairs*,
vol. 61, no. 1 (Winter 1984/5): 9–25.
"Roles, Politics, and the Survival of the V-22 Osprey" by Christopher M.
Jones. Updated for this edition by the author from "Roles, Politics, and
the Survival of the V-22 Osprey," *Journal of Political and Military Sociol-
ogy*, vol. 29, no. 1 (Summer 2001).
"NATO Expansion: The Anatomy of a Decision" by James M. Goldgeier.
Abridged and edited from "NATO Expansion: The Anatomy of a Deci-
sion," *Washington Quarterly*, vol. 21, no. 1 (Winter 1998): 85–102.
"Sources of Humanitarian Intervention: Beliefs, Information, and Ad-
vocacy in U.S. Decisions on Somalia and Bosnia" by Jon Western.
Adapted by the author from "Sources of Humanitarian Intervention:
Beliefs, Information, and Advocacy in U.S. Decisions on Somalia and
Bosnia," *International Security*, vol. 26, no. 4 (Spring 2002): 112–42.
"Last Stand" by Seymour M. Hersh. Slightly edited from "Last Stand,"
New Yorker, vol. 82, issue 21 (July 10 and 17, 2006): 42–43, 45–49.
"Obama: The Consequentialist" by Ryan Lizza. Abridged from "The
Consequentialist," *New Yorker*, vol. 87, issue 11 (May 2, 2011): 44–55.

Introduction

The Domestic Sources of American Foreign Policy

On November 4, 2008, Barack Obama won the presidency with 365 electoral votes and 53 percent of the popular vote. With that victory, he appeared to be foreshadowing significant change in America's foreign and domestic policy. Indeed, he called for a new direction in American foreign policy, one that would set his approach apart from the previous administration. Under his administration, the United States would pursue a foreign policy based on the promotion of American domestic values, but it would also seek greater cooperation (or partnership) with other nations in addressing pressing global issues. President Obama outlined some of the components of this approach in foreign policy addresses in Prague, Moscow, Cairo, and Accra during the first six months of his presidency: The United States would support the promotion of democracy around the world, but it would not impose it; the United States would seek cooperation with other states "to renew our prosperity" and "to provide for our common security"; and the United States would address "our [common] problems . . . through partnership" because "our progress must be shared."[1] In all, such an approach not only emphasized the importance of interdependence in addressing global problems but also reminded us of the inevitable nexus between foreign and domestic policy.

The linkage of foreign and domestic policy for the United States and other countries is hardly a new phenomenon, but those ties have accelerated in recent decades, largely fueled by the process of globalization. Globalization—the political, economic, and social forces that are drawing peoples together regardless of state boundaries—continues to increase dramatically in the first decade of the twenty-first century, and the distinctions between foreign and domestic policies across a broad spectrum of issues

1

are increasingly blurred. The expansion of intergovernmental organizations in the world, the rise of more and more nongovernmental organizations globally, and the growth of transnational linkages through the Information Revolution of cyberspace—all have reduced the significance of national boundaries and geographical distance in addressing many policy issues.[2]

Regional and global economic organizations—notably, the North American Free Trade Agreement, the European Union, the Asia-Pacific Economic Cooperation, the World Trade Organization, and the incipient Trans-Pacific Partnership—are increasingly important shapers of foreign and domestic politics of many states. Several political-military organizations— North Atlantic Treaty Organization, the ASEAN Regional Forum, and the Organization for Security and Cooperation in Europe—have expanded their agendas, enlarged their memberships, and impacted the behavior of individual states. The number and variety of nongovernmental organizations—ties principally between individuals and groups across states—continue to proliferate, and these actors also impact national behavior. As these economic, technological, and personal contacts across state boundaries continue to expand, few governments are immune from those globalizing pressures.

These differing kinds of globalization—whether economic, social, or political—are occurring at differing rates for countries across the world. The KOF Index of Globalization, for example, shows that economic globalization continues to outpace political and social globalization over the last several decades, although all three types have increased significantly during this period. In the context of the financial and economic crisis, however, economic and social globalization patterns have decelerated a bit for that Index's most recent data year (2008), although political globalization continues to increase worldwide.[3] In all, then, these differing networks of ties between states and peoples are an important feature of global politics today.

Even as the positive aspects of globalization continue, the negative sides of these globalizing processes are very not far behind. That is, the globalization process also facilitates the rapid transfer of drugs and crimes, the transmittal of diseases, and the export of terrorism on a global scale. The attacks of September 11 brought home to Americans this dark side of globalization in the most dramatic way. Using cell phones, rapid-fire financial transfers, and open borders—all propelled by globalization—a small band of terrorists wrought havoc on the American homeland. The "end of geography" and the "death of distance" took on wholly new meanings for Americans and their leaders. No state was beyond reach, especially by determined nonstate actors. No borders were impenetrable for those determined to do harm. The threat of international terrorism—whether the occurrence of terror attacks in London, Bali, Madrid, and Fort Hood, or attempted attacks in Detroit or New York—continuously reminds us of the negative aspects of globalization.

More recently, these global ties have also been an important vehicle for the spreading of the economic crisis worldwide. With the problems of the mortgage industry, the failure of major banks and investment houses, and the bankruptcy of major corporations, America's Great Recession of 2008 and beyond resulted in high unemployment, growing national debt, and economic uncertainty at home. Because of the centrality and the interconnectedness of the American economy to the rest of the world, other economies were not immune to these economic problems. Similarly, the economic turbulence in the European Union, and Eurozone countries more precisely, have produced a similar effect on the United States and indeed worldwide. The debt problems of Greece, Italy, and Spain, for example, cannot be isolated to these countries or even to the Eurozone nations. Witness, for example, the rise and fall of the American stock markets (and other international markets) in response to the changing maneuvers within Europe to its debt issue.

Another significant reaction to this globalization phenomenon, and its dislocations, has been the increasing fragmentation of the global community, as societies seek greater identity and security from more familiar surroundings. As a consequence, we have witnessed the emergence of more and more political, economic, and social forces driving people apart. Widespread ethnopolitical and sectarian conflicts have become commonplace, whether in Rwanda, Bosnia, Kosovo, or East Timor in past decade or so, or in Sudan, Somalia, Iraq, Lebanon, or Afghanistan during the current one. Similarly, democratization movements have also taken hold in various parts of the globe, propelled in part by these globalization forces. The "Arab Spring" in Tunisia, Egypt, and Libya is the most recent manifestation of this phenomenon, as this political awakening produced popular efforts to replace long-standing dictatorships with democratic institutions.

This shift in the focus of world politics from conflicts between states to conflicts and problems within them challenge the principle of state sovereignty and further erode any domestic/foreign policy distinction. The currency collapses in Mexico, Thailand, and Indonesia in the 1990s and the turmoil from the Great Recession of the late 2000s produced serious dislocations and economic hardships on peoples around the world. In the security sphere as well, concerns about the proliferation of weapons of mass destruction, whether in India and Pakistan previously or Iran and North Korea in the current era, have divided states and peoples. Fears of climate change stimulated by global warming, the impact of natural disasters epitomized by Hurricane Katrina in 2005 and the Japanese tsunami and earthquake in 2011, social dislocations and unrest tied to human rights violations in Darfur and elsewhere, and the growing numbers of migrants and refugees have fissured the global community as well. As a consequence, domestic politics and foreign policy are recognized as increasingly inseparable, and American foreign policy has been compelled to confront these complexly intertwined issues, often with seemingly different responses.

The events of September 11 and the Iraq War fueled one kind of response for the role of the United States in the world in the twenty-first century. In its 2002 national security strategy, the Bush administration argued that the United States ought to maintain a military sufficient to "assure our allies and friends; dissuade future military competition; deter threats against U.S. interests, allies, and friends; and decisively defeat any adversary if deterrence fails." Furthermore, the administration sought to build a "coalition of the willing" to defeat terrorists and tyrants globally, especially those with the potential to develop weapons of mass destruction. Also, it asserted that the United States reserved to itself "the option of preemptive actions to counter a sufficient threat to our national security."[4] With the initiation of wars in Afghanistan and Iraq, the Bush administration implemented these imperatives to fight international terrorism.

Another response, and largely in opposition to this "Bush Doctrine," came from that Obama administration. That administration advanced a new strategy that emphasized a cooperative and comprehensive involvement by the United States with the world, whether friend and foe, and that focused on strengthening the international order to solve common economic, political, and military problems. Put differently, the Obama administration's national security strategy approach, labeled a "strategy of engagement," sought to restore American leadership worldwide and to promote a "just and sustainable international order."

Specifically, the administration outlined several specific actions that must be taken to implement such a strategy and illustrate how domestic and foreign policy are closely intertwined with one another. First, and foremost, the administration argued, the United States must engage in "building our foundation" at home. Central to that task was renewing the American economy, "which serves as the wellspring of American power," and living our values at home so that we can credibly promote them abroad. Second, the United States must pursue "comprehensive engagement" with "nations, institutions, and peoples around the world on the basis of mutual interests and mutual respect." Such engagement would be with friends and allies, influential and emerging states, and hostile ones as well, both to address common problems and to address contentious ones. Third, the United States must engage with, and strengthen, the international order by recognizing "the rights and responsibilities of all nations," improving the "enforcement of international law," and modernizing "international institutions and frameworks." Such actions with international institutions, and those countries that belong to them, "will enhance international capacity to prevent conflict, spur economic growth, improve security, combat climate change, and address the challenges posed by weak and failing states."[5] The administration sought to implement these components through coopera-tive initiatives with an array of states and through increasingly turning to international institutions to address pressing political and economic issues. Still, like the Bush administration before it, the Obama administration has found that outlining a new strategy is often easier than implementing it.

Much as the dark side of globalization initially shaped debates among analysts about the future of American foreign policy, it also reshaped the potency of domestic participants in the foreign policy process. Foreign pol-icy was viewed as a sustained domestic concern, with increased public and media attention directed toward both global issues and homeland security. In that context, the American people were willing to afford the president a greater degree of latitude in shaping America's global posture in the im-mediate aftermath of 9/11. A decade later, that leeway has now diminished as a result of American actions in Iraq and Afghanistan, the perceived rise of China in global importance, and the economic difficulties experienced by the American people over the past several years. Instead, the public has become somewhat more circumspect about the role for the United States. Increasingly, the American public "overwhelming prefer to focus on fixing problems at home," even though they are not "backing away from their long-held commitment to take an active part in world affairs." Further, they remain committed to "a strong global military posture" and a fidelity to "alliances, international treaties and agreements, humanitarian interven-tions, and multilateral approaches to many problems." At the same time, the people increasingly accept the fact that the United States is "playing a less dominant role in the world," and they prefer a selective engagement approach for American involvement in "major conflicts . . . and long-term military commitments."[6]

In the immediate months after 9/11, Congress's foreign policy voice was muted and largely deferential to presidential direction. As the war in Iraq dragged on, public opposition grew, eventually resulting in the Democrats gaining control of both Houses of Congress in 2006. That institution then sought to reassert its foreign policy role. The Congress has continued to be more assertive toward the Obama administration, whether over the clos-ing of the U.S. prison at Guantanamo Bay, the approval of the New START Treaty, or the recent American policy toward Libya, as Louis Fisher in chap-ter 10 and James M. Lindsay in chapter 12 of this volume point out. Some interest groups also lost the prominence that they had gained following the collapse of the Berlin Wall and the implosion of the Soviet Union immedi-ately after the events of 9/11, but the proliferation of both the number and kind of foreign policy interest groups today are greater and more vocal than in perhaps any recent period.

In addition to the changing security environment impacting the domestic/foreign policy linkage, America's increasingly dense webwork of involvement in the world political economy, as we have suggested, has stimulated greater domestic pressures on the nation's foreign policies and policymaking processes. As the experience of other states confirms, interdependence compromises the sovereign autonomy of the state, blurs the distinction between foreign and domestic politics, and elevates the participation of domestically oriented government agencies in the policy process. As transnational economic exchanges accelerate, for example, they produce clear winners and losers. Yet such linkages also create greater uncertainty for transnational actors at home, as reflected by the Great Recession in recent years. In addition, these groups may also appeal to government officials for either policy continuity or changes to meet their concerns. The upshot of all these components of globalization is the continuation of, and, arguably, an increase in, the "domestication" of American foreign policy.

DOMESTIC POLITICS AND FOREIGN POLICY

The proposition that domestic politics explains foreign policy stands in sharp contrast to the realist tradition in the study of foreign policy. Political realism, a perspective that enjoyed widespread acceptance among policymakers and scholars during the Cold War and before, argues that foreign policy is primarily a function of what occurs outside national borders. In this tradition, states are the principal actors; power and national interests are the dominant policy considerations; and maintaining the balance of power among states is the principal policy imperative. Furthermore, all states—democratic and nondemocratic—operate on the same assumptions and respond similarly to changes in the international system. In short, from a realist perspective, domestic politics exerts little if any impact on state behavior.

While political realism provides valuable insights into the motivations and actions of states, particularly at times of heightened concern about national security, it surely underestimates the effects of the domestic environment, both historically and today. Even the Greek philosopher Thucydides, perhaps the first political realist, recognized the importance of domestic politics in shaping the external behavior of Athens and Sparta. In language with a decidedly contemporary ring, he observed that the actions leaders of Greek city-states directed toward one another often sought to affect the political climates within their own polities, not what happened between them.

Centuries later Immanuel Kant argued in his treatise *Perpetual Peace* that democracies are inherently less warlike than autocracies, because democratic leaders are accountable to the public, which restrains them from waging war. Because ordinary citizens would have to supply the soldiers and bear the human and financial costs of imperial policies, he contended, liberal democracies are "natural" forces for peace. History has been kind to Kant's thesis—democracies rarely fight one another. That theme highlighted the Clinton administration's foreign policy in the decade of the 1990s, which held that the spread of democratic market economies is good not only for peace but also for business and prosperity. The Bush administration embraced that theme as well. In his second inaugural address, for instance, George W. Bush declared that "it is the policy of the United States to seek and support the growth of democratic movements and institutions in every nature and culture, with the ultimate goal of ending tyranny in the world." Likewise, Barack Obama has emphasized the advancement of democracy as an important foreign policy objective of the United States. In his 2009 Cairo speech, President Obama acknowledged that "no system of government can or should be imposed by one nation by any other," but he went on to that such a stance "does not lessen my commitment . . . to governments that reflect the will of the people." Furthermore, he recognized that "each nation gives life to this principle in its own way, grounded in the traditions of its own people," and that "America does not presume to know what is best for everyone, just as we would not presume to pick the outcome of a peaceful election." Still, President Obama continued, "I do have an unyielding belief that all people yearn for certain things: the ability to speak your mind and have a say in how you are governed; confidence in the rule of law and the equal administration of justice; government that is transparent and doesn't steal from the people; the freedom to live as you choose."

The impact of domestic politics on foreign policy manifested itself in several ways in the post-9/11 environment for the Bush administration, and it continues to do so for the Obama administration a decade later. For example, it is difficult to explain France's reluctance to endorse the Bush administration's approach to Iraq without taking into account its perennial skepticism of American leadership in world affairs, grounded in its own history and experience, as well as its traditional ties with Iraq itself. Saudi Arabia's hesitance to grant access to military bases important for an attack on Iraq was closely tied to its Islamic heritage and foundations. Turkey, also with a large Muslim population, had similar concerns, with the added worry that its sizable Kurdish minority might use the war to carve a new Kurdistan out of parts of Turkey and Iraq.

The Obama administration faced similar constraints from abroad to its foreign policy initiatives, despite President Obama's initial global popularity. In Pew Research Center surveys across twenty-five and twenty countries, respectively, in 2009 and 2010, the "U.S. favorability rating" increased as did global perception that President Obama "will do the right thing in global affairs," compared to his predecessor. Yet this perception of support

did not necessarily translate into support for American policy. The publics
in most of the survey countries continued to oppose the administration's
handling of the Middle East, majorities or pluralities in half of the countries
opposed U.S. policy toward Iran, and majorities in several countries continued to oppose the Afghan War.[7] In all, personal popularity generally did
not remove the policy opposition to American actions abroad.

President Obama generally faced the same foreign policy challengers
in dealing with policymakers in allied and friendly countries. That is, the
leadership in NATO countries generally opposed the Obama administration's call for maintaining or increasing troops in Afghanistan, with some
countries deciding to withdraw their forces (e.g., Canada and the Netherlands). The leaders of several key G-20 nations opposed the Obama administration's call for stimulating economic growth prior to addressing budget
debt issues.[8] To be sure, the Obama administration was able to prod the
European Union to impose sanctions on Iran over its nuclear program in
2010, and it gained acquiescence (and abstention), if not support, in the
United Nations for a resolution to take actions again Muammar Qaddafi's
Libya in 2011. Still, domestic considerations and national interests undoubtedly governed the decisions of these states and their leaders—and the
Obama administration was not exempt from such constraints in pursuing
its foreign policy.

DOMESTIC POLITICS AND AMERICAN FOREIGN POLICY

America's post–Cold War and post-9/11 foreign policies are rife with examples of how domestic politics shapes its actions abroad. In the latter years
of the Clinton administration, for example, the president felt constrained
in dealing with various humanitarian crises abroad by an American public
reluctant to support sending U.S. ground forces to cope with them. Hence,
when Clinton announced his decision to bomb Serbian positions in Kosovo
in response to Serbia's mistreatment of its own Albanian minority there, he
explicitly excluded the option of sending ground forces from any military
action. Similarly, the administration's desire to ratify the Comprehensive
Test Ban Treaty was halted by a reluctant Senate, where less than a majority
approved it. Congress also stymied Clinton's hopes for further expanding
free trade agreements with other countries when it refused to grant him
"fast-track" trading authority. Also, both houses of Congress, controlled by
the opposition Republican Party, prodded Clinton to approve a national
missile defense bill that he had originally opposed.

Upon taking office, George W. Bush also confronted a public and Congress
not wholly supportive of his foreign policy plans. Early polls showed that
barely a majority of Americans supported his initial foreign policy designs.

An equally divided Congress also expressed skepticism about the unilateralism evident in many of the new administration's early pronouncements and actions. September 11 changed all of that, at least for a time. Congressional criticism became muted, and public enthusiasm for the president's agenda blossomed. By early 2003, however, the tides once again appeared to shift as war with Iraq loomed. While the initial success in Iraq brought some positive public reaction, that effect began to erode as reconstruction efforts in Iraq lagged and internal opposition and sectarian violence increased. Further, as American casualties increased, public support at home began to erode. While President Bush continued to hew to the policy line of "staying the course" in Iraq, the American public dealt a sharp rebuke to the administration's approach with the 2006 congressional elections.

As a result, a Democratic-controlled Congress quickly sought to challenge the president's approach to Iraq, especially after President Bush announced his new "surge" strategy for Iraq in early 2007. Hearings were held in both Houses of Congress on Iraq and American foreign policy generally, and other congressional bills and resolutions were initiated, albeit with limited results. Nonetheless, the existence of congressional opposition made it difficult for the administration to advance new foreign policy initiatives.

The Obama administration came into office on a wave of popular sentiment, but it, too, quickly faced opposition at home to its foreign policy initiatives. President Obama's efforts to close the American prison at Guantanamo Bay, Cuba, and transfer the "enemy combatants" there to a mainland facility met with both public and congressional resistance. Similarly, when President Obama's attorney general announced that some prisoners held in Guantanamo Bay would be given civilian trials in New York, public and congressional opposition arose once more. Ultimately, the Obama administration decided to utilize military tribunals and to keep some prisoners at Guantanamo Bay.

Other national security issues also sparked public or congressional opposition at various times. The decision to employ a "surge strategy" in Afghanistan sparked critiques from liberals and conservatives, albeit for differing reasons. The New START Treaty with Russia produced extended Senate debate over the wisdom of ratification and whether it imperiled America's nuclear arsenal. Although the administration ultimately gained that body's approval in late 2010, it did so only after extended negotiations. The administration's policy toward Iran and North Korea over their nuclear programs, and the seeming lack of successful action in halting those nuclear programs, remain a source of criticism. Similarly, the administration's position on the requirements for negotiations between Israel and the Palestinians in 2011 fostered sharp domestic criticism, especially by those with close ties to Israel. In all, the impact of domestic politics on foreign policy matters continues.

Given the nation's historical roots, the constraints domestic politics impose on American foreign policy should hardly be surprisingly. Since its founding, the United States has perceived itself as a different—indeed, as an exceptional—nation, one with a foreign policy driven more by domestic values than by the vagaries of international politics. Analysts who have examined the views of Thomas Jefferson and other founders conclude that they believed that "the objectives of foreign policy were but a means to the end of posterity and promoting the goals of domestic society."[9] That belief still permeates American society and its political processes.

Still, satisfying the requirements of domestic politics arguably became more critical for foreign policy over recent decades than at other times in the nation's history. Whether that is cause for concern may be debated, but it raises questions about the ability of a democratic society to pursue a successful foreign strategy. As the French political sociologist Alexis de Tocqueville observed over 150 years ago, "Foreign politics demand scarcely any of those qualities which a democracy possesses; they require, on the contrary, the perfect use of almost all those faculties in which it is deficient."

Although there may be broad agreement that domestic imperatives sometimes shape foreign policy, there is less agreement about the particulars and how they manifest themselves in the political process. For analytic purposes, we can begin our inquiry into the domestic sources of American foreign policy by grouping them into three broad categories: the nation's societal environment, its institutional setting, and the individual characteristics of its decision-makers and the policymaking positions they occupy.

Figure I.1 illustrates the relationship between each of the domestic explanatory categories and American foreign policy and their interrelationships with one another. The figure posits that domestic policy influences are inputs into the decision-making process that converts policy demands into foreign policy. (We can define "foreign policy" as the goals that a nation's officials seek to realize abroad, the values that give rise to them, and the means or instruments used to pursue them.) Conceptualized as the output of the process that converts policy demands into goals and means, foreign policy is typically multifaceted, ranging from discrete behaviors linked to specific issues to recurring patterns of behavior that define the continual efforts to cope with the environment beyond a state's borders.

Although we can easily identify many of the discrete variables that make up the domestic source categories, the lines between the categories themselves are not always clear cut. To help draw these larger distinctions as well as explicate the smaller ones, it is useful to think of the explanatory categories as layers of differing size and complexity.

THE SOCIETAL ENVIRONMENT

The broadest layer is the societal environment. The political culture of the United States—the basic needs, values, beliefs, and self-images widely shared by Americans about their political system—stands out as a primary societal source of American foreign policy. Minimally, those beliefs find expression in the kinds of values and political institutions American policymakers have sought to export to others throughout much of its history. Included is a preference for democracy, capitalism, and the values of the American liberal tradition-limited government, individual liberty, due process of law, self-determination, free enterprise, inalienable (natural) rights, the equality of citizens before the law, majority rule, minority rights, federalism, and the separation of powers.

With roots deeply implanted in the nation's history, elements of the political culture remain potent forces explaining what the United States does in its foreign policy. But as both the positive and negative aspects

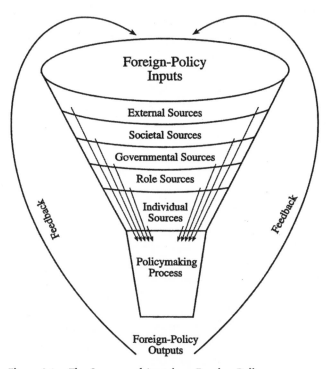

Figure I.1. The Sources of American Foreign Policy
Source: Charles W. Kegley Jr. and Eugene Wittkopf, *American Foreign Policy: Pattern and Process*, 5th ed. (New York: St. Martin's Press, 1996), 15.

of globalization are more fully recognized, the domestic roots of foreign policy may increasingly be found elsewhere. While industry, labor, and environmental interests seek to place their own stamp on U.S. responses to globalization issues (like wages, labor trafficking, and World Trade Organization dispute-settlement rulings), other entities, particularly ideological, ethnic, and single-issue groups, have expressed concern about American targets abroad in its anti-terror campaign and have sought to impose their imprint on policy positions.

Since the end of the Vietnam War, American opinion toward foreign policy issues has consistently revealed domestic divisions about what is the appropriate role of the United States in world affairs. While American opinion leaders and policymakers remain overwhelmingly internationalist in orientation, fissures have continued to be evident among the public over the nature of America's internationalism—and the involvements in the Afghanistan and Iraq Wars surely exacerbated those divisions. Indeed, while majorities of those who identify themselves as Republicans or Democrats still agree on most foreign policy issues, partisan differences on some are quite deep and persistent. These include sharp gulfs between Democrats and Republicans over the benefits of globalization, over the handling of immigration, and over the dangers of climate change. Party identifiers likewise differ by a wide margin on the utility of the United States going along with the decisions of international institutions to address global problems and the degree of support for a global institution to regulate financial bodies through international standards. These partisans also disagree on the degree of support for Israel and over the use of torture "to extract information from suspected terrorists."[10] Such divisions among the public can and do make it difficult for policymakers to fashion and carry out a foreign policy that meets public approval. In this sense, these divisions pose a significant difficulty in producing a foreign policy consensus and a clear direction in America's actions abroad. Yet the exact shape of America's involvement is likely to be more fully contested in the ensuing presidential and congressional elections, revealing once again the close linkage between foreign and domestic politics.

Historically, American leaders have been able to define the parameters of American involvement in the world and to count on public support for their choices. Especially important was the so-called Establishment, consisting of (largely male) leaders drawn from the corporate and financial world and later supplemented by faculty members from the nation's elite universities. With roots in the early twentieth century, the Establishment was a major force defining key elements of American foreign policy prior to World War II and in the decades of Cold War conflict that followed. Its role is consistent with the elitist model of foreign policymaking, which says that public policy is little more than an expression of elites' preferences—and the interests underlying them.

A long-standing belief that public opinion will not tolerate large losses of life in situations involving American troops is consistent with another tradition known as *pluralism*. Whereas the elitist model sees the process of policymaking as one flowing from the top downward, pluralism sees the process as an upward-flowing one. Mass public opinion, which enjoys greater weight in this model, finds expression through interest groups, whose ability to shape foreign policy has been enhanced in recent years.

The media figure prominently but quite differently in these competing policymaking models. From the elitist perspective, the media are largely the mouthpieces of elites, providing the conduit through which mass public opinion is manipulated and molded to fit elite preferences. From the pluralist perspective, on the other hand, the media comprise an independent force able to scrutinize what the government is doing and provide an independent assessment of its policies. Thus, the media appear less conspiratorial in the pluralist than in the elitist model, but their role is potent nonetheless. Indeed, to some the media are public opinion. Minimally, the media help to set the agenda for public discussion and often layout for the American people the range of interpretations about foreign policy issues from which they might choose. Thus, the media help to aggregate the interests of more discrete groups in American society.

Political parties also aggregate interests. In the two-party system of the United States, political parties are broad coalitions of ethnic, religious, economic, educational, professional, working-class, and other sociodemographic groups. One of the most important functions these broad coalitions serve is the selection of personnel to key policymaking positions. They can also serve as referenda on past policy performance. Increasingly, the two major political parties are pursuing differing foreign policy paths, a departure from the tradition of bipartisanship in foreign affairs and another indicator of the enhanced role of domestic division on American foreign policy.

What role foreign policy beliefs and preferences play in shaping citizens' choices on these broad issues is difficult to determine. On the one hand, most citizens are motivated not by foreign policy issues but by domestic ones. Their electoral choices typically reflect those preferences, something especially evident in recent presidential elections. Still, we cannot easily dismiss the role elections play in the expression and consequences of Americans' foreign policy preferences. In the 2002 and 2006 congressional elections and in the presidential election in 2004, an abundant of evidence suggested the foreign policy issues, especially terrorism and the war in Iraq, figured prominently in the voting calculus of many Americans. Moreover, as Miroslav Nincic reports in chapter 8, foreign policy has always been an issue across presidential elections and can be crucial, especially in a closely-contested election through the electoral college system. It is thus reasonable to hypothesize that the foreign policy preferences of Americans may have been pivotal in shaping the ultimate electoral outcome than we might suspect. In this sense, foreign policy issues can and do matter in presidential elections.

As these ideas suggest, the political culture, the foreign policy attitudes and beliefs of leaders and masses, and the role that the media, interest groups, and elections play in shaping Americans' political preferences and transmitting them to leaders may be potent explanations of what the United States does in the world.

THE INSTITUTIONAL SETTING

As we peel away the societal environment as a source of American foreign policy, a second category is revealed: the institutional setting, consisting of the various branches of government and the departments and agencies assigned responsibility for decision-making, management, and implementation. The category incorporates the diverse properties related to the structure of the U.S. government—notably its presidential rather than parliamentary form—that limit or enhance the foreign policy choices made by decision-makers and affect their implementation, thus revealing the linkages between the substance of foreign policy and the process by which it is made.

Broadly speaking, the American "foreign affairs government" encompasses a cluster of variables and organizational actors that influence what the United States does—or does not do—abroad. Most striking in this regard is the division of authority and responsibility for foreign policymaking between the Congress and the president. The Constitution embraces the eighteenth-century belief that the abuse of political power is controlled best not through centralization but by fragmenting it in a system of checks and balances. Hence, because authority and responsibility for American foreign policy is lodged in separate institutions sharing power, the Constitution is an "invitation to struggle."

The struggle for control over foreign policymaking between Congress and the president is most evident during periods when Congress and the presidency are controlled by different political parties (divided government). But even during periods when the government is not divided, conflict over foreign policymaking continues, often within the executive branch itself. There we find departments and agencies that grew in size and importance during nearly a half-century of Cold War competition with the Soviet Union. Each is populated by career professionals who fight both for personal gain and for what they view as the appropriate response of the United States to challenges from abroad. Not surprisingly, then, bureaucratic struggles over appropriate American policies have long been evident. They continue to leave their imprints on American foreign policy.

The growing interdependence of the United States with the world political economy reinforces these bureaucratic battles, as several executive branch departments seemingly oriented toward domestic affairs (e.g., Agriculture, Commerce, Justice, and Treasury) now are also stakeholders in the foreign policy game. This is especially evident in the fight against international terrorism. Foreign intelligence agencies (notably the CIA) and domestic law enforcement agencies (notably the FBI) are constrained by law and tradition to different policy and implementation tracks, yet today they find they must triangulate their efforts on common external threats, including not only terrorism in its physical sense but also cyberterrorism and such other challenges as trafficking in illicit drugs. While there have been numerous efforts to encourage such interdepartmental cooperation, the differing cultural traditions within these bureaucracies remain formidable, and conflicts continue.

Fragmentation of authority over policymaking within the executive branch itself is a product of the complexity and competition evident within the foreign affairs government. That characterization takes on a special meaning when we consider the often overlapping roles of the White House and National Security Council staffs, the State Department, the Defense Department, the Treasury Department, the intelligence community, and other decision-making units, including the Department of Homeland Security established in 2002. This last department's charge is particularly challenging, since it is directed to integrate intelligence-gathering and law-enforcement responsibilities now spread across many different departments and agencies. The 2004 legislation creating a national director of intelligence as a means to integrate the disparate elements of the intelligence community is yet another case in point of the festering problem of fragmentation within the foreign affairs government—and this effort at restructuring has not been without growing pains.

As more agencies have achieved places in the foreign affairs government, and as the domestic political support they enjoy has solidified, the management of policymaking by the president, whose role in the conduct of foreign affairs is preeminent, has become more difficult. To many, blame for the incoherence and inconsistency sometimes exhibited in American foreign policy lies here. Ironically, however, efforts to enhance presidential control of foreign policymaking by centralizing it in the White House have sometimes exacerbated rather than diminished incoherence and inconsistency, by encouraging competition and conflict between the presidency, on the one hand, and the executive branch departments and agencies constituting the permanent foreign affairs government, on the other.

In sum, understanding the institutional setting as a source of American foreign policy requires an examination of the responsibilities of numerous institutions and their relations with one another: the institutionalized presidency, the Congress, the cabinet-level departments, and other agencies with foreign affairs responsibilities. These, then, will be our concerns in part II.

DECISION-MAKERS AND
THEIR POLICYMAKING POSITIONS

When we peel away the institutional setting as a domestic source of American foreign policy, the people who make the policies, their policymaking positions, and the bureaucratic environments in which they work become the focus of our attention. The underlying proposition is that the personal characteristics of individuals (personality traits, perceptions, and psychological predispositions), the role responsibilities that the individual assumes within the decision process (as president, national security adviser, or secretary of the treasury), and the differing bureaucratic environments (the FBI versus the CIA, for instance) in which individuals operate affect policy choices. Still, and despite the combination of these forces, it is important to keep in mind that the individual decision-maker is the ultimate source of influence on policy, the final mediating force in the causal chain linking the other domestic sources to the ends and means of American foreign policy.

There are several ways in which personality and perceptual factors may impinge upon foreign policymaking. Ideas about communism and the Soviet Union instilled early in life, for example, likely affect the attitudes and behaviors of many now responsible for negotiating with the leaders of the post-Soviet states, including Russia. Similarly, policymakers' orientation toward decision-making may profoundly affect the nation's foreign policy strategies. It has been suggested, for example, that American leaders can be characterized as either crusaders or pragmatists. The hallmark of a crusader is a "missionary zeal to make the world better. The crusader tends to make decisions based on a preconceived idea rather than on the basis of experience. Even though there are alternatives, he usually does not see them." The pragmatist, on the other hand, "is guided by the facts and his experience in a given situation, not by wishes or unexamined preconceptions . . . . Always flexible, he does not get locked into a losing policy. He can change direction and try again, without inflicting damage to his self-esteem."[11] Woodrow Wilson is the preeminent twentieth-century crusader, Harry S. Truman the personification of the pragmatist. Others, including Ronald Reagan, Bill Clinton, George W. Bush, and Barack Obama could easily be characterized in these terms as well.

Personality factors also help to explain how presidents manage the conduct of foreign affairs. A president's approach to information processing, known as his or her "cognitive style," that person's orientation toward political conflict, and his or her sense of political efficacy are all important in understanding how he or she will structure the policymaking system and deal with those around the chief executive. In this case personal predispositions form a bridge between the institutional setting of American foreign policymaking and the process of decision-making itself.

Presidents sometimes engage in foreign policy actions not to affect the external environment but to influence domestic politics. Foreign policy can be used to mobilize popular support at home (the "rally 'round the flag" effect), to increase authority through appeals to patriotism, and to enhance prospects for reelection using macroeconomic policymaking tools or distributing private benefits through trade policy or other mechanisms, such as defense spending distributions. Again, the connection between domestic politics and foreign policy is apparent.

Although policymakers doubtless use foreign policy for domestic purposes, it is unclear whether they do so because of who they are or because of the positions they occupy. Because of the frequency with which policymakers in the United States and other countries alike allegedly engage in this type of behavior, it seems that leaders' role requirements, not their personal predilections, explain this behavior. Policymakers' positions thus appear to stimulate certain predictable patterns of behavior. Conversely, the position an individual holds may constrain the impact of personality on policymaking behavior. Institutional roles thus reduce the influence of idiosyncratic factors on policy performance.

Individuals can, of course, interpret the roles they occupy differently. That fact blurs the distinction between decision-makers and their policy positions as competing rather than complementary explanations of American foreign policy. Clearly, however, policymaking positions, or roles, severely circumscribe the freedom and autonomy of the particular individuals who occupy them and thus diminish the range of politically feasible choices. Hence, we must understand the relationship between the person and the position and how each separately and in combination affects policy outcomes. In no way can that conclusion be illustrated more clearly than with a simple aphorism drawn from bureaucratic politics: "Where you stand depends on where you sit."

In sum, a focus on decision-makers and their policy positions as a category of domestic influences on American foreign policy draws attention to the capacity of individuals to place their personal imprints on the nation's conduct abroad, while simultaneously alerting us to the need to examine the forces that constrain individual initiative. Principal among these are the role-induced constraints that occur within bureaucratic settings. Because the making and execution of American foreign policy is fundamentally a group or organizational enterprise, we can surmise that these constraints are considerable. The essays in part III will focus on these ideas and how they relate to American foreign policymaking.

NOTES

1. The quoted passages are taken from the Prague and Cairo speeches by President Barack Obama. See Barack Obama, "Remarks by President Barack Obama," Hradcany Square, Prague, Czech Republic, April 5, 2009, the White House, Office of the Press Secretary; and Barack Obama, "Remarks by the President on a New Beginning," Cairo University, Cairo, Egypt, June 4, 2009, the White House, Office of the Press Secretary.

2. On the information revolution, or what he labels the "Third Industrial Revolution," and the various ramifications of its impact on global politics, see Joseph S. Nye Jr., *The Future of Power* (New York: Public Affairs, 2011), 113–51.

3. For a discussion of the KOF Index of Globalization along these three dimensions and for the results released in 2011 for the 2008 data year, see http://globalization.kof.ethz.ch/static/pdf/press_release_2011_en.pdf.

4. The quoted passages are from *The National Security Strategy of the United States* (Washington, DC: The White House, September 17, 2002).

5. All the quoted passages in the two paragraphs on the Obama administration are from *The National Security Strategy* (Washington, DC: The White House, May 2010), at www.whitehouse.gov/sites/default/files/rss_viewer/national_security_strategy.pdf.

6. See Chicago Council on Global Affairs, *Constrained Internationalism: Adapting to New Realities, Results of a 2010 National Survey of American Public Opinion* (Chicago: Chicago Council on Global Affairs, 2010), 3, for the quoted passages and for a full report on current foreign policy attitudes.

7. For a fuller discussion of these Pew poll results and how the results for Muslim countries were generally much less supportive of President Obama, see James M. McCormick, "The Obama Presidency: A Foreign Policy of Change?" in Steven E. Schier, ed., *Transforming America: Barack Obama in the White House* (Lanham, MD: Rowman & Littlefield, 2011), 243–44.

8. McCormick, "The Obama Presidency," 244–45.

9. Robert W. Tucker and David C. Hendrickson, "Thomas Jefferson and American Foreign Policy," *Foreign Affairs* 69 (Spring 1990): 139.

10. See Chicago Council on Global Affairs, *Constrained Internationalism*, 77–81, for a complete discussion of these party differences and magnitude of the difference between Republicans and Democrats on these and other issues.

11. John G. Stoessinger, *Crusaders and Pragmatists: Movers of Modern American Foreign Policy* (New York: Norton, 1985), xiii–xiv.

I

THE SOCIETAL ENVIRONMENT

"Politics stops at the water's edge." That aphorism, popular during much of the Cold War, embraces the notion that domestic differences should not cloud American efforts abroad. The domestic unity implied by the phrase waned in the aftermath of the Vietnam War and, later, with the end of the Cold War as foreign policy disputes became frequent. The tragic events of September 11 seemingly resurrected this aphorism as the public rallied behind its leaders and partisan divisions were put aside to confront international terrorism. The Iraq War of 2003 and its tragic aftermath, the ongoing Afghanistan War, and the Great Recession of 2008 and beyond shattered this temporary unity, and the constraints of the societal environment once again were fully in evidence by the end of the decade.

The events of September 11, 2001, had a profound effect on public and partisan unity, and, indeed, politics stopped at the water's edge for a time. After 9/11, the public's foreign policy mood shifted perceptibly with Americans becoming more committed to an "active role" for the United States than at any time in recent decades.[1] Not surprisingly, terrorism topped the list when people were asked to name "one of the two or three biggest problems facing the country," and the American public embraced a greater willingness to endorse a series of military measures, such as American air strikes, the use of ground troops, and even assassination as antiterrorist means if accompanied by multilateral support.

The events of September 11 also altered partisan and ideological divisions on foreign policy among American policymakers. Within days of 9/11, for example, Congress, by overwhelming margins, passed Senate Joint Resolution 23, which authorized the president to employ force "against those nations, organizations, or persons, he determines planned, authorized, committed, or aided the terrorist attacks." A month later, Congress passed the USA Patriot Act, which granted even more discretion to the president in pursuing terrorist suspects, even to the extent of easing some civil liberty protections. And a year later Congress passed another joint resolution authorizing the president to use force "as he determines to be necessary and appropriate in order to defend the national security of the United States against the continuing threat posed by Iraq and enforce all relevant United Nations Security Council Resolutions regarding Iraq."

However, the Iraq War, initiated in March 2003, shattered this bipartisan unity and created a broad array of domestic challenges to the Bush administration's foreign policy. Although the toppling of the Iraqi regime occurred quite quickly, and Bush announced the end of combat on an American naval vessel standing before a banner proclaiming "Mission Accomplished," the challenge of the Iraq invasion, it turns out, was just beginning. The effort at reconstruction and reconciliation proved a daunting task. As the insurgent opposition and sectarian violence grew, as weapons of mass destruction could not be found in Iraq, and as the number of Americans killed in Iraq increased, domestic opposition did as well. The foreign policy unity of several months earlier began to erode. The Democratic opposition, of course, led these attacks, but dissent within the president's own Republican ranks emerged as well. Foreign policy—both the war in Iraq and the larger war on terrorism—became an important issue in both the 2004 presidential election and the 2006 congressional elections. Politics no longer stopped at the water's edge.

Congress was now engaged once again in the foreign policy debate. In this sense, much as 9/11 focused attention by Congress on supporting the president, the policy failures over Iraq have now drawn Congress back to focus on its responsibilities in the foreign policy arena. President Bush's party took a "thumping" in the 2006 congressional elections, as the president acknowledged, with the Democrats gaining control of both houses of Congress as a result. That election was widely seen as a referendum on the Iraq War and the Bush administration's handling of foreign policy. The new Congress sought to hold the president accountable for his actions in Iraq and elsewhere and attempted to put its own stamp on foreign policy, albeit with limited success. Still, the social environment for American foreign policy had seemingly changed quite perceptibly in the space of a few years and in response to a major foreign policy event.

With Barack Obama's victory in the 2008 presidential election, continuing Democratic control of Congress, and the president's call for bringing people together, the stage seemed set to move back to more domestic unity on foreign policy. Indeed, candidate Obama had pledged to bring a new style of American leadership, restore America's reputation in the world, and reverse some of the foreign policy actions of the Bush administration. President Obama issued three executive orders within two days of his inauguration dealing with terrorism issues—one calling for the closing of overseas prisons used by the Central Intelligence Agency to hold terrorist suspects and the ending of certain interrogation methods, a second directing the closing of the Guantanamo Bay detention camp within one year, and the third setting up a taskforce to identify legal ways for dealing with those individuals "captured or apprehended in connection with armed conflicts and counterterrorism operations." Efforts to close the Guantanamo Bay facility, however, almost immediately sparked congressional and public opposition. The public did not want these terrorist suspects housed near them and on American soil. One public opinion survey in 2010 indicated that 60 percent of the American public wanted the prisons at Guantanamo Bay to remain open. Congress ultimately passed legislation blocking funding to renovate a facility in Illinois.[2]

In December 2009, the Obama administration's adoption of a "surge strategy" toward the deteriorating situation in Afghanistan increased the war effort in that country, even as the American public was reducing its support for the war. That decision also sparked criticism from both sides of the political aisle. By the decision, thirty thousand additional American forces would be sent to Afghanistan, although the president also committed to begin to withdraw these forces by July 2011, "taking into account conditions on the ground." Those on the left were concerned about the commitment of additional troops and extending the stay in Afghanistan, while those on the right were concerned about whether the troops were sufficient and the contingency to begin to withdraw the troops by the middle of 2011.

Similarly, the Obama administration's decision to support a "no-fly zone" over Libya in March 2011 to halt Muammar Qaddafi's assaults on his people sparked domestic controversy as well. Some objected that no vital national interests were at stake in Libya, and the United States was yet again involving itself in an internal war of another nation. Members of Congress objected that the president was usurping its war powers under the Constitution by such action. Further, others noted that the president went to the United Nations Security Council for approval of this action, but he did not go to the U.S. Congress. In all, domestic debate over foreign policy continued.

In the context of these political-military issues, the American economy was deteriorating with the failure of several large banks and investment firms, the bankruptcy by major corporations (or the need for bailouts by the government to keep them operating), and the collapse of the housing industry. As a result, the domestic economy was eroding and America's position in global economy (and indeed in global politics) seemingly was in decline. Furthermore, according to polling data, the American public appeared largely acquiescent to this declining global role, and they supported a greater focus on America's domestic ills.

Understanding the changes in American foreign policy after September 11, after the Afghanistan and Iraq War, and after the Great Recession requires a fuller understanding of the domestic political and social environment in recent years. What are the competing societal forces shaping America's responses abroad today? Which among them play pivotal roles in charting the direction of foreign policy? How have these events of the past decade or more shaped and reshaped the societal environment and its impact on American foreign policy?

We begin our search for answers to these questions with three readings that focus on the broader societal environment and its impact on American foreign policy. The first two chapters address the standing of the United States in light of these events, and the two authors come to differing assessments about the degree of decline in American power and status and its likely position in the international system in the years ahead. Although both of these chapters focus on the international system, each also places considerable attention on the domestic social and political environment in reaching his conclusion. The third chapter focuses even more specifically on the domestic setting and the reaction of the American public to the Great Recession and its likely effect on American foreign policy in the future.

In "The Future of American Power: Dominance and Decline in Perspective," foreign policy analyst Joseph S. Nye Jr. addresses the question of American decline, especially in light of the financial crisis beginning in 2008, accesses projections of the loss of American dominance over the next two decades, and evaluates the impact of the rise of China. Nye generally remains skeptical of "declinism" analyses, since beliefs both in America's dominance and its decline have tended to be exaggerated over the years. American power, as he notes, "is not what it used to be, but it also never really was as great as assumed."

Nye readily acknowledges that China may be on the rise, but it "has a long way to go to equal the power resources of the United States." China, for example, must address a number of challenges of its own in order to continue this rise in global power. It has a large underdeveloped countryside that has not shared in its rise, serious demographic problems in light of its one-child policy that will hinder its future advance, and an authoritarian political system that may well meet resistance in the years ahead. Furthermore, a rising China may face resistance from its neighbors, particularly India and Japan, and that possibility will actually aid the United States in maintaining its global position.

Although Nye thus appears more circumspect about the rise of China than others, he is quick to catalog a number of societal issues that the United States faces and that will be crucial to America maintaining its leading global role in the future. These include fostering a sound immigration policy (since immigration has always been a source of U.S. strength in the past), improving the performance of the American economy, and addressing the issue of national debt. In addition, the political system is suffering from gridlock with both American politics and its political institutions more polarized. In this sense, the United States faces a problem of "power conversion—translating power resources into desired outcomes." Nonetheless, the United States still maintains several advantages in comparison to others. It generally has a well-educated work force, maintains leading universities and top-tier secondary schools (although primary education appears to be lagging), continues to make large investments in research and development, and exhibits an entrepreneurial spirit.

In all, Nye judges that the United States is not in absolute decline as some might suggest, and even in relative terms, it remains more powerful than any single state at present. The United States will continue to face the increase in the power resources of many other states, but "the problem of American power in the twenty-first century . . . is not one of decline but what to do in light of the realization that even the largest country cannot achieve the outcomes it wants without help of others." In this sense, we will not "see a post-American world," but the United States will need to pursue "a smart strategy that combines hard- and soft-power resources."

In contrast to Nye's views, Gideon Rachman in the second chapter argues that America's global decline is now a reality. In his "Think Again: American Decline," Rachman contends that the challenge from China is more serious than previous threats to U.S. global dominance from the Soviet Union and Japan. China's economic dynamism is more vigorous than the Soviet Union was ever able to develop and its population far surpasses that of Japan's. China is also becoming the "preferred partner of many African governments" and "the biggest trading partner" of new powers like Brazil and South Africa. Further, these new powers are often aligning themselves politically with China and against the United States on key issues.

Rachman readily acknowledges that China faces major economic challenges—a property bubble and inflation at home, and an undervalued currency abroad—as well as demographic and environmental challenges—an aging population, widespread pollution, and water shortages. Yet Rachman does not see these challenges as necessarily slowing down China's rise. "Sheer size and economic motivation mean that the Chinese juggernaut will keep rolling forward."

At the same time, Rachman agrees with Nye that the United States has important global advantages at the moment, but he is skeptical whether these will last. To be sure, the United States has the largest economy in the world, leading universities, numerous global corporations, a dominant military, "entrepreneurial flair," and "technological prowess." But if jobs are less readily available for graduates, if American firms continue to lose their global dominance to others, and if the military continues to be under the pressure of austerity, America's position will decline. Furthermore, the American economy is increasingly dependent upon China to purchase U.S. Treasury bills to support its budget deficit, further enlarging the potential vulnerability of the United States. Indeed, the former chairman of the U.S. Joint Chiefs of Staff pointedly identified the growing national debt as the fundamental threat to U.S. security.

Rachman also questions two popular theories about globalization and its impact on contributing to the spread of Western values and in turn continued U.S. global leadership. One theory—economic growth leads to democratization—appears not to be supported by the Chinese experience. China has had spectacular economic growth, but democratization has not followed. The other theory—that new democracies would be friendly and helpful to the United States—appears to falter, too, since new and developing democracies—India, Brazil, or Turkey, for example—have disagreed with the United States on important policy questions. In all, globalization and democratization are unlikely to sustain U.S. dominance.

Finally, Rachman argues that the globalization has not proved to be a positive sum game or a win-win situation for the United States. China has balked at reducing its protectionist policy or at devaluing its currency to move toward more equity in trade relations. Similarly, China continues to resist efforts to reach a global environmental accord, and it has been a halting partner on several foreign policy matters, including the nuclear weapons issues with Iran and North Korea. The overall result is that economic and political power is moving from West to East and "new international rivalries are inevitably emerging." In short, the United States "will never again experience the global dominance" that it enjoyed after the breakup of the Soviet Union.

In the next chapter, "The Tea Party, Populism, and the Domestic Culture of U.S. Foreign Policy," Walter Russell Mead identifies and discusses an important aspect of domestic political culture and its potential impact on American foreign policy today. Mead begins by outlining the background of the Tea Party movement and its recent activism in American politics, especially in the 2010 elections. At the same time, this movement—with its anti-government and anti-elite views—fits well with Jacksonian populism in American history. Such populism, Mead notes, "is more than an intellectual conviction in the United States; it is a cultural force." Thus, "the Tea Party movement is best understood as a contemporary revolt of Jacksonian common sense against elites perceived as both misguided and corrupt." In foreign policy, Jacksonian populism—and hence the Tea Party movement—supports highly nationalist policies, is committed to American exceptionalism to guide actions toward the rest of the world, and remains skeptical of American leaders seeking to build a liberal global order.

Since at least the Franklin Roosevelt administration, this Jacksonian strain within American political culture has always been a central challenge for the conduct of American foreign policy, and it remains so today. Although the anti-communism of the Cold War years garnered some support among Jacksonians, the other goals and aims of the American administrations during this period did not. With the end of the Cold War, Jacksonians support waned as American leaders sought to expand the liberal international order through the promotion of such initiatives as the Kyoto Protocol, the International Criminal Court, the North American Free Trade Agreement, and the World Trade Organization.

The events of September 11 reversed this Jacksonian skepticism, since an "external threat was immediate and real" for U.S. security. In this sense, the Bush administration's policies gained some support from the Jacksonians, but those policies went too far in not gaining the support of others. In response, the Obama administration's approach to foreign policy moved away from those preferred by these populists—"just as a confluence of foreign and domestic developments are creating a new Jacksonian moment in U.S. politics." As a result, the foreign policy challenge ahead is to "satisfy the Jacksonian requirements at home while seeking to work effectively in the international arena."

Uncertainty remains regarding how the Tea Party movement will shape future foreign policy. International events, of course, will be important, but Mead notes that the division within this movement—between the Palinite wing (followers of Sarah Palin) and the Paulite wing (followers of Ron Paul)—will also shape its impact. The former wing supports a more activist, albeit highly nationalist, involvement on some issues (e.g., terrorism, support for Israel), while the latter opts for a more neo-isolationist foreign policy. Yet both wings "are united in their dislike for liberal internationalism—the attempt to conduct international relations through multilateral institutions." Finally, as Mead concludes, today's Jacksonians "are unlikely to disappear" from the American political landscape. In this sense, this movement is an important shaper of American political culture, and this culture will affect American foreign policy.

The next three chapters address the impact of differing domestic interests on American foreign policy. One looks at the array of established and emerging ethnic interest groups and evaluates their current or potential impact on American foreign policy. A second looks at the role of the Jewish lobby and its impact on American foreign policy toward the Middle East. And the third examines how military experience impacts the attitudes and behaviors of political elites on their support for the use of American force abroad.

In the first of these three chapters, James M. McCormick analyzes the role of "Ethnic Interest Groups in American Foreign Policy." He begins his analysis by identifying the number and types of foreign policy interest groups today. Although the number of such groups is difficult to determine precisely, most estimates place them in the thousands, immediately suggesting the potential impact of such groups in the foreign policy process. These groups cover a broad array of interests—business, labor, agriculture, religious communities, veteran organizations, and a host of single-issue interest groups. Finally, and importantly, such groups include the oldest of these groups—ethnic interest groups. These groups are those "Americans who hold a particular concern for U.S. policy toward the particular country or region of their own or their ancestors' origin."

In the rest of the chapter, McCormick examines the principal and emerging ethnic groups and assesses the influence of each one on American foreign policy at the present time. To make this assessment, he utilizes four characteristics of these groups: (1) the group's ability to provide votes to candidates for office; (2) its ability to make campaign contribution; (3) the extent of its organizational structure to lobby public officials on key issues; and (4) the group's degree of domestic support among the American public.

By these criteria, the most effective ethnic interest group is the Jewish lobby, followed by the Cuban lobby. The former ethnic group possesses a highly effective organizational structure, has significant Jewish populations in key electoral states, and makes substantial contributions to political leaders nationally. Over the years, the Jewish community has also enjoyed widespread political support among the American people and across the political spectrum. The latter ethnic group, the Cuban lobby, does not have the kind of widespread support of the Jewish lobby, but this ethnic group is concentrated in a few key states (namely, Florida and New Jersey) and has a considerable intensity and fervor in carrying out its anti-Castro lobbying effort. Although its intensity and organizational unity has waned in the past decade or so, it remains an example of an effective ethnic interest group. Three other ethnic groups lobbies—the Greek, Turkish, and Armenian lobbies—have periodically enjoyed success on foreign policy issues related to the Middle East. Moreover, they may often find themselves in opposition to one another over these issues. Because these groups do not have the same organizational and political strength of the Jewish and Cuban lobbies, these groups do not enjoy the same degree of success.

In the last part of this chapter, McCormick surveys four emerging ethnic interest groups—the Mexican American, African American, Eastern European, and Indian American ethnic groups. Each has some of the crucial characteristics that may make them successful ethnic interest groups in the future. The Indian American ethnic lobby is the one that comes closest to matching—or even surpassing—some of the principal ethnic groups. Indeed, in terms of its organizational effectiveness, campaign contributions, and level of intensity, this lobby has been likened to the Jewish lobby in affecting American foreign policy. In recent years, the Indian American lobby has had some remarkable impact on American foreign policy on some targeted issues dealing with India.

In all, this chapter draws several conclusions about these ethnic groups and their role in foreign policy. First of all, these groups appear to matter in the foreign policy process, although some are more successful than others. The type of policy issues affects the success of individual groups, and occasionally, these groups work with one another to achieve their common goals. Finally, though, the crucial factor that appears to drive these groups and the intensity of their lobbying is the close personal identity that they have with the group and with issues at hand.

The next chapter, "The Israel Lobby," by John Mearsheimer and Stephen Walt, is an abridged version of a longer piece on this topic published in the *London Review of Books* in March 2006. Their argument is that American policy toward Israel and toward the Middle East is driven less by moral and strategic concerns and more by the impact of the domestic Jewish lobby. And this lobby has been very successful, in their estimate. The United States has provided Israel with substantial foreign assistance on a year-to-year basis, ensured "consistent diplomatic support" through the use of the veto in the UN Security Council on resolutions that were critical of Israel, and made available "top-drawer weaponry."

Mearsheimer and Walt claim that this substantial support cannot be accounted for by strategic or moral considerations. To be sure, Israel did prove an asset to the United States during the Cold War, but Israel also "complicated America's relations with the Arab world." In addition, Israel complicates the efforts against terrorism since America's close ties with Israel partly serve as a source of anti-U.S. terrorism. As a moral imperative, Mearsheimer and Walt do acknowledge that "there is a strong moral case for supporting Israel's existence, but that is not in jeopardy." Instead, they claim that, "viewed objectively," Israel's "past and present conduct offers no moral basis for privileging it over the Palestinians." They also question whether there is an imperative to support Israel so strongly simply because it is a fellow democracy, because of its isolated position in the Middle East, or because of its past history.

Instead, their explanation for the continued American support "is the unmatched power of the Israel Lobby." As they note, this lobby is a "loose coalition of individuals and organizations who actively work to steer U.S. foreign policy in a pro-Israel direction." As such, they map out the nature and extent of the lobby—the organizations and individuals associated with it. Moreover, they argue that its effectiveness is particularly tied to "its influence in Congress," but they also note its impact on the media, think tanks, and the academic community. Mearsheimer and Walt conclude by discussing whether the "Lobby's power can be curtailed." While they are skeptical about that prospect, they do call for more open debate on this topic. Perhaps needless to say, their analysis sparked considerable controversy and a series of exchanges among academics and the public on the issue of foreign policy lobbying.[3] By indirection, their analysis and the discussions also highlight the role that domestic groups—and especially domestic ethnic groups—play in the foreign policy process.

The next chapter, "American Veterans in Government and the Use of Force," by Peter D. Feaver and Christopher Gelpi, points to another kind of societal influence, the military, on one important aspect of American foreign policy—namely, the use of force abroad. In particular, they evaluate how military experience among policymakers affects the propensity of the United States to initiate and escalate the use of force abroad. To examine this relationship, Feaver and Gelpi first identify the number of "militarized disputes" that the United States initiated from 1816 to 1992 and the number of such disputes that were escalated. Next, they determine the degree of military experience among the executive and legislative branches since both branches may impact the use of force abroad. Feaver and Gelpi also consider the impact of the type of disputes abroad—disputes that affect the core values of the United States (what they call "realpolitik" targets) and disputes that do not ("interventionist" targets). Finally, Feaver and Gelpi also enter a number of other "control" variables into their analysis that might plausibly account for America's decision to use or escalate force.

The results "provide strong and striking support" for their argument that as the percentage of military veterans among policymakers increase, the United States is less likely to initiate the use of force abroad. They also found that, as the proportion of policymakers with military experience increases, the propensity to use force against interventionist targets is even less likely than against realpolitik targets. They also report that none of the control variables "can account for the impact of elite veterans" on their results. In addition, Feaver and Gelpi also find that, while policymakers with military experience may be reluctant to initiate force, elite veterans are more likely to support the escalation of American force once some forces have been initiated. In all, then, their results have important substantive implications for the future use of American force abroad, but they also point to the important role that a societal interest, the military, may have on American foreign policy.

The final two chapters in part I take a broader look at societal influences on foreign policy by examining how the public at large affects the foreign policy process. Adam J. Berinsky provides an explanation for public support or opposition to military conflict with particular emphasis on the Iraq War. His "elite cue" theory points to the importance of domestic politics, and particularly partisanship, as crucial for determining such support. In "External Affairs and the Electoral Connection," Miroslav Nincic evaluates how the electoral process and its outcomes can affect America's actions abroad.

In "Events, Elites, and American Public Support for Military Conflict," Adam J. Berinsky advances an explanation for when American public opinion will support or oppose a military conflict. The explanation is fundamentally rooted in domestic politics. His "elite cue" theory argues that the public's decision to support or oppose military actions turns on "listening to trusted sources—those politicians who share their political predispositions." In turn, Berinsky presents evidence from two surveys during the Iraq War to support his theory.

Berinsky's theory, of course, stands in contrast to other leading theories about public support or opposition to conflicts. One traditional view is the "casualties hypothesis" that has been used to account for the level of support or opposition to war. Put simply, as the number of American deaths increases, public support declines. A second conventional explanation points to the success of the mission as the crucial factor for public support. The clearer the objectives of the conflict and their probability of success, the greater the level of public support for American actions in a conflict. Yet Berinsky contends that such "event-response" theories, as he calls them, are problematic for at least three reasons. First, these theories assume more knowledge about politics than is warranted among the public. Second, these theories are based on aggregate analyses of public responses and do not provide any explanation for individual calculations of support or opposition to war. Third, these theories appear to leave out the partisan nature and the impact of *domestic politics* in accounting for war support or opposition.

He thus seeks to address these problems with his elite cue theory. Berinsky begins his theory by drawing on the work of political scientist John Zaller. Zaller argues that the balance of elite discourse on a particular policy position is important as to whether the public will support or oppose a policy. While this focus on elite discourse is important, it is also incomplete. Berinsky contends that the actors on both sides of "a controversy [may] provide persuasive messages." Hence, how does the public decide whether to support or oppose such a policy in this instance? Berinsky contends that it becomes a political choice for the public: "citizens could use the positions of prominent elites [to] . . . decide whether to support or oppose a policy." In this sense, Berinsky expects that day-to-day events about a conflict will have little effect on support or opposition. Instead, the "patterns of elite discourse—the stated positions of leading Democrat and Republican politicians—will play a large role in determining public support for war." In this way, the public take their cues from their preferred partisans, not from foreign events.

To test his theory, Berinsky reports on two surveys that he conducted on support and opposition to the Iraq War. In the first survey experiment, Berinsky's results show that the American public had considerable diffi- culty in estimating the number of war deaths in the Iraq War, and that the estimates individuals made were tied to their political views. In particular, those who are "overestimators" of battle deaths in Iraq tended to be Demo- crats, while "underestimators tend[ed] to be Republicans." Within this first survey, some respondents were provided correct information about the number of deaths for the "underestimators" and "overestimators." Yet such information did not affect their resultant attitudes to the war. In this sense, information about events was not crucial to their position on the war. In a second survey of the public a year later, Berinsky utilized six different survey question wordings, each with varying level of information about the costs and benefits of the Iraq war. Berinsky reports that these differing questions made virtually no difference in levels of support by the public. In this case, he argues that these results imply that the respondents had already decided on the war and that they were not influenced by events or information.

In sum, Berinsky concludes that event-response theories do not explain support or opposition to the Iraq War. Instead, partisanship, as the elite cue theory would predict, was the more likely explanation of the level of sup- port or opposition to the Iraq War. Furthermore, and by implication, this elite cue theory would operate for other conflicts as well.

In the last essay in this section, Miroslav Nincic argues that foreign pol- icy issues "have been a big part of national electoral campaigns since the country's rise to superpower status," and, in this sense, domestic politics and elections shape foreign policy. From the Cold War to today, foreign policy disputes have always figured in presidential campaigns, albeit to a different extent in each one. To demonstrate the importance of foreign policy to the electoral process, Nincic first shows that a significant portion of the public votes on foreign policy in elections and that significant differ- ences exist between Republicans and Democrats over the means and ends of American foreign policy. In the 2000 presidential election, for example, 10 percent of the American public indicated that foreign policy was the most important determinant of their voting choice. In 2004, after the events of 9/11 and during the Iraq War, Nincic reports that "fully half of the electorate considered foreign policy the most important influence on their presidential voting decision." In 2008, the impact of foreign policy reverted closely to the 2000 election, with 10 to 15 percent of the elector- ate considering foreign policy issues the most important issue. Moreover, these foreign policy effects will undoubtedly become more evident in the future, especially since Nincic also reports that Republicans and Democrats prefer different goals for the United States in world affairs. Republicans tend to have a "stronger preference for goals of the self-regarding type," such as "maintaining superior military power, controlling illegal immigration, and protecting American jobs." Democrats have a stronger preference for goals that are "other-regarding," such as "combating world hunger, protecting weak nations from aggression, and strengthening the United Nations." The parties also differ on the means of American foreign policy with Democrats tending to prefer multilateral means and a focus on diplomacy and Republicans tending to prefer unilateral means and a focus on military measures.

In the last part of the chapter, Nincic contends that elections have consequences for American foreign policy in at least two other ways. First, the outcome of elections can bring abrupt change, especially when a new president takes control. Nincic catalogs a series of policy changes across several presidents. This type of shift, Nincic argues, "often reflects the convictions and interests of the incumbent administration's core support groups." In this sense, foreign policy actions "often reflect the logic of domestic politics more closely than objective international reality." Second, important foreign policy decisions or actions by presidents often take the electoral cycle into account. The last year of a presidential term is unlikely to be one in which the president takes new initiatives, as Nincic illustrates by looking at presidential actions toward the Soviet Union during the Cold War and various military interventions since. Interestingly, as his data illustrate, only one American intervention occurred in the fourth year of a president's term (Carter in Iran in 1980), and that with disastrous results. On balance, then, foreign policy plays an important role in the electoral process in terms of both the candidates who are selected by the public and the changes in direction that an administration might undertake toward the rest of the world.

Editor's Note: At the end of each chapter is a series of discussion questions for use by the students and instructor.

NOTES

1. See Chicago Council on Foreign Relations, "A World Transformed: Foreign Policy Attitudes of the U.S. Public after September 11," http://worldviews.org/key_findings/us_911_report.htm, for the immediate results after 9/11. For recent results on American attitudes and how attitudes have changed and remained the same, especially on actions against terrorism, see Chicago Council on Global Affairs, *Constrained Internationalism: Adapting to New Realities, Results of a 2010 National Survey of American Public Opinion* (Chicago: Chicago Council on Global Affairs, 2010).

2. See David Welna, "Democrats Block Funding to Close Guantanamo," May 20, 2009, www.npr.org/templates/story/story.php?storyId=104334339; and Charles Savage, "Closing Guantanamo Fades as a Priority," *New York Times*, June 25, 2010, www.nytimes.com/2010/06/26/us/politics/26gitmo.html.

3. The original article generated so much debate that the *London Review of Books* sponsored a debate on September 28, 2006, at the Great Hall of the Cooper Union (see www.lrb.co.uk/v28/n06/mear9]1_html). *Foreign Policy* magazine devoted a substantial portion of its July/August 2006 issue to this topic as well.

1

The Future of American Power

Dominance and Decline in Perspective

Joseph S. Nye Jr.

The twenty-first century began with a very unequal distribution of power resources. With 5 percent of the world's population, the United States accounted for about a quarter of the world's economic output, was responsible for nearly half of global military expenditures, and had the most extensive cultural and educational soft-power resources. All this is still true, but the future of U.S. power is hotly debated. Many observers have interpreted the 2008 global financial crisis as the beginning of American decline. The National Intelligence Council, for example, has projected that in 2025, "the U.S. will remain the preeminent power, but that American dominance will be much diminished."

Power is the ability to attain the outcomes one wants, and the resources that produce it vary in different contexts. Spain in the sixteenth century took advantage of its control of colonies and gold bullion, the Netherlands in the seventeenth century profited from trade and finance, France in the eighteenth century benefited from its large population and armies, and the United Kingdom in the nineteenth century derived power from its primacy in the Industrial Revolution and its navy. This century is marked by a burgeoning revolution in information technology and globalization, and to understand this revolution, certain pitfalls need to be avoided.

First, one must beware of misleading metaphors of organic decline. Nations are not like humans, with predictable life spans. Rome remained dominant for more than three centuries after the peak of its power, and even then it did not succumb to the rise of another state. For all the fashionable predictions of China, India, or Brazil surpassing the United States in the next decades, the greater threat may come from modern barbarians and nonstate actors. In an information-based world, power diffusion may pose a bigger danger than power transition. Conventional wisdom holds that the state with the largest army prevails, but in the information age, the state (or the nonstate actor) with the best story may sometimes win.

Power today is distributed in a pattern that resembles a complex three-dimensional chess game. On the top chessboard, military power is largely unipolar, and the United States is likely to retain primacy for quite some time. On the middle chessboard, economic power has been multipolar for more than a decade, with the United States, Europe, Japan, and China as the major players and others gaining in importance. The bottom chessboard is the realm of transnational relations. It includes nonstate actors as diverse as bankers who electronically transfer funds, terrorists who traffic weapons, hackers who threaten cybersecurity, and challenges such as pandemics and climate change. On this bottom board, power is widely diffused, and it makes no sense to speak of unipolarity, multipolarity, or hegemony.

In interstate politics, the most important factor will be the continuing return of Asia to the world stage. In 1750, Asia had more than half the world's population and economic output. By 1900, after the Industrial Revolution in Europe and the United States, Asia's share shrank to one-fifth of global economic output. By 2050, Asia will be well on its way back to its historical share. The rise of China and India may create instability, but this is a problem with precedents, and history suggests how policies can affect the outcome.

HEGEMONIC DECLINE?

It is currently fashionable to compare the United States' power to that of the United Kingdom a century ago and to predict a similar hegemonic decline. Some Americans react emotionally to the idea of decline, but it would be counterintuitive and ahistorical to believe that the United States will have a preponderant share of power resources forever. The word "decline" mixes up two different dimensions: absolute decline, in the sense of decay, and relative decline, in which the power resources of other states grow or are used more effectively.

The analogy with British decline is misleading. The United Kingdom had naval supremacy and an empire on which the sun never set, but by World War I, the country ranked only fourth among the great powers in its share of military personnel, fourth in GDP, and third in military spending. With the rise of nationalism, protecting the empire became more of a burden than an asset. For all the talk of an American empire, the United States has more freedom of action than the United Kingdom did. And whereas the United Kingdom faced rising neighbors, Germany and Russia, the United States benefits from being surrounded by two oceans and weaker neighbors.

Despite such differences, Americans are prone to cycles of belief in their own decline. The Founding Fathers worried about comparisons to the Roman Republic. Charles Dickens observed a century and a half ago, "If its individual citizens, to a man, are to be believed, [the United States] always is depressed, and always is stagnated, and always is at an alarming crisis, and never was otherwise." In the last half century, belief in American decline rose after the Soviet Union launched Sputnik in 1957, after President Richard Nixon's economic adjustments and the oil shocks in the 1970s, and after the closing of rust-belt industries and the budget deficits in the Reagan era. Ten years later, Americans believed that the United States was the sole superpower, and now polls show that many believe in decline again.

Pundits lament the inability of Washington to control states such as Afghanistan or Iran, but they allow the golden glow of the past to color their appraisals. The United States' power is not what it used to be, but it also never really was as great as assumed. After World War II, the United States had nuclear weapons and an overwhelming preponderance of economic power but nonetheless was unable to prevent the "loss" of China, to roll back communism in Eastern Europe, to overcome stalemate in the Korean War, to stop the "loss" of North Vietnam, or to dislodge the Castro regime in Cuba. Power measured in resources rarely equals power measured in preferred outcomes, and cycles of belief in decline reveal more about psychology than they do about real shifts in power resources. Unfortunately, mistaken beliefs in decline—at home and abroad—can lead to dangerous mistakes in policy.

CHINA ON THE RISE

For more than a decade, many have viewed China as the most likely contender to balance U.S. power or surpass it. Some draw analogies to the challenge that imperial Germany posed to the United Kingdom at the beginning of the last century. A recent book (by Martin Jacques) is even titled *When China Rules the World: The End of the Western World and the Birth of a New Global Order*. Goldman Sachs has projected that the total size of China's economy will surpass that of the United States in 2027.

Yet China has a long way to go to equal the power resources of the United States, and it still faces many obstacles to its development. Even if overall Chinese GDP passed that of the United States around 2030, the two economies, although roughly equivalent in size, would not be equivalent in composition. China would still have a vast underdeveloped countryside, and it would have begun to face demographic problems from the delayed effects of its one-child policy. Per capita income provides a measure of the sophistication of an economy. Assuming a 6 percent Chinese GDP growth rate and only 2 percent American GDP growth rate after 2030, China would probably not equal the United States in per capita income until sometime around the middle of the century. In other words, China's impressive economic growth rate and increasing population will likely lead the Chinese economy to pass the U.S. economy in total size in a few decades, but that is not the same as equality.

Moreover, linear projections can be misleading, and growth rates generally slow as economies reach higher levels of development. China's authoritarian political system has shown an impressive capability to harness the country's power, but whether the government can maintain that capability over the longer term is a mystery both to outsiders and to Chinese leaders. Unlike India, which was born with a democratic constitution, China has not yet found a way to solve the problem of demands for political participation (if not democracy) that tend to accompany rising per capita income. Whether China can develop a formula that manages an expanding urban middle class, regional inequality, rural poverty, and resentment among ethnic minorities remains to be seen.

Some have argued that China aims to challenge the United States' position in East Asia and, eventually, the world. Even if this were an accurate assessment of China's current intentions (and even the Chinese themselves cannot know the views of future generations), it is doubtful that China will have the military capability to make this possible anytime soon. Moreover, Chinese leaders will have to contend with the reactions of other countries and the constraints created by China's need for external markets and resources. Too aggressive a Chinese military posture could produce a countervailing coalition among China's neighbors that would weaken both its hard and its soft power.

The rise of Chinese power in Asia is contested by both India and Japan (as well as other states), and that provides a major power advantage to the United States. The U.S.-Japanese alliance and the improvement in U.S.-Indian relations mean that China cannot easily expel the Americans from Asia. From that position of strength, the United States, Japan, India, Australia, and others can engage China and provide incentives for it to play a responsible role, while hedging against the possibility of aggressive behavior as China's power grows.

DOMESTIC DECAY?

Some argue that the United States suffers from "imperial overstretch," but so far, the facts do not fit that theory. On the contrary, defense and foreign affairs expenditures have declined as a share of GDP over the past several decades. Nonetheless, the United States could decline not because of imperial overstretch but because of domestic underreach. Rome rotted from within, and some observers, noting the sourness of current U.S. politics, project that the United States will lose its ability to influence world events because of domestic battles over culture, the collapse of its political institutions, and economic stagnation. This possibility cannot be ruled out, but the trends are not as clear as the current gloomy mood suggests.

Although the United States has many social problems—and always has—they do not seem to be getting worse in any linear manner. Some of these problems are even improving, such as rates of crime, divorce, and teenage pregnancy. Although there are culture wars over issues such as same-sex marriage and abortion, polls show an overall increase in tolerance. Civil society is robust, and church attendance is high, at 42 percent. The country's past cultural battles, over immigration, slavery, evolution, temperance, McCarthyism, and civil rights, were arguably more serious than any of today's.

A graver concern would be if the country turned inward and seriously curtailed immigration. With its current levels of immigration, the United States is one of the few developed countries that may avoid demographic decline and keep its share of world population, but this could change if xenophobia or reactions to terrorism closed its borders. The percentage of foreign-born residents in the United States reached its twentieth-century peak, 14.7 percent, in 1910. Today, 11.7 percent of U.S. residents are foreign born, but in 2009, 50 percent of Americans favored decreasing immigration, up from 39 percent in 2008. The economic recession has only aggravated the problem.

Although too rapid a rate of immigration can cause social problems, over the long term, immigration strengthens U.S. power. Today, the United States is the world's third most populous country; fifty years from now, it is likely to still be third (after India and China). Not only is this relevant to economic power, but, given that nearly all developed countries are aging and face the burden of providing for the older generation, immigration could also help reduce the sharpness of the resulting policy problem. In addition, there is a strong correlation between the number of H-1B visas and the number of patents filed in the United States. In 1998, Chinese- and Indian-born engineers were running one-quarter of Silicon Valley's high-tech businesses, and in 2005, immigrants were found to have helped start one of every four American technology start-ups over the previous decade.

Equally important are the benefits of immigration for the United States' soft power. Attracted by the upward mobility of American immigrants, people want to come to the United States. The United States is a magnet, and many people can envisage themselves as Americans. Many successful Americans look like people in other countries. Rather than diluting hard and soft power, immigration enhances both. When Singapore's Lee Kuan Yew concludes that China will not surpass the United States as the leading power of the twenty-first century, he cites the ability of the United States to attract the best and brightest from the rest of the world and meld them into a diverse culture of creativity. China has a larger population to recruit from domestically, but in his view, its Sinocentric culture will make it less creative than the United States, which can draw on the whole world.

However, a failure in the performance of the U.S. economy would be a showstopper. Keeping in mind that macroeconomic forecasts (like weather forecasts) are notoriously unreliable, it appears that the United States will experience slower growth in the decade after the 2008 financial crisis. The International Monetary Fund expects U.S. economic growth to average about two percent in 2014. This is lower than the average over the past several decades but roughly the same as the average rate over the past ten years.

In the 1980s, many observers believed that the U.S. economy had run out of steam and that Germany and Japan were overtaking the United States. The country seemed to have lost its competitive edge. Today, however, even after the financial crisis and the ensuing recession, the World Economic Forum has ranked the United States fourth (after Switzerland, Sweden, and Singapore) in global economic competitiveness. (China, in comparison, was ranked twenty-seventh.) The U.S. economy leads in many new growth sectors, such as information technology, biotechnology, and nanotechnology. And even though optimists tend to cite the United States' dominance in the production and use of information technology, that is not the only source of U.S. productivity. The United States has seen significant agricultural innovation, too, and its openness to globalization, if it continues, will also drive up productivity. Economic experts project that American productivity growth will be between 1.5 and 2.25 percent in the next decade.

In terms of investment in research and development, the United States was the world leader in 2007, with $369 billion, followed by all of Asia ($338 billon) and the European Union ($263 billion). The United States spent 2.7 percent of its GDP on research and development, nearly double what China spent (but slightly less than the 3 percent spent by Japan and South Korea). In 2007, American inventors registered about eighty thousand patents in the United States, or more than the rest of the world combined. A number of reports have expressed concern about problems such as high corporate tax rates, the flight of human capital, and the growing number of overseas patents, but U.S. venture capital firms invest 70 percent of their money in domestic start-ups. A 2009 survey by the Global Entrepreneurship Monitor ranked the United States ahead of other countries in opportunities for entrepreneurship because it has a favorable business culture, the most mature venture capital industry, close relations between universities and industry, and an open immigration policy.

Other concerns about the future of the U.S. economy focus on the current account deficit (whose current level indicates that Americans are becoming more indebted to foreigners) and the rise in government debt. In the words of the historian Niall Ferguson, "This is how empires decline. It begins with a debt explosion." Not only did the recent bank bailout and Keynesian stimulus package add to U.S. debt, but the rising costs of health care and entitlement programs such as Social Security, along with the rising cost of servicing the debt, will also claim large shares of future revenue. Other observers are less alarmist. The United States, they claim, is not like Greece.

The Congressional Budget Office calculates that total government debt will reach 100 percent of GDP by 2023, and many economists begin to worry when debt levels in rich countries exceed 90 percent. But as the *Economist* pointed out last June, "America has two huge advantages over other countries that have allowed it to face its debt with relative equanimity: possessing both the world's reserve currency and its most liquid asset market, in Treasury bonds." And contrary to fears of a collapse of confidence in the dollar, during the financial crisis, the dollar rose and bond yields fell. A sudden crisis of confidence is less the problem than that a gradual increase in the cost of servicing the debt could affect the long-term health of the economy.

It is in this sense that the debt problem is important, and studies suggest that interest rates rise 0.03 percent for every 1 percent increase in the debt-to-GDP ratio over the long term. Higher interest rates mean lower private-sector investment and slower growth. These effects can be mitigated by good policies or exacerbated by bad ones. Increasing debt need not lead to the United States' decline, but it certainly raises the long-term risk.

A well-educated labor force is another key to economic success in the information age. At first glance, the United States does well in this regard. It spends twice as much on higher education as a percentage of GDP as do France, Germany, Japan, and the United Kingdom. The London-based Times Higher Educations 2009 list of the top ten universities includes six in the United States, and a 2010 study by Shanghai Jiao Tong University places seventeen U.S. universities—and no Chinese universities—among its top twenty. Americans win more Nobel Prizes and publish more scientific papers in peer-reviewed journals—three times as many as the Chinese—than do the citizens of any other country. These accomplishments enhance both the country's economic power and its soft power.

American education at its best—many universities and the top slice of the secondary education system—meets or sets the global standard. But American education at its worst—too many primary and secondary schools, especially in less affluent districts—lags badly behind. This means that the quality of the labor force will not keep up with the rising standards needed in an information-driven economy. There is no convincing evidence that students are performing worse than in the past, but the United States' educational advantage is eroding because other countries are doing better than ever. Improvement in the country's K–12 education system will be necessary if the country is to meet the standards needed in an information-based economy.

POLITICS AND INSTITUTIONS

Despite these problems and uncertainties, it seems probable that with the right policies, the U.S. economy can continue to produce hard power for the country. But what about U.S. institutions? The journalist James Fallows, who spent years in China, came home worried less about the United States' economic performance than the gridlock in its political system. In his view, "America still has the means to address nearly any of its structural weaknesses. . . . That is the American tragedy of the early 21st century: a vital and self-renewing culture that attracts the world's talent and a governing system that increasingly looks like a joke." Although political gridlock in a period of recession looks bad, it is difficult to ascertain whether the situation today is much worse than in the past.

Power conversion—translating power resources into desired outcomes— is a long-standing problem for the United States. The U.S. Constitution is based on the eighteenth-century liberal view that power is best controlled by fragmentation and countervailing checks and balances. In foreign policy, the Constitution has always invited the president and Congress to compete for control. Strong economic and ethnic pressure groups struggle for their self-interested definitions of the national interest, and Congress is designed to pay attention to squeaky wheels.

Another cause for concern is the decline of public confidence in government institutions. In 2010, a poll by the Pew Research Center found that 61 percent of respondents thought the United States was in decline, and only 19 percent trusted the government to do what is right most of the time. In 1964, by contrast, three-quarters of the American public said they trusted the federal government to do the right thing most of the time. The numbers have varied somewhat over time, rising after 9/11 before gradually declining again.

The United States was founded in part on a mistrust of government, and its constitution was designed to resist centralized power. Moreover, when asked not about day-to-day government but about the underlying constitutional framework, Americans are very positive. If asked where the best place to live is, the overwhelming majority of them say the United States. If asked whether they like their democratic system of government, nearly everyone says yes. Few people feel the system is rotten and must be overthrown.

Some aspects of the current mood probably represent discontent with the bickering and deadlock in the political process. Compared with the recent past, party politics has become more polarized, but nasty politics is nothing new—as John Adams, Alexander Hamilton, and Thomas Jefferson could attest. Part of the problem with assessing the current atmosphere is that trust in government became abnormally high among the generation that survived the Depression and won World War II. Over the long view of U.S. history, that generation may be the anomaly. Much of the evidence for a loss of trust in government comes from modern polling data, and responses are sensitive to the way questions are asked. The sharpest decline occurred more than four decades ago, during the Johnson and Nixon administrations.

This does not mean that there are no problems with declining confidence in government. If the public became unwilling to pay taxes or comply with laws, or if bright young people refused to go into public service, the government's capacity would be impaired, and people would become more dissatisfied with the government. Moreover, a climate of distrust can trigger extreme actions by deviant members of the population, such as the 1995 bombing of a federal office building in Oklahoma City. Such results could diminish the United States' hard and soft power.

As yet, however, these fears do not seem to have materialized. The Internal Revenue Service has seen no increase in tax cheating. By many accounts, government officials have become less corrupt than in earlier decades, and the World Bank gives the United States a high score (above the 90th percentile) on "control of corruption." The voluntary return of census forms increased to 67 percent in 2000 and was slightly higher in 2010, reversing a thirty-year decline. Voting rates fell from 62 percent to 50 percent over the four decades after 1960, but the decline stopped in 2000 and returned to 58 percent in 2008. In other words, the public's behavior has not changed as dramatically as its responses to poll questions indicates.

How serious are changes in social capital when it comes to the effectiveness of American institutions? The political scientist Robert Putnam notes that community bonds have not weakened steadily over the last century. On the contrary, U.S. history, carefully examined, is a story of ups and downs in civic engagement. Three-quarters of Americans, according to the Pew Partnership for Civic Change, feel connected to their communities and say that the quality of life there is excellent or good. Another of the group's polls found that 111 million Americans had volunteered their time to help solve problems in their communities in the past twelve months and that 60 million volunteer on a regular basis. Forty percent said working together with others in their community was the most important thing they could do.

In recent years, U.S. politics and political institutions have become more polarized than the actual distribution of public opinion would suggest. The situation has been exacerbated by the recent economic downturn. As the

Economist noted, "America's political system was designed to make legislation at the federal level difficult, not easy. . . . So the basic system works; but that is no excuse for ignoring areas where it could be reformed." Some important reforms—such as changing the gerrymandered safe seats in the House of Representatives or altering Senate rules about filibusters—would not require any constitutional amendment. Whether the U.S. political system can reform itself and cope with the problems described above remains to be seen, but it is not as broken as implied by critics who draw analogies to the domestic decay of Rome or other empires.

DEBATING DECLINE

Any net assessment of American power in the coming decades will remain uncertain, but analysis is not helped by misleading metaphors of decline. Declinists should be chastened by remembering how wildly exaggerated U.S. estimates of Soviet power in the 1970s and of Japanese power in the 1980s were. Equally misguided were those prophets of unipolarity who argued a decade ago that the United States was so powerful that it could do as it wished and others had no choice but to follow. Today, some confidently predict that the twenty-first century will see China replace the United States as the world's leading state, whereas others argue with equal confidence that the twenty-first century will be the American century. But unforeseen events often confound such projections. There is always a range of possible futures, not one.

As for the United States' power relative to China's, much will depend on the uncertainties of future political change in China. Barring any political upheaval, China's size and high rate of economic growth will almost certainly increase its relative strength vis-à-vis the United States. This will bring China closer to the United States in power resources, but it does not necessarily mean that China will surpass the United States as the most powerful country—even if China suffers no major domestic political setbacks. Projections based on GDP growth alone are one-dimensional. They ignore U.S. advantages in military and soft power, as well as China's geopolitical disadvantages in the Asian balance of power.

Among the range of possible futures, the more likely are those in which China gives the United States a run for its money but does not surpass it in overall power in the first half of this century. Looking back at history, the British strategist Lawrence Freedman has noted that the United States has "two features which distinguish it from the dominant great powers of the past: American power is based on alliances rather than colonies and is associated with an ideology that is flexible. . . . Together they provide a core of relationships and values to which America can return even after it has overextended itself." And looking to the future, the scholar Anne-Marie Slaughter has argued that the United States' culture of openness and innovation will keep it central in a world where networks supplement, if not fully replace, hierarchical power.

The United States is well placed to benefit from such networks and alliances, if it follows smart strategies. Given Japanese concerns about the rise of Chinese power, Japan is more likely to seek U.S. support to preserve its independence than ally with China. This enhances the United States' position. Unless Americans act foolishly with regard to Japan, an allied East Asia is not a plausible candidate to displace the United States. It matters that the two entities in the world with per capita incomes and sophisticated economies similar to those of the United States—the European Union and Japan—both are U.S. allies. In traditional realist terms of balances of power resources, that makes a large difference for the net position of U.S. power. And in a more positive-sum view of power—that of holding power with, rather than over, other countries—Europe and Japan provide the largest pools of resources for dealing with common transnational problems. Although their interests are not identical to those of the United States, they share overlapping social and governmental networks with it that provide opportunities for cooperation.

On the question of absolute, rather than relative, American decline, the United States faces serious problems in areas such as debt, secondary education, and political gridlock. But they are only part of the picture. Of the multiple possible futures, stronger cases can be made for the positive ones than the negative ones. But among the negative futures, the most plausible is one in which the United States overreacts to terrorist attacks by turning inward and thus cuts itself off from the strength it obtains from openness. Barring such mistaken strategies, however, there are solutions to the major American problems of today. (Long-term debt, for example, could be solved by putting in place, after the economy recovers, spending cuts and consumption taxes that could pay for entitlements.) Of course, such solutions may forever remain out of reach. But it is important to distinguish hopeless situations for which there are no solutions from those that could in principle be solved. After all, the bipartisan reforms of the Progressive era a century ago rejuvenated a badly troubled country.

A NEW NARRATIVE

It is time for a new narrative about the future of U.S. power. Describing power transition in the twenty-first century as a traditional case of hegemonic decline is inaccurate, and it can lead to dangerous policy implications if it encourages China to engage in adventurous policies or the United States to overreact out of fear. The United States is not in absolute decline, and in relative terms, there is a reasonable probability that it will remain more powerful than any single state in the coming decades.

At the same time, the country will certainly face a rise in the power resources of many others—both states and nonstate actors. Because globalization will spread technological capabilities and information technology will allow more people to communicate, U.S. culture and the U.S. economy will become less globally dominant than they were at the start of this century. Yet it is unlikely that the United States will decay like ancient Rome, or even that it will be surpassed by another state, including China.

The problem of American power in the twenty-first century, then, is not one of decline but what to do in light of the realization that even the largest country cannot achieve the outcomes it wants without the help of others. An increasing number of challenges will require the United States to exercise power with others as much as power over others. This, in turn, will require a deeper understanding of power, how it is changing, and how to construct "smart power" strategies that combine hard- and soft-power resources in an information age. The country's capacity to maintain alliances and create networks will be an important dimension of its hard and soft power.

Power is not good or bad per se. It is like calories in a diet: more is not always better. If a country has too few power resources, it is less likely to obtain its preferred outcomes. But too much power (in terms of resources) has often proved to be a curse when it leads to overconfidence and inappropriate strategies. David slew Goliath because Goliath's superior power resources led him to pursue an inferior strategy, which in turn led to his defeat and death. A smart-power narrative for the twenty-first century is not about maximizing power or preserving hegemony. It is about finding ways to combine resources in successful strategies in the new context of power diffusion and "the rise of the rest."

As the largest power, the United States will remain important in global affairs, but the twentieth-century narrative about an American century and American primacy—as well as narratives of American decline—is misleading when it is used as a guide to the type of strategy that will be necessary in the twenty-first century. The coming decades are not likely to see a post-American world, but the United States will need a smart strategy that combines hard- and soft-power resources—and that emphasizes alliances and networks that are responsive to the new context of a global information age.

DISCUSSION QUESTIONS

1. What is the current distribution of power in the world today? Where does the United States land on those dimensions?
2. What is meant by "decline" and has the United States ever experienced or believed in decline previously?
3. How does Nye assess China's rise in power? Is it likely to surpass the United States? What are its problems?
4. What are some areas of America's "domestic decay"? How does immigration fit into the discussion of American power versus other nations?
5. What are American areas of strength in the global community?
6. What are two or three strengths and weaknesses in America's politics and its institutions?
7. To what extent has America experienced an absolute decline? a relative decline? Explain the difference.
8. What does Nye mean when he suggests the need for a "new narrative" about American power?

2

Think Again: American Decline

Gideon Rachman

"WE'VE HEARD ALL THIS ABOUT
AMERICAN DECLINE BEFORE"

This time it's different. It's certainly true that America has been through cycles of declinism in the past. Campaigning for the presidency in 1960, John F. Kennedy complained, "American strength relative to that of the Soviet Union has been slipping, and communism has been advancing steadily in every area of the world." Ezra Vogel's *Japan as Number One* was published in 1979, heralding a decade of steadily rising paranoia about Japanese manufacturing techniques and trade policies.

In the end, of course, the Soviet and Japanese threats to American supremacy proved chimerical. So Americans can be forgiven if they greet talk of a new challenge from China as just another case of the boy who cried wolf. But a frequently overlooked fact about that fable is that the boy was eventually proved right. The wolf did arrive—and China is the wolf.

The Chinese challenge to the United States is more serious for both economic and demographic reasons. The Soviet Union collapsed because its economic system was highly inefficient, a fatal flaw that was disguised for a long time because the USSR never attempted to compete on world markets. China, by contrast, has proved its economic prowess on the global stage. Its economy has been growing at 9 to 10 percent a year, on average, for roughly three decades. It is now the world's leading exporter and its biggest manufacturer, and it is sitting on more than $2.5 trillion of foreign reserves. Chinese goods compete all over the world. This is no Soviet-style economic basket case.

Japan, of course, also experienced many years of rapid economic growth and is still an export powerhouse. But it was a never a plausible candidate to be No. 1. The Japanese population is less than half that of the United States, which means that the average Japanese person would have to be more than twice as rich as the average American before Japan's economy surpassed America's. That was never going to happen. By contrast, China's population is more than four times that of the United States. The famous projection by Goldman Sachs that China's economy will be bigger than that of the United States by 2027 was made before the 2008 economic crash. At the current pace, China could be No. 1 well before then.

China's economic prowess is already allowing Beijing to challenge American influence all over the world. The Chinese are the preferred partners of many African governments and the biggest trading partner of other emerging powers, such as Brazil and South Africa. China is also stepping in to buy the bonds of financially strapped members of the eurozone, such as Greece and Portugal.

And China is only the largest part of a bigger story about the rise of new economic and political players. America's traditional allies in Europe—Britain, France, Italy, even Germany—are slipping down the economic ranks. New powers are on the rise: India, Brazil, Turkey. They each have their own foreign policy preferences, which collectively constrain America's ability to shape the world. Think of how India and Brazil sided with China at the global climate-change talks. Or the votes by Turkey and Brazil against America at the United Nations on sanctions against Iran. That is just a taste of things to come.

"CHINA WILL IMPLODE SOONER OR LATER"

Don't count on it. It is certainly true that when Americans are worrying about national decline, they tend to overlook the weaknesses of their scariest-looking rival. The flaws in the Soviet and Japanese systems became obvious only in retrospect. Those who are confident that American hegemony will be extended long into the future point to the potential liabilities of the Chinese system. In a recent interview with the *Times* of London, former U.S. president George W. Bush suggested that China's internal problems mean that its economy will be unlikely to rival America's in the foreseeable future. "Do I still think America will remain the sole superpower?" he asked. "I do."

But predictions of the imminent demise of the Chinese miracle have been a regular feature of Western analysis ever since it got rolling in the late 1970s. In 1989, the Communist Party seemed to be staggering after the Tiananmen Square massacre. In the 1990s, economy watchers regularly pointed to the parlous state of Chinese banks and state-owned enterprises. Yet the Chinese economy has kept growing, doubling in size roughly every seven years.

Of course, it would be absurd to pretend that China does not face major challenges. In the short term, there is plenty of evidence that a property bubble is building in big cities like Shanghai, and inflation is on the rise. Over the long term, China has alarming political and economic transitions to navigate. The Communist Party is unlikely to be able to maintain its monopoly on political power forever. And the country's traditional dependence on exports and an undervalued currency are coming under increasing criticism from the United States and other international actors demanding a "rebalancing" of China's export-driven economy. The country also faces major demographic and environmental challenges: The population is aging rapidly as a result of the one-child policy, and China is threatened by water shortages and pollution.

Yet even if you factor in considerable future economic and political turbulence, it would be a big mistake to assume that the Chinese challenge to U.S. power will simply disappear. Once countries get the hang of economic growth, it takes a great deal to throw them off course. The analogy to the rise of Germany from the mid-nineteenth century onward is instructive. Germany went through two catastrophic military defeats, hyperinflation, the Great Depression, the collapse of democracy, and the destruction of its major cities and infrastructure by Allied bombs. And yet by the end of the 1950s, West Germany was once again one of the world's leading economies, albeit shorn of its imperial ambitions.

In a nuclear age, China is unlikely to get sucked into a world war, so it will not face turbulence and disorder on remotely the scale Germany did in the twentieth century. And whatever economic and political difficulties it does experience will not be enough to stop the country's rise to great-power status. Sheer size and economic momentum mean that the Chinese juggernaut will keep rolling forward, no matter what obstacles lie in its path.

"AMERICA STILL LEADS ACROSS THE BOARD"

For now. As things stand, America has the world's largest economy, the world's leading universities, and many of its biggest companies. The U.S. military is also incomparably more powerful than any rival. The United States spends almost as much on its military as the rest of the world put together. And let's also add in America's intangible assets. The country's combination of entrepreneurial flair and technological prowess has allowed it to lead the technological revolution. Talented immigrants still flock to U.S.

shores. And now that Barack Obama is in the White House, the country's soft power has received a big boost. For all his troubles, polls show Obama is still the most charismatic leader in the world; Hu Jintao doesn't even come close. America also boasts the global allure of its creative industries (Hollywood and all that), its values, the increasing universality of the English language, and the attractiveness of the American Dream.

All true—but all more vulnerable than you might think. American universities remain a formidable asset. But if the U.S. economy is not generating jobs, then those bright Asian graduate students who fill up the engineering and computer science departments at Stanford University and MIT will return home in larger numbers. *Fortune's* latest ranking of the world's largest companies has only two American firms in the top ten—Walmart at No. 1 and ExxonMobil at No. 3. There are already three Chinese firms in the top ten: Sinopec, State Grid, and China National Petroleum. America's appeal might also diminish if the country is no longer so closely associated with opportunity, prosperity, and success. And though many foreigners are deeply attracted to the American Dream, there is also a deep well of anti-American sentiment in the world that al Qaeda and others have skillfully exploited, Obama or no Obama.

As for the U.S. military, the lesson of the Iraq and Afghan wars is that America's martial prowess is less useful than former defense secretary Donald Rumsfeld and others imagined. U.S. troops, planes, and missiles can overthrow a government on the other side of the world in weeks, but pacifying and stabilizing a conquered country is another matter. Years after apparent victory, America is still bogged down by an apparently endless insurgency in Afghanistan.

Not only are Americans losing their appetite for foreign adventures, but the U.S. military budget is also clearly going to come under pressure in this new age of austerity. The present paralysis in Washington offers little hope that the United States will deal with its budgetary problems swiftly or efficiently. The U.S. government's continuing reliance on foreign lending makes the country vulnerable, as Secretary of State Hillary Clinton's humbling 2009 request to the Chinese to keep buying U.S. Treasury bills revealed. America is funding its military supremacy through deficit spending, meaning the war in Afghanistan is effectively being paid for with a Chinese credit card. Little wonder that Adm. Mike Mullen, [former] chairman of the Joint Chiefs of Staff, has identified the burgeoning national debt as the single largest threat to U.S. national security.

Meanwhile, China's spending on its military continues to grow rapidly. The country will soon announce the construction of its first aircraft carrier and is aiming to build five or six in total. Perhaps more seriously, China's development of new missile and anti-satellite technology threatens the command of the sea and skies on which the United States bases its Pacific supremacy. In a nuclear age, the U.S. and Chinese militaries are unlikely to clash. A common Chinese view is that the United States will instead eventually find it can no longer afford its military position in the Pacific. U.S. allies in the region—Japan, South Korea, and increasingly India—may partner more with Washington to try to counter rising Chinese power. But if the United States has to scale back its presence in the Pacific for budgetary reasons, its allies will start to accommodate themselves to a rising China. Beijing's influence will expand, and the Asia-Pacific region—the emerging center of the global economy—will become China's backyard.

"GLOBALIZATION IS BENDING THE WORLD THE WAY OF THE WEST"

Not really. One reason why the United States was relaxed about China's rise in the years after the end of the Cold War was the deeply ingrained belief that globalization was spreading Western values. Some even thought that globalization and Americanization were virtually synonymous.

Pundit Fareed Zakaria was prescient when he wrote that the "rise of the rest" (i.e., non-American powers) would be one of the major features of a "post-American world." But even Zakaria argued that this trend was essentially beneficial to the United States: "The power shift . . . is good for America, if approached properly. The world is going America's way. Countries are becoming more open, market-friendly, and democratic."

Both George W. Bush and Bill Clinton took a similar view that globalization and free trade would serve as a vehicle for the export of American values. In 1999, two years before China's accession to the World Trade Organization, Bush argued, "Economic freedom creates habits of liberty. And habits of liberty create expectations of democracy. . . . Trade freely with China, and time is on our side."

There were two important misunderstandings buried in this theorizing. The first was that economic growth would inevitably—and fairly swiftly— lead to democratization. The second was that new democracies would inevitably be more friendly and helpful toward the United States. Neither assumption is working out.

In 1989, after the Tiananmen Square massacre, few Western analysts would have believed that twenty years later China would still be a one-party state—and that its economy would also still be growing at phenomenal rates. The common (and comforting) Western assumption was that China would have to choose between political liberalization and economic failure. Surely a tightly controlled one-party state could not succeed in the era of cell phones and the World Wide Web? As Clinton put it during a visit to China in 1998, "In this global information age, when economic success is built on ideas, personal freedom is . . . essential to the greatness of any modern nation."

In fact, China managed to combine censorship and one-party rule with continuing economic success over the following decade. The confrontation between the Chinese government and Google in 2010 was instructive. Google, that icon of the digital era, threatened to withdraw from China in protest at censorship, but it eventually backed down in return for token concessions. It is now entirely conceivable that when China becomes the world's largest economy—let us say in 2027—it will still be a one-party state run by the Communist Party.

And even if China does democratize, there is absolutely no guarantee that this will make life easier for the United States, let alone prolong America's global hegemony. The idea that democracies are liable to agree on the big global issues is now being undermined on a regular basis. India does not agree with the United States on climate change or the Doha round of trade talks. Brazil does not agree with the United States on how to handle Venezuela or Iran. A more democratic Turkey is today also a more Islamist Turkey, which is now refusing to take the American line on either Israel or Iran. In a similar vein, a more democratic China might also be a more prickly China, if the popularity of nationalist books and Internet sites in the Middle Kingdom is any guide.

"GLOBALIZATION IS NOT A ZERO-SUM GAME"

Don't be too sure. Successive U.S. presidents, from the first Bush to Obama, have explicitly welcomed China's rise. Just before his first visit to China, Obama summarized the traditional approach when he said, "Power does not need to be a zero-sum game, and nations need not fear the success of another . . . we welcome China's efforts to play a greater role on the world stage."

But whatever they say in formal speeches, America's leaders are clearly beginning to have their doubts, and rightly so. It is a central tenet of modern economics that trade is mutually beneficial for both partners, a win-win rather than a zero-sum. But that implies the rules of the game aren't rigged. Speaking before the 2010 World Economic Forum, Larry Summers, then Obama's chief economic advisor, remarked pointedly that the normal rules about the mutual benefits of trade do not necessarily apply when one trading partner is practicing mercantilist or protectionist policies. The U.S. government clearly thinks that China's undervaluation of its currency is a form of protectionism that has led to global economic imbalances and job losses in the United States. Leading economists, such as *New York Times* columnist Paul Krugman and the Peterson Institute's C. Fred Bergsten, have taken a similar line, arguing that tariffs or other retaliatory measures would be a legitimate response. So much for the win-win world.

And when it comes to the broader geopolitical picture, the world of the future looks even more like a zero-sum game, despite the gauzy rhetoric of globalization that comforted the last generation of American politicians. For the United States has been acting as if the mutual interests created by globalization have repealed one of the oldest laws of international politics: the notion that rising players eventually clash with established powers.

In fact, rivalry between a rising China and a weakened America is now apparent across a whole range of issues, from territorial disputes in Asia to human rights. It is mercifully unlikely that the United States and China would ever actually go to war, but that is because both sides have nuclear weapons, not because globalization has magically dissolved their differences.

At the G-20 summit in November 2010, the U.S. drive to deal with "global economic imbalances" was essentially thwarted by China's obdurate refusal to change its currency policy. The 2009 climate-change talks in Copenhagen ended in disarray after another U.S.-China standoff. Growing Chinese economic and military clout clearly poses a long-term threat to American hegemony in the Pacific. The Chinese reluctantly agreed to a new package of UN sanctions on Iran, but the cost of securing Chinese agreement was a weak deal that is unlikely to derail the Iranian nuclear program. Both sides have taken part in the talks with North Korea, but a barely submerged rivalry prevents truly effective Sino-American cooperation. China does not like Kim Jong-il's [now Kim Jong-un's] regime, but it is also very wary of a reunified Korea on its borders, particularly if the new Korea still played host to U.S. troops. China is also competing fiercely for access to resources, in particular oil, which is driving up global prices.

American leaders are right to reject zero-sum logic in public. To do anything else would needlessly antagonize the Chinese. But that shouldn't obscure this unavoidable fact: As economic and political power moves from West to East, new international rivalries are inevitably emerging.

The United States still has formidable strengths. Its economy will eventually recover. Its military has a global presence and a technological edge that no other country can yet match. But America will never again experience the global dominance it enjoyed in the seventeen years between the Soviet Union's collapse in 1991 and the financial crisis of 2008. Those days are over.

DISCUSSION QUESTIONS

1. How do the previous challengers to U.S. hegemony differ from China today?
2. What are some American foreign policy goals affected by the rise of China?
3. What issues are potential hindrances to China's rise?
4. In addition to having the world's largest economy, what are some other strengths of the United States?
5. How does Rachman question the Clinton/Bush assumptions about the impact of globalization and free trade on China?
6. What is the greatest threat to the United States today?
7. Can the United States take any effective actions to slow its decline?

3

The Tea Party, Populism, and the Domestic Culture of U.S. Foreign Policy

Walter Russell Mead

During the night of December 16, 1773, somewhere between 30 and 130 men, a few disguised as Mohawk Indians, boarded three merchant ships in Boston Harbor and destroyed 342 chests of tea to protest duties imposed by the British parliament. Samuel Adams was widely considered to be the ringleader of the demonstration. The historical record is ambiguous; he disclaimed all responsibility while doing everything possible to publicize the event. The next year, a more decorous "tea party" occurred in Edenton, North Carolina, when Mrs. Penelope Barker convened fifty-one women to support the colony's resistance to British taxation. Tea was neither destroyed nor consumed, but something even more momentous happened that day: Barker's gathering is believed to have been the first women's political meeting in British North America.

Both tea parties stirred British opinion. Although prominent Whigs, such as John Wilkes and Edmund Burke, supported the Americans against King George III and his handpicked government, the lawlessness of Boston and the unheard-of political activism of the women of Edenton seemed proof to many in the mother country that the colonials were violent and barbaric. The idea of a women's political meeting was shocking enough to merit coverage in the London press, where the resolutions taken by the Edenton activists were reprinted in full. The British writer Samuel Johnson published a pamphlet denouncing the colonials' tea parties and their arguments against imperial taxation, writing, "These antipatriotic prejudices are the abortions of folly impregnated by faction."

Today, tea parties have returned, and Johnson's objections still resonate. The modern Tea Party movement began in February 2009 as an on-air rant by a CNBC financial reporter who, from the floor of the Chicago Mercantile

Exchange, called for a Chicago tea party to protest the taxpayer-financed bailout of mortgage defaulters. Objecting to what they saw as the undue growth of government spending and government power under President Barack Obama, Republicans and like-minded independents (backed by wealthy sympathizers) soon built a network of organizations across the United States. Energized to some degree by persistently favorable coverage on Fox News (and perhaps equally energized by less sympathetic treatment in what the Tea Party heroine Sarah Palin has dubbed "the lamestream media"), Tea Party activists rapidly shook up American politics and contributed to the wave of anti-big-government sentiment that made the 2010 elections a significant Democratic defeat.

The rise of the Tea Party movement has been the most controversial and dramatic development in U.S. politics in many years. Supporters have hailed it as a return to core American values; opponents have seen it as a racist, reactionary, and ultimately futile protest against the emerging reality of a multicultural, multiracial United States and a new era of government activism.

To some degree, this controversy is impossible to resolve. The Tea Party movement is an amorphous collection of individuals and groups that range from center right to the far fringes of American political life. It lacks a central hierarchy that can direct the movement or even declare who belongs to it and who does not. As the Tea Party label became better known, all kinds of people sought to hitch their wagons to this rising star. Affluent suburban libertarians, rural fundamentalists, ambitious pundits, unreconstructed racists, and fiscally conservative housewives all can and do claim to be Tea Party supporters.

[Former] Fox News host Glenn Beck may be the most visible spokesperson for the Tea Party, but his religious views (extremely strong and very Mormon) hardly typify the movement, in which libertarians are often more active than social conservatives and Ayn Rand is a more influential prophet than Brigham Young. There is little evidence that the reading lists and history lessons that Beck offer[ed] on his nightly program appeal[ed] to more than a small percentage of the movement's supporters. (In a March 2010 public opinion poll, 37 percent of respondents expressed support for the Tea Party, suggesting that about 115 million Americans sympathize at least partly with the movement; Beck's audience on Fox averag[ed] 2.6 million.)

Other prominent political figures associated with the Tea Party also send a contradictory mix of messages. The Texas congressman Ron Paul and his (somewhat less doctrinaire) son, the newly elected Kentucky senator Rand Paul, come close to resurrecting isolationism. The conservative commentator Pat Buchanan echoes criticisms of the U.S.-Israeli alliance made by such scholars as John Mearsheimer. Palin, however, is a full-throated supporter of the "war on terror" and, as governor of Alaska, kept an Israeli flag in her office.

If the movement resists easy definition, its impact on the November 2010 midterm elections is also hard to state with precision. On the one hand, the excitement that Tea Party figures such as Palin brought to the Republican campaign clearly helped the party attract candidates, raise money, and get voters to the polls in an off-year election. The GOP victory in the House of Representatives, the largest gain by either major party since 1938, would likely have been much less dramatic without the energy generated by the Tea Party. On the other hand, public doubts about some Tea Party candidates, such as Delaware's Christine O'Donnell, who felt it necessary to buy advertising time to tell voters, "I am not a witch," probably cost Republicans between two and four seats in the Senate, ending any chance for a GOP takeover of that chamber.

In Alaska, Palin and the Tea Party leaders endorsed the senatorial candidate Joe Miller, who defeated the incumbent Lisa Murkowski in the Republican primary. Miller went on to lose the general election, however, after Murkowski organized the first successful write-in campaign for the U.S. Senate since Strom Thurmond was elected from South Carolina in 1954. If libertarian Alaska rejects a Palin-endorsed Tea Party candidate, then there are reasons to doubt the movement's long-term ability to dominate politics across the rest of the country.

But with all its ambiguities and its uneven political record, the Tea Party movement has clearly struck a nerve in American politics, and students of American foreign policy need to think through the consequences of this populist and nationalist political insurgency. That is particularly true because the U.S. constitutional system allows minorities to block appointments and important legislation through filibusters and block the ratification of treaties with only one-third of the Senate. For a movement of "No!" like the Tea Party, those are powerful legislative tools. As is so often the case in the United States, to understand the present and future of American politics, one must begin by coming to grips with the past. The Tea Party movement taps deep roots in U.S. history, and past episodes of populist rebellion can help one think intelligently about the trajectory of the movement today.

Historian Jill Lepore's book *The Whites of Their Eyes* makes the point that many Tea Party activists have a crude understanding of the politics of the American Revolution. Yet however unsophisticated the Tea Party's reading of the past may be, the movement's appeal to colonial history makes sense. From colonial times, resentment of the well-bred, the well-connected, and the well-paid has merged with suspicion about the motives and methods of government insiders to produce populist rebellions against the established political order. This form of American populism is often called

"Jacksonianism" after Andrew Jackson, the president who tapped this populist energy in the 1830s to remake the United States' party system and introduce mass electoral politics into the country for good. . . .

Jacksonian populism does not always have a clear-cut program. In the nineteenth century, the Jacksonians combined a strong aversion to government debt with demands that the government's most valuable asset (title to the vast public lands of the West) be transferred to homesteaders at no cost. Today's Jacksonians want the budget balanced—but are much less enthusiastic about cutting middle-class entitlement programs such as Social Security and Medicare.

Intellectually, Jacksonian ideas are rooted in the commonsense tradition of the Scottish Enlightenment. This philosophy—that moral, scientific, political, and religious truths can be ascertained by the average person—is more than an intellectual conviction in the United States; it is a cultural force. Jacksonians regard supposed experts with suspicion, believing that the credentialed and the connected are trying to advance their own class agenda. These political, economic, scientific, or cultural elites often want to assert truths that run counter to the commonsense reasoning of Jacksonian America. That federal deficits produce economic growth and that free trade with low-wage countries raises Americans' living standards are the kind of propositions that clash with the common sense of many Americans. In the not-too-distant past, so did the assertion that people of different races deserved equal treatment before the law. . . .

The Tea Party movement is best understood as a contemporary revolt of Jacksonian common sense against elites perceived as both misguided and corrupt. And although the movement itself may splinter and even disappear, the populist energy that powers it will not go away soon. Jacksonianism is always an important force in American politics; at times of social and economic stress and change, like the present, its importance tends to grow. Even though it is by no means likely that the new Jacksonians will gain full control of the government anytime soon (or perhaps ever), the influence of the populist revolt against mainstream politics has become so significant that students of U.S. foreign policy must consider its consequences.

In foreign policy, Jacksonians embrace a set of strongly nationalist ideas. They combine a firm belief in American exceptionalism and an American world mission with deep skepticism about the United States' ability to create a liberal world order. They draw a sharp contrast between the Lockean political order that prevails at home with what they see as a Hobbesian international system: in a competitive world, each sovereign state must place its own interests first. They intuitively accept a Westphalian view of international relations: what states do domestically may earn one's contempt, but a country should only react when states violate their international obligations or attack it. When the United States is attacked, they believe in total war leading to the unconditional surrender of the enemy. They are prepared to support wholesale violence against enemy civilians in the interest of victory; they do not like limited wars for limited goals. Although they value allies and believe that the United States must honor its word, they do not believe in institutional constraints on the United States' freedom to act, unilaterally if necessary, in self-defense. Historically, Jacksonians have never liked international economic agreements or systems that limit the U.S. government's ability to pursue loose credit policies at home.

Finding populist support for U.S. foreign policy has been the central domestic challenge for policymakers ever since President Franklin Roosevelt struggled to build domestic support for an increasingly interventionist policy vis-à-vis the Axis powers. The Japanese solved Roosevelt's problem by attacking Pearl Harbor, but his sensitivity to Jacksonian opinion did not end with the United States' entry into World War II. From his embrace of unconditional surrender as a war objective to his internment of Japanese Americans, Roosevelt always had a careful eye out for the concerns of this constituency. If he had thought Jacksonian America would have accepted the indefinite stationing of hundreds of thousands of U.S. troops abroad, he might have taken a harder line with the Soviet Union on the future of Eastern Europe.

The need to attract and hold populist support also influenced Harry Truman's foreign policy, particularly his approach to Soviet expansionism and larger questions of world order. Key policymakers in the Truman administration, such as Secretary of State Dean Acheson, believed that the collapse of the United Kingdom as a world power had left a vacuum that the United States had no choice but to fill. The United Kingdom had historically served as the gyroscope of world order, managing the international economic system, keeping the sea lanes open, and protecting the balance of power in the chief geostrategic theaters of the world. Truman administration officials agreed that the Great Depression and World War II could in large part be blamed on the United States' failure to take up the burden of global leadership as the United Kingdom declined. The Soviet disruption of the balance of power in Europe and the Middle East after World War II was, they believed, exactly the kind of challenge to world order that the United States now had to meet.

The problem, as policymakers saw it, was that Jacksonian opinion was not interested in assuming the mantle of the United Kingdom. The Jacksonians were ready to act against definite military threats and, after two world wars, were prepared to support a more active security policy overseas in the 1940s than they were in the 1920s. But to enlist their support for a far-reaching foreign policy, Truman and Acheson believed that it was necessary to define U.S. foreign policy in terms of opposing the Soviet Union and its communist ideology rather than as an effort to secure a liberal world order.

Acheson's decision to be "clearer than truth" when discussing the threat of communism and Truman's decision to take Senator Arthur Vandenberg's advice and "scare [the] hell out of the country" ignited populist fears about the Soviet Union, which helped the administration get congressional support for aid to Greece and Turkey and the Marshall Plan. Political leaders at the time concluded that without such appeals, Congress would not have provided the requested support, and historians generally agree.

But having roused the sleeping dogs of anticommunism, the Truman administration would spend the rest of its time in office trying (and sometimes failing) to cope with the forces it had unleashed. Once convinced that communism was an immediate threat to national security, the Jacksonians wanted a more hawkish policy than Acheson and his planning chief, George Kennan, thought was wise. The success of Mao Zedong's revolution in China—and the seeming indifference of the Truman administration to the fate of the world's most populous country and its network of missionary institutions and Christian converts—inflamed Jacksonian opinion and set the stage for Senator Joseph McCarthy's politics of paranoia in the 1950s.

Communism was in many ways a perfect enemy for Jacksonian America, and for the next forty years, public opinion sustained the high defense budgets and foreign military commitments required to fight it. The priorities of the Cold War from a Jacksonian perspective—above all, the military containment of communism wherever communists, or left-wing nationalists willing to ally with them, were active—did not always fit comfortably with the Hamiltonian (commercial and realist) and Wilsonian (idealist and generally multilateral) priorities held by many U.S. policymakers. But in general, the mix of policies necessary to promote a liberal world order was close enough to what was needed to wage a struggle against the Soviets that the liberal-world-order builders were able to attract enough Jacksonian support for their project. The need to compete with the Soviets provided a rationale for a whole series of U.S. initiatives—the development of a liberal trading system under the General Agreement on Tariffs and Trade; Marshall Plan aid tied to the promotion of European economic integration; development assistance in Africa, Asia, and Latin America—that also had the effect of building a new international system encompassing the noncommunist world.

This approach enabled the United States to win the Cold War and build a flexible, dynamic, and reasonably stable international system that, after 1989, gradually and for the most part peacefully absorbed the majority of the former communist states. It did, however, leave a political vulnerability at the core of the U.S. foreign policy debate, a vulnerability that threatens to become much more serious going forward: today's Jacksonians are ready and willing to do whatever it takes to defend the United States, but they do not believe that U.S. interests are best served by the creation of a liberal and cosmopolitan world order.

After the Soviet Union disobligingly collapsed in 1991, the United States endeavored to maintain and extend its efforts to build a liberal world order. On the one hand, these projects no longer faced the opposition of a single determined enemy; on the other hand, American leaders had to find domestic support for complex, risky, and expensive foreign initiatives without invoking the Soviet threat.

This did not look difficult at first. In the heady aftermath of the 1989 revolutions in Eastern Europe, it seemed to many as if the task would be so easy and so cheap that U.S. policymakers could cut defense and foreign aid budgets while a liberal world order largely constructed itself. No powerful states or ideologies opposed the principles of the American world order, and both the economic agenda of liberalizing trade and finance and the Wilsonian agenda of extending democracy were believed to be popular at home and abroad.

Clear domestic constraints on U.S. foreign policy began to appear during the 1990s. The Clinton administration devoted intense efforts to cultivating obstructionist legislators, such as Senator Jesse Helms of North Carolina, but it was increasingly unable to get the resources and support needed to carry out what it believed were important elements of the United States' agenda abroad. Congress balked at paying the country's UN dues in a timely fashion and, after the GOP congressional takeover in 1994, opposed a range of proposed and actual military interventions. The Senate recoiled from treaties such as the Kyoto Protocol and refused to join the International Criminal Court. The relentless decline in support for free trade after the bitter fights over the ratification of the North American Free Trade Agreement and U.S. entry into the new World Trade Organization in the early 1990s left U.S. diplomats negotiating within a tightening range of constraints, which soon led to a steady deceleration in the construction of a liberal global trading regime.

September 11, 2001, changed this. The high level of perceived threat after the attacks put U.S. foreign policy back to the position it had enjoyed in 1947–1948: convinced that an external threat was immediate and real, the public was ready to support enormous expenditures of treasure and blood to counter it. Jacksonians cared about foreign policy again, and the George W. Bush administration had an opportunity to repeat the accomplishment of the Truman administration by using public concern about a genuine security threat to energize public support for a far-reaching program of building a liberal world order.

Historians will be discussing for years to come why the Bush administration missed this opportunity. It may be that in the years after 9/11, the administration was so determined to satisfy domestic Jacksonian opinion that it constructed a response to terrorism—the kind of no-holds-barred total war preferred by Jacksonians—that would inevitably undercut its ability to engage with key partners at home and abroad. In any case, by January 2009, the United States was engaged in two wars and a variety of counterterrorism activities around the world but lacked anything like a domestic consensus on even the broadest outlines of foreign policy.

The Obama administration came into office believing that the Bush administration had been too Jacksonian and that its resulting policy choices were chaotic, incoherent, and self-defeating. Uncritically pro-Israel, unilateralist, indifferent to the requirements of international law, too quick to respond with force, contemptuous of international institutions and norms, blind to the importance of non-terrorism-related threats such as climate change, and addicted to polarizing, us-against-them rhetoric, the Bush administration was, the incoming Democrats believed, a textbook case of Jacksonianism run wild. Recognizing the enduring power of Jacksonians in U.S. politics but convinced that their ideas were wrong-headed and outdated, the Obama administration decided that it would make what it believed were the minimum necessary concessions to Jacksonian sentiments while committing itself to a set of policies intended to build a world order on a largely Wilsonian basis. Rather than embracing the "global war on terror" as an overarching strategic umbrella under which it could position a range of aid, trade, and institution-building initiatives, it has repositioned the terrorism threat as one among many threats the United States faces and has separated its world-order-building activities from its vigorous work to combat terrorism.

It is much too early to predict how this will turn out, but it is already clear that the Obama administration faces serious challenges in building support for its foreign policy in a polarized, and to some degree traumatized, domestic environment. The administration is trying to steer U.S. foreign policy away from Jacksonian approaches just as a confluence of foreign and domestic developments are creating a new Jacksonian moment in U.S. politics. The United States faces a continuing threat of terrorism involving domestic as well as foreign extremists, a threat from China that includes both international security challenges in Asia and a type of economic rivalry that Jacksonians associate with the economic woes of the middle class, and a looming federal debt crisis that endangers both the prosperity and the security of the country. The combination of these threats with the perceived cultural and social conflict between "arrogant" elites with counterintuitive ideas and "average" Americans relying on common sense creates the ideal conditions for a major Jacksonian storm in U.S. politics. The importance of the Jacksonian resurgence goes beyond the political problems of the Obama administration; the development of foreign policy strategies that can satisfy Jacksonian requirements at home while also working effectively in the international arena is likely to be the greatest single challenge facing U.S. administrations for some time to come.

Forecasting how this newly energized populist movement will influence foreign policy is difficult. Public opinion is responsive to events; a terrorist attack inside U.S. borders or a crisis in East Asia or the Middle East could transform the politics of U.S. foreign policy overnight. A further worsening of the global economic situation could further polarize the politics of both domestic and foreign policy in the United States.

Nevertheless, some trends seem clear. The first is that the contest in the Tea Party between what might be called its Palinite and its Paulite wings will likely end in a victory for the Palinites. Ron Paul represents an inward-looking, neo-isolationist approach to foreign policy that has more in common with classic Jeffersonian ideas than with assertive Jacksonian nationalism. Although both wings share, for example, a visceral hostility to anything that smacks of "world government," Paul and his followers look for ways to avoid contact with the world, whereas such contemporary Jacksonians as Sarah Palin and Fox News host Bill O'Reilly would rather win than withdraw. "We don't need to be the world's policeman," says Paul. Palin might say something similar, but she would be quick to add that we also do not want to give the bad guys any room.

Similarly, the Palinite wing of the Tea Party wants a vigorous, proactive approach to the problem of terrorism in the Middle East, one that rests on a close alliance between the United States and Israel. The Paulite wing would rather distance the United States from Israel as part of a general reduction of the United States' profile in a part of the world from which little good can be expected. The Paulites are likely to lose this contest because the commonsense reasoning of the American people now generally takes as axiomatic something that seemed much more controversial in the 1930s: that security at home cannot be protected without substantial engagement overseas. The rise of China and the sullen presence of the threat of terrorism reinforce this perception, and the more dangerous the world feels, the more Jacksonian America sees a need to prepare, to seek reliable allies, and to act. A period like that between 1989 and 2001, when Jacksonian America did not identify any serious threats from abroad, is unlikely to arise anytime soon; the great mass of Tea Party America does not seem headed toward a new isolationism.

Jacksonian support for Israel will also be a factor. Sympathetic to Israel and concerned about both energy security and terrorism, Jacksonians are likely to accept and even demand continued U.S. diplomatic, political, and military engagement in the Middle East. Not all American Jacksonians back Israel, but in general, rising Jacksonian political influence in the United States will lead to stronger support in Washington for the Jewish state. This support does not proceed simply from evangelical Christian influence. Many Jacksonians are not particularly religious, and many of the pro-Jacksonian "Reagan Democrats" are Roman Catholics. But Jacksonians admire Israeli courage and self-reliance—and they do not believe that Arab governments are trustworthy or reliable allies. They are generally untroubled by Israeli responses to terrorist attacks, which many observers deem "disproportionate." Jacksonian common sense does not give much weight to the concept of disproportionate force, believing that if you are attacked, you have the right and even the duty to respond with overwhelming force until the enemy surrenders. That may or may not be a viable strategy in the modern Middle East, but Jacksonians generally accept Israel's right to defend itself in whatever way it chooses. They are more likely to criticize Israel for failing to act firmly in Gaza and southern Lebanon than to criticize it for overreacting to terrorist attacks. Jacksonians still believe that the use of nuclear weapons against Japan in 1945 was justified; they argue that military strength is there to be used.

Any increase in Jacksonian political strength makes a military response to the Iranian nuclear program more likely. Although the public's reaction to the progress of North Korea's nuclear program has been relatively mild, recent polls show that up to 64 percent of the U.S. public favors military strikes to end the Iranian nuclear program. Deep public concerns over oil and Israel, combined with memories of the 1979 Iranian hostage crisis among older Americans, put Iran's nuclear program in Jacksonians' cross hairs. Polls show that more than 50 percent of the public believes the United States should defend Israel against Iran—even if Israel sets off hostilities by launching the first strike. Many U.S. presidents have been dragged into war reluctantly by aroused public opinion; to the degree that Congress and the public are influenced by Jacksonian ideas, a president who allows Iran to get nuclear weapons without using military action to try to prevent it would face political trouble. (Future presidents should, however, take care. Military engagements undertaken without a clear strategy for victory can backfire disastrously. Lyndon Johnson committed himself to war in Southeast Asia because he believed, probably correctly, that Jacksonian fury at a communist victory in Vietnam would undermine his domestic goals. The story did not end well.)

On other issues, Paulites and Palinites are united in their dislike for liberal internationalism—the attempt to conduct international relations through multilateral institutions under an ever-tightening web of international laws and treaties. From climate change to the International Criminal Court to the treatment of enemy combatants captured in unconventional conflicts, both wings of the Tea Party reject liberal internationalist ideas and will continue to do so. The U.S. Senate, in which each state is allotted two senators regardless of the state's population, heavily favors the less populated states, where Jacksonian sentiment is often strongest. The United States is unlikely to ratify many new treaties written in the spirit of liberal internationalism for some time to come.

The new era in U.S. politics could see foreign policy elites struggling to receive a hearing for their ideas from a skeptical public. "The Council on Foreign Relations," the pundit Beck said in January 2010, "was a progressive idea of, let's take media and eggheads and figure out what the idea is, what the solution is, then teach it to the media, and they'll let the masses know what should be done." Tea Partiers intend to be vigilant to ensure that elites with what the movement calls their "one-world government" ideas and bureaucratic agendas of class privilege do not dominate foreign policy debates. The United States may return to a time when prominent political leaders found it helpful to avoid too public an association with institutions and ideas perceived as distant from, and even hostile to, the interests and values of Jacksonian America.

Concern about China has been growing for some time in American opinion, and the Jacksonian surge makes it more likely that the simmering anger and resentment will come to a boil. Free trade is an issue that has historically divided populists in the United States (agrarians have tended to like it; manufacturing workers have not); even though Jacksonians like to buy cheap goods at Walmart, common sense largely leads them to believe that the first job of trade negotiators ought to be to preserve U.S. jobs rather than embrace visionary "win-win" global schemes.

More broadly, across a range of issues, both wings of the Tea Party will seek to reopen the discussion about whether U.S. foreign policy should be nationalist or cosmopolitan. The Paulite wing would ideally like to end any kind of American participation in the construction of a liberal world order. The Palinite wing leans toward a more moderate position of wanting to ensure that what world-order building Washington does clearly proceeds from a consideration of specific national interests rather than the world's reliance on the United States as a kind of disinterested promoter of the global good. Acheson, no friend of grandiose institutional schemes, might find something to sympathize with here; in any event, foreign policymakers should welcome the opportunity to hold a serious discussion on the relationship of specific U.S. interests to the requirements of a liberal world order.

There is much in the Tea Party movement to give foreign policy thinkers pause, but effective foreign policy must always begin with a realistic assessment of the facts on the ground. Today's Jacksonians are unlikely to disappear. Americans should rejoice that in many ways the Tea Party movement, warts and all, is a significantly more capable and reliable partner for the United States' world-order-building tasks than were the isolationists of sixty years ago. Compared to the Jacksonians during the Truman administration, today's are less racist, less antifeminist, less homophobic, and more open to an appreciation of other cultures and worldviews. Their starting point, that national security requires international engagement, is considerably more auspicious than the knee-jerk isolationism that Truman and Acheson faced. Even in the immediate aftermath of 9/11, there was no public support for the equivalent of the internment of Japanese Americans after Pearl Harbor, nor has there been anything like the anticommunist hysteria of the McCarthy era. Today's southern Republican populists are far more sympathetic to core liberal capitalist concepts than were the populist supporters of William Jennings Bryan a century ago. Bobby Jindal is in every way a better governor of Louisiana than Huey Long was—and there is simply no comparison between Senator Jim DeMint, of South Carolina, and "Pitchfork Ben" Tillman.

Foreign policy mandarins often wish the public would leave them alone so that they can get on with the serious business of statecraft. That is not going to happen in the United States. If the Tea Party movement fades away, other voices of populist protest will take its place. American policymakers and their counterparts overseas simply cannot do their jobs well without a deep understanding of what is one of the principal forces in American political life.

DISCUSSION QUESTIONS

1. What are the goals of the Tea Party movement? How successful has it been?
2. In what ways is the Tea Party movement reminiscent of the populism of Andrew Jackson?
3. What are the key foreign policy beliefs of the Jacksonians?
4. How does Mead suggest that Jacksonian populism affected the foreign policy of Roosevelt and Truman?
5. How does Jacksonian populism fit with the American effort to build a liberal world order? How was this managed during the Cold War and after?
6. How was the Bush foreign policy consistent with the Jacksonians and how have the new Jacksonians challenged the Obama administration's foreign policy?
7. What is the greatest single foreign policy challenge facing U.S. administrations in the years ahead?
8. What are the foreign policy differences of the Palinite and Paulite wings of the Tea Party movement?
9. Ultimately, what does Mead suggest is the important lesson to take from the Tea Party movement for the conduct of American foreign policy?

4

Ethnic Interest Groups in American Foreign Policy*

James M. McCormick

In March 2010, the House Committee on Foreign Affairs narrowly passed H. Res. 252 by a vote of 23–22 and sent the resolution to the full House for its consideration. The non-binding resolution called upon the president to acknowledge the Armenian genocide of 1915 by Turkey. Three years earlier, the same resolution passed the committee by a larger margin (27–21), but failed to reach a vote on the House floor. The Armenian Assembly and the Armenian National Committee of America, the key interest groups of the Armenian community in the United States, supported and lobbied for the 2007 and 2010 resolutions. Both resolutions elicited a large number of cosponsors from members of the House of Representatives, 143 for the 2010 resolution and 212 for the 2007 one. These two resolutions also sparked intense lobbying by Turkish interests, both within the United States and from abroad. The 2007 resolution "pitted Turkey's money and high-placed connections against a persistent and emotional campaign by Armenian-American citizens' groups," and the 2010 resolution stimulated "a full-page ad in the *Washington Post*" by Turkish groups and a visit of eight Turkish parliamentarians to Capitol Hill over the impending committee vote. Yet these resolutions caused more than just a clash between domestic interest groups and foreign lobbies on both sides of the issue; they also caused foreign policy difficulties between United States and Turkey. Just prior to the 2010 committee vote, for instance, Turkish President Abdullah Gul called President Obama apparently to seek his help in stopping this resolution, and Turkey subsequently recalled its ambassador to the United States in protest when the resolution passed in the Foreign Affairs Com-

---

*All endnotes have been deleted.

mittee. Turkish interests also made veiled threats about further disruption in U.S.-Turkish relations as a result of the passage of this resolution. In all, these nonbinding resolutions, advocated and opposed by competing ethnic interest groups, had the potential of disrupting foreign relations between the United States and Turkey.

To be sure, the Armenian and Turkish lobbies are relatively small in comparison to the size of other ethnic lobbies, and the nonbinding resolution may have more symbolic than substantive effect on foreign policy. Yet this episode exemplifies how organized and mobilized ethnic interest groups can affect foreign policy debate at home and may disrupt relations abroad. Is this the case for other ethnic groups as well, or is this an isolated instance of ethnic and foreign lobbies involved in U.S. foreign policymaking? Indeed, are other ethnic and foreign lobbies more consequential for the foreign policy process?

In this chapter, we address these and related questions. . . . [O]ur point of departure is to identify the number and type of foreign policy interest groups at the present time. Next, we evaluate several ethnic interest groups that have operated for some time and have had an impact on American foreign policy over the years. Then we turn to identify and assess the potential role of several new and emerging ethnic groups that have become active more recently. With all of these groups, we utilize several criteria for evaluating their effectiveness and judging their relative impact on U.S. foreign policy. We conclude by considering the overall influence of these kinds of interest groups on the conduct of American foreign policy.

NUMBER AND TYPES OF FOREIGN POLICY INTEREST GROUPS

The number and types of interest groups active on foreign policy today are indeed numerous, but identifying the precise number is difficult to do for several interrelated reasons. As the foreign policy agenda of the United States has expanded from its traditional emphasis on security concerns to one that now encompasses economic, environmental, and social issues, foreign policy interest groups have grown exponentially. As this agenda has expanded, the decision-making arena on foreign policy has as well. Now more policymaking involves Congress and the executive branch—and more foreign policy interest group involvement as well. Because such groups often form, lobby, and then disband, it is difficult to track their exact number at any particular time. Finally, and importantly, we have no single accounting mechanism or reporting requirement to identify the number or types of these foreign policy interest groups; instead, we necessarily must rely upon estimates from a variety of sources.

Yet the estimates of interest groups vary widely. One estimate judged that there were about 11,000 firms or groups lobbying in Washington, DC, and these firms employed about seventeen thousand individuals to seek to influence the policy process. Another estimate, based upon the growth of nongovernmental organizations, or NGOs, worldwide, placed the number anywhere from 5,600 to 25,000 and even to 100,000 such groups. These interest groups or NGOs are surely not all concerned with foreign policy (although the line is blurring between domestic and foreign policy concerns for many lobbying groups). In all, whatever the exact number, these estimates do illustrate how numerous and pervasive such groups have become today and thus have the potential to affect foreign policy.

As the number of foreign policy interest groups has increased in recent decades, the types of such groups have as well. Foreign policy interest groups include some traditional lobbying groups, such as business groups, labor unions and agricultural interests, with their principal focus on international trade issues (although increasingly these groups take stances on a broad array of other foreign policy concerns as well), and they now also include several newer groups that are active on foreign policy. These groups include religious communities, veteran organizations, academic think-tanks, ideological organizations (such as the Americans for Democratic Action (ADA), and single-issue interest groups (e.g., United Nations Association of the United States, Union of Concerned Scientists, and Americans against Escalation in Iraq).

Yet this listing does not include arguably the oldest foreign policy lobby, ethnic interest groups. Ethnic groups, or those groups of Americans who hold a particular concern for U.S. policy toward the particular country or region of their own or their ancestors' origin, are not only the oldest foreign policy lobby, but, in many ways, they also frequently turn out to be the most influential. In important ways, too, these ethnic groups are often tied to foreign country lobbies, or those groups that directly lobby the American government on behalf of another nation. (As a result of these international linkages, American ethnic groups may sometimes get extra scrutiny by the U.S. government to make certain that they are in compliance with the strictures in the Foreign Agents Registration Act and are not acting as foreign agents of another government.) These foreign lobbies, moreover, are increasingly numerous and consequential, and they often complement the work of ethnic groups. Foreign country lobbies can appeal to American ethnic groups that share their views on a particular issue to broaden their level of support, and ethnic groups can gain support from foreign lobbies (and particularly their domestic representatives) to aid in making their case to Congress or the executive branch on a particular issue.

PRINCIPAL ETHNIC LOBBIES

Although ethnic lobbies are increasingly numerous today, the level of activism and effectiveness of individual lobbies varies. Traditionally, Americans of Jewish, Irish, and Eastern European heritage have been the most active ethnic lobbies on foreign policy. Over the past several decades, however, Americans of African, Arab, Armenian, Cuban, Greek, Hispanic, Mexican, and Turkish descent have been increasingly active on foreign policy issues as well. Recently, yet another group, Indian Americans, has become increasingly involved in the foreign policy process. For these interest groups, their principal foreign policy concern is American policy toward the country or region of their origin. Hence, Jewish Americans are most often concerned with U.S. policy toward Israel, Irish Americans toward Ireland, Cuban Americans toward Cuba, and so on. Because of their singular focus on policy toward a particular country or region, these individual ethnic groups tend to be highly motivated in their lobbying effort, and that level of motivation often proves crucial in their effort to obtain their preferred policy from the American government. To be sure, some ethnic groups are more successful than others, and we discuss those first. With all of the ethnic groups that we discuss, we will identify several factors that account for their relative success as compared to others.

The Jewish Lobby

By virtually all assessments, the Jewish lobby, or the Israel lobby, is perhaps the most influential ethnic lobby today with the preponderance of its attention on issues related to the state of Israel and to the Middle East more generally. The Jewish lobby has been described as a "loose coalition of individuals and organizations that actively work to shape U.S. policy in a pro-Israel direction." This lobby has two umbrella organizations that coordinate its activities, the Conference of Presidents of Major American Jewish Organizations and the American-Israel Public Affairs Committee (AIPAC), but AIPAC is usually the organization most often identified with the Jewish lobbying efforts. AIPAC has a relatively large membership at about one hundred thousand activists, has "a network of 10 regional offices and nine satellite offices," and has a large and effective staff in its Washington office. AIPAC also provides a variety of services to its members in an effort to stimulate grassroots support for key issues. The organization's website, for example, provides a wealth of information that allow its members to participate in the foreign policy process: a summary of key issues under consideration by Congress; a congressional directory to facilitate those who want to contact their representatives; numerous policy statements on issues important to the organization; and a list of AIPAC policy achievements.

Furthermore, the website contains direct links, or buttons, for Capitol Hill staffers and for the press as additional ways to get its message out. Finally, and interestingly, AIPAC proudly proclaims its policy effectiveness: "The most important organization affecting America's relationship with Israel"— a descriptor provided by the *New York Times* some years ago.

The Jewish lobby, and AIPAC in particular, have indeed been successful in affecting the direction of American foreign policy toward Israel and the Middle East more generally over the years. AIPAC has largely been able to garner widespread support to promote legislation that it favors or to stop legislation that it opposes. In the 1970s, for example, it was able to obtain seventy-six Senate cosponsors for the Jackson-Vanik Amendment to the Trade Act of 1974 that prohibited most-favored-nation (MFN) status to any state without a free emigration policy—a bill focused on the Soviet Union's restriction on Jewish emigration at the time. In the same decade, it also obtained seventy-six senators to sign a letter urging President Ford to support Israel in any peace effort in the Middle East. In the 1980s, AIPAC was instrumental in forcing the Reagan administration to alter the composition of an arms sale to Saudi Arabia, and, in 1988, Saudi Arabia purchased $30 billion in arms from Britain rather than deal with congressional opposition from supporters of Israel. Currently, AIPAC points to several specific legislative actions to demonstrate the effectiveness of its lobbying: "passing more than a dozen bills and resolutions condemning and imposing tough sanctions on Iran," supporting numerous resolutions passed in Congress that "affirm congressional support for Israel's right to self-defense," and promoting legislation "requiring the administration to evaluate all future military sales to Arab states in the context of the need to maintain Israel's qualitative military edge over potential adversaries." . . . Undoubtedly the best single indicator of congressional support, and a measure of AIPAC's policy success in that body, has been the fact that Israel has continuously received the highest amount of U.S. foreign assistance of any country over the past three decades—at $3 billion annually.

What accounts for the success of this ethnic lobby—or indeed any ethnic lobby? After all, the number of Jewish Americans at 6.2 million constitutes less than 3 percent of America's population. How can this interest group seemingly be so influential? Political scientist Tony Smith in his *Foreign Attachments* begins to provide an answer for this group and others. Smith points to two general factors: (1) the structure of the American political system, and (2) the characteristics of ethnic groups themselves. The former factor refers to the plural nature of the American political system that allows interest groups access to the governmental process, while the latter refers to specific resources that ethnic groups can use to affect the process. The access that these groups have, Smith argues, is "at the local, grassroots level of party selection of officeholders during primaries," "in the divisions that naturally open between the executive and the legislature," and in "the divisions within the legislature itself in Washington." Although these points of access are obviously important, the ability of ethnic groups to take advantage of them is arguably even more crucial. To do that and thus to gain influence, ethnic groups, Smith argues, potentially possess three important resources: (1) their ability to provide votes in key areas, (2) their ability to make campaign contributions to office seekers, and (3) their ability to organize and lobby on key issues.

Applying these three criteria to the Jewish lobby, we begin to see how that lobby can be so effective. First of all, America's Jewish population tends to be concentrated in several key states. States along the east coast (New York, New Jersey, Florida, and to a lesser extent Maryland and Massachusetts) tend to have large concentrations of Jewish voters as do the states of California, Illinois, and Ohio. Further, and importantly, Jews tend to participate in the political process at a much higher rate than other groups in American society. As a result, presidential candidates will likely be sensitive to the interests of Jewish voters in these states, especially since these states have a large number of electoral votes and especially in years with closely-contested national elections. Second, the Jewish community and pro-Israel lobbying groups provide a large amount of campaign funding for congressional and presidential elections. According to the Center for Responsive Politics, pro-Israel groups provided some $13.8 million in campaign contributions in 2008 with 63 percent of those funds supporting Democratic candidates for office and 37 percent for Republican candidates. (AIPAC does not directly make campaign contributions, but it has close ties with political action committees [PACs] that can be used to make such contributions.) Moreover, the support or opposition of pro-Israel groups can be—and has been—crucial in the electoral fortunes of political candidates. . . . Third . . . AIPAC has an effective and efficient organizational structure operating within Washington, DC. With its large contingent of activists nationwide, AIPAC is well positioned to elicit a grassroots response to Congress and the executive branch at any particular time. Furthermore, AIPAC has effectively tied itself into the political decision-making network in Washington. One tangible, and important, indicator of its close linkage to the political leadership is the list of regular attendees and speakers at the annual AIPAC Policy conferences. . . . At the 2010 conference, Secretary of State Hillary Clinton gave a plenary address summarizing the Obama administration's continued support for Israel, but the delegates also heard presentations by public officials from across the political spectrum: Senators Charles Schumer (D-NY), Lindsey Graham (R-SC), and Evan Bayh (D-IN); Governors Martin O'Malley (D-MD) and Tim Pawlenty (R-MN); and House Majority Leader Steny Hoyer (D-MD) and House Republican Whip Eric Cantor (R-VA).

Beyond Smith's three criteria, another crucial factor also contributes to the effectiveness of any ethnic group. The late Senator Charles McC. Mathias identified that factor about three decades ago, albeit in an inverse way. "Foreign lobbies," he wrote, "that lack significant domestic support exert only limited influence on American foreign policy." A lack of domestic support is hardly the case for the Jewish lobby. Among the American public, the level of support for Israel remains very high. In February 2010, 63 percent of the American public expressed more sympathy with the Israelis than with the Palestinians, and such high levels of support have generally been the case for the past twenty years of Gallup polling data. Moral, ethical, and political considerations are the important reasons for this substantial support among the American public for Israel. . . .

A final important factor that impacts the effectiveness of any ethnic group is the extent to which a countervailing ethnic group is active on similar foreign policy issues. Three pro-Arab lobbies, the National Association of Arab Americans (NAAA) founded in 1972, the American-Arab Anti-Discrimination Committee (ADC) founded in 1980, and the Arab American Institute (AAI) founded in 1985, have tended not to be nearly as effective as the Jewish lobby over the years and thus have not served as effective counterweights. Indeed, the NAAA and ADC joined together in 2001, undoubtedly in an effort to increase their effectiveness. . . . Nonetheless, these groups cannot be judged as effective as the pro-Israel lobby. Part of the difficulty for these groups, based upon our earlier criteria for an interest group's success in gaining influence, is the lack of an effective voting bloc among the American public that they can directly appeal to for support, the limited campaign contributions that these groups (or their PACs) provide in election campaigns, and the relatively low public support for Arab states and the Palestinian Authority among the American people. . . . Perhaps the founder of ADC and former U.S. senator James Abourezk best summarized the challenge facing his group, and the Arab lobbies more generally: "To have influence in Congress you have to have money for candidates or control lots of votes. We're trying to build a grass-roots network; it's difficult for us to raise money."

Despite the Jewish lobby's success, it is not without controversy over its influence. In a recent controversial article, and later book, two political scientists John Mearsheimer and Stephen Walt raised questions about this lobby's undue influence on American foreign policy (see chapter 5). In particular, they contend that the strength of the Israel Lobby more fully accounts for American policy toward Israel than moral or strategic explanations by the public or its leaders, and they call for a more open discussion of the power of this particular ethnic lobby on American foreign policy. More recently, another book, *Transforming America's Israel Lobby*, appeared and it also assessed an array of Jewish lobbies, including AIPAC. Importantly, it argued that AIPAC did not wholly reflect the views of the American Jewish community.

Indeed, AIPAC policy positions—which are often seen as too hard-line and often wholly supportive of the Israeli government in power—has created a division within the Jewish community, and that division has now stimulated the emergence of an opposition group. In 2008, J Street was established. . . . Its goals are to give a "political voice to mainstream American Jews and other supporters of Israel who . . . believe that a two-state solution to the Israeli-Palestinian conflict is essential to Israel's survival." The organization not only hopes to promote this policy position but also seeks "to ensure a broad debate on Israel and the Middle East in national politics and the American Jewish community." Moreover, J Street has sought to broaden its base by joining with the Jewish Alliance for Justice and Peace in January 2010, and it now claims to have 150,000 supporters that it can call on to contact members of Congress. Still, one recent analysis raises questions about its staying power and its ability to maintain support among the Jewish community. . . .

The Cuban Lobby

A second influential ethnic group in recent years has been a Hispanic group, the Cuban Lobby. The Cuban American National Foundation (CANF), founded in 1981 by Jorge Mas Canosa, is the principal Cuban lobby. It originated with those Cuban émigrés who fled the Fidel Castro regime in Cuba after the 1959 revolution and also included some who had participated in the Bay of Pigs invasion of Cuba in April 1961. From the outset, its principal foreign policy aim was to affect U.S. policy toward Cuba. Over the years, this general aim has largely meant the maintenance of the American embargo against Cuba and the promotion of the return of democracy to that island nation as soon as possible. At present, CANF identifies its mission as directed toward producing "nonviolent and meaningful" change in Cuba, providing support to those seeking to effect change within Cuba, and "working to counteract the Castro regime's propaganda machine."

For a relatively small lobby, CANF has seemingly been remarkably successful in influencing the conduct of American foreign policy toward Cuba. The trade embargo against Cuba, originally imposed in the early 1960s by executive order, has remained in effect to this day. Indeed, the embargo was actually strengthened in the 1990s by two legislative actions. With the passage of the Cuban Democracy Act of 1992, the embargo was codified into law, rather than being dependent upon an executive order, and with the passage of the Helms-Burton Act (or more formally the Cuban Liberty and Democratic Solidarity Act) of 1996, the embargo was again codified into law and two important additional restrictions were placed upon interactions with Cuba. Title III of the Helm-Burton Act allowed Americans to sue foreign companies "trafficking in stolen property" in Cuba. That is, if a foreign company was operating on or doing business with property in Cuba that was previously owned by Americans before Castro's seizure of such property, that company could be sued. Title IV in the act would deny American visas to officials from such companies that were "trafficking" in stolen Cuban properties. . . .

The continuance of the embargo and the passage of these pieces of legislations represent important policy successes for CANF. Yet they are not the only ones reflecting its impact. CANF was instrumental in promoting the establishment of Radio Marti, a U.S. government–sponsored station to broadcast to Cuba during the Reagan administration. During the Clinton years, this lobby was important in stopping some administrative appointments to the State Department that it did not approve and in prodding the administration to respond to Cuba's shooting down of two unarmed planes of the "Brothers to the Rescue" organization in international waters off Cuba. In 2003, in fact, CANF called for the indictment of Fidel Castro over this episode. The George W. Bush administration did not change American policy during its tenure, and the Obama administration has not either. In this sense, there remains largely a status-quo approach to Cuba by the United States—and the CANF seems in part to be an important reason why.

If we apply our earlier criteria for ethnic group effectiveness to this group, we begin to see why this is the case. Although the Cuban American population (estimated at about 1.2 million) is relatively small within the United States, it is concentrated in some key electoral states (e.g., Florida and New Jersey), and CANF has been able to utilize that electoral clout to maintain influence. Furthermore, over the years, CANF was operating in a political environment in which there was public and leadership support to pressure the Cuban regime. During the Cold War years, relatively few political leaders were willing to propose the easing of the embargo against Cuba. Indeed, few leaders were willing to promote any policy that would be viewed as in any way accommodating Castro's communist regime in Cuba. In this sense, CANF's position was reinforced by Cold War politics. In addition, its leadership, especially under Jorge Mas Canosa, was well connected in official Washington and was able to provide some support to favored political candidates. Moreover, CANF was also regarded as an effective lobby in Congress when it needed to be. One member of Congress put it this way: "[CANF] uses difficult, difficult tactics whenever you disagree with them." Finally, and perhaps the most compelling factor for the Cuban lobby's success, there is the high degree of policy motivation and intensity among its members. Their antipathy toward the Castro regime and their determination to elicit change in Cuba have been critically important to the lobby's success.

In the last decade or so, CANF has in fact experienced some difficulty in maintaining this same level of intensity and unity—and influence. Several reasons account for this change: the death of CANF founder, Jorge Mas Canosa, in 1997; the generational divide between older Cuban Americans who experienced the Castro regime and younger Cuban Americans born in the United States without that direct experience; and the rise of other lobbying groups—some more inclined toward improving Cuban-American relations and others more inclined toward no accommodation with Castro's regime under any circumstance. Overall, though, and like the Jewish lobby, the Cuban lobby remains a formidable example of an ethnic group with an impact on foreign policy.

Greek, Turkish, and Armenian Lobbies

The Greek, Turkish, and Armenian lobbies are three other ethnic lobbies that have operated for some time. Each has sought to affect American policy toward southeast Europe and the Middle East. The issues of concern to these three groups are often similar, but each lobby's positions (and especially the Greek and Turkish lobbies) are often at odds with one another. Hence, the actions of these differing ethnic groups have often complicated American foreign policymaking on several key issues toward the countries of origin for these lobbies.

The first of these three groups is the Greek lobby, or the American Hellenic Institute (AHI). This organization was established in 1974, immediately after the Turkish invasion of Cyprus. A year later, the American Hellenic Institute Public Affairs Committee (AHIPAC) was created with the express goal to focus on lobbying on behalf of Greek Americans. The current foreign policy goals of this lobby focus primarily on American policy toward Greece, Cyprus, and the region surrounding these countries. Specifically, AHI seeks to strengthen American ties with Greece, remove the Turkish occupation from Cyprus, support sovereignty for Greece in the Aegean Sea, and oppose the use of "Macedonia" by the Former Yugoslav Republic of Macedonia in its name.

This lobby points to several important successes in affecting American foreign policy over the past four decades. Undoubtedly AHI's principal success was persuading Congress to impose an arms embargo against Turkey in 1975 over that country's invasion of Cyprus a year earlier and to sustain that embargo for some three years until June 1978. This American action was seen as punishment for Turkey's use of U.S. arms during its intervention and occupation of Cyprus, an action that directly violated the Foreign Military Sales Act. AHI also claims as important achievements the maintenance of American military assistance to Greece at 70 percent of the level of such assistance to Turkey, Congress's elimination of economic grant aid to Turkey in 1995, and the halting of direct trade by the United States with the Turkish-controlled northern sector of Cyprus. . . .

The strength of this lobby is partially tied to the number of Greek Americans (the estimates range from 1.38 million to 3 million). Despite their modest numbers within the American population, these Greek Americans tend to be concentrated in some urban areas, are active in politics, and well connected within their communities. Hence, they have the potential to exercise some electoral influence. Importantly, the American Hellenic Institute is also well organized and effective in its lobby activities, particularly on Capitol Hill. Its relative success as a lobbying organization has also been tied to a number of prominent Greek Americans who have held influential and leadership positions within Congress over the years. In addition, the House Congressional Caucus on Hellenic Issues provides yet another means for the Greek American community to influence the congressional process.

A countervailing group for the Greek . . . lobby is the Turkish lobby. The principal organization for promoting Turkish interests in the United States is the Turkish Coalition of America (TCA), although there is a broad array of other Turkish American groups in existence as well. The TCA is a relatively new organization, only established in 2007, and it has a number of social, cultural, and educational activities. It also engages in numerous political activities to advance issues important to Turkey and the Middle East region. Although Turkish interests have been heavily involved in seeking to stop the passage of the Armenian genocide resolution in the U.S. Congress, it has also been engaged over issues related to America's relationship with Greece, the issue of Cyprus, and sovereignty concerns in the Aegean Sea.

The impact of the Turkish lobby appears to come less from the size of the Turkish American population or its campaign contributions and more from its successful efforts to engage in lobbying on Capitol Hill. The Turkish American population is only about a tenth of the size of the Greek American population; hence, it is a substantially less significant voting bloc and source of campaign contributions than is the Greek American community. Instead, the Turkish lobbying must stress Turkey's strategic importance for the United States when seeking to advance its interests with Congress or the executive branch. . . . [T]he Turkish community can routinely work with the House Congressional Caucus on U.S.-Turkish Relations and Turkish Americans . . . but it also relies upon support from the Turkish government to lobby more directly with Congress or the executive branch. In this connection, the Turkish government itself has often been involved in defending its interests by employing prominent Americans as lobbyists on its behalf. At the time of the debate over the 2007 Armenian genocide resolution, for example, two prominent former members of Congress—Robert Livingston (R-LA), former Speaker of the House-designate, and Richard Gephardt

(D-MO), former majority leader of the House—were deeply involved in seeking to stop this resolution.

The third ethnic lobby seeking to affect American policy toward this region is the Armenian lobby. Its principal organizations are the Armenian Assembly and the Armenian National Committee of America. As we indicated earlier, this lobby has been extremely active and involved in seeking passage of the Armenian genocide resolution that targets Turkey. Yet it also works to advance a number of other aims regarding American foreign policy and Armenia. For instance, this lobby seeks to increase American assistance for Armenia and to obtain direct aid for Nagorno Karabakh. (Nagorno Karabakh is a territory wholly within Azerbaijan that is largely populated by Armenians. Since the breakup of the Soviet Union in particular, this territory has been contested between Azerbaijan and Armenia, including a war between the two countries that ended in 1994.) At the same time, it seeks to deny American aid to Azerbaijan, its regional rival, especially in light of the trade blockade by that nation toward Armenia. Finally, and importantly, this lobby promotes independence for Nagorno Karabakh. . . .

The Armenian lobby has had some success in obtaining these goals—or at least in making progress on them. American assistance to Armenia since its independence from the former Soviet Union has totaled nearly $2 billion, and Armenia has also received funding through the Millennium Challenge Account, a program initiated by the George W. Bush administration to aid selected countries that meet several key performance indicators. The United States has also provided some direct assistance to Nagorno Karabakh, much as the lobby desired.

This success of this lobby is somewhat surprising in that there is a relatively small population (446,000) claiming Armenian ancestry within the United States. However, that population is politically active and involved. Much of the Armenian American population is concentrated in the American West, and importantly in some congressional districts in California, and that fact aids the lobby's impact. The main sponsor of the Armenian genocide resolutions in Congress in 2007 and 2010 was Congressman Adam Schiff from the 29th district in California. That congressional district has an Armenian American population that totals sixty-seven thousand, more than 10 percent of its total size. Such a concentration of Armenian Americans in this district undoubtedly contributed to Rep. Schiff's interest in promoting this resolution (as it had done for his predecessor in that seat, former congressman James Rogan).

The Armenian National Committee of America (ANCA), however, remains politically active beyond this single district. It conducts national voter registration drives, endorses candidates for office, and issues "report cards" on members of Congress. In addition to its electoral efforts, the Armenian community has proved to be an effective lobbying organization in Washington with good connections on Capitol Hill. . . . Further, the Congressional Caucus on Armenian Issues, established in 1995, now has 150 members from the House of Representatives. This caucus thus provides yet another mechanism for keeping Armenian-related issues before political leaders and the public.

EMERGING ETHNIC LOBBIES

Over the last several decades, a number of other ethnic lobbies have also sought to engage in America's foreign policy process. These groups have not been as continuously active, organized, or influential as some of the ones that we have just discussed, but they may become increasingly consequential in the future. We focus on four of these new and emerging ethnic lobbies.

Mexican American Lobby

The Mexican American lobby is the first. The Mexican American community is a significantly larger Hispanic group than the Cuban American community, but it has generally been described as much less successful as an ethnic lobby. With at least 21 million and perhaps as many as 30 million Mexican Americans, this group potentially provides an enormous voting bloc, a significant source of campaign contributions, and a potent lobbying force. Part of the explanation for their lack of success is that this community is not as well organized to lobby or as committed on foreign policy issues as other ethnic groups—two important requirements for lobbying success as we pointed out earlier. . . . [Indeed, one analyst] was even more decisive about the effect of this ethnic lobby: "The Hispanic community exerts almost no systematic influence on U.S.-Latin American relations, or, for that matter, on U.S. foreign policy in general."

Such a conclusion, however, may need to be altered somewhat, especially on the issue of immigration and especially in light of recent Mexican American activism on state and national legislation related to that issue. Indeed, one analyst argues that the Mexican American community has "two effective national organizations in the National Council of La Raza and the Mexican American Legal Defense and Education Fund," and contends that this community was active in affecting the Immigration Reform and Control Act of 1986 and the Immigration Act of 1990. These measures "effectively blocked meaningful changes" over prevailing "migration patterns" and included "amnesty provisions" that "surely substantially accelerated" these patterns. More recently, as Congress was taking up immigration legislation in 2006 and beyond, several Mexican American organizations conducted nationwide demonstrations to protest this legislation. In 2010, this same community also became active over an immigration law passed by the state of Arizona. In this sense, on the immigration issue, the growing Mexican American population may well play a role in shaping U.S. policy in the future. On other foreign policy issues—the promotion of NAFTA and Mexican democracy, for example—this community has been judged as having a decidedly limited impact. Yet given the overall size of this community (particularly in some western states), the potential for foreign policy influence in the years ahead remains a distinct possibility.

The Rebirth of the Eastern European Lobby

Shortly after the implosion of the Soviet Union in 1991 and the gaining of independence of numerous states in the old Soviet empire, a new ethnic organization, the Central and Eastern European Coalition (CEEC), emerged in the United States to promote the interests of these new nations. This organization, established in 1994, was indeed a coalition—a collection of eighteen national organizations, representing Americans who traced their ancestry to Hungary, Latvia, Armenia, Belarus, Bulgaria, Czechoslovakia, Estonia, Georgia, Lithuania, Poland, and Ukraine. In a sense, this lobby might be thought of as the successor to the "captive nations" lobby of the 1950s that sought freedom and independence for those nations behind the iron curtain, albeit now with goals that seek greater stability and security for this region of the world. Supporters of the CEEC argue that the economic and security interests of the United States "demand an unwavering commitment to and sustained engagement with the Central and East European countries." In this sense, the well-being of these coalition nations and the United States should be wholly tied together.

To enhance this linkage, the coalition promotes and supports a number of ongoing American policies. CEEC, for example, has been a major proponent of NATO expansion and the incorporation of these new states in that organization to maintain their security and independence. It currently supports moving Georgia and Ukraine toward full NATO membership in accordance with the organization's Membership Action Plan (MAP). CEEC also strongly supports the principal aid and reform initiatives taken by the United States over the past three administrations—the Support for East European Democracy (SEED) dating back to 1989, the Freedom Support Act (FSA) of 1992, and the more recent Millennium Challenge Account (MCA) program of 2004—and views them as important mechanisms to advance democratic and market reforms in the countries of Central and Eastern Europe. Furthermore, the coalition promotes more vigorous action on the part of the United States "to counter Russia's neo-imperialism" both within Russia itself and within this region of the world.

American foreign policy generally comports with the principal goals of the coalition. In this sense, it is less clear how much effect the CEEC has had in shaping these policies as compared to the general political environment of the post–Cold War years. Still, CEEC has sought to keep its principal issues before America's political leaders through a variety of informational and educational activities. With its headquarters in Washington, DC, the CEEC and its affiliate organizations regularly hold events and discussion forums in Washington, on Capitol Hill, or even at the White House as important mechanisms for shaping the foreign policy debate about this region of the world. Furthermore, CEEC has developed a series of position papers that are routinely shared with members of the current American administration. Finally, supportive members of Congress have formed the Congressional Caucus on Central and Eastern Europe as yet another way to discuss these issues, although the impact of this caucus appears to be rather modest.

Through its member organizations, CEEC has the potential to reach the 22 million Americans who share an ancestry from this part of the world and serve as an important voting bloc. Since most Americans with central and eastern European heritage are concentrated in the Midwest, this region would seem especially ripe for electoral impact if these foreign policy issues were to dominate the campaign agenda. At the present time, however, the coalition does not appear to have a ready mechanism to mobilize them in the way that we have seen with some of the more successful ethnic lobbies. Overall, then, the CEEC cannot be judged as having the influential effect on foreign policy as either the Jewish, Cuban, Greek, or Armenian lobbies. . . . If issues pertaining to this region were to reemerge as central to American foreign policy, and with greater organizational development within CEEC, this lobby might be able to exert increased influence.

African American Lobby

A third ethnic lobby that has emerged over the past several decades is the African American lobby. TransAfrica (or the TransAfrica Forum) is the principal organization that promotes the interests of those with African heritage in the United States, the Caribbean, and parts of Latin America. It was founded in 1977 and pursues a number of goals relating to creating greater economic justice globally, reducing American militarism, and promoting democracy in Africa and among the African diaspora. To achieve such goals, TransAfrica has taken a number of actions to try to affect American foreign policy over the past four decades.

Its lobbying efforts began in the late 1970s, and it has continued to try to influence American foreign policy in this way during each succeeding decade. One of its initial actions focused on seeking to maintain U.S.

economic sanctions on white-ruled Rhodesia in southern Africa. By 1980, this activity, and a series of actions by a number of others, resulted in the creation of the state of Zimbabwe from this former British colony. A few years later, this organization lobbied the Reagan administration to impose economic sanctions on South Africa over its apartheid policy. In 1986, TransAfrica supported efforts by Congress to override a presidential veto and pass the Anti-Apartheid Act of 1986, a measure that strengthened the administration's executive order of 1985. By the early 1990s, TransAfrica was influential in prodding the Clinton administration to take stronger measures against those who had overthrown the democratic government in Haiti. In 1994, moreover, the Clinton administration did order an American intervention in Haiti, and the military rulers fled the country.

In the twenty-first century, this organization continued its lobbying effort, albeit with decidedly more mixed results. For instance, TransAfrica opposed the African Growth and Opportunity Act, which was enacted into law, over concern of how much it would aid Africa, and it also opposed the creation of the "Africa Command" within the American military structure because the organization viewed it as leading to a greater militarization within Africa. TransAfrica also worked to oppose the increasingly repressive Robert Mugabe government in Zimbabwe, also with limited success. At the present time, TransAfrica focuses on seeking relief for the substantial debt owed by Africa and the Caribbean countries, continues to oppose the militarization of Africa, and seeks to promote "human rights, fair trade, and self-determination of African peoples" as "the cornerstone of U.S. policy towards Africa."

Unlike many of the other ethnic lobbies that we have discussed, the African American lobby appears to do a great deal of its work with civil society groups abroad (in various countries in Africa and elsewhere) and with Americans of African ancestry at home. In this sense, there is potentially a substantial grassroots component to TransAfrica, but the extent of its following at home as a whole is not clear. Furthermore, it has a limited domestic electoral base and has not been a major campaign contributor to candidates for elective office. In this sense, TransAfrica does not possess some of the important characteristics that we identified as important for a successful ethnic lobby. . . . TransAfrica . . . has a natural ally in the Congressional Black Caucus (since its founding is linked to this caucus), and that tie helps it to gain access and influence in official Washington. Overall, though, this organization appears less well organized and influential than some of the other ethnic lobbies that we have discussed. Nevertheless, TransAfrica has the potential to appeal to the African American community within the United States, especially on issues related to Africa and on issues related to global social justice.

The Indian Lobby

The newest ethnic lobby, and the most influential of this group, is the Indian lobby. This lobby consists of those Americans whose ancestry is tied to the country of India. The number of Americans with Asian Indian ancestry totals between 1.7 and 1.9 million in the 2000 U.S. Census and was estimated at "over 2.5 million" in 2007. The total is probably somewhat larger today, but still, even with a modest increase, the percentage of Indian Americans represents less than 1 percent of the total U.S. population. Yet in one recent assessment, this lobby has been described as "the only lobby in Washington likely to acquire the strength of the Israel lobby."

How can this descriptor be possible for such a relatively small group? As was the case with other groups of relatively small size (e.g., the Cuban lobby, the Armenian lobby), an important part of the explanation rests with the substantial motivation of members of this community, the electoral clout—both through voting blocs and campaign contributions—that the lobby possesses in particular states and districts around the country, and the improved organizational structure that it has put into place in recent years. Finally—and hardly inconsequential—the changed international political environment over the past two decades has also aided the emergence of the Indian lobby.

Over the years, numerous disparate Indian American organizations have existed, but these organizations were often organized "along professional-occupational lines" (e.g., the American Association of Physicians of Indian Origin and the Asian American Hotel Owners Association). In 2002, however, the U.S. India Political Action Committee (USINPAC) was formed, established itself in the "K-Street neighborhood" in Washington, DC, hired a staff of professionals committed to advancing a series of important foreign and domestic policy goals, and put into place a comprehensive organizational structure for lobbying. Thus, this organization today is the principal lobbying organization for the Indian American community. . . .

USINPAC has a number of goals, both in foreign and domestic policy. In the foreign policy arena, USINPAC is primarily interested in strengthening U.S-Indian bilateral relations across the spectrum—defense, trade, and business. It is also interested in promoting "a fair and balanced policy on immigration" and addressing the issue of international terrorism. In the domestic arena, its concerns focus on protecting the civil rights of Indian Americans, promoting equal opportunity for members of this community, and advocating for small businesses as well. To achieve these goals, USINPAC has a broad array of activities including holding fundraisers for political candidates that it supports, hosting receptions and briefings on Capitol Hill, sponsoring trips to India for its supporters, and providing a listing of its key issues and events on its website. Furthermore, this organization and its associated groups work with two congressional caucuses dealing with India: the Congressional Caucus on India and Indian Americans in the House, and the Friends of India Caucus in the Senate. Finally, USINPAC also has a "National Outreach Program" that seeks to coordinate issue positions among affiliated groups, and it has been active in promoting Indian Americans who are competing for elective offices nationwide. In all, USINPAC in a relatively short period of time has established itself as a comprehensive and effective organization.

Other important characteristics of the Indian American community also facilitate its activism and impact. Indian Americans tend to be highly educated (with 64 percent over twenty-five with a college degree), economically successful (with a median income almost twice that of most Americans), and well connected. By one estimate, Indian Americans own "20 percent of all the companies in Silicon Valley" in California; and "the U.S.-India Business Council, which has a core committee of 200 companies that make up part of the United States' corporate elite, is closely allied with the India lobby." In this sense, the Indian lobby can reach out to a number of supporters beyond its core constituents to enhance its influence in the political process. Furthermore, and importantly, the Indian American community tends to be concentrated in particularly important electoral states (e.g., California, Washington, New York, Illinois, Texas, and Pennsylvania), and it has been increasingly a generous campaign contributor to its supporters in government. . . .

Although these organizational and individual characteristics account for a great deal of the rise of the Indian lobby, the political and economic environment surrounding U.S.-Indian relations over the past two decades also provided the occasion for this lobby to promote its foreign policy goals. First of all, with the end of the Cold War and the implosion of the Soviet Union, an opportunity developed for restarting U.S.-Indian relations, a relationship that had been decidedly cool with India's ties to the Soviet Union for so many years. Second, India is the world's largest democracy, and it is also one of the world's most dynamic economies. In this sense, India may well be America's new "ally" as Fareed Zakaria described it in *The Post-American World*. Third, in the post-9/11 era, India is also located in an important but volatile part of the world for the United States. Strong and productive relations with India are increasingly crucial for American foreign policy. For all of these reasons, then, the India lobby has had an opportunity to affect American foreign policy.

And the Indian lobby has done so. Perhaps the most important foreign policy achievement of this lobby was the passage of legislation in 2006 that lifted restrictions on nuclear fuels trade by the United States with India. Such restrictions had been in place for several decades as part of U.S. obligations under the Nuclear Nonproliferation Treaty (NPT) and domestic laws, dating back to India's "peaceful" nuclear explosion in 1974 and exacerbated by India's nuclear test in the late 1990s. Despite a skeptical Congress heading into an election in the fall of 2006 and a weakened Bush presidency from the Iraq War, both Houses of Congress gave approval to this legislation. One recent analysis argues that "Indian-American mobilization was *the* critical factor behind overwhelming congressional support" for this legislation approval.

ETHNIC LOBBIES AND THEIR INFLUENCE: SOME CONCLUSIONS

This survey of America's ethnic lobbies leads to several important conclusions about their impact on American foreign policy. First of all, ethnic groups matter. The Jewish lobby, the Cuban lobby, the Greek lobby, and, more recently, the Indian lobby have impacted American foreign policy in important ways, although their impact has primarily been tied to issues related to U.S. policy toward the country of each lobby's focus. In this sense, the lobbies may not appear to have a general effect on the overall conduct of American foreign policy. Yet, in fact, they do. . . . The more vexing question is how much the ethnic lobby shapes American policy toward a country or region compared to a variety of other factors.

Second, some lobbies have more influence on American foreign policy than others. This effectiveness is primarily due to a number of important group and organizational characteristics that we discussed throughout the chapter. The size of the ethnic community, the distribution of the group's population in particular congressional districts or states, and the group's political activism and involvement are important factors shaping an ethnic group's policy impact. Recall, for example, the size and involvement of the Jewish American and the Greek American communities compared to the Arab American or Turkish American communities. A large degree of motivation and commitment to a particular policy position, however, can often overcome an ethnic group's relative lack of size (e.g., the Armenian lobby). The ethnic group's organizational capacity and its skill in getting its message upward to policymakers and downward to its supporters are also important factors affecting its degree of policy effect. Note the organizational strength of the Jewish and the Indian lobbies as compared to that of the African American, Mexican, and Eastern European lobbies.

Third, the type of policy sought by an ethnic lobby affects its success. Lobbies that are seeking to change American foreign policy in some important way (e.g., the Armenian lobby, the Greek lobby, or the Indian lobby) often have a bigger challenge than those lobbies that are seeking to reinforce current policy or the status quo (e.g., the Cuban lobby, the Jewish lobby, or even the Central and Eastern European lobbies).

Fourth, an ethnic lobby that forms a coalition with other ethnic lobbies will likely have more effect on policy. The Armenian lobby, for example, has been able to work with the Greek lobby to oppose Turkish interests, while the Turkish lobby for a time gained support from the Jewish lobby. In this sense, the limited capacity of one group is leveraged with the assistance of another. In the future, in fact, we are likely to see more and more of this ethnic group cooperation as a mechanism to accomplish their goals.

In large measure, the conclusions discussed so far could reasonably be made about any type of interest group—ethnic or otherwise—but these ethnic groups also possess a quality that distinguishes them from other interest groups in one important way. That quality is the close personal identity that members of these ethnic groups feel toward the policy issues at hand. That is, the strong "identity politics" of ethnic group members, or, put differently, "the strong emotional bonds of large numbers of Americans to their cultural or ancestral homes," has been characterized as the "secret weapon" of these ethnic groups. Although these bonds can be beneficial to ethnic group members, they have also been criticized as having the potential of being carried to excess and thus proving "harmful to the national interest." . . .

Several years ago, noted political scientist Samuel Huntington certainly advanced that argument. He contended that "ethnic interests are generally transnational or nonnational," they "promote the interests of people and entities outside the United States," and they thus erode the pursuance of the national interest. The usual response is to argue that the national interest is not self-evident and that it is, in fact, the result of the competition among competing interests, including ethnic interests. Such a view, of course, fails to recognize the relative weight of some groups over others in this competition—and the resulting "national interest." In this connection, there is no doubt about the need to make certain that the ethnic lobbies continue to place their interests within the context of the collective interest of American foreign policy. Yet policymakers are aware of this dilemma, and much as they learned to manage the impact of the media on foreign policy (the so-called CNN effect), they are increasingly aware of, and seek to manage, the effects of ethnic lobbying. Yet the management of these lobbies is far from complete by policymakers. That is, these ethnic lobbies, often "experts" on a particular foreign policy issue, may combine with highly reputable reporters and media outlets to create what Bonardi and Keim describe as a "reputation cascade" for a "widely salient issue." By this process, both the public and policymakers have lost their decision latitude on an issue—and in this way, ethnic lobbies may continue to influence the direction of American foreign policy. . . .

DISCUSSION QUESTIONS

1. How large are foreign policy interest groups in the United States, and how varied are such groups?
2. What are ethnic interest groups, and do they differ from foreign lobbies?
3. What are the principal ethnic lobbies in the conduct of American foreign policy today?
4. What are the key characteristics that make ethnic interest groups effective in affecting foreign policy?
5. How well do the Jewish lobby and the Cuban lobby fit with the characteristics of successful ethnic lobbies?
6. How successful have the Greek, Turkish, and Armenian lobbies been in affecting U.S. foreign policy? What issues are of most interest and importance to these groups?
7. Among the emerging ethnic lobbies, which one appears to be the most effective? Why is that so, and on what issues is that group most influential?
8. What is the one quality that makes ethnic groups distinctive from other interest groups?
9. Are ethnic interest groups helpful or harmful to the conduct of American foreign policy?

5

The Israel Lobby

John Mearsheimer and Stephen Walt

For the past several decades, and especially since the Six-Day War in 1967, the centerpiece of U.S. Middle Eastern policy has been its relationship with Israel. The combination of unwavering support for Israel and the related effort to spread "democracy" throughout the region has inflamed Arab and Islamic opinion and jeopardized not only U.S. security but also that of much of the rest of the world. This situation has no equal in American political history. Why has the United States been willing to set aside its own security and that of many of its allies in order to advance the interests of another state? One might assume that the bond between the two countries was based on shared strategic interests or compelling moral imperatives, but neither explanation can account for the remarkable level of material and diplomatic support that the United States provides.

Instead, the thrust of U.S. policy in the region derives almost entirely from domestic politics, and especially the activities of the "Israel Lobby." Other special-interest groups have managed to skew foreign policy, but no lobby has managed to divert it as far from what the national interest would suggest, while simultaneously convincing Americans that U.S. interests and those of the other country—in this case, Israel—are essentially identical.

Since the October War in 1973, Washington has provided Israel with a level of support dwarfing that given to any other state. It has been the largest annual recipient of direct economic and military assistance since 1976, and is the largest recipient in total since World War II, to the tune of well over $140 billion (in 2004 dollars). Israel receives about $3 billion in direct assistance each year, roughly one-fifth of the foreign aid budget, and worth about $500 a year for every Israeli. This largesse is especially striking since

Israel is now a wealthy industrial state with a per capita income roughly equal to that of South Korea or Spain.

Other recipients get their money in quarterly installments, but Israel receives its entire appropriation at the beginning of each fiscal year and can thus earn interest on it. Most recipients of aid given for military purposes are required to spend all of it in the United States, but Israel is allowed to use roughly 25 percent of its allocation to subsidize its own defense industry. It is the only recipient that does not have to account for how the aid is spent, which makes it virtually impossible to prevent the money from being used for purposes the United States opposes, such as building settlements on the West Bank. Moreover, the United States has provided Israel with nearly $3 billion to develop weapons systems, and given it access to such top-drawer weaponry as Blackhawk helicopters and F-16 jets. Finally, the United States gives Israel access to intelligence it denies to its NATO allies and has turned a blind eye to Israel's acquisition of nuclear weapons.

Washington also provides Israel with consistent diplomatic support. Since 1982, the United States has vetoed thirty-two UN Security Council resolutions critical of Israel, more than the total number of vetoes cast by all the other Security Council members. It blocks the efforts of Arab states to put Israel's nuclear arsenal on the International Atomic Energy Agency's agenda. The United States comes to the rescue in wartime and takes Israel's side when negotiating peace. The Nixon administration protected it from the threat of Soviet intervention and re-supplied it during the October War. Washington was deeply involved in the negotiations that ended that war, as well as in the lengthy "step-by-step" process that followed, just as it played a key role in the negotiations that preceded and followed the 1993 Oslo Accords. In each case there was occasional friction between U.S. and Israeli officials, but the United States consistently supported the Israeli position. One American participant at Camp David in 2000 later said, "Far too often, we functioned . . . as Israel's lawyer." Finally, the George W. Bush administration's ambition to transform the Middle East was at least partly aimed at improving Israel's strategic situation.

This extraordinary generosity might be understandable if Israel were a vital strategic asset or if there were a compelling moral case for U.S. backing. But neither explanation is convincing. One might argue that Israel was an asset during the Cold War. By serving as America's proxy after 1967, it helped contain Soviet expansion in the region and inflicted humiliating defeats on Soviet clients like Egypt and Syria. It occasionally helped protect other U.S. allies (like King Hussein of Jordan), and its military prowess forced Moscow to spend more on backing its own client states. It also provided useful intelligence about Soviet capabilities.

Backing Israel was not cheap, however, and it complicated America's relations with the Arab world. For example, the decision to give $2.2 billion in emergency military aid during the October War triggered an OPEC oil embargo that inflicted considerable damage on Western economies. For all that, Israel's armed forces were not in a position to protect U.S. interests in the region. The United States could not, for example, rely on Israel when the Iranian Revolution in 1979 raised concerns about the security of oil supplies, and had to create its own Rapid Deployment Force instead.

The first Gulf War revealed the extent to which Israel was becoming a strategic burden. The United States could not use Israeli bases without rupturing the anti-Iraq coalition, and had to divert resources (e.g., Patriot missile batteries) to prevent Tel Aviv doing anything that might harm the alliance against Saddam Hussein. History repeated itself in 2003: although Israel was eager for the United States to attack Iraq, President Bush could not ask it to help without triggering Arab opposition. So Israel stayed on the sidelines once again.

Beginning in the 1990s, and even more after 9/11, U.S. support has been justified by the claim that both states are threatened by terrorist groups originating in the Arab and Muslim world, and by "rogue states" that back these groups and seek weapons of mass destruction. This is taken to mean not only that Washington should give Israel a free hand in dealing with the Palestinians and not press it to make concessions until all Palestinian terrorists are imprisoned or dead, but also that the United States should go after countries like Iran and Syria. Israel is thus seen as a crucial ally in the war on terror, because its enemies are America's enemies. In fact, Israel is a liability in the war on terror and the broader effort to deal with rogue states.

"Terrorism" is not a single adversary, but a tactic employed by a wide array of political groups. The terrorist organizations that threaten Israel do not threaten the United States, except when it intervenes against them (as in Lebanon in 1982). Moreover, Palestinian terrorism is not random violence directed against Israel or "the West"; it is largely a response to Israel's prolonged campaign to colonize the West Bank and Gaza Strip.

More important, saying that Israel and the United States are united by a shared terrorist threat has the causal relationship backwards: the United States has a terrorism problem in good part because it is so closely allied with Israel, not the other way around. Support for Israel is not the only source of anti-American terrorism, but it is an important one, and it makes winning the war on terror more difficult. There is no question that many al Qaeda leaders, including Osama bin Laden, are motivated by Israel's presence in Jerusalem and the plight of the Palestinians. Unconditional support for Israel makes it easier for extremists to rally popular support and to attract recruits.

As for so-called rogue states in the Middle East, they are not a dire threat to vital U.S. interests, except inasmuch as they are a threat to Israel. Even if these states acquire nuclear weapons—which is obviously undesirable—neither America nor Israel could be blackmailed, because the blackmailer could not carry out the threat without suffering overwhelming retaliation. The danger of a nuclear handover to terrorists is equally remote, because a rogue state could not be sure the transfer would go undetected or that it would not be blamed and punished afterward. The relationship with Israel actually makes it harder for the United States to deal with these states. Israel's nuclear arsenal is one reason some of its neighbors want nuclear weapons, and threatening them with regime change merely increases that desire.

A final reason to question Israel's strategic value is that it does not behave like a loyal ally. Israeli officials frequently ignore U.S. requests and renege on promises (including pledges to stop building settlements and to refrain from "targeted assassinations" of Palestinian leaders). Israel has provided sensitive military technology to potential rivals like China, in what the State Department inspector-general called "a systematic and growing pattern of unauthorized transfers." According to the General Accounting Office, Israel also "conducts the most aggressive espionage operations against the U.S. of any ally." In addition to the case of Jonathan Pollard, who gave Israel large quantities of classified material in the early 1980s (which it reportedly passed on to the Soviet Union in return for more exit visas for Soviet Jews), a new controversy erupted in 2004 when it was revealed that a key Pentagon official, Larry Franklin, had passed classified information to an Israeli diplomat. Israel is hardly the only country that spies on the United States, but its willingness to spy on its principal patron casts further doubt on its strategic value.

Israel's strategic value isn't the only issue. Its backers also argue that it deserves unqualified support because it is weak and surrounded by enemies; it is a democracy; the Jewish people have suffered from past crimes and therefore deserve special treatment; and Israel's conduct has been morally superior to that of its adversaries. On close inspection, none of these arguments is persuasive. There is a strong moral case for supporting Israel's existence, but that is not in jeopardy. Viewed objectively, its past and present conduct offers no moral basis for privileging it over the Palestinians.

Israel is often portrayed as David confronted by Goliath, but the converse is closer to the truth. Contrary to popular belief, the Zionists had larger, better equipped, and better led forces during the 1947–1949 War of Independence, and the Israel Defense Forces won quick and easy victories against Egypt in 1956 and against Egypt, Jordan, and Syria in 1967—all of this before large-scale U.S. aid began flowing. Today, Israel is the strongest military power in the Middle East. Its conventional forces are far superior to those of its neighbors, and it is the only state in the region with nuclear weapons. Egypt and Jordan have signed peace treaties with it, and Saudi Arabia has offered to do so. Syria has lost its Soviet patron, Iraq has been devastated by three disastrous wars, and Iran is hundreds of miles away. The Palestinians barely have an effective police force, let alone an army that could pose a threat to Israel. According to a 2005 assessment by Tel Aviv University's Jaffee Centre for Strategic Studies, "The strategic balance decidedly favours Israel, which has continued to widen the qualitative gap between its own military capability and deterrence powers and those of its neighbours." If backing the underdog were a compelling motive, the United States would be supporting Israel's opponents.

That Israel is a fellow democracy surrounded by hostile dictatorships cannot account for the current level of aid: there are many democracies around the world, but none receives the same lavish support. The United States has overthrown democratic governments in the past and supported dictators when this was thought to advance its interests—it has good relations with a number of dictatorships today.

Some aspects of Israeli democracy are at odds with core American values. Unlike the United States, where people are supposed to enjoy equal rights irrespective of race, religion, or ethnicity, Israel was explicitly founded as a Jewish state, and citizenship is based on the principle of blood kinship. Given this, it is not surprising that its 1.3 million Arabs are treated as second-class citizens, or that a recent Israeli government commission found that Israel behaves in a "neglectful and discriminatory" manner toward them. Its democratic status is also undermined by its refusal to grant the Palestinians a viable state of their own or full political rights.

A third justification is the history of Jewish suffering in the Christian West, especially during the Holocaust. Because Jews were persecuted for centuries and could feel safe only in a Jewish homeland, many people now believe that Israel deserves special treatment from the United States. The country's creation was undoubtedly an appropriate response to the long record of crimes against Jews, but it also brought about fresh crimes against a largely innocent third party: the Palestinians.

This was well understood by Israel's early leaders. David Ben-Gurion told Nahum Goldmann, the president of the World Jewish Congress,

> If I were an Arab leader I would never make terms with Israel. That is natural: we have taken their country. . . . We come from Israel, but two thousand years ago, and what is that to them? There has been anti-Semitism, the Nazis, Hitler, Auschwitz, but was that their fault? They only see one thing: we have come here and stolen their country. Why should they accept that?

Since then, Israeli leaders have repeatedly sought to deny the Palestinians' national ambitions. When she was prime minister, Golda Meir famously remarked that "there is no such thing as a Palestinian." Pressure from extremist violence and Palestinian population growth has forced subsequent

Israeli leaders to disengage from the Gaza Strip and consider other territorial compromises, but not even Yitzhak Rabin was willing to offer the Palestinians a viable state. Ehud Barak's purportedly generous offer at Camp David would have given them only a disarmed set of Bantustans under de facto Israeli control. The tragic history of the Jewish people does not obligate the United States to help Israel today no matter what it does.

Israel's backers also portray it as a country that has sought peace at every turn and shown great restraint even when provoked. The Arabs, by contrast, are said to have acted with great wickedness. Yet on the ground, Israel's record is not distinguishable from that of its opponents. Ben-Gurion acknowledged that the early Zionists were far from benevolent toward the Palestinian Arabs, who resisted their encroachments—which is hardly surprising, given that the Zionists were trying to create their own state on Arab land. In the same way, the creation of Israel in 1947–1948 involved acts of ethnic cleansing, including executions, massacres, and rapes by Jews, and Israel's subsequent conduct has often been brutal, belying any claim to moral superiority. Between 1949 and 1956, for example, Israeli security forces killed between 2,700 and 5,000 Arab infiltrators, the overwhelming majority of them unarmed. The Israel Defense Forces (IDF) murdered hundreds of Egyptian prisoners of war in both the 1956 and 1967 wars, while in 1967, it expelled between 100,000 and 260,000 Palestinians from the newly conquered West Bank, and drove 80,000 Syrians from the Golan Heights.

During the first intifada, the IDF distributed truncheons to its troops and encouraged them to break the bones of Palestinian protesters. The Swedish branch of Save the Children estimated that "23,600 to 29,900 children required medical treatment for their beating injuries in the first two years of the intifada." Nearly a third of them were aged ten or under. The response to the second intifada was even more violent, leading *Ha'aretz* to declare that "the IDF . . . is turning into a killing machine whose efficiency is awe-inspiring, yet shocking." The IDF fired one million bullets in the first days of the uprising. Since then, for every Israeli lost, Israel has killed 3.4 Palestinians, the majority of whom have been innocent bystanders; the ratio of Palestinian to Israeli children killed is even higher (5.7:1). It is also worth bearing in mind that the Zionists relied on terrorist bombs to drive the British from Palestine, and that Yitzhak Shamir, once a terrorist and later prime minister, declared that "neither Jewish ethics nor Jewish tradition can disqualify terrorism as a means of combat."

The Palestinian resort to terrorism is wrong but it isn't surprising. The Palestinians believe they have no other way to force Israeli concessions. As Ehud Barak once admitted, had he been born a Palestinian, he "would have joined a terrorist organization."

So if neither strategic nor moral arguments can account for America's support for Israel, how are we to explain it?

The explanation is the unmatched power of the Israel Lobby. We use "the Lobby" as shorthand for the loose coalition of individuals and organizations who actively work to steer U.S. foreign policy in a pro-Israel direction. This is not meant to suggest that the Lobby is a unified movement with a central leadership, or that individuals within it do not disagree on certain issues. Not all Jewish Americans are part of the Lobby because Israel is not a salient issue for many of them. In a 2004 survey, for example, roughly 36 percent of American Jews said they were either "not very" or "not at all" emotionally attached to Israel.

Jewish Americans also differ on specific Israeli policies. Many of the key organizations in the Lobby, such as the American-Israel Public Affairs Committee (AIPAC) and the Conference of Presidents of Major Jewish Organizations, are run by hard-liners who generally support the Likud Party's expansionist policies, including its hostility to the Oslo peace process. The bulk of U.S. Jewry, meanwhile, is more inclined to make concessions to the Palestinians, and a few groups—such as Jewish Voice for Peace—strongly advocate such steps. Despite these differences, moderates and hard-liners both favor giving steadfast support to Israel.

Not surprisingly, American Jewish leaders often consult Israeli officials, to make sure that their actions advance Israeli goals. As one activist from a major Jewish organization wrote, "It is routine for us to say: 'This is our policy on a certain issue, but we must check what the Israelis think.' We as a community do it all the time." There is a strong prejudice against criticizing Israeli policy, and putting pressure on Israel is considered out of order. Edgar Bronfman Sr., the president of the World Jewish Congress, was accused of "perfidy" when he wrote a letter to President Bush in mid-2003 urging him to persuade Israel to curb construction of its controversial "security fence." His critics said that "it would be obscene at any time for the president of the World Jewish Congress to lobby the president of the United States to resist policies being promoted by the government of Israel."

Similarly, when the president of the Israel Policy Forum, Seymour Reich, advised Condoleezza Rice in November 2005 to ask Israel to reopen a critical border crossing in the Gaza Strip, his action was denounced as "irresponsible": "There is," his critics said, "absolutely no room in the Jewish mainstream for actively canvassing against the security-related policies . . . of Israel." Recoiling from these attacks, Reich announced that "the word 'pressure' is not in my vocabulary when it comes to Israel."

Jewish Americans have set up an impressive array of organizations to influence American foreign policy, of which AIPAC is the most powerful and best known. In 1997, *Fortune* magazine asked members of Congress and their staffs to list the most powerful lobbies in Washington. AIPAC was ranked second behind the American Association of Retired People (AARP), but ahead of the AFL-CIO and the National Rifle Association. A *National*

Journal study in March 2005 reached a similar conclusion, placing AIPAC in second place (tied with AARP) in the Washington "muscle rankings."

The Lobby also includes prominent Christian evangelicals like Gary Bauer, Jerry Falwell, Ralph Reed, and Pat Robertson, as well as Dick Armey and Tom DeLay, former majority leaders in the House of Representatives, all of whom believe Israel's rebirth is the fulfillment of biblical prophecy and support its expansionist agenda; to do otherwise, they believe, would be contrary to God's will. Neo-conservative gentiles such as John Bolton; Robert Bartley, the former *Wall Street Journal* editor; William Bennett, the former secretary of education; Jeane Kirkpatrick, the former UN ambassador; and the influential columnist George Will are also steadfast supporters.

The U.S. form of government offers activists many ways of influencing the policy process. Interest groups can lobby elected representatives and members of the executive branch, make campaign contributions, vote in elections, try to mold public opinion, and so on. They enjoy a disproportionate amount of influence when they are committed to an issue to which the bulk of the population is indifferent. Policymakers will tend to accommodate those who care about the issue, even if their numbers are small, confident that the rest of the population will not penalize them for doing so.

In its basic operations, the Israel Lobby is no different from the farm lobby, steel or textile workers' unions, or other ethnic lobbies. There is nothing improper about American Jews and their Christian allies attempting to sway U.S. policy: the Lobby's activities are not a conspiracy of the sort depicted in tracts like the *Protocols of the Elders of Zion*. For the most part, the individuals and groups that compose it are only doing what other special interest groups do, but doing it very much better. By contrast, pro-Arab interest groups, in so far as they exist at all, are weak, which makes the Israel Lobby's task even easier.

The Lobby pursues two broad strategies. First, it wields its significant influence in Washington, pressuring both Congress and the executive branch. Whatever an individual lawmaker or policymaker's own views may be, the Lobby tries to make supporting Israel the "smart" choice. Second, it strives to ensure that public discourse portrays Israel in a positive light, by repeating myths about its founding and by promoting its point of view in policy debates. The goal is to prevent critical comments from getting a fair hearing in the political arena. Controlling the debate is essential to guaranteeing U.S. support because a candid discussion of U.S.-Israeli relations might lead Americans to favor a different policy.

A key pillar of the Lobby's effectiveness is its influence in Congress, where Israel is virtually immune from criticism. This in itself is remarkable because Congress rarely shies away from contentious issues. Where Israel is concerned, however, potential critics fall silent. One reason is that some key members are Christian Zionists like Dick Armey, who said in

September 2002, "My No. 1 priority in foreign policy is to protect Israel." One might think that the No. 1 priority for any congressman would be to protect America. There are also Jewish senators and congressmen who work to ensure that U.S. foreign policy supports Israel's interests.

Another source of the Lobby's power is its use of pro-Israel congressional staffers. As Morris Amitay, a former head of AIPAC, once admitted, "There are a lot of guys at the working level up here [on Capitol Hill] who happen to be Jewish, who are willing . . . to look at certain issues in terms of their Jewishness. . . . These are all guys who are in a position to make the decision in these areas for those senators. . . . You can get an awful lot done just at the staff level."

AIPAC itself, however, forms the core of the Lobby's influence in Congress. Its success is due to its ability to reward legislators and congressional candidates who support its agenda, and to punish those who challenge it. Money is critical to U.S. elections (as the scandal over lobbyist Jack Abramoff's shady dealings reminded us), and AIPAC makes sure that its friends get strong financial support from the many pro-Israel political action committees. Anyone who is seen as hostile to Israel can be sure that AIPAC will direct campaign contributions to his or her political opponents. AIPAC also organizes letter-writing campaigns and encourages newspaper editors to endorse pro-Israel candidates.

There is no doubt about the efficacy of these tactics. Here is one example: In the 1984 elections, AIPAC helped defeat Senator Charles Percy from Illinois, who, according to a prominent Lobby figure, had "displayed insensitivity and even hostility to our concerns." Thomas Dine, the head of AIPAC at the time, explained what happened: "All the Jews in America, from coast to coast, gathered to oust Percy. And the American politicians—those who hold public positions now, and those who aspire—got the message."

AIPAC's influence on Capitol Hill goes even further. According to Douglas Bloomfield, a former AIPAC staff member, "It is common for members of Congress and their staffs to turn to AIPAC first when they need information, before calling the Library of Congress, the Congressional Research Service, committee staff or administration experts." More important, he notes that AIPAC is "often called on to draft speeches, work on legislation, advise on tactics, perform research, collect co-sponsors and marshal votes."

The bottom line is that AIPAC, a de facto agent for a foreign government, has a stranglehold on Congress, with the result that U.S. policy towards Israel is not debated there, even though that policy has important consequences for the entire world. In other words, one of the three main branches of the government is firmly committed to supporting Israel. As one former Democratic senator, Ernest Hollings, noted on leaving office, "You can't have an Israeli policy other than what AIPAC gives you around here." Or as Ariel Sharon once told an American audience, "When people ask me how they can help Israel, I tell them, 'Help AIPAC.'"

Thanks in part to the influence Jewish voters have on presidential elections, the Lobby also has significant leverage over the executive branch. Although they make up less than 3 percent of the population, they make large campaign donations to candidates from both parties. The *Washington Post* once estimated that Democratic presidential candidates "depend on Jewish supporters to supply as much as 60 percent of the money." And because Jewish voters have high turn-out rates and are concentrated in key states like California, Florida, Illinois, New York, and Pennsylvania, presidential candidates go to great lengths not to antagonize them.

Key organizations in the Lobby make it their business to ensure that critics of Israel do not get important foreign policy jobs. Jimmy Carter wanted to make George Ball his first secretary of state, but knew that Ball was seen as critical of Israel and that the Lobby would oppose the appointment. In this way, any aspiring policymaker is encouraged to become an overt supporter of Israel, which is why public critics of Israeli policy have become an endangered species in the foreign policy establishment.

When Howard Dean called for the United States to take a more "even-handed role" in the Arab-Israeli conflict, Senator Joseph Lieberman accused him of selling Israel down the river and said his statement was "irresponsible." Virtually all the top Democrats in the House signed a letter criticizing Dean's remarks, and the *Chicago Jewish Star* reported that "anonymous attackers . . . are clogging the email inboxes of Jewish leaders around the country, warning—without much evidence—that Dean would somehow be bad for Israel."

This worry was absurd; Dean is, in fact, quite hawkish on Israel—his campaign cochair was a former AIPAC president, and Dean said his own views on the Middle East more closely reflected those of AIPAC than those of the more moderate Americans for Peace Now. He had merely suggested that to "bring the sides together," Washington should act as an honest broker. This is hardly a radical idea, but the Lobby doesn't tolerate even-handedness.

During the Clinton administration, Middle Eastern policy was largely shaped by officials with close ties to Israel or to prominent pro-Israel organizations, among them, Martin Indyk, the former deputy director of research at AIPAC and cofounder of the pro-Israel Washington Institute for Near East Policy (WINEP); Dennis Ross, who joined WINEP after leaving government in 2001; and Aaron Miller, who has lived in Israel and often visits the country. These men were among Clinton's closest advisers at the Camp David summit in July 2000. Although all three supported the Oslo peace process and favored the creation of a Palestinian state, they did so only within the limits of what would be acceptable to Israel. The American delegation took its cues from Ehud Barak, coordinated its negotiating positions with Israel in advance, and did not offer independent proposals. Not surprisingly, Palestinian negotiators complained that they were "negotiating with two Israeli teams—one displaying an Israeli flag, and one an American flag."

The situation was even more pronounced in the George W. Bush administration, whose ranks included such fervent advocates of the Israeli cause as Elliot Abrams, John Bolton, Douglas Feith, I. Lewis ("Scooter") Libby, Richard Perle, Paul Wolfowitz, and David Wurmser. These officials consistently pushed for policies favored by Israel and backed by organizations in the Lobby.

The Lobby doesn't want an open debate, of course, because that might lead Americans to question the level of support they provide. Accordingly, pro-Israel organizations work hard to influence the institutions that do most to shape popular opinion.

The Lobby's perspective prevails in the mainstream media: the debate among Middle East pundits, the journalist Eric Alterman writes, is "dominated by people who cannot imagine criticizing Israel." He lists sixty-one "columnists and commentators who can be counted on to support Israel reflexively and without qualification." Conversely, he found just five pundits who consistently criticize Israeli actions or endorse Arab positions. Newspapers occasionally publish guest op-eds challenging Israeli policy, but the balance of opinion clearly favors the other side. It is hard to imagine any mainstream media outlet in the United States publishing a piece like this one.

"Shamir, Sharon, Bibi—whatever those guys want is pretty much fine by me," Robert Bartley once remarked. Not surprisingly, his newspaper, the *Wall Street Journal*, along with other prominent papers like the *Chicago Sun-Times* and the *Washington Times*, regularly runs editorials that strongly support Israel. Magazines like *Commentary*, the *New Republic* and the *Weekly Standard* defend Israel at every turn.

Editorial bias is also found in papers like the *New York Times*, which occasionally criticizes Israeli policies and sometimes concedes that the Palestinians have legitimate grievances, but is not even-handed. In his memoirs, the paper's former executive editor Max Frankel acknowledges the impact his own attitude had on his editorial decisions: "I was much more deeply devoted to Israel than I dared to assert. . . . Fortified by my knowledge of Israel and my friendships there, I myself wrote most of our Middle East commentaries. As more Arab than Jewish readers recognized, I wrote them from a pro-Israel perspective."

News reports are more even-handed, in part because reporters strive to be objective, but also because it is difficult to cover events in the Occupied Territories without acknowledging Israel's actions on the ground. To discourage unfavorable reporting, the Lobby organizes letter-writing campaigns, demonstrations, and boycotts of news outlets whose content it considers anti-Israel. One CNN executive has said that he sometimes gets six thousand e-mail messages in a single day complaining about a story. In May 2003, the pro-Israel Committee for Accurate Middle East Reporting in America (CAMERA) organized demonstrations outside National Public Radio stations in thirty-three cities; it also tried to persuade contributors to withhold support from NPR until its Middle East coverage became more sympathetic to Israel. Boston's NPR station, WBUR, reportedly lost more than $1 million in contributions as a result of these efforts. Further pressure on NPR has come from Israel's friends in Congress, who have asked for an internal audit of NPR's Middle East coverage as well as more oversight.

The Israeli side also dominates the think tanks which play an important role in shaping public debate as well as actual policy. The Lobby created its own think tank in 1985, when Martin Indyk helped to found WINEP. Although WINEP plays down its links to Israel, claiming instead to provide a "balanced and realistic" perspective on Middle East issues, it is funded and run by individuals deeply committed to advancing Israel's agenda.

The Lobby's influence extends well beyond WINEP, however. Over the past twenty-five years, pro-Israel forces have established a commanding presence at the American Enterprise Institute, the Brookings Institution, the Center for Security Policy, the Foreign Policy Research Institute, the Heritage Foundation, the Hudson Institute, the Institute for Foreign Policy Analysis, and the Jewish Institute for National Security Affairs (JINSA). These think tanks employ few, if any, critics of U.S. support for Israel.

Take the Brookings Institution. For many years, its senior expert on the Middle East was William Quandt, a former NSC official with a well-deserved reputation for even-handedness. Today, Brookings's coverage is conducted through the Saban Center for Middle East Studies, which is financed by Haim Saban, an Israeli American businessman and ardent Zionist. The center's director is the ubiquitous Martin Indyk. What was once a nonpartisan policy institute is now part of the pro-Israel chorus.

Where the Lobby has had the most difficulty is in stifling debate on university campuses. In the 1990s, when the Oslo peace process was underway, there was only mild criticism of Israel, but it grew stronger with Oslo's collapse and Sharon's access to power, becoming quite vociferous when the IDF reoccupied the West Bank in spring 2002 and employed massive force to subdue the second intifada.

The Lobby moved immediately to "take back the campuses." New groups sprang up, like the Caravan for Democracy, which brought Israeli speakers to U.S. colleges. Established groups like the Jewish Council for Public Affairs and Hillel joined in, and a new group, the Israel on Campus Coalition, was formed to coordinate the many bodies that now sought to present

Israel's case. Finally, AIPAC more than tripled its spending on programs to monitor university activities and to train young advocates, in order to "vastly expand the number of students involved on campus . . . in the national pro-Israel effort."

The Lobby also monitors what professors write and teach. In September 2002, Martin Kramer and Daniel Pipes, two passionately pro-Israel neoconservatives, established a website (Campus Watch) that posted dossiers on suspect academics and encouraged students to report remarks or behavior that might be considered hostile to Israel. This transparent attempt to blacklist and intimidate scholars provoked a harsh reaction and Pipes and Kramer later removed the dossiers, but the website still invites students to report "anti-Israel" activity.

Groups within the Lobby put pressure on particular academics and universities. Columbia has been a frequent target, no doubt because of the presence of the late Edward Said on its faculty. "One can be sure that any public statement in support of the Palestinian people by the preeminent literary critic Edward Said will elicit hundreds of e-mails, letters, and journalistic accounts that call on us to denounce Said and to either sanction or fire him," Jonathan Cole, its former provost, reported. When Columbia recruited the historian Rashid Khalidi from Chicago, the same thing happened. It was a problem Princeton also faced a few years later when it considered wooing Khalidi away from Columbia. . . .

No discussion of the Lobby would be complete without an examination of one of its most powerful weapons: the charge of anti-Semitism. Anyone who criticizes Israel's actions or argues that pro-Israel groups have significant influence over U.S. Middle Eastern policy—an influence AIPAC celebrates—stands a good chance of being labeled an anti-Semite. Indeed, anyone who merely claims that there *is* an Israel Lobby runs the risk of being charged with anti-Semitism, even though the Israeli media refer to America's "Jewish Lobby." In other words, the Lobby first boasts of its influence and then attacks anyone who calls attention to it. It's a very effective tactic: anti-Semitism is something no one wants to be accused of. . . .

Can the Lobby's power be curtailed? One would like to think so, given the Iraq debacle, the obvious need to rebuild America's image in the Arab and Islamic world, and the recent revelations about AIPAC officials passing U.S. government secrets to Israel. One might also think that Arafat's death and the election of the more moderate Mahmoud Abbas would cause Washington to press vigorously and even-handedly for a peace agreement. In short, there are ample grounds for leaders to distance themselves from the Lobby and adopt a Middle East policy more consistent with broader U.S. interests. In particular, using American power to achieve a just peace between Israel and the Palestinians would help advance the cause of democracy in the region.

But that is not going to happen—not soon, anyway. AIPAC and its allies (including Christian Zionists) have no serious opponents in the lobbying world. They know it has become more difficult to make Israel's case today, and they are responding by taking on staff and expanding their activities. Besides, American politicians remain acutely sensitive to campaign contributions and other forms of political pressure, and major media outlets are likely to remain sympathetic to Israel no matter what it does.

The Lobby's influence causes trouble on several fronts. It increases the terrorist danger that all states face—including America's European allies. It has made it impossible to end the Israeli-Palestinian conflict, a situation that gives extremists a powerful recruiting tool, increases the pool of potential terrorists and sympathizers, and contributes to Islamic radicalism in Europe and Asia.

Equally worrying, the Lobby's campaign for regime change in Iran and Syria could lead the United States to attack those countries, with potentially disastrous effects. We don't need another Iraq. At a minimum, the Lobby's hostility towards Syria and Iran makes it almost impossible for Washington to enlist them in the struggle against al Qaeda and the Iraqi insurgency, where their help is badly needed.

There is a moral dimension here as well. Thanks to the Lobby, the United States has become the de facto enabler of Israeli expansion in the Occupied Territories, making it complicit in the crimes perpetrated against the Palestinians. This situation undercuts Washington's efforts to promote democracy abroad and makes it look hypocritical when it presses other states to respect human rights. U.S. efforts to limit nuclear proliferation appear equally hypocritical given its willingness to accept Israel's nuclear arsenal, which only encourages Iran and others to seek a similar capability.

Besides, the Lobby's campaign to quash debate about Israel is unhealthy for democracy. Silencing skeptics by organizing blacklists and boycotts—or by suggesting that critics are anti-Semites—violates the principle of open debate on which democracy depends. The inability of Congress to conduct a genuine debate on these important issues paralyzes the entire process of democratic deliberation. Israel's backers should be free to make their case and to challenge those who disagree with them, but efforts to stifle debate by intimidation must be roundly condemned.

Finally, the Lobby's influence has been bad for Israel. Its ability to persuade Washington to support an expansionist agenda has discouraged Israel from seizing opportunities—including a peace treaty with Syria and a prompt and full implementation of the Oslo Accords—that would have saved Israeli lives and shrunk the ranks of Palestinian extremists. Denying the Palestinians their legitimate political rights certainly has not made Israel more secure, and the long campaign to kill or marginalize a generation of Palestinian leaders has empowered extremist groups like Hamas and reduced the number of Palestinian leaders who would be willing to accept a fair settlement and able to make it work. Israel itself would probably be better off if the Lobby were less powerful and U.S. policy more even-handed.

There is a ray of hope, however. Although the Lobby remains a powerful force, the adverse effects of its influence are increasingly difficult to hide. Powerful states can maintain flawed policies for quite some time, but reality cannot be ignored for ever. What is needed is a candid discussion of the Lobby's influence and a more open debate about U.S. interests in this vital region. Israel's well-being is one of those interests, but its continued occupation of the West Bank and its broader regional agenda are not. Open debate will expose the limits of the strategic and moral case for one-sided U.S. support and could move the United States to a position more consistent with its own national interest, with the interests of the other states in the region, and with Israel's long-term interests as well.

DISCUSSION QUESTIONS

1. What are two possible explanations for the bond between the United States and Israel?
2. What do Mearsheimer and Walt argue is the actual reason that the countries are so closely tied?
3. What reasons do Mearsheimer and Walt give for questioning Israel's strategic value to the United States?
4. What are four reasons for questioning the moral basis of the United States' relationship with Israel?
5. What is the Jewish Lobby? What are its two broad strategies?
6. What is AIPAC and why is it important?
7. How has the Israel lobby extended its influence outside of Congress to media, think tanks, and universities?

6

American Veterans in Government and the Use of Force

Peter D. Feaver and Christopher Gelpi

In this chapter . . . we examine whether the prevalence of military experience among the policymaking elite affects the propensity of the United States to use military force. Because veteran opinion corresponds with military opinion, we use veteran presence in the political elite as a proxy for measuring the civil-military gap over time. Relying on a composite measure of military experience across the executive and legislative branches of government, we examine the impact of elite military experience on the U.S. propensity to initiate and to escalate militarized interstate disputes between 1816 and 1992.

The results of these analyses are striking. We find that as the percentage of veterans serving in the executive branch and the legislature increases, the probability that the United States will initiate militarized disputes declines. At the same time, however, once a dispute has been initiated, the higher the proportion of veterans, the greater the level of force the United States will use in the dispute. These results are statistically robust and are not spurious; they hold even when we control for other factors that are known to affect the propensity to use force. The civil-military gap matters, at least as far as the use of force goes. . . .

FROM BELIEFS TO BEHAVIOR: THE CIVIL-MILITARY GAP AND INTERSTATE CONFLICT

Although civilian and military preferences regarding the use of force may differ, civilians have had the final say regarding both when and how military force will be used throughout U.S. history. The American military has never openly challenged the fundamental principle of civilian control, and we do not anticipate that it will do so. Nonetheless, even under the basic rubric of civilian control, one can imagine varying levels of military influence (Feaver 2003).

Military preferences shape U.S. foreign policy to a greater or lesser extent through at least two significant mechanisms. First, while the military may not determine American policy, its advisory role is well respected and established. Given their obvious expertise regarding the use of force, military advisors will have the opportunity to persuade civilian policymakers to adopt views that reflect the beliefs and preferences of the military. Second, even if military advisors are unable to alter the views of policymakers, their preferences may constrain them because of the leverage that the military can give to competing civilian elites (that is, elite members of a competing political party or faction). The norms of civilian control may inhibit military leaders from openly and publicly challenging civilian decisions regarding the use of force, but competing civilian elites are under no such constraint. Research indicates that one of the keys to maintaining public support for the use of force is the existence of an elite consensus in support of the issue (Larson 1996). Should civilian leaders select policies that are contrary to military advice, however, competing civilian elites will be ready and willing to attack the leadership for ignoring such expert advice if the policy is eventually judged a failure. Thus military preferences may influence the civilian elite, despite the strong American norm of civilian control, to the extent that these views can either persuade or coerce civilian policymakers to alter their choices.

The linkage between military preferences and American conflict behavior may be further complicated by the fact that individuals' preferences over when and how to use military force are likely to be related to each other. That is, an individual's preferences regarding one dimension may be contingent on the policy outcome on the other dimension (Hinich and Munger 1997). For example, it would be entirely consistent for a realpolitik policymaker to oppose intervention in response to human rights abuses abroad, but also to argue that if the United States does intervene in such conflicts it should do so with a high level of force. . . .

First, state leaders must decide whether or not to use force. If they choose not to initiate, then no force is used and the status quo prevails. If the decision is made to initiate, however, then a second decision must be made regarding how much military force will be used. This decision tree has three end-nodes: (1) no force is used and the status quo prevails, (2) limited use of force, and (3) large-scale use of force. Our contention is that civilian and military elites have different preference rankings across these three outcomes. Moreover, preference rankings within each of these groups may vary depending upon the nature of the goal for which force is being contemplated.

The specific preferences of the relevant actors can be deduced from what is known about their views in general. Both previous case study research and our own survey research suggest that civilian elite nonveterans would most prefer a limited intervention. This preference for limited involvement appears to hold regardless of whether the goals of the military operation are realpolitik issues such as the defense of Kuwait or South Korea, or interventionist issues such as the civil war in Somalia or human rights abuses in Kosovo. However, nonveteran civilian rankings of the other two outcomes—do nothing and use large-scale force—appear to switch depending on the nature of the issue. That is, faced with realpolitik threats, nonveteran civilians seem likely to prefer large-scale force to doing nothing (for example, Kuwait and Korea). With regard to interventionist issues, however, it is arguable that nonveteran civilians would prefer doing nothing to escalating to the large-scale use of force (for example, in Kosovo and Somalia).

While nonveteran civilians' preferences are defined by their focus on limited force as the most attractive option, the military elite consistently ranks this as its least preferred outcome. This preference against limited military action is consistent across policy issues. The military's relative ranking of large-scale force and doing nothing, however, changes depending upon the nature of the issue at stake. With regard to realpolitik issues, the military's most preferred option is the large-scale use of force. It is important to note that some members of the military may have a rather restrictive conception of a realpolitik threat. Given that the military views an issue as a threat to American national security, however, its most preferred outcome is to use force on a large scale, while doing nothing ranks in between large scale and limited force. With regard to interventionist issues, however, the military's most preferred outcome is to do nothing, while large-scale force remains preferable to limited force.

Given these preference rankings, what kind of advice is the military likely to offer to civilian leaders? With regard to realpolitik issues, the military would like to counsel civilians to use force on a large scale. However, it will be wary of advising civilians to do so because of the fear that once the United States becomes involved in the conflict, civilians will place constraints on how force will be used. This subsequent choice would, of course, present the military with its least preferred outcome. The cautious and restrained nature of the military advice prior to the Gulf War may serve as an example of this pattern. Many in the military saw a threat to American security, but advised caution regarding the use of force partly out of fear that civilians would constrain the nature of the operation (Betts 1991).

With regard to interventionist issues, however, military advice is likely to be adamantly opposed to using force rather than merely cautious. In this case, the military's most preferred option is to do nothing, and it will attempt to persuade civilian elites to stay out. Military advisors should be particularly adamant in this regard because they are aware that while limited intervention is civilians' most preferred outcome, a large-scale use of force is their least favorite option. Thus a decision to use force on an interventionist issue such as Kosovo or Somalia will most likely present the military with its least preferred outcome: the limited use of force.

Not surprisingly, we expect that military preferences will have a greater influence on civilian policy choices when civilian leaders share preferences that are similar to those of the military. Moreover, our earlier findings indicate that civilians who have served in the military have preferences that are closer to those of the military than are the views of civilian nonveterans. Thus we expect that American conflict behavior will tend to reflect "military views" as the proportion of civilian policymakers with military experience increases.

Once the decision has been made to use military force, the nature of the military's advice to civilian policymakers becomes more straightforward. The military always prefers the large-scale use of force to the limited use of force. Indeed, the limited use of force is always the military's least preferred outcome. Thus once civilian policymakers have decided to use force (and the "do nothing" option disappears), military advisors will always counsel strongly for using force on a large scale. Once again, we expect this advice to be more influential when the civil-military gap is small.

Of course, the decision to use force is influenced by many factors, of which civil-military relations may not be the most important. The presence of these other factors presents a challenge for testing the influence of the civil-military opinion gap over time. Even so, it should be possible to isolate the impact of civil-military relations relative to other contributing factors that shape the use of force. The hypotheses that follow, then, are all subject to the ceteris paribus condition; controlling for all the other factors that affect the decision to use force, we expect that

Hypothesis 1: As the proportion of civilian policymakers with military experience increases, the probability that the United States will initiate militarized disputes will decrease.

Hypothesis 2: The impact of policymakers' military experience on American decisions to initiate militarized disputes will be more pronounced with regard to interventionist threats rather than realpolitik threats.

Hypothesis 3: As the proportion of civilian policymakers with military experience increases, the level of force the United States uses in disputes it initiates will increase.

MEASURING THE IMPACT OF THE CIVIL-MILITARY GAP ON AMERICAN CONFLICT BEHAVIOR

To test these hypotheses, we relate the civil-military gap to U.S. conflict behavior over the nineteenth and twentieth centuries while controlling, as far as possible, for other factors that are known to shape the use of force. We discuss the results of our analyses in the next section. . . .

Scope

We test for the impact of the elite civil-military gap on American decisions to use force with a cross-sectional time-series dataset composed of interstate dyads of which the United States was a member between 1816 and 1992. State membership is determined by the Correlates of War dataset's definition of membership in the international system. One difficulty in using such dyadic pooled time-series data is determining which states were capable of interacting. During the latter part of the twentieth century, this issue seems less salient because of the frequent opportunities for interaction among states. As we move back in time through the nineteenth century, however, it becomes less plausible to assume that all states were capable of fighting with one another. Following a number of prominent analyses of the use of force, we address this problem by analyzing only "politically relevant" dyads (Maoz and Russett 1993; Oneal and Russett 1997), which are defined as (1) any pair of states in which at least one of the states is a major power; or (2) any pair of states that share a border or are divided by less than 250 miles of water.

Since the United States became a major power (according to the Correlates of War Capabilities dataset) in 1898, this rule implies that we analyze all interstate dyads including the United States from 1898 onward. Prior to 1898, the rule implies that we analyze American relations with all of the major powers during that period as well as American interactions with Mexico. For the entire 177 years under study, there are 8,780 dyad-years involving the United States.

Dependent Variable (1): Initiation of Force by the United States

Our argument made specific predictions about how civil-military factors might affect two different aspects of the use of force. The first aspect is the *propensity* to initiate the use of force, and thus our first dependent variable is the propensity of the United States to initiate the use of force. We code American initiations of force on the basis of the Correlates of War (COW) Militarized Interstate Disputes (MIDs) dataset, which defines the initiation of militarized disputes as explicit threats to use force, displays of force, mobilizations of force, or actual uses of force (Jones, Bremer, and Singer 1996). This variable is coded on an annual basis for each dyad, set at 1 for each year that the United States initiated a militarized dispute against the other state in the dyad, and otherwise at 0. For the entire 177 years studied, there were 111 militarized disputes initiated by the United States. Over the same period, the United States was also involved in 132 other militarized disputes that were initiated by other states. But since our theory only addresses disputes initiated by the United States, we do not include them in our analysis.

Dependent Variable (2): Level of Force Used by the United States

We also predicted a relationship between civil-military factors and the *level* of force used (that is, whether unconstrained in keeping with the classical "military" preference or constrained in keeping with the classical "civilian" preference). Once again, we rely on the COW MIDs dataset for our measure of the second dependent variable, the level of force used by the United States in the disputes that it initiated. In the MIDs dataset the highest level of force used by each side in a dispute is coded on a five-point scale as follows: 1 = no militarized response to a MID initiation by the other state; 2 = threat of force; 3 = show of force; 4 = use of force; 5 = war. For our purposes, of course, the first category of this variable is irrelevant, for we analyze the level of force only if the United States initiated a dispute. Threats of force involve verbal actions that are not supported by militarized behavior. A show of force involves the actual movement and use of troops, but stops short of extended or direct combat. The use of force involves direct military hostilities but stops short of full-scale war. Wars are defined as military engagements in which the combatants suffer at least one thousand battle deaths. . . .

Key Explanatory Variable: The Elite Civil-Military Gap

We have no way of directly measuring the preferences of policymakers regarding the use of force across the span of American history. However, we can measure the military *experience* of American policymakers. That is, we can determine whether each of these policymakers ever served in the military. As we discussed above, this measure acts as a surrogate indicator for the presence of "military views" within the civilian policymaking elite.

Focusing on military experience as a measure of the gap fits nicely within the causal chain with which we link the civil-military gap to the use of force. We view the impact of the gap as a two-stage process. First, military experience shapes individuals' attitudes and preferences regarding the use of force. Second, these differing preferences, in turn, alter American conflict behavior.

That is, although our aggregate analysis of American conflict behavior draws a direct linkage between military experience and dispute behavior, we view attitudes as an intervening variable between military experience and American foreign policy.

Our approach requires us to assume that the link between opinions about the use of force and military/veteran status has been more or less constant over the time. We are not arguing that all elite civilians have always thought exactly the same way or that all elite military have always thought exactly the same way. Rather, we are assuming that the general structure of opinion has been relatively constant over time, and we believe that this assumption is both modest and plausible.

Our analyses in this chapter also treat all forms of military experience as the same. This assumption is perhaps more problematic, because intuitively there would seem to be a difference in perspective between a draftee who served his minimum tour and a career officer who rose to the highest military ranks before pursuing a political career. Likewise, it is plausible that there is a difference in perspective between serving during combat versus serving during peacetime, or serving in a combat unit versus serving as a cook, or serving in the reserves versus active duty.

For our present purposes, this limitation in the data biases our analysis *against* finding any effect. If variations in military experience matters in ways we are not able to capture, then it will show up as more noisy variation in the data, driving coefficients toward zero and lowering the likelihood of finding any statistically significant relationship. Put another way, our assumptions increase the likelihood that we will falsely reject a veteran's effect when there really is one, and decrease the likelihood that we will falsely accept a veteran's effect when there really is none.

The next issue is the determination of whose military experience might be relevant for predicting the use of force. The president's military experience should be an important aspect of this process, but should by no means be the only factor. The president inevitably relies on advice from members of his cabinet and his national security team, so surely their military experience will shape the views and the information they convey to him. In addition, the president must also be concerned about how other policymakers will respond to his decisions regarding whether and how to use force. Congress has often publicly debated American decisions to use force, and as we noted earlier, public support for a military operation may depend critically on the existence of an elite consensus in support of the operation (Larson 1996). Thus the president must be concerned with whether legislators will hold hearings or make public statements that question the administration's policy. Congress also retains an important budgetary and constitutional link to American uses of force, and the president may consult directly with prominent members of Congress who have expertise in foreign affairs.

Consequently, our measure of the military experience of policymakers encompasses the executive and legislative branches. We do not include the military experience of the Supreme Court or other aspects of the judiciary, because judges have not historically played a role in American decisions to use force or debated such decisions publicly. For the executive branch, we recorded the percentage of veterans serving in the cabinet for each year. Thus we include the military experience of the president, the vice president, and any other cabinet officers serving during that year. For Congress, we use the percentage of veterans serving in the House of Representatives for each year.

Secondary Explanatory Variable:
Interventionist Versus Realpolitik Uses of Force

One important aspect of our argument is that civilians differ from those with military experience in terms of their willingness to use military force to address issues that are outside the realpolitik scope of American security policy—especially those that involve intervention inside other states. To test this hypothesis, we divided dyads into two categories: states whose actions could represent a threat to the core bases of American security, and states whose actions could not represent such a threat. The former category we labeled "realpolitik" targets and the latter we labeled "interventionist." We defined interventionist targets as any state that (1) faced worse than a 99:1 disadvantage against the United States in terms of relative military capabilities and (2) was not allied with a competing major power. Such small, nonaligned states clearly do not have the capability to threaten American security in a realpolitik manner. Instead, disputes with such states were likely to involve U.S. intervention inside the minor state because of domestic turmoil or because the United States was dissatisfied with the policies or behaviors of the ruling government of such states. States that enjoyed less than a 99:1 disadvantage against the United States or were allied with a rival major power were coded as realpolitik targets. This coding rule results in approximately 51 percent of the dyad-years in our dataset being coded as interventionist. . . .

Control Variables

Because decisions to use force are multifaceted and complex, even if we did find a relationship between our measures of the civil-military gap and the propensity to use force, we would not expect it to be the only (or even the most important) factor influencing the use of force. A large body of literature on international conflict has already identified numerous factors that affect the use of force, including distance, military capabilities, and democracy, for example. To the extent that the elite military experience is correlated with any of these factors, the failure to include that factor in our analysis might bias our estimate of the impact of elite veterans. Control variables thus allow us to address many of the critiques we have encountered, most of which take the form of conceding a statistical correlation but denying a causal relationship on the grounds that some other factor is the true causal agent. As far as possible, we have controlled for every plausible alternative argument in our empirical analysis.

Including additional control variables cannot artificially inflate the estimated impact of our variable of interest. It can, however, introduce problems such as multicollinearity. Such problems would inflate the standard errors of the coefficients and could reduce the statistical significance of our results. Thus the inclusion of control variables can only provide a more stringent test of our hypotheses. Including these variables also allows us to compare the impact of elite military experience with the influence of other prominent causes of conflict. [*The control variables included are portrayed in tables 6.1 and 6.2, in addition to the principal explanatory variables.—Ed.*]

DOES THE CIVIL-MILITARY GAP INFLUENCE AMERICAN CONFLICT BEHAVIOR?

We conducted a logit analysis of every politically relevant interstate dyadic relationship in which the United States was a partner from 1816 to 1992. Table 6.1 presents our analysis of the propensity of the United States to initiate militarized disputes. Our results provide strong and striking support for hypotheses 1 and 2. As predicted, the negative coefficient for elite veterans is statistically significant, indicating that the more veterans there were in the political elite, the less likely the United States was to initiate the use of force. Also as predicted, the effect of veterans on the propensity to use force was even greater in interventionist cases. As indicated by column three of table 6.1, the coefficient for this variable for realpolitik dyads is only -0.19 ($p < .10$). With regard to interventionist dyads, in contrast, the coefficient is calculated by adding that value to the coefficient on the interaction between the percentage of veterans in the policy elite and an interventionist threat (-0.47, $p < .01$). Thus the overall effect of elite veterans for interventionist dyads is -0.66—more than three times the impact for realpolitik dyads.

Figure 6.1 displays the predicted probability that the United States would initiate a militarized dispute as the percentage of veterans in the cabinet and Congress ranged from its historical near-minimum of 10 percent to its historical near-maximum of 80 percent. When only one policymaker in ten had military experience, the probability that the United States would initiate a dispute within a given dyad was approximately 3.6 percent. At first glance, this might look like a relatively small risk. But because militarized disputes are rare events, a 3 percent probability of a dispute between a given pair of states actually indicates a relatively high risk. Moreover, the effect of a 3 percent probability is magnified by the large number of dyads in which the United States was involved each year. For large portions of our data set, the United States was engaged in over one hundred such dyads per year. Thus a 3 percent per dyad probability of a dispute yields a prediction that, holding all other factors that influence the decision to use force hypothetically constant, the United States might initiate several additional militarized disputes per year because so few policymakers had military experience.

Conversely, of course, as the percentage of policymakers with military experience increases, the probability of dispute initiation drops substantially. The impact of these changes is slightly nonlinear, with the greatest decreases in the probability of a dispute occurring as the percentage of veterans ranges between 10 percent and 67 percent. By the time the rate of military experience among policymakers reaches 67 percent, the probability that the United States would initiate a dispute within a given dyad drops from 3.6 percent to 0.7 percent—representing more than an 80 percent decrease from its previous value, which we call a reduction in relative risk. Further increases in elite military experience up to 80 percent reduce the probability of a dispute within a dyad to nearly 0.4 percent.

Also in figure 6.1, we compare the impact of elite veterans on the probability that the United States would initiate a crisis against realpolitik and interventionist threats. As one would expect from the results in table 6.1, the impact of elite veterans is much greater for interventionist cases. When few veterans are in office, the United States is less likely to initiate a dispute against realpolitik than interventionist targets. Specifically, when only 10 percent of policymakers are veterans, the probability of a U.S. initiation in a realpolitik dyad is 4.7 percent, and in an interventionist dyad it is approximately 6.0 percent. As the percentage of elite veterans increases, the probability of a dispute drops within both sets of dyads, but the decline is much steeper in the interventionist group. In fact, by the time the percentage of veterans reaches 50 percent, the United States is actually more than three times as likely to initiate force against a realpolitik threat. When the percentage of veterans nears its historical maximum, the probability of initiation against a realpolitik threat is 1 percent, while the probability of initiation against an interventionist threat is only 0.08 percent. These results are made all the more striking by the crude nature of our distinction between realpolitik and interventionist threats. More careful theorizing and empirical work on these categories would surely increase the decisiveness of this distinction.

Table 6.1. Elite Military Experience and American Militarized Dispute Initiation

Explanatory Variables	Elite Veterans Model	Elite and Mass Veterans Model	Realpolitik vs. Interventionist Threats
Percent Veteran in Cabinet and House	−0.032*** (0.011)	−0.031** (0.014)	−0.19* (0.011)
Elite Vets x Interventionist			−0.47*** (0.012)
Interventionist Threat			1.02** (0.46)
Ln of Previous War's Battle	−0.16*** −1.41**	−0.22** (0.092)	−0.17*** (0.056)
Percent Veteran in U.S. Public		−0.042 (0.059)	
Cold War Years	1.70*** (0.50)	2.17*** (0.76)	1.83*** (0.52)
Republican Administration	0.44 (0.28)	0.41 (0.31)	0.45 (0.28)
U.S. Involvement in Other	−0.070 (0.060)	−0.065 (0.063)	−0.061 (0.06)
Balance of Military Capabilities	−1.75*** (0.61)	−1.84*** (0.72)	−1.15 (0.74)
Alliance Similarity	−1.41** (0.65)	−1.36** (0.70)	−1.77** (0.79)
United States Is a Major Power	−0.39 (0.38)	−0.76 (0.69)	−0.61 (0.40)
Adversary Is a Major Power	−0.39 (0.69)	−0.43 (0.86)	−0.29 (0.70)
Adversary Level of Democracy	−0.045** (0.023)	−0.061** (0.026)	−0.037* (0.023)
Ln Distance between States	−0.30*** (0.029)	−0.30*** (0.031)	−0.28** (0.027)
Year since U.S. Initiation in Constant[a]	−1.29 (0.90)	−2.38 (1.80)	0.61 (1.04)
Number of Observations	8,739	8,464	8,739
Initial Log Likelihood	−594.92	−534.37	−594.92
Log-Likelihood at Convergence	−469.72	−419.82	−456.54
Chi-squared	601.74 (19d.f.)	727.95 (18d.f.)*	560.77 (19d.f.)*

* = p<.10, ** = p < .05, *** = p < .01

Note: Huber-White robust standard errors in parentheses. Standard errors allow for clustering by dyad.

[a]For reasons of space, the temporal dependence coefficients are not reported here. As expected, years since the previous U.S. initiation did have a significant and nonlinear effect on U.S. dispute initiation as predicted by Beck, Katz, and Tucker (1998).

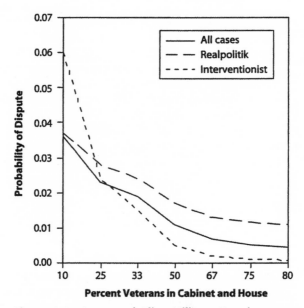

Figure 6.1. Impact of Elite Military Experience on U.S. Dispute Initiations: Realpolitik, Interventionist, and All Cases

Many of our control variables also have a significant impact on U.S. dispute initiation, but none of these effects can account for the impact of elite veterans. For example, our analysis supports the war-weariness hypothesis. The coefficient for the log of U.S. casualties in the previous war is negative and statistically significant, but it does not account for the impact of elite veterans. The percentage of veterans among the U.S. public, in contrast, has no significant effect. The fact that elite military experience matters while military experience among the public does not fits precisely with the elite-level causal mechanism that we hypothesized. The coefficient for Republican administrations was consistently positive, but did not quite achieve statistical significance (p < .11 for model in column one). Thus any possible association between the U.S. military and the Republican Party cannot account for the relationship between elite military experience and American conflict behavior. . . .

DOES THE CIVIL-MILITARY GAP INFLUENCE
HOW AMERICA USES FORCE?

Does elite military experience also have an impact on the American escalation of disputes? The answer to this question—displayed in table 6.2—appears to be an unqualified yes. Our results indicate that higher percentages of veterans

Table 6.2. Elite Military Experience and the Level of Military Force Used by the United States in a Dispute

Explanatory Variables	Coefficients and Standard Errors
Percent Veteran in the Cabinet and House	0.089***
	(0.024)
Republican Administration	−0.42
	(0.47)
Cold War Years	−4.31***
	(1.24)
Balance of Military Capabilities	−1.93
	(1.45)
Alliance Similarity Score	0.89
	(1.11)
U.S. Is a Major Power	1.91**
	(0.79)
Adversary Is a Major Power	−2.73***
	(1.01)
Adversary Level of Democracy	0.066
	(0.049)
U.S. Involvement in Other Disputes	−0.10
	(0.13)
Contiguous State	−0.68
	(1.016)
Distance between States	−0.0002
	(0.0002)
Adversary's Level of Force	0.61***
	(0.16)
Selection Effects Parameter	5.17*
	(3.15)
Threshold 1	−0.61
	(1.87)
Threshold 2	2.86*
	(1.90)
Threshold 3	7.08***
	(2.04)
Number of Observations	111
Initial Log-Likelihood	−112.54
Log-Likelihood at Convergence	−92.47
Chi-squared (10 d.f.)	40.13 (12 d.f.)***

Note: Huber-White robust standard errors for coefficients in parentheses.
* = $p < .10$, ** = $p < .05$, *** = $p < .01$.

in the political elite were associated with greater levels of force by the United States—if the United States did initiate the use of force. The coefficient for the percentage of veterans in the cabinet and in Congress is positive and statistically significant, and the impact of this variable is substantial.

Figure 6.2 indicates that as the percentage of veterans in the cabinet and Congress increases from 10 percent to 80 percent, the probability that the United States would engage in direct combat (use-of-force coding) increases from 2 percent to 73 percent. This same increase in the percentage of elite veterans increases the probability that the United States will escalate the dispute to the level of becoming a war from 0.06 percent to 9 percent. This latter increase is particularly substantial given the rarity of wars (0.2 percent of the dyad-years) and the gravity of escalating to such a level. Most of this impact is felt after the percentage of policymakers with military experience may well have favored something like an informal Powell Doctrine long before any such doctrine was articulated, far back in American history. . . .

Our measure of escalation is fairly crude and . . . developing more nuanced measures is a priority for future research. Nevertheless, it is striking that we find such statistically strong results in support of the theory's expectations, especially given the difficulties of measuring the phenomena

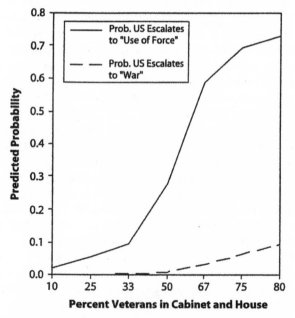

Figure 6.2. **Impact of Elite Military Experience on the Level of Force Used in Dispute**

involved. Moreover, note that the theory leads to opposite expectations from the veterans variable in these two stages of analysis: more veterans should lead to *fewer* dispute initiations but *higher* escalations. Nevertheless, the results support each apparently opposite dynamic, thus offering even stronger support for the underlying argument. . . .

CONCLUSION

Civil-military relations at the policymaking level often seem dominated by personalities. Contrast the problems of President Clinton with those of his war-hero predecessor, President Bush; compare the rumpled tenure of Secretary Les Aspin or the academic acerbity of Secretary Madeleine Albright with the no-nonsense corporate mentality of Secretary Donald Rumsfeld; or consider the unusual charisma and political clout of General and then Secretary Colin Powell. Personalities matter and may be decisive in certain cases. Nonetheless, the findings presented here suggest that, at least when it comes to the use of force, we can identify consistent civilian and military tendencies in policymaking, irrespective of personalities.

[Earlier we have] shown that elite civilians with military experience behave like "Colin Powells" and elite civilian nonveterans are like "Madeleine Albrights"—at least where opinions on the use of force are concerned. What creates these different types? Why do civilians without military experience tend to have foreign policy views that systematically differ from the views of those who have served? We cannot definitively answer that question. We would contend, however, that service in the U.S. military is an important socialization experience that shapes individuals' attitudes. The military teaches lessons about the role of military force in American foreign policy and lessons about how military force ought to be used. These lessons do not appear to be forgotten when individuals leave the military and enter civilian life. Of course, we cannot yet specify the precise mechanisms at work in this socialization process, and our data may be consistent with other explanations as well. Nonetheless, our results suggest that the relationship among military experience, foreign policy attitudes, and conflict behavior merits further attention.

Whatever the causes of this civil-military opinion gap, we have shown that the gap had a profound effect on American military behavior from 1816 to 1992. As expected, we found that the higher the proportion of American policymakers with military experience, the lower the probability that the United States would initiate a militarized dispute. Also as expected, we found that the impact of military experience on dispute initiation became even larger when we focused on states that represented interventionist rather than realpolitik threats to the United States. Finally, also as expected, we found that the veteran's effect showed up in the level of force as well; the higher the proportion of American policymakers with military experience, the higher the level of force used by the United States, given that it had already initiated a use of force. Throughout these analyses, the impact of elite military experience was substantively large and often outweighed the impact of variables that have received considerably more attention in the study of international conflict.

It may be "normal" for military personnel and civilians to develop distinctive views regarding the use of force, but when this divergence of views begins to have an impact on American conflict behavior, one cannot simply shrug off the difference and say, "Who cares?" The difference in views between those with and without experience in the American military is a profoundly important issue that is in need of public attention and discussion. In the wake of the Cold War, the United States is faced primarily with interventionist threats such as civil wars and the violation of human rights. Undoubtedly, debates over what ought to be done in future Kosovos, Haitis, and Rwandas will be shaped by this pervasive civil-military dynamic. If veteran representation in the political elite continues to decline, we can expect American involvement in many more Kosovos, Haitis, and Rwandas to come.

DISCUSSION QUESTIONS

1. What are the underlying questions or hypotheses that Feaver and Gelpi analyze in this study?
2. What are the two ways in which military preferences affect the shaping of U.S. foreign policy?
3. How do civilians and the military likely differ in their attitudes toward the use of force?
4. What relationship do Feaver and Gelpi find between the percentage of veterans in the Cabinet and the House of Representatives and the use of force?
5. How does this relationship differ for "realpolitik" cases and "interventionist" cases?
6. What is the relationship between the percentage of veterans in the Cabinet and the House of Representatives and the probability that there will be an escalation in the use of force or in the probability of an escalation to war?
7. What are the implications of this study for understanding the relationship between military experience and the conduct of U.S. foreign policy in the future?

REFERENCES

Beck, Nathaniel, Jonathan Katz, and Richard Tucker. 1998. "Taking Times Seriously: Time-Series-Cross-Section Analysis with a Binary Dependent Variable." *American Journal of Political Science* 42, no. 4: 1260–88.

Betts, Richard K. 1991. *Soldiers, Statesmen, and Cold War Crises*. New York: Columbia University Press.

Feaver, Peter. 2003. *Armed Servants: Agency, Oversight, and Civil-Military Relations*. Cambridge, MA: Harvard University Press.

Hinich, Melvin J., and Michael C. Munger. 1997. *Analytical Politics*. New York: Cambridge University Press.

Jones, Daniel M., Stuart A. Bremer, and J. David Singer. 1996. "Militarized Interstate Disputes, 1816–1992: Rationale, Coding Rules, and Empirical Patterns." *Conflict Management and Peace Science* 15, no. 2: 163–213.

Larson, Eric V. 1996. *Casualties and Consensus: The Historical Role of Casualties in Domestic Support for U.S. Military Operations*. Santa Monica, CA: Rand.

Maoz, Zeev, and Bruce M. Russett. 1993. Normative and Structural Causes of Democratic Peace." *American Political Science Review* 87, no. 3: 624–38.

Oneal, John R., and Bruce M. Russett. 1997. "The Classical Liberals Were Right: Democracy, Independence, and Conflict, 1950–1985." *International Studies Quarterly* 41, no. 2: 267–94.

7

Events, Elites, and American Public Support for Military Conflict*

Adam J. Berinsky

In recent years, a charitable view of the mass public has emerged in the public opinion and foreign policy literature. Increasingly, scholars have attributed "rationality" to public opinion concerning war. Many political scientists and policymakers argue that unmediated events—the successes and failures on the battlefield—determine whether the mass public will support military excursions. The public supports war, the story goes, if the benefits of action outweigh the costs of conflict and should therefore have a place at the policymaking table.

In this [chapter], I argue that military events may shape public opinion, but not in the straightforward manner posited by most scholars of public opinion and war. I draw upon and expand the work of scholars who contend that the balance of elite discourse influences levels of public support for war. Integrating research on heuristics and shortcuts with information-based theories of political choice, I demonstrate that patterns of conflict among partisan political actors shape mass opinion on war. It is not the direct influence of wartime events on individual citizens' decisions that determines public opinion, as "event response" theories of war support claim. Instead, consistent with the "elite cue" theory I advance in this [chapter], the nature of conflict among political elites concerning the salience and meaning of those events determines if the public will rally to war. To a significant degree citizens determine their positions on war by listening to trusted sources—those politicians who share their political predispositions.

I present evidence from . . . the second Iraq war to come to this common conclusion. . . . I find that significant segments of the mass public possessed

---

*All footnotes, in-text references, and references have been deleted.

little knowledge of the most basic facts of [this conflict]. Thus, there is little evidence that citizens had the information needed to make cost/benefit calculations when deciding whether to support or oppose military action. Instead, I find that patterns of elite conflict shaped opinions . . . during the Iraq conflict. When elites come to a common interpretation of a political reality, the public gives them great latitude to wage war. But when prominent political actors take divergent stands on the wisdom of intervention, the public divides as well. Furthermore, even in cases—such as the second Iraq war—where prominent political actors on one side of the partisan divide stay silent, the presence of a prominent partisan cue giver can lead to divergence in opinion. In sum, while members of the mass public are not lemmings—they have agency to determine their own opinion and may even, in the aggregate, reasonably react to changing events—in the realm of war, any apparent rationality arises largely through the process of elite cue taking, not through a reasoned cost/benefit analysis. The mass public is rational only to the extent that prominent political actors provide a rational lead.

THE POWER OF EVENTS?

The conventional wisdom that has emerged over the last thirty years in the public opinion and foreign policy literature holds that the course of events in a given conflict directly determines public support for war. The most prominent line of argument in this vein is what [James] Burk calls the "casualties hypothesis," the view that the American people will shrink from international involvement in the face of war deaths. This hypothesis grows out of [John] Mueller's contention that public support for war is inversely related to the log of casualties. Some modifications have been made to this basic theory over time. [Scott] Gartner and [Gary] Segura have, for instance, demonstrated the importance of local casualty rates in determining support for the war. Even so, the basic story advanced by Mueller remains a dominant view among both academics and policymakers.

Scholars have moved beyond simply investigating the impact of casualties to examine the effects of other events that affect the costs and benefits of military conflict. According to [Eric] Larson, the greater the perceived stakes, the clearer the objectives, and the higher the probability of success, the greater the level of public support for war. Building on this argument, other authors contend that the ongoing success of a mission—whether the war will come to a victorious end—determines public support for conflict. These theories differ in their particulars, yet all share the belief that "events" directly determine public support for war by altering the balance of costs and benefits related to a particular conflict. Thus, even for scholars who consider factors beyond casualties, the basic logic underlying Mueller's argument remains the dominant position: the collective mass public is rational and will support war if, and only if, the events of war ensure that the costs of military action are outweighed by the perceived benefits of a successful outcome.

Though "event-response" theories of public support for war have made important contributions, they have several potentially serious conceptual problems. First, these theories presume that members of the mass public at least implicitly incorporate knowledge of political developments into their political judgments. However, there is a long line of research that finds great heterogeneity in levels of political knowledge among the mass public. While researchers have long known that, on average, Americans know little about politics, knowledge levels are even dimmer when the focus turns to specific factual information. For instance, [Martin] Gilens found that the public's knowledge of specific policy-relevant information is low, even among those respondents who have high levels of general political knowledge.

Second, much research on the relationship between casualties and support for war has examined differences in collective public support for intervention across wars, not the differences among individuals within particular conflicts. With some important exceptions, analysis has proceeded at the aggregate level. Several existing theories, therefore, rest on untested notions of collective rationality. Larson, for instance, argues that the aggregate mass public will support war "if the aims are clear," but he does not describe the conditions under which individuals, much less the aggregate public, make such complex calculations. Thus, many existing theories of public support for military action fail to specify the mechanisms by which members of the mass public process information concerning the events of war and come to determine—both as individuals and collectives—either to support or oppose a given military operation. This aggregate-level work is certainly valuable, but it must be supplemented by individual-level analysis that accounts for individual-level variation on relevant political dimensions.

This leads to the final and most important point. Almost all the work described above ignores the partisan nature of the American political process. Treating the mass public as an undifferentiated whole—innocent of political and partisan attachments—leaves no room for the effect of domestic politics. Many researchers who study public opinion and war—even those scholars who conduct individual-level analysis—often talk about "the public" as if it were a monolithic entity. But foreign policy is often as contentious and partisan as domestic politics. Theories of war and politics must account for the effects of the domestic political process.

MEDIATED REALITY: THE PRIMACY OF
POLITICAL COMPETITION

In the early days of survey research, scholars argued that the public opinion concerning foreign policy was volatile and irrational—a fickle and changing "mood" in [Gabriel] Almond's words. However, the relative shortcoming of event-response theories does not mean that we must retreat to these dismal conclusions regarding public opinion and foreign policy. Event-response theories, after all, are not the only explanation for the dynamics of public support for war. Another possibility is to examine the influence of competition among political elites on public opinion.

The leading proponent of this theory in the context of foreign policy is [John] Zaller, who claims that elite discourse is the key to explaining war support. Zaller argues that the balance of persuasive messages carried in the political media determines the balance of opinion on a given policy controversy. Individuals who are most politically knowledgeable are most likely to receive political messages and accept those messages that accord with their personal political predispositions. The greater the volume of elite discourse favoring a particular policy position from elites of a particular political stripe, the more likely it is that the members of the mass public who share the political predispositions of those elites will adopt that position.

Zaller makes his case in the context of the Vietnam War, arguing that the decline in the support for that war was driven by a change in the balance of elite discourse across the 1960s. In the early phase of the war, when political elites were almost uniform in their support for the U.S. policy in Vietnam, Zaller found a monotonic relationship between political awareness and support for the war; those most attentive to elite discourse were most supportive of the current policy, regardless of their individual predispositions. Zaller terms this phenomenon the "mainstream pattern" of political support. On the other hand, in the later phases of the Vietnam War, when the mainstream consensus dissolved into elite disagreement, a "polarization pattern" emerged. Here, the effect of political awareness on support for the war was conditional on an individual's political values. Citizens attentive to politics followed the path of those leaders who shared their political views. For the Vietnam War, greater awareness led to higher levels of support among hawks and higher levels of opposition among doves. Zaller's story is not particular to Vietnam. [George] Belknap and [Angus] Campbell found a similar pattern of opinion during the Korean War; differences between Republican and Democratic identifiers were greatest among those respondents with high levels of political information, mirroring the corresponding differences among political elites.

The elite competition theory explicitly brings politics into the study of public opinion, allowing us to see how individuals with different political predilections react to different forms of elite discourse. At the same time, Zaller's explanation is somewhat incomplete. Zaller claims that the dynamics of opinion are driven exclusively by the net balance of partisan messages gleaned by individuals through political discourse. However, it is not clear if these messages are the only path to elite influence. Certainly, there are cases where political actors on both sides of a controversy provide persuasive messages, leading to polarized opinions among the mass public. But even in the absence of a balanced flow of discourse, individuals might have the information they need to come to a judgment regarding the fit between the policy options on the table and their political predispositions. Here the literature on cue taking and heuristics is instructive. Several studies have demonstrated that poorly informed citizens can make decisions that emulate the behavior of well-informed citizens by following the cues of politicians who share their political views. These studies suggest that even in the absence of specific policy messages, citizens can use the positions of elites to come to reasonable political decisions. We would therefore expect that citizens could use the positions of prominent elites as a reference point and decide whether to support or oppose a policy based on those positions, even in the absence of explicitly contradictory messages. In effect, citizens delegate the difficult process of arriving at an opinion on a complicated policy matter to trusted political experts. Presidents can serve as such cue givers, especially in the realm of foreign policy. For instance, if I am a Democrat, I need only know that George W. Bush supports a policy initiative to recognize that I should oppose such a course of action.

But to use this cue requires that citizens have knowledge of the positions of relevant political actors. Here is where Zaller's information-based theory can be brought into accord with cue-taking theories. As an individual's level of political information increases, their awareness of the positions of particular elites—and the distinctiveness of that position relative to other political actors—increases. Thus a pattern of opinion polarization could occur even in the absence of vocal opposition, provided a strong cue giver takes a clear position on that policy. As I will show below, this alternative mechanism of elite influence—what I call the elite cue theory—can explain the pattern of opinion in World War II, where both FDR and his Republican opponents took distinct positions. Moreover, unlike Zaller's original formulation, this theory can also explain the polarized pattern of opinion concerning the second war in Iraq, a situation where President Bush and Republican Party leaders took a strong pro-war position, but Democratic party leaders failed to express strong support or opposition.

EXPECTATIONS

Taken together, I have clear expectations regarding the relative role of events and elites in structuring opinion concerning war. Consistent with recent work on U.S. public opinion, but contrary to the expectations of scholars in the rationalist cost/benefit tradition, I expect that events will have little effect on the public's day-to-day judgments regarding the wisdom of war. This is not to say that events will never play a role in structuring opinion; certainly cataclysmic events, such as Pearl Harbor or the attacks of 9/11, can directly influence public opinion. But the events that many scholars of public opinion and war have examined—casualties and other mission indicators—play only a secondary role in determining public support for war. I therefore expect that knowledge of wartime events will not be widespread. Furthermore, correcting misperceptions of these events will have little effect on war support.

Conversely, I expect that patterns of elite discourse—the stated positions of leading Democrat and Republican politicians—will play a large role in determining public support for war. Individuals will use positions of prominent elites as a reference point, providing structure and guidance to opinions concerning war. Moreover, contrary to Zaller, I expect to find divergence without prominent elites speaking on both sides. The presence of prominent war-support cue givers can lead to a polarization of opinion as long as their political opponents do not also support war and vice versa. While citizens, in this view, do not rationally balance the costs and benefits of military action, neither do they blindly follow the messages disseminated by political elites. Rather they account for patterns of political leadership and partisan conflict to come to reasonable decisions that accord with their predispositions.

INDETERMINATE TESTS

Event-response theories, such as the casualties hypothesis (and its extensions) and the elite cue theory, which places the primary mechanism in the hands of partisan political actors, provide very different explanations for the dynamics of public support for war. These theories also carry very different normative implications: whether partisan political actors lead or follow opinion concerning war is a question with profound consequences for the practice of democracy. However, it has been difficult to assess the relative validity of the two approaches because scholars have focused on the Cold War and post–Cold War American experiences—namely, war failures and short-term military excursions. Consider, for instance, the Korea and Vietnam wars. Both the elite cue theory and the event-response theory predict that public support would decline as the conflicts unfolded. In the first view, as divisions among elites widened over time during both Korea and Vietnam, public opinion became polarized, thereby decreasing overall support for war. At the same time, since most scholars have used cumulative casualties as a measure of the war's cost, and cumulative casualties—as Gartner, Segura, and Wilkening note—are collinear with time, the casualties hypothesis predicts a secular decline in support for war over time. Thus, for both theories of public support, time is correlated with the explanatory variables of interest: real world events and how those events are discussed by elites. To distinguish the accuracy of these two theories, we need to look to new evidence.

In the rest of this [chapter], I draw upon [one case] to provide support for my elite cue theory. . . . I present evidence from two surveys I conducted concerning the war in Iraq to reveal that citizens do not incorporate information about wartime events into their political judgments. I find instead that partisanship and attentiveness to politics can explain patterns of opinion polarization as my theory of elite cue taking implies. . . .

THE WAR IN IRAQ

In March of 2003, the United States invaded Iraq, beginning a period of combat operations that continued through the 2006 election and beyond. Two facts about this war are particularly important for present purposes. First, dissemination of correct information about wartime events—especially the ongoing count of war dead—was prevalent in the media. We can therefore surmise that any misreporting in levels of war deaths by citizens is the result of faulty perceptions of reports of war deaths on the part of citizens, not faulty reports of the number of deaths by the media. Second, the positions of prominent cue givers regarding support for war were clear. As commander in chief, President Bush was strongly associated with support for the conflict. For much of this period, Republican Party elites followed his lead. The position of Democrats on this issue was less clear. A review of *Newsweek* articles on Iraq from February 2002 onward indicates that Democrats lacked a clear agenda for how to proceed on the Iraq question. For months after the initial invasion, there was limited dissent among Democrats. In the presidential campaign the notable dissenters on Iraq—Howard Dean and Wesley Clark—were quickly pushed aside by John Kerry, a senator who voted to authorize war in Iraq and, in line with other prominent Democrats, never took a clear position against the war. The question, then, is: Given the prominence of relevant information in media, which factor best explains variation in support for the war: casualties, as the event-response theory would suggest, or elite positions concerning the wisdom of that conflict, as the elite cue theory contends?

To answer this question, I conducted an experimental survey in the summer of 2004. My Iraq War Casualty Survey, conducted from July 23 to August 2, 2004, by Knowledge Networks, asked a random portion of a nationally representative sample of respondents the following:

> Please give your best guess to this next question, even if you are not sure of the correct answer. As you know, the United States is currently involved in a war in Iraq. Do you happen to know how many soldiers of the U.S. military have been killed in Iraq since the fighting began in March 2003?

At first glance, it appears that the public was informed about the level of troop deaths in Iraq. The mean estimate of deaths in the sample was 952 deaths, while the median response was 900 deaths. Both of these figures are extraordinarily close to the true casualty count, which rose from 901 to 915 over the span of the survey. The accuracy of the median respondent, however, disregards large variation in the casualty estimates. Respondents gave answers ranging from 0 deaths to 130,000 deaths. Even setting aside the extreme responses (casualty guesses under 10 and over 10,000), the standard deviation of the casualty estimate was 802.

A simple tabulation of the estimates illuminates the pattern of responses to the casualty question. Underestimating the casualty level of the war is a qualitatively different response than overestimating casualties. Thus, simply predicting the casualty estimate, or the absolute error of the estimate, is not informative. Instead, I created a three-category casualty estimate scale. I scored those respondents who estimated the number of war deaths to be between 801 and 1,015 (the true estimate +/- 100 deaths) as "correct." Those who gave an estimate of 800 or lower were scored as "underestimators," while those who guessed higher than 1,015 were considered "overestimators." The modal response (47 percent) was a correct answer. However, nearly as many respondents (42 percent) underestimated the number of war deaths (11 percent overestimated the number of deaths). The pattern of knowledge of casualties found in this survey extends to knowledge of the rate of American deaths in Iraq from around the same time. The Pew Research Center conducted a survey in September 2004 that asked respondents, "What's your impression about what's happened in Iraq over the past month? Has the number of American military casualties been higher, lower, or about the same as in other recent months?" Though a plurality of 46 percent gave the correct answer of "higher," a majority of respondents either gave an incorrect answer or were unable to provide an answer to the question. These knowledge levels certainly compare favorably to knowledge of other political facts, such as the percentage of budget devoted to foreign aid, but given the prominence of war deaths in the news, these studies demonstrate that even in a high salience environment, great variation existed in knowledge about events on the ground in Iraq.

More important for the purposes of this [chapter], this variation was not random; elite cues played a significant role in biasing the recall of knowledge. I examined the determinants of perceived level of casualties using measures of political engagement and partisan political leanings. I ran a multinomial logit (MNL) using the three-category casualty estimate scale (underestimator/correct/overestimator) as the dependent variable and the respondents' partisanship to account for the patterns of cue taking from partisan political actors. I also included as independent variables the amount of attention the respondent paid to news about Iraq, how much the respondent watched Fox News, and the respondent's general political information, education, and gender. The result of this analysis is presented in table 7.1. The coefficients in the second column are the effect of a given variable on the probability of underestimating the number of casualties versus correctly estimating the number of casualties. In the third column, the estimates are the effect on the probability of being an "overestimator," as compared to giving the correct answer.

Since the MNL coefficients can be difficult to interpret directly, I generated predicted probabilities of choosing the different response categories for the extreme values of the partisanship for the "typical" member of the public. These results are presented in table 7.2. As expected, compared to strong Republicans, strong Democrats are less likely to underestimate and are slightly more likely to overestimate casualty levels. By way of comparison, the effect of partisanship on the probability of underestimating casualty levels is roughly equal to the effect of moving from low information to high information. This finding is consistent with the Pew data on casualty rates described above. Among independents, 47 percent correctly stated that casualty rates were higher in the current month than in the previous

Table 7.1. MNL Analysis of Determinants of Estimates of War Deaths

Variable	*Correct Answer vs. Underestimate*	
	Coefficient (SE)	*Coefficient (SE)*
Constant	1.67 (.45)*	−.08 (.70)
Information	−.94 (.31)*	−1.44 (.48)*
Education	.10 (.09)	.06 (.15)
Gender	.03 (.18)	−.02 (.29)
Follow Iraq News	−2.06 (.38)*	−1.33 (.61)*
Watch Fox News	−.14 (.53)	.42 (.85)
Party Identification (Strong Dem High)	−.51 (.26)*	.11 (.43)

N = 621.
LL = -544.58.
*=p < .05.

Table 7.2. Predicted Probability of Causality Estimates

Information	Pr (Underestimate)	Pr (Correct Answer)	Pr (Overestimate)
Low Information	.51	.31	.18
High Information	.36	.56	.07
Difference	*−.15*	*+.25*	*−.11*
Strong Republican	.48	.44	.08
Strong Democrat	.35	.54	.12
Difference	*−.13*	*+.10*	*+.04*

month. Democrats were even more likely to say that casualties were higher—54 percent gave the correct answer—and Republicans were less likely to say that casualties were increasing—only 36 percent gave the correct answer. In short, perceptions of war deaths are influenced not only by information and engagement with political news, but also by the individual's political predispositions. Having demonstrated that the respondents' perceptions of events in the Iraq war were influenced by partisanship, I next move to the more important question of whether the casualty estimates had any influence on options concerning war.

Embedded in the Iraq war survey was an experiment in which one half of those respondents who were asked to estimate how many soldiers died in Iraq were then told, "Many people don't know the answer to this question, but according to the latest estimates, 901 soldiers have been killed in Iraq since the fighting began in March 2003." In other words, one-half of the respondents who were asked to estimate the number of American deaths were given a "treatment" of correct information. This experimental design allows me to compare levels of support for the war between two comparable groups: (1) the respondents in the "estimate war deaths" condition who underestimate casualties but were not told the correct number of war deaths; and (2) the respondents in the "corrected" condition who underestimate war deaths but were then told the number of U.S. soldiers who died. I can make a similar comparison for respondents who overestimate casualties. This is a powerful comparison, because the "correct information" treatment was randomly assigned. The only difference between the "estimate" group and the "corrected" group is that respondents in the "corrected" condition were subsequently told the true casualty rates. Thus, by comparing these two groups, I can assess the effect of introducing the correct information on support for war for individuals who are similarly misinformed about casualty rates.

I measured attitudes toward the Iraq war with two common measures of war support. The first question asked, "Do you think the U.S. made the right decision or the wrong decision in using military force against Iraq?"

The second question asked, "All in all, considering the costs to the United States versus the benefits to the United States, do you think the current war with Iraq has been worth fighting, or not?" The results of these analyses are presented in table 7.3. There were no reliably significant differences between the respondents in the two conditions in either a substantive or a statistical sense. Furthermore, the direction of the treatment effect is in the incorrect direction for both the "worth fighting" and the "right decision" questions—respondents who were told that the number of war deaths was larger than they had believed were *more* supportive of the war (though the difference is small and statistically insignificant by a wide margin). Among overestimators, the effect of the treatment was in the expected direction for the "worth fighting" question only and is statistically insignificant.

THE HUMAN AND MONETARY COSTS OF WAR

One of the best-known findings from the survey research literature is that seemingly minor alterations in the wording of particular questions can lead to large changes in the answers respondents give to surveys. Recent

Table 7.3.   Effect of Information Treatment on Support for War in Iraq

Among Underestimators	
Did the United States Make the Right Decision in Using Military Force against Iraq?	*United States Made Right Decision*
Estimate War Deaths Condition	52%
Corrected Information Condition	56%
N = 252; x2(l) = .40 Pr =.53	
Has the Current War in Iraq Been Worth Fighting?	*Worth Fighting*
Estimate War Deaths Condition	42%
Corrected Information Condition	47%
N = 253; x2(l) = .71 Pr = .40	
Among Overestimators	
Did the United States Make the Right Decision in Using Military Force against Iraq?	*United States Made Right Decision*
Estimate War Deaths Condition	58%
Corrected Information Condition	58%
N =57; x2(l) = .00 Pr = .95	
Has the Current War in Iraq Been Worth Fighting?	*Worth Fighting*
Estimate War Deaths Condition	42%
Corrected Information Condition	48%
N =57; x2(l) = .26 Pr = .61	

advances in theories of the survey response have helped researchers to predict when opinion changes might occur. As Zaller argues, "Individuals do not typically possess 'true attitudes' on issues, as conventional theorizing assumes, but a series of partially independent and often inconsistent ones." Answers to survey questions are, therefore, in part determined by the balance of arguments made salient by survey questions.

Bringing additional pieces of information—to use Zaller's terminology, "considerations"—to mind alters the base of information that individuals use to come to particular decisions. From this point of view, highlighting negative information—such as the human and monetary costs of war—should cause individuals to focus on the downside of war. In the aggregate, questions that contain information about casualties and the costs of war should therefore yield lower levels of support for war than questions that omit such information.

Somewhat surprisingly, in two separate experiments, I did not find this predicted pattern of results. The design of the 2004 Iraq War Casualty Survey allowed me to directly test the effect of introducing casualty information on support for war. The Iraq War Casualty Survey was a 2 x 2 experimental design. Only one-half of the respondents were asked to estimate the number of casualties, as described above. The other half of the sample permitted a further experimental test. In the "control" condition of the survey, respondents were neither asked nor given any information concerning the casualty rates in Iraq; they were simply asked their level of support for the conflict. In the "information only" condition, respondents were not asked to provide an estimate of war deaths, but they were told the correct casualty rates. I found no statistically significant difference in the answers to the war support questions between these two conditions. Making salient a negative consideration—the scope of the human cost of war—and providing specific information about that cost did not change the aggregate shape of opinion on the war.

In the fall of 2005, I collected additional data to assess the effects of event-specific information on opinions concerning the Iraq war. Respondents to an omnibus survey were randomly assigned to one of six conditions: a "baseline" condition, a "standard survey question" condition, or one of four information conditions.

> *Form 1* (baseline): "All in all, do you think the war with Iraq was worth fighting, or not?"
>
> *Form 2* (standard survey question): "All in all, considering the costs to the United States versus the benefits to the United States, do you think the war with Iraq was worth fighting, or not?"
>
> *Form 3*: "As you may know, since the war in Iraq began in March 2003, many American soldiers have been killed. All in all, considering the

costs to the United States versus the benefits to the United States, do you think the war with Iraq was worth fighting, or not?"

Form 4: "As you may know, since the war in Iraq began in March 2003, almost 2,000 American soldiers have been killed. All in all, considering the costs to the United States versus the benefits to the United States, do you think the war with Iraq was worth fighting, or not?"

Form 5: "As you may know, since the war in Iraq began in March 2003, the United States has spent a large amount of money on operations in Iraq. All in all, considering the costs to the United States versus the benefits to the United States, do you think the war with Iraq was worth fighting, or not?"

Form 6: "As you may know, since the war in Iraq began in March 2003, the United States has spent almost 200 billion dollars on operations in Iraq. All in all, considering the costs to the United States versus the benefits to the United States, do you think the war with Iraq was worth fighting, or not?"

The first (baseline) condition presented a neutral stimulus; respondents were simply asked whether or not they support the war. In the second (standard survey question) condition, respondents were explicitly asked to consider the costs and benefits of the Iraqi invasion, following the convention of poll questions asked by the *Washington Post* and Gallup. Respondents in the other four conditions were asked forms of the questions that highlighted specific information about the human and financial costs of the Iraq war, in either general (forms 3 and 5) or specific (forms 4 and 6) terms.

Given the vast amounts of research on question wording effects, we would expect to find large differences across conditions based on the types of information presented in the question. But this is not the case. In fact, as table 7.4 demonstrates, there are almost no differences in levels of support across conditions.

Why, in the face of strong negative information, did these treatments have no effect? The lack of an effect is probably not because respondents

Table 7.4.   Effect of Information Treatment on Support for War in Iraq

Has the Current War in Iraq Been Worth Fighting	*United States Made Right Decision*
Baseline	40%
Standard Survey	42%
Many Soldiers Died	43%
2,000 Soldiers Died	41%
U.S. Spent a Lot of Money	40%
U.S. Spent $200 Billion	37%

N = 1,168; x2(10) = 9.48 Pr = .49.

had already incorporated the information into their judgments. As the 2004 Iraq War Survey demonstrates, many respondents did not know the correct casualty figures. Instead, I did not find substantive difference among the conditions because respondents had already made up their minds on Iraq. Citizens discounted new information in favor of more important considerations—their attachments to particular political leaders.

ELITE CUES

Though event-response theories cannot explain differences in support for war, models that account for the influence of partisan cues strongly predict patterns of war support. Recall that the elite cue theory hypothesizes that members of the mass public will look to prominent political actors as guides for their positions on the war. In the context of Iraq, the Bush administration's clear stance on the war—and the general unity of the Republican Party for much of this time—provides such a guide. Even though Democratic leaders had not taken a consistent and strong antiwar stance at the time of the survey, both Republicans and Democrats who were attentive to politics could use the strong support of the war by George Bush and Republican party leaders as a cue to influence their position on the war.

As noted above, partisanship has a larger effect on support for the war than does casualty information. More tellingly, support for the Iraq conflict followed the polarization pattern, as the elite cue theory predicts. The "polarization pattern" of political support emerges when prominent political actors take a clear position on the necessity of military action and their counterparts across the political aisle do not follow suit. Under these circumstances, citizens who are more informed will follow those political actors who share their views. If, on the other hand, elite discourse is unified in support of intervention, public opinion should be characterized by the "mainstream pattern"; more informed citizens should be more supportive of government policy, regardless of their political predispositions. To determine whether the mainstream pattern or the polarization pattern best characterizes public opinion, we need individual-level measures of three quantities: support for the war, political predispositions, and levels of political information (which, following Zaller, proxies attentiveness to elite discourse). The Iraq War Casualty Survey contains all of these quantities. Following Zaller, I ran a probit of the measures of support for war on partisanship, information, the interaction between information and partisanship, and several control variables. [*The full regression results are omitted here.—Ed.*] Figure 7.1 presents the results of an analysis of the effects of political information levels on support for the war. As the figure demonstrates,

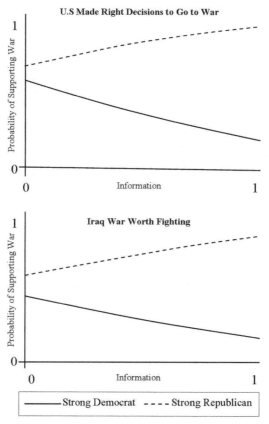

Figure 7.1. Patterns in Polarization in Iraq War Attitudes, August 2004

as a modal respondent's attention to political discourse increases, he adopts diametrically opposed positions on the war, depending on whether he is a Democrat or a Republican.

Although there is a gap between Democrats and Republicans at the lowest information levels, this gap grows as information levels increase, indicating that differences in elite positions are reflected in individuals' positions on war.

All told, these results provide support for elite-centered views of war support. Perceptions of war deaths are influenced by the respondent's partisan attachments. Furthermore, perceptions of war deaths do not influence attitudes toward war, and correcting respondents' misperceptions has little effect on support for war. Whatever inconsistent effects arise from presenting correct information pale in comparison to the effects of partisanship. . . .

DISCUSSION QUESTIONS

1. What is the usual "conventional wisdom" that is relied upon to explain the American public's support for war?
2. What is the "casualties hypothesis" in explaining war support?
3. According to the author, what are some problems with "event-response" theories of public support for war?
4. How does the competition among political elites affect public opinion and support or opposition to war?
5. What is the "elite cue" theory of public opinion?
6. What are the expectations that the author has regarding the interaction of events and elites in structuring opinion concerning support for war?
7. How does the author go about testing the impact of events, information, and partisanship with the data from the second Iraq war?
8. How does the author show that partisanship is more important than other factors in support or opposition to the second Iraq war?

8

External Affairs and the Electoral Connection

Miroslav Nincic

The dictum that politics should stop at water's edge, when international affairs are involved, reflects neither reality nor core principles of U.S. democracy. Except at times of extreme and immediate threat to values all Americans embrace, foreign policy, like all policy, is a product of domestic politics, for very good reasons. External policy is about the pursuit of the national interest, which, in the vast majority of cases, is not an objective datum on which all can agree but the resultant of often discrepant vectors of domestic interest and preference; and it is most appropriately defined through national debate and electoral competition. Accordingly, foreign policy has been a big part of national electoral campaigns since the country's rise to superpower status, presidential elections differing only in the range of foreign policy and national security issues that have been subject to electoral politicization.

A HISTORY OF POLITICIZED FOREIGN POLICY

Although it is assumed that splendid bipartisan consensus marked the coldest years of the Cold War, elections were not, even then, immune to political wrangling. During the 1952 campaign, denunciation of Truman's foreign policy was a principal theme of Eisenhower's electoral strategy, Truman being excoriated for weakness toward the Soviet Union. John F. Kennedy's campaign is remembered for his hammering away at the theme of a "missile gap" to America's disadvantage that Republicans had allowed to develop. The 1972 presidential election and to some extent that of 1968 were largely fought around the Vietnam War, a war justified by a Cold War rationale. Relations between the United States and the Soviet Union were central to the 1976 and 1980 election campaigns. In 1976, the assault was led by Ronald Reagan in his bid to wrest the Republican president nomination from Gerald Ford. In 1980, Reagan declared that President Carter's policy, by "bordering on appeasement," could be inviting another world war.[1]

Cold War and post–Cold War years differed only in the range of issues on which disagreements could be voiced. At the height of the Cold War, no dissent was possible on the nature of the threat or the character of the adversary; all that could be debated was the mode of pursuing the rivalry (e.g., rollback or containment) and the actual balance of power between the superpowers (e.g., was there, or was there not, an ICBM gap). As Vietnam and the Cold War's demise shattered much of the bipartisanship of earlier years, the character of the debate and thus its role in major national elections changed.

Despite a hiatus on foreign policy partisanship in the early 1990s, a period when post–Cold War hopes of a new world order decreased the salience of external affairs, partisan divisions were soon revived. Thus, foreign aid for Third World population control programs, the Comprehensive Test Ban Treaty, Kosovo, the Kyoto Protocol, and so forth have been the object of vigorous electoral debates. In one view, the main causes of the growing disharmony have been the demise of the Soviet Union, allowing for a broader discussion on the ends and means of U.S. foreign policy and the tendency of politicians to seek to energize their core supporters by exaggerating policy differences.[2] These new divisions and their electoral consequences were especially stark in 2004 as both George W. Bush and John Kerry battled to impress the electorate with their own interpretations of the Iraq War's challenges and the proper way of addressing them. The 2008 election shifted the focus somewhat, from U.S. involvement in Iraq to the country's growing entanglement in Afghanistan, and it focused, on Hillary's Clinton's side during the primaries and John McCain's during the general election, on the need to elect a leader experienced in the conduct of foreign affairs.

While foreign policy has always been a major issue around which contenders for the presidency (sometimes for Congress and the Senate) have structured their campaigns, this would not affect electoral outcomes if there were no significant discord within the body of the electorate on international matters. Moreover, if, at least between elections, politics did stop at water's edge, the impact on the actual conduct of foreign policy would rarely be felt. We ask, therefore, two questions: (1) Does foreign policy really affect electoral outcomes in the United States? (2) Do these outcomes shape the actual conduct of the nation's external affairs?

THE IMPACT OF FOREIGN POLICY ON NATIONAL ELECTIONS

The actual electoral impact of international politics should hinge on two circumstances: first, whether voters care enough about external affairs to vote accordingly, especially when important domestic issues loom; and, second, whether there are characteristic partisan rifts in voter preferences in this area, rifts that could be exploited by candidates competing for their support.

Do Americans Vote Their Foreign Policy Preferences?

Although the behavior of politicians suggests that Americans care enough about foreign policy to let it shape their voting decisions, some may find this surprising. Many people don't seem interested in world politics, largely because the consequences cannot easily be linked to their personal interests and, in any case, the electorate's generally scant understanding of politics and policy is especially deficient where international issues are concerned. Nevertheless, foreign policy does matter sufficiently to a large enough percentage of the electorate to have a significant electoral impact. Although the impact rarely is irrelevant, it stands to be greater when international storms brew than when conditions are calm. Let us compare, in this regard, the presidential elections of 2000, 2004, and 2008.

2000 Election

The 2000 election occurred at a time when no major foreign threat confronted the United States, as the world adapted to post–Cold War conditions, to the reintegration of Eastern Europe into the community of nations, and to the multifaceted impact of economic globalization. The wars in the Balkans had pretty much ended, and the 1999 intervention of the North Atlantic Treaty Organization (NATO) on behalf of Kosovo Albanians had produced its desired outcome. Table 8.1 describes how important, in these relatively serene conditions, various policy issues were to voting decisions in 2000. The first column lists a number of issues, and the second reveals the percentage of respondents considering it the issue most important to their voting decision.

A first observation is that domestic issues mattered more than foreign policy. Circumstances like the economy and education have a direct impact on the lives of voters, who usually know and care more about them. Despite the primacy of the domestic, 10 percent of the electorate deemed foreign policy *the* most important issue. If this does not seem much, it must

Table 8.1. The Impact of Issue Categories on the 2000 Presidential Vote

Type of Issue	% Considering the Issue Most Important
Education	20
The Economy	16
Taxes	15
Social Security	15
Health Care	12
Foreign Policy	10
Prescription Drugs	5
Other	5
Don't Know	2

Source: Washington Post tracking poll, October 2000

be remembered that, in the United States, presidential elections often are determined by thin margins. Between 1968 and 2004, the average gap in the percentage of the vote received by the Democratic and Republican candidates was 7.7 percent, and three of these elections were won by less than 3 percent.[3] The 2008 election was carried by Barack Obama by 7.2 percent. This means that external affairs could make the difference between victory and defeat since even voters who do not consider foreign policy the *most* important issue often deem it important enough to affect their voting decision. For example, one poll conducted in the run-up to this election revealed that 21.5 percent of the respondents considered foreign affairs to be "one" of the issues most important to their vote for president, while fully 60.4 percent said it was "somewhat important."[4]

2004 Election

The election year 2004 was powerfully dominated by international issues, including terrorism-associated security threats and the U.S. invasion of Iraq. While the list of questions in table 8.2 is not quite identical to that of table 8.1, the electoral importance of foreign policy issues is evident.

As before, education and the economy (and, here, moral and ethical issues) top the list. While "foreign affairs," as such, was considered most important by only 5 percent of the respondents, the picture changes with the specific matters of terrorism and Iraq (both intimately related to international policy). With these counted in the total, fully half the electorate considered foreign policy the most important influence on their presidential voting decision. Efforts by both John Kerry and George W. Bush to establish their credibility on such issues reflected the interest they held for many American voters. As election day approached, the salience of Iraq and the war on terror progressively increased, actually overtaking the traditionally dominant issues of jobs and the economy (see table 8.4).

Table 8.2. The Impact of Issue Categories on the 2004 Presidential Vote

Type of Issue	% Considering the Issue Most Important
Moral/ethical values	40
Jobs/economy	33
Terrorism/homeland security	29
Situation in Iraq	16
Education	15
Social issues such as abortion and gay marriage	15
Taxes	9
Health care	9
Foreign affairs	5
Social security	5
Medicare/prescription drugs	3

Source: Los Angeles Times exit poll, November 2004.

It is noteworthy that while, by September, John Kerry was thought likely to do a better job on the economy (by 49 to 43 percent), the ultimate winner, George W. Bush, was deemed apt to do a better job on Iraq and the war on terror (51 to 39 percent).

2008 Election

In 2008, external threats to the United States appeared slighter than in 2004 and Americans seemed less worried about international affairs: memories of 9/11 were not as raw and the U.S. involvement in Iraq was tapering off. Although the nation's leaders fretted about the nuclear programs of Iran and North Korea, these were not issues on the minds of many voters. Accordingly, foreign policy's electoral weight resembled more closely that of 2000 than of 2004, as revealed in table 8.3, suggesting that, absent major crises, foreign policy issues dominate the electoral calculus of 10–15 percent of U.S. voters. In this case, John McCain was generally considered to

Table 8.3. The Impact of Issue Categories on the 2008 Presidential Vote

Type of Issue	% Considering the Issue Most Important
The Economy	50
Iraq	10
Terrorism	5
Energy policy	3
Health care	10
Something else	21
No opinion	1

Source: ABC News/Washington Post, October 30–November 2, 2008. Asked of likely voters.

offer somewhat stronger leadership on Iraq and terrorism, whereas Obama had a very commanding lead on the economy (the issue that mattered most to most voters). Foreign policy does not easily trump economic considerations, but it is very likely that McCain's support would have been even lower without the foreign policy advantage—a difference perhaps equal to the margin (over 7 percent) by which Obama won.

The bottom line: During halcyon times, foreign policy can affect the electoral balance in a tight election; in troubled times, it may play a decisive role.

International affairs also seem to influence the outcome of congressional elections. In 2002, one national survey established that whereas 50 percent of the respondents would vote for a congressional candidate on the basis of domestic issues, fully 46 percent would be guided by foreign policy and national security issues, such as terrorism and the war in Afghanistan.[5] Asked in April 2006 how important the situation in Iraq would be in determining the respondent's vote for Congress in the fall, 83 percent declared it to be "one of the most important" or a "very important" issue.[6] In 2010, 48 percent of the respondents declared that they would be more likely to vote for a congressional candidate who supported withdrawing U.S. troops from Afghanistan (regardless of whether conditions were getting better or worse).[7]

DO FOREIGN POLICY DIVISIONS CHARACTERIZE THE AMERICAN ELECTORATE?

If the electorate considers international affairs in its voting decisions, this could have a meaningful impact on electoral decisions only if significant fissures mark the foreign policy preferences of voters: these differences could lend themselves to electoral politicization only if they fall within predictable partisan categories, which they do.

While relatively muted at the height of the Cold War,[8] partisan cleavages developed in the wake of Vietnam. By the 1980s, they became especially

Table 8.4. Iraq and the Economy as 2004 Campaign Issues: Which Is More Important? *(Base: Likely voters)*

	June (%)	August (%)	September (%)
The Economy and jobs	52	50	47
Iraq and the war on terror	41	43	48
Neither/not sure	7	7	4

Note: Question wording: "If the presidential election were held today, which would be more important to you in deciding who to vote for—issues related to the economy and jobs or issues related to Iran and the war on terror?
Source: Harris Poll no. 68, September 23, 2004.

apparent, encompassing a broad range of both domestic and international issues.[9] In 2004, the Pew Research Center for the People and the Press computed composite attitude scales on twenty-four questions concerning political and policy issues and seventeen involving social and personal attitudes.[10] Examination of the two trends since 1987 revealed that the partisan gap had widened and that it was even greater for political and policy attitudes than for social and personal stances. Though domestic issues came to the forefront of concerns at the end of the decade, differences on foreign affairs and national security remained very pronounced.[11] These positions have not escaped partisan polarization, and one comprehensive study found hardening and increasingly divergent positions between conservatives and liberals and between Republicans and Democrats on most matters of international and security policy.[12]

The dilemma is how best to characterize these increasingly divergent worldviews, and we will begin by examining the kinds of foreign policy objectives that Americans tend to consider very important, asking whether there are clusters of goals preferred by supporters of either major party. An overview of these goals is provided by surveys regularly conducted for the Chicago Council on Foreign Relations, which presents its respondents with a set of external aims, asking whether they consider them "very important," "somewhat important," or "not at all important." The 2004 survey questions are presented in the first column of table 8.5.

Within this list of foreign policy objectives, do we see certain characteristic features that would make certain aims naturally cluster together? If so, this might tell us whether there is a systematic difference in the *type* of foreign policy ends Republicans and Democrats prefer. We are helped here by a statistical technique called "factor analysis," which searches for commonalities among variables, defining those that seem to hang together as sharing common "factors," implying that they lie astride a common dimension.

Numerical values were assigned to the importance accorded by respondents to the goals mentioned in the survey,[13] and the results were subjected to factor analysis.[14] The "loading" of each variable (here, each foreign policy objective) on the factor tells us how highly each is, in a sense, correlated with that factor—that is, how big a part of that factor it represents. These loadings are presented in the second and third columns of table 8.5.

The results indicate that there are, indeed, two distinct factors that characterize the examined objectives and that there is a systematic difference in the types of variables (foreign policy objectives) that load highly on each. The higher loadings on the first factor involve objectives such as "maintaining superior military power," "controlling illegal immigration," "protecting American jobs," and so on. The higher loading on the second factor is associated with goals such as "combating world hunger," "protecting weak

Table 8.5. Partisan Dimension of Foreign Policy Priorities

Foreign Policy Objective	Self-Regarding (Factor 1)	Other-Regarding (Factor 2)
Protecting weak nations from aggression	0.35	0.51
Strengthening the United Nations	−0.001	0.41
Combating world hunger	0.07	0.66
Combating international terrorism	0.63	0.14
Maintaining superior military power	0.63	−0.01
Promoting democracy abroad	0.32	0.41
Securing adequate energy supplies	0.38	0.16
Controlling illegal immigration	0.40	−0.13
Improving the living standards of less developed countries	0.05	0.75
Improving the global environment	0.05	0.43
Preventing the spread of nuclear weapons	0.57	0.21
Stopping the flow of illegal drugs to the United States	0.31	0.12
Protecting American business	0.37	0.18
Protecting American jobs	0.23	0.04
Eigenvalue	3.19	1.32

nations from aggression," and "strengthening the United Nations." The first group includes ends that primarily and directly benefit the United States; goals in the second group seek benefits of a broader international sort. Let us designate objectives loading highly on factor 1 as "self-regarding" objectives and those that load substantially on factor 2 as "other-regarding" goals. A preference for one or another type of goal presumably reflects a person's political philosophy. Do Republicans and Democrats differ systematically in their preference for one or another category of goal?

To answer this question, we calculate "factor scores" for the survey respondents, which provide a measure of how highly they rate on each factor, and we ask whether there is a meaningful difference in the scores of Republicans and Democrats. Table 8.6 displays the results.

There is, indeed, a major gap between Republicans and Democrats with regard to the type of foreign policy they prefer. Republicans have a stronger preference for goals of the self-regarding type, and Democrats are more committed to ends of the other-regarding sort. This probably stems from a major difference in basic worldviews associated with liberal and conservative political ideology,[15] and there is evidence that the corresponding partisan gap has been increasing.[16] The gap defines, in part, foreign policy goals apt to attract the votes of Republicans and Democrats and thus the practical consequences of their votes: as candidates tailor policies to the preferences of their core constituencies and as the distance between these constituen-

Table 8.6.   Average Factor Scores by Party Affiliation

	Self-Regarding Factor	Other-Regarding Factor
Democrats	–0.29	0.11
Republicans	0.05	–0.25

cies grows. Republican administrations, this implies, will lean toward self-regarding goals, and Democratic administrations will show more sympathy for other-regarding goals.

Republicans and Democrats differ not only on the aims they assign to foreign policy but also on how they think these should be pursued. One choice is whether to act in multilateral partnerships, where decisions and responsibilities are shared with other nations, or unilaterally, hoping that others will follow but carrying on regardless. One might expect that those preferring self-regarding ends would also favor unilateral means, while those more committed to other-regarding goals would tend toward the multilateral option. Such is indeed the case. When queried, in 2004, "When dealing with international problems, the United States should be more willing to make decisions within the United Nations even if this means that the United States will sometimes have to go along with a policy that is not its first choice," 78 percent of the Democratic respondents agreed, and only 52 percent of the Republicans.[17] Similarly, when asked (the same year) whether, if a situation like Iraq arose in the future, it would be essential, before using force, to secure the approval of (1) the United Nations, (2) NATO, or (3) our main European allies, substantially more Democrats opted for the multilateral solution. In a more recent survey (November 2009), Americans were asked whether or not they agreed that "The United States should cooperate fully with the United Nations." The results, shown in table 8.7, display the partisan breach.

Partisanship also is associated with relative preference for armed force or diplomacy as tools of foreign policy, and we might think that those preferring multilateralism would also incline toward diplomacy and vice versa. This is confirmed by surveys in which people were asked whether (1) "good

Table 8.7.   Partisan Support for the United Nations

The United States should cooperate fully with the United Nations	Republican	Democrat	Independent
Agree	39%	65%	47%
Disagree	53%	22%	43%
Don't know/refused	8%	13%	9%

Source: Pew Research Center for the People and the Press/Pew Forum on Religion and Public Life.

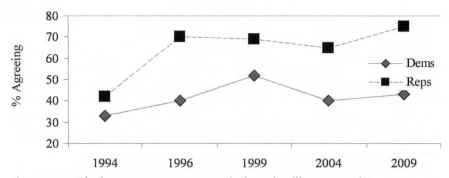

Figure 8.1. "The best way to ensure peace is through military strength"
Source: Pew Research Center for the People and the Press

diplomacy is the best way to ensure peace" or (2) "military strength is the best way to ensure peace." While in 2004 a slight majority of 55 percent of all Americans chose diplomacy as the surest path to peace, the difference between Republicans and Democrats was significant. While only 32 percent of Republicans concurred with that view, more than twice as many Democrats did. At the same time, Republicans have been far more likely to endorse military force as the surest path to peace. While 62 percent of Republicans opted for military force in 2004, that number for Democrats was 33 percent (see figure 8.1).[18] By 2009 the difference was 75 percent and 43 percent.[19] Clearly, there is a major gap between supporters of the nation's two major parties when it comes to their preferred tools of foreign policy, and the difference has been increasing in recent years.

Whether ends or means of foreign policy are concerned, Democrats and Republicans have different worldviews: the former with a greater relative preference for other-regarding goals, multilateralism, and diplomacy; the latter favoring self-regarding goals, unilateralism, and military force. To the extent that candidates for national office seek the support of core constituencies, they shape their platforms accordingly; and because victors can't totally neglect their own promises, the substance of foreign policy depends on who is elected.

THE CONSEQUENCES OF
THE ELECTORAL CONNECTION

Two categories of consequences follow from foreign policy's electoral connections. The first involves discontinuities in the way the country conducts its external affairs, and the second bears on periodicities imparted to this conduct by the electoral cycle.

Foreign Policy Discontinuities

During the Cold War, and especially since, discontinuities in U.S. foreign policy often followed elections that brought a new administration to office. Abrupt policy changes flow from gaps between positions of challengers and incumbents and between Republican and Democratic voters, positions that harden and gaps that widen in electoral campaigns. Consequently, foreign policy shifts often reflect the logic of domestic politics more closely than objective international reality, making it harder for friends and adversaries to anticipate the course of America's policies and to adjust their behavior accordingly.

Thus, President Eisenhower's limited interest in developing nations was replaced by President Kennedy's virtual obsession with the Third World as an arena of East-West conflict. Whereas the Nixon and Ford administrations' pragmatic approach to geopolitics left little room for concern with human rights, President Carter initially made it a cornerstone of his foreign policy. His step-by-step approach to a Middle East settlement was dropped in the Reagan administration's unsuccessful attempt to sweep regional differences under the carpet and create an anti-Soviet alliance of pro-Western states in that part of the world. George H. W. Bush's hands-off attitude regarding the conflict in the Balkans was replaced by Bill Clinton's active interventionism in the region and so forth.

George W. Bush's accession to power dramatically altered the nation's way of dealing with the international community, a shift that can be linked to the widening partisan chasm and to the administration's notion of where the base of its electoral support was located. The government's attitude toward the use of armed force was one expression of the new foreign policy philosophy.

The 2001 military action in Afghanistan was driven by a clear imperative in the wake of 9/11: attacking al Qaeda's infrastructure and dismantling the regime that provided it with a safe base of operations. While it is unlikely that the Democratic candidate in 2000, Al Gore, would have acted any differently had he been elected, and though support was firm on both sides of the congressional aisle, subsequent actions are much more closely connected to partisan worldviews. Thus, the 2003 invasion of Iraq followed no pressing security imperative, and the arguments by which it was justified (Saddam Hussein's quest for weapons of mass destruction and his links to al Qaeda) were subsequently proven false.[20] At the same time, the invasion placed in sharp relief the administration's greater faith in military force than diplomatic engagement and its readiness to act unilaterally when significant portions of the international community disagreed with its course. (Several members of the UN Security Council urged further diplomatic efforts to ascertain whether the Iraqi regime was, indeed, pursuing weapons of mass destruction, and this body did not endorse the invasion.) Similarly, the president's decision to embrace a doctrine of preemptive military action, whenever the administration felt this to be in the nation's security interests,[21] represented, at least at the level of declared policy, a sharp break from the past and a further embrace of military force as the premier tool of foreign policy.

Other actions underscored the predilection for self-regarding ends and unilateral means. The administration rejected the Kyoto Protocol, designed to reduce greenhouse emissions, even though the United States was their largest producer, mainly because it would create economic difficulties for many of the country's industrial producers. Similarly, the treaty establishing the International Criminal Court, initially signed by the Clinton administration, was repudiated, the objection being that it might subject U.S. soldiers to politically motivated prosecutions. An attempt to strengthen the Biological Weapons Convention with a new protocol designed to strengthen verification also was spurned in large part because it might impede America's own bio-weapons program and harm the interests of domestic drug companies.

Barack Obama's electoral victory in 2008, signaled a return to earlier traditions of U.S. multilateralism, a (somewhat hesitant) realignment with other developed countries on environmental matters, and an increasing commitment to diplomacy as a tool of U.S. foreign policy.

The point is that electoral outcomes produce powerful consequences for U.S. foreign policy, which, far from stopping at water's edge, often reflects the convictions and interests of the incumbent administration's core support groups. Lamentable though some consider this, it flows from the fact that the national interest is not (except at its outer margins) an objective given but rather the product of national dialogue and political competition,[22] a large part of which occurs in the context of national elections.

Foreign Policy Periodicities

Apart from the consequences for the substance of U.S. international activity, elections also make themselves felt in the periodicities they impart to policymaking. Partly, this is seen in the manner in which incumbents and challengers divide their attention between international and domestic matters. When external relations are going well, incumbents try to focus voters' attention on international relations, while challengers seek to draw that attention toward domestic matters. By contrast, when foreign policy is more problematic, challengers turn the spotlight on the incumbents' conduct of foreign affairs, while the latter try to focus attention on the domestic realm.[23] Some periodicities show even greater structure, as has been illustrated in America's policy toward the Soviet Union during the Cold War and in its pattern of resorting to military force abroad.

COLD WAR POLITICS

During the Cold War, presidential contenders tended to compete in asserting their uncompromising toughness toward Moscow while questioning the wisdom of their rivals' positions. At the same time, the unease of much of the electorate with excessive saber rattling and inflammatory rhetoric as well as the need to curb the escalatory risks associated with the rivalry meant that constructive policies had to coexist with firmness—the result was a cyclical quality to progress in U.S.-Soviet relations. In the fourth year of a typical four-year cycle, the need to establish staunch anti-Soviet credentials for electoral purposes made it unlikely that cooperative gestures would be made toward the Kremlin, making these the years of some of the most bellicose Cold War rhetoric. Because of the uncompromising attitudes adopted in election years, a movement toward cooperation was not usually possible in their immediate aftermath, implying that little progress in U.S.-Soviet relations could be expected during the first year of the next four-year cycle. Accordingly, the first constructive steps often were witnessed during the cycle's second year, and, because initiatives rarely bear immediate fruit, tangible achievements were not likely before the third year. After this, election-year pressures typically precluded further progress in the near term and so on.[24]

This was illustrated in a number of ways. Average increases in U.S. strategic spending (almost all of which was directed against the Soviet Union) were highest during the fourth and first years of the cycle, lower during the second year, and lowest during the third year. By far the greatest number of arms control agreements were signed during the third year, the fewest in the first and fourth years. In addition, most superpower summits—the occasions for improving bilateral relations—occurred during third years.[25] It is also significant that U.S. policy toward the Soviet Union was considerably more cooperative during second presidential terms than during first terms: arms control agreements were more frequent, summits were more often held, and strategic spending was more likely to decline than to increase. One reason is that second-term presidents worried less about the electoral implications of important foreign policy decisions.

Thus, even one of the most momentous aspects of U.S. postwar foreign policy was, in the periodicities it exhibited and perhaps in its overall tenor, driven by the rhythms of electoral politics.

MILITARY INTERVENTION

Voters are very attentive to the risks of armed involvements abroad, and while surges in presidential popularity may accompany short and successful actions, inconclusive and costly military engagements—as, for example, the intervention in Lebanon in the early 1980s, the Somalia imbroglio a decade later, and the entanglement in Iraq—can dissolve popular support and magnify electoral risks. The problem is that it is not always possible to anticipate how successful military force will be at attaining its policy goals, and interventions often acquire a dynamic of their own, meaning that their costs and duration may far exceed what initially had been expected. Under the circumstances, a very different impact of the electoral cycle on military intervention would be anticipated depending on how risk-acceptant or risk-averse political leaders were thought to be. If risk-acceptant, incumbents might wish to benefit from the expected surge in public approval associated with brief and successful intervention, timing armed incursions to coincide with the fourth year of the election cycle, when the incumbent (if a first-term president) or his party's designated successor might derive the most electoral benefit from the action. If risk-averse, the fear of a costly and inconclusive venture might make intervention less likely in close proximity to election years and relatively more so at the beginning of the four-year cycle (when the chances of extrication before the next election are better).

As not every show of force or bit of saber rattling is of interest to us, our standard of military "intervention" will be the employment in combat of U.S. forces over a period of at least twenty-four hours and involving at least one American casualty. By this standard, fifteen interventions since World War II have satisfied the definitional requirement. Table 8.8 lists these interventions along with the year within the electoral cycle when the action was initiated.

Table 8.8.   U.S. Military Intervention and the Electoral Cycle

Intervention	Year in Cycle
Korea (1950)	2
Lebanon (1958)	2
Vietnam (1965)	1
Dominican Republic (1965)	1
Mayaguez rescue (1975)	3
Iran hostage rescue (1980)	4
Lebanon (1982)	2
Grenada (1983)	3
Libya (1986)	2
Panama (1989)	1
Persian Gulf (1991)	3
Somalia (1993)	1
Yugoslavia (1999)	3
Afghanistan (2001)	1
Iraq (2003)	3

The evidence supports a view of risk-averse politicians. Although the incidence of U.S. military engagement is fairly evenly spread across the first three years of the cycle, a *single* instance is encountered during a fourth year—it being four or five times more likely in any one of the other three years. Note, too, that the only example of a fourth-year intervention—the Iran hostage rescue attempt in 1980—was an unambiguous failure that contributed to President Carter's defeat. Again—and other things being equal—electoral considerations do shape the timing with which a principal instrument of U.S. foreign policy is used. This is pretty much in line with what occurs in other democracies. As the best available study of the election-war relation observes, "When elections are approaching, democratic states have avoided wars. After elections, they have tended to enter more wars."[26]

CONCLUSION

American foreign policy reflects domestic politics, elections in particular. Except when external threats are stark and immediate (a rare occurrence), much about how the United States deals with the international community flows from partisan politics and electoral calculations. Because partisan differences have increased since the Cold War's demise and especially in recent years, the conduct of international affairs has become tightly enmeshed in presidential (even congressional) campaigns, the outcomes of which can produce considerable lurches in policy, which are, in addition, linked to periodicities associated with the electoral cycle. Plainly, this does not coincide with the ideal of a country presenting a united front when dealing with the outside world. It is, however, consistent with the fact that, given its international reach and consequences, many aspects of U.S. foreign policy affect the values and interests of its citizens, allowing for different conceptions of the national interest and implying that an operative definition can emerge only from a political dialogue mediated by the rough-and-tumble of electoral politics. Under the circumstances, it is important to understand what characteristic policy preferences undergird political partisanship and what the consequences of electoral choices are likely to be.

DISCUSSION QUESTIONS

1. To what extent has foreign policy reflected bipartisanship historically?
2. How important was foreign policy in affecting the outcome of elections in 2000, 2004, and 2008?
3. How do Democrats and Republicans differ in the foreign policy goals for the United States?

4. How do Democrats and Republicans differ on the foreign policy tools that the United States should use?
5. What are some examples of the foreign policy consequences of elections?
6. How did the electoral cycle affect the foreign policy actions of differing American administrations during the Cold War?
7. How does the election cycle affect American military interventions abroad?

NOTES

1. "Reagan Is Stressing a Tough U.S. Stance in Foreign Affairs in Bid to Gain Ground," *Wall Street Journal*, January 31, 1980.

2. James M. Lindsay, "The New Partisanship: The Changed Politics of American Foreign Policy," *Foreign Policy Agenda*, September 2000. See also Robert Y. Shapiro and Yaeli Bloch-Elkon, "Partisan Conflict, Public Opinion, and U.S. Foreign Policy" (paper presented at the Inequality and Social Policy Seminar, John F. Kennedy School of Government, Harvard University, December 12, 2005).

3. Calculated on the basis of Joseph A. Pike and John A. Maltese, *The Politics of the Presidency* (Washington, DC: Congressional Quarterly Press, 2004), 428–29. The 2004 update is by the author.

4. Program on International Policy Attitudes, Center for International and Security Studies, University of Maryland, October 2000.

5. Time/CNN/Harris Interactive Poll, May 22–23, 2002.

6. ABC News/Washington Post Poll, April 6–9, 2006.

7. Survey by Bloomberg, October 2010. Reported by the Roper Center public opinion archives.

8. As one of the leading students of public opinion on foreign policy observed, "For two decades, spanning the Truman, Eisenhower, Kennedy, and Johnson administrations . . . whatever differences divided the American public on foreign policy rarely fell along a cleavage defined by partisan loyalties." Ole Holsti, *Public Opinion and American Foreign Policy* (Ann Arbor: University of Michigan Press, 1996), 133.

9. Geoffrey C. Layman and Thomas M. Carsey, "Party Polarization and Conflict Extension in the American Electorate," *American Journal of Political Science* 46, no. 4 (October 2002): 286–303.

10. Pew Research Center for the People and the Press, "Evenly Divided and Increasingly Polarized," survey report (2004).

11. Pew Research Center for the People and the Press, "Beyond Red vs. Blue: The Political Typology" (May 4, 2011).

12. Shapiro and Bloch-Elkon, "Partisan Conflict, Public Opinion."

13. "Very important" = 1; "somewhat important" = 2; "not at all important" = 3.

14. The factors are orthogonally rotated.

15. For a closer examination of the gap and its ideological sources, see Miroslav Nincic and Jennifer Ramos, "Ideological Structures and Foreign Policy Preferences" *Journal of Political Ideologies* 15, no. 2 (June 2010): 119–41.

16. See Miroslav Nincic, "Divided We Stand: Political Partisanship and Military Force," in Harvey Starr, ed., *Approaches, Levels, and Methods of Analysis in International Relations: Crossing Boundaries* (New York: Palgrave Macmillan, 2006).

17. Chicago Council on Foreign Relations, "American Public Opinion and U.S. Foreign Policy," survey conducted by Knowledge Networks, July 16–12, 2004, question 90.

18. Pew Research Center for the People and the Press, "Politics and Values in a 51%–48% Nation," survey report, January 2005, p. 2.

19. Pew Research Center for the People and the Press, "2009 Values Survey," March 2009.

20. On this, see U.S. Senate, Select Committee on Intelligence, *Postwar Findings about Iraq's WMD Programs and Links to Terrorism and How They Compare with Prewar Assessments*, 109th Cong., 2d sess., September 8, 2006.

21. The preemptive doctrine was developed in the government's document titled *National Security Strategy of the United States of America* (Washington, DC: September 20, 2002).

22. See Miroslav Nincic, "The National Interest and Its Interpretation," *Review of Politics* 61, no. 1 (Winter 1999): 29–55.

23. Kurt Taylor Gaubatz, "Elections and Foreign Policy: Strategic Politicians and the Domestic Salience of International Issues" (unpublished manuscript, 2002).

24. This is developed in Miroslav Nincic, "U.S. Soviet Policy and the Electoral Connection," *World Politics* 42, no. 3 (April 1990): 370–96.

25. Nincic, "U.S. Soviet Policy."

26. Kurt Taylor Gaubatz, *Elections and War: The Electoral Incentive in the Democratic Politics of War and Peace* (Stanford, CA: Stanford University Press, 1999), 147.

II

THE INSTITUTIONAL SETTING

Foreign policy is a product of the actions officials take on behalf of the nation. Because of this, the way the government is structured for policymaking also arguably affects the conduct and content of foreign affairs. Thus, we can hypothesize that a relationship exists between the substance of policy and the institutional setting from which it derives. The proposition is particularly compelling if attention is directed not to the foreign policy goals the nation's leaders select but to the means they choose to satisfy particular objectives.

A salient feature of the American institutional setting is that the president and the institutionalized presidency—the latter consisting of the president's personal staff and the Executive Office of the President—are preeminent in the foreign policymaking process. This derives in part from the authority granted the president in the Constitution and in part from the combination of judicial interpretation, legislative acquiescence, personal assertiveness, and custom and tradition that have transformed the presidency into the most powerful office in the world. The crisis-ridden atmosphere that characterized the Cold War era also contributed to the enhancement of presidential authority by encouraging the president to act energetically and decisively when dealing with global challenges. The widely shared consensus among American leaders and the American public that the international environment demanded an active world role also contributed to the felt need for strong presidential leadership. Although this viewpoint was sometimes vigorously debated in the years following American involvement in Vietnam, the perceived need for strong presidential leadership was generally accepted throughout the Cold War.

Because of the president's key role in foreign policymaking, it is useful to consider the institutional arrangements that govern the process as a series of concentric circles that effectively alter the standard government organization chart so as to draw attention to the core, or most immediate source of the action (see figure II.1).

Thus, the innermost circle in the policymaking process consists of the president, his immediate personal advisers, and such important political appointees as the secretaries of state and defense, the director of central intelligence, and various under, deputy, and assistant secretaries who bear responsibility for carrying out policy decisions. Here, in principle, is where the most important decisions involving the fate of the nation are made.

The second concentric circle comprises the various departments and agencies of the executive branch. If we exclude from that circle the politically appointed heads of agencies and their immediate subordinates, who are more properly placed in the innermost circle, we can think of the individuals within the second circle as career professionals who provide continuity in the implementation of policy from one administration to the next. Their primary tasks—in theory—are to provide top-level policymakers with the information necessary for sound decision-making and to carry out the decisions policymakers reach. As noted in the introduction to this book, the

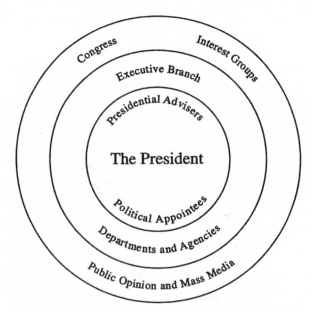

Figure II.1. The Concentric Circles of Policymaking
Source: Adapted from Roger Hilsman, *To Move a Nation* (New York: Doubleday, 1967), 541–44.

involvement of the United States in a complex web of interdependent ties with other nations in the world has led to the involvement in foreign affairs of many organizations the primary tasks of which are seemingly oriented toward the domestic environment. The Treasury Department and the U.S. Trade Representative have become especially visible in recent years as the globalization of the world political economy has increased the salience of economic issues as foreign policy issues. The Departments of Agriculture, Commerce, and Justice (including the FBI) have also figured prominently as globalization and international terrorism have blurred the distinction between foreign and domestic politics and policy. The creation of the Department of Homeland Security in 2002 epitomizes the linking of the domestic and international arenas within one organization. While the department, as its name implies, has the explicit duty of protecting citizens at home, it also has the responsibility to gather and analyze intelligence information about foreign threats and to deter and protect against such attacks as occurred on September 11, 2001.

The departments of state and defense and the intelligence community continue to command center stage among the dozens of executive branch departments and agencies now involved in foreign affairs. The State Department's role derives from being the only department charged (in theory, at least) with responsibility for the whole range of America's relations with other nations. The Defense Department and the intelligence community, especially the CIA, on the other hand, in the Cold War years derived their importance from the threatening and crisis-ridden atmosphere; they often had ready alternatives from which top-level policymakers could choose when diplomacy and negotiation seemed destined to fail. While both bureaucracies played a diminished role in the post–Cold War world, both appear to have especially important parts to play in the post-9/11 world. Indeed, the intelligence community immediately received congressional and executive branch scrutiny over the analytic failures surrounding 9/11 and Iraq and its alleged weapons of mass destruction during the Bush years. More recently, during the Obama administration, the intelligence community has also received additional scrutiny over its handling of the attempted bombings in Detroit on Christmas Day 2009 and in New York's Times Square a few months later. The intelligence community, composed of agencies from sixteen departments, has been restructured, and a director of national intelligence and a National Counterterrorism Center have been created to provide unity to the organization, although the effectiveness of these changes has remained a subject of debate.

Moving beyond the departments and agencies of the executive branch, the third concentric circle consists of Congress. Although technically a single institutional entity, Congress often appears to embrace many different centers of power and authority—ranging from the House and Senate leadership to the various coalitions operative in the legislative branch and from the various committees and subcommittees in which Congress does its real work to the individual senators and representatives who often vie with one another for publicity as well as power. Of all the institutions involved in foreign policymaking, Congress is least engaged in the day-to-day conduct of the nation's foreign relations, as reflected in its placement in the outermost circle.

Does this stylized description of the relative influence of various institutions and actors involved in foreign policymaking continue to hold in the wake of September 11, the turbulence of the Iraq and Afghanistan wars, and the Great Recession more recently? Roger Hilsman, who first suggested this institutional conceptualization some four decades ago in his *To Move a Nation*, even then cautioned against a too facile reliance on this description. Although the institutional setting may affect the form and flow of policy, the politicking inherent in the process by no means conforms to the neatly compartmentalized, institutionalized paths implied by Hilsman's framework. What the nation chooses to do abroad is more often the product of an intense political struggle among the prominent players in the policymaking process, the policymaking positions or roles occupied by the key decision-makers, and the characteristics of those individuals. The changed and changing nature of the international system is also pertinent to the contemporary institutional setting. As the constraints and opportunities in the twenty-first century unfold, the character and responsiveness of institutions largely formed during the decades of Cold War can be expected to change. It is a viewpoint we examine in the chapters in part II.

Beginning with the innermost concentric circle, a case can be made that the post-9/11 changes in the global environment have strengthened the presidency and increased its centrality in the governmental setting. Indeed, the *Economist* proclaimed shortly after September 11 that "the United States is witnessing the most dramatic expansion in presidential power for a generation."[1] In effect, we seemed to be witnessing a return of the "imperial presidency" of the Vietnam era. As the Iraq War has dragged on, as public opinion increasingly opposed presidential actions, and as Congress came under the control of the opposition party in 2006, presidential power came under more and more scrutiny and constraint. Barack Obama sought to restore the authority to the presidential office with his sweeping 2008 victory and his seeming charismatic style. Yet he also soon faced the opposition party gaining control of the House of Representatives in the 2010 congressional elections, and his deliberative leadership style and personal characteristics came under scrutiny as well.[2]

As Michael Nelson argues in the first chapter in part II, "Person and Office: Presidents, the Presidency, and Foreign Policy," it is really a combination of the characteristics of the presidency and characteristics of the individual occupying the presidency that provides the fullest understanding of that institution. The presidency, as Nelson notes, possesses several important constitutional powers, although their exact operation was never made clear by the framers. Indeed, "it took well over a century for parchment to become practice" and "for all the constitutionally enumerated powers of the presidency to come to life." The activation of these powers actually came sooner in foreign policy than in domestic policy with Washington's proclamation of neutrality in the war between France and England and the declaration of the Monroe Doctrine. These (and other early unilateral actions by presidents) were defended by citing the nature of the presidency, with its unity of office and its election by the entire country. In the modern era, these arguments for presidential leadership were strengthened with the emergence of the Cold War and with the reluctance of Congress to challenge executive prerogatives in foreign affairs. Despite congressional passage of the War Powers Resolution in the aftermath of the Vietnam War, for example, succeeding presidents have not "complied with the letter, much less the spirit," of that law. Throughout much of the history of the Republic, the Supreme Court has routinely backed the executive's prerogatives in foreign affairs.

Another dimension of the office that aids presidential dominance is the president's dual role as chief of state and chief of government. The former role allows the president to represent the nation externally; the latter allows the president to lead the nation internally. Importantly, both roles afford the president the opportunity to lead the public, thus enhancing his ability to use his popularity to promote his policy.

The experiences, the personality, and the skills that an individual brings to the office are also important for understanding presidents' conduct of foreign policy. Some presidents served as secretary of state prior to assuming office, but recent ones more often come with backgrounds as state governors. As a result, recent presidents have had less experience in foreign affairs than as chief executives. The degree of self-confidence and the degree of consistency in their actions, Nelson points out, may also be helpful in understanding presidents' behavior. Finally, the leadership skills of a president—his management of authority within his own staff, his tactical political skills in dealing with Congress, and his presentation of self to the public—appear to be crucial in making the presidency function effectively as an institution.

In "Presidents Who Initiate Wars," Louis Fisher is pessimistic about the prospects of altering the balance of executive-legislative influence in foreign policy, even on issues involving the use of American force abroad. In this critical policy arena, presidents continue to act unilaterally. "Instead of coming to Congress for authority," as the Constitution calls for, "presidents are more likely to justify military actions either on the commander in chief clause . . . or on decisions reached by the UN Security Council and the North Atlantic Treaty Organization (NATO)."

President Truman encouraged this process early in the Cold War by first promising to obtain congressional approval for any use of U.S. troops as part of a UN operation but then ignoring Congress when he sent American troops to Korea in June 1950. Presidents George H. W. Bush and Bill Clinton continued that tradition in the immediate post–Cold War years. "Instead of seeking authority from Congress [to prosecute the war against Saddam Hussein], Bush created a multinational alliance and encouraged the [United Nations] Security Council to authorize the use of military force." Even when Bush finally asked Congress to vote on the use of force in the Gulf, he was asking for their "support," not their "authority."

In sending American forces to Haiti and Bosnia and using American air power in Kosovo, Clinton followed a similar strategy. To deal with Haiti, he sought and obtained a Security Council resolution authorizing an invasion and explicitly denied that he needed congressional support: "I have not agreed that I was constitutionally mandated to obtain the support of Congress." In Bosnia, he invoked authority under Article 2 of the Constitution and the NATO Treaty to deploy American forces as part of the Dayton Accords of November 1995, and he again denied that he needed congressional approval for his actions. Before the Kosovo campaign, Clinton again looked to NATO to authorize action, and he made that decision unilaterally ("I decided that the United States would vote to give NATO the authority to carry out military strikes against Serbia").

In early 2002 when George W. Bush first began discussing war against Iraq, there was little mention of going to Congress to request its support— or even going to an international forum, as his father and Clinton had done to justify earlier interventions. By the fall of that year, the administration had changed its mind and asked the Congress to pass a resolution on Iraq prior to the 2002 congressional elections. In this highly partisan atmosphere and because of the popularity of the president, Bush easily succeeded in obtaining a resolution to use force against Iraq at his discretion. While a U.S. victory over Iraqi forces occurred quickly, the reconstruction of Iraq proved extraordinarily difficult, and sectarian violence was difficult to control.

In the case of Libya in 2011, President Obama followed the same practice as past presidents. As Fisher writes, "he decided to embark on a new war in Libya without seeking or obtaining authority from Congress." Instead, President Obama relied upon the passage of a United Nations Security Council Resolution (1973) to justify this action. He did notify Congress of his actions, but he did not seek their approval. His actions did result in several efforts by the members of Congress, including the passage of a resolution offered by the Speaker of the House John Boehner (R-OH) admonishing the president for failing "to provide Congress with a compelling rationale" for the actions in Libya and seeking a detailed report within fourteen days. The president did send such a report, and he invoked his powers as commander in chief and as chief executive to take such actions. Fisher categories a series of other efforts over the next several months by Congress, but those efforts did not produce any real changes in executive behavior. Moreover, Congress was not able to enact any decisive actions against the president.

In all these cases—Korea, the Persian Gulf, Haiti, Bosnia, Kosovo, Iraq, and Libya—Congress acquiesced in presidential encroachment on its powers. Indeed, Fisher argues that "Congress . . . not only fails to fight back but even volunteers fundamental legislative powers, including the war power and the power of the purse." While partisan politics partially explains Congress's acquiescence, members of both political parties often support presidential prerogatives. In the end, Fisher worries that the process "undermines public control, the system of checks and balances, and constitutional government."

Another important institutional mechanism within the first concentric circle of foreign policymaking is the National Security Council (NSC) system. It consists of the formal National Security Council, the complex of interagency committees that carry on its work, and the NSC staff, which serves the president, his advisers, and the committees making up the NSC system. The NSC staff is headed by the president's assistant for national security affairs, who has assumed a position of prominence in recent decades. Similarly, the NSC system and staff have become crucial mechanisms within the institutionalized presidency used by the White House to ensure its control of policymaking and to enhance prospects for policy coherence and consistency with presidential wishes.

Often the visibility and power of the national security assistant has been cause for conflict with other key participants in the process, notably the secretary of state. That was especially apparent during the Nixon and Carter presidencies. During the Reagan presidency, the role of the NSC staff became more contentious—indeed, infamous—as the staff engaged in the abuse of power: Lieutenant Colonel Oliver L. North undertook covert operational activities designed to divert profits from the sale of arms to Iran to the Contras fighting the Sandinista regime in Nicaragua, in apparent contravention of congressional prohibitions.

Steps were later taken to ensure that the NSC staff would no longer engage in operational activities, and both the first Bush and the Clinton presidencies were marked by the absence of public squabbles between their respective secretaries of state (James A. Baker for Bush, Warren Christopher and later Madeleine Albright for Clinton) and national security advisers (Brent Scowcroft for Bush, Anthony Lake and then Samuel Berger for Clinton). Still, Scowcroft, Lake, and Berger were powerful players in the policy process, exercising decisive influence in supporting Bush's determination to evict Iraqi forces from Kuwait and pressing Clinton to intervene in Haiti and to support the expansion of NATO.

Under President George W. Bush, the pattern of a strong and influential national security adviser continued. Condoleezza Rice, according to one assessment, played "a critical, if largely hidden, role in the overall direction of the president's foreign policy." Her successor as national security adviser in the Bush administration's second term was Stephen Hadley, her deputy from 2001 to 2004. He exercised perhaps a less public role than Rice, but he continued to be an important shaper of foreign policy. President Obama's first national security adviser, James Jones, a retired general, did not directly fit this mode in terms of dominating policymaking. After he resigned in November 2010, he was replaced by his deputy, Tom Donilon, a long-time political and foreign policy operative, who appears to be a more effective shaper of foreign policy, although Secretary of State Hillary Clinton plays a prominent role as well.

In the next chapter, I. M. (Mac) Destler provides a closer look at the role of the national security adviser in the foreign policy process. In his "How National Security Advisers See Their Role," he draws directly on the results of two roundtables with individuals who served in this position over the past four decades or so and his long experience as an observer of this position. Destler begins his analysis by identifying the reasons the role of the national security adviser has expanded since its inception. The primary reason is what they call "the president's need for close-in foreign policy support," but other factors have aided this expansion as well. As the NSC staff increased and became institutionalized, it assumed new functions in the policy process (e.g., crisis management). As the foreign policy agenda expanded, the NSC adviser and staff also took on more intermestic issues. As "U.S. politics no longer ends at the water's edge," the NSC, acting as the White House's surrogate, assumed responsibility to monitor the political aspects of foreign policy actions.

Within the context of these expanded responsibilities, Destler identifies three principal roles that the national security adviser undertakes: managing the foreign policy decision-making process, undertaking operational matters, and assuming public responsibilities. The most important of these is the first one, managing the decision process. In this role, the adviser needs "to ensure both that those with strong stakes are involved and that all realistic policy options are fully considered." He or she must also make certain that choices are made in a "timely manner" and must oversee "the implementation of the decisions made by the president and his or her advisers."

The operational and public roles of the national security advisers have less importance than the managerial one, but they have become increasingly used in recent years. As we have seen, in the aftermath of the Iran-Contra scandal in the mid-1980s, the NSC and its staff formally rejected an operational role. In practice, as Destler point outs, the national security adviser and the NSC staff continue to play an operational role. This role occurs for several reasons: other governments have counterparts to the adviser and require this kind of direct interaction, the traditional foreign policy bureaucracies have not been responsive to the president's directives, or the president wants to signal a fundamental shift in foreign policy through the adviser's action. The public role of the national security adviser has emerged largely with the increased politicization of foreign policy over the past three or four decades and with the expansion of media outlets, which have required that an administration have "all the bases . . . covered" in addressing foreign affairs. With this public role, demands for more accountability of the advisers have increased, including requiring Senate confirmation of these appointments, which is not currently done.

If the institutions in the innermost (presidential) concentric circle have seemingly become more powerful since the events of September 11, that is clearly not the case with Congress during the past several years. First, it reverted to a foreign policy role reminiscent of the early years of the Cold War, with substantial deference to the president. As the war in Iraq soured, Congress then sought to be more assertive on foreign policy, and that posture has continued during the Obama administration. In "The Shifting Pendulum of Power: Executive-Legislative Relations on American Foreign Policy," James M. Lindsay surveys the changes in congressional attitudes toward the foreign policy process, especially during the past decade or so. In 2002, Lindsay notes, the concern was that "Congress looked to have surrendered its constitutional role in foreign policymaking to the White House." By 2007, however, "Congress recovered its voice on foreign policy," and this "resurgent interest" in foreign policy has continued during the Obama administration. His explanation for this congressional volte-face lies not within "the realm of law" but within "the realm of politics." The crucial political questions for Congress are whether the country is threatened internationally and whether the president's policies are working ("Presidents who succeed find themselves surrounded by admirers; presidents who don't find themselves targeted by critics").

While the Constitution provides the framework for both Congress and president to exercise influence in the conduct of foreign policy, the political arena has often been the determinant of whether the Congress actually exercises its authority. Lindsay argues that the ebbs and flows of congressional actions in foreign affairs turn largely on the perceived threat from abroad. Congressional deference was particularly evident in the immediate post–World War II years, for example, but it came "to a crashing halt" with the Vietnam War. Later, "the end of the Cold War accelerated the trend toward congressional activism." Indeed, the Clinton administration faced a series of congressional foreign policy challenges, and, more often than not, Congress prevailed.

September 11 changed that again, as "the pendulum of power swung sharply back toward the White House." Not only did members of Congress promptly provide the president with sweeping authority to retaliate against terrorism, but they also reversed policy stances that they had previously adopted. They quickly agreed to pay overdue UN dues to facilitate coalition building through that body, they lifted sanctions against Pakistan that had been imposed since the military coup in that country in 1999, and they were prepared to increase defense spending sharply. Congressional criticism of the war on terrorism was muted, and criticism that did arise was quickly challenged on patriotic grounds. By 2006, however, both Democrats and Republicans in Congress questioned the failing Iraq policy, and the stunning congressional defeats in the House and the Senate for the president's party embolden this foreign policy opposition. By early 2007, congressional criticism of foreign policy was in full throat—and across party lines—and for the balance of the Bush administration.

Congressional opposition on foreign policy continued with the Obama administration—whether over seeking to close the U.S. prison at Guantanamo Bay, Cuba, trying to pass cap-and-trade legislation, or ratifying the New START Treaty negotiated by the administration. Similarly, President Obama's action toward Libya in 2011 produced a chorus of congressional criticism, prompted by the belief that the president was usurping Congress's war powers. Although Congress may not always be successful in these efforts to overturn presidential actions, that may not ultimately be necessary. As Lindsay points out, "Congress influences foreign policy not just by what it does, but what it can persuade the White House not to do."

What, Lindsay asks, is the "proper balance between activism and deference" by Congress? His judgment is that both have costs and benefits. Congressional activism forces the president and his advisers to think through their policy options, and it affords the Congress the opportunity to debate and legitimate the chosen course with the American public. Yet such activism has its downside. It makes the process more cumbersome and time consuming, and it may also lead to an incoherent policy if the two branches differ on the direction of policy. While congressional deference may avoid such problems, it may contribute to presidential "overreach" on policy. Because "presidents and their advisers are not infallible," congressional checks and balances can aid in their choices of the best policies for the nation.

According to the Constitution, the president and Congress are coequal partners in foreign policymaking. Both are elected by the American people. In practice, however, the bureaucratic organizations of the permanent foreign affairs government depicted in the second concentric circle in figure II.1 provide continuity from one administration to the next and through the continuing presidential and congressional electoral cycles. Not surprisingly, then, the organizations constituting the foreign affairs government are often described as "the fourth branch of government."

People who work in the "fourth branch" often spend their entire careers managing the routine affairs that constitute America's relations with other countries. Indeed, these career professionals and the organizations they work for are expected to be the government's "eyes and ears," searching for incipient global changes and assessing American needs and interests abroad. Thus, these key institutions can be expected to change as global challenges and opportunities change. As the last five chapters in part II suggest, organizations central to American diplomatic, military, intelligence, and economic policymaking are, in fact, responding to the changing global environment, especially after 9/11. How well they have adapted is, however, a matter of sometimes contentious political debate, as the previous chapters dealing with congressional-executive relations suggest.

The first of our selections on these important bureaucracies is by the Obama administration's secretary of state, Hillary Rodham Clinton. In "Leading through Civilian Power," Clinton outlines how America needs to change its diplomacy, how diplomacy and development should be tied together, and how greater civilian involvement can play an important role in solving global challenges. The vehicle that she used for outlining these changes was the first Quadrennial Diplomacy and Development Review (QDDR). This review of the Department of State and the United States Agency for International Development (USAID) focused on how "to make diplomacy and development coordinated, complementary, and mutually reinforcing." The recommendations that resulted from this review aimed at "modernizing and coordinating diplomacy" within federal agencies, emphasizing sustainable development, and establishing a strong link between diplomacy and development but also "better coordination with partners in the military, in conflict zones and [in] fragile states."

Although traditional American diplomacy remains an important component of the work of the Department of State, Clinton also emphasizes that diplomacy must increasingly involve agencies that seemingly were only confined to the domestic arena. Domestic agencies with responsibilities to address economic, environmental, and criminal justice issues increasingly have a foreign policy role as well. Many embassies abroad have already incorporated a number of domestic agencies, and the Department of State has increasingly worked with those in federal agencies at home. For instance, the American dialogue with India involved twenty-two government agencies and the Strategic and Economic Dialogue with China involved more than thirty such agencies. By more fully integrating domestic agencies and Foreign Service personnel, Clinton argues, "the United States can build a global civilian service of the same caliber and flexibility as the U.S. military."

This civilian engagement, however, must go beyond the realm of state-to-state contact. Public diplomacy, in which U.S. government officials engage with the host country's population, must also be part of the new kind of involvement abroad. In addition, the civilian power of the American government must incorporate nonstate actors such as business and citizen groups in its outreach. These groups, moreover, can often do tasks that the government cannot perform. In recent years, such public-private cooperative efforts, for example, proved successful in responding to the earthquake in Haiti.

The American diplomacy must also promote "high-impact development," because it "is one of the best tools to enhance the United States' stability and prosperity." Development does so by bolstering failing states, strengthening states that may assist the United States in addressing key issues, and promoting democratic reforms around the world. At the same time, and in the context of scarce resources, the United States must be strategic in targeting countries, and sectors within those countries, that have the real potential for sustained development. The Obama administration approach also seeks to create partnerships with countries on key initiatives, such as through its Global Health Initiative and its Feed the Future initiative, as yet other means to foster development. Just as American diplomacy can assist these development efforts through greater dialogue with other countries and greater integration of its work with other U.S. government agencies, USAID must also streamline and reform its operations as well. In all, Clinton calls for the Department of State and USAID to work more closely together and broaden its relationship.

In particular, the State Department and USAID officials must work together in two key arenas: conflict zones and fragile states. Whether in Iraq, Afghanistan, Pakistan, or Yemen, the civilian power of the United States is crucial in addressing the efforts to stabilize and advance these states. "Properly trained and equipped, civilians are force multipliers," but these civilians need to work with others across agencies of the U.S. government and outside the government to maximize their effectiveness. In this way, and "with the right balance of civilian and military power," Clinton concludes that "the United States can advance its interests and values, lead and support other nations in solving global problems, and forge strong diplomatic and development partnerships with traditional allies and newly emerging powers."

The American military as a foreign and national security policy institution has hardly been immune from the impact of dramatic events of the past decade or more, and it has not been immune from calls for significant change. Just after George W. Bush took office, for example, the U.S. Commission on National Security/Twenty-First Century (the Hart-Rudman Commission) argued that the Pentagon "needs to be overhauled" and that "strategy should once again drive the design and implementation of U.S. national security policies." More recently, and especially with the increasing budgetary difficulties of the American government and with the wars in Iraq and Afghanistan winding down during the Obama administration, the Department of Defense, and the defense budget in particular, have become primary targets for possible change in missions and funding.

In "A Leaner and Meaner Defense," Gordon Adams and Matthew Leatherman address these kinds of issues and set out their views on how the military should be transformed. In particular, Adams and Leatherman argue that the United States "faces a watershed moment" in regard to its military spending and missions. For too long, they argue, the United States has relied on sustained military engagement. Now it must decide "which defense missions to undertake"; it must "exercise restraint in defense planning and budgeting," and it must "bring tough management practices to the Pentagon."

The wars in Afghanistan and Iraq expanded the Pentagon's military missions to include "nation building, stabilizing fragile states, counterinsurgency, and strengthening the security capacities of other countries." Defense spending has likewise been enlarged to where it accounts for 56 percent of the discretionary spending on the part of the federal government. These expansions have come about, Adams and Leatherman argue, despite the fact that "United States had never been more secure militarily." Even with some projected changes as the wars in Afghanistan and Iraq end, including some reductions in the size of the force, and proposed programmatic changes, the defense budget by FY2018 "would be well above the Cold War average."

As a consequence, Adams and Leatherman argue that much more dramatic cuts in missions and spending are needed at this time. Some missions, such as dismantling al Qaeda and addressing cybersecurity, are crucial and should remain, but even aspects of these two missions can be accomplished by the civilian side of government or the private sector. Homeland security can assist in dealing with the former, and the private sector can assist in dealing with the latter. Spending on nuclear and large-scale conventional combat, however, can be significantly restrained, since these two areas are "improbable dangers" for the United States. Further, although policy planners at the Pentagon still seem to be driven by changing Chinese capabilities or by the prospects of future Afghanistan or Iraq wars, these factors should not now be the guide for future defense policy, Adams and Leatherman judge.

Instead, they argue that by more careful setting of defense priorities, the overall size of the military could be reduced substantially, and by eliminating particular missions as high priorities for the United States, the number of ground troops could be cut. A different assessment, for example, of the requirement for nuclear deterrence and conventional warfare would make possible troop reductions in Europe and Asia, even while tilting more forces toward the latter region. U.S. forces could be reduced still further by trimming the tail, or support forces, of the active-duty forces in comparison to the tooth, or combat forces. Specifically, Adams and Leatherman estimate that one hundred thousand active-duty forces could be removed from excess overhead support forces. In all, they envision a reduction in the size of the total force by 19 percent to 1.21 million over a five-year period, resulting in significant savings in military spending.

In turn, more focus should be placed on priority missions and away from those that are less central or less likely. In this context, the focus should be on strengthening cargo aircraft and sealift capabilities to allow rapid deployment of American forces and on placing additional investments in unmanned surveillance capabilities, missile strikes, and support for ground forces. With a change in priorities, Adams and Leatherman proceed to identify several major programs "to cut, curtail, or delay." These include a new fighter aircraft, the F-35, the V-22 Osprey, a cruise-missile surveillance system, and a new air defense system in development. They also identify a series of other programs that should be reconsidered and propose a reduction in military research and development (R&D) as yet another way to achieve savings. Further, they propose a substantial review and overhaul of the pay system in the military "to generate the right combination of needed specialties and skills," a revamping of the health care system used by the Department of Defense, and several revisions in the military's retirement program. Finally, and importantly, they propose that intelligence funding, with roughly 80 percent of its funds located in the Department of Defense budget, and currently totally some $80 billion, be trimmed.

Although their recommendations for such a broad-gauge overhaul of spending and missions for the Department of Defense may appear a bit draconian to some, Adams and Leatherman argue that "the remaining U.S. military force would still be superior to any other in technology and capability," and that the U.S. defense budget would, as a result, "help solve the United States' fiscal problems."

The intelligence community is the third major foreign policy institution in the second concentric circle of policymaking. It, too, has been buffeted by recent changes in world politics. While the intelligence community has long come under criticism for its failures in intelligence estimates, the impact of September 11 produced a firestorm of criticism within Congress, as did the failures over assessing whether Saddam Hussein possessed weapons of mass destruction prior to the war with Iraq. Calls were heard for investigations of the presumed failures that had allowed the events to happen, and the 9/11 Commission offered a series of recommendations of how the intelligence community should be restructured and how changes in its operation should occur.[3] Further, Congress passed and the president signed the National Intelligence Security Reform Act of 2004, creating a new director of national intelligence to oversee and provide unity to the far-flung intelligence community.

Despite these changes, the new structure of the intelligence community has continued to have its difficulties. The attempted bombing of an airline by the "underwear bomber" on Christmas Day in 2009 and the failed terrorist attack on Times Square in 2010 raised questions anew about the effectiveness of intelligence. To be sure, the intelligence community's (and the military's) success in killing Osama bin Laden in Pakistan in May 2011 and Anwar al-Awlaki in Yemen in September 2011 muted this criticism somewhat. Nonetheless, problems continue to exist between policymakers and the intelligence community over the quality and timeliness of information.

In chapter 15, "Why Intelligence and Policymakers Clash," political scientist Robert Jervis outlines some of these issues. In particular, he shows how the differing needs and views between policymaking and intelligence officials "guarantee conflict between them." Jervis notes that policymakers, for "both political and psychological reasons," tend "to oversell their policies" and, in doing so, they seemingly pressure the intelligence community to reinforce their policy views. Such pressure clashes with the fundamental role of intelligence—to produce information "to support better policy" and not to support a particular position of a policymaker. In all, the preferred position of policymakers for reinforcing intelligence clashes with the intelligence community's objective to produce accurate assessments. The rest of the chapter skillfully analyzes the conflicting positions of these organizations in more detail.

The run-up to the Iraq War in 2003 illustrates these competing pressures between these two important actors. The Bush administration had one view of Saddam Hussein, Iraq's nuclear weapons program, and the costs of a war with that nation. For psychological and political reasons, the Bush administration tended to link all these views together into a coherent policymaking package. Although the community believed that Iraq had a weapons of mass destruction (WMD) program, the intelligence community's view on Saddam Hussein and the linkage with al Qaeda and on the costs of a war with Iraq was much more differentiated. In particular, the intelligence community was more skeptical of any link between Iraq and al Qaeda than Bush administration policymakers, and it doubted the ease of postwar reconstruction in that country. In essence, intelligence "did not feel the psychological need to bolster the case for war, [and] it did not have to pull other perceptions into line."

Beyond this fundamental tension, a series of factors may exacerbate the conflict between policymakers and the intelligence community. Jervis systematically goes through each of them and uses a series of historical examples to illustrate each one. First, policymakers are reluctant to consider an alternative option (Plan B) when a preferred option (Plan A) is not working. Yet the intelligence community, without the same stake in Plan A as policymakers, can more quickly "detect signs that the policies are failing." Jervis points to "perseverance" and "confidence" on the part of policymakers as important explanations for policymakers sticking with Plan A, even when intelligence might suggest an alternate option. That is, policymakers believe that if they stay with a policy long enough, it will succeed. Alternately, because policymakers have "confidence" in their policy choice, they are reluctant to abandon it for psychological and political reasons. Second, "cognitive predisposition" on the part of both policymakers and the intelligence community make it difficult for the two communities to work together. Each group, Jervis argues, often comes to a policy situation with differing worldviews. As such, they may have difficulty in reconciling the information that they are receiving and processing. Third, timing is crucial with intelligence assessments and policymakers, and the intelligence community often has difficulty making the two agree. That is, intelligence "must arrive at the right time." Intelligence that arrives "too early" will be ignored by policymakers, while intelligence arriving "too late" may be put aside. Hence, to resolve this dilemma, Jervis suggests that intelligence should operate "on questions that are important, but not immediately pressing" for the policymakers. In this way, intelligence has the best prospect of making a difference. Suffice it to say, timing remains a real challenge for both participants.

Finally, Jervis tackles the issue of attempted politicization of intelligence by policymakers and discusses how that can also produce added friction between the two parties. Politicization may be attempted by policymakers in a variety of ways—from telling the intelligence community the desired conclusions in an assessment requested to demoting an official for a wrong answer to not seeking evaluations on some topics over fear of the answer. Jervis readily acknowledges that many of these efforts at politicization are ambiguous and difficult to untangle, and that fact complicates the relationship even more. Indeed, both sides have important reasons for taking differing actions that may be viewed as advancing politicization or resisting information requests. That is, policymakers want to probe for more thorough intelligence assessments (and thus they could be accused of politicizing an issue), while intelligence does not want to be pushed in a direction that they do not want to go (and they could be accused of being unresponsive to policymakers). As such, these issues "are rarely easy to settle," and tensions between the two continue.

In all, Jervis concludes where he began by arguing that "the two groups are doomed to work together and to come into conflict." And the reason is a fundamental one: "The needs and missions of leaders and intelligence officials are very different."

While intelligence reform is an important component for enhancing America's security, the Hart-Rudman Commission in early 2001, prior to 9/11, recommended that a "new, cabinet-level National Homeland Security Agency" be established. Immediately after September 11, President Bush created by executive order an Office of Homeland Security, but he initially balked at a separate cabinet post for this function. Prodded by members of Congress, Bush changed his mind and embraced the idea of a new cabinet agency, which became the Department of Homeland Security in late 2002. The new department consolidated twenty-two agencies and nearly 170,000 workers into the third-largest bureaucracy in the federal government, with responsibilities in the areas of border and transportation security, emergency preparedness, science and technology, and information analysis related to terrorist threats. With such a broad mandate and an uncertain structure, the department was immediately criticized "as a management challenge without precedent." Fears were also raised about whether its unwieldy nature may "divert [it] from its central mission of safeguarding the American public from terrorist attacks."[4] Moreover, these concerns remain, especially with homeland security's requirements of trying to address domestic and foreign issues and with the need to integrate various levels of government—national, state, and local—in carrying out its multiple missions.

In "Intermestic Politics and Homeland Security," Philip A. Russo and Patrick J. Haney examine some of the growing pains associated with homeland security and how multiple goals, multiple actors, and funding issues remain as important challenges. They begin their analysis by explaining the origins of the "intermestic" concept—issues that are both domestic and international in content—and how the pursuance of homeland security, especially after the events of September 11, fit that characterization. In turn, they explain several dimensions of homeland security to explain the problems of its operation.

The long-standing embargo against Cuba provides their initial illustration of the intermestic nature of homeland security. Although the embargo has long had numerous government agencies involved in its enforcement, these same agencies (and others) in the post-9/11 era now have the additional responsibility for ensuring homeland security against terrorism and related threats. As Russo and Haney note, these differing policy responsibilities may (and do) come into conflict in light of the limited human and material resources available to these agencies. In addition, the agencies have placed differing importance on these goals. Indeed, the older foreign policy goal (the enforcement of the embargo) with its longstanding domestic political implications has seemingly crowded out the newer foreign policy goal (the enforcement of anti-terrorist activities), even with its domestic concerns for the latter goal. Thus, these competing goals, and the competing domestic constituencies involved with each one, demonstrate how homeland security has become captive of domestic politics, albeit in differing ways.

Yet providing homeland security does not just involve officials at the national level—it also involves utilizing officials at the state and local levels. Building off former Speaker of the House Thomas P. "Tip" O'Neill's famous aphorism that "all politics is local," Russo and Haney note, correctly, that "all security is local." In that sense, the task is to coordinate homeland security activities across different layers of government. In so doing, homeland security has introduced a whole series of new domestic actors with foreign policy responsibilities. Complicating this mosaic of actors from the national to the local level is the congressional mandate that the Department of Homeland Security utilize an "all-hazards" model of homeland security. Such a model requires that officials embrace both terrorist activities and natural disasters as their responsibilities. In this sense, foreign policy and domestic policy concerns are even more fully intertwined for national, state, and local officials. As such, as one analyst noted, this arrangement truly makes for "an intergovernmental system under stress."

In an effort to address this complexity, seventy-two "Fusion Centers" have been created across the United States, but, with such centers, difficulties remain. Such centers are largely funded through the Homeland Security Grant Program, presumably to coordinate activities uniformly in the nation. As Russo and Haney point out, however, the sustained and systematic funding of these centers remains problematic. Questions have also been raised about the funding of some centers over others due to possible political influence. Although Russo and Haney appear to distance themselves from this latter concern, the issues of policy coordination and funding demonstrate not only how homeland security operates today, but also how this seeming foreign policy issue is highly intermestic.

Recent American administrations have made trade policy a central focus of their foreign policy agendas. During the Clinton administration, for example, numerous bilateral and multilateral trade agreements (e.g., the North American Free Trade Agreement and the World Trade Organization [WTO]) were negotiated and entered into force. The Bush administration continued this process with the negotiation of several bilateral free-trade agreements around the world. The Obama administration has continued this process with its own ambitious trade policy agenda. The administration has declared that its "trade policy will support more American jobs and better jobs as we open world markets for Made in America products."[5] Trade policy, however, can be controversial, at home and abroad as the Clinton, Bush, and Obama administrations learned. Clinton faced substantial opposition at home in 1993 in seeking congressional approval for

NAFTA and massive demonstrations by environmental, labor, and anti-globalization groups protesting against international trade regulations at the 1999 WTO meeting in Seattle. Bush had to deal with similar protests in Quebec City, Canada, over the Free Trade Area of the Americas in April 2001 and with opposition in Congress over several free-trade agreements. Obama similarly confronted sustained congressional opposition over previously signed free-trade agreements with Panama, Colombia, and South Korea (although ultimately prevailing in October 2011). In all, foreign economic issues remain divisive in domestic and foreign policy, and the trade process and trade politics remain crucial issues in American foreign policy.

In the last chapter in part II, "American Trade Policymaking: A Unique Process," trade analyst I. M. (Mac) Destler tackles these issues by providing a careful assessment of the trade policymaking process over the history of the Republic and by analyzing the current domestic politics of trade policy. He begins his analysis by noting that historically trade policymaking was centered in the Congress and the principal issue was the tariff on importation. Indeed, the tariff issue dominated the trade agenda until the early twentieth century, reaching its apex with the passage of the Smoot-Hawley Act of 1930 that raised the average tariff to 60 percent. Such a punitive tariff, and similar ones across the world, deepened the Depression and "contributed to a fundamental change in U.S. trade policy, substantively and institutionally." Substantively, the policy turn was to lower tariffs, and institutionally, the process turn was a greater role for the executive branch in initiating trade policy.

The principal vehicle for the shift in policymaking and policy results was the Reciprocal Trade Agreements Act of 1934. Under this act, as Destler explains, the executive branch would negotiate trade tariffs under authority granted by Congress, and, in this way, the executive tends to lower rather than raise tariffs. By the end of World War II, moreover, this pattern continued beyond bilateral negotiations to include multilateral agreements as well.

Still, Congress was not entirely pleased with this arrangement, especially since the Department of State primarily carried out these negotiations and some members of Congress believed that State did not wholly understanding the requirements of business. Hence, when President Kennedy sought greater negotiating authority, Congress provided it to him in the Trade Expansion Act of 1962, but it did so by creating the office of the "President's Special Representative for Trade Negotiations (STR)" within the White House. In doing so, the president (or his representative) gained even more authority over trade policymaking.

By the Trade Act of 1974, Congress transformed the STR into a statutory office and, five years later, the position was changed yet again, "renaming the STR the Office of the *United States* Trade Representative (USTR) and broadening its authority." In 1988, the Omnibus Trade and Competitiveness Act increased the power of the USTR yet again to where it is presently. As a result, the USTR "typically leads and manages on major trade issues" and "heads a statutory interagency coordinating committee structure that operates at cabinet and sub-cabinet levels."

Yet the USTR is not the sole agency involved in the formulation and implementation of U.S. trade policy. In conjunction with the United States International Trade Commission, the Department of Commerce determines whether U.S. industries have suffered "injury" by the trade actions of foreign countries. If it so determines, Commerce has the responsibility to impose countervailing duties and enforce anti-dumping laws for the United States on behalf of these firms. Importantly, Commerce also operates the U.S. and Foreign Commercial Service, the principal agency for promoting U.S. businesses around the world. Finally, as Destler points out, the Department of Agriculture also has trade policymaking responsibilities when issues related to agricultural trade liberalization arise.

The executive branch thus has important responsibilities in the formulation of trade policy, but the approval of Congress is still needed to implement actions. An important and recent innovation in improving interbranch coordination over formulation and implementation has been the "fast-track procedures" (later called "trade promotion authority"). Under this arrangement, the president (or more accurately, the USTR) negotiates a trade agreement with another country, and Congress agrees to vote on the negotiated agreement, without amendment, within ninety days of its submittal to Congress. At the same time, and as part of this process, the USTR is required to consult with Congress and private-sector advisory groups during the course of its negotiations. Moreover, as Destler points out, this procedure has been very important in the completion of trade agreements by the United States. Yet it also allows Congress to maintain ultimate control over the trade policy process.

Much as the process for formulating trade policy has changed over the past century, the domestic politics of trade has as well. In particular, Destler discusses two important changes in the trade policy environment that affects the effort to move toward a more open trading system. First, American business and industries have largely moved from a protectionist to a free-trade stance, hence supporting more openness, while organized labor has moved in the opposite direction, from espousing free trade to a more protectionist posture, hence seeking to slow down market openness. Second, an "anti-globalization" movement emerged in the 1990s—composed of labor unions, environmentalists, and some nongovernmental organizations—that also is skeptical of free trade and its impact at home, on developing countries, and the environment. This movement has complicated the passage of free-trade agreements (FTAs) negotiated by the Bush administration, and it has further exacerbated partisan divisions over trade policy. Although a congressional compromise was negotiated in 2007 (the "May 10 agreement") to bridge the gaps between the two parties of these free-trade pacts, the agreement worked imperfectly. Instead, and as we noted earlier, it took several years to get previously negotiated agreements (e.g., Colombia, Panama, Korea) approved by the Congress in late 2011. As a result, and as Destler concludes, "the most likely near-term scenario is a kind of trade policy stasis" in which the United States will pursue "full economic openness," but "not quite reaching it." In this sense, America's trade policy remains constrained by the requirements of domestic politics.

Editor's Note: At the end of each chapter is a series of discussion questions for use by the students and instructor.

NOTES

1. "The Imperial Presidency," *Economist*, November 3, 2001, 39.

2. For an example of President Obama's deliberative decision-making, especially over decision-making on Afghanistan, see Bob Woodward, *Obama's Wars* (New York: Simon and Schuster, 2010), and for an analysis of President Obama's personality and personal identity, see Stanley A. Renshon, *Barack Obama and the Politics of Redemption* (New York: Routledge, 2012).

3. *The 9/11 Commission Report* (New York: Norton, 2004).

4. Philip Senon, "Establishing New Agency Is Expected to Take Years and Could Divert It from Mission," *New York Times*, November 20, 2002, A12.

5. Ambassador Ron Kirk (Office of the United States Trade Representative), "President's 2011 Trade Policy Agenda Focuses on American Jobs," March 1, 2011, www.ustr.gov/about-us/press-office/press-releases/2011/presidents-2011-trade-policy-agenda-focuses-american-jobs.

9

Person and Office

Presidents, the Presidency, and Foreign Policy

Michael Nelson

Henry Jones Ford, in his classic work *The Rise and Growth of American Government*, quoted Alexander Hamilton's prediction to a friend that the time would "assuredly come when every vital question of the state will be merged in the question, 'Who shall be the next president?'" Ford cited this remark to support his argument that in creating the presidency, the Constitutional Convention of 1787 had "revived the oldest political institution of the race, the elective kingship."

Although there is much truth in Ford's evaluation of the presidency, it also displays a certain measure of ambivalence on a fundamental issue. Is the presidency best understood as a person ("Who shall be the next president?") or an office (an "elective kingship")?

Political scientists in the twentieth and twenty-first centuries have continued to grapple with Ford's conundrum. Most of them probably would agree that the best answer to the person-or-office question is some combination of both: person and office, president and presidency. The office has become important mostly because its constitutional design suited it well for national leadership in the changing circumstances of history. But because the Constitution invested so much responsibility in the person who is the president, that person's background, personality, and leadership skills are consequential as well.

Modern political scientists also tend to agree on a second matter—namely, that the presidency and the presidents who occupy the office are never more important than in the making of foreign policy. George W. Bush, a president who was more narrowly elected (2000) and reelected (2004) than any of his predecessors, showed that this is especially true of issues and challenges that concern the national security. Bush launched

179

wars in Afghanistan and Iraq and, despite the latter's severe unpopularity by 2006, was able to increase the American military commitment even after suffering a major defeat in the midterm congressional elections. Bush's successor, Barack Obama, won a more convincing victory in 2008 and immediately faced the challenge of trying to bring the wars that Bush began to a reasonably successful conclusion. Obama faced many obstacles in doing so, but none of these originated in Congress or domestic politics.

OFFICE

The Constitutional Convention created a government marked less by separation of powers than, in political scientist Richard Neustadt's apt phrase, by "separated institutions sharing powers." Institutional separation meant that in stark contrast to parliamentary governments, which typically draw their executive leaders from the legislature, the president was forbidden by Article 1, Section 6, of the Constitution to appoint any sitting member of Congress to the cabinet or White House staff. These severely separated branches were, however, constitutionally enjoined to share in the exercise of virtually all the powers of the national government. Congress is empowered to "make all laws," but the president may veto them. The Senate may (or may choose not to) give "Advice and Consent" concerning presidential appointments to the executive branch and the judiciary. In matters of war, the president is "Commander in Chief of the Army and Navy," but Congress has the power to "declare war," to "raise and support Armies," and to "provide and maintain a Navy." In matters of peace, no treaty proposed by a president can take effect unless two-thirds of the Senate votes to ratify it.

Powers alone do not define power. Through history, the presidency has become much more powerful than at its inception, even though the formal powers of the office have remained the same. A second cluster of constitutional decisions, those concerning the number and selection of the executive, provides much of the explanation for the presidency's expanding influence. The framers of the Constitution, after much debate, created the presidency as a unitary, not a plural or committee-style, office and provided that the president would be elected by the entire nation, independently of Congress and the state governments. In doing so, they made the president the only national officer who can plausibly claim both a political mandate to speak for the people and their government and an institutional capacity to lead with what the Pennsylvania delegate James Wilson described as "energy, unity, and responsibility."

Lead, that is, when and in such areas of public policy as national leadership is sought—which, during the nineteenth century, usually was not in the domestic realm. Historically, it took well over a century for parchment to become practice—that is, for all of the constitutionally enumerated powers of the presidency to come to life. Congress seized the lion's share of the government's shared powers in domestic policy nearly from the beginning, dominating even the executive appointment process. When it came to legislation, members of Congress treated with scorn most early presidential efforts to recommend or influence their consideration of bills and resolutions. Nor, until Andrew Jackson in the 1830s, were presidents able to exercise the veto power without provoking a politically disabling storm of opposition on Capitol Hill.

Although presidential disempowerment was long lived, it was not eternal. The weakness of the presidency in domestic matters was a function of the weak national government that generally prevailed during the nineteenth century. The country, then a congeries of local economies and cultures, was not seeking what the presidency was constitutionally designed to provide—namely, energetic leadership on behalf of national initiatives. But the conditions that sustained weak government began to change around the turn of the century. The widespread dissemination of railroads and telegraph lines made all but inevitable the development of a national economy, and with this transformation came demands that the national government take measures to facilitate the spread (while taming the excesses) of the new and massive corporations. Early twentieth-century presidents Theodore Roosevelt and Woodrow Wilson roused a popular mandate for the president to make full use of the office's constitutional powers to lead Congress and the executive branch. Franklin D. Roosevelt, during the Great Depression of the 1930s, and more recent presidents, such as Lyndon B. Johnson, Ronald Reagan, and Barack Obama, also played the role of chief legislator on a grand scale.

In contrast to the slow awakening of the presidency's constitutional powers concerning domestic policy, on matters of foreign policy the powers of the office were activated early. In 1793, George Washington issued the Proclamation of Neutrality on his own authority, declaring that the United States would not take sides in the war between England and France. Critics declared that he lacked that authority. Because a declaration of war must be approved by Congress, they argued, so must a declaration not to go to war. Secretary of the Treasury Alexander Hamilton, writing as "Pacificus," replied in a series of pseudonymous newspaper articles that the president's constitutional powers were sufficient. Unlike the vesting clause of Article 1, which states, "All legislative Powers herein granted shall be vested in a Congress of the United States," the vesting clause for the president lacks the words "herein granted," stating instead, "The executive Power shall be vested in a President of the United States of America." The omission of these two words, Hamilton claimed, meant that the president had constitutional powers beyond those specified by name, especially in foreign policy. Washington's proclamation stood.

Although presidents had to struggle to invigorate the domestic powers of their office during the nineteenth and early twentieth centuries, they usually were able to get their way when deciding how the United States should deal with other countries. In 1823 an otherwise weak president, James Monroe, issued the Monroe Doctrine on his own authority. The doctrine declared that the Americas were off-limits to any attempts at European colonization. James K. Polk secretly negotiated for the annexation of Texas during the mid-1840s and, by sending troops into disputed territory, provoked war with Mexico. Without congressional consultation, Presidents William McKinley, William Howard Taft, Woodrow Wilson, and Calvin Coolidge dispatched American forces into foreign countries.

Similarly, beginning with the Washington administration, presidential decisions about which foreign governments to recognize have gone uncontested as a proper exercise of the president's constitutional authority to "receive Ambassadors." Treaties gradually gave way to executive agreements as the main form of contract between the United States and other countries.

When criticized for their assertiveness in foreign policy, presidents invariably invoked the institutional nature of their office, especially its unitary character and election by the entire country. In his book *The Decline and Resurgence of Congress*, James Sundquist summarized the standard (and politically persuasive) response of presidents to their critics: "Quick decision was imperative; . . . the move had to be made, or negotiations conducted, in secret, and only the executive could maintain confidentiality; . . . only the president has the essential information; . . . effective intercourse with other nations requires the United States to speak with a single voice, which can only be the president's."

Arguments such as these became especially compelling in the post–World War II era. As in previous wars, vast temporary powers had been granted to the president during the World War II. What made this war different was its aftermath. Instead of lapsing into relative isolation from world political affairs, the United States entered into a Cold War with the Soviet Union. New technologies of warfare, especially nuclear weapons and intercontinental delivery systems, raised the specter of instant and global destruction.

These developments made the president's number- and selection-based constitutional strengths appear even more significant than during past wars. Increased reliance not only on executive agreements but also on secrecy in all diplomacy made the conduct of postwar foreign policy a shared power with Congress in only the most nominal sense. The Republican Eightieth Congress (1947–1949) was angrily partisan on domestic issues, but it readily assented to Democratic president Harry S. Truman's far-reaching foreign policy initiatives, including the Marshall Plan and the North Atlantic Treaty Organization (NATO). Congress supported the American intervention in the Korean War, which it was never asked to declare, with annual military appropriations. It provided similar support for the war in Vietnam during the 1960s and early 1970s. In the years between these two wars, Congress wrote virtual blank checks in advance support of whatever actions the administrations of Dwight D. Eisenhower and John F. Kennedy might decide to take in the Middle East, Berlin, Cuba, and elsewhere.

Much was made in the post-Vietnam era of Congress's newfound assertiveness in foreign policy. In 1973, for example, Congress enacted the War Powers Resolution over President Richard Nixon's veto. The resolution requires the president to consult with Congress "in every possible instance" before sending American forces into hostile or dangerous situations. After committing the armed forces, the president is then charged to remove them within sixty (or, by special presidential request, ninety) days unless Congress votes to authorize their continued involvement.

Every president since the War Powers Resolution was enacted has questioned its constitutionality. A number of military operations have been undertaken—by presidents Gerald Ford (the *Mayaguez* rescue), Jimmy Carter (the attempted Iranian hostage rescue), Ronald Reagan (the Grenada invasion), George H. W. Bush (the Panama invasion and the Persian Gulf War), Bill Clinton (the stationing of peacekeeping troops in Somalia, Haiti, and Bosnia), and George W. Bush (the wars in Afghanistan and Iraq). In few instances have these presidents complied with the letter, much less the spirit, of the War Powers Resolution. Yet Congress has seldom voted to start the sixty-day clock—and never when it mattered. The main lesson of more than three decades of experience under the resolution is that law cannot substitute for political will if Congress is to curb the president's role in war making.

Congress's weakness in foreign policymaking can be partially explained by its institutional character: large, diverse, unwieldy, and slow. As Sundquist observed, Congress can "disrupt the policy that the president pursues, but it cannot act affirmatively to carry out a comprehensive substitute policy of its own." Congress also is constrained by the public's expectations of its members. Voters want their representatives and senators to concern themselves more with local than national interests, which leaves out most foreign policies. Not surprisingly, Congress is most assertive on those few global issues that have a clear domestic policy coloration, such as trade policy and support for nations, especially Israel, that have large and well-organized domestic lobbies.

As for the Supreme Court, although it occasionally rebukes a president for exceeding the constitutional authority of the office, on the whole it has defended presidents' expansive interpretations of their powers. In *Hamdan v. Rumsfeld* (2006), the court slapped down George W. Bush's claim that the president could establish military tribunals to try suspected foreign terrorists. But no Supreme Court decision has challenged the Court's most important ruling concerning presidential power in foreign affairs. In *United States v. Curtiss-Wright Export Corp.* (1936), the Court echoed Pacificus in declaring that "the President is the sole organ of the federal government in the field of international relations." The president, the Court continued, "not Congress, has the better opportunity of knowing the conditions which prevail in foreign countries, and especially is this true in time of war." The Court's strong defense of presidential power in foreign affairs was all the more remarkable because at the time of the decision, the justices were reining in the president's powers in domestic policy.

One other aspect of the presidential office merits special attention. In making the presidency a unitary office elected by its own national constituency, the framers of the Constitution unwittingly combined the normally separate executive leadership roles of chief of government and chief of state into one office. As chief of government, the president is called on to act as a partisan political leader in the manner of, for example, the British prime minister. As chief of state, the president is the equivalent of the British monarch—the ceremonial leader of the nation and the living symbol of national unity.

The significance of the chief of state role has little to do with the insignificant formal powers that accompany it or the activities it requires. Rather, it lies in the emotions the role arouses in citizens. Long before they have any knowledge of what the president does, young children already have positive feelings about the president's seemingly boundless power and benevolence. The death of a president causes adults to react in an equally emotional way. Surveys taken shortly after the Kennedy assassination found Americans displaying symptoms of grief that otherwise appear only at the death of a close friend or family member. Similar outpourings seem to have accompanied the deaths in office, whether by assassination or natural causes, of all presidents, whether they were young or old, popular or unpopular. In Great Britain, it is royal deaths, such as King George V's in 1936 and Princess Diana's in 1997, that occasion such deep emotions. It is the monarch whom children think of as powerful and good, not the prime minister.

The public's attachment to the president as chief of state sometimes has strong implications for the president's powers as chief of government, especially in foreign policy. In particular, the often-observed "rally 'round the flag effect" is a way in which the president benefits politically from being the nation's living symbol of unity. A rally effect is the sudden and substantial increase in public approval of the president that occurs in response to dramatic international events involving the United States. These include sudden military interventions, major diplomatic actions, and attacks on the United States. Richard Nixon's public approval rating rose twelve percentage points after his October 1969 "Vietnamization" speech. Gerald Ford's jumped eleven points after he dispatched troops to rescue the *Mayaguez*. Carter added twelve points to his approval rating as a result of the Camp David summit that achieved peace between Israel and Egypt. Reagan's approval rating leaped eight points when he invaded Grenada. George H. W. Bush's rating soared higher than any previous president's after the American victory against Iraq in the Gulf War. His record was broken by his son, George W. Bush, after he launched the war on terrorism in September 2001. The younger Bush's approval rating rose from 51 to 90 percent and remained above 75 percent for nearly a year, strengthening his hand as he directed the course of American policy toward Afghanistan and Iraq. Obama's rating improved in January 2011 after he persuaded the Senate to ratify the New START nuclear arms reduction treaty with Russia.

PERSON

Because the presidency is important, so is the person who is president. What kinds of experience do presidents typically bring with them into office? What manner of personality? What skills of leadership?

Concerning experience, presidents almost always have been drawn from the ranks of high government officials: vice presidents, members of Congress, governors, cabinet members, or generals. Yet in more recent elections, the roster of presidential candidates has been confined largely to governors, vice presidents, and senators.

The disappearance of cabinet members, generals, and members of Congress from the presidential talent pool has reduced the likelihood that the president will be experienced in foreign policy before taking office. Early in the nation's history, service as secretary of state was the main stepping-stone to the presidency. Four of the first six presidents—Thomas Jefferson, James Madison, James Monroe, and John Quincy Adams—had previously served as secretary of state. Generals in successful wars, such as Andrew Jackson (War of 1812), Zachary Taylor (Mexican-American War), Ulysses S. Grant (Civil War), and Dwight D. Eisenhower (World War II) sometimes have been elected president, but not in the modern era of warfare. In the four elections from 1960 to 1972, every major party nominee was a senator or a former senator. But in the anti-Washington political climate that has dominated presidential elections since the Vietnam War and the Watergate scandal, not a single senator has been elected president (with the exception of Senator Barack Obama in 2008).

Instead of secretaries of state, generals, and senators, state governors have dominated the ranks of the presidency in recent years. Of the six presidents elected since the mid-1970s, four were governors: Jimmy Carter of Georgia in 1976, Ronald Reagan of California in 1980 and 1984, Bill Clinton of

Arkansas in 1992 and 1996, and George W. Bush of Texas in 2000 and 2004. (The only exceptions were Vice President George H. W. Bush in 1988 and Senator Barack Obama.) Although international concerns came to dominate the administrations of all of these presidents, nearly everything they knew about foreign policy, the elder Bush excepted, came from election-year cramming and on-the-job experience.

The personality, or psychological character, that a president brings to the White House is, considering the power of the office and the pressures that weigh on its occupant, of obvious importance. In 1972, James David Barber drew scholarly attention to this concern. In his book *The Presidential Character*, Barber offered a theory that places each president into one of four character types. The most dangerous of these is the "active negative," the president who is attracted to politics by a lack of self-esteem that can be compensated for psychologically only by dominating others through the wielding of official power. When active-negative presidents feel that their hold on power is threatened, they react in rigidly defensive ways, persisting in ineffective and destructive courses of action and treating critics as enemies. In Barber's view, Wilson's failure to compromise with Senate critics on the League of Nations treaty and Johnson's unwillingness to change course in Vietnam were the products of active-negative psychological characters.

Critics have taken Barber to task for a number of fundamental weaknesses in his theory. At root, the psychological study of personality is still too murky a field to explain, much less to predict, the presidential character. But public concern remains high. For example, in 2000 doubts about character went a long way toward explaining the outcome of the presidential election. Democratic candidate Al Gore carried a reputation into the campaign as an aggressive, experienced, and skillful debater, a reputation that his Republican opponent, George W. Bush, lacked. Yet Bush ended up benefiting considerably more from their three nationally televised debates than Gore did. In the first debate, Gore treated his opponent with disdain, often speaking condescendingly when it was his turn and sighing and grimacing while Bush spoke. Chastened by the adverse public response, Gore was deferential, almost obsequious, during the second debate. He hit his stride in the third debate, but the inconsistency of his behavior from one debate to the next fed voters' doubts about who Gore really was. Bush was not strongly impressive in any of the debates, but voters saw the same person in all three of them. Gore, who had entered the debate season leading Bush by around five percentage points in the polls, left it trailing by five points.

The skills of leadership that a president requires may be more confidently described than the presidential character. In relations with the rest of the executive branch, the president is called on to be an adroit *manager of authority*, both of lieutenants on the White House staff (whose chronic sycophancy toward the president and hostility toward the president's critics perennially threaten to overwhelm the good effects of their loyalty, talent, and hard work) and of the massive departments and agencies of the bureaucracy, whose activities lie at the heart of the president's role as chief executive. For example, as a new president, George W. Bush went a long way toward reassuring foreign policy experts who doubted his understanding of international issues by appointing veteran Washington hands to important executive positions, especially Richard Cheney as vice president, Colin Powell as secretary of state, and Donald Rumsfeld as secretary of defense. Experience proved no sure guide in office, however. Cheney's and Rumsfeld's failure to anticipate the difficulties of occupying Iraq were the source of innumerable difficulties after American-led forces toppled Iraqi dictator Saddam Hussein in 2003. Nevertheless, Obama emulated Bush in appointing experienced leaders to major foreign policy positions: Joseph Biden as vice president, Hillary Rodham Clinton as secretary of state, and Robert Gates (Rumsfeld's replacement during Bush's final two years) as secretary of defense.

Presidential leadership of Congress requires different, more *tactical political skills*. Senators and representatives, no less than the president, are politically independent and self-interested. No one has described the challenge of leading them more pithily and precisely than Neustadt in his book *Presidential Power*. To lead, Neustadt argued, is to persuade; to persuade is to bargain; and to bargain is to convince members of Congress that their interests and the president's are (or can be made to be) the same.

Ultimately, a president's standing with Congress and the bureaucracy rests on the bedrock of public opinion, which makes the *presentation of self* (a phrase invented by the sociologist Erving Goffman) to the American people an important category of leadership skills. Presentation of self involves not just speechmaking, press conferences, and other forms of rhetoric but dramaturgy as well. During Richard Nixon's first term, for example, he reinforced a televised speech appealing for the support of the "silent majority" of blue-collar workers and their families by dramatically donning a hard hat before a cheering crowd (and a battery of cameras) at a New York City construction site. Bill Clinton, concerned that neither the military nor the American people regarded him as a confident commander in chief, learned from studying videotapes of Ronald Reagan how to transform limp, offhand salutes on ceremonial occasions into shoulders-back posture and crisp salutes. George W. Bush used rhetoric and dramaturgy to reassure a worried nation two days after the September 11 attacks. Standing in the midst of New York's Ground Zero with his arm around a rescue worker, Bush answered listeners who said they could not hear him by declaring, "I can hear you. The rest of the world hears you. And the people who knocked these buildings down will hear all of us soon." In December 2009 Obama chose West Point as the setting in which to launch his new, two-pronged approach to the war in Afghanistan: an immediate infusion of new troops in 2010 followed by troop withdrawals starting in 2011.

Perhaps a president's most important leadership skill involves a *strategic sense* of the historical possibilities of the time. These possibilities are defined both by objective conditions (the international situation, the budget, the health of the economy, and so on) and by the public mood. Above all, the president must have a highly developed aptitude for what Woodrow Wilson called "interpretation"—that is, the ability to understand and articulate the varying, vaguely expressed desires of the American people for change or quiescence, material prosperity or moral challenge, isolation from or intervention in the problems of the world, and so on.

In the end, the background, personality, and leadership skills of the president are important because of the ways in which the Constitution and changing historical circumstances have made the presidency important. Person and office, although defined and often discussed separately, are in essence one.

DISCUSSION QUESTIONS

1. What are the constitutional powers of the presidency?
2. What does Nelson mean when he says "powers alone do not define power"?
3. How have the actions of past presidents affected the powers of the office?
4. How have presidential powers changed over time?
5. What are the key personal characteristics of a president that may affect his approach to the presidency and foreign policy?
6. What are some of the drawbacks to using a president's personality to determine his foreign policy approach?

10

Presidents Who Initiate Wars

Louis Fisher

In March 2011, Barack Obama became the most recent president to decide that he, and he alone, could take the country from a state of peace to a state of war without seeking or obtaining congressional authority. Without any threat or attack from Libya, he initiated military force against Libya on the basis of a UN Security Council resolution and the support of NATO allies, the Arab League, and the "Libyan people." He did not bother to attract the support of Congress or the American people. Through unconvincing legal and constitutional analysis, his administration argued that the military activities in Libya did not amount to "war" or "hostilities." His decision to concentrate the war power in the hands of one person provoked a backlash from the House of Representatives. The Senate, supposedly the leading branch of Congress in matters of foreign affairs and national security, was largely passive and deferential to presidential power. Details of the war in Libya are included later in this chapter.

From 1789 to 1950, all major military initiatives by the United States were decided by Congress, either by a formal declaration of war or by a statute authorizing the president to use military force. There were some notable exceptions, such as the actions by President James Polk that led to hostilities between the United States and Mexico. Even on this occasion Polk knew that the Constitution required him to come to Congress to seek authority. Presidents also used military force for various "life and property" actions, but they were typically limited, short-term engagements. By and large, the first century and a half followed the framers' expectations that matters of war and peace would be vested in the government's representative branch—Congress.

The record since 1950 has been dramatically different. Presidents over the past half century have felt increasingly comfortable in acting unilaterally when using military force against other countries. Instead of coming to Congress for authority, they justify military actions either on the commander-in-chief clause in the Constitution or on decisions reached by the UN Security Council and the North Atlantic Treaty Organization (NATO). Even with these departures, however, only two major U.S. wars have been entered into without a congressional declaration or authorization of war: Korea in 1950 and Yugoslavia in 1999.

CONSTITUTIONAL PRINCIPLES

When the American Constitution was drafted in 1787, the framers were aware that existing models of government placed the war power and foreign affairs solely in the hands of the king. Thus, matters of treaties, appointment of ambassadors, the raising and regulation of fleets and armies, and the initiation of military actions against other countries had been vested in the king. Accordingly, John Locke and William Blackstone, whose writings deeply influenced the framers, assigned war powers and foreign affairs exclusively to the executive branch.

This monarchical model was expressly rejected at the Philadelphia convention. As revealed in the historical records of the Constitutional Convention,[1] Charles Pinckney said he was for "a vigorous Executive but was afraid the Executive powers of [the existing] Congress might extend to peace & war &c which would render the Executive a Monarchy, of the worst kind, to wit an elective one." Although John Rutledge wanted the executive power placed in a single person, "he was not for giving him the power of war and peace." James Wilson supported a single executive but "did not consider the Prerogative of the British Monarch as a proper guide in defining the Executive powers. Some of these prerogatives were of a Legislative nature. Among others that of war & peace &c." Edmund Randolph worried about executive power, calling it "the foetus of monarchy."

The framers recognized that the president would need unilateral power in one area: defensive actions to repel sudden attacks, especially when Congress was not in session to legislate. An early draft of the Constitution empowered Congress to "make war." Charles Pinckney objected that legislative proceedings "were too slow" for the safety of the country in an emergency since he expected Congress to meet but once a year. James Madison and Elbridge Gerry moved to insert "declare" for "make," leaving to the president "the power to repel sudden attacks."

Debate on the Madison-Gerry amendment underscored the limited grant of authority to the president. Pierce Butler wanted to give the president the power to make war, arguing that he "will have all the requisite qualities, and will not make war but when the Nation will support it." Roger Sherman objected: "The Executive shd. be able to repel and not to commence war." Gerry said he "never expected to hear in a republic a motion to empower the Executive alone to declare war." George Mason spoke "agst giving the power of war to the Executive, because not [safely] to be trusted with it; . . . He was for clogging rather than facilitating war."

Similar statements were made at the state ratifying conventions. In Pennsylvania, James Wilson expressed the prevailing sentiment that the system of checks and balances "will not hurry us into war; it is calculated to guard against it. It will not be in the power of a single man, or a single body of men, to involve us in such distress; for the important power of declaring war is vested in the legislature at large."[2] The framers also took great pains to separate the purse and the sword. They were familiar with the efforts of English kings to rely on extra-parliamentary sources of revenue for military expeditions. After a series of monarchical transgressions, England lurched into a bloody civil war. The origin and vigor of democratic government is directly related to legislative control over the purse.

The U.S. Constitution states, "No Money shall be drawn from the Treasury, but in Consequences of Appropriations made by Law." In *Federalist* No. 48, Madison explained that "the legislative department alone has access to the pockets of the people." The Constitution empowers Congress to lay and collect taxes, duties, imposts, and excises; to borrow money on the credit of the United States; and to coin money and regulate its value. The power of the purse, Madison said in *Federalist* No. 58, represents the "most compleat and effectual weapon with which any constitution can arm the immediate representatives of the people, for obtaining a redress of every grievance, and for carrying into effect every just and salutary measure."

In making the president the commander in chief, Congress retained for Congress the important check over spending. Madison set forth this tenet: "Those who are to *conduct a war* cannot in the nature of things, be proper or safe judges, whether *a war ought* to be *commenced, continued,* or *concluded.* They are barred from the latter functions by a great principle in free government, analogous to that which separates the sword from the purse, or the power of executing from the power of enacting laws." At the Philadelphia convention, George Mason counseled that the "purse & the sword ought never to get into the same hands (whether Legislative or Executive)."

Throughout the next century and a half, major military actions were either declared by Congress (the War of 1812, the Mexican War of 1846, the Spanish-American War of 1898, World War I, and World War II) or authorized by Congress (the Quasi-War against France from 1798 to 1800 and the Barbary Wars during the administrations of Thomas Jefferson and

James Madison). In either case, presidents regularly came to Congress to seek authority to initiate offensive actions against another country.

That pattern was radically changed in 1950 when President Harry Truman ordered American troops to Korea without ever coming to Congress for authority, either before or after. He based his actions in part on resolutions adopted by the UN Security Council, but nothing in the history of the UN Charter implies that Congress ever contemplated placing in the hands of the president the unilateral power to wage war. Truman's initiative became a model for President George H. W. Bush in going to war against Iraq in 1991 and President Bill Clinton in threatening to invade Haiti in 1994. In addition, Clinton cited NATO as authority for air strikes in Bosnia and sending ground troops to that region. In 1999, he relied on NATO to wage war against Yugoslavia. But the legislative histories of the United Nations and NATO show no intent on the part of Congress to sanction independent presidential war power.

THE UNITED NATIONS AND NATO

In 1945, during Senate debate on the UN Charter, President Truman sent a cable from Potsdam stating that all agreements involving U.S. troop commitments to the United Nations would first have to be approved by both houses of Congress. He pledged without equivocation, "When any such agreement or agreements are negotiated it will be my purpose to ask the Congress for appropriate legislation to approve them."[3] By "agreements" he meant the procedures that would permit UN military force in dealing with threats to peace, breaches of the peace, and acts of aggression. All UN members would make available to the Security Council, "on its call and in accordance with a special agreement or agreements," armed forces and other assistance for the purpose of maintaining international peace and security.

The UN Charter provided that these agreements, concluded between the Security Council and member states, "shall be subject to ratification by the signatory states in accordance with their respective constitutional processes." Each nation would have to adopt its own procedures for meeting their international obligations.

After the Senate approved the UN Charter, Congress had to decide the meaning of "constitutional processes." What procedure was necessary, under the U.S. Constitution, to bring into effect the special agreements needed to contribute American troops to UN military actions? That issue was decided by the UN Participation Act of 1945, which stated without the slightest ambiguity that the agreements "shall be subject to the approval of the Congress by appropriate Act or joint resolution." The agreements between the United States and the Security Council would not result from unilateral executive action, nor would they be brought into force only by the Senate acting through the treaty process. Action by both houses of Congress would be required.

At every step in the legislative history of the UN Participation Act—hearings, committee reports, and floor debate—these elementary points were underscored and reinforced. Executive officials repeatedly assured members of Congress that the president could not commit troops to UN military actions unless Congress first approved.

During this time the Senate also approved the NATO treaty of 1949, which provides that an armed attack against one or more of the parties in Europe or North America "shall be considered an attack against them all." In the event of an attack, member states could exercise the right of individual or collective self-defense recognized by Article 51 of the UN Charter and assist the country or countries attacked by taking "such action as it deems necessary, including the use of armed force." However, Article 11 of the treaty states that it shall be ratified "and its provisions carried out by the Parties in accordance with their respective constitutional processes." The Southeast Asia Treaty of 1954 also stated that the treaty "shall be ratified and its provisions carried out by the Parties in accordance with their respective constitutional processes."

These treaties do not grant the president unilateral power to use military force against other nations. First, it is well recognized that the concept in mutual security treaties of an attack on one nation being an attack on all does not require from any nation an immediate response. Each country maintains the sovereign right to decide such matters by itself. As noted in the Rio Treaty of 1947, "no State shall be required to use armed force without its consent." In the U.S. system, who decides to use armed forces?

During hearings in 1949 on NATO, Secretary of State Dean Acheson told the Senate Foreign Relations Committee that it "does not mean that the United States would automatically be at war if one of the other signatory nations were the victim of an armed attack. Under our Constitution, the Congress alone has the power to declare war." Of course, he was merely saying what is expressly provided for in the Constitution. However, nothing in the legislative history of NATO gives the president any type of unilateral authority in the event of an attack. That the president lacks unilateral powers under the UN Charter or NATO should be obvious from the fact that both are international treaties entered into by way of a presidential proposal and Senate advice and consent. The president and the Senate cannot use the treaty process to strip the House of Representatives and future Senates of their prerogatives over the use of military force.

In the words of one scholar, the provisions in the NATO treaty that it be carried out according to constitutional processes was "intended to ensure that the Executive Branch of the Government should come back to the Congress when decisions were required in which the Congress has a constitutional responsibility." The NATO treaty "does not transfer to the President the Congressional power to make war."[4] Those predictions would be eroded by practices during the Clinton administration.

TRUMAN IN KOREA

With these treaty and statutory safeguards supposedly in place to protect legislative prerogatives, President Truman nonetheless sent U.S. troops to Korea in 1950 without ever seeking or obtaining congressional authority. How could this happen? How could so many explicit executive assurances to Congress and explicit statutory procedures be ignored and circumvented?

On June 26, Truman announced that the UN Security Council had ordered North Korea to withdraw its invading forces to positions north of the thirty-eighth parallel and that "in accordance with the resolution of the Security Council, the United States will vigorously support the effort of the Council to terminate this serious breach of the peace." The next day he ordered U.S. air and sea forces to provide military support to South Korea. It was not until the evening of June 27 that the Security Council actually called for military action. In his memoirs, *Present at the Creation*, Dean Acheson admitted that "some American action, said to be in support of the resolution of June 27, was in fact ordered, and possibly taken, prior to the resolution."

Truman violated the statutory language and legislative history of the UN Participation Act, including his own assurance from Potsdam that he would first obtain the approval of Congress before sending U.S. forces to a UN action. How was this possible? He simply ignored the special agreements that were supposed to be the guarantee of congressional control. Indeed, no state has ever entered into a special agreement with the Security Council—and none is ever likely to do so.

Truman exploited the UN machinery in part because of a fluke: the Soviet Union had absented itself from the Security Council during two crucial votes taken during the early days of the crisis. It is difficult to argue that the president's constitutional powers vary with the presence or absence of Soviet (or other) delegates to the Security Council. As Robert Bork noted in 1971, "The approval of the United Nations was obtained only because the Soviet Union happened to be boycotting the Security Council at the time, and the president's Constitutional powers can hardly be said to ebb and flow with the veto of the Soviet Union in the Security Council."[5]

Truman tried to justify his actions in Korea by calling it a UN "police action" rather than an American war. That argument was suspect from the start and deteriorated as U.S. casualties mounted. The United Nations exercised no real authority over the conduct of the war. Other than token support from a few nations, it remained an American war—measured by troops, money, casualties, and deaths—from start to finish. The euphemism "police action" was never persuasive. As a federal court concluded in 1953, "We doubt very much if there is any question in the minds of the majority of the people of this country that the conflict now raging in Korea can be anything but war."[6]

BUSH IN IRAQ (1990–1991)

Truman's initiative in Korea became a precedent for actions taken in 1990 by President George H. W. Bush. In response to Iraq's invasion of Kuwait on August 2, Bush sent several hundred thousand troops to Saudi Arabia for defensive purposes. Over the next few months, the size of the American force climbed to five hundred thousand, giving Bush the capability for mounting an offensive strike.

Instead of seeking authority from Congress, Bush created a multinational alliance and encouraged the UN Security Council to authorize the use of military force. The strategic calculations have been recorded by James A. Baker III, who served as secretary of state in the Bush administration. In his book *The Politics of Diplomacy*, Baker says he realized that military initiatives by Presidents Reagan in Grenada and Bush in Panama had reinforced in the international community the impression that American foreign policy followed a "cowboy mentality." In response to those concerns, Bush wanted to assemble an international political coalition. Baker notes, "From the very beginning, the president recognized the importance of having the express approval of the international community if at all possible." It is noteworthy that Bush would seek the express approval of other nations but not the express approval of Congress.

On November 20, Bush said he wanted to delay asking Congress for authorization until after the Security Council considered a proposed resolution supporting the use of force against Iraq. About a week later, on November 29, the Security Council authorized member states to use "all necessary means" to force Iraqi troops out of Kuwait. "All necessary means" is code language for military action. To avoid war, Iraq had to withdraw from Kuwait by January 15, 1991. Although the Security Council "authorized" each member state to act militarily against Iraq, the resolution did not compel or obligate them to participate. Instead, member states were free to use (or refuse) force pursuant to their own constitutional systems and judgments about national interests.

What procedure would the United States follow in deciding to use force? When Secretary of Defense Dick Cheney appeared before the Senate Armed

Services Committee on December 3, 1990, he said that President Bush did not require "any additional authorization from the Congress" before attacking Iraq. Through such language, he implied that authorization from the United Nations was sufficient.

The Justice Department argued in court that President Bush could order offensive actions against Iraq without seeking advance authority from Congress. On December 13, 1990, in *Dellums v. Bush*, the court expressly and forcefully rejected the sweeping interpretation of presidential war power advanced by the Justice Department. If the president had the sole power to determine that any offensive military operation, "no matter how vast, does not constitute war-making but only an offensive military attack, the congressional power to declare war will be at the mercy of a semantic decision by the Executive." But, having dismissed the Justice Department's interpretation, the court then held that the case was not ripe for adjudication.

On January 8, 1991, President Bush asked Congress to pass legislation supporting the UN position. The next day, reporters asked whether he needed authority from Congress. His reply: "I don't think I need it. . . . I feel that I have the authority to fully implement the United Nations resolutions." The legal crisis was avoided on January 12 when Congress authorized offensive actions against Iraq. In signing the bill, Bush indicated that he could have acted without legislation: "As I made clear to congressional leaders at the outset, my request for congressional support did not, and my signing this resolution does not, constitute any change in the longstanding positions of the executive branch on either the president's constitutional authority to use the Armed Forces to defend vital U.S. interests or the constitutionality of the War Powers Resolution." Despite his comments, the bill expressly authorized the action against Iraq. A signed statement does not alter the contents of a public law.

CLINTON IN HAITI

During the 1992 presidential campaign, Bill Clinton projected himself as a strong leader in foreign affairs and indicated a willingness to resort to military action. Criticizing Bush's foreign policy, he said he was prepared to use military force—in concert with other nations—to bring humanitarian aid to the citizens of Bosnia and Herzegovina. While saying he did not relish the prospect of sending Americans into combat, "neither do I flinch from it."[7] He accused the Bush administration of "turning its back" on "those struggling for democracy in China and on those fleeing Haiti."

Once in office, Clinton's position on what to do about the military regime in Haiti fluctuated from month to month, depending on shifting political pressures. Jean-Bertrand Aristide, the island's first democratically elected president, had been overthrown in a military coup on September 30, 1991. Political repression by the military rulers produced a flood of refugees trying to reach the United States.

Because of the refugee crisis, pressure mounted on Clinton to intervene militarily. In October 1993 he sent a contingent of six hundred U.S. soldiers to Haiti to work on roads, bridges, and water supplies. A group of armed civilians, opposed to U.S. intervention, prevented them from landing. Lightly armed, the U.S. troops were instructed by their commanders not to use force but to leave the area. The retreat in the face of tiny Haiti was widely interpreted as a humiliation for the United States.

Clinton soon began threatening the use of military force. By late July 1994, rumors began to circulate about an imminent Security Council resolution that would authorize the invasion of Haiti. A memo written by a U.S. official described the political calculations within the Clinton White House. Presidential advisers believed that an invasion of Haiti offered political benefits because it would highlight for the American public "the president's decision making capability and the firmness of leadership in international political matters."[8]

On July 31 the UN Security Council adopted a resolution "inviting" all states, particularly those in the region of Haiti, to use "all necessary means" to remove the military leadership in that island. At a news conference on August 3, Clinton denied that he needed authority from Congress to invade Haiti: "Like my predecessors of both parties, I have not agreed that I was constitutionally mandated to obtain the support of Congress." In a nationwide television address on September 15, Clinton told the American people that he was prepared to use military force to invade Haiti, referring to the Security Council resolution and expressing his willingness to lead a multilateral force "to carry out the will of the United Nations." No mention at all of the will of Congress.

The public and a substantial majority of legislators assailed the planned invasion. Criticized in the past for currying public favor and failing to lead, Clinton now seemed to glory in the idea of acting against the grain. He was determined to proceed with the invasion: "But regardless [of this opposition], this is what I believe is the right thing to do. I realize it is unpopular. I know it is unpopular. I know the timing is unpopular. I know the whole thing is unpopular. But I believe it is the right thing." Apparently there was no consideration of doing the legal thing, the authorized thing, or the constitutional thing.

Clinton emphasized the need to keep commitments: "I'd like to mention just one other thing that is equally important, and that is the reliability of the United States and the United Nations once we say we're going to do something." But who is the "we"? It was not Congress or the American public. It was a commitment made unilaterally by a president acting in concert with the UN Security Council.

An invasion of Haiti proved unnecessary. Clinton sent former president Jimmy Carter to negotiate with the military leaders in Haiti. They agreed to step down to permit the return of Aristide. Initially, nearly twenty thousand U.S. troops were dispatched to occupy Haiti and provide stability. Both houses passed legislation stating that "the president should have sought and welcomed Congressional approval before deploying United States Forces to Haiti."

INTERVENTION IN BOSNIA

In concert with the United Nations and NATO, the Bush and Clinton administrations participated in humanitarian airlifts in Sarajevo and helped enforce a "no-fly zone" (a ban on unauthorized flights over Bosnia-Herzegovina). In 1993, Clinton indicated that he would have to seek support and authorization from Congress before ordering air strikes. On May 7 he stated, "If I decide to ask the American people and the United States Congress to support an approach that would include the use of air power, I would have a very specific, clearly defined strategy." He anticipated asking "for the authority to use air power from the Congress and the American people."

Later in the year he began to object to legislative efforts to restrict his military options. Instead of seeking authority from Congress, Clinton now said he would seek from Congress advice and support. He was "fundamentally opposed" to any statutory provisions that "improperly limit my ability to perform my constitutional duties as Commander-in-Chief." He would operate through NATO, even though NATO had never used military force during its almost half century of existence.

In 1994, Clinton announced that decisions to use air power would be taken in response to UN Security Council resolutions, operating through NATO's military command. There was no more talk about seeking authority from Congress. Curiously, by operating through NATO, Clinton would seek the agreement of England, France, Italy, and other NATO allies but not Congress. NATO air strikes began in February 1994 and were followed by additional strikes throughout the year and into the next. The authorizing body was a multinational organization, not Congress.

The next escalation of U.S. military action was Clinton's decision to introduce ground troops into Bosnia. When reporters asked him on October 19, 1995, if he would send the troops even if Congress did not approve, he replied, "I am not going to lay down any of my constitutional prerogatives here today." On the basis of what he considered sufficient authority under

Article 2 of the Constitution and under NATO, he ordered the deployment of American ground troops to Bosnia without obtaining authority or support from Congress. In an address on November 27, 1995, he said that deployment of U.S. ground troops to Bosnia was "the right thing to do," paralleling his justification for invading Haiti. It was the right thing, he said, even if not the legal thing.

On December 21, Clinton expected that the military mission to Bosnia "can be accomplished in about a year." A year later, on December 17, 1996, he extended the troop deployment for another eighteen months. At the end of 1997 he announced that the deployment would have to be extended again but this time without attempting to fix a deadline. In 2007, U.S. troops were still in Bosnia.

THE WAR IN YUGOSLAVIA

In October 1998, the Clinton administration was again threatening the Serbs with air strikes, this time because of Serb attacks on the ethnic Albanian majority in Kosovo. At a news conference on October 8, Clinton stated, "Yesterday I decided that the United States would vote to give NATO the authority to carry out military strikes against Serbia if President Milosevic continues to defy the international community." An interesting sentence—"*I* decided that the United States." Whatever Clinton personally decided would be America's policy.

Clinton's chief foreign policy advisers went to Capitol Hill to consult with lawmakers but not to obtain their approval. Although Congress was to be given no formal role in the use of force against Serbs, legislatures in other NATO countries took votes to authorize military action in Yugoslavia. The Italian Parliament had to vote approval for the NATO strikes, and the German Supreme Court ruled that the Bundestag, which had been dissolved with the election that ousted Chancellor Kohl, had to be recalled to approve deployment of German aircraft and troops to Kosovo.

With air strikes imminent in March 1999, the Senate voted 58–41 in support of military air operations and missile strikes against Serbia. On April 28, after the first month of bombing, the House took a series of votes on war in Yugoslavia. A vote to authorize the air operations and missiles strikes lost on a tie vote, 213–213. Several resolutions were offered in the Senate to either authorize or restrict the war, but they were tabled. The Senate chose procedural remedies rather than voting on the merits.

During the bombing of Serbia and Kosovo, Rep. Tom Campbell (R-CA) went to court with twenty-five other House colleagues to seek a declaration that President Clinton had violated the Constitution and the War Powers Resolution by conducting the air offensive without congressional authorization. A district judge held that Campbell did not have standing to raise his claims. Although each House had taken a number of votes, Congress had never as an entire institution ordered Clinton to cease military operations. In that sense, there was no "constitutional impasse" or "actual confrontation" for the court to resolve.[9]

THE IRAQ RESOLUTION IN 2002

When the Bush administration first began talking about war against Iraq in 2002, the White House cautioned that President George W. Bush was carefully studying a number of options. On August 21, stating that "we will look at all options," Bush said the country was too preoccupied with military action against Iraq. Yet five days later, Vice President Dick Cheney delivered a forceful speech that implied that only one option existed: going to war. He warned that Saddam Hussein would "fairly soon" have nuclear weapons and that it would be useless to seek a Security Council resolution requiring Iraq to submit to weapons inspectors. Newspaper editorials concluded that Cheney's speech left little room for measures short of destroying Hussein's regime through preemptive military action. What happened to the options carefully being weighed by Bush?

The meaning of "regime change" shifted with time. On April 4, 2002, Bush said that he had made up his mind "that Saddam needs to go. . . . The policy of my Government is that he goes." Yet when Bush addressed the United Nations on September 12, he laid down five conditions (including inspections) that could lead to a peaceful settlement. If Hussein complied with those demands, he could stay in power. What had happened to the policy of regime change?

Four days after the September 12 speech, Iraq agreed to unconditional inspections. At that point, the administration began to belittle the importance of inspections. If they were of little use, why have Bush go to the United Nations and place that demand on Iraq and the Security Council?

Initially, the White House concluded that Bush did not need authority from Congress. However, for one reason or another, Bush decided in early September to seek authorization from Congress. There was pressure on lawmakers to complete action on the authorizing resolution before they adjourned for the elections, inviting partisan exploitation of the war issue. Several Republican nominees in congressional contests made a political weapon out of Iraq, comparing their "strong stand" on Iraq to "weak" positions by Democratic campaigners.

The administration released various accounts to demonstrate why Iraq was an imminent threat. On September 7, Bush cited a report by the International Atomic Energy Agency that the Iraqis were "six months away from developing a weapon. I don't know what more evidence we need." However, the report did not exist. The administration promoted a story about Mohamed Atta, the 9/11 leader, meeting with an Iraqi intelligence officer in Prague in April 2001. Yet Czech president Vaclav Havel was convinced that there was no evidence that the meeting ever took place.

The administration tried to make a link between Iraq and al Qaeda, but the reports could never be substantiated. Similar unproven claims were made about Iraq seeking uranium ore from a country in Africa, using aluminum tubes to advance its nuclear weapons program, deploying mobile labs capable of generating biological weapons, and having a stock of unmanned planes (drones) able to disperse chemical and biological agents. Those claims were unproven before the vote on the Iraq Resolution in October 2002 and utterly repudiated after the war began the following March.

There was little doubt that Bush would gain House support for the resolution. The question was whether the vote would divide along party lines. The partisan issue blurred when House Minority Leader Dick Gephardt (D-MO) broke ranks with many in his party and announced support for a slightly redrafted resolution. He said, "We had to go through this, putting politics aside, so we have a chance to get a consensus that will lead the country in the right direction." Of course, politics could not be put aside. The vote on the resolution was inescapably and legitimately a political decision. Lawmakers would be voting on whether to commit hundreds of billions of dollars to a war stretching over a period of years. Their actions would stabilize or destabilize the Middle East, strengthen or weaken the war against terrorism, enhance or debase the nation's prestige.

Why were Democrats so worried about being labeled "antiwar"? They had supported military operations against Afghanistan after 9/11. Going to war is a grave matter, requiring informed decisions on whether the use of military force is necessary and is in the nation's interest. Polls indicated that 63 percent of the public preferred to wait to give UN inspectors time to complete their work. A *Washington Post* story on October 8 noted that the public's enthusiasm for war against Iraq "is tepid and declining."

On October 10, the House passed the Iraq resolution, 296–133. That evening, the Senate voted 77–23 for the resolution. It would have been better for Congress as an institution, and for the country as a whole, to have Bush request the Security Council to authorize inspections in Iraq and then to come to Congress after the elections (as was done in 1990–1991). Congress would have been in the position at that point to make an informed choice. It chose, instead, to vote under partisan pressures, with inadequate information, and thereby abdicated its constitutional duties to the president. In passing the resolution, lawmakers decided only that President Bush should decide. After the Security Council voted on November 8 that

Iraq must allow inspectors into the country, the judgment on whether war would be necessary was in the hands of Bush, not Congress.

On March 19, 2003, President Bush notified the nation of the deployment of combat forces to Iraq. American forces triumphed over Iraqi troops in less than a month, but the quick victory proved to be an illusion. Instead of confronting the vastly superior U.S. army, the opposition decided to melt away and prepare for a long guerrilla war. American commanders soon recognized that insurgents had ready access to weapons and were determined to make the United States pay a heavy price for the occupation. There were never sufficient U.S. troops to provide political stability in Iraq. As a result, government buildings were looted, violence spread across the country, and reconstruction projects were either delayed or abandoned. Iraq, which had provided a secular check on Islamic fundamentalism in the Middle East, deteriorated into a civil war between Shia and Sunni and even factional contests within those two groups. The Bush administration had planned to install a model democratic government in Iraq, capable of spreading those ideals to neighboring states. Instead, the chief victor in the Middle East was the growing power and influence of Iran.

The congressional elections in 2006 demonstrated that public opposition to the Iraq War was the central issue across the country. Voters returned Democrats to power in both the House and the Senate. Throughout 2007, members of Congress explored ways to place restrictions on U.S. military operations in Iraq and speed the return of American troops. Even with U.S. forces withdrawn and redeployed, the future of Iraq is highly uncertain. Will the contending Iraqi forces reach a political settlement that places the national interest first, or will the majority Shia drive Sunnis out of the country and install an Islamic state? On that fundamental question, the Bush administration had little control. Having opened a Pandora's box, it had few tools of control and influence. As with the Vietnam War, the administration learned that superior and overwhelming military force was not a winning card.

OBAMA'S WAR IN LIBYA

Barack Obama entered the White House with the intention to wind down the war in Iraq and escalate the war in Afghanistan. By the spring of 2011, he decided to embark on a new war in Libya without seeking or obtaining authority from Congress. On March 17, 2011, the Security Council passed Resolution 1973 to establish a ban on "all flights in the airspace of the Libyan Arab Jamahiriya in order to help protect civilians." Of course, the ban did not apply to "all" flights. It covered only those by the Libyan government. Military flights by coalition forces would be necessary to enforce the ban. Passage of Resolution 1973 came only after the Arab League had agreed to support a no-fly zone over Libya. Russia and China, prepared to veto the resolution, abstained, as did Germany, India, and Brazil.

On March 21, President Obama notified Congress that, two days earlier, U.S. forces "at my direction," commenced military operations against Libya "to assist an international effort authorized by the United Nations (U.N.) Security Council."[10] As explained earlier in this chapter, authority can come only from Congress. The U.S. Constitution does not permit transferring congressional powers to outside bodies, including the UN and NATO. However, acting under Resolution 1973, coalition partners began a series of strikes against Libya's air defense systems and military airfields. Obama promised that the strikes would be "limited in their nature, duration, and scope," but the military commitment deepened on March 21 when he announced at a news conference, "It is U.S. policy that Qaddafi needs to go." The initial no-fly zone policy now added regime change. Also, the administration said that it would ask Congress for legislative authority to shift some of the $30 billion in Libyan frozen assets to assist the rebels.

In a March 28 address to the nation, Obama described his Libyan actions in this manner: "The United States has done what we said we would do."[11] His reference to "the United States" and "we" was misleading. There was no joint agreement between the executive and legislative branches. Obama alone made the military commitment. He identified certain supporting institutions: "We had a unique ability to stop that violence: an international mandate for action, a broad coalition prepared to join us, the support of Arab countries, and a plea for help from the Libyan people themselves." Absent from this picture were Congress and the American people.

On April 1, the Office of Legal Analysis (OLC) in the Justice Department released a fourteen-page legal defense titled "Authority to Use Military Force in Libya." It spoke about "widespread popular demonstrations" throughout the Middle East beginning in mid-February, seeking government reform.[12] President Obama thus had time to inform Congress of the developing program and seek legislative authorization. Instead, he devoted time and energy in attracting support from allies, Arab nations, and the Security Council, not from the legislative branch. OLC looked to the Security Council resolution for authorization, but UN actions are not constitutional substitutes for congressional support. OLC cited a number of earlier actions by presidents taken without legislative authorization, but the precedents (missions of goodwill, rescue, or protecting American lives and property) have no connection to the military action against Libya.

Obama's failure to respect the constitutional role of Congress in the exercise of the war power led to strong challenges in the House of Representatives. Both Democrats and Republicans regarded his conduct as offensive. On June 3, the House debated and voted on two resolutions that criticized

Obama for not seeking legislative authorization for the war in Libya. One resolution, introduced by Rep. Dennis Kucinich (D-OH) with Republican cosponsors, directed the removal of U.S. forces from Libya within fifteen days of the resolution's adoption. It failed 148–265. Introduced as a concurrent resolution, it would not have been legally binding. At most, it would have expressed the sentiments of the two chambers.

The second resolution was introduced by Speaker John Boehner (R-OH) and adopted 268–145. It noted that Obama had "failed to provide Congress with a compelling rationale" for military activities in Libya and directed Obama within fourteen days to describe "in detail" U.S. security interests and objectives in Libya and explain why he did not seek "authorization by Congress for the use of military force in Libya." Obama submitted his report to Boehner on June 15. By that time, the military action in Libya had exceeded the sixty-day clock of the War Powers Resolution of 1973 and neared the final ninety-day deadline—the first time a president had exceeded the ninety-day limit.

How would the administration respond? Would it recognize that the ninety-day limit was binding on the president, requiring Obama to obtain statutory authorization? Would it announce that the War Powers Resolution was unconstitutional and its clock had no application? It chose to do neither. Instead, on page 25 of the June 15 report, it continued to insist that President Obama "had constitutional authority, as Commander in Chief and Chief Executive and pursuant to his foreign affairs powers, to direct such limited military operations abroad." Moreover, it held that the clock started only with the existence of "hostilities," and that no hostilities existed in Libya for this reason: "U.S. operations do not involve sustained fighting or active exchanges of fire with hostile forces, nor do they involve the presence of U.S. ground troops, U.S. casualties or a serious threat thereof, or any significance chance of escalation into a conflict characterized by those factors." In other words, if the United States conducted military operations by dropping bombs at thirty-thousand feet, launching Tomahawk missiles from ships in the Mediterranean, and using unmanned armed drones, there would be no "hostilities" in Libya under the terms of the War Powers Resolution, provided U.S. casualties were minimal or nonexistent. According to this legal analysis, a nation could pulverize a weaker country with nuclear weapons and there would be neither war nor hostilities.[13]

On June 24, the House responded to this report by debating two other measures that rebuked Obama. The chamber voted down a resolution that would have authorized U.S. military action in Libya. The vote: 123–295. Seventy Democrats joined Republicans in voting against the resolution. A separate measure, to provide limited funding for the war, was also rejected, 180–238. Only thirty-six Democrats favored this bill. Critics of the House action called the two votes a "mixed message." Yet the legislative communication was quite clear on the fundamental point of whether to authorize and fund the war. On both counts: No.

On July 7, the House again passed restrictive language on military activities in Libya. It adopted, 225–201, an amendment to bar funding for training, equipping, or advising the rebel forces fighting against Colonel Qaddafi. An amendment to bar the use of any funds for military force in Libya fell on a vote of 199–229. A total of 132 Republicans and 67 Democrats voted for this restriction. A shift of thirteen votes would have meant, in the House, a total bar to funding the war.

The Senate, throughout this period, was nearly silent on the war. On March 1, it passed S. Res. 85, which urged the Security Council "to take such further action as may be necessary to protect civilians in Libya from attack, including the possible imposition of a no-fly zone over Libyan territory." The bill was introduced that day and passed late in the afternoon with no debate and only thirty-five seconds for Senate action. The no-fly provision was added late in the afternoon with inadequate notice to senators. As a Senate resolution, it had no legal meaning.[14]

On May 23, the Senate introduced S. Res. 194, again another non-binding Senate resolution. It expressed no concern about the lack of congressional authorization for the war in Libya. It merely requested President Obama "to consult regularly with Congress regarding United States efforts in Libya." The war power of Congress is diminished—or extinguished—when a president need only "consult" with a few members. The Constitution requires a declaration of authorization by Congress when the country goes from a state of peace to a state of war. The Senate took no action on S. Res. 194.

On June 28, the Senate Foreign Relations Committee held hearings on "Libya and War Powers." In the afternoon it marked up a bill, S. J. Res. 20, to authorize the war. As a joint resolution it would be legally binding. The committee planned to bring the resolution to the floor for Senate action on July 5, but it was withdrawn in favor of debate on the debt-limit crisis. No further action was taken in July and it appeared doubtful that anything would occur in August. Because of its constitutional role with treaties and appointment of ambassadors, the Senate supposedly has a more prominent role in foreign affairs than the House. But the House acted first on Libya and its legislative actions were significantly stronger in terms of defending institutional interests.[15]

A FAILURE OF CHECKS AND BALANCES

The framers of the Constitution assumed that each branch of the government would protect its own prerogatives. Efforts by one branch to encroach on another would be beaten back. As Madison explained in *Federalist* No.

51, "The great security against a gradual concentration of the several powers in the same department, consists in giving to those who administer each department the necessary constitutional means and personal motives to resist encroachments of the others. . . . Ambition must be made to counter ambition." To some extent, this theory has worked well. The president and the judiciary invoke a multitude of powers to protect their institutions.

Congress, on the other hand, not only fails to fight back but also volunteers to surrender fundamental legislative powers, including the war power and the power of the purse. Members of Congress seem uncertain about the scope of their constitutional powers. Some claim that Congress can limit funds for presidential actions that were taken in the past but never for future actions. There is no constitutional support for that position. The decision to use military force against other nations is reserved to Congress, other than for defensive actions. Members may restrict a president's actions prospectively as well as retrospectively.

Some legislators suggest that a cutoff of funds would leave American soldiers stranded and without ammunition. During debate in 1995 on prohibiting funds from being used for the deployment of ground forces to Bosnia and Herzegovina, Congressman Porter Goss said, "I cannot support a complete withdrawal of funds and support for the United States troops who are already on the ground in the former Yugoslavia. These men and women are wearing the uniform of the U.S. military and obeying orders, and we cannot leave them stranded in hostile territory." Congressman George Gekas added, "I cannot vote under any circumstances to abandon our troops. Not to fund them? Unheard of. I cannot support that. Not to supply them with foods, material, ammunition, all the weapons that they require to do their mission?"[16] Cutting off funds would not have that effect. A funding prohibition would force the withdrawal of whatever troops were in place and prevent the deployment of any other troops to that region. Rather than place U.S. soldiers at risk, they are redeployed to more secure locations.

Theories of presidential war power that would have been shocking fifty years ago are now offered as though they were obvious and free of controversy. Instead of the two branches working in concert to create a program that has broad public support and understanding, with some hope of continuity, presidents take unilateral steps to engage the country in military operations abroad. Typically, they not only justify their actions on broad interpretations of the Constitution but also cite "authority" granted by multinational institutions in which the United States is but one of many state actors. This pattern does not merely weaken Congress and the power of the purse. It also undermines public control, the system of checks and balances, and constitutional government.

DISCUSSION QUESTIONS

1. On what "legal" grounds do U.S. presidents justify their unilateral decisions to use U.S. forces against other countries?
2. Why did the "framers" empower Congress to "declare war" but not to "make war"?
3. Why are the UN Participation Act of 1945 and Article 11 of the NATO Treaty important to U.S. participation in international military operations?
4. How did President Truman manage to circumvent congressional approval for sending troops to Korea in 1950?
5. What was the situation in Haiti in the early and mid-1990s, and why did President Clinton contemplate use of military force without express congressional authorization?
6. On what basis did President Clinton claim that he had the authority to send troops to Bosnia in 1995?
7. What strategies did George W. Bush employ to demonstrate that Iraq was an imminent threat?
8. Why does Fisher say that by voting for the Iraq Resolution under partisan pressure, Congress "abdicated its constitutional duties to the president"?
9. On what basis did President Obama direct action to be taken in Libya in March 2011? How did Congress respond? Did it restrict presidential action in any way?
10. In the end, why does Congress systematically defer to executive decisions regarding the use of U.S. forces abroad?

NOTES

1. See Max Farrand, ed., *The Records of the Federal Convention of 1787* (New Haven, CT: Yale University Press, 1937), especially 1:64–66, and 2:318–19.

2. Jonathan Eliot, ed., *The Debates in the Several State Conventions, on the Adoption of the Federal Constitution* (Washington, DC: 1836–1845), 2:528.

3. 91 *Cong. Rec.* 8185 (1945).

4. Richard H. Heindel et al., "The North Atlantic Treaty in the United States Senate," *American Journal of International Law* 43 (1949): 649–50.

5. Robert H. Bork, "Comments on the Articles on the Legality of the United States Action in Cambodia," *American Journal of International Law* 65 (1971): 81.

6. *Weissman v. Metropolitan Life Ins. Co.*, 112 F. Supp. 420, 425 (S.D. Cal. 1953).

7. *New York Times*, June 28, 1992, 16; *New York Times*, August 14, 1992, A15.

8. Louis Fisher, *Presidential War Power*, 2nd ed. (Lawrence: University Press of Kansas, 2004), 181–82.

9. *Campbell v. Clinton*, 52 F. Supp. 2d 34 (D.D.C. 1999), aff'd, *Campbell v. Clinton*, 203 F. 3d 19 (D.C. 2000).

10. www.whitehouse.gov/the-press-office/2011/03/21/letter-president-regarding-commencement-operations-libya.

11. www.whitehouse.gov/the-press-office/2011/03/28/remarks-president-address-nation-libya.

12. www.justice.gov/olc/2011/authority-military-use-in-libya.pdf.

13. Louis Fisher, "Parsing the War Power," *National Law Journal* (July 4, 2011): 51–52.

14. See pages 6–7 of testimony by Louis Fisher before the Senate Foreign Relations committee on June 28, 2011, available at http://foreign.senate.gov/imo/media/doc/Fisher_Testimony.pdf.

15. Louis Fisher, "Senate Should Protect War Powers on Libya," *Roll Call* (July 29, 2011): 17.

16. 141 *Cong. Rec.* H14820, H14822 (daily ed. December 13, 1995).

11

How National Security Advisers See Their Role

I. M. (Mac) Destler

Over the past half century, the assistant to the president for national security affairs (as the national security adviser is formally known) has emerged as the most important foreign policy aide to the president.[1] Whether the job is performed largely outside of public view, as by Brent Scowcroft (1975–1977, 1989–1993) and Stephen Hadley (2005–2009), or in a highly prominent manner, as was true for Henry Kissinger (1969–1975), Zbigniew Brzezinski (1977–1981), and Condoleezza Rice (2001–2005), almost every national security adviser since McGeorge Bundy (1961–1966) has emerged as a principal player in the foreign policy arena. And those who did not so emerge—Richard Allen (1981); James Jones (2009–2010)—have typically found themselves replaced by persons better able to connect to their presidents.

Yet despite the enormous power they have wielded, there has been insufficient attention to the role these advisers play in the formulation and implementation of foreign policy. Unlike the jobs of their cabinet counterparts, their position is neither rooted in law nor accountable to Congress. As the White House point person on foreign policy, the national security adviser serves at the pleasure of the president. Moreover, while the adviser heads an important staff, his or her managerial duties are modest compared to the huge departmental responsibilities of the secretaries of state, defense, treasury, and other principal foreign policymakers. And though some advisers have not shunned the limelight, their public responsibilities are far more limited than those of, say, the secretary of state, who is the president's principal foreign policy spokesperson at home and abroad.

Nonetheless, the national security adviser and the National Security Council (NSC) staff have become central foreign policy players. Indeed, over the years the NSC staff has expanded from a small group of less than fifteen policy people in the early 1960s to what is today a fully ensconced, agency-like organization of well over two hundred people, including over one hundred substantive professionals. This organization has its own perspective on the myriad of national security issues confronting the government. It has become less like a staff and more like an operating agency. With its own press, legislative, communication, and speechmaking offices, the NSC conducts ongoing relations with the media, Congress, the American public, and foreign governments.

The reasons for this expansion are many. The foundation, of course, has been presidents' need for close-in foreign policy support, and advisers' success in meeting this need. Beyond this, three developments stand out. First, as can be expected of any organization that has operated for decades, the NSC has become institutionalized and even bureaucratized. The White House Situation Room, established under Kennedy, has become the focal point for crisis management. The NSC communications system, also inaugurated under Kennedy, has grown in sophistication with the advance of technology. It allows staff to monitor the overseas messages sent to and from the State Department, to have access to major intelligence material, and to communicate directly and secretly with foreign governments. Over time, these capacities, together with continuing presidential need, have built the NSC into a strong, entrenched, and legitimate presidential institution.

Second, the kinds of foreign policy issues that need to be addressed have both expanded in number and become more complex in nature. With the end of the Cold War, national security issues now involve more dimensions, each linked to proponents somewhere in the executive branch. The traditional and long-recognized dividing lines—between foreign and domestic policy, and between the "high-politics" issues of war and peace and the "low-politics" issues of social and economic advancement—have blurred. As a result, the number and type of players concerned with each issue have grown as well—placing a premium on effective organization and integration of different interests. Of all the players in the executive branch, only the White House has the recognized power necessary to manage these disparate interests effectively. And within the White House, only the NSC has the demonstrated capacity to do so. (The National Economic Council [NEC], established by President Clinton, plays this role to some extent on issues linking domestic and international economics.)

Third, U.S. politics no longer ends at the water's edge—it continues right on into the mainstream of foreign affairs. Aside from extraordinary events like the war against al Qaeda in response to September 11, few issues are easily separated from domestic political turmoil—not military intervention, not diplomatic relations, and certainly not trade and economic interactions with the outside world. The necessity to provide political oversight of executive action—to ensure not only that policy is executed in the best manner possible but also that the political consequences of doing so have been considered—naturally falls to the White House, and to the NSC acting as its surrogate.

Yet while the national security adviser and the NSC staff have grown in importance, their specific roles and significance remain unclear not only to the American public, but also to many of the most avid followers of foreign policy in Congress, the media, and academia. Two roundtables with former national security advisers help elucidate their roles.[2] In freewheeling discussions, which ranged historically from the Eisenhower administration in the 1950s to the George W. Bush administration in the new century, former advisers recounted their experiences, debated their responsibilities, and reflected on the proper role of the national security adviser under present circumstances. The discussions centered on three issues: the adviser's role in managing the foreign policy decision-making process, the adviser's operational role and responsibility, and the adviser's public responsibilities, especially with respect to Congress.

MANAGING THE DECISION-MAKING PROCESS

Aside from staffing the president in his personal foreign policy role—by making sure he gets the necessary information and is briefed prior to meetings, visits, and negotiations—the most important role of the national security adviser is to manage the decision-making process effectively. This involves three steps. First is guiding governmental deliberations on major foreign and national security issues to ensure both that those with strong stakes in the issue are involved in the process and that all realistic policy options are fully considered—including options not favored by any agency—before these issues reach the president and his senior advisers for decision. Second is driving this process to make real choices in a timely manner. Third is overseeing the implementation of the decisions made by the president and his advisers.

Managing this process effectively is demanding in a number of ways. There is, first of all, the inherent tension between the need of the national security adviser to be an effective and trustworthy honest broker among the different players in the decision-making process and the desire of the president to have the best possible policy advice, including advice from his closest foreign policy aide. The roles are inherently in conflict. Balancing them is tricky and possible only if the adviser has earned the trust of the other key players. As Sandy Berger argued, "You have to be perceived by your colleagues as an honest representative of their viewpoint, or the system breaks down." Walt Rostow agreed: "The national security advisor ought to be able to state the point of view of each member the president consults, with sympathy. He may disagree with it, but if a cabinet member ever looks at what is in the summary paper, nothing is more gratifying to a national security adviser than to have him say, 'The State Department couldn't have done any better itself.'" And Zbigniew Brzezinski suggested that

> one would have to be awfully stupid to misrepresent the views of one's colleagues to the president, because you know that if the issue is important, there will be a discussion. The president will go back and discuss it, in your presence or even your absence, with his principal advisers, be they secretary of state or secretary of defense. And it would very quickly be evident that you distorted their views if you did. So you have to be absolutely precise and present as persuasively as you can the arguments that they have mustered in favor of their position.

Brent Scowcroft aptly summarized the matter in the Brookings-Maryland roundtable:

> It's always more exciting to be the adviser, but if you are not the honest broker, you don't have the confidence of the NSC. If you don't have their confidence, then the system doesn't work, because they will go around you to get to the president. . . . So in order for the system to work, you first have to establish yourself in the confidence of your colleagues to convince them you are not going to pull fast ones on them. That means when you are in there with the president alone, which you are more than anybody else, that you will represent them fairly. . . . And after you have done that, then you are free to be an adviser.

Once the national security adviser has gained the trust of his colleagues, it is also important that the president receive his unvarnished advice. And while a good White House staff person would do well to follow "empirical rule number one" of the Eisenhower administration (which Goodpaster recalled as "The president is always right!") at least in public, it is equally important to tell the president when he is wrong. As Berger maintained, "I think the national security advisor often has to be the one that says the president's wrong. I always felt it was my particular obligation to give the president the downsides of a particular step he was about to take or to simply state to him—there may be a consensus among his decision-makers, but this consensus does not reflect another serious point of view that he should consider."

In short, the national security adviser must balance the roles of adviser and honest broker by both earning the trust of colleagues in presenting their views fully, fairly, and faithfully to the president and giving the president his or her best advice on every issue (even—indeed, especially—if it has not been asked for), in order to ensure the president is aware of all possible points of view. Such advice, however, should be given privately in person or by memo; in public, the national security adviser must stand with the president at all times. As Brzezinski recalls,

> While I do agree that the president's always right in public—whenever there's a group, he's right, because the national security adviser is helping him—in private, you have the obligation to tell him that he's wrong. And I did that repeatedly, and the president wanted me to. There was only one time that he finally sent me a little note saying, "Zbig, don't you know when to stop?" when I went back several times, trying to argue that this was not right.

Of course, even in providing the president with unvarnished advice—including advice he may not like to hear—the national security adviser also must make sure that the president's own perspective and preferences are brought into the decision-making process at an early stage. After all, the president is the only person in the executive branch actually elected by the people—everyone else serves at his pleasure alone. Condoleezza Rice emphasized this role in an interview with the *New York Times*, saying of President George W. Bush, "This president has a very strong anchor and compass about the direction of policy, about not just what's right and what's wrong, but what might work and what might not work."[3] Her job, she maintained, was to translate these presidential instincts into policy.

Managing the process is also important at the sub-cabinet level. Scowcroft was particularly good at empowering his deputy, Robert Gates, to perform this function. And Tom Donilon was so skilled at coordinating from the deputy position that when President Barack Obama decided to replace General Jones in 2010, Donilon was the natural successor.

A second balancing requirement concerns making demands on the president's time—his most precious commodity. There are many, many demands—meetings with aides, meetings with members of Congress, public ceremonies, issues other than foreign policy, and so on and so forth—and only twenty-four hours in a day. A key responsibility of the national security adviser is therefore to try to minimize imposition on the president's time. Of course, many issues require his involvement and attention—but not all. Deciding where and when the president should be involved is an issue that must preoccupy any national security adviser.

To minimize imposing on the president's time, the adviser will often seek to forge a consensus on policy among the different players and interests. As Berger suggests, the objective is often to "try to bring the secretary of defense, the secretary of state and others to what I used to call the highest common denominator. If there was not a consensus at a fairly high level, it was better to bring the president two starkly different points of view. But some of this is a function of trying to clear the underbrush of decisions before they get to the president." Frank Carlucci recalls a similar process, in which, when he was secretary of defense, he met with his successor at the NSC, Colin Powell, and the secretary of state, George Shultz, every morning at seven o'clock, without substitutes or agendas "to lay out the day's events and see if we could reach agreement. And invariably, we reached agreement. And the number of decisions that had to go to the president was greatly reduced by that process."

Of course, while it is important to try to preserve the president's time, it is also important not to create a policy process that presents the president with *faits accomplis* on important policy issues. A decision-making process that is geared toward consensus will often lead to lowest, rather than highest, common denominator policies, which invariably lack boldness or even clear direction. Equally pernicious, a consensus process can result in delays in decision-making in order to allow time for disagreements to be resolved—enhancing the prospect for ad hoc and reactive policymaking and needlessly limiting the options that could logically be considered if decisions were made at an earlier stage. Finally, a consensus process increases the likelihood that mistakes will go uncorrected, as the need for maintaining bureaucratic comity outweighs the requirement to reexamine policy.

What can complicate matters is a headstrong president, certain in his convictions about the right course to follow. Because a president's advisers serve at his pleasure and can be effective only if they retain his confidence, it is often very difficult for any of them to go against a consensus that has formed around the president's policy preference. This appears to have been the case with President George W. Bush and Iraq. Not long after the September 11 attacks and the subsequent rapid ouster of the Taliban from Afghanistan, the president concluded that Saddam Hussein had to be ousted from power—most likely through the use of force. There never was a formal debate within his administration, or even a process by which to assess the pros and cons of such a far-reaching action. Instead, the president decided this was necessary and a consensus to that effect guided policymaking from that point onward. By the time the downsides of this decision had become clear, it was too late to shift course.

To avoid consensus leading to costly inaction, it may be necessary for the national security adviser to act more forcefully to challenge the consensus that exists, even when the president doesn't want such a challenge. At the Brookings-Maryland roundtable, Anthony Lake recalled his early "mistake the first six months when I tried too much to be just an honest broker. I remember Colin Powell coming to me and saying that I needed to give my own views more push . . . you have to drive the process, and you have to understand that only the NSC can do that." At the same time, when consensus is achieved rapidly and with little debate, the adviser needs to be skeptical of the outcome, to make sure all aspects of a policy have been thought through, and must, furthermore, be ready to be the devil's advocate to ensure the consensus reflects the best course. As the tapes of the Cuban Missile Crisis meetings have revealed, McGeorge Bundy saw it as his role to challenge any emerging consensus, no matter whether hawkish or dovish, to ensure all the consequences of a particular action had been considered. By all accounts, Condoleezza Rice failed to play a similarly constructive role with respect to Iraq—not just on the decision to go to war, but also on plans to bring stable governance after the invasion was completed.

One final consideration in managing the decision-making process concerns the kinds of issues that should fall within the NSC's coordination purview. The NSC exists for the purpose of integrating a government organized among large stovepipes, among which there is insufficient interaction. The national security adviser will have to decide which issues will have to be coordinated among these different stovepipes, how, and at what level. Too little coordination, confined to too high a level, will likely result in the exclusion of relevant issues. Too much coordination at too low a level will invariably involve the NSC in micromanaging the policy process in ways that will soon overwhelm the capacity of the staff. For that reason, Brzezinski suggested that "coordination has to take place at the presidential level. That is to say, when the decisions are of a presidential-level type decisions, then NSC coordination is necessary."

Berger disagreed, insisting that among the "important functions of the National Security Council staff is to coordinate decision-making, particularly at the working level, between the various agencies." Citing the case of Bosnia, Berger asserted,

> There were day-to-day decisions that needed to be made, that were not at the presidential level, but were critically important, generally made at the assistant secretary level or above. . . . In those issues that are high priority and fast-moving, it is often useful, although I think you can't generalize, for the NSC to be convening the Defense Department, the State Department and others because the institutional tensions between State and Defense often are such that without a third party in the chair, things fall back on bureaucratic instinct.

The difference between Brzezinski and Berger probably cannot be resolved except on a case-by-case basis. On those issues that require presidential input or decision, NSC involvement is, of course, a must. But not all others can be left solely to the departments to resolve, for they typically have neither the incentive nor the mechanisms necessary to do so. Bureaucratic stalemate or, possibly worse, pursuit of conflicting policies that reflect departmental rather than presidential preferences, can often result. Conversely, however, an NSC staff that insists on coordinating each and every issue will soon become mired in details and incapable of concentrating on the big picture. Moreover, the temptation for the adviser or an NSC staff member will often be to seize control of an issue, even to the point of becoming responsible for policy implementation. That, as history tells us, can sometimes be highly effective—and also exceedingly dangerous.

The other major question with regard to the issues that need to be covered by the NSC and the adviser concerns the breadth of issue competence. The NSC was originally founded to concern itself with foreign policy and defense issues—whence the restriction of its membership to the secretaries of state and defense as well as the president and vice president. However, over time, and especially in the last two decades, the issues affecting foreign policy have grown in number and complexity, and so has the need for effective policy coordination. By the end of the Clinton administration, the national security adviser had to deal not only with traditional issues of defense and regional diplomacy, but also with energy, the environment, international finance, terrorism, drug trafficking, human rights and disaster relief, and even, it was felt, Gulf War illnesses. The policy coordinating task therefore included the traditional NSC agencies of State, Defense, and the military and intelligence communities, as well as Treasury, Justice, Transportation, and even Health and Human Services.

The Bush administration entered office in 2001 with the view that the NSC competence had been stretched too far and too thin. Rice cut the NSC staff by more than 30 percent, and she ordered her staff to cease coordinating policy with the domestic government agencies, including Justice and the FBI. The National Security Council would once again focus on the hard-power issues of defense and diplomacy involving the great powers. The September 11 attacks underscored that in an age of transnational threat, dividing the world and policymaking neatly between foreign and domestic policy is increasingly difficult. Yet the Bush administration tried just that— assigning the NSC the role of coordinating counter-terrorism abroad while setting up a new structure (the Office of Homeland Security) to coordinate anti-terrorism policy at home. The Obama administration reversed this by consolidating homeland security staff under the NSC.

HOW OPERATIONAL SHOULD THE NSC BE?

A perennial issue for every national security adviser is the question of the NSC's operational involvement in executing policy. The consensus view, especially after the Iran-Contra affair, is that the NSC performs a coordinating and oversight and advisory function but should never become operational. That was the view expressed in 1987 by the Tower Commission, established to review the causes of that fiasco, and it has been faithfully repeated since. Yet the national security adviser and staff have repeatedly been operationally involved in the twenty-five years since the Iran-Contra affair became public.

Advisers have traveled on solo missions abroad. They have met with foreign diplomats and ministers on an almost daily basis. As Scowcroft recalled, "Somebody from the NSC always traveled with the secretary of state or the secretary of defense," and NSC staff members often serve as members of negotiating delegations abroad. So the question is not really whether the NSC should have an operational role, but, rather, what kind and to what extent.

It is important to understand why the president might wish the national security adviser to be operationally involved. On one level, it is the result of a basic degree of confidence, comfort, and trust. Presidents know their national security advisers well and have confidence in the advisers' staffs. The same is not always true for the secretary of state and certainly not for the State Department generally, which is largely staffed by career officials. Some presidents come to power with—or develop—a distinct distrust of the State Department (Kennedy, Nixon, and George W. Bush come to mind); others want to run foreign policy out of the White House to secure a central personal role for themselves (Carter and George H. W. Bush, as well as Kennedy and Nixon). In either case, the NSC is the bureaucratic beneficiary of the president's desires. As Brzezinski puts it,

> If you have a president who comes to office intent on making foreign policy himself, on a daily basis, you have a different role than if the president comes to office, let's say, more interested in domestic affairs and more inclined to delegate foreign policy authority to his principal advisors. In the first instance, the national security advisor is the inevitable bureaucratic beneficiary of deep presidential involvement.

In addition, as Anthony Lake noted, an operational NSC role is "necessary because of the way other governments are structured. For the same reasons it's happening here, other governments more and more are revolving around presidencies, prime ministers, etc., and the international contacts between them. As Brent knows, I inherited his phone with the direct lines to our counterparts all around the world who simply had to be engaged."

Aside from presidential intent and international governmental evolution, the normal ebb and flow of events will also tend to influence the nature and extent of the NSC's operational involvement. One major factor propelling such involvement is the lack of bureaucratic responsiveness to presidential direction. As Bud McFarlane recalled in an oblique reference to Iran-Contra, there is the "frustration a president can experience as someone who is there for four years wanting to get something done, to be able to demonstrate leadership in X or Y area, and with the frustration of not seeing that the Department of State or others in his administration moving in that direction." The temptation in these situations is for the national security adviser or even the president to force the issue by having the NSC implement the policy as the president wants it implemented. It is a temptation that

McFarlane warns the national security adviser to resist. It should not "lead the National Security Council or the adviser to go beyond the line and take on an operational role. You simply don't have the resources, and you don't have the mandate in law to do that. So that's a big mistake."

A further reason why the national security adviser may become operationally involved is to effect a fundamental shift in policy that, if left to the State Department to implement, would risk being derailed in bureaucratic entanglement. This, of course, was the cited reason for the most famous and productive operational engagement by a national security assistant: Henry Kissinger's secret diplomacy with China (over opening relations), North Vietnam (to negotiate a peace agreement), and the Soviet Union (over arms control and détente). There also may be other occasions when it is logical for the president to send his national security adviser on a quiet diplomatic mission—both to keep the actual mission out of public view and to underscore the president's own commitment to the issue in question. Zbigniew Brzezinski recalled four such missions during his time in office: to normalize relations with China, address a particular Middle East peace issue with Egypt, to reassure the Europeans over the Euromissile question, and to organize a regional response to the Soviet invasion of Afghanistan (the first of these did not prove to be very secret). Brent Scowcroft traveled twice to Beijing in the aftermath of the Tiananmen Square massacres. Tony Lake undertook two trips to Europe in connection with Bosnia, and a trip to China to help repair badly frayed relations in 1996. Sandy Berger traveled to Moscow to gauge Russia's interest in an arms control deal. Rice also went to Moscow, arriving there even before the secretary of state had visited. And Stephen Hadley traveled to Iraq as well as to India and Pakistan. In each case, however, the actual trip was coordinated within the U.S. government. Unlike in Kissinger's diplomacy, carried out largely without the knowledge of Secretary of State William P. Rogers, the secretary of state was kept fully informed of these missions and often a senior state department representative would travel along with the president's own adviser.

Clearly, then, the national security adviser has a unique operational role to play under certain circumstances. What makes them unique, however, is not just the issue at hand, but also the fact that such engagement is exceptional rather than routine.

THE PUBLIC ROLE OF THE NATIONAL SECURITY ADVISER

In recent years, the national security adviser has emerged as a prominent public spokesperson on foreign policy. Whereas Brent Scowcroft once counseled that the national security adviser "should be seen occasionally and heard even less," the reverse is increasingly the case. Now, a Sandy Berger and a Condoleezza Rice seem to be everywhere—giving speeches of major import, being quoted in newspapers and newsmagazines as a result of frequent press briefings and even more frequent media interviews, and appearing on the Sunday-morning talk show circuit.

The reason for the public emergence of the national security adviser appears to be twofold. First, the increasing politicization of foreign policy has made defense of the president's policies by the person most directly associated with the president politically more important. It is not coincidental, therefore, that four of the most recent national security advisers (Tony Lake, Sandy Berger, Condoleezza Rice, and Stephen Hadley) were all key advisers to the president during his campaign for office. In contrast, with the exception of Zbigniew Brzezinski and Richard Allen, prior national security advisers were not politically associated with the incoming president. The second reason for the greater public exposure of the national security adviser in recent years is changes in the media—especially proliferation in the number of media outlets. The need to cover all the bases requires a larger number of spokespeople to engage, including, by extension, the national security adviser. As Berger argues, "The pace of the news cycle is now almost continuous, and the breadth of the media tends to pull the national security adviser out more as part of a team of people who goes out, but always with the secretary of state at the lead."

One of the consequences of the public emergence of the national security adviser is the demand for increased accountability, especially on Capitol Hill, where congressmen and senators get to ask questions of the department heads but are unable to demand answers from the president's closest foreign policy adviser. As former congressman Lee Hamilton put it to the panel of former national security assistants, "I think the national security advisor occupies a very special place. He is, if not the principal advisor, among the two or three principal advisors to the president on foreign policy. You're perfectly willing to go before all of the TV networks anytime they give you a ring, if you want to go. Why should you discriminate against the Congress?" Told by a number of the former advisers that they always were willing to meet with members in their offices, Hamilton continued: "But it is not the same thing for a national security advisor to come into the private office and meet behind closed doors with members of Congress. That's not the same thing as going into a public body and answering questions, in my judgment. They're two different things."

The absence of congressional accountability sometimes leads to the suggestion that the national security adviser should be confirmed—a suggestion reviewed, and rejected, by the Tower Commission. The former advisers all rejected that possibility. They offered a variety of reasons:

- It would prove a major diversion, because with confirmation comes the requirement to testify on the Hill. Brzezinski: "If you get confirmed you also have to testify a lot, you have to go down to the Hill a lot. The schedule demands on you are so enormous already that that would be an additional burden. Moreover, it would greatly complicate the issue we talked about earlier, namely, who speaks for foreign policy in the government besides the president? The answer should be the secretary of state. If you are confirmed, that would become fuzzed and confused."

- It would compromise the ability of the national security adviser to provide confidential advice to the president. Berger: "One benefit of not having confirmation is that you can say no to a congressional committee. In fact, most presidents have taken the view that under executive privilege their national security advisor, just like their chief of staff, can't be compelled to go up on the Hill."
- It would have a negative impact on the policy formation process. Carlucci: "If you make the national security advisor subject to Senate confirmation, you're going to degrade the process significantly. The president will have a very difficult time implementing a coherent foreign policy. I think the president would simply name another staff person to do what the national security advisor does and let this confirmed official run around on the Hill."
- It is unnecessary because there is accountability in the system. Carlucci: "These are staff people to the president. And we had a case where the president was almost brought down because of the actions of National Security Council staff—Ronald Reagan. So there is an accountability system, and the president should be free to pick whomever he wants to give him advice."

The modern national security adviser has been a staple of the American foreign policymaking process for half a century. Although the role will evolve with each president and with the growing complexity of the world, the fundamental tasks are unlikely to change all that much—to staff the president and manage the foreign policy formulation and implementation process. The demands and dilemmas each occupant has faced in meeting these tasks will also surely continue. It is in reflecting on how others have handled these challenges in the past that future occupants may prove able to do a job that, by any standard, has become difficult indeed.

President Obama signaled the importance he gave to the NSA position by selecting a senior military officer, retired General James L. Jones. The former marine commandant and NATO commander was widely admired for his integrity, and in his first prominent press interview he declared that the Obama NSC would be "dramatically different" from its predecessors in scope and impact. Within months, however, his influence was being discounted by Washington insiders, and he did not last through Obama's second year.

In retrospect, the Obama-Jones relationship was doomed from the start. To be effective, a national security adviser must be personally close to the president and in sync with his operating style. Jones was neither. The president barely knew him, and by his own admission, the general "'wasn't very good at' being an aide."[4] As a military man accustomed to the prerogatives of rank and to formal, hierarchical decision structures, Jones acted as if issues should come to him in an orderly manner, rather than assuring that he was the one who brought issues to the president. Meanwhile, the lawyer-professor-politician who was now president worked informally with other trusted aides, fashioning his own ad hoc decision process. One of those aides was deputy national security adviser Tom Donilon, who coordinated a range of issues through a very active interagency NSC Deputies Committee.

Interestingly, however, Jones's non-success highlighted the importance of the national security adviser position, for it was widely noticed, and it generated continuing pressure for corrective action. Obama took such action in October 2010, replacing Jones with Donilon. The move was perhaps accelerated by evidence that Jones had talked too freely to Bob Woodward for the journalist's detailed description and critique of presidential decision-making on Afghanistan. In any case, the move had the virtue of placing in the position the man who was already doing a substantial share of the NSC's task of high-level policy coordination. Donilon was much more adept than Jones as a staff aide, and much more in tune with the president's style and priorities.

This president carries a substantial share of the process management burden himself. His engagement in detail was evident in his protracted decision process on Afghanistan in 2009, and it has continued. But the presence of Donilon as assistant to the president for national security affairs has brought organizational continuity with past White Houses, not just in form but in practice as well. And it has underscored, once again, the importance of the position first brought to prominence by McGeorge Bundy a half-century before.

DISCUSSION QUESTIONS

1. What are two or three major reasons for the expansion of the role of the national security adviser in the foreign policy process?
2. What are some specific responsibilities of the national security adviser? What are the three different roles that national security advisers play today?
3. In Destler's view, what is the most important role of the national security adviser?

4. What does the author mean when he states that "the national security adviser must balance the roles of advisor and honest broker"?
5. In the author's opinion, why would the president want the National Security Council not only to perform advisory and coordinating functions but also to become operational?
6. Why has the national security adviser more recently emerged as a prominent voice on U.S. foreign policy?
7. Why do former national security advisers believe that the national security adviser should not be subject to congressional confirmation?
8. How has the role of the national security adviser been affirmed during the Obama administration with the replacement of General Jones by Tom Donilon?

NOTES

1. This chapter was adapted and updated from a previous version coauthored with Ivo Daalder, who is now serving as U.S. ambassador to NATO.

2. One roundtable, convened by the Brookings-Maryland project on the National Security Council on October 25, 1999, featured Richard Allen (1981–1982), Frank Carlucci (1986–1987), Walt Rostow (1966–1969), Anthony Lake (1993–1997), and Brent Scowcroft. The other, convened by the Woodrow Wilson Center for International Scholars and the Baker Institute at Rice University on April 12, 2001, featured Samuel Berger (1997–2001), Zbigniew Brzezinski, Frank Carlucci, Robert (Bud) McFarlane (1983–1985), Rostow, and Andrew Goodpaster, who was staff secretary to President Dwight Eisenhower (1954–1961), and as such performed many of the tasks of day-to-day national security policy management carried out by national security advisers from the Kennedy administration onward. The transcript of the Brookings-Maryland Roundtable is available at www.cissm.umd.edu/papers/files/the_role_of_the_national_security_adviser.pdf, which also includes transcripts of interviews with Samuel Berger, Robert McFarlane, Colin Powell (1987–1989), and John Poindexter (1985–1987). The transcript of the Wilson Center/Rice roundtable is available at www.wilsoncenter.org/sites/default/files/nsa.pdf. Unless otherwise noted, all quotations are drawn from these transcripts.

3. Quoted in Elisabeth Bumiller, "A Partner in Shaping Foreign Policy," *New York Times*, January 7, 2004.

4. Quoted in Bob Woodward, *Obama's Wars* (New York: Simon and Schuster, 2010), 37.

12

The Shifting Pendulum of Power

Executive-Legislative Relations on American Foreign Policy

James M. Lindsay

In 2002, Congress looked to have surrendered its constitutional role in foreign policymaking to the White House. After voting nearly unanimously a year earlier to attack Afghanistan for harboring the plotters behind the 9/11 attacks, many lawmakers were privately questioning President George W. Bush's handling of the war on terrorism and especially his mounting push to overthrow Saddam Hussein. But few lawmakers aired their criticisms publicly. When President Bush asked Congress to give him authority to wage war on Iraq, Congress quibbled with some of the language of the draft resolution. Nonetheless, the revised bill, which the House and Senate passed overwhelmingly, amounted to a blank check that the president could cash as he saw fit. When asked why congressional Democrats had not done more to oppose a resolution so many thought unwise or premature, Senate Majority Leader Tom Daschle (D-SD) replied, "The bottom line is . . . we want to move on."[1] Congress's eagerness to delegate its war power to the president drew the ire of Senator Robert Byrd (D-WV), a veteran of five decades of service on Capitol Hill: "How have we gotten to this low point in the history of Congress? Are we too feeble to resist the demand of a president who is determined to bend the collective will of Congress to his will?"[2]

Five years later, however, Congress recovered its voice on foreign policy. In January 2007, President Bush unveiled a proposal to send 21,500 additional U.S. troops to Iraq in a bid to stop escalating sectarian violence there. Rather than applauding the president, members of Congress from both parties assailed the plan and his overall handling of the Iraq War. Senator Russell D. Feingold (D-WI) accused the administration of committing "quite possibly the greatest foreign policy mistake in the history of our nation."[3]

Senator Chuck Hagel (R-NE), a decorated Vietnam War veteran, called the troop increase proposal "a dangerous foreign policy blunder."[4] Members in both the House and Senate rushed to submit bills to limit the president's ability to send more troops to Iraq. Senator Olympia Snowe (R-Maine) captured the new mood on Capitol Hill: "Now is the time for the Congress to make its voice heard on a policy that has such significant implications for the nation, the Middle East, and the world."[5]

Congress's resurgent interest in foreign policy carried over into Barack Obama's presidency. Stiff congressional opposition forced him to abandon his plans to close down the prison at Guantanamo Bay that held foreign terrorists and to start a nation-wide program to reduce the emission of greenhouse gases. His effort to win Senate approval of the New START Treaty, which lowered the limit on the number of strategic nuclear warheads that Russia and United States could deploy, met strong Republican opposition. Unlike the case with the initial military actions in Afghanistan and Iraq, his decision to launch Operation Odyssey Dawn, the military operation intended to protect Libyan civilians from the Muammar Qaddafi's military forces, drew sharp criticism on Capitol Hill. Some members of Congress lambasted him for moving too slowly, while others complained that he had overstepped his constitutional authorities.

The change in the tone of executive-legislative relations between the beginning of the decade and end of it was dramatic. It was not, however, unprecedented. The pendulum of power on foreign policy has swung back and forth between Congress and the president many times over the course of American history. The reason does not lie in the Constitution. Its formal allocation of foreign policy powers, which gives important authorities to both Congress and the president, has not changed since it was drafted. Rather, the answer lies in politics. How aggressively Congress exercises its foreign policy powers turns on two critical questions: Does the country see itself as threatened or secure? Are the president's policies working or not? Times of peace favor congressional activism, while times of war favor congressional deference. Successful presidents have more followers than failed ones do.

The George W. Bush and Obama presidencies illustrate an equally important lesson about Congress and foreign policy: resurgent congressional activism does not always equal greater congressional influence. Even when Congress chooses to exercise its powers it may not get its way. Bush ultimately sent more troops to Iraq, the Senate eventually approved the New START Treaty, and Congress failed to stop the U.S. military intervention in Libya. Presidents typically defend their policy choices against congressional criticism, and many times they succeed.

Does it matter whether Congress exercises its foreign policy powers? The answer to this question lies in the eyes of the beholder. Americans can and do disagree over what constitutes the "national interest" and which policies will do the most to achieve them. What is certain, though, is that the balance of power between the two ends of Pennsylvania Avenue will continue to ebb and flow with the political tides.

THE CONSTITUTION AND FOREIGN POLICY

Ask most Americans who makes foreign policy in the United States and their immediate answer is the president. And to a point they are right. But even a cursory reading of the Constitution makes clear that Congress also possesses extensive powers to shape foreign policy. Article 1, Section 8, assigns Congress the power to "provide for the common Defence," "To regulate Commerce with foreign Nations," "To define and punish Piracies and Felonies committed on the high Seas," "To declare War," "To raise and support Armies," "To provide and maintain a Navy," and "To make Rules for the Government and Regulation of the land and naval Forces." Article 2, Section 2, specifies that the Senate must give its advice and consent to all treaties and ambassadorial appointments. And Congress's more general powers to appropriate all government funds and to confirm cabinet officials provide additional means to influence foreign policy.

These powers can have great consequence. To begin with, they enable Congress—or, in the case of the treaty power, the Senate—to specify the substance of American foreign policy. The most popular vehicle for doing so is the appropriations power, which, while not unlimited in scope, is nonetheless quite broad. (The Supreme Court has never struck down any use of the appropriations power as an unconstitutional infringement on the president's authority to conduct foreign policy.) Dollars are policy in Washington, DC, and the president generally cannot spend money unless Congress appropriates it. Thus, by deciding to fund some ventures and not others, Congress can steer the course of U.S. defense and foreign policy. Congress can also specify the substance of foreign policy by regulating foreign commerce. One notable instance in which it used its trade power this way was a 1986 bill that placed sanctions on South Africa in order to pressure Pretoria to end its policy of apartheid. The Senate's treaty power can have similar effects. When the Senate rejected the Treaty of Versailles after World War I, it blocked U.S. membership in the League of Nations and preserved the traditional U.S. policy of avoiding entangling alliances.

Congress's power to establish and direct the business of the federal bureaucracy (e.g., to provide and maintain a navy) also enables it to influence foreign policy by changing the procedures that the executive branch must follow in making decisions. The premise underlying such procedural legislation is that changing the rules governing how the executive branch makes decisions will change the decisions it makes. In trade policy, for example, U.S. law requires the White House to consult with a wide range of consumer, industry, and labor groups whenever it is negotiating an international trade agreement. The law's sponsors calculated that including these groups in decision-making would make it more likely that U.S. trade policy would reflect U.S. economic interests. Likewise, over the years, Congress has directed the State Department to set up special offices to handle issues such as democracy, counterterrorism, and trafficking in persons. In each instance, the idea was that the executive branch would be more likely to address the issue in question if someone in the bureaucracy had clear responsibility for it.

Congress's broader powers to hold hearings, conduct investigations, and debate issues also give it the ability to *indirectly* shape the course of foreign policy. What is said—and what is not said—on Capitol Hill influences public opinion. That, in turn, helps determine how much leeway presidents have to act. A Congress that applauds a president's proposals makes it all but certain that the public will rally behind the White House. Conversely, a Congress that condemns presidential initiatives fuels public skepticism and forces the White House to pay a higher—and possibly unacceptable— political price to get its way.

The overarching lesson here is that when it comes to foreign affairs, Congress and the president *both* can claim ample constitutional authority. The two branches are, in Richard Neustadt's oft-repeated formulation, "separated institutions *sharing* power."[6] The question of which branch should prevail as a matter of principle when their powers conflict has been disputed ever since Alexander Hamilton and James Madison squared off two centuries ago in their famed Pacificus-Helvidius debate. (Hamilton argued the president was free to exercise his powers as he saw fit; Madison argued the president could not exercise his authority in ways that constrained Congress's ability to exercise its powers.) And while the president exercises some foreign affairs powers that are off-limits to Congress—with the power to negotiate on behalf of the United States being the most prominent—the fact that the Constitution grants Congress extensive authority in foreign policy means that most executive-legislative disputes do not raise constitutional issues.

To say that Congress *can* put its mark on foreign policy, however, is not the same as saying that it *will* do so. To understand why congressional activism and influence on foreign policy varies over time, it is necessary to leave the realm of law and enter the realm of politics.

POLITICS AND FOREIGN POLICY

The explanation for why Congress's say in foreign policy ebbs and flows lies first in an observation that the famed French commentator on American life Alexis de Tocqueville made more than 150 years ago. Surprised to find that the pre–Civil War Congress played a major role in foreign policy, he speculated that congressional activism stemmed from the country's isolation from external threat. "If the Union's existence were constantly menaced, and if its great interests were continually interwoven with those of other powerful nations, one would see the prestige of the executive growing, because of what was expected from it and of what it did."[7]

Why might perceptions of threat affect how Congress behaves? When Americans believe they face few external threats—or think that international engagement could itself produce a threat—they see less merit in deferring to the White House on foreign policy and more merit to congressional activism. Debate and disagreement are not likely to pose significant costs; after all, the country is secure. But when Americans believe the country faces an external threat, they quickly convert to the need for strong presidential leadership. Congressional dissent that was previously acceptable suddenly looks to be unhelpful meddling at best and unpatriotic at worst. Members of Congress are themselves likely to feel the same shifting sentiments toward the wisdom of deferring to the president as well as being profoundly aware that being on the wrong side of that shift could hurt them come the next election.

A second factor shaping executive-legislative interactions on foreign policy is how well the president's policies are faring. Presidents who succeed find themselves surrounded by admirers; presidents who don't find themselves targeted by critics. The reason is easy to understand. It is difficult to argue with success. When things go well for a White House, friends on Capitol Hill applaud and critics bite their tongues. But when policies fail, critics step up their attacks and friends worry about their own political futures. That is precisely what happened to President George W. Bush in 2006 and 2007; as the death toll of U.S. soldiers in Iraq mounted, so too did domestic criticism of his policies. The statement that President Kennedy made when he took responsibility for the disastrous U.S. effort to foment Castro's overthrow by landing Cuban exiles at the Bay of Pigs in 1961 captures the underlying political reality: "Victory has a hundred fathers and defeat is an orphan."[8]

Throughout American history, power over foreign policy has flowed back and forth between the two ends of Pennsylvania Avenue according to these two basic dynamics. In the second half of the nineteenth century, the United States was as secure from foreign attack as at any time in American history. This was also a time when Congress so dominated foreign policy that it has been called the era of "congressional government," "congressional supremacy," and "government-by-Congress." When the United States entered World War I, the pendulum of power swung to the White House. Woodrow Wilson experienced few congressional challenges during his war presidency. But once the war ended, Congress—and the Senate in particular—reasserted itself. Congressional activism persisted into the 1930s and even intensified. Convinced that America would be safe only as long as it kept out of Europe's political affairs, "isolationist" lawmakers in Congress fought bitterly to prevent President Franklin Roosevelt from doing anything that might involve the United States in the war that was brewing across the Atlantic.

Japan's bombing of Pearl Harbor punctured the argument against non-intervention and greatly expanded Roosevelt's freedom to conduct foreign policy. He made virtually all his major wartime decisions without reference to or input from Capitol Hill. When World War II ended, Congress began to reassert itself. Senior members of the House Foreign Affairs Committee and the Senate Foreign Relations Committee helped draft the UN Charter, the peace treaties for the Axis satellite states, and the NATO Treaty.

But growing concerns about the Soviet Union slowed the shift of power away from the White House. As Americans became convinced in the late 1940s that hostile communist states threatened the United States and the rest of the free world, they increasingly came to agree on two basic ideas: the United States needed to resist communist expansion, and achieving this goal demanded strong presidential leadership. Most members of Congress shared these two basic beliefs (and helped promote them); those who disagreed risked punishment at the polls. The process became self-reinforcing. As more lawmakers stepped to the sidelines on defense and foreign policy over the course of the 1950s, others saw it as increasingly futile, not to mention dangerous politically, to continue to speak out. By 1960, the "imperial presidency," the flip side of a deferential Congress, was in full bloom.[9] As one senator complained in 1965, members of Congress were responding to even the most far-reaching presidential decisions on foreign affairs by "stumbling over each other to see who can say 'yea' the quickest and loudest."[10]

The era of congressional deference to an imperial president came to a crashing halt when public opinion soured on the Vietnam War. Many Americans became convinced that communist revolutions in the Third World posed no direct threat to core U.S. security interests and that the United States could find a way to coexist peacefully with the Soviet Union. With the public more willing to question administration policies, so too were members of Congress. Many lawmakers had substantive disagreements with the White House over what America's vital interests were and how best to advance them. Moreover, members of Congress had less to fear politically by the early 1970s in challenging the White House than they had only a few years earlier. Indeed, many lawmakers calculated that challenging the president's foreign policies could actually help at the ballot box by enabling them to stake out positions that their constituents favored. The result was a surge in congressional activism. Presidents Carter and Reagan received far less cooperation from Capitol Hill than Presidents Eisenhower and Kennedy did.

Activist members of Congress did not always succeed, however, in putting their stamp on foreign policy in the 1970s and 1980s. Knee-jerk support of the president was gone, but elements of congressional deference persisted among senior lawmakers (who had come of age during the era of congressional deference) and moderates (who worried that defeating the president could harm the country's credibility). Presidents from Richard Nixon through George H. W. Bush often prevailed on major issues because they could rally congressional support with a simple argument: the administration's policy might not be perfect, but rejecting the president's request would damage his standing abroad, perhaps embolden Moscow to act more aggressively, and ultimately harm American interests. Yet the mere fact that the post-Vietnam presidents had to make this argument showed how much had changed from the days of the imperial presidency.

THE FALL OF THE BERLIN WALL

The end of the Cold War accelerated the trend toward greater congressional activism that Vietnam triggered. With the Soviet Union relegated to the ash heap of history, most Americans looked abroad and saw no threat of similar magnitude on the horizon. When asked to name the most important problem facing the United States, polls in the 1990s rarely found that more than 5 percent of Americans named a foreign policy issue. That was a steep drop from the upward of 50 percent who named a foreign policy issue during the height of the Cold War. Moreover, many Americans had trouble identifying *any* foreign policy issue that worried them. One 1998 poll asked people to name "two or three of the biggest foreign-policy problems facing the United States today." The most common response by far, at 21 percent, was "don't know."[11]

These public attitudes meant that members of Congress who challenged the White House on foreign policy ran almost no electoral risks. With the public not caring enough to punish them for any excesses, lawmakers went busily about challenging Bill Clinton's foreign policy. In April 1999, for instance, during the Kosovo War, the House refused to vote to support the bombing. Not to be outdone, the Senate voted down the Comprehensive Test Ban Treaty in October 1999 even though President Clinton and sixty-two senators had asked that it be withdrawn from consideration. These episodes were major departures from past practice. When members of Congress had squared off against the White House in the latter half of the Cold War on issues like Vietnam, they had vocal public support. On Kosovo and the test ban, however, few Americans were urging Congress to challenge Clinton. To the extent that they had opinions—and many did not—most Americans sided with the president.

Just as important, the once powerful argument that members of Congress should defer to the White House on key issues lest they harm broader American interests fell on deaf ears. In 1997 the Clinton administration sought to convince Congress to give it "fast-track" negotiating authority for international trade agreements. (With fast-track authority, or what is now called "trade-promotion authority," Congress agrees to approve or reject any trade agreement the president negotiates without amendment. This simplifies trade negotiations because other countries do not have to worry that Congress will rewrite any trade deal.) When it became clear that he lacked the votes needed to prevail, President Clinton escalated the stakes by arguing that the fast track was needed because "more than ever, our economic security is also the foundation of our national security."[12] The decision to recast a trade issue as a national security issue—a tried and true Cold War strategy—changed few minds, however. Recognizing defeat, Clinton asked congressional leaders to withdraw the bill from consideration, marking the first time in decades that a president had failed to persuade Congress to support a major trade initiative.

THE DEFERENTIAL CONGRESS RETURNS

Congress's assertiveness in the first post–Cold War decade rested on the public's belief that what happened outside America's borders mattered little for their lives. September 11 punctured that illusion and ended America's decade-long "holiday from history."[13] Foreign policy suddenly became a top priority with the public. Not surprisingly, the pendulum of power swung sharply back toward the White House.

The impact of September 11 on American public opinion was dramatic. Shortly after the attacks, Gallup found that two out of every three Americans named terrorism, national security, or war as the most important problem facing the United States. Foreign policy had reached this level of political salience only twice since the advent of scientific polling—during the early stages of both the Korean and Vietnam wars. President George W. Bush's public approval ratings soared to 90 percent—a figure seen only once before when his father waged the Gulf War. And while the elder Bush's public approval ratings quickly returned to their prewar levels, the younger Bush's remained high for months.

Members of Congress similarly rallied behind the president. Three days after the attack, all but one member of Congress voted to give the president open-ended authority to retaliate against those responsible, authorizing him "to use all necessary and appropriate force against those nations, organizations, or persons he determines planned, authorized, committed, or aided the terrorist attacks that occurred on September 11, 2001, or harbored such organizations or persons." In short, Congress effectively declared war and left it up to President Bush to decide who the enemy was.

Over the next few months, Congress reversed key policy stands that administration officials said interfered with its conduct of the war on terrorism. For several years, conservative legislators had blocked a bipartisan plan to pay much of the outstanding U.S. dues to the United Nations. President Bush argued that these back dues hindered his efforts to assemble a multinational coalition to prosecute the war on terrorism, so Congress appropriated the long-delayed funds without opposition. Congress did something else that had been unthinkable only a month earlier—it allowed President Bush to lift the sanctions that the United States had imposed on Pakistan to protest General Pervez Musharraf's seizure of power in 1999. When President Bush proposed increasing defense spending by $38 billion in 2003—a sum equal to Great Britain's entire military budget and three-quarters of China's—Congress quickly voted to appropriate the funds. Lawmakers' enthusiasm for the spending increase was not diminished by the fact that most of the new money went to fund defense programs that had been on the drawing boards before September 11 rather than to meet the needs of the war on terrorism.

Congress retreated from confrontations with the president on other issues as well. Senate Democrats dropped their plans to make the administration's proposals to build a missile defense and withdraw from the 1972 Anti-Ballistic Missile Treaty the centerpiece of foreign policy debate. Congress also voted to give President Bush what it had denied President Clinton: fast-track negotiating authority (by now renamed trade-promotion authority). When the White House set up special military commissions to try captured Taliban and al Qaeda officials, lawmakers did not ask whether the Constitution in fact gave the president power to set up his own judicial system. (The U.S. Supreme Court subsequently ruled in *Hamdan v. Rumsfeld* that he did not.)

The willingness of members of Congress to defer to President Bush on foreign policy after 9/11 stemmed in good part from a basic principled motive—the crisis demanded less "second guessing" of the White House. But lawmakers who might have preferred different policies quickly understood that discretion was the greater part of valor. They worried that if they challenged a popular wartime president, they risked being accused of playing politics with national security. This was not an idle fear. When Senate Majority Leader Tom Daschle (D-SD) said in February 2002 that the

Bush administration's efforts to expand the war lacked "a clear direction," Republican leaders questioned his patriotism. One went as far as to accuse him of "giving aid and comfort to our enemies," which happens to be the legal definition of treason.[14]

Party reputations reinforced Congress's instinct to defer to the White House. Because President Bush was a Republican, challenges to his foreign policy stewardship would more likely come from congressional Democrats than congressional Republicans. But Democrats had a problem in trying to criticize a popular Republican president on foreign policy—most Americans lacked confidence in their ability to handle national security issues. Ever since the Vietnam War, Americans had given Republicans far higher marks than Democrats on defense and foreign policy. In times of peace and prosperity, like the 1990s, these perceptions did not create insurmountable obstacles for Democrats. In a wartime context, however, they left Democrats such as Daschle, who offered even mild criticisms of the White House, open to charges of being unpatriotic.

A desire not to give the Republicans a campaign issue, perhaps more than agreement on the substance, explains why many Democrats embraced President Bush's call in the fall of 2002 for a resolution authorizing him to wage war on Iraq. Leading congressional Democrats privately believed the request was both premature and unwise.[15] Most of America's traditional allies publicly opposed the White House's policy of regime change in Iraq. Moreover, while few lawmakers doubted that the U.S. military could capture Baghdad, most feared that the ouster of Saddam Hussein could have tremendous unintended and undesirable consequences. Finally, in asking Congress to act, President Bush said he had not made up his mind whether to wage war against Iraq. Lawmakers knew, however, that the war power was a use-it-and-lose-it authority. Once they gave President Bush authority to wage war, he could exercise it as he saw fit, even if most members of Congress (or most Americans) thought the circumstances no longer warranted it.

But with the 2002 midterm congressional elections looming, most Democratic political strategists looked at the polling data and urged their candidates to support the White House. They calculated that rallying around the president would deny Republicans the opportunity to question Democrats' patriotism. It would also get Iraq off the front pages and shift the national debate back to domestic policy, where Democratic positions were more popular with the voters. In the end, political calculations trumped. Congress did something unprecedented in American history—it authorized a war against another country before the United States itself had been attacked and even before the president had publicly made up his mind to wage war.

CONGRESS REGAINS ITS VOICE

Four years after Congress authorized the invasion of Iraq, many Democrats and more than a few Republicans wished they could take back their votes. The speedy U.S. conquest of Baghdad had given way to a protracted and bloody occupation. By the start of 2007, more than three thousand U.S. troops had died, and many times that had been wounded. Rather than forging a new democracy, Iraq looked to be spiraling into a civil war. With the death toll mounting and the prospects for a stable Iraq, let alone a democratic one, receding, George W. Bush discovered what Lyndon Johnson learned more than three decades earlier on Vietnam—the fact that members of Congress defer to the White House on the takeoff in foreign policy does not mean they will be deferential when it crashes.

A major blow to the Bush White House came when Democrats retook control of both houses of Congress in the 2006 midterm elections. No one doubted that the Republicans' stunning defeat reflected the public's unhappiness with the war in Iraq. Empowered by their status as the new majority party, Democrats held hearings and pursued investigations critical of the Bush administration. Even more troubling for the White House, the once solid Republican support for Bush's policies began to crack. The defections partly reflected doubts that the president's policies would work. "I've gone along with the president on this, and I bought into his dream," remarked Senator George V. Voinovich (R-OH), "and at this stage of the game, I don't think it's going to happen."[16] But Republican dissatisfaction also reflected political calculations. Rep. Ray LaHood (R-IL) put the White House's problem bluntly: "People are worried about their political skins."[17]

In seeking to regain a say in foreign policy, members of Congress quickly discovered that authority once given away is hard to reclaim. Because Congress had approved the FY 2007 defense budget in 2006, the Bush administration already had sufficient funds to finance the major new policy initiative it unveiled in January 2007: the dispatch of 21,500 additional U.S. troops to Iraq. That funding decision could be reversed only if Congress passed a new funding bill by a veto-proof majority. And that Congress failed to do. In May 2007, President Bush vetoed a bill that would have begun the withdrawal of U.S. troops from Iraq. Congressional leaders subsequently acknowledged that while they could pass symbolic, non-binding resolutions criticizing the administration's Iraq policy, they lacked the votes needed to override the president's veto.

Barack Obama learned that Capitol Hill could be equally unwelcoming to a Democratic president. On his third day in office, he fulfilled one of his campaign promises by ordering the closure of the U.S. prison at Guantanamo Bay, Cuba, which housed foreign fighters captured in the war on terror. However, fierce congressional criticism ultimately forced him to reverse his decision. Obama had also campaigned on a promise to establish a so-called cap-and-trade-system for curtailing the emission of the greenhouse gases driving climate change. The House passed the legislation needed to start the program, but the Senate refused to act on it. After a year of fruitless efforts to spur Senate action, Obama acknowledged politically reality and abandoned the cap-and-trade initiative.

Another of Obama's foreign policy priorities was negotiating a new arms control agreement with Russia to succeed the START Treaty, which expired in December 2009. Obama and Russian President Dmitri Medvedev eventually signed the New START Treaty in April 2010. The White House anticipated rapid Senate approval. After all, a who's who of military leaders and foreign policy luminaries, including former Republican secretaries of state Henry Kissinger, James Baker, Lawrence Eagleburger, and Colin Powell as well as Republican national security adviser Brent Scowcroft endorsed the agreement. Instead, a group of Senate Republicans, led by Senate Minority Leader Mitch McConnell (R-KY) and Senate Minority Whip Jon Kyl (R-AZ), fought to kill the treaty. The Senate approved it in the end, but only after a protracted White House lobbying effort. The administration's legislative push included promising something that many of the treaty's critics wanted: a commitment to spend billions of dollars modernizing the U.S. nuclear weapons arsenal.

Obama's decision to launch Operation Odyssey Dawn, the military operation to protect Libyan civilians from the Muammar Qaddafi's military forces, also faced congressional opposition. Some lawmakers criticized Obama for acting too slowly and ineffectively to topple the Libyan dictator. However, far more lawmakers argued that by attacking a country that had not attacked the United States or even threatened to, Obama had usurped Congress's war power. The White House argued that the 1973 War Powers Resolution gave the president the authority to use military force for up to ninety days without prior congressional authorization. When the military operations continued past the ninety-day mark, the House of Representatives voted overwhelmingly not to authorize continued air strikes against Libya. Meanwhile, the White House continued with the air strikes but carefully limited U.S. air operations and repeatedly refused to consider sending U.S. ground troops to Libya in order to avoid antagonizing Congress further.

The surge in Iraq and Operation Odyssey Dawn show that a more assertive Congress does not necessarily get its way. When presidents are intent on exercising their constitutional authorities—and willing to pay the price for doing so—they may carry the day. This is most likely to happen in situations in which presidents can act *until* Congress stops them. This was precisely the case with Bush in Iraq and Obama in Libya. With the federal courts historically reluctant to intervene in disputes between the

White House and Congress over decisions to use military force, Congress could impose its will only by passing a law with enough support that it would withstand the inevitable presidential veto. As Iraq shows, that is enormously difficult to do. Conversely, the advantage shifts to Congress when the Constitution or existing legislation bars the president from acting *unless* he gets congressional approval. In these situations, the difficulties in assembling congressional majorities work against the president, witness the failure of the effort to create a cap-and-trade system.

Although a more assertive Congress may not win a showdown with the White House, its willingness to resist presidential initiatives can still shape foreign policy. Presidents worry about how they spend their time, energy, and political capital. They may decide against pursuing policies that Congress is likely to oppose because they are not confident they will win or they judge that the political costs of winning are too high. For example, the fierce resistance Senate Republicans put up against the New START Treaty persuaded the Obama administration not to ask the Senate to vote on an even more controversial arms control agreement, the Comprehensive Test Ban Treaty. As a result, Congress influences foreign policy not just by what it does, but also by what it can persuade the White House not to do.

CONCLUSION

The framers of the Constitution created a political system that gives Congress substantial powers to shape the course of American foreign policy. Congress's willingness to exercise those powers has ebbed and flowed over time according to the vicissitudes of politics. When Americans are at peace and believe themselves secure, congressional assertiveness grows. When Americans find themselves at war or fear great peril, congressional deference to the president comes to the fore. At the same time, how much deference the president can expect from Capitol Hill depends on whether presidential policies are seen to be succeeding. Successful presidents can push Congress to the sidelines, while struggling presidents see their policies challenged on Capitol Hill.

Is there any reason to believe that America's foreign policy is better served by an assertive Congress or deferential one? This question is easy to ask and impossible to answer. No objective standard exists for judging the proper balance between activism and deference. The temptation is always to judge Congress in light of whether one likes what the president wants to do. As one Reagan administration official commented, "I have been a 'strong president man' when in the executive branch and a 'strong Congress man' when out of the government in political opposition."[18] That answer hardly satisfies those who have different partisan preferences.

What is clear is that activist and deferential congresses pose different mixes of costs and benefits. Although congressional activism usually looks unhelpful from the vantage point of the White House, it has several merits. For the same reason that an upcoming test encourages students to study, the possibility that Congress might step into the fray encourages administration officials to think through their policy proposals more carefully. Members of Congress also bring different views to bear on policy debates, views that can provide a useful scrub for administration proposals. When Capitol Hill is more hawkish than the White House, congressional activism strengthens the president's hand overseas. And congressional debate helps to legitimate foreign policy with the public. This latter virtue should not be underestimated; the success of the United States abroad ultimately depends on the willingness of Americans to accept the sacrifices asked of them.

But if congressional activism can be helpful, it can also be harmful. At a minimum, it makes an already cumbersome decision-making process even more so. More people need to be consulted, and more opportunities to derail a policy are created. Such inefficiency is not inherently disastrous—after all, the maxim "he who hesitates is lost" has its counterpoint in "decide in haste, repent at leisure." It does, however, increase the burdens on the time and energy of executive branch officials, potentially keeping them from other duties, and it can strain relations with allies that don't understand why Washington is so slow in acting. At its worst, congressional activism may render U.S. foreign policy incoherent as members of Congress push issues they do not fully understand and pursue narrow interests rather than national ones.

A deferential Congress avoids these problems but can easily create others. Presidents unburdened by congressional second-guessing find it easier to exploit the advantages of "decision, activity, secrecy, and dispatch" that Alexander Hamilton long ago hailed as the great virtues of the presidency.[19] But presidents and their advisers are not infallible. They can choose unwisely, and the lack of domestic checks can tempt them to overreach. President George W. Bush's critics would offer up his handling of the Iraq War as a case in point. But he was hardly the only American president to find his foreign policy plans go awry. It was the imperial presidency, after all, that gave America the Bay of Pigs and the Vietnam War.

A decade after 9/11, the political winds on foreign policy blew briskly in the direction of Capitol Hill. How long the new period of congressional assertiveness lasts and how far Congress will go to put its mark on foreign policy depends on events abroad and the consequences of White House policies. Only one thing is for certain: the pendulum of power will continue to swing back and forth between the two ends of Pennsylvania Avenue.

DISCUSSION QUESTIONS

1. According to James Lindsay, who makes foreign policy? How much power does Congress possess?
2. According to Lindsay, what are the conditions under which Congress exercises its foreign policy powers?
3. What are some legal tools that Congress possesses for directing foreign policy?
4. What are some examples of the ebbs and flows in congressional-executive relations?
5. What was the impact of the end of the Cold War on Congress's involvement in foreign affairs?
6. What happened to congressional involvement in foreign affairs after 9/11? Has Congress regained its "voice" today?
7. To what extent has Congress affected the foreign policy actions of the Obama administration?

NOTES

1. Quoted in Frank Rich, "It's the War, Stupid," *New York Times*, October 12, 2002.

2. Robert C. Byrd, "Congress Must Resist the Rush to War," *New York Times*, October 10, 2002.

3. Quoted in Thom Shanker and David S. Cloud, "Bush's Plan for Iraq Runs into Opposition," *New York Times*, January 12, 2007.

4. Shanker and Cloud, "Bush's Plan for Iraq."

5. Quoted in Carl Hulse, "Measure in Senate Urges No Troop Rise in Iraq," *New York Times*, January 18, 2007.

6. Richard E. Neustadt, *Presidential Power and the Modern Presidents: The Politics of Leadership from Roosevelt to Reagan* (New York: Free Press, 1990), 29.

7. Alexis de Tocqueville, *Democracy in America* (New York: Anchor Books, 1969), 126.

8. Quoted in Arthur M. Schlesinger Jr., *A Thousand Days* (Boston: Houghton Mifflin, 1965), 289–90.

9. Arthur M. Schlesinger Jr., *The Imperial Presidency* (Boston: Houghton Mifflin, 1973).

10. Quoted in James L. Sundquist, *The Decline and Resurgence of Congress* (Washington, DC: Brookings Institution, 1981), 125.

11. John E. Reilly, "Americans and the World: A Survey at Century's End," *Foreign Policy* 114 (Spring 1999): 111.

12. Quoted in John M. Broder, "House Postpones Trade-Issue Vote," *New York Times*, November 8, 1997.

13. Charles Krauthammer, "The Hundred Days," *Time*, December 31, 2001, 156.

14. Rep. Tom Davis (R-VA), quoted in Helen Dewar, "Lott Calls Daschle Divisive," *Washington Post*, March 1, 2002.

15. See Elizabeth Drew, "War Games in the Senate," *New York Review of Books*, December 5, 2002, 66–68.

16. Quoted in Michael Abramowitz and Jonathan Weisman, "Bush's Iraq Plan Meets Skepticism on Capitol Hill," *Washington Post*, January 12, 2007.

17. Quoted in David Rogers, "Groundwork for a War Debate," *Wall Street Journal*, January 17, 2007.

18. John Lehman, *Making War: The 200-Year-Old Battle between the President and Congress over How America Goes to War* (New York: Scribner, 1992), xii.

19. Alexander Hamilton, "Federalist No. 70," in Alexander Hamilton, James Madison, and John Jay, *The Federalist Papers*, ed. Garry Wills (New York: Bantam Books, 1982), 356.

13

Leading through Civilian Power

Hillary Rodham Clinton

REDEFINING AMERICAN
DIPLOMACY AND DEVELOPMENT

Today's world is a crucible of challenges testing American leadership. Global problems, from violent extremism to worldwide recession to climate change to poverty, demand collective solutions, even as power in the world becomes more diffuse. They require effective international cooperation, even as that becomes harder to achieve. And they cannot be solved unless a nation is willing to accept the responsibility of mobilizing action. The United States is that nation.

I began my tenure as U.S. secretary of state by stressing the need to elevate diplomacy and development alongside defense—a "smart power" approach to solving global problems. To make that approach succeed, however, U.S. civilian power must be strengthened and amplified. It must, as U.S. Secretary of Defense Robert Gates has argued, be brought into better balance with U.S. military power. Gates said, "There has to be a change in attitude in the recognition of the critical role that agencies like State and AID play . . . for them to play the leading role that I think they need to play."

This effort is under way. Congress has already appropriated funds for 1,108 new Foreign Service and Civil Service officers to strengthen the State Department's capacity to pursue American interests and advance American values. The United States Agency for International Development (USAID) is in the process of doubling its development staff, hiring 1,200 new Foreign Service officers with the specific skills and experience required for evolving development challenges, and is making better use of local hires at our overseas missions, who have deep knowledge of their countries. The

Obama administration has begun rebuilding USAID to make it the world's premier development organization, one that fosters long-term growth and democratic governance, includes its own research arm, shapes policy and innovation, and uses metrics to ensure that our investments are cost-effective and sound.

But we must do more. We must not only rebuild but also rethink, reform, and recalibrate. During my years on the Senate Armed Services Committee, I saw how the Department of Defense used its Quadrennial Defense Review to align its resources, policies, and strategies for the present—and the future. No similar mechanism existed for modernizing the State Department or USAID. In July 2009, I launched the first Quadrennial Diplomacy and Development Review (QDDR), a wholesale review of the State Department and USAID to recommend how to better equip, fund, train, and organize ourselves to meet current diplomatic and development priorities and how to begin building the people, structures, processes, and resources today to address the world's challenges in the years ahead.

The QDDR is not simply a review. It defines how to make diplomacy and development coordinated, complementary, and mutually reinforcing. It assesses what has worked in the past and what has not. And it forecasts future strategic choices and resource needs.

Although the State Department and USAID have distinct roles and missions, diplomacy and development often overlap and must work in tandem. Increasingly, global challenges call for a mix of both, requiring a more holistic approach to civilian power.

Diplomatic objectives are often secured by gains in development. The resumption of direct talks between the Israelis and the Palestinians over the summer of 2010 was the handiwork of talented and persistent diplomacy. But progress at the negotiating table will be directly linked to progress in building strong and stable institutions for a Palestinian state and providing Israel with the security it needs. And development objectives are often secured by diplomatic engagement. The impact of the Feed the Future global hunger program and the Global Health Initiative will turn in part on the promotion of policy reforms in partner countries; the Millennium Challenge Compacts are in part the product of sustained political engagement designed to create positive conditions for development. In many places, including Afghanistan and Iraq, the need for mutually reinforcing diplomatic and development strategies stems from the combined causes and effects of violent conflict, instability, and weak states.

The two *D*s in QDDR reflect the world as the State Department sees it today—and as it envisions it in the future. The review process relied on the wisdom and talent of exceptional people in the State Department and USAID who worked tirelessly to produce a blueprint for reforms that will be implemented over the next four years and will have an impact for much longer. This year's inaugural QDDR identifies new approaches and skill sets for diplomats and development experts, sets budget priorities, establishes planning procedures, revises promotion incentives, and recommends organizational reforms. It focuses on three main areas: modernizing and coordinating diplomacy across U.S. government agencies, ensuring that development work creates a lasting and sustainable impact, and creating a stronger nexus between diplomacy and development, as well as better coordination with partners in the military, in conflict zones and fragile states.

A GLOBAL CIVILIAN SERVICE

Diplomacy has long been the backbone of U.S. foreign policy. It remains so today. The vast majority of my work at the State Department consists of engaging in diplomacy to address major global and regional challenges, such as confronting Iran's nuclear ambitions, facilitating negotiations between the Israelis and the Palestinians, enhancing stability on the Korean Peninsula, and working with other governments to bring emergency relief to Haiti. And President Barack Obama and I certainly relied on old-fashioned diplomatic elbow grease to hammer out a last-minute accord at the Copenhagen conference on climate change. . . .

In annual strategic dialogues with a range of key partners—including China, India, Indonesia, Nigeria, Pakistan, Russia, and South Africa—the United States aims to deepen and broaden its relationships and to establish a stronger foundation for addressing shared problems, advancing shared interests, and managing differences. The United States is investing in strengthening global structures such as the G-20 and regional institutions such as the Organization of American States and the Association of Southeast Asian Nations. This is part of a commitment to building a new global architecture of cooperation that includes not only the East and the West but also the North and the South.

Although traditional diplomacy will always be critical to advancing the United States' agenda, it is not enough. The State Department must expand its engagement to reach and influence wider and more diverse groups using new skills, strategies, and tools. To that end, the department is broadening the way it conceives of diplomacy as well as the roles and responsibilities of its practitioners.

The original Foreign Service, as its name implies, consisted of people trained to manage U.S. relations with foreign states, principally through consultations with their counterparts in government. This has been the main function of U.S. ambassadors and embassies, as well as the staff at the State Department. But increasing global interconnectedness now necessitates reaching beyond governments to citizens directly and broadening the U.S. foreign policy portfolio to include issues once confined to the domestic sphere, such as economic and environmental regulation, drugs and disease, organized crime, and world hunger. As those issues spill across borders, the domestic agencies addressing them must now do more of their work overseas, operating out of embassies and consulates. A U.S. ambassador in 2010 is thus responsible not only for managing civilians from the State Department and USAID but also for operating as the CEO of a multiagency mission. And he or she must also be adept at connecting with audiences outside of government, such as the private sector and civil society.

Consider the U.S. embassy in Islamabad. The mission includes 800 staff members; about 450 are diplomats and civil servants from the State Department, and 100 are from USAID. A large portion of the work there consists of traditional diplomacy—Foreign Service officers helping Americans traveling or doing business in the region, issuing visas, and engaging with their Pakistani civilian and military counterparts. But the U.S. ambassador there also leads civilians from eleven other federal agencies, including disaster relief and reconstruction experts helping to rebuild after . . . historic floods; specialists in health, energy, communications, finance, agriculture, and justice; and military personnel working with the Pakistani military to bolster Pakistani capacities and to help in the fight against violent extremists.

Back in Washington, my responsibility as secretary is to ensure that the Foreign Service and Civil Service personnel within the State Department and USAID are working together and with their colleagues across the federal government. The United States' strategic dialogue with Pakistan involves ten separate working groups that bring together cabinet secretaries and experts from a range of agencies in both governments. The U.S. dialogue with India engages twenty-two different agencies, and when U.S. Treasury Secretary Timothy Geithner and I traveled to Beijing . . . for the second round of the Strategic and Economic Dialogue, our delegation included civilians from over thirty agencies.

Foreign Service officers, Civil Service personnel, and local staff at the State Department and USAID form the backbone of our global engagement. By drawing on the pool of talent that already exists in U.S. federal agencies and at overseas posts, the United States can build a global civilian service of the same caliber and flexibility as the U.S. military. With staff members and experts from a variety of institutions—including the State Department, USAID, the Millennium Challenge Corporation, the Overseas Private Investment Corporation, the Export Import Bank, the Department of Justice, the Department of the Treasury, the Department of Agriculture, the Centers for Disease Control and Prevention, the Peace Corps, and many others—the U.S. foreign policy apparatus must reward teamwork, promote collaboration, and support interagency rotations.

Engagement must go far beyond government-to-government interactions. In this information age, public opinion takes on added importance even in authoritarian states and as nonstate actors are more able to influence current events. Today, a U.S. ambassador creates ties not only with the host nation's government but also with its people. The QDDR endorses a new public diplomacy strategy that makes public engagement every diplomat's duty, through town-hall meetings and interviews with the media, organized outreach, events in provincial towns and smaller communities, student exchange programs, and virtual connections that bring together citizens and civic organizations. Indeed, in the twenty-first century, a diplomat is as likely to meet with a tribal elder in a rural village as a counterpart in a foreign ministry, and is as likely to wear cargo pants as a pinstriped suit.

Public diplomacy must start at the top. In Indonesia and Turkey, I conducted bilateral meetings with government officials, but I also met with civil-society leaders and appeared as a guest on popular television talk shows. I have held town-hall meetings with diverse groups of citizens on every continent I have visited, as I have done throughout my career. Public events such as these are as much a part of my job as secretary of state as my meetings in foreign ministries, because the durability of the United States' partnerships abroad will depend on the attitudes of the people as well as the policies of their governments.

In Washington as well, the State Department is streamlining and modernizing the way it conceives of and conducts public diplomacy. We are shifting away from traditional platforms and instead are building connections to foreign publics in regions once considered beyond the United States' reach. It makes no sense to allocate the greatest amount of resources to parts of the world where the United States' ties are already strong and secure and to minimize efforts where engaging the public is critical to success.

We can also leverage civilian power by connecting businesses, philanthropists, and citizens' groups with partner governments to perform tasks that governments alone cannot. Technology, in particular, provides new tools of engagement. One great success . . . was a partnership forged almost overnight among U.S. and Haitian cell-phone companies, the Red Cross, social entrepreneurs, the U.S. Coast Guard, and, eventually, the U.S. Marines to create a platform that used text messaging to broadcast the locations of earthquake victims in need of rescue. The State Department also launched a program to facilitate the texting of $10 donations to the Red Cross for Haiti, which drew contributions from 31 million Americans. At the State Department and USAID, we continue to develop new ways to use the world's 4.6 billion cell phones to improve the lives of people living in remote areas and arduous circumstances. . . .

Looking down the road to the forces that will shape global politics tomorrow, it becomes clear how the material conditions of people's lives can affect U.S. national security objectives. While USAID leads U.S. development work overseas, State Department employees today—from ambassadors to Civil Service experts—must be better versed and more engaged in development issues. For this reason, I called for a broad review of U.S. aid programs in Afghanistan and Pakistan to ensure that they were aligned with U.S. strategic objectives and sent two experienced ambassadors to coordinate foreign assistance in Kabul and Islamabad.

This comprehensive approach is essential to U.S. engagement in many regions. In Mexico, for example, the United States continues to support law enforcement efforts to arrest and prosecute members of drug cartels, but it has also begun the next phase of the Merida Initiative, working with Mexican partners—in government, business, and civil society—to strengthen justice systems and promote a "culture of legality" in local communities.

When the diverse elements of U.S. civilian power work cohesively—as in many embassies around the world, and on the best days in Washington—the potential impact of a global civilian service becomes evident. There is no guarantee that this comprehensive approach will achieve every goal, especially where the challenges are as entrenched and complex as they are in places such as Haiti, Pakistan, or Yemen. But it is the best alternative we have, and one we must pursue.

HIGH-IMPACT DEVELOPMENT

I am sometimes asked why development matters to U.S. foreign policy and why the United States should spend money on people overseas when it has economic challenges at home. As counterintuitive as it may seem, the answer is that development, when done effectively, is one of the best tools to enhance the United States' stability and prosperity. It can strengthen fragile or failing states, support the rise of capable partners that can help solve regional and global problems, and advance democracy and human rights.

At the same time, it is important to acknowledge that although the world's problems are vast, the United States' resources are not. As stewards of American taxpayer dollars, the State Department and USAID must be strategic in pursuing the most critical needs and in making decisions based on hard evidence to ensure that investments deliver results. And we must also stay focused on the long term—not simply addressing the urgent needs of people today but also building the foundations for a more prosperous future. With this in mind, the Presidential Policy Directive on Development that President Obama issued in September [2010]—the first by a U.S. president—emphasizes the importance of targeting countries with responsible governments and favorable conditions for development and working in a smaller number of targeted sectors in each country for maximum impact. It affirms that assistance must be coordinated with trade, finance, investment credits, and other economic policies to bolster emerging markets and to foster widespread and sustainable economic growth. Economic growth is the surest route out of poverty, and expanding and strengthening middle classes around the world will be key to creating the just and sustainable international order that lies at the heart of the United States' national security strategy.

The QDDR embraces development as a process of assisted self-help in the furtherance of American interests and values. A developing country must be in charge and set its own goals for meeting the needs of its people. The U.S. government comes to the table as a partner, not a patron, lending resources and expertise and, eventually, putting itself out of business when a host country is self-sustaining.

Today, the Obama administration is putting that partnership model into practice in two signature initiatives that it announced over the past year: the Global Health Initiative and Feed the Future, part of the administration's broader global food-security initiative.

The Global Health Initiative recognizes that the landscape for health in many developing countries has improved over the years, due in part to George W. Bush's President's Emergency Plan for AIDS Relief (PEPFAR), his President's Malaria Initiative (PMI), and the contributions of many other countries and organizations. But this more crowded landscape does not necessarily improve health outcomes efficiently or for the long term.

The fundamental purpose of the Global Health Initiative is to put an end to isolated and sporadic care by tying individual health programs— PEPFAR, the PMI, and programs regarding maternal and children's health, family planning, neglected tropical diseases, and other critical health areas—together in an integrated, coordinated, and sustainable system of care, with the affected countries themselves in the lead.

The Feed the Future initiative is based on the same principles. To give one example, Bangladesh is developing its own food-security investment plan based in part on consultations in a public forum with more than five hundred representatives from civil society, academia, think tanks, and the private sector. The strategy has been reviewed by independent technical experts and is being further refined by national leaders and other experts. The U.S. government is now developing an investment plan in support of Bangladesh's strategy, in full collaboration with other governments and international donors.

This is what partnership looks like in practice. Partner governments will almost certainly choose to do things differently from how the United States might, or they might outline different priorities. Vetting and investing in

these governments' plans may take longer than delivering services ourselves. But the result promises a sustainable strategy that will continue even
after U.S. assistance has ended.

The QDDR also focuses on the diplomatic side of effective development
policy, arguing for building much stronger and more systematic links between the State Department and USAID both in Washington and in the
field.

Diplomacy can support development policy in different ways. The United
States' most important diplomatic effort with China in recent years—the
Strategic and Economic Dialogue—includes high-level discussions about
development and about what it means to the two countries' respective and
collective efforts in Africa and elsewhere. Before the 2009 meeting of the G-8
in L'Aquila, Italy, high-level engagement with partner governments enabled
the United States to secure a $20 billion international commitment to pro-
moting food security, building a coalition of countries willing to contribute.
And at the 2009 Summit of the Americas, President Obama launched the
Energy and Climate Partnership of the Americas, bringing together all the
democratically elected governments in the hemisphere to work toward a
shared goal of clean, renewable, and inexpensive energy sources. As part of
that effort, the United States and Brazil are helping seven energy-poor Central American and Caribbean countries develop their own biofuels. This will
promote sustainable economic development and regional integration and
help reduce dependence on imported Venezuelan oil.

But diplomacy and development can only be mutually reinforcing if the
U.S. government also get its own house in order. The first step is to move
beyond agency "stovepiping" and use all the talent and expertise within the
federal government. The Global Health Initiative, for example, is jointly
led by the USAID administrator, the U.S. global AIDS coordinator, and the
director of the Centers for Disease Control and Prevention. Their agencies,
along with the Department of Health and Human Services, the National
Institutes of Health, and the Peace Corps, work together under my overall
guidance and direction. This unique leadership structure strengthens coordination at every level, from the White House down.

The QDDR also recommends specific internal reforms within USAID,
some of which have already begun. USAID Administrator Rajiv Shah has
laid out an aggressive set of operational priorities called USAID Forward,
which are designed to make the agency more effective, accountable, and
transparent. In coordination with other QDDR recommendations, USAID
Forward concentrates on procurement, people, and policy.

Procurement reform has as its goal the building of local capacities in
the countries where the United States works by drawing on the talent and
expertise of small businesses and nongovernmental organizations. Senegal,
for example, has more than 1,400 so-called health huts, where local health

workers trained by USAID provide basic and often lifesaving treatments, lowering costs and moving the country closer to the day when U.S. aid will no longer be necessary.

To reform policy, USAID has already created the new Bureau of Policy, Planning and Learning. Evidence-based development must be more than a notion; it must become reality. We will measure our investments not by the number of programs run but by the number of children nourished or vaccinated and by the number of people benefiting from clean water, electricity, teachers, medicine, or jobs. We will also make sure that taxpayer dollars are well spent, by gathering baseline data, surveying development indicators before projects are launched, and then measuring those same indicators over the lives of the projects. Where our approaches are successful, we will replicate them and scale them up. Where they are not, we will admit it, learn from our failures, and come up with a better idea.

USAID will also rely on the innovations of science and technology to help it work better, cheaper, and faster in the pursuit of high-impact development. Cell phones have already transformed the lives of countless people in sub-Saharan Africa. Imagine what the world would look like if off-grid renewable energy provided illumination to billions of people now living in the dark or if more kinds of drought-resistant seeds existed for farmers in the developing world. The QDDR endorses USAID's creation of Development Innovation Ventures, by which creative solutions will be funded, piloted, and brought to scale. . . .

As the State Department and USAID undertake these efforts, we will broaden our partnerships. Twenty years ago, the development community did not exist far beyond the walls of USAID. Today, it includes corporate leaders, philanthropists, foundations, and advocates, all of whom add new skills and perspectives. Equally important are the grass-roots leaders: the religious groups, the students, and other activists who lend their passion and energy to humanitarian efforts. These advocates and entrepreneurs are willing to challenge old orthodoxies and bring a new mindset to their work. We will partner with them to get results.

BUILDING PEACE AND STABILITY

American civilians have long operated in conflict zones and fragile states. But now, U.S. diplomats and development experts are being asked to undertake missions of a scale and a scope never seen before. The United States' task in Iraq is to lead a broad mission in support of the Iraqi people as they build a multiethnic democratic state.

At the same time, the United States is responsible in Afghanistan for helping reduce the strength of the insurgency there, improve governance, and promote stability that will last after U.S. troops return home. In Pakistan, Washington is assisting a government and a society buffeted by the global economic recession, natural disasters, and regional instability, while supporting a counterterrorism and counterinsurgency campaign. Today, 20 percent of the U.S. diplomatic corps and nearly 10 percent of U.S. development professionals are stationed in these three countries—where democracy is young, institutions are struggling to serve local populations, society is ethnically or religiously divided, and security is an ongoing challenge. Beyond those countries, the United States is working to stabilize fragile states from Somalia and Sudan to Haiti and Kyrgyzstan. . . .

Properly trained and equipped, civilians are force multipliers. One effective diplomat or development expert can leverage as many as ten local partners, and when local partners build their own capacities and networks, communities become stronger and more resilient.

Civilian leadership in addressing conflict and instability also depends on marshaling and leveraging the varied assets of the U.S. government as a whole. Under the leadership of strong ambassadors and agency representatives, collaboration among American civilians from across the government has reached new levels in Afghanistan, Haiti, Iraq, Pakistan, and elsewhere. Washington is pooling the expertise of civilians at the State Department and USAID, as well as at the Departments of Justice, Commerce, the Treasury, Homeland Security, and Health and Human Services; the Centers for Disease Control and Prevention; and other agencies. The United States cannot succeed in these fragile states if these agencies are not working together. That means organizing the internal branches of the U.S. government with a focus on integration, cohesion, and problem solving. For example, the Office of the Special Representative for Afghanistan and Pakistan—in which sixteen agencies are represented—was created to overcome agency compartmentalization and achieve a comprehensive strategy.

The QDDR also draws on the talents of the Civilian Response Corps, which has identified hundreds of civilian experts across the government who can be quickly deployed to conflict zones or fragile states. I sent the CRC's expeditionary conflict and security experts to Southern Sudan, where the United States [was] mounting a civilian surge around the southern capital of Juba to prepare for the January 2011 referendum [to determine] whether Southern Sudan secedes from the North.

The QDDR recommends building rapid-response diplomatic teams and cultivating specially trained experts who can operate effectively over the longer term amid conflict and instability. Since the end of the Cold War, the State Department and USAID have steadily taken on more missions in difficult and dangerous places, from Lebanon to Bosnia to East Timor. Moving forward, both agencies will create a joint operating framework and response plan that will allow them to work more effectively together and with other agencies. Within this framework, the State Department will lead in complex political crises, and USAID will lead in disaster response, building on its ability to get relief supplies and recovery workers into the field within twenty-four hours after a disaster strikes.

In Yemen, the U.S. embassy is working to address poor economic conditions and the ravages of poverty in a country that has recently faced a secessionist movement in the south, a rebellion in the north, and a persistent threat from al Qaeda on the Arabian Peninsula. Through the Friends of Yemen—a forum of countries and multilateral organizations working with the government of Yemen to identify practical solutions to the country's problems—and through concentrated efforts to stabilize fragile local communities and to create opportunities for economic growth, the United States is trying to help the Yemeni government provide better services for its citizens and to prevent conflict. The QDDR anticipates more situations requiring rapidly deployable civilian teams of diplomats, stabilization and reconstruction experts, and development professionals that can meet U.S. needs in places such as Sudan or Yemen while also mounting larger efforts in other countries at the same time.

Poverty and repression do not automatically engender terrorism, but countries that are impoverished, corrupt, lawless, or mired in recurring cycles of conflict are more prone to becoming havens for terrorists and other criminals. Al Qaeda first operated out of Sudan and bombed U.S. embassies in Kenya and Tanzania before migrating to Afghanistan, then a country notable for its poverty, high infant mortality, and repressive Taliban government. It is no coincidence that al Qaeda is most active today in underdeveloped nations such as Mali, Mauritania, Niger, Pakistan, Somalia, and Yemen. Beyond terrorism and violent extremism, drug cartels, criminal gangs funded by the illicit exploitation of natural resources, and gender-based sexual violence can also dramatically undermine governments in ways that can have dangerous consequences for an entire region.

On the positive side, civilian power has worked effectively with military forces to impede conflict and to contribute to stability. In Liberia, as fighting between rebel groups and government forces under the leadership of Charles Taylor intensified and as the humanitarian situation deteriorated, the United States undertook intense diplomatic efforts, including public calls for Taylor's resignation, as well as military deployments, to the region, to help shore up the peacekeeping efforts of the Economic Community of West African States. Taylor's resignation paved the way for a comprehensive peace agreement that led to the end of Liberia's conflict and set the stage for Liberia's stabilization and reconstruction efforts. Both the United Nations and the United States continue to partner with Liberia as it rebuilds social and economic infrastructure destroyed by years of conflict. Achieving a more stable and peaceful world depends on the success of all these types of missions—from Iraq and Afghanistan to West Africa—and on the United States' and other countries' ability to mount more of them.

The American people must understand that spending taxpayer dollars on diplomacy and development is in their interest, especially when those investments support missions in conflict zones, fragile states, and states that can play a responsible role in their regions and in the world. And Congress, which has a long tradition of bipartisan support for traditional diplomacy and development, must appreciate the scale and scope of the reconstruction and stabilization missions that U.S. civilians are being asked to undertake.

The House and the Senate have appropriated hundreds of billions of dollars for the military missions in Afghanistan and Iraq. The diplomatic and development activities there represent a fraction of that cost, yet the funding often gets bogged down in old debates over foreign aid. It is time to move beyond the past and to recognize diplomacy and development as national security priorities and smart investments in the United States' future stability and security. These missions can succeed, but only with the necessary congressional leadership and support. Congress must provide the necessary funding now.

THE DIVIDENDS OF CIVILIAN POWER

An emphasis on civilian power is in keeping with America's history and traditions. The Marshall Plan was a civilian development initiative undertaken with European governments. Eleanor Roosevelt chaired the drafting committee that produced the Universal Declaration of Human Rights. Decades before the term "soft power" was coined, President John F. Kennedy founded the Peace Corps to show the world a different face of the United States. The American scientist Norman Borlaug was responsible for the "green revolution" that fed millions of hungry people. U.S. diplomats helped negotiate the reunification of Europe in 1991 without a shot fired. Meanwhile, Americans have enjoyed the world's admiration because of their spirit of innovation, their abundant goodwill, and their audacious belief that technological, social, and political advances can and must be used to improve the lives of human beings around the world.

The men and women who volunteer for the United States armed forces exemplify this spirit. So do the growing number of people who work for the civilian agencies that advance U.S. interests around the world. With the right balance of civilian and military power, the United States can advance its interests and values, lead and support other nations in solving global problems, and forge strong diplomatic and development partnerships with traditional allies and newly emerging powers. And we can rise to the challenges of the world in the twenty-first century and meet the tests of America's global leadership.

DISCUSSION QUESTIONS

1. What does Hillary Clinton say must be done to enhance America's effort to solve global problems?
2. What are the aims of the Quadrennial Diplomacy and Development Review (QDDR)? How do diplomacy and development work hand in hand?
3. Why is traditional diplomacy not sufficient? How is the Department of State broadening its view of diplomacy?
4. How does public engagement form part of this new diplomacy?
5. What is meant by high-impact development? What are some examples of this approach?
6. What are some ways for USAID, the State Department, and other agencies to cooperate in solving global challenges?
7. What are the benefits of civilian power for American foreign policy?

14

A Leaner and Meaner Defense

Gordon Adams and Matthew Leatherman

The United States faces a watershed moment: it must decide whether to increase its already massive debt in order to continue being the world's sheriff or restrain its military missions and focus on economic recovery. Military power has dominated the United States' global engagement over the last decade, but it is now clear that the country overreached. Americans are questioning whether pursuing a defense strategy focused on counterinsurgency and nation building, supported by a defense budget that is growing continuously, makes sense at a time of severe economic and fiscal challenges. . . . The U.S. government must make difficult choices about which defense missions to undertake, exercise restraint in defense planning and budgeting, and bring tough management practices to the Pentagon.

U.S. military missions and the defense budget that supports them have grown without discipline over the past decade, largely as a consequence of the wars in Afghanistan and Iraq. Various administrations and Congresses have neglected the imperative of setting priorities. This has allowed the Department of Defense to undertake an ever-growing array of tasks, adding to traditional missions, such as conventional and nuclear deterrence, sea-lane patrol, and disaster relief, a suite of new ones: nation building, stabilizing fragile states, counterinsurgency, and strengthening the security capacities of other countries. The 2010 Quadrennial Defense Review reinforced this trend by overstating the world's dangers and advocating the elimination of all possible risks. The U.S. government's ambitions now outstrip its capacities at home and its welcome abroad.

The national defense budget accounts for 56 percent of all U.S. federal discretionary spending. Defense is now one of the country's "Big Four" accounts, consuming roughly the same share of federal spending as do each

253

of Social Security, income-based entitlements (such as welfare), and the total nondefense discretionary budget. And the United States was expected to spend over $700 billion on national defense in 2011—twice as much as it spent in 2001, more in real dollars than for any year since the end of World War II, and as much as is spent by the rest of the world's militaries combined.

Defense missions have expanded and spending has soared even though the United States has never been more secure militarily. It has no close competitor, a strategic nuclear exchange is highly improbable, major conventional combat on land is unlikely, and it maintains significant dominance at sea. Al Qaeda and its allies remain active, but their capacity to launch attacks and their support base in Afghanistan have eroded. The U.S. deployment in Iraq [ended in December 2011, and U.S. forces in Afghanistan started leaving in July 2011].

Meanwhile, economic and fiscal challenges are center stage. As Admiral Mike Mullen, chairman of the Joint Chiefs of Staff, said in August 2010, "The single biggest threat to our national security is our debt." Overcoming that threat will require making tough choices to control all federal revenues and spending, including national defense costs.

The Congressional Budget Office currently projects that between fiscal year (FY) 2012 and FY 2018, the U.S. government will spend over $5.54 trillion on defense. In addition to any reductions stemming from the United States' withdrawal from Afghanistan and Iraq, gradual cuts could lower the defense budget over those seven years by more than $788 billion, to about $4.75 trillion—a reduction of more than 14 percent. This would involve reducing the active-duty force by 275,000 troops to 1.21 million (yielding $166 billion in savings); cutting programs that are redundant, underperforming, or linked to low-priority missions ($354 billion in savings); restraining military compensation, health care, and retirement costs ($148 billion in savings); and reforming the intelligence community ($120 billion in savings).

Even with these reductions, and after adjusting for inflation, U.S. defense spending in FY 2018 would be well above the Cold War average. The United States would remain the world's dominant military power and as able as it is today to deploy its military force globally, fight al Qaeda, respond to present and future security challenges, and act as a peacekeeper and a major deterrent force. Befitting its priority missions, the U.S. military would have fewer ground troops, continuing air superiority, a large naval capability, and a force more focused overall on combat—and it would better ensure the security of the United States. And by choosing to undertake only tailored missions and to fund them with disciplined budgets, the Pentagon would also be contributing vitally to the country's broader fiscal health.

MISSIONS: IMPOSSIBLE

[Former] defense secretary Robert Gates . . . proposed eliminating the Joint Forces Command and two Pentagon bureaucracies (the Business Transformation Agency and the Office of the Assistant Secretary of Defense for Networks and Information Integration), canceling several military hardware programs, and reforming the defense contracting process. Efficiency gains such as these are always helpful. But Gates also argued that "the task before us is not to reduce the department's top-line budget; rather, it is significantly to reduce its excess overhead costs and apply the savings to force structure and modernization." In other words, instead of contributing to a disciplined and well-planned reduction of the United States' debt, Gates wanted to keep existing funds in the Pentagon and maintain both the military's current size and most of the Pentagon's planned investment programs. The FY 2011 budget propose[d] to increase the defense budget, despite its already historic level, and Gates ha[d] widely advertised that he hoped to achieve 1 percent real growth in the defense budget in the years after FY 2011.

More effort will be necessary to discipline defense missions and reduce the Pentagon's spending. The last substantial drawdown, which started with the Balanced Budget and Emergency Deficit Control Act of 1985 and proceeded through the end of the Cold War, is a clear historical precedent: it proves that major reductions are possible and can make the force even stronger. At the same time as other cuts were being made across the national budget, between FY 1989 and FY 1998, the Department of Defense decreased its total budget by 28 percent in constant dollars (this included a 50 percent reduction in funds for the procurement of military hardware). The number of civilians employed by the Department of Defense fell from 1.13 million to 747,000, and the Pentagon reduced active-duty troops from 2.2 million to 1.47 million. And this reduced force was still able to help bring peace to the Balkans in the 1990s, topple the Taliban in 2001, and overrun the Iraqi military in 2003.

Reducing the deficit and controlling debt today will require the U.S. government to make similarly tough calls—and start setting priorities among missions rather than simply layering on additional missions, as proposed in the 2010 Quadrennial Defense Review. Spending less on defense means doing fewer things, and that means making firm choices in precisely the areas that Gates said he wanted to protect from budget cutbacks, including the size of the military itself. Force size drives the defense budget: it has a direct impact on the cost of operations, investment in hardware, and the cost of payroll. Thus, budget discipline requires mission discipline. Not all tasks are equal; some are more critical or more urgent, or demand more forces. A sober evaluation of missions' relative importance would lead to a smaller and more focused military, with budget savings as a result. Dismantling al

Qaeda's core, including capturing or killing its leaders, should be the top priority. But this will require far fewer forces than the global campaign against terrorism; it will primarily require special operators such as the Army Rangers, Delta Force, the Special Forces, and the Navy SEALS, of which there are already enough for the mission. In addition, many aspects of the fight against al Qaeda, such as homeland security and law enforcement, fall on the civilian side of the U.S. government. Rather than increasing the military's size, it will be important to invest both in other countries' development (in order to assist them with building governance institutions) and in law enforcement efforts to prosecute terrorists and control U.S. borders (in order to increase the United States' resiliency).

Cybersecurity is another critical priority. Controlling information and communications networks enables the military's missions, both offensive and defensive. As Deputy Secretary of Defense William Lynn wrote [in fall 2010], describing a breach of the U.S. Central Command's systems by an infected flash drive, this challenge is very real. At the same time, the Department of Defense's activities surely include plans to observe, redirect, or even disable its adversaries' communications. Yet although this mission is crucial, the threat to which it responds is not existential, its ambit is focused, and it does not require significant forces—much like the mission to dismantle the al Qaeda network. As the RAND cybersecurity expert Martin Libicki put it . . . "Almost 99.9 percent of that stuff [cyberattacks] is just espionage going back and forth." And when it comes to the country's civilian infrastructure, the private sector, and especially industry, is most responsible for securing its networks, both for its own sake and for that of the public. This is especially true with respect to cyber-espionage because industry is very experienced in defending its trade secrets. In the less frequent instances of outright cyberwar, it falls largely on the civilian institutions of government, such as the Department of Homeland Security, to ensure protection. Preventing and preparing for such attacks will require the Pentagon to concentrate its investment more narrowly—according to the military-specific mission of Cyber Command—and transition much of the cyber-protection currently executed by the National Security Agency to the Department of Homeland Security.

Meanwhile, several threats to which the U.S. military has traditionally devoted considerable resources are now less likely to occur than in the past or would be less consequential if they did. The end of the Cold War brought an unprecedented level of security to the United States. Since then, both nuclear and large-scale conventional combat have become improbable dangers. Spending in these areas should be sufficient to hedge against risk, but they should not drive the budget.

Some people point to China as a successor to the Soviet Union and cite it as a reason why preventing and preparing for nuclear or large-scale conventional war should remain priority missions. They highlight the risk of a

U.S.-Chinese conflict over Taiwan or the possibility that China will deny the U.S. military access to the western Pacific. Of course, China is a rising power that is making increasingly substantial investments in defense. But it is important not to overreact to this fact. Focusing on China's military capabilities ought not replace a broader strategy. As the United States determines how to engage China and how to protect its interests in Asia generally, it must balance the diplomatic, economic, and financial, as well as military, elements of its policy. Most defense analysts estimate that China's military investments and capabilities are decades behind those of the United States, and there is very little evidence that China seeks a conventional conflict with the United States. There is substantial evidence that China's economic and financial policy is a more urgent problem for the United States, but one of the best ways for the United States to respond to that is to get its fiscal house in order.

The prospect of a major war with other states is even less plausible. Defense planning scenarios in the 1990s were built around the possibility of two conflicts. The one involving Iraq is now off the table. A conflict with North Korea was the second, but although that country's military is numerically impressive, South Korea's state-of-the-art armed forces can manage that challenge without needing the assistance of U.S. troops. The United States can now limit its contribution to strategic nuclear deterrence, air support, and offshore naval balancing in the region. The prospect of a conventional war with Iran is not credible. Iran's vast size, to say nothing of the probability that the population would be hostile to any U.S. presence there, means that anything more than U.S. air strikes and Special Forces operations targeting Iranian nuclear capabilities is unlikely.

Given the stakes, some hedging for these exceedingly low-probability risks is reasonable. But even a smaller U.S. force and budget than today's would be ample because many of these risks are less likely than ever and the United States' allies now enjoy unprecedented military and strategic advantages. The most vexing missions are those at the heart of the Quadrennial Defense Review: counterinsurgency, nation building, and the building of other countries' security sectors, among others. And these, alongside competition with China, motivated Gates and other planners at the Pentagon, despite Gates's acknowledgment . . . that "the United States is unlikely to repeat a mission on the scale of those in Afghanistan or Iraq anytime soon—that is, forced regime change followed by nation building under fire." Such planned missions are based on a misguided premise: that the U.S. campaigns in Afghanistan and Iraq foreshadow the need for a large U.S. military force to increasingly intervene in failing states teeming with insurgents and terrorists. But Gates's effort to nonetheless tailor U.S. military capabilities to such tasks suggests that there is still significant support for them in the Pentagon. According to General George Casey, [now former] army chief of staff, for example, the United States is in an "era of persistent conflict." Yet the United States is very unlikely to embark on another regime-change and nation-building mission in the next decade—nor should it. Indeed, in the wake of its operations in Afghanistan and Iraq, the demand for the United States to act as global policeman will decline.

Pakistan is often cited as a state that might require such an intervention. Clearly, it is the case that Gates had in mind when he worried about "a nuclear-armed state [that] could collapse into chaos and criminality." But even if Pakistan collapsed, the U.S. government would probably not send in massive forces for fear of facing widespread popular opposition and an armed resistance in the more remote parts of the country. More likely, the U.S. government would resort to air power and Special Forces in order to secure Pakistan's nuclear arsenal. After the invasions of Afghanistan and Iraq, it is clear that U.S. forces are not suited to lengthy occupations, especially when they involve a stabilization mission, governance reform, and economic development.

TOOTH AND TAIL

Setting priorities will make it possible to reduce the size of the U.S. military while retaining a sufficiently large and superior force for critical missions. Eliminating counterinsurgency, stabilization, and nation building as first-order tasks would allow for cuts in the number of ground forces. In particular, the buildup in ground troops that President George W. Bush announced in his 2007 State of the Union address—an addition of 92,000 soldiers and marines for operations in Afghanistan and Iraq—could be reversed.

Moreover, a revised assessment of the United States' needs in terms of nuclear deterrence and conventional warfare would allow for an additional drawdown of permanently stationed U.S. forces. In Europe, where the chances of a military conflict continue to decrease—and where military planners are consequently reducing and restructuring their forces—the U.S. presence could shrink by 50,000, from approximately 70,000 down to 20,000 troops. Deployments in Asia could be halved, from 60,000 to 30,000, to refocus the United States' presence in the region on its comparative advantage: strategic nuclear deterrence and naval operations. These changes would also rebalance the United States' permanent deployments overseas toward Asia, where war, although still very unlikely, is more possible than in Europe. The United States' air and naval forces in Asia would be largely unaffected, leaving ample capacity to counter any threat from China or North Korea as well as guarantee the United States' access to the Pacific and reassure U.S. allies that it will continue to play an important military role in the region.

U.S. forces could be trimmed even further by reducing the size of the military's "tail," or overhead, relative to its "tooth," or combat forces. According to a report by the consulting firm McKinsey & Company in spring 2010, the U.S. military's tooth-to-tail ratio is more skewed toward the tail than are these ratios for the militaries of nearly all other industrialized countries. In an October 2008 study, the Defense Business Board found that 42 percent of the Pentagon's budget goes to overhead—including training, departmental management, and the general health program for service members and their families. These tasks are the primary duties of roughly 35 percent of the active-duty force, or approximately 500,000 people. A July 2010 study by the Defense Business Board found that 560,000 troops have never been deployed, despite the demand of the operations in Afghanistan and Iraq.

This overhead must be streamlined. Some 100,000 active-duty forces should be cut from the back office across the services. This is a conservative estimate of the number of positions that could be cut through attrition alone over five years. The vacancies created would not need to be filled again by civilians or contractors because if missions were prioritized, the Pentagon's overall personnel needs would shrink. These cuts should come on top of the several thousand positions that will be saved by closing the Joint Forces Command. Together with the reduction of the 92,000 ground troops that were added for the operations in Afghanistan and Iraq and the 80,000 troops to be withdrawn from Europe and Asia, the total cuts would amount to about 275,000 fewer personnel, or a 19 percent reduction in the force's total size. The cuts would take place gradually over a five-year period, starting in FY 2012, and would leave the United States with a total force of 1.21 million and one rebalanced toward combat. With roughly $1.2 billion saved annually for every 10,000 forces cut, and the 275,000 troop reduction implemented over five years, total savings would amount to $166 billion between FY 2012 and FY 2018.

THE RIGHT STUFF

Setting priorities would also help the Pentagon make better investment decisions. Emphasis should be placed on spending that supports priority missions and that is adapted to the specific tasks that U.S. forces are likely to undertake in carrying out those missions. For example, cargo aircraft and sealift capabilities make rapid deployment possible, which can justify having a smaller permanent force overseas. Increased investments in unmanned aerial vehicles for surveillance, missile strikes, and support for ground forces would advance multiple missions, from conventional deterrence to modern special operations, and thereby decrease the need for high-cost fighter jets. Additionally, investments in hardware should be assessed according to whether they create excess capability, are too costly for the capability they deliver, and perform as expected.

With these criteria in mind, five major investment programs currently under way should be cut, curtailed, or delayed. They are excessive both because the mission that justifies them, conventional war, is extremely improbable and because the United States' existing capabilities for waging such a war are already significantly superior to those available to its potential adversaries. Moreover, the production lines for current-generation programs remain open, which means that more equipment could always be acquired later should it become necessary.

The F-35 Lightning II program, which is expected to cost a total of $260 billion starting FY 2012, well exceeds current and foreseeable needs. According to the U.S. Air Force and the U.S. Navy, the military's current fourth-generation fighters—the F-15, the F-16, and the F-18—are superior to Chinese and Russian aircraft, and they are less expensive than the F-35. The V-22 Osprey, a tilt-rotor aircraft designed to fly like a plane and take off and land like a helicopter, offers new and attractive capabilities, but its cost per unit has ballooned well beyond expectations, and its performance in Afghanistan and Iraq has been disappointing. Rather than spend an additional $18 billion on the V-22 starting in FY 2012, as planned, refocusing on more affordable and effective helicopter programs that already exist would be an adequate and more fiscally disciplined alternative. The blimp-carried cruise missile surveillance system known as JLENS, for which $6 billion is slated when production starts in FY 2012, should not be pursued, because the United States is very unlikely to face a cruise missile attack and has numerous other well-performing surveillance options at its disposal. The Medium Extended Air Defense System, due to enter service in FY 2018, is designed to intercept shorter-range missiles. Developed in cooperation with Germany and Italy, the program persists because it symbolizes successful interstate relations. Yet it is redundant with the Patriot system and, by the army's own accounting, does "not address current and emerging threats." That assessment makes the program's total price tag starting FY 2012—$28 billion—completely unaffordable. The Marine Corps' program for the Expeditionary Fighting Vehicle, which is designed for amphibious assault, should also be terminated. Costs per unit have grown by 177 percent since 2000, to $24 million. The vehicle's performance record is questionable, and in any case, no amphibious landing has been executed under combat circumstances in decades. [*The Expeditionary Fighting Vehicle was cancelled in mid-2011.—Ed.*]

Two other investment programs need to be reconsidered. Plans to add forty-two vessels to the existing fleet of next-generation attack submarines—at a cost of $2.76 billion each starting in FY 2012—would provide excess capability. Deferring the purchase of seven of those ships until the mid-2020s would more adequately reflect the exceedingly low likelihood that the United States will need to engage in all-out submarine warfare over the next two decades. Even more extravagant is the program for ballistic missile defense. Projected costs for the program between FY 2012 and FY 2015 are $29 billion, and the program has already cost over $130 billion since it began in the 1980s. Reducing this funding by half would incentivize the Missile Defense Agency to concentrate on more effective and cheaper technologies, which could function as a hedge against any threat of a ballistic missile attack in the near term. Foremost among those technologies is the Aegis system mounted on U.S. Navy destroyers.

Based on figures in the Pentagon's Selected Acquisition Report for the fall of 2009 and other government analyses of recent budgets, canceling the five hardware-purchase programs, deferring the construction of some submarines, and reducing funding for ballistic missile defense research would yield $164 billion in savings between FY 2012 and FY 2018.

Yet discipline in the Department of Defense's investment budgets will need to go deeper; major investment programs such as these account for less than half of the total defense procurement budget each year. The remainder of defense procurement—for example, for transportation and construction equipment; such items as radios, rifles, and night-vision goggles; and some services contracting—is rarely subjected to close scrutiny even though it consumes 60 percent of the procurement budget. The amount of spending on this category of investments closely mirrors the size of the force. Consistent with the proposed 19 percent reduction in the force's size, funding for minor procurement of this kind should be cut by $103 billion between FY 2012 and FY 2018.

The budget for research and development (R&D), which has grown in real terms by 60 percent since 2001, should also be reduced. There is no obviously "right" level of funding for R&D, but with the current overall U.S. military R&D investment exceeding China's entire defense budget for 2009, it would be safe to cut it by 19 percent between FY 2012 and FY 2018. Such a reduction would yield roughly $87 billion in savings while keeping the United States' level of military R&D far above that of any other country. This cut, in addition to the other proposed reductions in total defense investments, would generate savings of $354 billion.

PAID AS YOU GO

The Department of Defense has struggled for years to control its budgets for pay and health-care and retirement benefits as the real cost of these expenses has grown and the population eligible for them has expanded. Congress has exacerbated the problem by continually increasing existing benefits and creating new ones. As Gates himself has pointed out, these expenses are now "eating the Defense Department alive." Yet reining them in has proved to be a political third rail. Congress has already received and rejected proposals for such cuts, but that does not change the fact that the country's important obligation to its military personnel needs to be balanced with fiscal discipline. The newly elected members of Congress in November 2010 campaigned on their resolve to tackle unrealistic entitlements for civilians, and their zeal might extend to equally unrealistic military benefits.

The U.S. military's pay system has become increasingly disconnected from its primary purpose: developing a compensation system that produces the mix of personnel that can get the work done most effectively. By this standard, the key indicator of the adequacy of military pay is whether recruitment and retention targets are being met, particularly for tasks requiring critical skills. The Congressional Budget Office has determined that overall military pay, including cash and in-kind compensation, presently exceeds compensation for comparable work by civilians by at least 11 percent. This is the result of the Pentagon's long-standing tradition of maintaining morale by paying members of equal rank and grade roughly the same, irrespective of the demand for particular skills, as well as of Congress's routine practice of authorizing pay increases above those requested by the Pentagon.

A much more refined pay model is needed, one that replaces across-the-board pay raises with a more tailored approach that would allow supply and demand to generate the right combination of needed specialties and skills. This would involve much greater use of targeted bonuses and special pay for key required specializations or jobs, such as assignments to hazardous stations and language or technological skills. Importantly, current pay increases based on promotions or longevity would not be affected, nor would the special compensation given to combat troops for hazardous duties. Across-the-board pay increases should be suspended as military forces are reduced and reorganized according to the cuts suggested here. This adjustment could take two years or more, at which point the general pay increase question could be revisited. This could save roughly $40 billion between FY 2012 and FY 2018.

Likewise, the Department of Defense's health-care system, TRICARE, badly needs discipline. Defense health-system costs grew from $19 billion in FY 2001 to over $50 billion in FY 2010. The pool of eligible personnel has expanded since Congress created TRICARE in 1995: TRICARE Reserve Select was introduced for reservists and their dependents, and TRICARE for Life was added for Medicare-eligible retirees and their dependents.

There are two types of retirees in the TRICARE system: those who are eligible for Medicare and those who are not, typically because they remain in the work force and have not reached the age of eligibility for Medicare. TRICARE was founded with the expectation that beneficiaries who had not yet reached the age of eligibility for Medicare would pay approximately 27 percent of the overall cost of the program through enrollment fees and co-pays. But the premiums and the cost-sharing system have not changed since then. This has attracted a large number of military retirees still in the work force to TRICARE and away from alternative, civilian health-care plans. Now only 11 percent of the program's costs are covered by beneficiaries not yet eligible for Medicare.

This must be corrected. Retirees who are eligible for Medicare and their dependents should share in the costs of TRICARE. For other retired beneficiaries, the enrollment fees and copays should be increased to 27 percent of costs, as was intended when the program was created. According to figures from the Congressional Budget Office, such changes could save $48 billion between FY 2012 and FY 2018.

Finally, the military's retirement program should be revised. It is an unfair system for those employees who leave the service before twenty years, the term after which they become eligible for the program. And it frustrates Pentagon managers, who could more easily encourage departures to match the military's personnel needs if a retirement option before twenty years of service were available. The system should be revised wholesale, using the civilian Federal Employees Retirement System (FERS) as a model. FERS benefits become vested after five years, the program includes Social Security and a defined benefit plan, and employee contributions are matched by the employer. Eligibility for a full pension should be delayed until the retirement age set by Social Security, but a one-time lump-sum payment to ease the transition to civilian life should be provided to service members whenever they leave the service. Personnel who already have over fifteen years of service at the time of the transition to the new system should be exempt from it. An analysis of similar proposals developed by the Department of Defense suggests that $60 billion could be saved between FY 2012 and FY 2018 from such a reform. Forgoing across-the-board military pay increases for two years, modernizing the TRICARE cost-sharing system for working military retirees, and reforming the military retirement savings plan could generate $148 billion in savings between FY 2012 and FY 2018.

SMART MONEY

Funding for intelligence, 80 percent of which falls under the responsibility of the secretary of defense, should also be reconsidered. In 2004, Congress created the Office of the Director of National Intelligence to provide a stronger central direction for the intelligence community's sixteen other agencies and impose budgetary discipline on them. Intelligence activities, programs, and agencies have expanded rapidly since 2001 and at a significantly increased cost. According to James Clapper, the director of national intelligence, the intelligence budget for FY 2010 exceeded $80 billion. Size may now be the intelligence community's most significant problem.

Duplication in information technology, security procedures, human resource systems, and purchasing could be eliminated and overall management simplified. More savings still could be found by decreasing spending on government satellite imagery, which duplicates commercially available imagery, and by no longer vacuuming up more intelligence signals than are needed or can be processed. Helping the policymakers across the government who consume intelligence better communicate their needs to intelligence providers would also eliminate a sizable amount of unused analysis and the costs of generating it. Analysts with considerable internal management experience in the intelligence community think it reasonable to assume that such initiatives could save U.S. taxpayers $120 billion between FY 2012 and FY 2018.

Defense missions, plans, and budgets have been largely exempt from scrutiny over the last decade. Yet the lessons of the wars in Afghanistan and Iraq, the necessity for internal management discipline at the Pentagon, and the United States' severe fiscal problems all point to the need to make fundamental choices about national security priorities and the funds that support them. These proposals would save $788 billion between FY 2012 and FY 2018 and yet would leave in place a U.S. military fully ready to fulfill the priority missions it should conduct after the wars in Afghanistan and Iraq are concluded. Should the cuts be implemented, the remaining U.S. military force would still be superior to any other in technology and capability. It would be the only force capable of patrolling the world's oceans, deploying hundreds of thousands of ground forces anywhere on the planet, dominating airspace, and managing intelligence and logistics worldwide. These reductions would result not only in a more focused and more efficient U.S. military capability but also in a defense budget that, although still very large, would help solve the United States' fiscal problems.

DISCUSSION QUESTIONS

1. What are the two choices for the United States in military affairs at the moment?
2. How do the authors characterize the growth in the military mission and the defense budget?
3. How do the authors summarize the current threat environment?
4. What are the authors' projections of likely defense spending in the future at the current pace?

5. What do the authors identify as some key factors in considering cuts to the defense budget? How will the nature of military missions be affected by such cuts?
6. What are some changes in military missions that the authors suggest to reduce the military budget?
7. How should the issues of cybersecurity be addressed? To what extent should it be a military responsibility only?
8. To what extent do the authors believe that nuclear and large-scale conventional combat drive the military budget? Why do they adopt that view?
9. To what extent should China be a focal point of America's military spending?
10. Where do the authors suggest reductions in U.S. forces worldwide?
11. What is meant by reducing the military's "tail" relative to its "tooth"?
12. What are some of the major investment programs that "should be cut, curtailed, or delayed"?
13. What are some of the changes recommended in the military pay system and benefit packages?
14. Can American military spending be cut as outlined in this chapter and America's safety be maintained?

15

Why Intelligence and Policymakers Clash*

Robert Jervis

INTELLIGENCE AND POLICYMAKERS

Policymakers say they need and want good intelligence. They do need it, but often they do not like it, and are prone to believe that when intelligence is not out to get them, it is incompetent. Richard Nixon was the most vocal of presidents in wondering how "those clowns out at Langley" could misunderstand so much of the world and cause his administration so much trouble. Unfortunately, not only will even the best intelligence services often be wrong, but even (or especially) when they are right, they are likely to bring disturbing news, and this incurs a cost. As director of central intelligence (DCI) Richard Helms said shortly after he was let go in 1973, he was "the easiest man in Washington to fire. I have no political, military or industrial base." Although DCI James Woolsey's view was colored by his bad relations with President Bill Clinton, he was not far off the mark in saying that the best job description for his position was "not to be liked."

For the general public, intelligence is not popular, for the additional reasons that its two prime characteristics of secrecy and covert action clash, if not with American traditions, then with the American self-image, and even those who applaud the results are likely to be uncomfortable with the means. It is telling that discussions of interventions in others' internal politics, and especially attempts to overthrow their regimes, are couched in terms of Central Intelligence Agency (CIA) interventions despite the fact that the CIA acts under instructions from the president. Critics, even those on the left, shy away from the correct label, which is that it is a U.S.

---

*All footnotes have been deleted.

government intervention. Political leaders see little reason to encourage a better understanding.

A New York clothing store has as its slogan "An educated consumer is our best customer." Intelligence can say this as well, but its wish for an educated consumer is not likely to be granted. Many presidents and cabinet officers come to the job with little knowledge or experience with intelligence and with less time to learn once they are in power. Even presidents like Nixon, who were more informed and who doubted the CIA's abilities, often held unreasonable expectations about what intelligence could produce. Henry Kissinger sometimes knew better, as revealed by what he told his staff about the congressional complaints that the United States had failed to anticipate the coup in Portugal:

> . . . I absolutely resent—anytime there's a coup you start with the assumption that the home government missed it. . . . Why the hell should we know better than the government that's being overthrown. . . . I mean what request is it to make of our intelligence agencies to discover coups all over the world?

Although Kissinger was right, even he sometimes expected more information and better analysis than was likely to be forthcoming and displayed the familiar schizophrenic pattern of both scorning intelligence and being disappointed by it.

DECISION-MAKERS' NEEDS AND HOW INTELLIGENCE CONFLICTS WITH THEM

The different needs and perspectives of decision-makers and intelligence officials guarantee conflict between them. For both political and psychological reasons, political leaders have to oversell their policies, especially in domestic systems in which power is decentralized, and this will produce pressures on and distortions of intelligence. It is, then, not surprising that intelligence officials, especially those at the working level, tend to see political leaders as unscrupulous and careless, if not intellectually deficient, and that leaders see their intelligence services as timid, unreliable, and—often—out to get them.

Although it may be presumptuous for the CIA to have chiseled in its lobby "And ye shall know the truth and the truth will make you free," it can at least claim this as its objective. No decision-maker could do so, as the more honest of them realize. When Secretary of State Dean Acheson said that the goal of a major National Security Council document was to be "clearer than truth," he understood this very well. Some of the resulting tensions came out when Porter Goss became DCI and told the members of the CIA that they should support policymakers. Of course, the job of intelligence is to inform policymakers and in this way to support better policy. But support can also mean providing analysis that reinforces policies and rallies others to the cause. The first kind of support fits with intelligence's preferred mission, the one that decision-makers pay lip service to. But given the political and psychological world in which they live, it is often the latter kind of support that decision-makers seek. They need confidence and political support, and honest intelligence unfortunately often diminishes rather than increases these goods by pointing to ambiguities, uncertainties, and the costs and risks of policies. In many cases, there is a conflict between what intelligence at its best can produce and what decision-makers seek and need.

Because it is axiomatic that a good policy must rest on an accurate assessment of the world, in a democracy policies must be—or at least be seen as being—grounded in intelligence. Ironically, this is true only because intelligence is seen as proficient, a perception that developed in the wake of the technologies in the 1960s, and the pressures on intelligence follow from its supposed strengths. When Secretary of State Colin Powell insisted that DCI George Tenet sit right behind him when he laid out the case against Iraq before the United Nations Security Council, he was following this imperative in a way that was especially dramatic but not different in kind from the norm. It is the very need to claim that intelligence and policy are in close harmony that produces conflict between them.

In principle, it could be different. President George W. Bush could have said something like this: "I think Saddam is a terrible menace. This is a political judgment, and I have been elected to make difficult calls. While I have listened to our intelligence services and other experts, this is my decision, not theirs." In other cases, the president could announce, "The evidence is ambiguous, but on balance I believe that we must act on the likelihood that the more alarming possibilities are true." But speeches that clearly separate themselves from intelligence will seem weak and will be politically unpersuasive, and it is not surprising that leaders want to use intelligence to bolster not only their arguments but also their political standing.

CONFLICTING PRESSURES

For reasons of both psychology and politics, decision-makers want to minimize not only actual value trade-offs but also their own perception of them. Leaders talk about how they make hard decisions all the time, but like the rest of us, they prefer easy ones and will try to convince themselves and others that a particular decision is, in fact, not so hard. Maximizing political support for a policy means arguing that it meets many goals, is supported by many considerations, and has few costs. Decision-makers, then, want to portray the world as one in which their policy is superior to the alternatives in many independent dimensions. For example, when a nuclear test ban was being debated during the Cold War, proponents argued both that atmospheric testing was a major public health hazard and that a test ban was good for American national security and could be verified. It would have undercut the case for the ban if its supporters had said, "We must stop atmospheric testing in order to save innocent lives even though there will be a significant cost in terms of national security."

Psychological as well as political dynamics are at work. To continue with the test ban example, proponents who were deeply concerned about public health did not like to think that they were advocating policies that would harm national security. Conversely, those who felt that inhibiting nuclear development would disadvantage the United States came to also believe that the testing was not a health hazard. They would have been discomfited by the idea that their preferred policy purchased American security at the cost of hundreds of thousands of innocent lives. Decision-makers have to sleep at night, after all.

The run-up to the war in Iraq is an unfortunately apt illustration of these processes. In its most general form, the Bush administration's case for the war was that Saddam Hussein was a great menace and that overthrowing him was a great opportunity for changing the Middle East. Furthermore, each of these two elements had several supporting components. Saddam was a threat because he was very hard to deter, had robust weapons of mass destruction (WMD) programs, and had ties to terrorists, whom he might provide with WMD. The opportunity was multifaceted as well: the war would be waged at low cost, the postwar reconstruction would be easy, and establishing a benign regime in Iraq would have salutary effects in the region by pushing other regimes along the road to democracy and facilitating the resolution of the Arab-Israeli dispute. Portraying the world in this way maximized support for the war. To those who accepted all components, the war seemed obviously the best course of action, which would justify supporting it with great enthusiasm; and people could accept the policy even if they endorsed only a few of the multiple reasons. Seeing the world in this way also eased the psychological burdens on decision-makers, which were surely great in ordering soldiers into combat and embarking on a bold venture. What is crucial in this context is not the validity of any of these beliefs but the convenience in holding them all simultaneously when there was no reason to expect the world to be arranged so neatly. This effect was so strong that Vice President Dick Cheney, who previously had recognized that removing Saddam could throw Iraq into chaos, was able to convince himself that it would not. There was no logic that prohibited the situation from presenting a threat but not an opportunity (or vice versa), or for there to have been threat of one kind—that is, that Saddam was on the verge of getting significant WMD capability—but not of another—for example, that he had no connection to al Qaeda. Logically, Cheney's heightened urgency about overthrowing Saddam should not have changed his view on what would follow. But it did.

The contrast with the intelligence community (IC) was sharp. While it did believe that Saddam had robust WMD programs, because it did not feel the psychological need to bolster the case for war, it did not have to pull other perceptions into line and so gave little support to the administration on points where the evidence was to the contrary. And this is where the friction arose. Intelligence denied any collaboration between Saddam and al Qaeda, and it was very skeptical about the possibility that Saddam would turn over WMD to terrorists. So it is not surprising that here the administration put great pressure on intelligence to come to a different view and that policymakers frequently made statements that were at variance with the assessments. It is also not surprising, although obviously it was not foreordained, that the intelligence here was quite accurate.

Intelligence also painted a gloomy picture of the prospects for postwar Iraq, noting the possibilities for continued resistance and, most of all, the difficulties in inducing the diverse and conflicting groups in the country to cooperate with one another. Because this skepticism did not receive public attention, these estimates were subject to less political pressure, although the fact that the administration not only ignored them but also frequently affirmed the opposite must have been frustrating to the analysts. Fortunately for them, however, on these points, the administration was content to assert its views without claiming that they were supported by intelligence, probably because the judgments were of a broad political nature and did not rely on secret information. Later, when the postwar situation deteriorated and intelligence officials revealed that they had, in fact, provided warnings, the conflict heightened as the administration felt that intelligence was being disloyal and furthering its own political agenda.

It is tempting to see the browbeating and ignoring of intelligence as a particular characteristic of the George W. Bush administration, but it was not. Although available evidence does not allow anything like a full inventory, it does reveal examples from other administrations. Because Bill Clinton and his colleagues were committed to returning Haiti's Jean-Bertrand Aristide to power after he had been ousted in a coup, they resented and resisted intelligence analysis that argued that he was unstable and his governing would not be effective or democratic. Neither the administration of Dwight D. Eisenhower nor that of John F. Kennedy, both of which favored a test-ban agreement, was happy with analyses that indicated that verification would be difficult. Although on many issues liberals are more accepting of value trade-offs than are conservatives and many liberals like to think of themselves as particularly willing to confront complexity, once they are in power, they, too, need to muster political support and live at peace with themselves.

Intelligence does not feel the same pressures. It does not carry the burden of decision but "merely" has to figure out what the world is like. If the resulting choices are difficult, so be it. It also is not the duty of intelligence to build political support for a policy, and so even intelligence officials who do not oppose a policy will—or should—feel no compulsion to portray the world in a helpful way. In many cases, good intelligence will then point out the costs and dangers implicit in a policy. It will make it harder for policy-makers to present a policy as clearly the best one and will nurture second thoughts, doubts, and unease. It is not that intelligence usually points to policies other than those the leaders prefer, but only that it is likely to give decision-makers a more complex and contradictory view than fits with their political and psychological needs. Ironically, it can do this even as it brings good news. One might think that Lyndon Johnson would have welcomed the CIA telling him that other countries would not fall to Communism even if Vietnam did, but since his policy was justified (to others and probably to himself) on the premise that the domino theory was correct, he did not.

RESISTANCE TO FALLBACK POSITIONS
AND SIGNS OF FAILURE

The same factors that lead decision-makers to underestimate trade-offs make them reluctant to develop fallback plans and inclined to resist information that their policy is failing. The latter more than the former causes conflicts with intelligence, although the two are closely linked. There are several reasons why leaders are reluctant to develop fallback plans. It is hard enough to develop one policy, and the burden of thinking through a second is often simply too great. Probably more important, if others learn of the existence of Plan B, they may give less support to Plan A. Even if they do not prefer the former, its existence will be taken as betraying the leaders' lack of faith in their policy. It may also be psychologically difficult for leaders to contemplate failure.

Examples abound. Clinton did not have a Plan B when he started bombing to induce Serbia's Slobodan Milosevic to withdraw his troops from Kosovo. Administration officials thought such a plan was not needed, because it was obvious that Milosevic would give in right away. In part, they believed this because they thought it had been the brief and minor bombing over Bosnia that had brought Milosevic to the table at Dayton, an inference that, even if it had been correct, would not have readily supported the conclusion that he would give up Kosovo without a fight. The result was that the administration had to scramble both militarily and politically and was fortunate to end the confrontation as well as it did. The most obvious and consequential recent case of a lack of Plan B is Iraq. Despite intelligence to the contrary, top administration officials believed that the political and economic reconstruction of Iraq would be easy and that they needed neither short-term plans to maintain order nor long-term preparations to put down an insurgency and create a stable polity. Thinking about a difficult postwar situation would have been psychologically and politically costly, which is why it was not done.

Having a Plan B means little unless decision-makers are willing to shift to it if they must; this implies a need to know whether the policy is working. This, even more than the development of the plan, involves intelligence, and so here the clashes will be greater. Leaders tend to stay with their first choice for as long as possible. Lord Salisbury, the famous British statesman of the end of the nineteenth century, noted that "the commonest error in politics is sticking to the carcasses of dead policies." Leaders are heavily invested in their policies. To change their basic objectives will be to incur very high costs, including, in some cases, losing their offices if not their lives. Indeed the resistance to seeing that a policy is failing is roughly proportional to the costs that are expected if it does. Iraq again provides a clear example. In early 2007, Senator John McCain explained, "It's just so hard for me to contemplate failure that I can't make the next step," and President Bush declared that American policy in Iraq would succeed "because it has to." This perseverance in what appears to be a losing cause may be rational for the leaders, if not for the country, as long as there is any chance of success and the costs of having to adopt a new policy are almost as great as those for continuing to the bitter end. An obvious example is Bush's decision to increase the number of American troops in Iraq in early 2007. The previous policy was not working and would have resulted in a major loss for the United States and for Bush, and even a failed "surge" would have cost him little more than admitting defeat and withdrawing without this renewed effort. Predictions of success or failure were not central to the decision. In most cases, however, predictions are involved, and it is hard for decision-makers to make them without bias.

Intelligence officials do not have such a stake in the established policies, and thus it is easier for them to detect signs that the policies are failing. The fact that the leaders of the Bush administration saw much more progress in Iraq than did the IC is not unusual. . . . The civilian intelligence agencies were quick to doubt that bombing North Vietnam would either cut the supply lines or induce the leadership to give in; they issued pessimistic reports on the pacification campaign and gave higher estimates of the size of the adversary's forces than the military or Johnson wanted to hear.

Leaders are not necessarily being foolish. The world is ambiguous, and indicators of success are likely to be elusive. If it were easy to tell who would win a political or military struggle, it would soon come to an end (or would not start at all), and Vietnam is not unique in permitting a postwar debate

on the virtues of alternative policies. Although it was a pernicious myth
that Germany lost World War I because of a "stab in the back," Germany
could have gained better peace terms if the top military leaders had not lost
their nerve in the late summer of 1918. Furthermore, leaders can be correct
even if their reasoning is not. The classic case is that of Winston Churchill
in the spring of 1940. He prevailed over strong sentiment in his cabinet for
a peace agreement with Germany in the wake of the fall of France by arguing that Britain could win because the German economy was badly over-
stretched and could be broken by a combination of bombing and guerrilla
warfare. This was a complete fantasy; his foreign secretary had reason to
write in his diary that "Winston talked the most frightful rot. It drives one
to despair when he works himself up into a passion of emotion when he
ought to make his brain think and reason." Fortunately, Churchill's emotion and force of character carried the day; intelligence can get no credit. But
regardless of who is right, we should expect conflict between leaders and
intelligence over whether Plan B is necessary.

CONFIDENCE AND PERSEVERANCE

We should perhaps not underestimate the virtues of perseverance, as pig-
headed as it may appear to opponents and to later observers when it fails.
Not a few apparently hopeless cases end well. This may prove to be true
in Iraq, and despite widespread opinion to the contrary, the mujahedeen
in Afghanistan were able to force the Soviets out of the country. Similarly,
two scientists spent over twenty years working on what almost everyone
else believed was a misguided quest to understand the workings of the
hypothalamus, producing no results until they independently made the
breakthroughs that earned them Nobel Prizes. Albert Hirschman points to
the "hiding hand" in many human affairs. If we saw the obstacles in our
path, we would not begin many difficult but ultimately successful endeav-
ors. For example, how many scholars would have started a dissertation had
they known how long and arduous it would be?

Confidence is necessary for perseverance and for embarking on any difficult venture. While it can be costly, it also is functional in many situations,
which helps explain why people are systematically overconfident. Although
it might seem that we would be better off if our confidence better matched
our knowledge, it turns out that the most mentally healthy people are
slightly over optimistic, overestimating their skills and ability to control
their lives. This is probably even more true for decision-makers, who carry
heavy burdens. As Henry Kissinger says, "Historians rarely do justice to
the psychological stress on a policymaker." A national leader who had no
more confidence than an objective reading of the evidence would permit

probably would do little or would be worn down by mental anguish after each decision. Dean Acheson understood this when he told the presidential scholar Richard Neustadt, "I know your theory [that presidents need to hear conflicting views]. You think Presidents should be warned. You're wrong. Presidents should be given confidence."

There is little reason to think that President Bush was being less than honest when he told Bob Woodward, "I know it is hard for you to believe, but I have not doubted what we're doing [in Iraq]." He was aware that a degree of self-manipulation, if not self-deception, was involved: "[A] president has got to be the calcium in the backbone. If I weaken, the whole team weakens. . . . If my confidence level in our ability declines, it will send ripples throughout the whole organization. I mean, it's essential that we be confident and determined and united." During the air campaign phase of the Gulf War, when the CIA estimated that the damage being inflicted was well below what the Air Force reported and what plans said was needed to launch the ground attack, the general in charge, Norman Schwarzkopf, demanded that the CIA get out of his business. His reasoning was not that the CIA was wrong but that these estimates reduced the confidence of the men and women in uniform on which success depended.

Of course, there are occasions on which intelligence can supply confidence. The breaking of German codes in World War II not only gave allied military and civilian leaders an enormous amount of information that enabled them to carry out successful military operations but also provided a general confidence that they could prevail. At the height of the Cuban Missile Crisis in 1962, Kennedy was given confidence by the report from his leading Soviet expert that Nikita Khrushchev would be willing to remove the missiles the Soviets had installed in Cuba without an American promise of a parallel withdrawal from Turkey. In most cases, however, intelligence is likely to provide a complicated, nuanced, and ambiguous picture.

When they are not prepared to change, leaders are prone both to reject the information and to scorn the messenger, claiming that intelligence is unhelpful (which in a real sense it is), superficial (which is sometimes the case), and disloyal (which is rare). Intelligence may lose its access or, if the case is important, much of its role. Thus, in the 1930s, when a unit in the Japanese military intelligence showed that the China campaign, far from leading to control over needed raw materials, was draining the Japanese economy, the army reorganized and marginalized it. Something similar was attempted in Vietnam by the U.S. military, which responded to the pessimistic reporting from the Department of State's Bureau of Intelligence and Research (INR) by having Secretary of Defense Robert McNamara insist that INR should not be permitted to analyze what was happening on the battlefield.

It might be comforting to believe that only rigid individuals or organizations act in this way, but what is at work is less the characteristics of the organization and the personalities of the leaders than the desire to continue the policy, the need for continuing political support, and the psychological pain of confronting failure. When the research arm of the U.S. Forest Service turned up solid evidence that the best way to manage forests was to permit if not facilitate controlled fires, the unit was abolished, because the founding mission and, indeed, identity of the service was to prevent forest fires.

TOO EARLY OR TOO LATE

For intelligence to be welcomed and to have an impact, it must arrive at the right time, which is after the leaders have become seized with the problem but before they have made up their minds. This is a narrow window. One might think that early warning would be especially useful because there is time to influence events. But in many cases, decision-makers will have an established policy, one that will be costly to change, and early warnings can rarely be definitive.

Intelligence about most of the world is irrelevant to leaders because they are too busy to pay attention to any but the most pressing concerns. Intelligence on matters that are not in this category may be useful for building the knowledge of the government and informing lower-level officials but will not receive a hearing at the top. This was the case with intelligence on domestic politics in Iran before the fall of 1978, when it became clear that the troubles facing the Shah were serious. Intelligence was badly flawed here, rarely going beyond inadequate reports from the field or assessing the situation in any depth. But even better analysis would not have gained much attention, because the president and his top assistants were preoccupied with other problems and projects, most obviously the attempt to bring peace to the Middle East that culminated in President Jimmy Carter's meeting with President Anwar Sadat and Prime Minister Meacham Begin at Camp David. As one CIA official said to me, "We could not give away intelligence on Iran before the crisis." Almost as soon as the crisis hit, however, it was too late. Top officials quickly established their own preferences and views of the situation. This is not unusual. On issues that are central, decision-makers and their assistants are prone to become their own intelligence analysts.

Perhaps intelligence can have the most influence if it operates on questions that are important but not immediately pressing. In the run-up to the war in Iraq, there was nothing that intelligence could have reasonably told President Bush that would have affected the basic decisions. But things might have been different if intelligence in the mid-1990s had been able to see that Saddam had postponed if not abandoned his ambitions for WMD. Had this been the standard view when Bush came to power, he and his colleagues might have accepted it because they were not then far down the road to war.

As a policy develops momentum, information and analyses that would have mattered if received earlier now will be ignored. This can be seen quite clearly in military operations, because it is relatively easy to mark the stages of the deliberation. At the start, the focus is on whether the operation can succeed, which means paying careful attention to the status of the adversary's forces and the possibilities of gaining surprise. But as things move ahead, new information is likely to be used for tactical purposes rather than for calling the operation into question. The greater the effort required to mount it and the greater the difficulty in securing agreement to proceed, the greater the resistance will be to new information that indicates it is not likely to succeed.

A clear example is Operation Market Garden in the fall of 1944. After the leading British general, Bernard Montgomery, was rebuffed by Eisenhower in his arguments for concentrating all Allied forces behind his thrust toward Berlin, political as well as military reasons led Eisenhower to agree to a bold but more limited attack deep into German-held territory, culminating at Arnhem. The need for allied unity and for conciliating Montgomery, combined with the fact that Eisenhower had been urging him to be more aggressive, meant that "once he was committed, retreat for Ike was all but impossible." Shortly before the attack was to be launched, code breaking revealed that the Germans had more and better-trained forces in the area than the allies had anticipated. Had they known this earlier, the operation would not have been approved. But once the basic decision was made, the political and psychological costs of reversing it were so high that the intelligence was disregarded, to the great cost of the soldiers parachuted onto the final bridge. The refusal or inability of a leading British general to heed the intelligence indicating that the British move into Greece in 1941 would almost surely fail can be similarly explained, as can the fact that pessimistic CIA assessments about the planned American invasion of Cambodia in 1971 were not forwarded to the president when DCI Helms realized that Nixon and Kissinger had made up their minds and would only be infuriated by the reports, which turned out to be accurate.

IMPORTANCE OF COGNITIVE PREDISPOSITIONS

Intelligence often has its own strongly held beliefs, which can operate at multiple levels of abstraction, from general theories of politics and human nature to images of adversaries to ideas about specific situations. These need not be uniform, and the IC, like the policymaking community, often is divided and usually along the same lines. During the Cold War, some factions were much more worried about the USSR than were others, and the China analysts were deeply divided in their views about the role of Mao Zedong and about how internal Chinese politics functioned. In these cases, analysts, like policymakers, were slow to change their views and saw most new information as confirming what they expected to see. This is true on the level of tactical intelligence as well. A striking case was the accidental shooting down of an Iranian airliner by the USS *Vincennes* toward the end of the Iran-Iraq War. One of the key errors was that the radar operator mis-read his screen as indicating that the airplane was descending toward the ship. What is relevant here is that the *Vincennes*'s captain had trained his crew very aggressively, leading them to expect an attack and giving them a mindset that was conducive to reading—and misreading—evidence as indicating that one was under way. A destroyer that was in the vicinity had not been drilled in this way, and its operator read the radar track correctly.

Differing predispositions provide another reason why decision-makers so often reject intelligence. The answers to many of their most important questions are linked to their beliefs about world politics, the images of those they are dealing with, and their general ideas, if not ideologies. Bush's view of Saddam rested in large measure on his beliefs about how tyrants behave, for example. If intelligence had explained that Saddam was not a major threat, being unlikely to aid terrorists or to try to dominate the region, this probably would not have been persuasive to Bush, and not just because he was particularly closed-minded. This kind of intelligence would have been derived not only from detailed analysis of how Saddam had behaved but from broad understandings of politics and even of human nature. Here, it is both to be expected and legitimate for decision-makers to act on their views rather than those propounded by intelligence. It is often rightly said that "policymakers are entitled to their own policies, but not to their own facts." Facts do not speak for themselves, however, and crucial political judgments grow out of a stratum that lies between if not beneath policies and facts.

Although it was not appropriate for a member of the National Security Council staff to ask whether the Baghdad station chief who produced a gloomy prognosis in November 2003 was a Democrat or Republican, it would not have been illegitimate to have inquired as to the person's general political outlook, his predisposition toward optimism or pessimism, his general views about how insurgencies could be put down, and his beliefs about how difficult it would be to bring stability to a conflicted society. Not only is it comforting for decision-makers to listen to those who share their general values and outlook, but it also makes real sense for them to do so. They are right to be skeptical of the analysis produced by those who see the world quite differently, because however objective the analysts are trying to be, their interpretations will inevitably be influenced by their general beliefs and theories.

It is, then, not surprising that people are rarely convinced in arguments about central issues. The debate about the nature of Soviet intentions went on throughout the Cold War, with few people being converted and fewer being swayed by intelligence or competing analysis. Without going so far as to say that everyone is born either a little hawk or a little dove, to paraphrase Gilbert and Sullivan, on the broadest issues of the nature and intentions of other countries and the existence and characteristics of broad historical trends, people's beliefs are determined more by their general worldviews, predispositions, and ideologies than they are by the sort of specific evidence that can be pieced together by intelligence. The reason why DCI John McCone expected the Soviets to put missiles into Cuba and his analysts did not was not that they examined different evidence or that he was more careful than they were, but that he strongly believed that the details of the nuclear balance influenced world politics and that Khrushchev would therefore be strongly motivated to improve his position. Similarly, as early as February 1933, Robert Vansittart, the United Kingdom's permanent undersecretary in the Foreign Office, who was to become a leading opponent of appeasement, said that the Germans were "likely to rely for their military power . . . on the mechanical weapons of the future, such as tanks, big guns, and above all military aircraft." Eighteen months later, when criticizing the military for being slow to appreciate the rise of Nazi power, he said, "Prophecy is largely a matter of insight. I do not think the Service Departments have enough. On the other hand they might say that I have too much. The answer is that I know the Germans better." Although contemporary decision-makers might not refer to intuition, they are likely to have deeply ingrained beliefs about the way the world works and what a number of countries are like, and in this sense, they will be prone to be their own intelligence analysts.

The discrepancy between the broad cognitive predispositions of the IC and those of political leaders explains why conflict has tended to be higher when Republicans are in power. With some reason, they see intelligence analysts as predominantly liberals. Their suspicions that intelligence has sought to thwart and embarrass the administration are usually false, but to the extent that the worldviews of most intelligence officers are different from those of the Republicans, the latter are justified in being skeptical of IC analysis on broad issues. For their part, intelligence analysts, like everyone else, underestimate the degree to which their own interpretations of specific bits of evidence are colored by their general predispositions and so consider the leaders' rejection of their views closed-minded and ideological. Although not all people are equally driven by their theories about the world, there is a degree of legitimacy to the leaders' position that members of the IC often fail to grasp. President Ronald Reagan and his colleagues, including DCI Bill Casey, probably were right to believe that the IC's assessments that the Soviet Union was not supporting terrorism and was not vulnerable to economic pressures were more a product of the IC's liberal leanings than of the evidence. They therefore felt justified in ignoring the IC when they did not put pressure on it, which in turn led to charges of politicization, a topic to which I will now turn.

Politicization of intelligence can take many forms, from the most blatant, in which intelligence is explicitly told what conclusions it should reach, to the less obvious, including demoting people who produce the "wrong" answer, putting in place personnel whose views are consistent with those of the top leaders, reducing the resources going to units whose analyses are troubling, and the operation of unconscious bias by analysts who fear that their careers will be damaged by producing undesired reports. Even more elusive may be what one analyst has called "politicization by omission": issues that are not evaluated because the results might displease superiors. Also subtle are the interactions between pressures and degrees of certainty in estimates. I suspect that one reason for the excess certainty in the Iraq WMD assessments was the knowledge of what the decision-makers wanted. Conversely, analysts are most likely to politically conform when they are uncertain about their own judgments, as will often be the case on difficult and contentious questions.

Only rarely does one find a case like the one in which President Johnson told DCI Helms, "Dick, I need a paper on Vietnam, and I'll tell you what I want included in it." Almost as blatant was Kissinger's response when CIA experts told Congress that intelligence did not believe that the new Soviet missile with multiple warheads could menace the American retaliatory force, contrary to what policymakers had said. He ordered the reports to be revised, and when they still did not conform, told Helms to remove the offending paragraph on the grounds that it was not "hard" intelligence but merely speculation on Soviet intentions, a subject on which intelligence lacked special qualifications.

Even this case points to the ambiguities in the notion of politicization and the difficulties in drawing a line between what political leaders should and should not do when they disagree with estimates. Intelligence said that "we consider it highly unlikely [that the Soviets] will attempt within the period of this estimate to achieve a first-strike capability." This prediction was reasonable—and turned out to be correct—but it rested in part on judgments of the Soviet system and the objectives of the Soviet leaders, and these are the kinds of questions that the top political leadership is entitled to answer for itself. On the other hand, to demand that intelligence keep silent on adversary intentions would be bizarre, and indeed, when the hard-liners forced an outside estimate at the end of the Gerald Ford administration, the group of selected hawks who formed "Team B" strongly criticized the IC for concentrating on capabilities and ignoring intentions.

So it is not surprising that arguments about whether politicization oc-curred are rarely easy to settle. In some cases, the only people with firsthand knowledge will have major stakes in the dispute, and in others, even a vid-eotape of the meeting might not tell us what happened. Was the office chief bemoaning the fact that an estimate would cause him grief with policymak-ers, or was he suggesting that it be changed? Was the DCI's assistant just doing his job when he strongly criticized a draft paper, arguing that the evi-dence was thin, alternatives were not considered, and the conclusion went beyond the evidence, or was he exerting pressure to get a different answer? When people in the vice president's office and the office of the secretary of defense told the IC analysts to look again—and again—at the evidence for links between Saddam and al Qaeda and repeatedly pressed them on why they were discounting sources that reported such links, were they just doing due diligence? Are analysts being oversensitive, or are leaders and managers being overassertive? Winks and nods, praise and blame, promotions and their absence are subject to multiple causes and multiple interpretations. In many of these cases, I suspect that one's judgment will depend on which side of the substantive debate one is on, because commentators, as well as the participants, will bring with them their own biases and reasons to see or reject claims of pressure.

Ironically, while many of the critics of the IC's performance on Iraqi WMD highlighted the dangers of politicization, some of the proposed reforms (ones that appear after every failure) show how hard it is to distinguish a good intelligence process from one that is driven by illegitimate political concerns. It is conventional wisdom that good analysis questions its own assumptions, looks for alternative explanations, examines low-probability interpretations as well as ones that seem more likely to be correct, scrutinizes sources with great care, and avoids excessive conformity. The problem in this context is that analysts faced with the probing questions that these pre-scriptions imply may believe that they are being pressured into producing a different answer. The obvious reply is that consumers and managers must apply these techniques to all important cases, not just when they object to the initial answers. There is something to this, and it would make sense to look back at previous cases in which politicization has been charged and see whether only those estimates that produced the "wrong" answers were sent back for further scrutiny.

But even this test is not infallible. If I am correct that political leaders and top intelligence managers are entitled to their own broad political views, then they are right to scrutinize especially carefully what they think are incorrect judgments. Thus, the political leaders insisted that the IC con-tinually reassess its conclusion that there were no significant links between Saddam and al Qaeda not only because they wanted a different answer but also because their feeling for how the world worked led them to expect such a connection, and they thought that the IC's assessment to the contrary was based less on the detailed evidence than on the misguided political sensibility that was dominant in the IC. It is not entirely wrong for policymakers to require a higher level of proof from intelligence when the evidence cuts against their desired policy. This means that the greater probing of the grounds for judgments and the possible alternatives that are the objectives of good intelligence procedures may increase the likelihood both of politicization and of analysts' incorrectly levying such a charge.

CONCLUSION

Decision-makers need information and analysis, and intelligence gets its significance and mission from influencing those who will make policy. But this does not mean that relations between the two groups will be smooth. The grievances of the IC are several but less consequential because it has much less power than the intelligence consumers. Members of the IC often feel that policymakers shun complicated analysis, cannot cope with uncertainty, will not read beyond the first page, forget what they have been told, and are quick to blame intelligence when policy fails. In response, members of the IC grumble a great deal among themselves and, when sufficiently provoked, leak their versions to the media.

For their part, policymakers not only overestimate the subversive activities of intelligence, but also frequently find it less than helpful. This is true in two senses. First, they find that only on a few occasions can intelligence light a clear path. The evidence that can be gathered by other than supernatural methods is limited and ambiguous, and in many significant cases, other states may not even know what they will do until the last minute. Even when intentions are long-standing, they and the associated capabilities often can be disguised, and the knowledge that deception is possible further degrades the available information. Even without this problem, it is difficult for intelligence officials to see the world as others see it and to penetrate minds that think quite differently than they do. This is especially true when the other side has beliefs and plans that, even when they become known later, make very little sense.

Leaders find intelligence less than completely helpful in another sense as well. Leaders want to understand the world in which they are operating, but above all, need to act and sustain themselves psychologically and politically. These requirements often conflict with the sort of analysis that intelligence is likely to provide. Leaders need confidence and political support, and all too often, intelligence undermines both. In many cases, intelligence will increase rather than reduce uncertainty as it notes ambiguities and alternative possibilities. Even worse, intelligence can report that the policy to which the leader is committed is likely to entail high costs with dubious prospects for success. Occasionally intelligence can point to opportunities that the country can seize or to signs that the difficulties confronting a policy are only temporary. But more often, it will indicate that the preferred path is not smooth, and may be a dead end.

No leader can have risen to the top without having frequently taken risks that others would shun and found success where others expected failure. Experience will have taught them to place faith in their own judgments. But they will still seek sources of reassurance. Psychologically, they will not want to face the full costs and risks of their policies lest they become fearful, inconsistent, and hesitant. The political problems are even greater, as they need to rally others at home and abroad. The exposure of the gaps in the information, the ambiguities in its interpretation, and the multiple problems the policy is likely to confront will not be politically helpful.

The frictions between particular American presidents and the IC are often attributed to special circumstances or the personality quirks of the former and the intellectual failures of the latter. These all do abound, but the problem goes much deeper. The needs and missions of leaders and intelligence officials are very different, and the two groups are doomed both to work together and to come into conflict.

DISCUSSION QUESTIONS

1. What are some of the attitudes that policymakers have toward intelligence and those that produce it?
2. What are two differing kinds of support that intelligence can provide policymakers?
3. How does the Iraq War illustrate the conflicting pressures on policymakers and the intelligence community?
4. Why does intelligence give policymakers "a more complex and contradictory view" than policymakers may like?
5. Why are policymakers reluctant to develop a Plan B in various situations? Why do they stick with Plan A for so long?
6. How do confidence and perseverance explain policymakers' commitment to policy? How does intelligence help or hinder such confidence?
7. When must intelligence arrive for policymakers to have an impact on policy?
8. What are some factors that make policymakers resistant to new information?
9. What does Jervis mean by the "cognitive predispositions" of intelligence analysts and policymakers?

10. To what extent does Jervis argue that policymakers are more con-
    vinced by their general world view than by intelligence assessments
    that they receive?
11. What are the different ways in which politicization of intelligence
    can occur?
12. Ultimately, why are policymakers and the intelligence community
    likely to come into conflict?

16

Intermestic Politics and Homeland Security

Philip A. Russo and Patrick J. Haney

The purpose of this chapter is to examine the increasingly "intermestic" nature of U.S. foreign policy, using homeland security policy—and some of the dynamics and trade-offs associated with it—for illustration. We pursue this discussion in two key ways. First, after introducing the "intermestic" concept, we examine some interesting trade-offs that exist between what are sometimes competing policy priorities: defending the homeland and implementing the long-standing embargo of Cuba. We use this as an example of the range of issues at the national level that include significant elements of "domestic" and "foreign" policy at the same time, and that also may come into conflict. Second, we draw attention to the way that homeland security policy has introduced a new range of actors to the foreign policy domain, actors that we would traditionally consider "domestic" actors at the sub-national level. In the "all hazards" approach to securing the homeland, local and state officials are often now also important "foreign policy" actors. The pursuit of homeland security—which exists right at the nexus between domestic politics and international security—has fully incorporated and is built upon our system of federalism, with important implications.

INTERMESTIC POLITICS

Bayless Manning, who was the first president of the venerable Council on Foreign Relations as well as a former dean of Stanford Law School, introduced the term "intermestic politics" thirty-five years ago in the pages of *Foreign Affairs* magazine (Manning 1977). This is the same place where three decades earlier a U.S. diplomat in the Soviet Union, George F. Kennan—writing under the pseudonym "Mr. X"—published "The Sources of Soviet Conduct" and introduced to broad public view the policy of "containment" that would so dominate the Cold War. *Foreign Affairs* is, as the name suggests, a magazine focused on "foreign policy" issues, not matters of domestic politics. Manning, however, argued that the lines between policies that had previously been categorized as exclusively either international or domestic in nature were becoming increasingly blurry. An increasing number of policies, he suggested, were both foreign and domestic in nature; they were, in short, "intermestic."

Manning noted that other issues, like tariffs, had in the American past "visibly intermingled" foreign affairs and domestic politics, but that such issues were the exception not the rule. "But the exception has now become preponderant. The issues of the new international agenda strike instantly into the economic and political interests of domestic constituencies" (Manning 1977, 309). Manning argued that economic interdependence was one factor driving this trend; he also argued that the agenda of modern diplomacy included many issues that are enmeshed with domestic interests. "These new issues are thus simultaneously, profoundly and inseparably both domestic and international. If I may be permitted a coinage whose very cacophony may help provide emphasis—these issues are "intermestic" (Manning 1977, 309). Most would argue that these dynamics are even more pervasive today than they were in the 1970s, when the energy crisis in particular brought these intermestic issues into focus. Especially in the post–Cold War world, foreign policymaking has been subjected to the kind of "political gaming and strategizing long dominant in domestic politics" (Nacos, Shapiro, and Isernia 2000, 14).

Modifying Manning's formulation somewhat, Brenner, Haney, and Vanderbush argue that rather than thinking of the issues themselves as intermestic, it might be more useful to think of the factors shaping a policy as themselves intermestic; for example, "U.S. presidents act simultaneously as domestic political actors and as international figures" (Brenner, Haney, and Vanderbush 2008, 78; see also Barilleaux 1985). It is the same with other actors that try to steer the ship of state: they increasingly are simultaneously foreign and domestic policy actors, coping with issues that have both foreign and domestic policy content. The ability of the president and a small group of elite advisers to control the foreign policy process is a thing of the past. As James Lindsay and Randall Ripley note, the "central players of the past no longer exclusively determine the agenda" (Lindsay and Ripley 1997, 36).

Just as an increasing number of issues have both a foreign and domestic policy content, so, too, are actors both domestic and international at the same time. The domestic competition for control over policy in the "foreign" policy space is increasing. Furthermore, as the case of homeland security policy highlights, there are now a host of new actors at the state and even local level vying for agenda control and who have been thrust into the limelight by the emergence of the homeland security policy space. Below we try to illustrate these developments by showing the intermestic nature of homeland security policy at the national level and also in terms of the intergovernmental relations upon which homeland security now rests.

A VIEW FROM ABOVE: POLICY TRADE-OFFS, POLITICS, AND SECURING THE HOMELAND

One way to think about the intermestic nature of homeland security policy is to consider the interesting tensions that have emerged in recent years between the steps taken to secure the homeland and the requirements of another top national foreign and policy priority: the embargo of Cuba. At first glance it might appear that these two policy goals are mostly in harmony: steps taken to keep terrorists out of the country should also be helpful in keeping Cuban cigars out of the country; and efforts to enforce some of the financial elements of the embargo should complement efforts to track down the sources of terrorist financing, for example. It turns out that in practice things are more complicated—and political—than that. Here we use the Cuban embargo as just one example of the intermestic nature of homeland security policy, an example that illustrates the policy trade-offs, competing interests, and broad range of actors involved in this policy space that exist at the national level—a "view from above."

First, some definitional issues. The Cuban embargo has been around in one form or another since the Eisenhower administration. It includes several elements, many of which have been altered over time in order to make the embargo more or less strict. Key elements of the embargo include a prohibition on imports from Cuba (including a total ban on American access to Cuban cigars, even when in a third country, such as Canada); severe restrictions on exports to Cuba, with some limited sales of food and medicine allowed under certain circumstances; a ban on Americans traveling to Cuba except under specific circumstances (so called licenses for journalists or academic research, for example); a policy for deciding whether Cubans fleeing the island can gain entry to the United States (the so-called wet foot/ dry foot policy); the lack of normal diplomatic relations between the two countries; and restrictions on Cuban Americans' ability to travel to visit family on the island and to send aid, or "remittances," to their families. Most of the embargo existed in several executive orders until the 1990s, when Congress passed several laws that codified much of the embargo as a matter of law rather than just a presidential order (which could easily be changed).

On the front lines of enforcement of the Cuban embargo are a host of separate agencies, including Customs and Border Protection (CBP) and the Coast Guard (which now reside inside the Department of Homeland Security), the Office of Foreign Assets Control (which is part of the Treasury Department), and elements of the Justice and Commerce departments. These same agencies contribute significantly to the homeland security mission as well. The Cuban embargo is a nice example to use here for two related reasons. First, the embargo mission existed before the emergence of "homeland security" as an operational and organizational construct, and when these agencies of the federal government were tasked with the homeland security mission, that mission was a net addition to their work. There was no subtraction, just addition. While there has been some increase in resources to homeland security, with the exception of the federalization of airport screeners and the birth of the Transportation Security Administration (TSA), most of the new resources were pushed down to the state and local level for "first responders," an issue to which we turn in the next section. These agencies mostly just had more on their plates after 9/11. These competing priorities, as we explore below, have perhaps had a negative impact on both missions.

The second reason it is an interesting example is that it illustrates the way "domestic" politics can drive priority setting. With the exception of a small group of Americans who might prioritize the embargo over the homeland security mission, most would assign a higher importance to defending the homeland (and it would also seem, from the outside, that these two missions would actually fit nicely together). However, it turns out that enforcement of the embargo may actually be "crowding out" the homeland security mission in important ways (Haney and Russo 2009).

In 2004 a report emerged from the Treasury Department indicating that far more Office of Foreign Assets Control (OFAC) agents had been tasked with tracking violations of the Cuban embargo than were focused on tracking al Qaeda's money. Through 2003, only four agents were apparently on the al Qaeda case, while twenty-one stalked the embargo (Solomon 2004). Bipartisan furor followed. Senator Charles Grassley (R-IA) commented, "OFAC obviously needs to enforce the law with regard to U.S. policy on Cuba, but the United States is at war against terrorism, and al-Qaida is the biggest threat to our national security. . . . Cutting off the blood money that has financed Saddam Hussein and Osama bin Laden must be a priority when it comes to resources" (quoted in Solomon 2004). Senators Max Baucus (D-MT) and Mike Enzi (R-WY) argued in strident terms in a newspaper editorial (2004), "Rather than fussing over a few cigars and wasting precious resources to enforce an outdated and ineffective embargo and travel ban against Cuba, let us direct our attention instead to cutting off the flow of money to terrorists who would attack our troops or sneak a bomb onto an airplane. The security of this nation depends on it."

Even after this burst of publicity, little appeared to have changed by 2007 when the Government Accountability Office (GAO) issued a report finding that significant competition among priorities continued to exist for the agencies on the frontlines of the homeland security mission.

The GAO focused on the Departments of the Treasury, Justice, Homeland Security, and Commerce, and examined the efforts of these four key federal agencies that are at the intersection of both our homeland security mission and enforcement of the Cuban embargo. The GAO concluded that the embargo's enforcement efforts indeed come with serious (if unintended) consequences. Increased efforts by Homeland Security and Treasury have placed a heavy strain on the government's inspection resources, with the bulk of the agencies' investigation activities focusing on "targeted minor violations" (GAO 2007).

Focusing on workload and performance data from 2000 to 2006, GAO analysts found that, of the more than seventeen thousand total OFAC investigations into suspected violations of all U.S. sanctions programs, 61 percent were specifically focused on infractions of the Cuban embargo. Perhaps even more troubling, the GAO found that, on average, U.S. CBP agents engage in "intensive" passenger inspections for approximately 20 percent of all travelers arriving at the Miami International Airport from Cuba. At the same time, CBP inspects no more than 3 percent of all passengers arriving from all other international points of departure. Miami International—admittedly a centerpiece for daily tensions between enforcing the embargo and searching for terrorists—was not the only place where the study discovered problems; indeed, the GAO "found weaknesses in CBP's inspections capacity at key U.S. ports of entry nationwide" (GAO 2007).

Airports are just one of several key platforms that are a focus of homeland security, though the one that is most visible given the nature of the 9/11 attacks. Getting that job right on its own is an extremely difficult task. A 2009 study showed that TSA screeners on average fail to detect weapons on passengers about 50 percent of the time, with some airports showing failure scores as high as 80 percent (Zeller 2009). In addition, there have been high-profile stories of spectacular failure, such as the recent case of dozens of screeners who were fired from the Honolulu airport for regularly not screening bags for explosives before loading them on airplanes (CNN 2011).

The mission is made more complicated when the daily job for those who are tasked with securing our airports has multiple components. Terrorism is not the only threat at airports; indeed, while it may be the most high-impact event, it is also perhaps the lowest probability event, meaning other missions compete with the terrorist mission. TSA's new "behavioral assessment" program, which is designed to spot terrorists at airports by evaluating the behaviors of travelers, has come under fire by whistleblowers who claim that the members of the behavioral detection unit in Hawaii targets Mexicans who may be in the country illegally, rather than focusing on potential terrorists (Kelleher 2011), although an investigation later cleared the TSA (Kelleher 2012). It is also worth remembering that airports are not the only portals through which a terrorist may try to enter the country or through which to send a bomb. In the high-profile effort to secure airports, however, other portals have received relatively less attention—perhaps making them more attractive to terrorists—such as our seaports. Indeed, recent congressional testimony shows that while there has been a $4 billion investment in technologies to detect nuclear smuggling at U.S. ports since 2005, the system is not particularly robust and also suffers from bureaucratic struggles among multiple federal actors, including CBP (Aloise and Caldwell 2010).

A final point is worth noting as well. The cost of the technological investments that have been made at air and sea ports since 2001 is very high, and there are multiple companies competing for lucrative contracts to develop and deploy these technologies, whether they are explosive- or radiation-detecting units, bomb screeners, or other biometric devices. As a result, the money spent by these companies on their lobbying operation in Washington, DC, has expanded tremendously in recent years (Schouten 2010). Adding all of these factors up, one must come to appreciate the inherently political nature of implementing homeland security policy, and the intermestic nature of that politics.

A VIEW FROM BELOW:
THE NEW GROUP OF FOREIGN POLICY ACTORS

The previous section discussed how thinking of homeland security policy as being driven in part by intermestic politics is visible among competing national priorities, carried out by actors at the federal level of government who are simultaneously domestic and foreign policy actors. Here we shift attention to the nature of American federalism upon which our homeland security system has been built. If the previous section takes the "national" perspective, this seeks to look up from below on the intermestic politics of homeland security policy so as to see the broad range of local officials who are now, by definition, also actors in security policy.

Since the end of the Cold War and at an accelerating pace since 9/11, thousands of state and local officials have been positioned within the intermestic policy space of Homeland Security at least in part because, as former

Speaker of the United States House of Representatives Thomas P. "Tip" O'Neill (D-MA) famously said, "all politics is local." Speaker O'Neill thus stated succinctly a fundamental characteristic of the dynamics of America's representative democracy: national policy goals may, in part, be understood as an aggregation of the plethora of needs, wants, and values of citizens that are attended to and transmitted by their elected "representatives" in the federal government. This "view from below" recognizes and underscores the interdependence of "local" and "national" considerations that policymakers incorporate into their domestic and foreign policy preferences.

Recognizing that *all politics is local*, homeland security policy also means it is important to understand also that *all security is local* because at the end of the day, all terrorism is local and all disasters are local. Soon after the 9/11 attacks, President George W. Bush created the Office of Homeland Security inside the Executive Office of the President, and appointed Pennsylvania Governor Tom Ridge as his homeland security advisor. In his cover letter to a report issued by the White House in July 2002, Ridge declared,

> All disasters are ultimately state and local events. A key objective of the National Strategy for Homeland Security is to develop a framework that ensures vertical coordination between local, state, and federal authorities so that our actions are mutually supportive and communities receive the assistance they need to develop and execute comprehensive counter-terrorism plans. (Ridge 2002)

In November of 2002 Congress passed the Homeland Security Act, which created the cabinet-level Department of Homeland Security (DHS) with Ridge as the first secretary of homeland security (see Hastedt 2005). In designing the new department, Congress did two things: First, it repackaged and recombined almost two dozen discrete agencies under one cabinet level structure. Added to the new Transportation Security Administration (TSA) were diverse agencies such as the Federal Emergency Management Agency (FEMA), Immigration and Customs Enforcement (ICE), Customs and Border Protection (CBP), the Secret Service, and the U.S. Coast Guard. This new department had to *coordinate* a wide range of technological and service delivery cultures.

Second, Congress mandated that DHS embrace the "all-hazards" model for homeland security. This framework defines homeland security in terms of both terrorist activities (e.g., the 9/11 attacks) and natural disasters (e.g., Hurricane Katrina). "In general, the all-hazards approach involves developing comprehensive capabilities for responding to a range of disasters, including natural disasters and terrorist attacks, rather than developing separate and distinct capabilities to respond to one type of disaster" (Canada 2003, 8). The all-hazards approach satisfied the predisposition of congressional actors to be *inclusionary* of security issues that were "national" (immigration and border protection) but at the same time decidedly "local" (public health and safety—police, fire, medical emergency services, and critical infrastructure and emergency management). Thus, with the policy space of homeland security structured as the problem of coordination of federal efforts *and* inclusion of local interests, some have argued that we created a "diffuse policy arena" that is characterized by a diverse community of *national and local* interests at the crossroads of domestic and international, or intermestic politics (see Eisinger 2006; Koski and May 2011).

Since all security is local because all terrorism is local, the intermestic politics of homeland security give rise to the participation of a wide (and practically dizzying) range of federal, state, and local actors and interests. Consequently, the intergovernmental (vertical and horizontal) dynamics of the all-hazards policy may range from a process characterized as "top-down" or "bottom-up" to even simply one marked by "confusion" (Schneider 1990). More recently, the dynamics of the intergovernmental "partnership" in homeland security have been described as "strained" due to the defects of "imperfect federalism" (Eisinger 2006). Other observers are more hopeful about this approach, suggesting a "network model" of the intergovernmental system of homeland security is needed because too frequently "homeland security discussions are dominated by dichotomies—local vs. national; military vs. civilian, emergency management vs. homeland security, among many others" (Scavo, Kearney, and Kilroy 2008, 103).

At the end of the day, according to Donald Kettl (2006), the homeland security architecture is "an intergovernmental system under stress." It is an intergovernmental system that is characterized as an arena in which there are not just new and more actors, but also new and more actors with increasingly diverse perspectives and interests. Indeed, as Light (2007) argues, the success of the homeland security mission now hinges on intergovernmental relations and actors. This multitude of actors with diverse perspectives and interests in the homeland security "network" has a direct impact on the nation's foreign policy, certainly at the margins if not more centrally. Consider any one of a range of current policy debates, such as immigration, alternative energy, border patrol, critical infrastructure, national ID cards, police, fire, and emergency medical services—all these policy issues are shaped by both national and local politics. They are all fully infused with issues of representation, election and reelection, policy and technological expertise, and bureaucratic territoriality (Clovis 2008). It is, in short, a contested political space.

As we discussed earlier, the intermestic politics of homeland security and the Cuban embargo is quite apparent, both in terms of the domestic politics components of that foreign policy and also because of the way competing actors and interests at the federal level confront trade-offs between that policy and others (like homeland security). The politics of the embargo's enforcement has, in fact, led to a debate about the value of confiscating contraband Cuban cigars at the cost of securing the homeland (GAO 2007). Similarly, considering the "view from below," the diverse intergovernmental actors and interests that are part of the intermestic politics of homeland security have led several analysts to ask, how secure is the homeland? Are we safer?

One way to try to gain some leverage over these questions is (to quote an old line from the Watergate scandal) to "follow the money." It is perhaps not surprising that there are budgetary battles involved in homeland security policy. As Clarke and Chenowith point out, "Budgetary struggles between Congress and the executive branch are unexceptional features of national political processes. To find them complicating homeland security initiatives is unsurprising but for the exceptional character of this policy issue" (2006, 97). Do these battles over resources—battles that are perhaps inherent in the all-hazards and intergovernmental nature of this policy space—have a negative impact on homeland security?

In a 2011 report, the GAO concluded that ten years after the attacks of 9/11, "more work remains for DHS to address gaps and weaknesses in its current operational and implementation efforts, and to strengthen the efficiency and effectiveness of those efforts to achieve its full potential" (GAO 2011, 8). Specifically, the report concluded that various homeland security issues such as border security, aviation security, emergency and disaster preparedness, maritime security, and protection from chemical-biological-nuclear threats are all hampered by recurring problems of *coordination* and *competition* among key federal, state, and local stakeholders.

Over the decade that has passed since 9/11, the all-hazards model has tried to "fuse" anti-terrorism initiatives with other forms of disaster preparedness and emergency management under the rubric of homeland security. Both congressional actions and presidential initiatives have emphasized the need for more and better coordination of information and interests among the varied intergovernmental actors across the landscape of homeland security. Several pieces of legislation, including the USA Patriot Act, the Homeland Security Act of 2002, and the Intelligence Reform and Terrorism Prevention Act of 2004, have positioned the federal government as lead actor in homeland security policy, but also laid the foundation for significant inclusion of state and local governments. Similarly, presidential actions reinforced and mandated the coordination of these intergovernmental efforts, but, most importantly, required a coordination of information among federal, state, and local actors in the homeland security network. Executive orders 13356 and 13388 and a presidential memorandum on December 16, 2005 (Bush 2005), all led to the creation of the Information Sharing Environment (ISE), which was implemented through the establishment of fusion centers at the state and local levels of government (for a discussion of the history of ISE, see www.ise.gov/background-and-authorities).

There are currently seventy-seven fusion centers, one for each of the fifty states plus each of the twenty-two major urban areas (plus some secondary centers) in the United States. Various federal, state, and local officials ranging from local police, fire, and emergency management to National Guard, FBI, Drug Enforcement Administration (DEA), and DHS personnel staff these centers. "National strategy states that fusion centers will serve as the primary focal points within states and localities for the receipt and sharing of terrorism-related information" (GAO 2010, 2). They are at the center of the homeland security policy space, and in that sense they provide an interesting window into the intermestic nature of homeland security policy.

In 2010, the GAO evaluated the performance of homeland security fusion centers and the intergovernmental funding decisions and patterns that constitute the primary resources that are directed toward homeland security policy goals. According to the GAO, the principal source of funding for fusion centers is through the Homeland Security Grant Program (HSGP) administered by DHS. "DHS's HSGP awards funds to states, territories, and urban areas to enhance their ability to prepare for, prevent, protect against, respond to, and recover from terrorist attacks and other major disasters" (GAO 2010, 11).

The evolution of and reliance on a system of intergovernmental grants is a defining characteristic of contemporary American federalism. It is a dynamic fiscal relationship in which the national government provides fiscal resources to state and local governments to participate in the integration and implementation of national policy goals. The dynamics of this fiscal federalism constitute the political economy of the distribution of "benefits" and "burdens," winners and losers, in American politics. Many observers of fiscal federalism contend that the system of intergovernmental grants is an arena in which national, state, and local actors engage in the competitive politics of redistribution, or "pork-barrel politics" (Peterson 1995). Federal grants that subsidize highly specialized or localized public works projects, the location of defense facilities and military bases, or fiscal rewards in the form of agriculture commodities subsidies are desirable "pork" that political actors see as important for satisfying constituents' interests and ensuring political support. These intergovernmental fiscal transfers "inefficiently" shift burdens and benefits (revenues and expenditures) in a pattern that benefits few in the population and burdens many. While the inefficiency of pork may violate the principle of fairness, it has substantial negative consequences for the achievement of national interests and overall policy goals.

According to the GAO, across all fifty states and twenty-two regions, "fusion centers compete with other state homeland security, law enforcement, and emergency management agencies and missions for a portion of the total amount of HSGP funding awarded to the SAA (State Asministrative Agency), which decides what portion of the total funding centers will receive. This process has generated long-standing concerns in the fusion center community about the lack of a longer term, predictable funding source for the centers" (GAO 2010, 21).

It is this competition, to which the GAO refers, that definitively shapes the "intermestic" politics of homeland security in this view from below: more actors, more interests, and more competition—for position, power, and resources. The cooperative approach to intergovernmental behavior takes a back seat to the competitive approach. State and local public safety actors compete for more and better equipment; emergency management actors compete for "command and control" resources; and medical and health actors compete for "medical assets and inventory." And while individual actors (such as a local police force) may experience a net increase in equipment, training, and/or authority, the overall goals of national homeland security and terrorism prevention may not be realized.

In part because this intermestic politics sits squarely in the center of the dynamics of American fiscal federalism, a debate has emerged over whether what we have really produced in the last ten years has been homeland *insecurity* (see also Friedman 2011; Zegart 2011). For example, some analysts maintain that "despite the urgency and immediacy of terrorism threats, we find Congress allocating funds more on the basis of traditional formulae than vulnerabilities assessment. Concerns persist that the patterns of domestic homeland security expenditures continue to reflect pork barrel politics rather than patterns of risk and vulnerability" (Clarke and Chenowith 2006, 98).

Other studies have concluded that congressional "tinkering" with the formula for the distribution of federal homeland security funds to states and local governments centers on trying to balance factors of "politics" and "risk." Even changes to the formula that try to focus more on "risk" appear to have not succeeded (see, for example, Gilliard-Matthews and Schneider 2010). Moreover, this "misallocation" of homeland security funding on the basis of politics rather than risk assessment has the consequence of producing "a less than optimal level of security in America" (de Rugy 2005).

Not all research finds a politically driven uncoupling of funding patterns, risk assessment, and desired homeland security outcomes (see, for example, Prante and Bohara 2008). Consequently, we should not view the fiscal policies of homeland security as an unfettered system for the distribution of largesse. Homeland security policy, and the funding that undergirds that policy, is not, in our view, simply an opportunity for political actors to exploit the need for a homeland security infrastructure as the "new pork." Nor do we argue that the behavior of policy actors in this policy space is motivated simply by the imperative to "bring home the bacon." However, what we do wish to emphasize in this discussion is the need to recognize the increasingly intermestic nature of U.S. foreign and homeland security policy. The case of homeland security is instructive if policy problems, foreign and domestic, are to be appropriately structured and policy goals effectively implemented. On the morning of September 11, 2001, U.S. foreign policy toward international terrorism intersected at the heart of the domestic politics of public health and safety, and emergency preparedness—giving rise to a unique policy space: the intermestic policy space of U.S. homeland security.

CONCLUSION

The development of intermestic politics has been a long time in coming. It was growing economic interdependence, highlighted by the oil shocks of the 1970s, that led Bayless Manning to coin the phrase and to note that "foreign" policies are no longer only international but also "inter-local" (1977, 309). Manning may not have predicted, however, that security policy would come to be defined by these same dynamics, or at least not as quickly as they have since his writing. The terrorist attacks of September 11 have had far-reaching consequences for the United States and the world. We have argued that these consequences include the introduction of homeland security into a contested political space and the injection of our federal and intergovernmental system into security policy. Understanding these dynamics is important both for citizens and analysts but also is an important part of the puzzle for policymakers in their effort to build a secure and resilient homeland.

DISCUSSION QUESTIONS

1. What is meant by "intermestic politics," and how is homeland security an intermestic issue?
2. How does the enforcement of the embargo against Cuba illustrate the intermestic nature of homeland security?
3. What is meant by the phrase "all security is local"? How has that notion created new foreign policy actors?
4. What is the "all hazards" model in operating the Department of Homeland Security?
5. Why do the authors seem to agree with Donald Kettl that the architecture of homeland security is "an intergovernmental system under stress"?
6. What are fusion centers, and how do they serve to coordinate homeland security? What are some issues that these centers face?

7. How has funding for the fusion centers and for homeland security generally been handled? Has such funding been on the basis of need or has domestic politics entered into the process?

REFERENCES

Aloise, Gene, and Stephen L. Caldwell. (2010). "Combating Nuclear Smuggling: Inadequate Communication and Oversight Hampered DHS Efforts to Develop an Advanced Radiography System to Detect Nuclear Materials." Statement for the Record to the Committee on Homeland Security and Governmental Affairs, U.S. Senate. Washington, DC: Government Accountability Office, GAO-10-1041T.

Barilleaux, Ryan J. (1985). "The President, 'Intermestic' Issues, and the Risks of Policy Leadership." *Presidential Studies Quarterly* 15 (4): 754–67.

Baucus, Max, and Mike Enzi. (2004). "As Terrorists Plot, Uncle Sam Pays to Halt Cuban Cigars." *Los Angeles Times*, May 19, 2004.

Brenner, Philip, Patrick J. Haney, and Walt Vanderbush. (2008). "Intermestic Interests and U.S. Policy toward Cuba." In Eugene R. Wittkopf and James M. McCormick, eds. *The Domestic Sources of American Foreign Policy*, 5th ed., 65–80. Lanham, MD: Rowman & Littlefield.

Bush, George W. (2005). "Memorandum for the Heads of Executive Departments and Agencies. Subject: Guidelines and Requirements in Support of the Information Sharing Environment." www.fas.org/sgp/news/2005/12/wh121605-memo.html.

Canada, Ben. (2003). "Department of Homeland Security: State and Local Preparedness Issues." Report RL31490. Washington, DC: Congressional Research Service.

Chenoweth, Erica, and Susan E. Clarke. (2010). "All Terrorism Is Local: Resources, Nested Institutions, and Governance for Urban Homeland Security in the American Federal System." *Political Research Quarterly* 63 (3): 495–507.

Clarke, Susan E., and Erica Chenoweth. (2006). "The Politics of Vulnerability: Constructing Local Performance Regimes for Homeland Security." *Review of Policy Research* 23:95–114.

Clovis, Samuel H., Jr. (2008). "Promises Unfulfilled: The Sub-optimization of Homeland Security National Preparedness." *Homeland Security Affairs* 4 (3). www.hsaj.org/?article=4.3.3.

CNN. (2011). "TSA Fires 28 over Improper Luggage Screening at Honolulu Airport." *CNN*, September 18, 2011. http://articles.cnn.com/2011-09-18/travel/travel_tsa-screeners_1_tsa-officers-tsa-administrator-john-pistole-bags?_s=PM:TRAVEL. Accessed November 15, 2011.

de Rugy, Veronique. (2005). "What Does Homeland Security Spending Buy?" American Enterprise Institute Working Paper No. 107, April 1, 2005. www.aei.org/files/2005/04/01/20050408_wp107.pdf.

Eisinger, Peter. (2006). "Imperfect Federalism: The Intergovernmental Partnership for Homeland Security." *Public Administration Review* 66: 537–45.

Friedman, Benjamin H. (2011). "Managing Fear: The Politics of Homeland Security." *Political Science Quarterly* 126 (1): 77–106.

Gilliard-Matthews, Stacia, and Anne L. Schneider. (2010). "Politics or Risks? An Analysis of Homeland Security Grant Allocations to the States." *Journal of Homeland Security and Emergency Management* 7 (1), article 57.

Government Accountability Office (GAO). (2011). "Department of Homeland Security: Progress Made and Work Remaining in Implementing Homeland Security Missions 10 Years after 9/11." Publication no. GAO-11-919T. www.gao.gov/new .items/d11919t.pdf.

Government Accountability Office (GAO). (2010). "Information Sharing: Federal Agencies Are Helping Fusion Centers Build and Sustain Capabilities and Protect Privacy, but Could Better Measure Results." Publication no. GAO-10-972. www .gao.gov/new.items/d10972.pdf.

Government Accountability Office (GAO). (2007). "Economic Sanctions: Agencies Face Competing Priorities in Enforcing the U.S. Embargo on Cuba." Publication no. GAO-08-80. www.gao.gov/new.items/d0880.pdf.

Haney, Patrick J., and Philip A. Russo. (2009). "When Do I Get My Cubanos? The Curious Connection between Cigars and U.S. Homeland Security." *Cigar Magazine* (Winter): 78–85.

Hastedt, Glenn. (2005). "Creation of the Department of Homeland Security." In Ralph G. Carter, ed. *Contemporary Cases in U.S. Foreign Policy: From Terrorism to Trade*, 2nd ed., 149–80. Washington, DC: CQ Press.

Kelleher, Jennifer Sinco. (2011). "TSA Probes Profiling Allegations in Honolulu." BloombergBusinessWeek, December 2, 2011. www.businessweek.com/ap/ financialnews/D9RCDOV00.htm.

Kelleher, Jennifer Sinco. (2012). "AP NewsBreak: TSA Finds No Profiling at Honolulu." MSNBC, April 13, 2012. www.msnbc.msn.com/id/47046768#.T5czU -1Kf6k.

Kettl, Donald F. (2006). *System under Stress: Homeland Security and American Politics*, 2nd ed. Washington, DC: CQ Press.

Koski, Chris, and Peter J. May. (2011). "Addressing Diffuse Problems: Fostering Communities of Interest." Prepared for the 11th National Public Management Research Conference, Syracuse, New York, June 2–4, 2011. www.maxwell.syr .edu/uploadedFiles/conferences/pmrc/Files/KoskiMayPRMC2011_Addressing %20Diffuse%20Problems%20-%20Fostering%20Communities%20of%20Interest .pdf.

Light, Paul C. (2007). "The Homeland Security Hash." *Wilson Quarterly* 31 (2): 36–44.

Lindsay, James M., and Randall B. Ripley. (1997). "U.S. Foreign Policy in a Changing World." In Randall B. Ripley and James M. Lindsay, eds. *U.S. Foreign Policy after the Cold War*, 3–20. Pittsburgh, PA: University of Pittsburgh Press.

Manning, Bayless. (1977). "The Congress, the Executive and Intermestic Affairs: Three Proposals." *Foreign Affairs* 55: 306–24.

Nacos, B. L., R. Y. Shapiro, and P. Isernia. (2000). "Old or New Ball Game? Mass Media, Public Opinion, and Foreign Policy in the Post–Cold War World." In Brigette L. Nacos, Robert Y. Shapiro, and Pierangelo Isernia, eds. *Decisionmaking in a Glass House: Mass Media, Public Opinion, and American and European Foreign Policy in the 21st Century*. Lanham, MD: Rowman & Littlefield.

Peterson, Paul E. (1995). *The Price of Federalism*. Washington, DC: Brookings Institution Press.

Prante, Tyler, and Alok K. Bohara. (2008). "What Determines Homeland Security Spending? An Econometric Analysis of the Homeland Security Grant Program." *Policy Studies Journal* 36: 243–56.

Ridge, T. (2002). *State and Local Actions for Homeland Security*. The White House: Office of Homeland Security. www.ncs.gov/library/policy_docs/State_and_Local_Actions_for_Homeland_Security.pdf.

Scavo, Carmine P., Richard C. Kearney, and Richard J. Kilroy. (2008). "Challenges to Federalism: Homeland Security and Disaster Response." *Publius* 38 (1): 81–110.

Schattschneider, E. E. (1960). *The Semi-Sovereign People*. New York: Holt, Rinehart, and Winston.

Schneider, Saundra K. (1990). "FEMA, Federalism, Hugo, and 'Frisco." *Publius* 20 (3): 97–115.

Schouten, F. (2010). "Body Scanner Makers Doubled Lobbying Case over 5 Years." *USAToday*, October 23, 2010. www.usatoday.com/news/washington/2010-11-22-scanner-lobby_N.htm.

Solomon, J. (2004). "More Agents Track Castro than Bin Laden." Associated Press, April 29, 2004. www.commondreams.org/headlines04/0429-12.htm.

Zegart, Amy B. (2011). "The Domestic Politics of Irrational Intelligence Oversight." *Political Science Quarterly* 126 (1): 1–25.

Zeller, Shawn. (2009). "Dismal Security Score." *CQ Weekly Reports*, June 29, 2009.

17

American Trade Policymaking

A Unique Process

I. M. (Mac) Destler

Trade policy in the United States flows from a process quite different from that for mainstream foreign policy or national security. Rooted in the constitutional grant of authority to the Congress, it has evolved with changes in American trade policy goals, in the structure of the U.S. economy, and in the character of domestic politics.

CONSTITUTIONAL FRAMEWORK

Trade policy centers on the regulation of imports of goods and services entering the United States. Should they be treated the same as those produced domestically, or should they be taxed or otherwise constrained to "protect" U.S. businesses and workers? Concern over this issue dates from the origins of the Republic. In fact, it arose among the original thirteen colonies as well. The framers of the Constitution were concerned about their restricting trade with one another, and the grant of authority over "commerce" to Congress in Article I, Section 8, includes that "among the several states" as well as "with foreign nations."

This power was conveyed, of course, within the overall structure of independent executive and legislative branches—what the late Richard Neustadt famously called "separated institutions sharing powers."[1] Their intertwining means that serious policy action in the United States almost always requires major contributions from both Congress and the president.

Through most of U.S. history, however, Congress was dominant on trade policy. The issue was "the tariff," which "more than any other single topic . . . engrossed Congressional energies for more than a hundred years."[2]

301

Tariffs were also the primary source of federal income until early in the twentieth century, when they were supplanted by the income tax. The issue divided the political parties, with Republicans seeking more protection and Democrats less. The former usually controlled the government from the Civil War to the Great Depression. Members of Congress were generally responsive to interests within their districts, and Republicans responded particularly to producer interests. This, plus log-rolling among such interests, brought tariffs higher and higher, culminating in the Smoot-Hawley Act of 1930.[3] That now-infamous law brought tariffs on dutiable imports to an average of 60 percent.

Smoot-Hawley was replicated across the advanced industrial world, and the consequence of multiple nations closing their markets was a deepening of the Great Depression. This contributed to a fundamental change in U.S. trade policy, substantively and institutionally. Policy shifted from a persistent tendency to raise import barriers to an equally steady inclination to lower them. And the process changed as well—Congress abruptly stopped enacting comprehensive tariff bills, with the initiative shifting to the executive branch.

The change was inaugurated in the administration of Franklin D. Roosevelt. Democrats had won large majorities in Congress, but rather than cut tariffs directly—as they had the power to do—they established a process that they hoped could outlast their existing partisan advantage. Specifically, the United States would negotiate reciprocal barrier-reducing agreements with nations that were our primary trading partners, and the president would use delegated authority from Congress to enact the lower rates. This was accomplished through the Reciprocal Trade Agreements Act of 1934. The Reciprocal Trade Agreements Act fundamentally altered the political dynamic. Though presidents were not immune to protectionist pressures, they generally pursued broader interests. In addition, the international negotiating process brought export interests into the trade policy game to balance those of trade-threatened domestic producers.

In the decades that followed, Congress frequently limited executive leeway in barrier reduction—exempting certain products, always imposing time limits. But the central question changed from how much Congress would raise a tariff, to how much the president's negotiators would bargain it down. After World War II, moreover, the negotiating arena shifted—from bilateral talks, with tariff reductions then generalized under the most-favored-nation (MFN) principle, to multilateral "rounds" under the General Agreement on Tariffs and Trade (GATT) negotiated in 1947.

In the prewar and postwar years, these negotiations were conducted by the Department of State. Indeed, Roosevelt's secretary—Cordell Hull—was the driving force behind the initiation of the new policymaking process. But members of Congress grew increasingly restive with a process where a department distant from U.S. economic interests was responsible for key decisions affecting them. So when, in 1962, President John F. Kennedy sought unprecedentedly broad and flexible authority to negotiate new barrier reductions with the recently formed European Economic Community, this concern surfaced with a vengeance. Wilbur Mills (D-AR) was then chair of the House Ways and Means Committee, which had jurisdiction over trade policy and hence the proposed legislation. He favored the proposed negotiations. He also respected the competence of State Department officials, but he didn't think they knew much about U.S. business. Commerce Department officials, by contrast, knew a lot about business but weren't as smart, Mills believed—moreover, they didn't know much about agriculture. Harry Byrd (D-VA), chair of the Ways and Means counterpart committee in the Senate, had similar reservations. Kennedy's response was to acquiesce, reluctantly, in placing responsibility for the new trade negotiations in the White House.

THE UNITED STATES TRADE REPRESENTATIVE: ESTABLISHMENT, EVOLUTION

The Trade Expansion Act of 1962 established the office of President's Special Representative for Trade Negotiations (STR) to conduct the multilateral trade talks that became known as the "Kennedy Round." In the course of those negotiations, the task of the representative's small office was to balance foreign and domestic economic interests, coordinate the executive branch, and bargain with both Congress and foreign governments. The arrangement proved successful, and the round produced cuts in U.S. tariffs averaging 35 percent—this on top of those achieved by earlier negotiations. Congress liked both the process and the product, and took regular steps to protect and strengthen the White House–based trade office.

When President Richard M. Nixon's administration showed interest in 1973 in subsuming STR under another White House economic office, Congress made it a statutory entity and gave its head a cabinet-level salary in the Trade Act of 1974. Five years later, when Congress insisted on a strengthening of executive branch trade policy institutions, President Jimmy Carter responded with a reorganization plan renaming STR the Office of the *United States* Trade Representative (USTR) and broadening its authority. When President Ronald Reagan proposed to replace it with a Department of Trade in 1983, the Senate resisted. When House members thought the president wasn't using his trade powers aggressively enough, they used the 1988 trade legislation to shift certain authorities from him to the USTR. When aides to President-elect George W. Bush spoke, during the 2000–2001 transition, of rescinding the USTR's cabinet status, a chorus of congressional and business voices led them to reconsider.[4]

As these events illustrate, the USTR has acquired enduring constituencies—in Congress, and in the trade-minded business community. Central to these constituencies have been the trade committees: House Ways and Means, and the Senate Committee on Finance. They come by this authority through their broad jurisdiction over revenues (tariffs are taxes), and their writ extends to such major governmental enterprises as Social Security and Medicare. This makes them powerful within their chambers, which in turn attracts ambitious and competent legislators to their ranks. When U.S. trade policy has been effective, it has typically reflected cooperation between these committees and the office they saw as "their" agent within the executive branch. Presidents weren't always eager to buy into this arrangement, and retaining presidential support has been a recurrent problem for the USTR. But the basic system has now endured for fifty years, and there is no strong current pressure to change it.

Formally, the USTR is housed in the Executive Office of the President (EOP). It is, in the words of the Carter executive order of 1980, responsible for "international trade policy development, coordination, and negotiation." Coordination of trade policy with other concerns is the responsibility of the National Economic Council (NEC)—established by President Clinton, retained by his successors—and, intermittently, of the much more established National Security Council on which the NEC is modeled. But the USTR typically leads and manages on major trade issues. It is politically attuned—to Congress, to interested industries. But even in a highly partisan era it has retained a priority in technical competence and a preference to work across party lines. Lawyers are prominent among its staff, some of whom move back and forth to the staffs of the Congressional committees. And former USTR officials are prominent in the Washington trade bar.

Within the trade policy sphere, the USTR heads a statutory interagency coordinating committee structure that operates at cabinet and sub-cabinet levels. Other important members of these committees—and trade policy participants—include the Departments of Commerce, Agriculture, Treasury, and State, and Executive Office of the President units such as the Council of Economic Advisers.

Among these other U.S. agencies, second to the USTR in importance on trade is the U.S. Department of Commerce, which the Carter order made "the focus of nonagricultural operational trade responsibilities." Commerce assumed, in 1980, authority to administer the countervailing duty and antidumping laws, enacted and periodically strengthened by Congress to give producers recourse against "unfair" imports either subsidized by foreign governments or "dumped" at less than it costs to produce them. Commerce wields this authority with dense technical expertise in a petitioner-friendly manner that reflects congressional desires. That department also houses the U.S. and Foreign Commercial Service, which works with private business in

Washington and overseas to promote U.S. exports. Overall, Commerce is the federal agency deepest in expertise in trade and the industries involved.

For most matters, the USTR-Commerce division of labor is relatively clear. One place where coordination can fail is at the top. For trade is the most prominent of Commerce's generally unexciting set of responsibilities, and it is not untypical for the secretary of commerce to have closer links to the president than the USTR who is supposed to lead him. Secretaries Maurice Stans (under Nixon) and Malcolm Baldrige (under Reagan) sought government-wide leadership on trade. Secretaries Robert Mosbacher (under George H. W. Bush) and Don Evans (who served George W. Bush) were also closer to their presidents than the USTRs of their time. It was Baldrige's power struggle with USTR Bill Brock in 1981–1984 that caused the greatest problems for trade policy. Baldrige was aided by the fact that some major steel negotiations involved antidumping and countervailing duty cases before his department. Interestingly, though the commerce secretary retained Reagan's support through the period, Brock eventually won out due to his strong backing on Capitol Hill.

Another consequential institution is the United States International Trade Commission (USITC). The USITC is a regulatory body, independent of the president, with six members appointed by him and confirmed by Congress. No more than three can be members of the same political party. The USITC determines whether firms petitioning Commerce for trade relief have suffered economic "injury," with an affirmative finding being a prerequisite for the relief. In escape clause (Section 201) cases, where neither subsidies nor dumping are alleged, the commission also recommends to the president the most appropriate form of import relief, though he need not follow the recommendation. (On subsidy and dumping cases, the relief is specified in statute.)

The United States Department of Agriculture (USDA) plays an important role within its sphere due to its responsibility for farm programs that are prominent in international negotiations. When USTRs advance agricultural trade liberalization proposals, they typically do so jointly with the USDA. (When the Doha talks broke down in July 2006, for example, USTR Susan Schwab and Agriculture Secretary Mike Johanns explained it together in a joint "press availability.") Treasury plays a strong role when the negotiating issue involves financial institutions, when exchange rates are a problem, or when its secretary (such as James Baker III under Reagan) is the effective overall economic policy leader of the government.

Societal economic interests are consulted regularly, particularly the interests of producers, because advancing them is an important function of trade negotiations, and because their support is needed for agreements reached. Formally, communication takes place through a statutory network of industry and labor advisory committees, which must report to Congress their views on pending trade agreements. In recent years, committees have been added and representatives appointed to reflect the interests of civil society groups—environmentalists in particular.

Senior officials in the USTR and the departments are, of course, appointed by the president and confirmed by Congress. It is through these appointments that the chief executive exercises his strongest impact on trade policy. A strong designee (Robert Strauss under Carter) brings effectiveness and priority to trade. A delayed appointment (typical for most first-term presidents) generates doubts for the same reasons. An appointee generally perceived as weak (Ron Kirk under Obama) makes an administration's overall trade policy less effective.

COORDINATING WITH CONGRESS: "FAST TRACK"

The executive branch process is significant, but the most important coordination for U.S. trade policy is that between the two branches. The USTR cannot be effective if Congress undercuts him, or if foreign or domestic interlocutors believe that it will. And the structure of "separated institutions" makes this highly likely in the absence of processes designed to promote cooperation and shared responsibility.

When trade negotiations were limited to tariffs, as was the case from the 1930s through the 1960s, coordination was straightforward: Congress told the president, through legislation, what his agents could and could not negotiate, specifically how far they could bargain down tariffs, generally and specifically. Operating within these constraints, the president could implement tariff reductions through his delegated authority and proclaim the new rates. But problems arose when U.S. negotiators struck deals that went beyond tariffs, for then implementation required detailed statutory language whose enactment could not be delegated to the president in advance. Congress refused, in fact, to implement two Kennedy Round deals negotiated by the Johnson administration in the 1960s—one on antidumping, the second on how certain U.S. duties were calculated. Other nations then withdrew concessions they had made to Washington, and declared the United States an unreliable negotiating partner.

Thus when the Nixon administration sought authority for the Tokyo Round negotiations (launched in 1973), where non-tariff barriers would be central, it faced acute skepticism abroad as well as at home. In particular, it had to assuage foreign doubts about whether the United States could deliver on the deals its negotiators struck. The challenge was to establish executive credibility while maintaining Congressional authority. The answer was a major innovation, which became known as the "fast-track procedures." When Congress authorized a trade negotiation, it would commit itself to act on the results, as submitted by the president, within a limited time period—ninety legislative days. It would make this commitment through rules binding on each of its two chambers. Unlike on a tariff agreement—when Congress had no ratification role—other nations could still not be certain that the United States would deliver on its commitments. Congress could, after all, reject a trade deal. But U.S. negotiating partners *could* be confident that Congress would vote on them, and would not alter them in the process. And in most circumstances, assuming the executive did its political homework, a positive vote could be expected.

The fast-track procedures were incorporated in the Trade Act of 1974, and they have governed, essentially, all major and minor barrier-reducing agreements entered into since that time, up to and including free trade agreements (FTAs) voted on in October 2011. The sequence is as follows: the president seeks and Congress grants authority to engage in trade negotiations, with objectives defined in statute; the USTR and other officials consult with Congress (the trade committees in particular) and private-sector advisory groups during the course of the negotiations; Congress and the advisory groups are notified of the content of an agreement 90 (or 120) days prior to its signing; the groups make independent reports to Congress recommending approval or rejection; the president, after further consultation with Congress, provides draft implementing legislation (introduced without change by congressional leaders); Congress then acts on this legislation within a limit of ninety legislative days.[5]

The first test came with the Tokyo Round, and the procedures were adapted in practice when leaders of the Senate Committee on Finance pressed USTR Robert Strauss for a role in drafting the president's implementing bill. ("You do want it to pass, don't you?") He agreed, launching what became known as "non-markups"—meetings of congressional committees with executive officials where the legislators discussed and agreed on draft language. These were followed, for the Tokyo Round and typically thereafter, by a "non-conference," where Finance and Ways and Means committee leaders met to reconcile their differences. President Carter submitted the agreed-upon result with few changes, and the legislation passed overwhelmingly (just seven representatives and four senators voted "nay"). The procedures also worked effectively in implementing three subsequent major trade agreements: the Canada-U.S. Free Trade Agreement of 1988, the North American Free Trade Agreement (NAFTA) approved in 1993, and the Uruguay Round/WTO accord ratified in 1994. Essentially, they replicated the legislative process insofar as the statutory language was concerned, though the substance of the bills was, of course, constrained by what the executive branch had negotiated.

The processes favored the committees over other members of congress, and trade "insiders" over those outside the trade policy mainstream. They were condemned by some critics as undemocratic. But from the Tokyo Round through the Uruguay Round, they proved effective. They maintained congressional authority without sacrificing executive negotiating credibility.

A NEW TRADE POLITICS:
(1) BUSINESS CHANGES ITS SPOTS

The prime political purpose of the trade policymaking system launched in 1934 was to counter broad business protectionism. American industry had grown strong behind tariff walls, and many of its leaders were committed to maintaining them. By changing the game from unilateral tariff-setting to international trade bargaining, and by shifting the locus of initiative away from the branch most vulnerable to particularist pressures, the system made possible the steady opening up of the American economy.

In the decades after World War II, the need for such institutions and processes seemed to grow. After a brief period of war-generated industrial dominance, U.S. producers began to face fierce international competition—first from Europe, then from a resurgent Japan. Traditionally protectionist sectors like textiles and shoes and steel were joined by newly threatened producers of television sets, machine tools, even automobiles. Organized labor, in the free-trade camp during the first half-century, moved to the trade-restrictive side. Many Democrats followed, though this was offset by Republicans moving in the free-market direction. And when, in the early and mid-eighties, a suddenly strong dollar generated huge surges in imports and record trade deficits, members of both parties grew increasingly aggressive in demanding forceful responses. Responding to this pressure, Ronald Reagan—committed in principle to free trade—was driven, in the words of his treasury secretary, to "grant more import relief to U.S. industry than any of his predecessors in more than half a century."[6] And his administration, at congressional insistence, grew far more active in pressing foreign governments to lift what U.S. law labeled "unreasonable and unjustifiable" barriers to U.S. trade.

But while Congress insisted on passing broad trade legislation in 1988, its content was moderated after the dollar had declined sharply in value and the trade balance improved with a surge in exports. And when imports surged again in the late 1990s, at rates comparable to the Reagan period, there was no comparable protectionist response. Only the steel industry mobilized for import relief, which it finally received (for twenty-one months) in the first George W. Bush administration. The politically weakened textile industry, by far the most potent force for trade protection from the 1950s through the 1980s, acceded to globalization. Fabric producers now focused on shaping "rules of origin" in bilateral FTAs to assure that clothing shipped here from partner nations used made-in-USA cloth. With such rules in place, the industry actually came out in support of the politically controversial NAFTA agreement.

More generally, U.S. business became globalized. For the U.S. economy as a whole, trade averaged—in 2000—roughly 30 percent of the value of total national goods production, up from about 10 percent in 1970. This meant not only that producers were exporting a larger share of what they made, but also that they were importing many of the inputs into their final products. They now depended on open access to world markets. At mid-century, business protectionism had been the main concern of trade policymakers. By 2000, business was being attacked from the left for its open-market stance.

A NEW TRADE POLITICS: (2) THE RISE OF SOCIAL ISSUES AND PARTISANSHIP

This attack was an element in a broad anti-globalization movement that arose in the 1990s and persisted thereafter. So if business as a whole no longer impeded trade liberalization, other concerns rose to slow its progress. A loose coalition on the left—labor, environmentalists, some nongovernmental organizations (NGOs)—came to argue that trade, and business more generally, imposed serious social costs. Products from third-world nations came from factories that exploited workers, they declared. And this "unfair" competition drove down wages in advanced countries. Moreover, environmental conditions in these plants were often egregious. Not only was this bad for the poor countries themselves, but it also threatened an environmental "race to the bottom" as developed country competitors sought loosening of regulations at home so that they could better compete in the global marketplace.

For some advocates, these concerns were sufficient to justify full-blown opposition to new trade agreements—for their own sake, and (for some in the labor movement) because they provided "cover" for narrower economic interests. Others took a more qualified position—agreements could be beneficial *if* they included measures that addressed these social harms. Bill Clinton gave this stance visibility and credibility in the 1992 election campaign, when he declared he supported NAFTA (negotiated under President George H. W. Bush) but would not send it to Congress for approval unless and until there were appended to it side agreements on labor and the environment.

Clinton's USTR, Mickey Kantor, negotiated such agreements, and the president then sent NAFTA to Congress and won the uphill battle for its ratification. The coalition opposing it—labor, elements of the environmental community, and their allies—was bested in this battle, but they were determined it would not be the last. Through the rest of Clinton's presidency, they resisted new trade initiatives, bringing about failure of his effort to renew fast-track trade negotiating authority in 1997, and contributing to the breakdown of the Seattle ministerial conference of the World Trade Organization (WTO) convened to launch a new round of global trade negotiations. Their resistance also undercut progress on other ambitious undertakings to which Clinton was committed—a Free Trade Area of the Americas (FTAA), and an open trade regime among members of the Asia-Pacific Economic Cooperation (APEC) group.

The administration was able, in 2000, to win congressional approval of permanent normal trade relations with China, an indispensable element of that nation's joining the WTO. But Clinton bequeathed to his successor a polity divided over trade in general and the new social issues in particular. Most Democrats favored, at minimum, strong labor and environmental standards incorporated in the text of any future FTAs. Most Republicans, backed by business, wanted such standards minimized if included at all. This partisan polarization was relatively new to trade policy. But it reflected, and was reinforced by, broader trends in American politics.

In substantive views and voting behavior, the House of Representatives was becoming steadily more divided along partisan lines. One picture may not tell it all, but it shows a lot. Figure 17.1 shows the ideological distribution of liberal and conservative members (measured by voting record) in 1969–1970, when there was considerable overlap between the two parties, and 1999–2000, when there was virtually none.[7] The causes were several and are addressed by the author in detail elsewhere.[8] But two were prominent.

The first was the sorting out of political party memberships that made them ideologically more cohesive. After the civil rights revolution, southern Democrats became Republicans—and/or their children did. And liberal northeastern Republicans turned into Democrats. As a result, the Republican Party became, predominantly, the conservative party, and the Democrats, substantially, the liberal party.

The second change was the onset of decennial House redistricting, after the Supreme Court ruled that members must represent constituencies of equal size. This meant redrawing the lines after every census, and state legislatures—under pressure from House members—drew them primarily so as to protect incumbents, and only secondarily (if they controlled both branches of the state government) to increase the number elected from their own party. This produced Representatives safe from challenge by the other party, but vulnerable to challenge within their own party if they strayed too far from the party line.

As substantive polarization deepens, the political party becomes more than a convenient association for politicians seeking election—it becomes

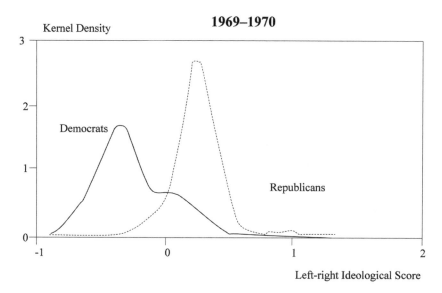

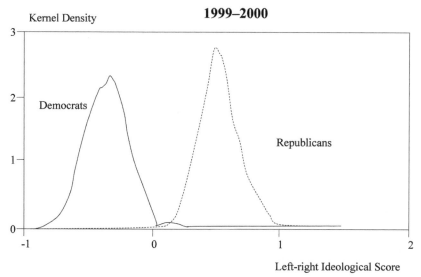

Figure 17.1. Ideological Distribution of the Parties in the U.S. House, 1969–1970 and 1999–2000

a group of like-minded individuals seeking to move public policy in specific, preferred directions. Within Congress, the group is represented by the party leadership and the party caucus, which seeks to shape substantive legislation at the expense of the committees. And the committee majorities are pressed to act in a partisan manner lest they lose power. In the process, members come to communicate mainly with their own kind, and seldom with those on the other side of the aisle. As communication fades, so does trust.

Substantive positions on trade policy do not fit comfortably into this new partisan mold. For decades, Republicans had been growing more pro-trade and Democrats, particularly labor Democrats, more skeptical. But the normal trade liberalization coalition remains a centrist one, as illustrated by the fact that extreme anti-trade sentiment appears almost equally at the fringes of both parties. In 2000 and 2005, for example, the House voted, as required by law, on whether the United States should withdraw from the World Trade Organization. Both resolutions were overwhelmingly rejected. The first withdrawal resolution won support from 21 Democrats—and 33 Republicans! The second was backed by 46 Democrats and 39 Republicans. General views on trade also do not differ fundamentally between these parties' rank and file—a poll taken in the heat of the Central America Free Trade Agreement (CAFTA) debate found 51 percent of Democrats in favor—and 50 percent of Republicans![9]

Perhaps for these reasons, it took a while for party polarization to infect trade policy. Through the 1970s and, for the most part, the 1980s, the Ways and Means and Finance committees handled trade on a bipartisan basis. There were occasions when the majority Democrats excluded the minority and/or used trade to advance partisan purposes, but they were the exception. Chairman Dan Rostenkowski maintained the bipartisan tradition at Ways and Means into the early 1990s, resisting House Democratic Caucus pressure to operate in a more partisan manner.

But gradually, growing partisan rancor made trade compromise increasingly difficult to reach in the U.S. House of Representatives. This was reinforced by the fact that labor and environmental issues—unlike trade liberalization—*are* classic issues of liberal versus conservative. When the George W. Bush administration came to power in 2001 determined to pursue an active trade policy agenda, therefore, it and the House Republican leadership faced a choice. As they moved in 2001 for renewal of fast-track, now renamed "Trade Promotion Authority," they could seek compromise on these issues with leading Democrats. Or they could rely instead on their majority control of the chamber, "whipping" an overwhelming majority of their members into line (even though, in recent major votes, one-fourth to one-third of Republicans had voted against trade liberalization).[10]

Pushed by the House leadership, they chose the latter course. Ways and Means Chairman Bill Thomas (R-CA) refused, on more than one occasion, to meet with Democratic counterpart Charles Rangel (D-NY) to determine whether common ground could be found, even though President Bush had encouraged serious compromise talks.[11] The result was that essentially centrist legislation—it did include modest labor and environmental provisions—was adopted in a highly partisan process. With Democrats alienated, Republicans had to pressure their own. Driven by "the Hammer" (a.k.a. Majority Whip Tom DeLay [R-TX]), they extended the December 2001 vote on Trade Promotion Authority for twenty minutes beyond the time that the rules allowed, then had the speaker bang the gavel when one last reluctant Republican was dragged (and bought) into line, and Trade Promotion Authority survived, 215–214. In all, they were able to squeeze the number of "nay" votes from their party down to 23 (out of 217). Out of 210 Democrats, 21 voted in favor. After Senate approval and two more narrowly won House procedural votes, it became law in August 2002. The bill was named, ironically, the Bipartisan Trade Promotion Authority Act.

Bush's first-term trade representative, Robert Zoellick, used the new authority aggressively—not just for the newly launched Doha Round of multilateral trade talks, but also for an unprecedented number of bilateral and regional FTAs. Most were with relatively uncontroversial trading partners, with whom labor and environmental issues were not paramount— deals with Chile, Singapore, Australia, and Morocco won easy bipartisan approval. However, the Central America–Dominican Republic Free Trade Agreement (CAFTA-DR), signed in late 2003, brought back the partisan divisions. The vote was delayed until July 2005. With Democratic support down to fifteen votes, the Republican leadership replicated the 2001 process, holding the ballot open for more than an hour beyond the time decreed by House rules, until it was clear exactly how many GOP votes would be required. CAFTA-DR was approved 217–215, with three additional Republican votes available just in case.

Then, suddenly, the string ran out. Republicans faced defeat in the 2006 midterm election; Tom DeLay was under investigation and forced to resign his post. A new FTA was completed with Peru in December 2005, but Democrats found its labor-environmental provisions wanting, and Republicans no longer could roll it through the House on their own.

2007 AND AFTER: COMPROMISE AND DELAY

As Democrats prepared to assume power in the House in January 2007, USTR Susan C. Schwab recognized the need for a broader political base. She was completing an FTA with Colombia, and negotiations were well advanced on agreements with Panama and Korea. For these to have a chance in the new political environment, the split over labor and environmental standards needed to be resolved. Ways and Means Democrats were willing to deal, so she negotiated with now-Chairman Rangel what became known as the May 10 agreement. Endorsed by Speaker Nancy Pelosi, it specified provisions that would be added to the Peru and Colombia deals, and negotiated with Panama and Korea. On labor standards, for example, the executive-congressional agreement met the longstanding Democratic demand that trading partners commit themselves to the five core labor standards endorsed in the landmark June 1998 International Labor Organization Declaration on Fundamental Principles and Rights at Work: freedom of association, the right to bargain collectively, elimination of forced labor, effective abolition of child labor, and elimination of employment discrimination. Environmental provisions included pledges to adopt and enforce the obligations under major international environmental agreements and not to lower their own environmental standards.[12]

Business endorsed the agreement. Though it did not accord with the preferences of their members, organizations like the Business Roundtable and the Chamber of Commerce recognized the value of removing what had been, on its face, the primary impediment to bipartisan cooperation on trade over the past decade.

Schwab hoped that the May 10 deal would pave the way for approval of all four FTAs. But Ways and Means Democrats had additional problems with Colombia (on the security of labor leaders) and Korea (on the provisions for autos). Korea was also proving difficult on beef imports—a top priority for Montana Senator Max Baucus, who chaired the Senate Committee on Finance. And Panama developed problems with the United States on other issues. So only the Peru agreement won approval during the Bush years. Moreover, the Schwab-Rangel deal did not generate any momentum for extension of Trade Promotion Authority, which expired at the end of June 2007. Schwab could have used this to strengthen her hand in the Doha negotiations, which would fail to reach a conclusion during her tenure.

Meanwhile, a 2008 episode underscored the shakiness of bipartisan cooperation on trade and the fast-track procedures. President Bush was deeply committed to the Colombia FTA, wishing to reward a stalwart regional ally that was winning its fight against internal insurrection and drug violence. For months, his trade and economic officials sought to strike a deal with Pelosi allowing that FTA to be voted on and approved. Pelosi temporized, not willing to challenge organized labor, which vehemently opposed the pact. With time running out, Bush did what the procedures empowered him to do—he sent to legislation implementing the Colombia FTA to Congress for the requisite up-or-down vote.

Never had a president done this without the cooperation of the House leadership, and Pelosi responded by exploiting fast-track's Achilles heel, its foundation on the rules of each chamber. These were subject to change by majority vote, and Pelosi took the unusual step of having the House vote to remove the time limit as it applied to Colombia. This exposed a fact well known to trade cognoscenti but not to many others—that the seemingly ironclad promise of expeditious Congressional action was not so ironclad after all.

In his campaign, candidate Barack Obama expressed reservations about the Colombia and Korea FTAs as negotiated. In his first fifteen months, President Obama gave priority to domestic legislation—a record economic stimulus bill to counter the Great Recession, and comprehensive health care legislation. It was not until 2010 that he began to move. His January State of the Union address called for improving trade relations with Colombia, Korea, and Panama—though it fell short of mentioning the FTAs themselves. Obama and Korean President Lee Myung-bak met in June and committed themselves to renegotiate sensitive issues, especially the auto provisions. In December they announced agreement: specifically, changes in how Korea would liberalize car imports, and delays in the reduction of tariffs for that nation's vehicles entering the U.S. market. In the spring of 2011, a deal was reached with Colombia on an enhanced program to combat violence against labor leaders. Outstanding issues with Panama were resolved as well.

Since fast-track rules do not limit the time period between completion of an agreement and its submission for legislative action, the Korea and Panama FTAs could be sent to Congress under them—even though the deadline for concluding new agreements under fast-track was June 30, 2007. Colombia had to be considered under normal rules, because of its prior submission in 2008. But with Republicans overwhelmingly supportive, the way seemed clear for enactment. Yet action was delayed for months over a related issue—the extension of the Trade Adjustment Assistance (TAA) program for workers displaced by imports. Important provisions of this law had expired at the end of 2010, and the White House and congressional Democrats wanted them extended. Their major leverage with the House, now returned to Republican control, was to hold back on submitting the FTAs until agreement was reached on substance and timing. Resolution was delayed by lack of trust across partisan lines, but in the end an understanding was struck. After years of delay, the House and Senate conducted a total of seven trade votes on the same day—October 12. The lower chamber approved the three FTAs and the TAA legislation. The Senate, which had already voted the latter, approved the three agreements as well. None of the votes were close.

The Obama administration had one other important trade initiative— the Trans-Pacific Partnership (TPP) negotiation. Originated in Bush's last year, these talks involved nine nations (Australia, Brunei, Chile, Malaysia, New Zealand, Peru, Singapore, the United States, and Vietnam) seeking to conclude a comprehensive FTA. By early 2012, substantial progress had been made, but much work remained. And the story was complicated when

Japan's prime minister announced, with shaky domestic support, the desire for his country to enter the talks.

STASIS IN TRADE POLICY?

As Americans approach the 2012 election, Congress and the Obama administration have at last finished most of the work the Bush administration began. The large exception is the Doha Round, which marked the end of its tenth year with little prospect of a fruitful conclusion. In the spring of 2011, Schwab put in writing what many had been thinking, labeling the negotiation as "doomed" and urging nations to move beyond it.[13]

Obama has been moving beyond it with TPP, but these talks would certainly stretch over into 2012 and probably into the next presidential term. Meanwhile, the politics of U.S. trade seemed to be stuck in a holding pattern. There was little serious protectionism, but also little impetus for moving forward.[14] Ongoing partisan rancor has undercut consensus-building—whichever party controls the White House or the Congress—but its roots lie outside trade policy and grow deeper as the years go by. The credibility of the TPA/fast-track process was undercut by the Bush-Pelosi confrontation in 2008, but the United States nonetheless delivered on its negotiated FTA commitments three years later. Renewing the authority for the future, however, does not seem near the top of the administration's policy agenda. Nor, with anti-government sentiment rampant and deficit-cutting the order of the day, is there much near-term prospect for enactment of truly robust social policies that would offer broad support and recourse for workers that the forces of globalization have driven from their jobs.[15]

The most likely near-term scenario is a kind of trade policy stasis: for the United States to hover near full economic openness, not quite reaching it, but still deriving large benefits from economic interaction with the world. The only force that might give new energy to U.S. trade policy is the challenge of China, already generating legislative action against its policy of keeping its currency undervalued and running large trade surpluses. TPP is an important response to that challenge. It should be accompanied by a comprehensive set of home-based "policies . . . to make the United States a more attractive location for the production of world-competitive goods and services."[16] Whether either TPP or this broader policy goal will be realized, only time will tell.

DISCUSSION QUESTIONS

1. Which branch of government has been dominant in trade policy over the history of the country, and what was the dominant issue that shaped such policy?

2. What precipitated the shift in trade policymaking in the 1930s? What was the significance of the Reciprocal Trade Agreements Act of 1934?
3. How did the President's Special Representative for Trade Negotiations develop, and how did that representative evolve into the present-day USTR?
4. What role does the USTR play in trade policymaking today? Is the USTR an executive office or a congressional office? Explain.
5. What are the functions of the Department of Commerce, USITC, and the Department of Agriculture in trade policymaking?
6. What is meant by the fast track procedure, or trade promotion authority? How does this procedure work in practice?
7. What are two important changes in trade policy since World War II that have changed the groups that support and challenge the freeing up of international trade by the United States?
8. What factors does Destler point to in explaining the new divisions on trade policy in the U.S. Congress?
9. What was the May 10 agreement and how did it seek to address the congressional stalemate over free-trade agreements negotiated by recent presidents?
10. How does Destler judge the direction of American trade policy in the near term?

*This chapter draws on the author's *American Trade Politics*, fourth edition (Washington, DC: Institute for International Economics, 2005).

NOTES

1. Richard E. Neustadt, *Presidential Power: The Politics of Leadership* (New York: Wiley, 1960).

2. James L. Sundquist, *The Decline and Resurgence of Congress* (Washington, DC: Brookings Institution, 1981), 99.

3. E. E. Schattschneider, *Politics, Pressures, and the Tariff* (New York: Prentice-Hall, 1935).

4. For more on these specific episodes, see I. M. Destler, *Making Foreign Economic Policy* (Washington, DC: Brookings Institution, 1980); and I. M. Destler, *American Trade Politics*, 4th ed. (Washington, DC: Institute for International Economics, 2005).

5. For more detail on fast track and how the process functioned through 1996, see I. M. Destler, "Renewing Fast-Track Legislation," Policy Analysis No. 50, Institute for International Economics (September 1997). The procedures were renamed Trade Promotion Authority (TPA) by the George W. Bush administration in 2001.

6. Remarks of secretary of the treasury James A. Baker III at the Institute for International Economics, Washington, DC, September 14, 1987.

7. This chart (in Destler, *American Trade Politics*, 283) is reprinted with permission from Sarah A. Binder, *Stalemate: Causes and Consequences of Legislative Gridlock* (Washington, DC: Brookings Institution, 2003), 24–25. Binder's liberal-conservative scores draw upon Nolan M. McCarty et al., *Income Redistribution and the Realignment of American Politics* (Washington, DC: American Enterprise Institute, 1997).

8. Destler, *American Trade Politics*, chap. 11.

9. *Americans on CAFTA and U.S. Trade Policy*, a PIPA/Knowledge Networks study, July 11, 2005.

10. On the Uruguay Round agreements approved in 1994, Republicans split 121–56. On the China/WTO vote, the division was 164–57.

11. I address this matter in detail in "Trade Promotion Authority in 2001: The Bargain That Wasn't," appendix A to Destler, *American Trade Politics*, 331–42.

12. For details, see I. M. Destler, *American Trade Politics in 2007: Building Bipartisan Compromise*, Peterson Institute Policy Brief No. 07-5, May 2007.

13. Susan C. Schwab, "After Doha: Why the Negotiations Are Doomed and What We Should Do About It," *Foreign Affairs* (May/June 2011): 104–17.

14. Craig VanGrasstek, "Dereliction of Duties," draft manuscript (2011).

15. Calls for a "new social compact" were prevalent in the middle of the past decade. For a summary, see Destler, *American Trade Politics*, chapter 2. For a proposal to the Obama administration, see "A New Trade Policy for the United States: A Report to the President-Elect and the 111th Congress from the Trade Policy Study Group," Peterson Institute for International Economics (December 2008). The 2009 stimulus bill included a substantial broadening of trade adjustment assistance, but the sweeping Republican victory in 2010 took the momentum from this achievement and forced its proponents to play defense.

16. "U.S. Trade and Investment Policy," Independent Task Force Report No. 67, Council on Foreign Relations (September 2011).

III

DECISION-MAKERS AND THEIR POLICYMAKING POSITIONS

Foreign policy choices are often made by a remarkably small number of individuals, the most conspicuous of whom is the president. As Harry S. Truman exclaimed, "I make American foreign policy."

Because of the president's power and preeminence, it is tempting to think of foreign policy as determined exclusively by presidential preferences and to personalize government by identifying a policy with its proponents. "There is properly no history, only biography" is how Ralph Waldo Emerson dramatized the view that individual leaders are the makers and movers of history. This "hero-in-history" model finds expression in the practice of attaching the names of presidents to the policies they promulgate (e.g., the Truman Doctrine, the Kennedy Round, the Bush Doctrine, the Obama Doctrine), as if the men were synonymous with the nation itself and of routinely attributing foreign policy successes and failures to the administrations in which they occur.

The conviction that the individual who holds office makes a difference is one of the major premises underlying the electoral process. Thus, each new administration seeks to distinguish itself from its predecessor and to highlight policy departures as it seeks to convey the impression that it has engineered a new (and better) order. The media's tendency to label presidential actions "new" abets those efforts. Hence, leadership and policy are portrayed as synonymous, and changes in policy and policy direction are often perceived as the results of the predispositions of leaders themselves.

Clearly, leaders' individual attributes exert a potentially powerful influence on American foreign policy, and no account of policy sources would be complete without a discussion of them. Still, many scholars question the accuracy of this popular model. They argue that the hero-in-history, or idiosyncratic, model is misleading and simplistic, that it ascribes too much influence to the individuals responsible for the conduct of American foreign policy and implicitly assumes that this influence is the same for all leaders in all circumstances.

That individuals make a difference is unassailable, but it is more useful to ask (1) under what circumstances the idiosyncratic qualities of leaders exert their greatest impact, (2) what types of institutional structures and management strategies different leaders are likely to follow, and (3) what policy variations are most likely to result from different types of leaders. These questions force us to examine how individual characteristics find expression in foreign policy outcomes and how the policymaking roles that leaders occupy may circumscribe their individual influence.

When we consider the mediating impact of policymakers' roles, we draw attention to the fact that many different people, widely dispersed throughout the government, contribute to the making of American foreign policy. In part II, we examined some of the departments and agencies of government involved in the process. Here, in part III, the concern is with decision-makers and how the roles created by the government's foreign policy–related organizational structures influence the behavior of the policymakers occupying these roles and, ultimately, American foreign policy itself. As a rival hypothesis to the hero-in-history image of political leadership, "role theory" posits that the positions and the processes rather than the characteristics of the people who decide influence the behavior and choices of those responsible for making and executing the nation's foreign policy. Furthermore, in this view, changes in policy presumably result from changes in role conceptions rather than from changes in the individuals who occupy these roles.

Role theory also leads us to other perspectives on how policymakers make foreign policy choices. Considerable evidence, drawn from foreign policy case studies, points toward the pressures for conformity among those responsible for choosing among competing foreign policy alternatives, pressures that may lead to less than optimal choices. Furthermore, the principal actors in the foreign affairs government often compete with one another as they consider competing policy alternatives, with their respective bargaining positions dictated by organizational preferences rather than national interests. In particular, the "bureaucratic politics" model of decision-making stresses the importance of the roles individuals occupy in large-scale organizations and the struggles that occur among their constituent units. Proponents of the model claim it captures the essence of the highly politicized foreign policy decision-making process more accurately than does the model of rational behavior, which assumes that the government operates as a single, unitary actor. That popular decision-making model maintains that policymakers—notably the president and his principal advisers—

devise strategies and implement plans to realize goals "rationally"—that is, in terms of calculations about national interests based on the relative costs and benefits associated with alternative goals and means.

Graham Allison's book *Essence of Decision*, a study of the 1962 Cuban Missile Crisis, is the best-known effort to articulate and apply the bureaucratic politics model as an alternative to the rational actor model. Allison developed two alternative strands of the bureaucratic politics model. One, which he calls the *organizational process* paradigm, reflects the constraints that organizational procedures and routines place on decision-makers' choices. The other, which he calls *governmental politics*, draws attention to the "pulling and hauling" that occurs among the key bureaucratic participants in the decision process.[1]

How, from the perspective of organizational processes, do large-scale bureaucracies affect policymaking? One way is by devising standard operating procedures for coping with policy problems when they arise. For example, when the George W. Bush administration began talking about options for dealing with weapons of mass destruction in mid-2002, the absence of large forces-in-being in situ constrained its choice of military options. Over the next several months, the administration began deploying large military forces to the Middle East as a prelude to a war with Iraq. Ground forces were moved into Kuwait and surrounding countries; naval forces were dispatched to the Persian Gulf, the Indian Ocean, and the Mediterranean Sea; and reserve forces at home were mobilized to replace and supplement those sent abroad. The deployments' purpose was to maximize the military options available to the administration even as it pursued diplomatic strategies. Still, it is reasonable to assume that the deployments themselves and planning for various military options followed previously rehearsed routines, much as they had more than a decade earlier as a prelude to the Persian Gulf War. The organizational routines of the various units deployed arguably shaped what was possible and what was not (could missiles placed near Islamic mosques be destroyed from the air without also destroying the mosques?), thus constraining the menu of choice available not only to military leaders but also to the president and his civilian advisers.

The Bush administration, for example, faced the same organizational constraints when considering military options against possible other targets. With as many as 180,000 American troops tied down in Iraq and Afghanistan, with 500,000 military personnel needed for training purposes, and with another 150,000 personnel assigned worldwide, the administration had little flexibility in pursuing military options against perceived nuclear threats, such as Iran and North Korea, even if it were inclined to do so.[2] By early 2007, the administration acknowledged as much when President Bush in his State of the Union Address called for an increase of 92,000 active-duty personnel for the army and the Marine Corps.

The Obama administration faced the same kind of organizational constraints when it was considering the "surge strategy" over Afghanistan in late
2009. The logistics of transferring American military forces to that country
rapidly and efficiently were undoubtedly a part of the calculation that went
into the decision-making process. Further, when the Obama administration was considering the implementation of a "no-fly zone" over Libya
in response to the actions of Muammar Qaddafi's government against its
people, the availability of American military personnel for such an operation, with two ongoing wars elsewhere, was undoubtedly one consideration
(among others) in the decision-making. Moreover, the Obama administration opted to provide support for that operation, although leaving most
of the enforcement of this "no-fly zone" to other NATO nations. In short,
organizational processes shape and constrain foreign policy options.

Governmental politics, the second strand in the bureaucratic politics
model as articulated by Allison, draws attention to the way individuals act
in organizational settings. Not surprisingly, and as role theory predicts, the
many participants in the deliberations that lead to foreign policy choices
often define issues and favor policy alternatives that reflect their organizational affiliations. "Where you stand depends on where you sit" is a favorite
aphorism reflecting these bureaucratic (role) imperatives. Furthermore,
because the players in the game of governmental politics are responsible
for protecting the nation's security, they are "obliged to fight for what they
are convinced is right." The consequence is that "different groups pulling
in different directions produce a result, or better a resultant—a mixture of
conflicting preferences and unequal power of various individuals—distinct
from what any person or group intended."[3]

Sometimes, however, these bureaucratic differences can lead to policy
conflict and stalemates, as witnessed by the Bush administration during
the summer of 2002 when options about possible actions toward Iraq were
considered. While some within the administration favored quick action to
remove Saddam Hussein because of his development and use of weapons
of mass destruction, others, including Secretary of State Colin Powell and
his deputy, Richard Armitage, contended that that approach had "risks
and complexities" that needed more review.[4] Opinion was also reportedly
divided within the Department of Defense, with civilian officials favoring
military action more than military officers. Furthermore, members of Congress and officials from the earlier George H. W. Bush administration also
argued against rapid escalation to military action. Policy development was
thus stalled for a time, and the administration pursued resolutions in the
UN Security Council and Congress to garner more support for more vigorous action against Saddam Hussein.

The Obama administration experienced the same kind of internal policy
dispute over the direction of American policy in Afghanistan in 2009. In the

spring of 2009, the American commander in Afghanistan, General Stanley McChrystal, was ordered to conduct a policy review and make a recommendation to the president by the end of the summer. His recommendation called for the addition of American troops and the pursuance of a counterinsurgency strategy, an approach much like the one pursued by the Bush administration in Iraq in 2007. These recommendations set off an extended bureaucratic debate within the national security team. Vice President Biden, for example, opposed the commitment of more troops and favored a counterterrorism, not a counterinsurgency, strategy in Afghanistan, and the president's special representative to Afghanistan and Pakistan, Richard Holbrooke, largely opposed the sending of more American troops. The uniformed military, including General David Petraeus, and Secretary of Defense Robert Gates backed the recommendations in the McChrystal report; Secretary of State Hillary Clinton came to support that position as well. Nonetheless, the bureaucratic debate went on for several months before a presidential decision was announced on December 1, 2009, at West Point.[5]

The examples are consistent with the logic of the bureaucratic politics model, suggesting that sometimes the explanation for why states make the choices they do lies not in their behavior in terms of one another but because they are constrained by the disputes within their own governments. Furthermore, rather than presupposing the existence of a unitary actor, as the rational model does, the bureaucratic politics model suggests that "it is necessary to identify the games and players, to display the coalitions, bargains, and compromises, and to convey some feel for the confusion" in the policymaking process.[6]

In virtually every situation in which the United States has contemplated the use of force in recent years—in the Persian Gulf, Afghanistan, Somalia, Bosnia, Rwanda, Haiti, Kosovo, and Iraq—policymakers and critics alike have worried about the specter of Vietnam and the "lessons" it taught. In part this is because the protracted series of decisions that took the United States into Vietnam—and eventually out of it, on unsatisfactory terms after years of fighting and the loss of tens of thousands of lives—is fertile ground for probing how American foreign policy is made and implemented.

Part III of this book begins with an account, informed by role theory and bureaucratic politics, of how the United States became involved in and conducted the prolonged war in Southeast Asia. "How Could Vietnam Happen?" asks James C. Thomson Jr., almost rhetorically. The failure in Vietnam, Thomson contends, was the failure of America's policymaking process, not of its leadership. Vietnam shows that some of the most catastrophic of America's foreign policy initiatives have been the result not of evil or stupid people but of misdirected behaviors encouraged by the nature of the policymaking system and the roles and bureaucratic processes embedded in the way the government's foreign policy system is organized.

Thomson's argument, however disturbing, provides insight into the milieu of decision-making and identifies many syndromes crucial to understanding how the roles created by the decision-making setting influence the kinds of decisions that leaders make and that bureaucracies are asked to implement.

With the Vietnam experience as a backdrop, the next series of policymaking cases examines the impact of role theory, bureaucratic politics, and individuals in accounting for the actions taken more recently. For the individual analyses, the cases point to the impact of the position held by policymakers and to the personal characteristics that they bring to the policy process as explanations. The illustrative cases span several recent administrations—the Carter decision-making over the effort to rescue American hostages in the late 1970s, the George H. W. Bush administration's actions over Somalia and Bosnia in the early 1990s, the decision to expand the North Atlantic Treaty Organization (NATO) by the Clinton administration in the mid-1990s, the bureaucratic struggle over the V-22 Osprey primarily during the first Bush administration, and American policy options toward Iran in light of its seeming efforts to develop nuclear weapons during the George W. Bush administration. We conclude by considering the evolving worldview and the decision-making style of Barack Obama as he considered American foreign policy options during the "Arab Spring" in 2011. While all the cases highlight the impact (and limitations) of the bureaucratic setting, several of them also highlight the need to consider other factors, including individual mindsets and beliefs, the availability of information, and idiosyncratic characteristics of individual policymakers, in explaining these foreign policy decisions.

As noted previously, "Where you stand depends on where you sit" is a central maxim of the bureaucratic politics model. The aphorism purports to explain why participants in the deliberations that lead to foreign policy choices often define issues and favor policy alternatives that reflect their organizational affiliations. In "Policy Preferences and Bureaucratic Position: The Case of the American Hostage Rescue Mission," Steve Smith assesses this aphorism and its applicability to individuals working at the highest level of government during the Carter administration. Smith examines the process that led the Carter administration to the fateful decision to attempt a covert, paramilitary rescue of American diplomats held hostage by Iran beginning in late 1979. Like Vietnam, this is a tale of policy shortcomings—of policy failure. How did it happen? Smith does not attempt a complete answer to this question, but he does show that the key participants in the decision process acted in accordance with what the bureaucratic politics approach would suggest: namely, that the national security adviser, the secretary of defense, the chairman of the Joint Chiefs of Staff, and the director of the CIA would support military action; the secretary of state and, in his absence, his deputy would oppose it; those individuals who were bureaucratically tied to the president (the vice president, the press secretary, and the political adviser) would be fundamentally concerned with what was best for the Carter presidency; and President Carter, although clearly more than just another bureaucratic actor, would act in a way that reflected bureaucratically derived as well as personal influences.

Smith's analysis is compelling not only as a study of an important episode in American foreign policy but also as an illustration of the logic of the bureaucratic politics model. It is important also because it shows the pitfalls as well as promises of the perspective and why we must examine both policymaking roles and policymakers themselves. Smith's conclusions are important in this respect: "Role, in and of itself, cannot explain the positions adopted by individuals. . . . Yet role occupiers do become predisposed to think in certain bureaucratic ways, and for a variety of psychological reasons they tend to adopt mindsets compatible with those of their closest colleagues. In addition, individuals are often chosen for a specific post *because* they have certain kinds of worldviews." In the final analysis, then, to understand the impact of decision-makers and their policymaking positions on American foreign policy, we must understand both.

While Smith shows that the bureaucratic politics model applies to individuals working inside the government, does it also apply to organizations, both inside and outside government? The next chapter, "Roles, Politics, and the Survival of the V-22 Osprey," by Christopher M. Jones, begins to provide an answer to the inquiry. Drawing explicitly on Graham Allison's work, he extends the model to show how bureaucratic organizations' roles and interests and those of other policy actors predict their policy stands. The case examined is that of the V-22 Osprey, an innovative tilt-rotor transport plane that the Marine Corps wanted to replace its helicopters. Although Jones outlines the survival of the production of this aircraft to the present day— despite various attempts to cancel the program over the years—he concentrates his case analysis on the period from 1989 to 1992 and particularly its survival during the George H. W. Bush administration. During that period, despite "two separate crashes . . . the falsification of maintenance records . . . and unfavorable reports concerning the V-22's safety and reliability," the Osprey's supporters deflected efforts by the government to cancel it. Its survival, Jones argues, is explained by "a diverse but durable group of political actors" who worked to save it despite having "different reasons based on their distinct organizational roles and interests"—an analysis much in accord with the bureaucratic model.

Four principal players were involved in the decision. Support came from members of Congress, the Marine Corps, and the plane's contractors. The principal opposition came from the Office of the Secretary of Defense (OSD) within the Pentagon, whose civilian staff are the principal advisers to the secretary of defense, and from the secretary himself.

The Program Analysis and Evaluation office within the OSD had long been opposed to the V-22 on cost grounds, and its opposition was enhanced when Dick Cheney became secretary of defense. Indeed, Cheney actually announced the cancellation of the plane in April 1989, but he was unable to make that decision stick because of the other actors involved. Cheney's opposition focused on the plane's high cost and his belief that the transport mission of the plane "could be accomplished by less expensive helicopters." To support its position, the OSD regularly proposed alternatives to the Osprey in its annual budget messages to Congress; tried to "transfer, defer, or rescind V-22 appropriations"; and even "refused to spend money Congress had appropriated." OSD used other tactics as well to undermine the V-22 program, but all of them failed. Ultimately, the Bush administration "dropped its opposition and indicated that it would not stand in the way of spending $1.5 billion on the program."

The OSD and the Bush administration lost this bureaucratic battle because of the sustained support that the V-22 received from the other players. Congress, as noted, was a supporter of the plane. Its support "was not unanimous," Jones acknowledges, but "it was pervasive, encompassing conservative Republicans as well as liberal Democrats." Key states (e.g., Texas and Pennsylvania) with lots of jobs and votes at stake were involved in the production of the Osprey, for example, but that was only part of the reason. Members of Congress were also able to muster numerous arguments to support the program. Their arguments ranged from the cutting-edge technology that the plane represented to its flexible and multiple uses, from war fighting to drug interdiction, and to its safety, speed, and range. While policy arguments were important in the battle between the executive and legislative branches, Jones also points out that interbranch conflict was evident, with Congress seeking to protect its "power of the purse" and its right to legislate in the military area.

The two other actors involved also aided these congressional arguments. The position of the Marine Corps, the leading proponent of the Osprey within the executive branch, was based largely on its "role and interests." The Marines Corps saw this new transport plane as an important way to meet its organizational mission. Even after the Bush administration announced its opposition to the Osprey, the marines were still able to undertake "a vigorous, behind-the-scenes campaign on Capitol Hill" on behalf of the aircraft.

The contractors for the Osprey, Bell Helicopter Textron and Boeing, were "active and aggressive proponents." These manufacturers took several actions to widen support for the plane, expanding its domestic appeal by subcontracting out production components and engaging in public relations measures to gain greater support. The manufacturers, of course, were motivated by economic benefits, which distinguished them from the Marine Corps or members of Congress, but the three groups' shared interests were enough to ensure the survival of the Osprey—despite the opposition of the executive branch and the Pentagon leadership.

James Goldgeier, in his "NATO Expansion: The Anatomy of a Decision," supports the argument about the crucial importance of individuals in molding policy and illustrates the limitation on bureaucracies in shaping it. On the basis of extensive interviews with officials knowledgeable or involved in the initial NATO expansion decision during the Clinton administration, Goldgeier demonstrates that bureaucracies—and the individuals in those bureaucracies—can shape debate over an issue and can "pull" and "haul" to promote different positions, but they cannot determine policy. Instead, the issue of whether NATO membership would formally expand or whether the Partnership for Peace option would continue ultimately depended on President Clinton. Not until Clinton made a series of speeches in Brussels, Prague, and Warsaw did bureaucratic differences start to be settled. As Clinton stated, "The question is no longer whether NATO will take on new members but when and how."

The NATO case illustrates the importance of individuals in other ways. For example, Anthony Lake, the national security adviser at the time, and other foreign policy principals were able to move Clinton to make statements that seemingly committed the United States to NATO expansion. They in turn used his remarks as the basis for establishing a working group that set forth an "action plan," thus demonstrating the influence that individuals are sometimes able to exercise in the face of bureaucratic resistance. Particularly interesting is how Richard Holbrooke, assistant secretary of state for European affairs, became the "enforcer" of the NATO expansion decision within the interagency process. Invoking the president's wishes with the argument "either you are on the president's program or you are not," he was able to crystallize the president's key role in the policy choice.

The mindsets, the perceptions of reality, and the information that policymakers possess also affect the nature of the policy choices they pursue. In "Sources of Humanitarian Intervention: Beliefs, Information, and Advocacy in U.S. Decisions on Somalia and Bosnia," Jon Western argues that the initial decisions of the administration of George H. W. Bush in these cases were primarily functions of the belief systems among key policymakers and of their ability to use information and advocacy to shape those policy decisions. Yet Western's case study also demonstrates how information and advocacy can change the direction of American policy, as the Bush administration did in late 1992 toward Somalia.

Prior to its 1992 policy shift, Western argues, the Bush administration's policies toward Bosnia and Somalia were a function of the pervasive perception among key officials (the president, his key aides, and especially the Joint Chiefs of Staff) that the events in those two countries did not affect

U.S. national interests and American interventions "could only lead to a Vietnam-style quagmire." This perception of the "selective engagers" stood in contrast to the views of the "liberal humanitarians," who sought to intervene to prevent the human tragedies, massive killings, and wholesale starvation then occurring in Bosnia and Somalia. In addition, the perceptions of the key policymakers dominated the policy process because the administration controlled much of the information and more of the policy advocacy machinery. As Western notes, "The U.S. media . . . had little expertise in the Balkans," and "there was no galvanizing force that either linked disparate humanitarian organizations or mobilized the press corps." In short, the selective engagers had a clear edge over the liberal humanitarians in the policy process.

By the summer of 1992, however, perceptions began to change as both the media and liberal humanitarians "gradually developed and dedicated more resources for their own information-collection efforts to challenge the administration's framing of the two conflicts." Most notable were a report by the U.S. ambassador to Kenya about his visit to a refugee camp on the Somali-Kenyan border and a fact-finding visit by two U.S. senators to Somalia. At about the same time, reports surfaced about radical Serb nationalist and paramilitary forces "committing horrific atrocities" and about Serb-run concentration camps in Bosnia. These and other revelations began to challenge seriously the thinking of the selective engagers within the Bush administration, as did the challenge from presidential candidate Bill Clinton, who argued for more robust American actions in Bosnia.

Later that year, the Bush administration began to modify its position. Although President Bush "ordered his team to contest the liberal humanitarian view that U.S. intervention could quickly break the siege of Sarajevo with little cost to American lives," he ordered the Air Force to provide assistance in transporting relief to Somalia and agreed to American funding for Pakistani peacekeepers in that county. Western argues that this shift occurred because of increased political pressure on the administration regarding its policies in Somalia and Bosnia.

The change in policy direction continued even as selective engagers and liberal humanitarians continued their propaganda campaigns. After his victory in early November, Clinton visited Washington for various briefings, contributing to what Western calls the "cumulative pressure" on the selective engagers to change course. Within days, the Joint Chiefs of Staff reversed their opposition to intervention in Somalia. President Bush followed suit a few days later. Western attributes the policy reversal to the "mobilized political opposition" and its ability "to challenge the administration's framing of the crisis."

In "Last Stand," *New Yorker* contributor Seymour M. Hersh explores policymaking in the George W. Bush administration over the emerging nuclear threat with Iran. In particular, he examines the policymaking over the Bush administration's decision to plan for a possible military response if Iran were to develop nuclear weapons capability. While Hersh focuses on the bureaucratic debate—and especially the concerns of the military—he also outlines the concerns of other countries regarding this policy proposal. What is important to note about this analysis is the extent to which the military dissent on this bombing proposal is both among the services and between the services and their civilian leaders.

The military, as Hersh explains, is concerned by the difficulty that the bombing task poses—"The target array in Iran is huge, but it's amorphous," one general told Hersh; the lack of adequate intelligence on Iran's nuclear program, especially after the failures in Iraq on weapons of mass destruction; and the consequence of such an attack both for the United States and for the region. In all these areas, the top military leadership has serious doubts about the advisability of such actions since American ships in the Persian Gulf or Americans in Iraq might well be targets of Iranian retaliation. Further, America might also have to face the cutoff of oil shipments in the Persian Gulf or the Strait of Hormuz by Iranian actions. Finally, as Hersh notes, the Gulf States (e.g., Qatar) are uneasy about such planning since they would become ready targets for Iran, and the Europeans would be unlikely to support this kind of action. Only Israel seems supportive of this action, and it may feel compelled to act if the United States fails to do so.

To be sure, the military itself is divided on such actions, with the Air Force more supportive than any of the other branches, but there are limits within this bureaucratic setting over how persuasive the services can be. After all, they are subject to civilian leadership. As a former Air Force colonel quoted by Hersh says, "Plans are more and more being directed and run by civilians from the Office of the Secretary of Defense," and "the military is increasingly upset about not being taken seriously by [then-Secretary] Rumsfeld and his staff." While the military "achieved a major victory" when it convinced the White House to drop "its insistence that the plan for a bombing campaign include the possible use of a nuclear device," it still has serious limits on its actions. Yet, as Hersh concludes, "the generals will, of course, follow their orders" if the "administration decides on military action."

Several important messages about the bureaucratic politics model emerge from this chapter. First, it illustrates the role constraints that operate on the military. Since by tradition and law the military is always under civilian leadership, military disagreements with their civilian bosses in the American system always must be subsumed to civilian control. Second, this episode is a useful illustration of how individual preferences of military personnel are subject to the requirements (and limitations) of role responsibility in a bureaucratic setting. Third, not all the "players" in the bureaucratic process are equal since role requirements may constrain some players, such as the military in this instance, from fully impacting the policy process.

In "Obama: The Consequentialist," Ryan Lizza outlines the foreign policy beliefs of President Barack Obama and uses them to analyze his actions over the first part of his term, with particular emphasis on the period of the "Arab Spring." Moreover, Lizza ends up characterizing the foreign policy approach of President Obama as neither realist nor idealist; rather, he concludes that his approach is to decide "his response to every threat on its own merits." In this sense, he has become a foreign policy "consequentialist."

Such an approach developed over time for Senator Obama and then President Obama. Indeed, he came to Washington with limited foreign policy experience after winning election to the Senate. Although he had lived in Indonesia for a time in his childhood and had traveled abroad during his college-age years, he was not particularly knowledgeable about foreign affairs. As a result, he initially gravitated to the foreign policy views espoused by the left, particularly those of Harvard professor and author Samantha Power and Princeton professor Anne-Marie Slaughter. Yet as Obama began to entertain the idea of running for president, he reassessed his foreign policy views and thus called for "a strategy no longer driven by ideology and politics, but one that is based on a realistic assessment of the sobering facts on the ground and our interests in the region." He judged that "this kind of realism has been missing since the very conception of this [Iraq] war." In this vein, Obama reached out for advice and counsel from Zbigniew Brzezinski, former national security adviser to President Carter and a foreign policy realist.

As a result, Lizza contends that foreign policy realists ruled in the White House after President Obama's inauguration and that the administration's foreign policy priorities reflected that emphasis. The priorities were to end the wars in Iraq and Afghanistan, rebuild America's leadership, and focus more on Asia, the global economy, and nuclear nonproliferation. By contrast, human rights and democratic promotion were not a focus. Indeed, the reluctance of the administration to speak out during the Green Revolution in Iran (and indeed seeking to silence a State Department operative who sought to take action in the direction of support for democratic change) is one indicator of this focus, but the decision to support the "surge" strategy in Afghanistan in late 2009 is another. As Lizza writes, the State Department and Secretary of State Hillary Clinton, ironically in light of her realist leaning, were actually the forces keeping foreign policy idealism alive.

By mid-2010, some change in foreign policy appeared to be developing. President Obama called for an assessment of pursuing political reform in the Middle East and North Africa and asked his staff to develop new strategies, including those thinking outside the box. By the time that his staff had finished their work on this request, events were unfolding in the Middle East, and those events quickly became labeled the "Arab Spring": a series of democratic movements across the region. Lizza then analyzes, in considerable detail, the development of America's policy toward these movements, first with regard to Egypt and then with regard to Libya. In both instances, President Obama moved away from his initial realist impulse, and he eventually adopted more idealist positions. Both policy decisions were done on a case-by-case assessment, though, and his positions evolved rather than were decisively announced in each instance.

In the case of Egypt, President Obama initially seemed "to talk like an idealist while acting like a realist" as he sought to balance calling for political transition in that country and not seeking to abandon President Mubarak. Ultimately, though, President Obama moved to support the change emerging in the streets of Cairo and "aligned with the policy views of the idealists." With the Libyan case, and the emerging revolution there, President Obama faced the same ideological dilemma—exacerbated somewhat by the division at home between his secretary of state and secretary of defense over the proper policies to pursue. The president thus chose to "lead from behind" by letting other countries be out front, but working hard to get regional and United Nations support for the subsequent action of imposing a "no-fly" zone on Libya. Further, and ultimately, the administration secured passage of a UN Security Council resolution with a felicitous phrase allowing even more vigorous action by the allied countries. Indeed, President Obama went on to call for regime change in Libya. In this sense, the Libyan case illustrates this swing back to idealism and the promotion of the "responsibility to protect" doctrine by the international community for those people being harmed by their own government.

Still, Lizza concludes that these actions represent less an Obama Doctrine and more the choice of the president to decide on policy based on facts on the ground. Indeed, Lizza notes the president's own statement on this matter: "When you start applying blanket policies on the complexities of the current world situation, you're going to get yourself into trouble."

Editor's Note: At the end of each chapter entry is a series of discussion questions for use by the students and instructor.

NOTES

1. See Graham T. Allison, *Essence of Decision: Explaining the Cuban Missile Crisis* (Boston: Little, Brown, 1971), and Graham T. Allison and Philip Zelikow, *Essence of Decision: Explaining the Cuban Missile Crisis*, 2nd ed. (New York: Longman, 1999).

2. Edward Luttwak, "Change Course: It's the First Rule of the Re-elected," *Sunday Telegraph*, November 14, 2004, 22.

3. Allison, *Essence of Decision*, 145.

4. Todd S. Purdom and Patrick E. Tyler, "Top Republicans Break with Bush on Iraq Strategy," *New York Times*, August 16, 2002.

5. For an extended discussion of the internal debate over Afghanistan policy during the first year of the Obama administration, see Bob Woodward, *Obama's Wars* (New York: Simon & Schuster, 2010). Also see James M. McCormick, "The Obama Presidency: A Foreign Policy of Change?" in Steven E. Schier, ed., *Transforming America: Barack Obama in the White House* (Lanham, MD: Rowman & Littlefield, 2011), 235–66.

6. Allison, *Essence of Decision*, 146.

18

How Could Vietnam Happen?

An Autopsy

James C. Thomson Jr.

As a case study in the making of foreign policy, the Vietnam War will fasci-
nate historians and social scientists for many decades to come. One question that will certainly be asked: How did men of superior ability, sound
training, and high ideals—American policymakers of the 1960s—create
such a costly and divisive policy?

As one who watched the decision-making process in Washington from
1961 to 1966 under Presidents Kennedy and Johnson, I can suggest a
preliminary answer. I can do so by briefly listing some of the factors that
seemed to me to shape our Vietnam policy during my years as an East Asia
specialist at the State Department and the White House. I shall deal largely
with Washington as I saw or sensed it, and not with Saigon, where I spent
but a scant three days, in the entourage of the vice president, or with other
decision centers, the capitals of interested parties. Nor will I deal with other
important parts of the record: Vietnam's history prior to 1961, for instance,
or the overall course of America's relations with Vietnam.

Yet a first and central ingredient in these years of Vietnam decisions
does involve history. The ingredient was *the legacy of the 1950s*—by which
I mean the so-called loss of China, the Korean War, and the Far East policy
of Secretary of State Dulles. This legacy had an institutional by-product
for the Kennedy administration: In 1961 the U.S. government's East Asian
establishment was undoubtedly the most rigid and doctrinaire of Washington's regional divisions in foreign affairs. This was especially true at the
Department of State, where the incoming administration found the Bureau
of Far Eastern Affairs the hardest nut to crack. It was a bureau that had been
purged of its best China expertise, and of farsighted, dispassionate men,
as a result of McCarthyism. Its members were generally committed to one

policy line: the close containment and isolation of mainland China, the harassment of "neutralist" nations that sought to avoid alignment with either Washington or Peking, and the maintenance of a network of alliances with anticommunist client states on China's periphery.

Another aspect of the legacy was the special vulnerability and sensitivity of the new Democratic administration on Far East policy issues. The memory of the McCarthy era was still very sharp, and Kennedy's margin of victory was too thin. The 1960 Offshore Islands TV debate between Kennedy and Nixon had shown the president-elect the perils of "fresh thinking." The administration was inherently leery of moving too fast on Asia. As a result, the Far East Bureau (now the Bureau of East Asian and Pacific Affairs) was the last one to be overhauled. Not until Averell Harriman was brought in as assistant secretary in December 1961 were significant personnel changes attempted, and it took Harriman several months to make a deep imprint on the bureau because of his necessary preoccupation with the Laos settlement. Once he did so, there was virtually no effort to bring back the purged or exiled East Asia experts.

There were other important by-products of this "legacy of the 1950s."

The new administration inherited and somewhat shared a *general perception of China-on-the-march*—a sense of China's vastness, its numbers, its belligerence; a revived sense, perhaps, of the Golden Horde. This was a perception fed by Chinese intervention in the Korean War (an intervention actually based on appallingly bad communications and mutual miscalculation on the part of Washington and Peking, but the careful unraveling of the tragedy, which scholars have accomplished, had not yet become part of conventional wisdom).

The new administration inherited and briefly accepted *a monolithic conception of the communist bloc*. Despite much earlier predictions and reports by outside analysts, policymakers did not begin to accept the reality and possible finality of the Sino-Soviet split until the first weeks of 1962. The inevitably corrosive impact of competing nationalisms on communism was largely ignored.

The new administration inherited and to some extent shared the "*domino theory*" about Asia. This theory resulted from profound ignorance of Asian history and hence ignorance of the radical differences among Asian nations and societies. It resulted from a blindness to the power and resilience of Asian nationalisms. (It may also have resulted from a subconscious sense that since "all Asians look alike," all Asian nations will act alike.) As a theory, the domino fallacy was not merely inaccurate but also insulting to Asian nations.

Finally, the legacy of the 1950s was apparently compounded by an uneasy sense of a worldwide communist challenge to the new administration after the Bay of Pigs fiasco. A first manifestation was the president's traumatic Vienna meeting with Khrushchev in June 1961; then came the Berlin crisis of the summer. All this created an atmosphere in which President Kennedy undoubtedly felt under special pressure to show his nation's mettle in Vietnam—if the Vietnamese, unlike the people of Laos, were willing to fight.

In general, the legacy of the 1950s shaped such early moves of the new administration as the decisions to maintain a high-visibility Southeast Asia Treaty Organization (SEATO; by sending the secretary of state himself instead of some underling to its first meeting in 1961), to back away from diplomatic recognition of Mongolia in the summer of 1961, and, most important, to expand U.S. military assistance to South Vietnam that winter on the basis of the much more tentative Eisenhower commitment. It should be added that the increased commitment to Vietnam was also fueled by a new breed of military strategists and academic social scientists (some of whom had entered the new administration) who had developed theories of counterguerrilla warfare and were eager to see them put to the test. To some, "counterinsurgency" seemed a new panacea for coping with the world's instability.

So much for the legacy and the history. Any new administration inherits both complicated problems and simplistic views of the world. But surely among the policymakers of the Kennedy and Johnson administrations there were men who would warn of the dangers of an open-ended commitment to the Vietnam quagmire?

This raises a central question at the heart of the policy process: Where were the experts, the doubters, and the dissenters? Were they there at all, and if so, what happened to them?

The answer is complex but instructive.

In the first place, the American government was sorely *lacking in real Vietnam or Indochina expertise*. Originally treated as an adjunct of Embassy Paris, our Saigon embassy and the Vietnam Desk at State were largely staffed from 1954 onward by French-speaking Foreign Service personnel of narrowly European experience. Such diplomats were even more closely restricted than the normal embassy officer—by cast of mind as well as language—to contacts with Vietnam's French-speaking urban elites. For instance, Foreign Service linguists in Portugal are able to speak with the peasantry if they get out of Lisbon and choose to do so; not so the French speakers of Embassy Saigon.

In addition, the *shadow of the "loss of China"* distorted Vietnam reporting. Career officers in the department, and especially those in the field, had not forgotten the fate of their World War II colleagues who wrote in frankness from China and were later pilloried by Senate committees for critical comments on the Chinese nationalists. Candid reporting on the strengths of the Viet Cong and the weaknesses of the Diem government was inhibited by the memory. It was also inhibited by some higher officials, notably Ambassador Nolting in Saigon, who refused to sign off on such cables.

In due course, to be sure, some Vietnam talent was discovered or developed. But a recurrent and increasingly important factor in the decision-making process was the *banishment of real expertise*. Here the underlying cause was the "closed politics" of policymaking as issues become hot: The more sensitive the issue, and the higher it rises in the bureaucracy, the more completely the experts are excluded while the harassed senior generalists take over (that is, the secretaries, undersecretaries, and presidential assistants). The frantic skimming of briefing papers in the back seats of limousines is no substitute for the presence of specialists; furthermore, in times of crisis such papers are deemed "too sensitive" even for review by the specialists. Another underlying cause of this banishment, as Vietnam became more critical, was the replacement of the experts, who were generally and increasingly pessimistic, by men described as "can-do guys": loyal and energetic fixers unsoured by expertise. In early 1965, when I confided my growing policy doubts to an older colleague on the National Security Council (NSC) staff, he assured me that the smartest thing both of us could do was to "steer clear of the whole Vietnam mess"; the gentleman in question had the misfortune to be a "can-do guy," however, and [was subsequently] highly placed in Vietnam, under orders to solve the mess.

Despite the banishment of the experts, internal doubters and dissenters did indeed appear and persist. Yet as I watched the process, such men were effectively neutralized by a subtle dynamic: *the domestication of dissenters*. Such "domestication" arose out of a twofold clubbish need: on the one hand, the dissenter's desire to stay aboard; and on the other hand, the nondissenter's conscience. Simply stated, dissent, when recognized, was made to feel at home. On the lowest possible scale of importance, I must confess my own considerable sense of dignity and acceptance (both vital) when my senior White House employer would refer to me as his "favorite dove." Far more significant was the case of the former under-secretary of state George Ball. Once Mr. Ball began to express doubts, he was warmly institutionalized: He was encouraged to become the in-house devil's advocate on Vietnam. The upshot was inevitable: The process of escalation allowed for periodic requests to Mr. Ball to speak his piece; Ball felt good, I assume (he had fought for righteousness); the others felt good (they had given a full hearing to the dovish option); and there was minimal unpleasantness. The club remained intact; and it is, of course, possible that matters would have gotten worse faster if Mr. Ball had kept silent, or left before his final departure in the fall of 1966. There was also, of course, the case of the last institutionalized doubter, Bill Moyers. The president is said to have greeted his arrival at meetings with an affectionate "Well, here comes Mr. Stop-the-

Bombing." Here again the dynamics of domesticated dissent sustained the relationship for a while.

A related point—and crucial, I suppose, to government at all times—was *the "effectiveness" trap*, the trap that keeps men from speaking out, as clearly or as often as they might, within the government. And it is the trap that keeps men from resigning in protest and airing their dissent outside the government. The most important asset that a man brings to bureaucratic life is his "effectiveness," a mysterious combination of training, style, and connections. The most ominous complaint that can be whispered of a bureaucrat is "I'm afraid Charlie's beginning to lose his effectiveness." To preserve your effectiveness, you must decide where and when to fight the mainstream of policy; the opportunities range from pillow talk with your wife, to private drinks with your friends, to meetings with the secretary of state or the president. The inclination to remain silent or to acquiesce in the presence of the great men—to live to fight another day, to give on this issue so that you can be "effective" on later issues—is overwhelming. Nor is it the tendency of youth alone; some of our most senior officials, men of wealth and fame, whose place in history is secure, have remained silent lest their connection with power be terminated. As for the disinclination to resign in protest, while not necessarily a Washington or even American specialty, it seems more true of a government in which ministers have no parliamentary back-bench to which to retreat. In the absence of such a refuge, it is easy to rationalize the decision to stay aboard. By doing so, one may be able to prevent a few bad things from happening and perhaps even make a few good things happen. To exit is to lose even those marginal chances for "effectiveness."

Another factor must be noted: As the Vietnam controversy escalated at home, there developed *a preoccupation with Vietnam public relations as opposed to Vietnam policymaking*. And here, ironically, internal doubters and dissenters were heavily employed. For such men, by virtue of their own doubts, were often deemed best able to "massage" the doubting intelligentsia. My senior East Asia colleague at the White House, a brilliant and humane doubter who had dealt with Indochina since 1954, spent three-quarters of his working days on Vietnam public relations: drafting presidential responses to letters from important critics, writing conciliatory language for presidential speeches, and meeting quite interminably with delegations of outraged Quakers, clergymen, academics, and housewives. His regular callers were the late A. J. Muste and Norman Thomas; mine were members of the Women's Strike for Peace. Our orders from above: Keep them off the backs of busy policymakers (who usually happened to be nondoubters). Incidentally, my most discouraging assignment in the realm of public relations was the preparation of a White House pamphlet titled

"Why Vietnam," in September 1965; in a gesture toward my conscience, I fought—and lost—a battle to have the title followed by a question mark.

Through a variety of procedures, both institutional and personal, doubt, dissent, and expertise were effectively neutralized in the making of policy. But what can be said of the men "in charge"? It is patently absurd to suggest that they produced such tragedy by intention and calculation. But it is neither absurd nor difficult to discern certain forces at work that caused decent and honorable men to do great harm.

Here I would stress the paramount role of *executive fatigue*. No factor seems to me more crucial and underrated in the making of foreign policy. The physical and emotional toll of executive responsibility in State, the Pentagon, the White House, and other executive agencies is enormous; that toll is, of course, compounded by extended service. Many Vietnam policymakers had been on the job for from four to seven years. Complaints may be few, and physical health may remain unimpaired, though emotional health is far harder to gauge. But what is most seriously eroded in the deadening process of fatigue is freshness of thought, imagination, a sense of possibility, a sense of priorities and perspective—those rare assets of a new administration in its first year or two of office. The tired policymaker becomes a prisoner of his own narrowed view of the world and his own clichéd rhetoric. He becomes irritable and defensive—short on sleep, short on family ties, short on patience. Such men make bad policy and then compound it. They have neither the time nor the temperament for new ideas or preventive diplomacy.

Below the level of the fatigued executives in the making of Vietnam policy was a widespread phenomenon: *the curator mentality* in the Department of State. By this I mean the collective inertia produced by the bureaucrat's view of his job. At State, the average "desk officer" inherits from his predecessor our policy toward Country X; he regards it as his function to keep that policy intact—under glass, untampered with, and dusted—so that he may pass it on in two to four years to his successor. And such curatorial service generally merits promotion within the system. (Maintain the status quo, and you will stay out of trouble.) In some circumstances, the inertia bred by such an outlook can act as a brake against rash innovation. But on many issues, this inertia sustains the momentum of bad policy and unwise commitments—momentum that might otherwise have been resisted within the ranks. Clearly, Vietnam [was] such an issue.

To fatigue and inertia must be added the factor of internal confusion. Even among the "architects" of our Vietnam commitment, there was persistent *confusion as to what type of war we were fighting* and, as a direct consequence, *confusion as to how to end that war*. (The "credibility gap" [was], in part, a reflection of such internal confusion.) Was it, for instance, a civil war, in which case counterinsurgency might suffice? Or was it a war of international aggression? (This might invoke SEATO or UN commitment.) Who was the aggressor—and the "real enemy"? The Viet Cong? Hanoi? Peking? Moscow? International communism? Or maybe "Asian communism"? Differing enemies dictated differing strategies and tactics. And confused throughout, in like fashion, was the question of American objectives; your objectives depended on whom you were fighting and why. I shall not forget my assignment from an assistant secretary of state in March 1964: to draft a speech for Secretary McNamara which would, inter alia, once and for all dispose of the canard that the Vietnam conflict was a civil war. "But in some ways, of course," I mused, "it *is* a civil war." "Don't play word games with me!" snapped the assistant secretary.

Similar confusion beset the concept of "negotiations"—anathema to much of official Washington from 1961 to 1965. Not until April 1965 did "unconditional discussions" become respectable, via a presidential speech; even then the secretary of state stressed privately to newsmen that nothing had changed, since "discussions" were by no means the same as "negotiations." Months later that issue was resolved. But it took even longer to obtain a fragile internal agreement that negotiations might include the Viet Cong as something other than an appendage to Hanoi's delegation. Given such confusion as to the whos and whys of our Vietnam commitment, it is not surprising, as Theodore Draper has written, that policymakers found it so difficult to agree on how to end the war.

Of course, one force—a constant in the vortex of commitment—was that of *wishful thinking*. I partook of it myself at many times. I did so especially during Washington's struggle with Diem in the autumn of 1963 when some of us at State believed that for once, in dealing with a difficult client state, the U.S. government could use the leverage of our economic and military assistance to make good things happen, instead of being led around by the nose by foreign dictators. If we could prove that point, I thought, and move into a new day, with or without Diem, then Vietnam was well worth the effort. Later came the wishful thinking of the air-strike planners in the late autumn of 1964; there were those who actually thought that after six weeks of air strikes, the North Vietnamese would come crawling to us to ask for peace talks. And what, someone asked in one of the meetings of the time, if they don't? The answer was that we would bomb for another four weeks, and that would do the trick. And a few weeks later came one instance of wishful thinking that was symptomatic of good men misled: In January 1965, I encountered one of the very highest figures in the administration at a dinner, drew him aside, and told him of my worries about the air-strike option. He told me that I really shouldn't worry; it was his conviction that before any such plans could be put into effect, a neutralist government would come to power in Saigon that would politely invite us out. And finally, there was the recurrent wishful thinking that sustained many of us through the trying months of 1965–1966 after the air strikes had begun: that surely, somehow, one way or another, we would "be in a conference in six months," and the escalatory spiral would be suspended. The basis of our hope: "It simply can't go on."

As a further influence on policymakers, I would cite the factor of *bureaucratic detachment*. By this I mean what at best might be termed the professional callousness of the surgeon (and indeed, medical lingo—the "surgical strike," for instance—seemed to crop up in the euphemisms of the times). In Washington the semantics of the military muted the reality of war for the civilian policymakers. In quiet, air-conditioned, thick-carpeted rooms, such terms as "systematic pressure," "armed reconnaissance," "targets of opportunity," and even "body count" seemed to breed a sort of games theory detachment. Most memorable to me was a moment in the late 1964 target planning when the question under discussion was how heavy our bombing should be, and how extensive our strafing, at some midpoint in the projected pattern of systematic pressure. An assistant secretary of state resolved the point in the following words: "It seems to me that our orchestration should be mainly violins, but with periodic touches of brass." Perhaps the biggest shock of my return to Cambridge, Massachusetts, was the realization that the young men, the flesh and blood I taught and saw on these university streets, were potentially some of the numbers on the charts of those faraway planners. In a curious sense, Cambridge [was] closer to this war than Washington.

There is an unprovable factor that relates to bureaucratic detachment: the ingredient of *cryptoracism*. I do not mean to imply any conscious contempt for Asian loss of life on the part of Washington officials. But I do mean to imply that bureaucratic detachment may well be compounded by a traditional Western sense that there are so many Asians, after all; that Asians have a fatalism about life and a disregard for its loss; that they are cruel and barbaric to their own people; and that they are very different from us (and all look alike?). And I *do* mean to imply that the upshot of such subliminal views is a subliminal question of whether Asians, and particularly Asian peasants, and most particularly Asian communists, are really people—like you and me. To put the matter another way: Would we have pursued quite such policies—and quite such military tactics—if the Vietnamese were white?

It is impossible to write of Vietnam decision-making without writing about language. Throughout the conflict, words were of paramount importance. I refer here to the impact of *rhetorical escalation* and to the *problem of oversell*. In an important sense, Vietnam became of crucial significance to us *because we said that it was of crucial significance*. (The issue obviously relates to the public relations preoccupation described earlier.)

The key here is domestic politics: the need to sell the American people, press, and Congress on support for an unpopular and costly war in which

Hard to sell the war to the ppl.

the objectives themselves [were] in flux. To sell means to persuade, and to persuade means rhetoric. As the difficulties and costs mounted, so did the definition of the stakes. This is not to say that rhetorical escalation is an orderly process; executive prose is the product of many writers, and some concepts—North Vietnamese infiltration, America's "national honor," Red China as the chief enemy—entered the rhetoric only gradually and even sporadically. But there [was] an upward spiral nonetheless. And once you have *said* that the American Experiment itself stands or falls on the Vietnam outcome, you have thereby created a national stake far beyond any earlier stakes.

Crucial throughout the process of Vietnam decision-making was a conviction among many policymakers that Vietnam posed a *fundamental test of America's national will.* Time and again I was told by men reared in the tradition of Henry L. Stimson that all we needed was the will, and we would then prevail. Implicit in such a view, it seemed to me, was a curious assumption that Asians lacked will, or at least that in a contest between Asian and Anglo-Saxon wills, the non-Asians must prevail. A corollary to the persistent belief in will was a *fascination with power* and an awe in the face of the power America possessed as no nation or civilization ever before. Those who doubted our role in Vietnam were said to shrink from the burdens of power, the obligations of power, the uses of power, the responsibility of power. By implication, such men were soft-headed and effete.

Finally, no discussion of the factors and forces at work on Vietnam policymakers can ignore the central fact of *human ego investment.* Men who have participated in a decision develop a stake in that decision. As they participate in further, related decisions, their stake increases. It might have been possible to dissuade a man of strong self-confidence at an early stage of the ladder of decision; but it is infinitely harder at later stages since a change of mind there usually involves implicit or explicit repudiation of a chain of previous decisions.

To put it bluntly, at the heart of the Vietnam calamity was a group of able, dedicated men who were regularly and repeatedly wrong—and whose standing with their contemporaries, and more important, with history, depended, as they saw it, on being proven right. These were not men who could be asked to extricate themselves from error.

The various ingredients I have cited in the making of Vietnam policy created a variety of results, most of them fairly obvious. Here are some that seem to me most central.

Throughout the conflict, there was *persistent and repeated miscalculation* by virtually all the actors, in high echelons and low, whether dove, hawk, or something else. To cite one simple example among many, in late 1964 and early 1965, some peace-seeking planners at State who strongly opposed the projected bombing of the North urged that, instead, American ground

forces be sent to South Vietnam; this would, they said, increase our bargaining leverage against the North—our "chips"—and would give us something to negotiate about (the withdrawal of our forces) at an early peace
conference. Simultaneously, the air-strike option was urged by many in the
military who were dead set against American participation in "another land
war in Asia"; they were joined by other civilian peace-seekers who wanted
to bomb Hanoi into early negotiations. By late 1965, we had ended up with
the worst of all worlds: ineffective and costly air strikes against the North,
spiraling ground forces in the South, and no negotiations in sight.

Throughout the conflict as well, there [was] *a steady give-in to pressures for
a military solution* and only minimal and sporadic efforts at a diplomatic and
political solution. In part this resulted from the confusion (earlier cited)
among the civilians—confusion regarding objectives and strategy. And in
part this resulted from the self-enlarging nature of military investment.
Once air strikes and particularly ground forces were introduced, our investment itself had transformed the original stakes. More air power was needed
to protect the ground forces; and then more ground forces to protect the
ground forces. And needless to say, the military mind develops its own momentum in the absence of clear guidelines from the civilians. Once asked to
save South Vietnam, rather than to "advise" it, the American military could
not but press for escalation. In addition, sad to report, assorted military
constituencies, once involved in Vietnam, had a series of cases to prove: for
instance, the utility not only of air power (the Air Force) but also of super-
carrier-based air power (the Navy). Also, Vietnam policy suffered from one
ironic by-product of Secretary McNamara's establishment of civilian control
at the Pentagon: In the face of such control, interservice rivalry [gave] way to
a united front among the military—reflected in the new but recurrent phenomenon of Joint Chiefs of Staff unanimity. In conjunction with traditional
congressional allies (mostly Southern senators and representatives) such a
united front would pose a formidable problem for any president.

Throughout the conflict, there [were] *missed opportunities, large and small,
to disengage ourselves from Vietnam on increasingly unpleasant but still acceptable
terms.* Of the many moments from 1961 onward, I shall cite only one, the
last and most important opportunity that was lost: In the summer of 1964
the president instructed his chief advisers to prepare for him as wide a range
of Vietnam options as possible for postelection consideration and decision.
He explicitly asked that all options be laid out. What happened next was,
in effect, Lyndon Johnson's slow-motion Bay of Pigs. For the advisers so
effectively converged on one single option—juxtaposed against two other,
phony options (in effect, blowing up the world, or scuttle-and-run)—that
the president was confronted with unanimity for bombing the North from
all his trusted counselors. Had he been more confident in foreign affairs,

had he been deeply informed on Vietnam and Southeast Asia, and had he raised some hard questions that unanimity had submerged, this president could have used the largest electoral mandate in history to de-escalate in Vietnam, in the clear expectation that at the worst a neutralist government would come to power in Saigon and politely invite us out.

In the course of these years, another result of Vietnam decision-making [was] *the abuse and distortion of history.* Vietnamese, Southeast Asian, and Far Eastern history was rewritten by our policymakers, and their spokesmen, to conform to the alleged necessity of our presence in Vietnam. Highly dubious analogies from our experience elsewhere—the "Munich" sellout and "containment" from Europe; the Malayan insurgency and the Korean War from Asia—[were] imported in order to justify our actions. And later events [were] fitted to the Procrustean bed of Vietnam. Most notably, the change of power in Indonesia in 1965–1966 has been ascribed to our Vietnam presence, and virtually all progress in the Pacific region—the rise of regionalism, new forms of cooperation, and mounting growth rates—has been similarly explained. The Indonesian allegation is undoubtedly false (I tried to prove it, during six months of careful investigation at the White House, and had to confess failure); the regional allegation is patently unprovable in either direction (except, of course, for the clear fact that the economies of both Japan and Korea profited enormously from our Vietnam-related procurement in these countries, but that is a costly and highly dubious form of foreign aid).

There is a final result of Vietnam policy I would cite that holds potential danger for the future of American foreign policy: *the rise of a new breed of American ideologues who saw Vietnam as the ultimate test of their doctrine.* I have in mind those men in Washington who have given a new life to the missionary impulse in American foreign relations, who believe that this nation, in this era, has received a threefold endowment that can transform the world. As they see it, that endowment is composed of, first, our unsurpassed military might; second, our clear technological supremacy; and third, our allegedly invincible benevolence (our "altruism," our affluence, our lack of territorial aspirations). Together, it is argued, this threefold endowment provides us with the opportunity and the obligation to ease the nations of the earth toward modernization and stability: toward a full-fledged *Pax Americana Technocratica.* In reaching toward this goal, Vietnam was viewed as the last and crucial test. Once we succeeded there, the road ahead [was seen to be] clear.

Long before I went into government, I was told a story about Henry L. Stimson that seemed to me pertinent during the years that I watched the Vietnam tragedy unfold—and participated in that tragedy. It seems to me more pertinent than ever.

In his waning years Stimson was asked by an anxious questioner, "Mr. Secretary, how on earth can we ever bring peace to the world?" Stimson is said to have answered, "You begin by bringing to Washington a small handful of able men who believe that the achievement of peace is possible. You work them to the bone until they no longer believe that it is possible. And then you throw them out—and bring in a new bunch who believe that it is possible."

DISCUSSION QUESTIONS

1. What is meant by "the legacy of the 1950s"?
2. What were some of the "by-products" of this legacy?
3. Why were the "experts" unable to fully comprehend what was happening in Vietnam?
4. What does Thomson mean when he discusses the "'effectiveness' trap" and the "curator mentality"?
5. What were some key mistakes that Thomson identifies in American policy toward Vietnam?
6. How much impact did role factors or bureaucratic structures have on policymaking in this case?
7. How would you judge the role of individual factors in affecting policy?
8. What appeared to be the consequences of Vietnam policymaking for American foreign policy, according to Thomson?

19

Policy Preferences and Bureaucratic Position

The Case of the American Hostage Rescue Mission*

Steve Smith

Within two days of the seizure by student revolutionaries of the American embassy in Tehran on November 4, 1979, planning began on a possible rescue mission. Initial estimates of the probability of success were "zero," given the severe logistical problems involved in getting to the embassy in Iran and back out of the country without losing a large number of the hostages as casualties. Nevertheless, as negotiations dragged on with very little promise of success, and as the 1980 American presidential election campaign approached, the decision was made to undertake a very bold rescue mission. Photographs of the charred remains of the burned-out helicopters in the Dasht-e-Kavir desert provide the most vivid image of the failure of that mission.

The decisions about the mission were taken at three meetings on March 22, April 11, and April 15, 1980, by a very small group of people (on average, there were nine participants). Since 1980, the hostage rescue mission has received considerable coverage in the press and in the memoirs of the participants in that decision-making process. As such, it is an excellent case study for one of the most widely cited but rarely tested theories of foreign policy behavior: the bureaucratic politics approach.

THE THEORETICAL BACKGROUND

The dominant theories of why states act as they do derive from the basic assumption of rationality. Most theories of foreign policy are based on the premise that states act in a more or less monolithic way: Foreign policy

---

*All notes have been deleted.

is, accordingly, behavior that is goal-directed and intentional. Of course, many practitioners and academics quickly move away from the monolith assumption, but they can rarely command the kind of detailed information that would enable them to assess precisely what the factions are and how the balance of views lies in any decision-making group. It is, therefore, very common to talk of states as entities and to analyze "their" foreign policies according to some notion of a linkage between the means "they" choose and the ends these must be directed toward. Since practitioners and academics do not literally "know" why State X undertook Action Y, it becomes necessary to impute intentions to the behavior of states. The rationality linkage makes this task much easier; hence the popularity of the idea of the national interest, which incorporates very clear and powerful views on what the ends of governments are in international society and, therefore, on how the behavior can be linked to intentions. The most important attack on this viewpoint has been the "bureaucratic politics approach," most extensively outlined by Graham Allison in his *Essence of Decision*. According to this approach, foreign policy is the result of pulling and hauling between the various components of the decision-making process. Foreign policy may, therefore, be better explained as the outcome of bureaucratic bargaining than as a conscious choice by a decision-making group. As Allison puts it, the outcome of the decision-making process is not really a result but "a resultant—a mixture of conflicting preferences and unequal power of various individuals—distinct from what any person or group intended." The critical point is that these conflicting preferences are determined, above all, by bureaucratic position. Foreign policy, according to this perspective, is therefore to be explained by analyzing the bureaucratic battleground of policymaking, rather than imputing to something called the state a set of motives and interests. On the bureaucratic battleground, the preferences of the participants are governed by the aphorism . . . "where you stand depends on where you sit." . . .

The decision of the United States government to attempt a rescue of the fifty-three American hostages held in Iran offers an excellent opportunity . . . to test . . . Allison's claims about bureaucratic position and policy preference. . . .

The planning process for the rescue mission began on November 6, 1979, just two days after the hostages were seized in Tehran. During the winter and spring the planning continued, focusing on the composition and training of the rescue force, on the precise location of the hostages and the nature and location of their captors, and on the enormously complex logistical problems involved in mounting the mission. These preparations continued in secret alongside an equally complex process of negotiation for the release of the hostages with the various elements of the Iranian government (including a secret contact in Paris). Bargaining was also under way with the United States' allies, in an attempt to persuade them to impose sanctions on Iran. As noted above, there were three key meetings at which the rescue plan was discussed (on March 22, April 11, and April 15, 1980), although the actual decision to proceed, taken on April 11 and confirmed on April 15, was in many ways only the formal ratification of what had by then become the dominant mode of thinking among President Carter's most senior advisors. There were two schools of thought in the initial re-action to the seizure of the hostages: first, that the United States should impose economic sanctions on Iran; and second, that it should make use of international public opinion and international law to force the Iranian government to release the hostages. As these measures appeared less and less likely to succeed, the U.S. government became involved in attempts to persuade its allies to join in economic sanctions—a move that succeeded just two days before the rescue mission.

President Carter's initial reaction to the seizure was to stress the impor-tance of putting the lives of the hostages first. He declared on December 7, 1979, "I am not going to take any military action that would cause blood-shed or cause the unstable captors of our hostages to attack or punish them." Yet leaks from the White House indicated that military plans were being considered. By late March 1980, President Carter and his advisers were be-coming convinced that negotiations were not going to be successful, a view confirmed by the secret source in the Iranian government. At a meeting held on March 22 at Camp David, the president agreed to a reconnaissance flight into Iran to find an initial landing site for the rescue force (Desert One). The plan called for eight RH-53 helicopters from the aircraft carrier *Nimitz* to fly nearly six hundred miles, at a very low altitude and with radio blackout, from the Arabian Sea to Desert One. There, they would meet the rescue force of ninety-seven men (code named "Delta Force") who would have arrived from Egypt via Oman on four C-130 transport aircraft. The helicopters would refuel from the C-130s and then take Delta Force to a second location (Des-ert Two) some fifty miles southeast of Tehran, where Central Intelligence Agency (CIA) agents would meet them and hide the rescue force at a "moun-tain hideout." Delta Force would remain hidden during the day before being picked up by CIA operatives early the next night and driven to a location known as "the warehouse" just inside Tehran. From there they would attack the embassy and the Foreign Ministry where three of the hostages were held, rescue the hostages, and take them to a nearby soccer stadium, where the helicopters would meet them and transfer them to a further airstrip at Mon-zariyeh, to be taken to Egypt by the C-130s. The planning process had meant that very definite deadlines had emerged: By May 1 there would only be sixteen minutes of darkness more than required for the mission; by May 10, the temperature would be so high that it would seriously hamper helicopter performance. The latest feasible date for the mission appeared to be May 1, and by late March the planners were recommending April 24 for the mission (primarily because a very low level of moonlight was expected that night). But the rescue mission failed. It never got beyond Desert One. Of the eight helicopters assigned to the mission, one got lost in a dust storm and returned to the *Nimitz* and two suffered mechanical breakdowns. This left only five helicopters in working order at Desert One, whereas the plan had called for six to move on to Desert Two. The mission was subsequently aborted, and, in the process of maneuvering to vacate Desert One, one of the helicopters hit a C-130, causing the deaths of eight men.

It is critical, in any discussion of the applicability of the bureaucratic politics approach, to focus on the actual decisions that led to this mission and to review the positions adopted by the participants. We know that the three meetings of March 22, April 11, and April 15 were the decisive ones, and we know who took part and what they said. The key meeting in terms of the actual decision was on April 11, when the "go-ahead" was given. The meeting on March 22 was important because at it President Carter gave permission for aircraft to verify the site for Desert One. The meeting of April 15 was important because Cyrus Vance, the secretary of state, presented his reservations about the decision. As Zbigniew Brzezinski, President Carter's national security adviser, pointed out, "In a way, the decision [on April 11] had been foreshadowed by the discussion initiated at the March 22 briefing at Camp David. From that date on, the rescue mission became the obvious option if negotiations failed—and on that point there was almost unanimous consent within the top echelons of the Administration." A virtually identical set of people were present at those meetings. On March 22, there attended President Carter, Walter Mondale (the vice president), Cyrus Vance (the secretary of state), Harold Brown (the secretary of defense), David Jones (the chairman of the Joint Chiefs of Staff), Stansfield Turner (the director of the CIA), Zbigniew Brzezinski (the national security adviser), Jody Powell (the press secretary), and David Aaron (the deputy national security adviser). On April 11, the same participants convened, except that Warren Christopher, the deputy secretary of state, replaced Cyrus Vance, and Carter's aide Hamilton Jordan replaced Aaron. The final meeting on April 15 was attended by the same people who attended on April 11, except that Vance replaced Christopher.

In order to outline the positions adopted by the participants in this decision-making group, the participants can be divided into four subgroups: President Carter, "hawks," "doves," and "presidential supporters." (These terms are only intended as analytical shorthand.) . . . Although there is a risk of fitting evidence to a preconception, the conclusion . . . is that these groups acted in accordance with what the bureaucratic politics approach would suggest: namely, that the national security adviser, the secretary of defense, the chairman of the Joint Chiefs of Staff, and the director of the CIA would support military action . . . the secretary of state, and in his ab-

sence his deputy, would oppose it; those individuals who were bureaucratically tied to the president (the vice president, the press secretary, and the
political adviser) would be fundamentally concerned with what was best
for the Carter presidency; and President Carter, although clearly more than
just another bureaucratic actor, would act in a way that reflected bureaucratically derived as well as personal influences.

PRESIDENT CARTER

The key to understanding President Carter's position lies in the interaction
between his desire to avoid the blatant use of American military power
and the great pressure on him to satisfy his public and "do something."
From the earliest days of the crisis, he was attacked in the press and by the
Republican party for failing to act decisively. The year 1980 was, of course,
a presidential election year, the president's public opinion rating was poor,
and he was being challenged strongly for the Democratic party's nomination. His promise not to campaign for the election so long as the hostages
were in Iran made his situation worse. He was advised by his campaign staff
that decisive action was needed (especially after the fiasco of the morning
of the Wisconsin primary, on April 1, when the president announced that
the hostages were about to be released). That inaccurate assessment was
seen by many as a reflection of his lack of control over events; it was also
portrayed as manipulating the issue for his own political ends.

Another factor that added to the president's frustration was the desire to
make the allies go ahead with sanctions against Iran. It later turned out that
the allies' belief that the U.S. administration was planning military action
was their main incentive to join in the sanctions, in the hope of forestall-
ing it. But the critical moment came when the president felt that the only
alternative to military action was to wait until, possibly, the end of the year
for the release of the hostages by negotiation. That was the impression he
gained in the early days of April: Information coming out of Tehran indicated that the release of the hostages would be delayed for months by the
parliamentary elections due to be held in Iran on May 16. Indeed, by the
time the rescue mission was undertaken, the favorite estimate of how long
the new government in Iran would take to negotiate was five or six months.
So, as a result of fear that the hostages might be held until the end of 1980,
President Carter determined on a change in policy: "We could no longer
afford to depend on diplomacy. I decided to act." In fact, the president
threatened military action on April 12 and 17, unless the allies undertook
economic sanctions. This action (which, he said, had not been decided on
yet) would involve the interruption of trade with Iran. (This was widely
interpreted as meaning a naval blockade or the mining of Iranian harbors.)

Of course, this was a deliberate smokescreen. Accordingly, when on April 23 the European countries agreed to the imposition of sanctions on Iran, the White House let it be known that this would delay any military action until the summer.

Yet the desire of the president for drastic action is only part of the story. It is evident that he was also extremely concerned to limit the size of the operation, in order to avoid unnecessary loss of life. At the briefing with the mission commander, Colonel Beckwith, on April 16, Carter said, "It will be easy and tempting for your men to become engaged in gunfire with others and to try and settle some scores for our nation. That will interfere with your objective of getting our people out safely. In the eyes of the world, it is important that the scope of this mission be seen as simply removing our people." William Safire has argued that the reason why the mission was unsuccessful was precisely because Carter wanted the rescue to be a humanitarian rather than a combat mission and stipulated only a small force with very limited backup. Hence, in explaining President Carter's position on the rescue mission, two factors seem dominant: a personal concern to ensure that the mission was not to be seen as a punitive military action and a role-governed perception that American national honor was at stake. . . .

Carter's actions were, of course, a response to a number of factors. The bureaucratic politics approach draws our attention to certain of these: specifically, his desire for reelection and his perception of his responsibility as the individual charged with protecting American national honor. Clearly, Carter's personality was an important factor . . . but the bureaucratic politics approach seems much more useful in identifying the kinds of considerations that would be important to Carter than concentrating on notions of what would be most rational for the American nation. This is not to imply that bureaucratic factors are the only important ones in explaining what Carter did, but it is to claim that a bureaucratic perspective paints a far more accurate picture of what caused Carter to act as he did than any of the rival theories of foreign policymaking.

THE HAWKS

The leading political proponents of military action throughout the crisis were Brzezinski and Brown. Drew Middleton wrote, "For months, a hard-nosed Pentagon view had held that the seizure of the hostages itself was an act of war and that the United States was, therefore, justified in adopting a military response." Indeed, just two days after the hostages were taken, Brzezinski, Brown, and Jones began discussing the possibilities of a rescue mission. Their discussions led to the conclusion that an immediate mission was impossible, but Brzezinski felt that "one needed such a contingency scheme in the event . . . that some of the hostages either were put on trial and then sentenced to death or were murdered. . . . Accordingly, in such circumstances, we would have to undertake a rescue mission out of a moral as well as a political obligation, both to keep faith with our people imprisoned in Iran and to safeguard American national honor." In fact, Brzezinski felt a rescue mission was not enough: "It would [be] better if the United States were to engage in a generalized retaliatory strike, which could be publicly described as a punitive action and which would be accompanied by the rescue attempt. If the rescue succeeded, that would be all to the good; if it failed, the U.S. government could announce that it had executed a punitive mission against Iran." This punitive action, he thought, could take the form of a military blockade along with air strikes. In the earliest days of the crisis, Brzezinski, Turner, Jones, and Brown began to meet regularly in private and discuss military options; Brzezinski alone took (handwritten) notes. It was this group which directed the planning for the mission (which used military and CIA personnel) and gave the eventual plan its most detailed review. Similarly, it was Brzezinski who pressed for the reconnaissance flight into Iran, agreed on March 22, and the same group of four who proposed the rescue plan at the April 11 meeting, led by Brown and Jones. But it is clear from the available evidence that Brzezinski was the political force behind military action.

As early as February, Brzezinski felt increasing pressure from the public and from Congress for direct action to be taken against Iran. Brzezinski thought there were three choices: to continue negotiations, to undertake a large military operation, or to mount a small rescue mission. What swung him away from his earlier first choice, a punitive military operation, was the consideration that, after the Soviet intervention in Afghanistan in December 1979, any military action might give the Soviet Union additional opportunities for influence in the Persian Gulf and Indian Ocean: "It now seemed to me more important to forge an anti-Soviet Islamic coalition. It was in this context that the rescue mission started to look more attractive to me." As negotiations failed, Brzezinski sent a memorandum to Carter on April 10 in which he argued that a choice must be made between a punitive military action or a rescue mission. Given his fears about the spread of Soviet influence, Brzezinski recommended the latter option, concluding, "We have to think beyond the fate of the 50 Americans and consider the deleterious effects of a protracted stalemate, growing public frustration, and international humiliation of the U.S." At both the April 11 and April 15 meetings, Brzezinski spoke forcefully in favor of the mission.

Brown and Jones were the main advocates of the actual rescue plan. . . . These two men presented the plan to the April 11 meeting and conducted the detailed private briefing with Carter on April 16; it was Harold Brown who gave the detailed account, and defense, of the mission to the press after its failure. It was also Brown who spoke against the Christopher/Vance position at the April 11 and April 15 meetings. Finally, both Brown and Brzezinski spoke very strongly in justification of the mission after its failure, stating that it had been morally right and politically justified. Brzezinski was said to be "downright cocky about it [the mission] in private and insisting that military action might be necessary in the future." He also warned America's opponents: "Do not scoff at America's power. Do not scoff at American reach."

Turner, the director of the CIA, was also very much in favor of the mission, so much so that it appears that he did not voice the very serious doubts about the mission which had been expressed in a report by a special CIA review group, prepared for him on March 16, 1980. According to this report, the rescue plan would probably result in the loss of 60 percent of the hostages during the mission: "The estimate of a loss rate of 60 percent for the AmEmbassy hostages represents the best estimate." The report also estimated that the mission was as likely to prove a complete failure as a complete success. Yet it was exactly at this time that the review of the plan was undertaken by Brzezinski's small group. To quote Brzezinski again: "A very comprehensive review of the rescue plan undertaken by Brown, Jones, and me in mid-March led me to the conclusion that the rescue mission had a reasonably good chance of success though there probably would be some casualties. *There was no certain way of estimating how large they might be* [emphasis added]." Turner was involved in the detailed briefings of the president; at the meeting of April 11 he even said, "The conditions inside and around the compound are good." The evidence does not suggest that he made his agency's doubts public at any of these meetings, either in the small group or in the group of nine.

To sum up, the positions adopted by those classified here as "hawks" could have been predicted in advance. What is striking about the evidence is the consistency with which these four men—Brown, Brzezinski, Jones, and Turner—proposed policies that reflected their position in the bureaucratic network. . . . To the extent that the bureaucratic politics approach explains the policies adopted by these individuals, it illustrates the weaknesses of rationality-based theories of U.S. foreign policy.

PRESIDENTIAL SUPPORTERS

The next group to consider are those who do not fit into the traditional "hawks-doves" characterization of U.S. government. These are individuals whose primary loyalty is to the president and who would, therefore, be expected to adopt positions that promised to bolster the president's domestic standing. Unlike those groups discussed so far, the first concern of this group is not the nature of U.S. relations with other states, but, rather, the domestic position of the president. Mondale, Powell, and Jordan seem to have been neither "hawks" nor "doves" in their views of the Iranian action; rather, their policy proposals show that their concern was first and foremost with the effect of the crisis on the Carter presidency. This can be seen very clearly in Jordan's memoirs, which reveal both a loyalty to Carter and an evaluation of the rescue mission in terms of how it helped Carter out of a domestic political problem. "I knew our hard-line approach would not bring the hostages home any sooner, but I hoped that maybe it would buy us a little more time and patience from the public." The rescue mission was "the best of a lousy set of options." Throughout his memoirs, at every juncture of the mission's planning, failure, and consequences, Jordan's position is consistently one in which he advocates what he believed would benefit the president. This determined his reaction to Vance's objections (Vance was failing to support the president when he needed it, thereby putting Carter in an uncomfortable position), to the failure of the mission (Congress's reaction would be to concentrate on the lack of consultation, and it might accuse Carter of violating the War Powers Resolution), and to Vance's resignation and his replacement by Ed Muskie (the former created a problem for Carter; the latter was a vote of confidence in Carter's political future).

The evidence also unambiguously supports the contention that Mondale and Powell were motivated above all by an awareness of the president's domestic standing and their perceptions of how it might be improved. Brzezinski notes that Powell, Mondale, and Jordan "were feeling increasingly frustrated and concerned about rising public pressures for more direct action against Iran." All of them seemed to think that direct action was needed to stem this public pressure, especially after the Wisconsin primary announcement on April 1. As Powell put it on April 1, "We are about to have an enormous credibility problem. The combination of not campaigning and that early-morning announcement has made skeptics out of even our friends in the press." Salinger argues that Carter's "campaign for reelection registered the frustrations of the American public. While his political fortunes had risen after the taking of the hostages, he was beginning to slip in the polls and had lost a key primary in New York to Senator Kennedy. Jimmy Carter was now in the midst of a fight for his political life, and it looked as if he was losing. A military operation that freed the hostages would dramatically alter the odds." The position of the "presidential supporters" was summed up in Mondale's contribution to the April 11 meeting, when he said, "The rescue offered us the best way out of a situation which was becoming intolerably humiliating."

The "presidential supporters" then proposed policies that reflected their own bureaucratic position. Mondale, Powell, and Jordan had no vast

bureaucratic interests to represent, nor was their chief concern the relationship between U.S. foreign policy and other states. Each of them owed
their influence to their position vis-à-vis President Carter (as, of course,
did Brzezinski), and their concern was to act so as to aid his presidency,
above all his domestic political fortunes. In contemporary press reports,
it was these three men who voiced concern about the president's relations
with Congress and his chances of reelection. This was in contrast to both
the "hawks" and the "doves" who were far more concerned with Carter's
relations with Iran, the Soviet Union, and U.S. allies. As in the case of the
"hawks," the policy preferences of the "presidential supporters" seem to
have been predominantly determined by their bureaucratic role.

THE DOVES

The evidence that bureaucratic role determines policy stance is strongest of
all in the case of the "doves": Cyrus Vance, the secretary of state, and Warren
Christopher, the deputy secretary of state. Not only did the two men take
virtually identical stands on the subject of the rescue mission, but, as will
be discussed below, Christopher did not know what Vance's position was
when he attended the April 11 meeting.

From the earliest days of the crisis Vance had advised against the use
of military force. At the meeting on March 22, Vance agreed that a reconnaissance flight should go ahead in case a rescue mission should prove
necessary (in the case of a threat to the hostages' lives), but argued against
"the use of any military force, including a blockade or mining, as long as
the hostages were unharmed and in no imminent danger. In addition to
risking the lives of the hostages, I believed military action could jeopardize
our interests in the Persian Gulf. . . . Our only realistic course was to keep
up the pressure on Iran while we waited for Khomeini to determine that
. . . the hostages were of no further value. As painful as it would be, our
national interests and the need to protect the lives of our fellow Americans
dictated that we continued to exercise restraint." After this meeting, Vance
felt there was no indication that a decision on the use of military force was
imminent, and on April 10 he left for a long weekend's rest in Florida.

But on the very next day the meeting was held that made the decision
to go ahead with the rescue mission. Jody Powell explained to the press
later that Cyrus Vance was on a well-earned vacation and that "Vance was
not called back because it would have attracted too much attention when
the operation had to remain secret." There is no evidence as to why the
meeting was called in his absence, but it is clear that Vance did not know
that the mission was being so seriously considered and that everyone else
involved knew that Vance would disagree. Tom Wicker argues that Vance

was deliberately shunted aside from the critical meeting in order to weaken his (and the State Department's) ability to prevent the mission from proceeding. All the Carter, Brzezinski, and Jordan memoirs say is that Vance was on "a brief and much needed vacation" (Carter); "on vacation" (Brzezinski); and "in Florida on a long overdue vacation" (Jordan). In many ways the exclusion of Vance can be interpreted as a symptom of what Irving Janis calls "groupthink"; other symptoms can also be determined in this case study of the phenomenon, which refers to the tendency for groups to maintain amiability and cohesiveness at the cost of critical thinking about decisions.

The president opened the meeting of April 11 by saying that he was seriously considering undertaking a rescue mission, and he invited Brown and Jones to brief those present on the planned mission. At this point, Jordan turned to Christopher and said, "What do you think?" "I'm not sure. Does Cy know about this?" "The contingency rescue plan? Of course." "No, no—does he realize how far along the President is in his thinking about this?" "I don't know. . . . I assume they've talked about it." When the briefing finished, Christopher was first to speak. He outlined a number of alternatives to a rescue mission: a return to the UN for more discussions, the blacklisting of Iranian ships and aircraft, the possibility of getting European support for sanctions against Iran. Brown immediately dismissed these as "not impressive," and he was supported by Brzezinski, Jones, Turner, Powell, and Jordan, all of whom wanted to go ahead. Christopher was alone in his opposition to the plan. He declined to take up a formal position on the rescue mission since he had not been told about it in advance by Vance; he therefore felt that Vance had either accepted the plan or had felt that the State Department could not really prevent its going ahead. His impression was reinforced when Carter informed the meeting that Vance "prior to leaving for his vacation in Florida, had told the President that he opposed any military action but if a choice had to be made between a rescue and a wider blockade, he preferred the rescue." Christopher knew that Vance had opposed the use of military force, but it is logical to assume that he felt all he could do was to offer nonbelligerent alternatives (they were, after all, State Department people being held hostage) to any use of military force, but remain silent on the actual mission; particularly as it had been strongly suggested that Vance had already agreed to it. In support of this conclusion, it is interesting to note that Christopher did not contact Vance on holiday to tell him what had happened. . . .

Vance's reaction to the news was "that he was dismayed and mortified." Vance writes, "Stunned and angry that such a momentous decision had been made in my absence, I went to see the President." At this meeting Vance listed his objections to the mission, and Carter offered him the opportunity to present his views to the group which had made the original decision in the meeting to be held on 15 April. Vance's statement at that meeting focused on issues almost entirely dictated by his bureaucratic position. He said, first, that to undertake the mission when the United States had been trying to get the Europeans to support sanctions on the explicit promise that this would rule out military action would look like deliberate deception; second, the hostages, who were State Department employees, were in no immediate physical danger; third, there were apparently moves in Iran to form a functioning government with which the United States could negotiate; fourth, even if it succeeded, the mission might simply lead to the taking of more American (or allied) hostages by the Iranians; fifth, it might force the Iranians into the arms of the Soviet Union; and, finally, there would almost certainly be heavy casualties (he cited the figure of fifteen out of the fifty-three hostages and thirty out of the rescue force as a likely death toll).

After Vance's comments, Brown turned to him and asked him when he expected the hostages to be released; Vance replied that he did not know. No one supported Vance: his objections were met by "a deafening silence." Although Vance said later that, after the meeting, a number of participants told him that he had indeed raised serious objections, no one mentioned them at the time—an example of "groupthink"? Carter noted that Vance "was alone in his opposition to the rescue mission among all my advisers, and he knew it." In their memoirs, Carter and Brzezinski put Vance's subsequent resignation down to tiredness: "He looked worn out, his temper would flare up, his eyes were puffy, and he projected unhappiness. . . . Cy seemed to be burned out and determined to quit" (Brzezinski); "Vance has been extremely despondent lately . . . for the third or fourth time, he indicated that he might resign . . . but after he goes through a phase of uncertainty and disapproval, then he joins in with adequate support for me" (Carter). Even worries expressed by Vance about the details of the plan at the April 16 briefing were dismissed on the grounds that they reflected his opposition to the raid in principle. On April 21, Vance offered his resignation to Carter; it was accepted, with the agreement that it would not be made public until after the rescue mission, whatever the outcome. Vance duly resigned on April 28. The press reports about his resignation suggested that opposition to the mission was only the last incident in a long line and that Vance's resignation stemmed from his battle with Brzezinski over the direction of U.S. foreign policy. As a White House aide said, it had been "clear for some time that Mr. Vance was no longer part of the foreign policy mainstream in the Carter administration."

That Vance and Christopher opposed the rescue mission is not, in itself, proof of the applicability of the bureaucratic politics approach. What is critical is that their opposition was generated *not* simply from their personal views, but more as a result of their bureaucratic position (although there is a problem in weighting these). These factors warrant this conclusion. First,

Christopher, without knowing Vance's position on the rescue mission, and having been told (erroneously) that Vance supported it, still outlined alternatives. In fact, his opposition to the mission was on the same grounds as Vance's, even though he was led to believe that his superior had given the go-ahead. Second, Vance's statement at the April 15 meeting very clearly reflected State Department concerns. The response of Brown and Brzezinski did not address the problems Vance had outlined (for example, the position of the allies), but stressed issues such as national honor and security. These are role-governed policy prescriptions. Third, Vance was not opposed to a rescue mission as such, but only to one at a time when negotiation was still possible; his objection did not simply reflect a personal attitude toward violence. . . .

CONCLUSION

In the three key meetings that led to the decision to undertake the hostage rescue mission, the evidence presented here suggests that the participants adopted positions that reflected their location in the bureaucratic structure. The influence of bureaucratic structure makes it possible to explain the change in policy that occurred between the March 22 meeting and that of April 11. In each case, the same group proposed a rescue mission, and the same group (Vance on March 22, Christopher on April 11) opposed it. The change came about because the "presidential supporters" and President Carter himself felt that the situation had altered significantly. While this alteration was due in part to external events (the breakdown of negotiations), the evidence suggests that an even stronger reason was the extent of domestic criticism of Carter's inaction (especially after the Wisconsin primary fiasco). The "presidential supporters" felt it was "time to act." For similar reasons, Cyrus Vance's inability to change the rescue decision at the April 15 meeting is also explicable from a bureaucratic political standpoint. In the event, of course, his doubts were only too clearly vindicated. What this case study shows, therefore, is the limitations of an attempt to explain foreign policy decision-making as if the state were monolithic and as if "it" had interests. Such an approach makes policymaking appear rational, and this is a major reason for the popularity of such a perspective; but the case of the hostage rescue mission amply demonstrates the limitations of such conceptions of rationality, in that the key decisions are more powerfully explained by the bureaucratic politics perspective.

However, this conclusion requires some qualification since it raises fundamental problems about the precise claims advanced by proponents of the bureaucratic politics approach. . . . The question that must be addressed is whether bureaucratic position alone leads to the adoption of certain policy positions. As it stands, the bureaucratic politics approach is rather mechanical and static; it commits one to the rather simplistic notion that individuals will propose policy alternatives because of their bureaucratic position. Two problems emerge when this is applied to a case study such as this one. The first is that the bureaucratic politics approach lacks a causal mechanism; it cannot simply be true that occupying a role in a bureaucratic structure leads the occupant to hold certain views. The second relates to the wider issue of belief systems, in that certain individuals are "hawkish" irrespective of their precise position in a bureaucracy. The latter problem is most clearly illustrated by the case of Brzezinski, since it is arguable that whatever position he had occupied in Carter's administration, he would have adopted roughly similar views. Together, these problems force us to focus on one issue—namely, the exact meaning of the notion of role in the context of the bureaucratic politics approach.

This issue has been dealt with . . . in the work of Alexander George and of Glenn Snyder and Paul Diesing. George is concerned with the ways in which U.S. decision-makers use (and abuse) information and advice in the policy process. He examines in some depth the ways in which individuals and bureaucracies will select information to assist their rather parochial goals. In other words, through his study of the use of information, George arrives at precisely the same kind of concern that this study has led to— namely, the relationship between individuals and their policy advocacy. More salient, in their comprehensive survey of crisis decision-making, Snyder and Diesing discuss the psychological makeup of those groups of individuals named in their study (as in this) "hawks" and "doves." They believe that "hard and soft attitudes are more a function of personality than of governmental roles," and they offer a very useful summary of what the worldviews of hard- and soft-liners are. As such, the works of George and of Snyder and Diesing are the best available discussions of the impact of role on belief and of belief on information processing. . . .

While it is clear that it is simplistic to assume that bureaucratic position per se causes policy preference, it is equally clear that bureaucratic position has some impact. Role, in and of itself, cannot explain the positions adopted by individuals; after all, the very notion of role implies a certain latitude over how to play the role. Further, a role does not involve a single goal, and there is, therefore, significant room for maneuver and judgment in trading off various goals against each other. Thus, for example, it is not a sufficient explanation of Vance's position just to say that he was secretary of state. There was a complex interplay between his role, his personality, the decision under consideration, and other personal and bureaucratic goals. Yet role occupiers do become predisposed to think in certain bureaucratic ways, and for a variety of psychological reasons they tend to adopt mindsets compatible with those of their closest colleagues. In addition, individuals are often chosen for a specific post *because* they have certain kinds of world-views. So for reasons of selection, training, and the need to get on with colleagues, it is not surprising that individuals in certain jobs have certain worldviews. . . . Thus, while it is clearly the case that Brzezinski was a hawk, it is accurate neither to say that this was because he was national security adviser (since this would not in and of itself cause hawkishness), nor to say that his views were simply personal (since it is surely the case that, had he been secretary of state, he would have had to argue for courses of action other than those he did argue for—given the State Department's concern with getting the allies to agree on sanctions).

This case study, therefore, leaves us with some critical questions unanswered. On the one hand, the empirical findings are important in that they illustrate the weaknesses of the rational actor approach as an explanation of foreign policy behavior. States are not monoliths, and we might impute very misleading intentions to them if we assume that decisions are rational in this anthropomorphic way. The evidence indicates that the bureaucratic politics approach is very useful in explaining the decision to make an attempt to rescue the hostages. The linkage between the policy preferences of those individuals who made the decision and their bureaucratic position is a more powerful explanation of that decision than any of the alternatives. But . . . the bureaucratic politics approach overemphasizes certain factors and underemphasizes others. On the other hand, the theoretical implications of this case study force us to consider the issue of the sources of the beliefs of decision-makers. The "hawks-doves" dichotomy is brought out very strongly in this case study; and yet the bureaucratic politics approach as it stands is not capable of supporting a convincing mechanism for linking position and worldview. . . . What is needed is to link the concept of individual rationality with the structural influence of bureaucratic position. This chapter, therefore, points both to the utility of the bureaucratic politics approach and to its theoretical weaknesses. The very fact that bureaucratic position was so important in determining policy preference over the decision to attempt to rescue the hostages makes the clarification of the nature of bureaucratic role all the more important.

DISCUSSION QUESTIONS

1. What was the political and international context that necessitated the hostage rescue mission?
2. What is meant by the bureaucratic politics approach? How is it different from other kinds of policymaking?
3. The author delineates four different groups involved in the decision-making process concerning the rescue of hostages. What were the

main objectives of each of these groups? Were they all equal in power and authority?

4. How did the different interests shape the final policy decision?
5. To what extent does bureaucratic politics explain the decision to try to rescue the American hostages?
6. In the end, whose interests triumphed in this decision?
7. Were bureaucratic politics and its decision process responsible for the outcome?
8. How do individual positions also explain bureaucratic outcomes?

20

Roles, Politics, and the Survival of the V-22 Osprey

Christopher M. Jones

After a problem-plagued and politically controversial development period that extended more than two decades, the V-22 Osprey—a tilt-rotor plane designated to replace the Marine Corps' aging helicopter fleet—reached a series of important milestones. In September 2005, the Department of Defense approved full-rate production of the aircraft, whose futuristic design allows it take off and land vertically like a helicopter but fly like a plane. Two years later, a squadron of Ospreys was deployed to Iraq, marking its first use in a combat theater. Then, in March 2008, a $10.4 billion, multiyear procurement contract was awarded to build 167 planes to supplement the existing 216 V-22s (Reuters 2008). This arrangement positioned the program closer to the long-standing goal of the Marines buying a total of 360 Ospreys to transport troops and equipment and the Navy and Air Force procuring 98 planes for search and rescue, special warfare, logistics support, and special operations. The total cost of building the 458 aircraft is estimated to be over $50 billion in 2005 dollars (Gertler 2011, 6).

Despite these positive developments, the V-22 Osprey program was soon in a place where it has been many other times in its checkered history: under scrutiny and a source of political disagreement. In May 2009, the Government Accountability Office (GAO) issued a report that questioned whether the Osprey could meet the full range of missions associated with the helicopters that it is slated to replace, including performance in high-threat areas of operations. The report also raised concerns about the high cost of the V-22 and recommended reconsidering less expensive alternatives (GAO 2009). In April 2010, the first Osprey was lost in combat, six months after the planes were deployed to Afghanistan. Most troubling to the Marine Corps and other V-22 proponents was the National Commission on Fiscal

Responsibility and Reform's suggestion that ending procurement of the plane would be a prudent cost-saving measure. In a December 2010 document, the commission outlined that only 288 of the planned 458 Ospreys be acquired and that cheaper, less capable helicopters be purchased for less demanding military missions (National Commission on Fiscal Responsibility and Reform 2010, 18). However, when a measure to cut fiscal year (FY) 2011 funding for the V-22 came before the U.S. House of Representatives in February 2011, it was soundly defeated by a vote of 326–105 (Gertler 2011, 1). Yet this result was hardly a surprise to those observers familiar with the program.

Over the course of its more than twenty-year development and testing period, the V-22 demonstrated a remarkable ability to endure serious trouble. During the 1990s the program experienced intense political opposition, the crashes of two prototypes, a fire in another model, the resignation of the chief test pilot, and the deaths of seven crewmembers. At the same time, the Osprey's per unit cost rose steadily as the program fell farther behind schedule and the original plan to procure 913 aircraft was cut in half.

A decade later, there were again serious doubts over the program's future. The deaths of twenty-three marines in two separate crashes in 2000, the falsification of maintenance records, unexpected landings, and unfavorable reports concerning the V-22's safety and reliability focused new attention on arguably the most controversial weapons system of the last thirty years. These events prompted intense media coverage, a review by an independent panel of experts, a seventeen-month grounding of the program, major design modifications, and three additional years of flight-tests. Moreover, these problems constituted a harsh reminder that the V-22 program had absorbed nearly $20 billion of federal funding without producing a single plane for regular military use (see Bolkcom 2005).

However, past difficulties and more recent setbacks have not led to the plane's demise. A diverse but durable group of political actors has worked consistently and effectively to ensure its survival as a viable weapons procurement program. The cohesiveness of this coalition can be attributed to a common policy goal that the participants have strongly supported for different reasons based on their distinct organizational roles and interests.

To fully understand the members, motivations, and effectiveness of this political alliance, one need only look to the period when the V-22 faced and ultimately survived its greatest challenge—four years of intense opposition from the Office of the Secretary Defense (OSD). The program was initiated during President Ronald Reagan's defense build-up, and while the Clinton administration devoted less funding to the project through a low-rate production commitment than V-22 supporters preferred, it honored a 1992 campaign pledge to build the plane. The George W. Bush and Obama administrations also did not take actions to undermine the program. However, the George H. W. Bush administration tried repeatedly to cancel the Osprey. Each year, money to develop the aircraft was removed from the president's proposed defense budget. And each year, Congress, the Marine Corps, and the primary contractors, the Boeing Company and Bell Helicopter Textron, fought jointly and effectively to restore it. Clearly congressional budget authority was critical to the coalition's success. But given the intensity of executive branch opposition, which included a refusal to spend appropriations, V-22 proponents on Capitol Hill would have had difficulty sustaining the program without the steady commitment of the marines and the political skill of the manufacturers.

Drawing upon interviews, congressional testimony, private documents, and other available material, this analysis carefully reconstructs the decision to develop the V-22 Osprey from 1989 through 1992. In doing so it seeks to provide a clear basis for understanding the actors and interests that have protected the program in the past and will work to ensure its survival for the foreseeable future. Further, it employs the bureaucratic politics literature to argue that organizational mission provides a compelling explanation of the participants' policy preferences and the politics that shaped a significant national security decision with long-term fiscal and military implications. Lastly, the case suggests that the key assumptions of the bureaucratic politics literature, which have long been used to explain the behavior of the executive branch, can be applied to legislative and societal actors. The finding lends support to scholars who have advocated the need to broaden and refine the bureaucratic politics frameworks developed four decades ago.

THEORETICAL BACKGROUND

Of the theories available for understanding defense policy behavior, the bureaucratic politics paradigm (Allison and Halperin 1972) provides a compelling explanation of the four-year battle over the V-22 Osprey. Since the actors and interests supporting the program have not changed since the 1989–1992 period, it provides insight into the forces that have safeguarded the plane more recently and will protect it in the years to come.

The framework views the actions of government as political resultants. The resultants emerge from a defense policy process, characteristic of a game, where multiple players holding different conceptions of the national interest struggle, compete, and bargain over the substance and conduct of policy. The policy positions taken by the decision-makers are determined largely by their own organizational roles and interests. The final outcome either represents a compromise between the actors or reflects outright the policy preferences of the actors who won the political game. The presence and effective use of bargaining advantages, including the formal authority to control the decision-making process or *action-channel* ("a regularized means of taking government action on a specific kind of issue" [Allison and Zelikow 1999, 300]), are critical to determining which actors prevail.

Allison and Zelikow (1999, 255–324) is the most recent statement of the bureaucratic politics approach. For the purposes of this study, however, Allison and Halperin's earlier work offers a distinct advantage. They argue it is appropriate to treat organizations as well as individuals as single policy actors (1972, 47). In these instances, an organization's mission (like a decision-maker's bureaucratic position or job title) becomes a strong predictor of its policy stand on a particular issue. The "organizations as unitary actors" assumption is particularly useful in the case under study, because the documentary record reveals that the participants' behavior within the V-22 policy process was remarkably consistent over time.

Before proceeding further, some theoretical points are in order. For example, this study diverts from most applications of the bureaucratic politics approach by focusing on a decision-making process that extends beyond the executive branch to include other actors, such as Congress and private companies. While proponents of the approach do not highlight legislative and societal actors within their theoretical statements or case studies, nothing within their work precludes the involvement of such participants. In fact, they recognize this possibility by referring to such actors as *ad hoc players* (e.g., Allison and Halperin 1972, 47; Allison and Zelikow 1999, 296).

In addition, the bureaucratic politics explanation offered by this study should not be interpreted as a statement that other theories, especially those commonly used to understand weapons procurement decisions, are inapplicable to the V-22 episode. For instance, an iron triangle or structural policymaking pattern between congressional, bureaucratic, and private-sector actors is distinguishable in the case under study. However, an explanation based solely on the cooperative politics of the iron triangle model would not capture the executive-legislative or interbranch conflict, which also shaped the V-22 decision. Further, it would not draw proper attention to the OSD's involvement and role-based behavior.

A bureaucratic politics explanation also does *not* preclude the presence of rational behavior. Actors are rational in an instrumental sense if they can form preferences and select the most preferred outcome when confronted with multiple options (see Zagare 1990, 239–43). This conception of rationality has two implications. On the one hand, it allows decision-makers to be purposeful or goal-directed without being pure utility-maximizers. Thus, it is rational for actors to prefer one policy alternative to another based on their bureaucratic roles and interests. On the other hand, the assumption that individuals or organizations arrive at policy preferences through instrumental rationality does not prevent the final decision or action from being politically determined. We can assume, for instance, a two-step process. Actors will initially and independently prefer a particular policy option based on their specific organizational roles. Then, the policy stands of the various actors within the decision-making process will be aggregated politically through such means as bargaining, coalition building, logrolling, and compromise. This perspective would account for the politics within the V-22 case as well as participants' statements, such as "[O]ur behavior within the budget process was rationally driven" (O'Keefe 1997).

After a brief background section, the remainder of this study illustrates the presence of role-based behavior and, therefore, the utility of bureaucratic politics paradigm in explaining the case of the V-22 Osprey, 1989–1992. It demonstrates how the four central actors' policy positions and supporting arguments were directly related to their distinct roles and interests. Each player's organizational mission predisposed it to have a different conception of the national interest and, therefore, a different reason for supporting or opposing the development of the V-22. The case further illustrates how specific actors, bargaining advantages, and political interactions were critical in shaping the final policy outcome.

CONTEXT OF THE DECISION

In April 1989, shortly after the first flight of an Osprey prototype, Secretary of Defense Richard Cheney announced the cancellation of the V-22 program. His decision was not a complete surprise. Serious discussions about postponing or eliminating major weapons programs started within the Bush transition team. The incoming administration's search for budget savings was driven by the reality that the massive defense spending of the Reagan era could not continue. After all, the Soviet threat was waning; the federal budget deficit was soaring; the president-elect had pledged "no new taxes"; and the Congress was eager to reduce overall defense spending. It was within this environment that the new administration scrutinized several expensive weapons programs, including the V-22.

Once President George H. W. Bush took office, the pressure to make significant defense cuts intensified. In April 1989, the Republican president and leaders of the Democratic-controlled Congress convened a budget summit in an effort to meet a legally mandated deficit reduction target. The subsequent bipartisan agreement led to a $10 billion reduction in the FY 1990 defense budget, which was $4 billion deeper than Cheney's original proposal. As a result, the FY 1990 defense budget fell from President Reagan's request of $305.6 billion to $295.6 billion. Secretary Cheney decided to address this decline by ordering the navy "to absorb almost half of the $10 billion" with the major casualty being naval aviation (Aviation Week

& Space Technology Staff Report 1989; also see Moore 1989; Wilson 1989). As part of the Department of the Navy, the marines were impacted in the worst possible way when the V-22 was placed at the top of the hit list.

Executive branch opposition to the Osprey, while more widespread in the Bush administration, was not a new phenomenon. In fact, critics emerged shortly after the navy launched the program in 1982. The most consistent opposition came from Program Analysis and Evaluation (PA&E), which was the office within OSD responsible for monitoring the design and cost of weapons. Given its role and relative success throughout the 1970s, PA&E was unpopular with the service departments. Yet this disdain was negligible, because the watchdog office enjoyed the backing of consecutive secretaries of defense.

To the delight of the military services, PA&E's importance came to an abrupt end when the Reagan administration took control of the Pentagon in 1981. Seeing PA&E as an obstacle to the administration's massive defense build-up, including his plan for a six-hundred-ship navy, Secretary of Defense Caspar Weinberger "muted its role, downgrading the office head's title from assistant secretary to office director. Moreover, his controversial decentralization of the Pentagon seriously reduced the influence of PA&E as well as other central offices" (Griffiths 1986, 84). Thus, when the head of PA&E, David S. C. Chu, argued that modified CH-53E and UH-60 helicopters could perform the same multi-service mission as the Osprey at half the cost, he was ignored.

However, PA&E and its quest to eliminate the V-22 program were given new life when Mr. Cheney became secretary of defense in March 1989. He assumed the post belatedly after the first nominee, Senator John Tower (R-TX), failed to win Senate confirmation in early March. Mr. Tower, who was from one of the two states where the Osprey was being built, was a major supporter of the plane. Faced with a new position and confronted with the challenge of having to reduce the FY 1990 budget by $10 billion, Mr. Cheney turned to PA&E for assistance. David Chu, who had served in the Congressional Budget Office when Mr. Cheney was a representative from Wyoming, happily obliged. It was an opportunity for PA&E to regain its influence and strike back at the services, which in its view were spending far too much money on the wrong types of weapons.

Mr. Chu had opposed the V-22 since 1983, when it was awarded a preliminary design contract. Thus it came as little surprise that the plane was one of the first weapons systems he advised Cheney to cut. Specifically, Chu and his colleagues "recommended the marines substitute a 950 mix of CH-53E and UH-60 [helicopters] for 552 V-22s" (Flanagan 1990, 42). The Marine Corps, however, was quick to point out that Chu's plan was more expensive. So Chu responded by changing his proposal to 650 helicopters. This adjustment brought the cost below the V-22 package, but "these numbers were inadequate to lift the Marines and tonnage required" (AW&ST Staff Report 1989). After a number of confrontations with the Marine Corps over costs and military requirements, Chu softened his position and "recommended a one-year slip in the program" (Flanagan 1990, 42). However, Chu's willingness to delay a final decision on the Osprey came too late. Constrained by the budget summit agreement and Bush's preferred weapons projects (e.g., the B-2 bomber and Strategic Defense Initiative), Mr. Cheney saw no alternative. He acted on Chu's earlier advice and cancelled the V-22.

THE OFFICE OF THE SECRETARY OF DEFENSE

From 1989 through 1992, OSD was the most vigorous opponent of the Osprey. Its policy stand and corresponding arguments in favor of eliminating the plane were related to its organizational role. The traditional mission of the Defense Department is to ensure the defense and security of the United States and its allies. As the secretary of defense's principal staff unit for exercising civilian authority over the Pentagon, OSD must ensure defense policy reflects presidential priorities and corresponds to available fiscal resources. A key element of OSD's officially prescribed role is to "provide oversight to assure the effective allocation and efficient management of resources consistent with [administration] approved plans and programs" (U.S. Department of Defense 2001). Since OSD may choose to forgo certain military capabilities to save or redirect money, it has the potential to clash with the armed services.

To promote its policy stand against the Osprey, OSD drew on a number of bargaining advantages. For instance, OSD had the power to initiate the annual defense budget process, compelling Congress to react to its cancellation of the Osprey each year. OSD was also aided by a wealth of expertise generated from its own bureaus, the military services, and other executive departments. In addition, Secretary Cheney had the support of the president on this issue until August 1992, when the Bush administration abruptly dropped its opposition to the program. Furthermore, given OSD's opposition to the program and the lines of authority within the Pentagon, the marines were prevented from lobbying publicly on behalf of the plane (discussed below). Of course, the budget authority of the Congress overshadowed these assets.

Within the budget process, OSD's central reason for opposing the plane was its high cost relative to helicopters. As Cheney stated in 1991, "Cost is the driving issue, and the V-22 is too costly. . . . At these budget levels . . . we can afford to deploy operational systems embodying only those technologies that offer the greatest combat capability payoff per dollar invested. The

V-22 is not such a system" (U.S. Congress, House Armed Services Committee 1991a, 104, hereafter USHASC). In April 1989, Cheney also told Congress, "[We cannot] justify spending the amount of money . . . proposed
. . . when we are just getting ready to move into procurement of the V-22
to perform a very narrow mission I think can be performed . . . by using
helicopters" (Cooper 1991, 3). This statement captures three points OSD
would reiterate throughout the four-year period. First, the V-22's primary
mission, ship-to-shore transport, could be accomplished by less expensive
helicopters. Second, while the Osprey possessed greater speed and range
than helicopters, it would not add much to the Marine Corps' capacity to
fight. For instance, Cheney argued the marines would rarely, if ever, be
asked to conduct operations like the 1980 Iranian hostage rescue mission,
which proponents of the plane said the V-22 was well suited to perform.
Third, with the army's decision to leave the program in 1987, the V-22
would not be the multi-service, multi-mission aircraft it was intended to be.

Given who was to use the Osprey and what it was to be used for, OSD
believed the program was not cost-effective. At no time did the civilian
leadership of the Pentagon dispute the marines' contention that their helicopters need to be replaced. Similarly, there was no criticism of the Osprey's
capabilities or the tilt-rotor concept. Instead, OSD consistently approached
the development of the V-22 from the perspective of affordability. Sean
O'Keefe, the Pentagon's comptroller, best captured OSD's policy stand in
1991: "The V-22 may appear to be superior to existing helicopters. . . . But
our goal is to find ways of performing our most critical mission acceptably,
at a funding level that does not draw excessively from our many other critical military missions" (USHASC 1991b, 146).

In addition to arguments, OSD sought to advance its policy position
through a number of actions. For instance, it continually proposed modified or redesigned helicopters as a prudent alternative to the Osprey. Each
year the Bush administration submitted a defense budget to Congress
that included a request for helicopters rather than the V-22. In addition,
Deputy Secretary of Defense Donald J. Atwood challenged congressional
budget authority in December 1989 by ordering the Department of Navy
to terminate the V-22's production contracts. In his memorandum, Mr.
Atwood indicated that it was not in the "public fiscal interest" to spend
advanced procurement funds when OSD had no intention of moving
beyond the Osprey's research and development phase. Further, Secretary
Cheney made several unsuccessful attempts during the four-year period to
transfer, defer, or rescind V-22 appropriations. Moreover, OSD obstructed
a Cost Operational Effectiveness Analysis (COEA) of V-22 alternatives
commissioned by the Congress and conducted by the Institute for Defense
Analyses (IDA)—an organization funded by the Defense Department but
technically independent. Defying the language of the previous year's ap-

propriations act, OSD failed to submit the study with its FY 1991 budget proposal in February 1990. It also ignored subsequent requests to send the document to Capitol Hill. When the IDA study was finally released in June and revealed that in the long run the Osprey was the most cost-effective and capable option for satisfying the marines' need and the navy's search-and-rescue mission, OSD immediately challenged its findings. Secretary Cheney told Congress, "The investment cost to procure [the V-22] remains too high. In the current era of declining defense budgets, we must give up certain capabilities" (Cooper 1991, 6).

Last, OSD refused to spend money Congress had appropriated for the V-22. Angered by this pattern of defiance and the need to issue annual orders to release funds, members of Congress, including some with no interest in the Osprey, declared in 1992 that the Pentagon was illegally impounding $790 million. Some lawmakers went so far as "to intimate that they might go to court to challenge the right of Cheney . . . to override a line item in an appropriations act" (Forman 1994). After all, Congress had inserted special language in the FY 1992 Appropriations Act to ensure the money was spent. OSD argued its actions were not motivated by defiance, but by an inability to implement another portion of the same appropriations act. The law called for the "development, manufacture, and operational test of three production representative V-22 aircraft" by December 31, 1996. OSD maintained that limited funds, time constraints, and engineering problems precluded this goal (USHASC 1992b, 3, 6).

The U.S. Comptroller General's subsequent ruling that OSD had violated the law by impounding Osprey funding led Secretary Cheney to offer a compromise. On July 2, 1992, he told Congress he would release $1.5 billion to build six production representative aircraft *if* he were allowed to use some of the money to explore other options. The alternatives included updated models of existing helicopters, a new medium-lift helicopter, and a modified, less costly version of the V-22. Cheney also asked that the requirement to produce three production representative Ospreys by December 1996 be relaxed. Knowing the contractors were not ready to manufacture the planes, Congress agreed.

This good faith, however, quickly dissipated. In late July 1992, the Pentagon took three actions that appeared to contradict Cheney's earlier commitment. First, it ordered the marines to reexamine their medium-lift requirement and suggested performance standards could be lowered. Second, the Defense Department's Joint Requirements Oversight Council (JROC) decided the medium-lift replacement no longer had to meet the speed and long-range requirements necessary for special operations and search-and-rescue missions. Third, JROC rejected a Marine Corps statement of operational requirements corresponding to the V-22's capabilities. Instead, it retained a statement of requirements that could be met by existing helicopters. The Osprey's congressional allies were outraged. They charged that OSD's actions amounted to nothing more than an attempt to remove the V-22 from the medium-lift replacement competition (Morrocco 1992, 25). In a special hearing on the matter in August 1992, OSD countered its latest efforts were not "duplicitous," but were simply aimed at finding the most capable and affordable replacement for the marines' aging helicopters (USHASC 1992b, 3, 21).

The controversy continued after the hearing, but soon became irrelevant. In late August 1992, the Bush administration dropped its opposition to the V-22 and indicated it would not stand in the way of spending $1.5 billion on the program. Even though the policy reversal coincided with a similar announcement related to the army's M-1 Tank and a decision to sell $9 million worth of fighter jets to Taiwan and Saudi Arabia, the administration denied there was any connection to the upcoming presidential election. Instead, it took the position that the Osprey now complemented the emerging post–Cold War military strategy of projecting force in "hot spots." Political calculations, however, were salient. The Bush administration recognized it lacked the political support and constitutional authority to win the battle over the Osprey. Congress was intent on funding the program. Thus as the presidential election approached, the White House considered its public backing of the plane, including a visible contract announcement, a prudent political tactic. Texas and Pennsylvania were not only the sites of the two V-22 plants but also large electoral states.

THE CONGRESS

From 1989 through 1992, the Congress was a firm proponent of the Osprey. Support for the plane within the House and Senate was not unanimous, but it was pervasive, encompassing conservative Republicans as well as liberal Democrats. Two letters sent to President Bush regarding the V-22, one from 218 representatives and another signed by 40 senators, were indications of the program's broad bipartisan support. This strong backing was the product of role-based behavior on the part of lawmakers who approached the issue from either a political or policy perspective.

On the one hand, representatives and senators are politicians who want to be reelected to their offices. In order to attain this goal, they seek to secure benefits for their constituents. Thus, it is no surprise that some V-22 supporters were attracted to the program for what it offered their districts and states. Since the Osprey was being built in Texas and Pennsylvania, the senators and large congressional delegations from those states were firmly behind the program. Surely, Representatives Pete Geren (D-TX) and Curt Weldon (R-PA), who each had a V-22 plant in their district, backed the program for the jobs it would create and sustain. In August 1992, the primary contractors estimated a production rate of three or four Ospreys a month would employ between 2,000 and 3,000 people at each of the two production facilities (Ferguson 1992). Further, there is reason to believe members of Congress from other states also sought to protect or expand local employment. The engineering and manufacturing development (EMD) phase, for instance, involved an estimated 1,800 to 2,000 subcontractors (Harrison 1994). As of October 1994, nearly $353 million in subcontracts had been distributed to businesses in forty-two states and 258 congressional districts. Twenty-five states had purchase orders or letter contracts in excess of $500,000. Bell and Boeing calculated that there were ten thousand jobs tied to subcontracts (Arnold 1994; Bell-Boeing 1994a and 1994b).

On the other hand, members of Congress are policymakers, who must defend their policy positions on a daily basis. Through legislative experience, committee service, and consultations with staff, they develop a capacity to evaluate public policy and communicate it effectively to their constituents. In the case of the V-22, many lawmakers simply determined there were valid policy reasons for favoring the program. Some backed the plane because they were proponents of a strong national defense or traditional supporters of the Marine Corps. Others found compelling, non-military justifications for developing the aircraft (discussed below). Relatedly, many legislators were not beneficiaries of major subcontract awards or the roughly fifteen thousand estimated V-22-related jobs. Yet they still chose to back the project.

Congressional arguments on behalf of the Osprey embraced a far broader range of substantive issues than OSD's financial rationale or the marines' military perspective. Depending on the particular senator or representative, these diverse policy concerns enabled lawmakers to mask parochial concerns, counter OSD opposition, persuade undecided colleagues, and justify the program to constituents. Moreover, the range of possible policy reasons for building the V-22 explains why congressional support was so extensive and sustainable.

In some instances, legislators advocated the V-22 on the same issue OSD used to oppose it. That is, they challenged the Pentagon's contention the Osprey (when compared to helicopter alternatives) was too expensive to develop and procure. For instance, Rep. Curt Weldon (R-PA) stated in May 1989, "The Navy and Marine Corps presented data to the Secretary [of Defense] showing him that in fact over the 20-year life cycle the V-22 was the most cost-effective solution" (USHASC 1989, 282). However, it was more common for lawmakers to discuss how the Osprey's cutting-edge technology was capable of enhancing military performance, revolutionizing civilian aviation, and improving the country's trade balance.

Members of Congress employed a number of militarily oriented arguments related to the plane's tilt-rotor technology. First, both the age of existing helicopters and the fact that they were based on 1940s technology were referenced. Second, lawmakers argued the plane's speed, range, and operational flexibility complemented the military challenges of the post–Cold War era, including the need to project U.S. military power in the developing world. Third, congressional supporters reinforced the marines' view of the program. Rep. James Bilbray (D-NV) commented, "I have never met a Marine yet from the pilot that is a second lieutenant . . . to some of the top people in the Marine Corps that did not whisper in my ear . . . the V-22 . . . is the plane we want" (USHASC 1992a, 203). Last, the Osprey was advocated on the basis of safety, with an emphasis on how aging helicopters were plagued by maintenance problems and a restricted set of training maneuvers.

Another set of congressional arguments encompassed problems beyond the Marine Corps' medium-lift need. For instance, some senators and representatives claimed the Osprey would aid national security and law enforcement agencies with drug interdiction. Other legislators were convinced a government funded, tilt-rotor program would spawn civilian models that would revolutionize domestic air travel. On one hand, "with its ability to lift off from downtown helipads, they argue[d] the new plane could relieve the growing traffic jams at municipal airports" and better protect the environment (Waller 1989). On the other hand, lawmakers, such as Senator Ted Stevens (R-AK), a powerful member of the Senate Appropriations Committee, argued the V-22's speed and range would make rural and remote areas of the country more accessible. The Osprey, therefore, was championed as a national asset, capable of relieving two transportation problems without the construction of new runways or airports.

Besides the promise of improving civil aviation, congressional arguments focused on the relationship between tilt-rotor technology and the nation's economic well-being. For example, civilian spin-offs of the V-22 were seen as a way to boost the domestic economy by keeping the U.S. aerospace industry competitive in the international marketplace. Members of Congress also made it clear if the United States did not develop and produce tilt-rotor aircraft, then other countries would. Rep. Curt Weldon (R-PA) stated, "The Japanese and Europeans want to take this away from us, because they see the tilt-rotor as the next generation of commercial aviation. We are not going to let that happen" (ABC News 1993; also see USHASC 1990, 102). This was a particularly strong argument, because both a Japanese conglomerate and a consortium of European firms had designed tilt-rotor aircraft. Lawmakers, therefore, argued that thousands of actual and potential American jobs would be sacrificed if the Osprey and a subsequent civilian program were not pursued. This issue even won over "deficit hawks," such as Rep. John Kasich (R-OH) and Senator Warren Rudman (R-NH).

Congressional support for the V-22 was not confined to policy arguments. It also included actions. For instance, lawmakers made it clear that they were fully committed to production. Rep. James Bilbray (D-NY) told Deputy Secretary of Defense Atwood in April 1992, "[Y]ou can go back to the Marines or to the Navy and [tell them to] come up with an alternative, but you are going to come back to this subcommittee and find out [it] is going to continue with the V-22" (USHASC 1992a, 202). Also, members of Congress openly and repeatedly questioned whether OSD really had a legitimate alternative to the Osprey. Many believed its search for "other options" was simply a delay. Further, legislators countered OSD opposition by frequently reprising the findings of the Pentagon's IDA study, which indicated the V-22 was the most cost-effective option for replacing Marine Corps helicopters. Lastly, Congress was not receptive to OSD's annual refusal to spend appropriations earmarked for the V-22. In April 1991, Rep. Marilyn Lloyd (D-TN) remarked, "The Department's actions, in my judgment, amount to an unconstitutional attempt to exercise a line-item veto. This is not acceptable" (USHASC 1991b, 220). Lloyd's anger was not unique. Lawmakers, including those with no interest in the V-22 program, supported two actions. Beginning in 1990, special language was inserted into each appropriations act to ensure V-22 funds were obligated without delay. Then, in 1992, the House Armed Services Committee decided that for every month appropriations went unspent, the Pentagon comptroller's budget would be reduced by five percent.

Thus the battle surrounding the Osprey had two dimensions. On the one hand, Congress and OSD were engaged in a policy dispute over the future of the program. At the center of this controversy was the issue of whether the plane's assets outweighed the high cost of development and procurement. On the other hand, there was an interbranch conflict over the Pentagon's disregard for the legislative power of the purse. This second dimension served to solidify and broaden support for the V-22 on Capitol Hill. In the end, Congress won the programmatic and constitutional conflicts because it possessed two valuable bargaining advantages. First, it had the formal authority to control the budget authorization and appropriation process and, therefore, the ultimate fate of the V-22. Second, legislative backing would not have remained as cohesive and well organized without the Marine Corps' unwavering commitment to the program and the political skill of the contractors. This assistance was critical given the president's wishes, OSD's ardent opposition, and the reality that congressional support for the plane was strong but not unanimous.

THE MARINE CORPS

Over the four-year period, the marines were the strongest proponents of the V-22 within the executive branch. Like the other actors in the case, their policy stand was related to their role and interests. In fact, the Osprey was actually a means for improving the performance of the Marine Corps' organizational mission. As an amphibious, expeditionary, "national force in readiness," the marines are called upon to move rapidly to faraway places to perform a variety of military duties. Moreover, the regional and nontraditional security threats of the post-9/11 world will require a more mobile and flexible military posture, including an active Marine Corps.

For decades, helicopters were critical to fulfilling the marines' demanding responsibilities. By the late 1960s, however, it was determined that time and new combat circumstances would increasingly render existing helicopters obsolete. Consequently, "the Marine Corps first defined a requirement for a replacement helicopter in 1968" (Forman 1994, 2). Of course, this need was not met immediately. Nearly two decades passed before the V-22 program was approved in 1982 and a full-scale development contract was awarded in 1986. This delay made the marines truly eager, if not desperate, for the plane. Limited speed, noise, maintenance problems, and an inability to transport the necessary tonnage or conduct evasive maneuvers plagued their aging helicopter fleet. Moreover, the marines were drawn to the Osprey's impressive capabilities, which include the capacity to carry 24 fully equipped combat troops internally or up to 15,000 pounds of cargo externally at a speed of more than 250 knots over a distance of 200 nautical miles. With less personnel and cargo, the Osprey's ferrying range extends to 2,100 nautical miles, enabling it to fly independently to military bases, aircraft carriers, and "hot spots" through the world (Dady 1998).

Consequently, just months before Cheney cancelled the Osprey in 1989, Marine Corps General A. M. Gray told Congress, "[The V-22] is the most important advance in military aviation since the helicopter. . . . It is my number one aviation priority" (Scharfen 1990, 180). Shortly thereafter, the marines offered to forgo procurement of the M-1 tank to save the Osprey. The proposal, which was rejected, illustrated the organization's acute aviation needs. It also demonstrated a strong desire to acquire a weapons system that would enhance its mission as well as distinguish it from the army at a time when the armed services were competing for post–Cold War duties. Thus the V-22 was not merely critical to the Marine Corps' standing as an over-the-horizon strike force, but essential to its very existence.

Secretary Cheney's rejection of the marines' offer marked a transition in their behavior. Throughout the Reagan years and during the first few months of the Bush administration, the Marine Corps pushed strongly and openly for the Osprey. But when it became clear Cheney was determined to cancel the program, the marines employed a quieter approach. The marines were likely told by the Pentagon's leadership that they were not to make statements or take actions in public that contradicted OSD's position. During authorization hearings, members of Congress referred to "the gag order" and "the subtle pressures" on the Marine Corps (USHASC 1992a, 126–28; USHASC 1992b, 13). Also, the marines feared a public campaign on behalf of the V-22 would anger Cheney and affect how they fared in the interservice conflict over post–Cold War roles and missions. Given the level of congressional support, however, the marines were confident they could refrain from public lobbying and the program would still survive.

A number of bargaining advantages reinforced the marines' conviction that Congress would promote its policy preference. As part of the Department of the Navy, for instance, the marines have a congressional liaison staff that is far larger than the OSD contingent. There is also a strong tradition of support for the organization among senators and representatives who were once active-duty marines. In terms of the V-22 case, two of the most notable members of this formidable group were Senator John Glenn (D-OH), an influential member of the Senate Armed Services Committee, and Congressman Jack Murtha (D-PA), chairman of the Subcommittee on Defense and Appropriations. Further, there is a general perception on Capitol Hill that the Marines Corps is "conservative, realistic, and above all, honest in defining its needs" (Forman 1994, 7–8). Last, the Congress considers the Marines Corps to be the underdog of the four services because its needs are often overridden by the budget priorities of the army, navy, and air force. Consequently, when marines ask for the same budget item over an extended period, the request is usually honored.

These factors, however, did not preclude the Marine Corps from playing an important role in the case. There is evidence to suggest the organization engaged in a vigorous, behind-the-scenes campaign on Capitol Hill. More important, the marines demonstrated a clear commitment to the program through candid congressional testimony. Consistent with their organizational mission, they employed a number of militarily oriented arguments related to combat realities and the V-22's impressive speed, range, and operational flexibility. Even though this backing came in the form of answers to questions, it was critical in maintaining widespread legislative support. In fact, lawmakers often countered OSD opposition by referencing the statements of the Marine Corps leaders (discussed above).

For most of the four-year period, the Pentagon had one official position on the Osprey. According to OSD, the V-22 was unaffordable, and therefore subject to cancellation. The marines, cognizant of the lines of authority within the Defense Department and perhaps fearing retaliation by Secretary Cheney, publicly supported this policy stand by avoiding unsolicited statements or action on behalf of the program. When testifying before Congress and maneuvering behind-the-scenes, however, the marines made it clear there was a serious need to replace the service's aging helicopter fleet and the V-22 was the most capable option. Thus the official Pentagon position was accompanied by an unofficial Marine Corps stand in favor of the plane.

THE CONTRACTORS

With the exception of a few zealots in Congress, the most active and aggressive proponents of the V-22 Osprey were its manufacturers—Bell Helicopter Textron and the Boeing Company. Like the other actors in the case, their policy stand and corresponding behavior were consistent with their roles. Bell and Boeing, as economic actors, saw the plane as a way to guarantee profits and employment in an era of shrinking defense budgets. In addition to the economic benefits associated with military procurement, the contractors soon discovered there was considerable interest, both at home and abroad, in the civilian application of tilt-rotor technology. The V-22 program, therefore, held the potential to generate long-term business for both companies. Not surprisingly, this commercial stake compelled the Bell-Boeing Team to take a number of actions to protect and promote the Osprey.

One sign of the contractors' political acumen was their effort to control development and production costs. For example, in an effort to keep the V-22 program on schedule, the Bell-Boeing Team began full-scale development without a contract and with its own funds in 1985. The contractors also invested in the initial production tooling for the Osprey. This expenditure simultaneously reduced the government's up-front costs and demonstrated the companies' long-term commitment to the project. In addition, a fixed-priced development contract was signed in May 1986 by the two companies and the Department of the Navy (the contracting service for the Marine Corps). In the pact, Bell-Boeing agreed to absorb all costs over the ceiling price of $1.825 billion (USHASC 1991b). This arrangement transferred the financial risk of development to the contractors. Furthermore, when the Osprey enters full production, Bell and Boeing (which were cooperative development partners) will each have the ability to manufacture the entire plane. This capacity will ensure the government receives a more cost-effective V-22, because the two contractors will compete for production lots. Last, the Bell-Boeing Team improved its manufacturing and assembly techniques to make production more efficient and affordable.

Besides these efforts to control costs, the contractors widened the plane's domestic constituency. Among the strongest actions Bell-Boeing took was the distribution of subcontracts to nearly two thousand companies. Two hundred of these companies were major or first-tier subcontractors.

Examples include Grumman Aerospace (tail section), Lockheed Martin (flight control system), and IBM (avionics). Thus, the number of states with an economic interest in the Osprey grew from two (Pennsylvania and Texas) to over forty. Once part of the large Bell-Boeing Team, V-22 suppliers were encouraged to make their congressional representatives aware of the program's impact on local employment (Arnold 1994; Uchitelle 1992). Yet the subcontractors were only one part of the constituency Bell-Boeing strategists built. For instance, labor unions were involved. Organizations, such as the United Auto Workers and AFL-CIO, lobbied Congress, because thousands of their members had jobs related to the Osprey program. Another significant patron of the V-22 was the Federal Aviation Administration (FAA). In 1985, the contractors realized that if the Osprey was to be billed as a civilian asset, then FAA backing was critical (Forman 1994, 10–11). Two years later, Bell-Boeing convinced the FAA to cosponsor a civil tilt-rotor study and to participate in the Osprey's test-flight program. FAA endorsement activated other interested parties, such as the California Department of Transportation and the Port Authority of New York and New Jersey. Lastly, the contractors were instrumental in establishing the Tilt-Rotor Technology Coalition—a collection of contractors, subcontractors, members of Congress, retired Marines, and private-sector groups—which became a unified lobbying force.

The final means the contractors employed to promote the Osprey were public relations activities. For example, Bell-Boeing began a guest pilot program for members of Congress, the marines, and the private sector. The goal was to create an affinity for the plane among members of the policy community (Forman 1994, 9–10). In addition, the contractors launched a congressional awareness program that included events such as "Tilt-Rotor Appreciation Day" and the landing of a demonstrator aircraft on Capitol Hill. The *Osprey Fax* newsletter, full-page advertisements in newspapers and magazines, and television commercials during the Sunday morning talk shows were also aimed at building legislative and public support. Last, Bell-Boeing kept information about the Osprey freely available. This flow of information enabled the contractors to attract support, counter criticism and misinformation, and demonstrate to the media and public the V-22 was worthy of finite defense dollars.

Like the other actors involved in the V-22 case, the contractors employed arguments to support their policy stand. In fact, they used every conceivable justification for continuing the program. It was actions rather than arguments, however, that made the Bell-Boeing Team such an invaluable member of the Osprey coalition. Through its political skill, Bell-Boeing was able to make the V-22 appealing to a diverse group of actors and interests. Instead of simply promoting the Osprey as a badly needed weapons system, it was packaged as a national asset, which would complement post–Cold

War military strategy, create jobs, remedy domestic transportation problems, and become an attractive export.

CONCLUSION

Consistent with the central assumptions of the bureaucratic politics paradigm, the decision to fund the development of the V-22 Osprey from 1989 through 1992 emerged from a policy process pervaded by role-based politics. The major actors within this decision-making environment, the Office of the Secretary of Defense, Congress, the Marine Corps, and contractors, held policy positions on the plane that were directly related to their organizational missions. These distinct roles caused the actors to have different interests and, therefore, disparate reasons for supporting or opposing the V-22 program. Conflict arose between the executive and legislative branches, because OSD and Congress had competing interests as well as diametrically opposed policy goals. The disagreement grew wider and more intense when OSD challenged congressional budget authority by refusing to spend V-22 appropriations.

Despite four years of ardent opposition by OSD, Congress won the programmatic and constitutional battles related to the Osprey. As noted, its success was largely the result of two bargaining advantages. First, Congress had enough formal authority through its "power of the purse" to control the "action-channel" or budget process and, therefore, the ultimate fate of the Osprey. Second, a committed Marine Corps and a politically skillful team of contractors backed Congress. These actors ensured congressional support remained broad, cohesive, and well organized. In essence, it was the strength of this tripartite coalition that overrode OSD's policy stand and saved a program with potentially long-term military, fiscal, and economic implications.

This case study extends to the present, because the coalition of actors and interests that protected the plane in the George H. W. Bush administration (1989–1992) has not disappeared. In fact, there is reason to believe this political alliance is stronger today, because it has more at stake. Congress has invested billions of dollars; the contractors and subcontractors have thousands of jobs deeply tied to building the Osprey and designing civilian spin-off models; and Marine helicopters have aged to a point where they are near the end of their life cycle with no ready replacement except the V-22. The ongoing military campaign in Afghanistan has intensified this need, as helicopters have been lost to crashes, enemy fire, and the normal wear of war. These actors, therefore, have a strong interest in ensuring the program's survival. Even if the aircraft's rising cost (now conservatively estimated at $70 million per unit) coupled with new problems or an unforeseen mishap were to lead to the program's demise, one would still have to marvel at this program's capacity to survive for decades. The Osprey's longevity is testimony to its supporters' effectiveness and the difficulty of stopping a weapons project once it is under development.

Finally, a note about theory is in order. The case clearly shows that actors can be rational, in an instrumental sense, and still behave politically. Moreover, the applicability of the theory's key assumptions to legislative and nongovernmental actors suggests the importance of devoting attention to the development of a political decision-making approach that recognizes the true diversity of players, interests, and processes capable of shaping defense and foreign policy. One possibility is a "governmental politics paradigm" encompassing multiple analytical models. On one level, the models might share a common set of assumptions capturing the general characteristics of governmental politics: fragmented power, multiple actors, instrumental rationality, role-based policy stands, different interests, and politically generated outcomes. On another level, each model could be distinguished by a specific type of governmental politics defined by particular actors, forms of politics, action-channels, and other procedural characteristics. These assumptions might vary with the salience of the issue or the locus of decision-making. For instance, there might be different models to explain defense and foreign policy made by (1) the president and senior-level advisors, (2) bureaucracies, (3) the executive and legislative branches, and (4) executive, legislative, and private-sector actors. With further refinement, such a framework would build upon the valuable work of Allison and Halperin while addressing the legitimate concerns of their critics.

DISCUSSION QUESTIONS

1. What was the background to the V-22 Osprey? What was previous experience with this aircraft prior to, and after, the decisions during the George H. W. Bush administration between 1989 and 1992? How has the decision on this aircraft changed in the most recent period?
2. How does Jones describe the key components of the bureaucratic politics model, and why does it appear to fit this case?
3. Who were the principal participants in the decisions surrounding the Osprey?
4. What were the rationales for and against this aircraft presented by the various groups?
5. Which groups joined together to be successful in maintaining the Osprey program? Which ones lost out? Why?
6. Is this case a more convincing case of bureaucratic politics explaining a foreign policy decision than the previous one (see chapter 19)?

7. How might the bureaucratic politics model be adjusted in light of this case?

REFERENCES

ABC News. 1993. "Your Money, Your Choice." *World News Tonight,* March 3.

Allison, G., and M. Halperin. 1972. "Bureaucratic Politics: A Paradigm and Some Policy Implications." *World Politics* 24:40–80.

Allison, G., and P. Zelikow. 1999. *Essence of Decision: Explaining the Cuban Missile Crisis.* New York: Longman.

Arnold, T. 1994. Manager, Tiltrotor Communications, Bell Helicopter Textron. Telephone interview and follow-up correspondence, November 21.

Aviation Week & Space Technology (AW&ST) Staff Report. 1989. "Naval Aviation Modernization Hit Hard by Pentagon Cuts." *Aviation Week & Space Technology,* April 24.

Bell-Boeing. 1994a. "Status of V-22 Subcontracts (Including EMD and Uprated Drive System)." Internal memorandum and attachments, October 12. Distributed to author.

———. 1994b. "U.S. Map, V-22 EMD Supplier Dollars." Internal memorandum. Bell Helicopter Textron, October 12.

Bolkcom, C. 2005. "CRS Issue Brief for Congress: V-22 Osprey Tilt-Rotor Aircraft." Congressional Research Service: Washington, DC, January 7.

Cooper, B. 1991. "CRS Issue Brief for Congress: V-22 Tilt-Rotor Aircraft (Weapons Fact)." Congressional Research Service: Washington, DC, February 25.

Dady, G. 1998. "V-22" Public Affairs Office, U.S. Department of Navy. Telephone interview and follow-up correspondence, December 7.

Ferguson, D. W. 1992. "V-22 Production Employment." Internal memorandum. Bell Helicopter Textron, August 25. Distributed to author.

Flanagan, R. 1990. "The V-22 Is Slipping Away." *U.S. Naval Institute Proceedings* 116: 39–43.

Forman, B. 1994. "The V-22 Tiltrotor Osprey: The Program That Wouldn't Die." Paper distributed to author by Bell-Boeing Team.

Gertler, J. 2011. "CRS Report for Congress: V-22 Osprey Tilt-Rotor Aircraft: Background and Issues for Congress." Congressional Research Service: Washington, DC, March 10.

Government Accountability Office (GAO). 2009. *V-22 Osprey Aircraft: Assessments Needed to Address Operational and Cost Concerns to Define Future Investments.* GAO-09-692T. Washington, DC.

Griffiths, D. 1986. "Weinberger Puts Muzzle on Pentagon Watchdog." *Business Week,* September 5.

Harrison, M. 1994. Internal memorandum. Boeing Space Group, Helicopter Division, December 12. Distributed to author.

Moore, M. 1989. "Pentagon May Lose Weapons." *Washington Post,* April 15.

Morrocco, J. 1992. "Pentagon Narrows V-22 Mission, Reaffirms Medium-Lift." *Aviation Week & Space Technology,* July 27.

National Commission on Fiscal Responsibility and Reform. 2010. "$200 Billion in Illustrative Savings." Draft document, www.fiscalcommission.gov/sites/fiscalcommission.gov/files/documents/Illustrative_List_11.10.2010.pdf, November 12.

O'Keefe, S. 1997. Former secretary of the Navy and Department of Defense comptroller. Telephone interview, January 13.

Reuters. 2008. "Hamilton Sundstrand Announces Multi-year Procurement for V-22 Electric Systems." Press release, www.reuters.com, April 16.

Scharfen, J. 1990. "U.S. Marine Corps in 1989." *U.S. Naval Institute Proceedings* 116: 178–89.

Uchitelle, L. 1992. "An Odd Aircraft's Tenacity Shows Difficulty of Cutting Arms Budget." *New York Times*, November 2.

U.S. Congress, House Armed Services Committee. 1989. Navy Program Review. *Hearings on National Defense Authorization Act for Fiscal Year 1990—H.R. 2461 and Previously Authorized Programs*. 101st Congress, 1st Session, May 11, Washington, DC.

———. 1990. Department of the Navy and U.S. Marine Corps FY 1991 RTD&E Budget Request. *Hearings on National Defense Authorization Act for Fiscal Year 1991—H.R. 4753 and Oversight of Previously Authorized Programs*. 101st Congress, 2nd Session, March 7, Washington, DC.

———. 1991a. Fiscal Years 1992–1993 National Defense Authorization Request. *Hearings on National Defense Authorization Act for Fiscal Years 1992 and 1993—H.R. 2100 and Oversight of Previously Authorized Programs*. 102nd Congress, 1st Session, February 7, Washington, DC.

———. 1991b. V-22 Osprey Program Review. *Hearings on National Defense Authorization Act for Fiscal Years 1992 and 1993—H.R. 2100 Oversight of Previously Approved Programs*. 102nd Congress, 1st Session, April 11, Washington, DC.

———. 1992a. Procurement and Military Nuclear Systems Subcommittee Hearings. *Hearings on National Defense Authorization Act for Fiscal Year 1993—H.R. 5006 and Oversight of Previously Authorized Programs*. 102nd Congress, 2nd Session, April 28, Washington, DC.

———. 1992b. *The Status of the V-22 Tiltrotor Aircraft Program*. 102nd Congress, 2nd Session, August 5, Washington, DC.

U.S. Department of Defense. 2001. "Office of the Secretary of Defense Mission Statement." www.defenselink.mil/osd, February 5.

Waller, D. 1989. "Will the Osprey Ever Fly?" *Newsweek*, July 24.

Wilson, G. 1989. "Cheney Outlines $10 Billion in 'Painful' Defense Cuts." *Washington Post*, April 26.

Zagare, F. 1990. "Rationality and Deterrence." *World Politics* 42: 238–60.

21

NATO Expansion

The Anatomy of a Decision*

James M. Goldgeier

In deciding to enlarge the North Atlantic Treaty Organization (NATO), Bill Clinton's administration followed through on one of its most significant foreign policy initiatives and the most important political-military decision for the United States since the collapse of the Soviet Union. The policy . . . involved a difficult trade-off for the administration between wanting to ensure that political and economic reform succeeded in Central and Eastern Europe and not wanting to antagonize Russia, which had received billions of dollars to assist its transition to a democratic, market-oriented Western partner. Skeptics of the NATO expansion policy within the government also worried about its costs, its effect on the cohesiveness of the Atlantic Alliance, and the wisdom of extending security guarantees to new countries. How did President Clinton, often criticized for a lack of attention to foreign policy and for vacillation on important issues, come to make a decision with far-reaching consequences for all of Europe at a time when NATO faced no military threat and in the context of diminishing resources for foreign policy?

This [chapter] analyzes the process the U.S. government followed that led to this major foreign policy initiative. I have based my findings largely on interviews I conducted in 1997 with several dozen current and former U.S. government officials, from desk officers deep inside the State and Defense Departments all the way up to President Clinton's foreign policy advisers. The interviews reveal that the administration decided to expand NATO despite widespread bureaucratic opposition, because a few key people wanted it to happen, the most important being the president and his national security adviser, Anthony Lake. Other senior officials—particularly those

---

*Some notes have been deleted; others have been renumbered.

in the State Department—became important supporters and implementers of NATO expansion, but Lake's intervention proved critical early in the process. Keenly interested in pushing NATO's expansion as part of the administration's strategy of enlarging the community of democracies, Lake encouraged the president to make statements supporting expansion and then used those statements to direct the National Security Council (NSC) staff to develop a plan and a timetable for putting these ideas into action. The president, once convinced that this policy was the right thing to do, led the alliance on this mission into the territory of the former Warsaw Pact and sought to make NATO's traditional adversary part of the process through his personal relationship with Russian president Boris Yeltsin.

Rather than being a story of a single decision, this policy initiative came about through a series of decisions and presidential statements made during three key phases of the process in 1993 and 1994. During the summer and fall of 1993, the need to prepare for Clinton's January 1994 summit meetings in Brussels pushed the bureaucracy into action. The product of this bureaucratic activity was the October 1993 proposal to develop the Partnership for Peace (PFP), which would increase military ties between NATO and its former adversaries. In the second phase, which culminated in his January 1994 trip to Europe, Clinton first signaled U.S. seriousness about NATO expansion by saying the question was no longer "whether" but "when." The final phase discussed here encompasses the period from April to October 1994, when key supporters of NATO expansion attempted to turn this presidential rhetoric into reality. At the end of this period, the newly installed assistant secretary of state for European affairs, Richard Holbrooke, bludgeoned the bureaucracy into understanding that expansion was presidential policy, and an idea that had been bandied about for a year and a half finally started to become reality.

PHASE 1: BUREAUCRATIC DEBATE AND ENDORSEMENT OF THE PARTNERSHIP FOR PEACE

In the first few months of his administration, President Clinton had not given much thought to the issue of NATO's future. Then, in late April 1993, at the opening of the Holocaust Museum in Washington, he met one-on-one with a series of Central and Eastern European leaders, including the highly regarded leaders of Poland and the Czech Republic, Lech Walesa and Vaclav Havel. These two, having struggled so long to throw off the Soviet yoke, carried a moral authority matched by few others around the world. Each leader delivered the same message to Clinton: Their top priority was NATO membership. After the meetings, Clinton told Lake how impressed he had been with the vehemence with which these leaders spoke, and Lake says Clinton was inclined to think positively toward expansion from that moment.

At the June 1993 meeting of the North Atlantic Council (NAC) foreign ministers in Athens, Greece, U.S. Secretary of State Warren Christopher said enlarging NATO's membership was "not now on the agenda." But Christopher understood that NATO needed to assess its future, and with White House endorsement, he pushed his fellow foreign ministers to announce that their heads of state would meet six months later, in January 1994.[1] This announcement set in motion a process back in Washington to discuss the contentious issue of expansion. At the White House, Lake wrote in the margins of Christopher's statement, "Why not now?" and his senior director for European affairs, Jenonne Walker, convened an interagency working group (IWG) to prepare for the January 1994 meeting in Brussels and to recommend what the president should do there. The working group involved representatives from the NSC staff, the State Department, and the Pentagon. According to several participants, Walker informed the group at the start that both the president and Lake were interested in pursuing expansion.

On September 21, 1993, nine months into the Clinton administration, Lake gave his first major foreign policy speech, in which he developed ideas on promoting democracy and market economies that Clinton had enunciated during his campaign. Clinton had stressed the theme that democracies do not go to war with one another and thus that U.S. foreign policy strategy should focus on promoting democracy. Lake had helped to develop this approach, which leading campaign officials saw as a foreign policy initiative behind which different wings of the Democratic Party could rally. In the 1993 speech, Lake argued that "the successor to a doctrine of containment must be a strategy of enlargement—enlargement of the world's free community of market democracies." And he added, "At the NATO summit that the president has called for this January, we will seek to update NATO, so that there continues behind the enlargement of market democracies an essential collective security."[2]

Although Lake tried rhetorically to push the process along, the bureaucracy greatly resisted expanding the alliance. Officials at the Pentagon unanimously favored the PFP proposal developing largely through the efforts of General John Shalikashvili and his staff, first from Shalikashvili's perch as Supreme Allied Commander in Europe and then as chairman of the Joint Chiefs of Staff. PFP proponents sought to foster increased ties to all the former Warsaw Pact states as well as to the traditional European neutrals, and to ensure that NATO did not have to differentiate among its former adversaries or "draw new lines" in Europe. Every state that accepted its general principles could join the PFP, and the countries themselves could decide their level of participation. Many officials viewed the partnership as a means of strengthening and making operational the North Atlantic Cooperation Council (NACC), which had been NATO's first formal outreach effort to the East, undertaken in 1991. From the Pentagon's standpoint, it did not make sense to talk about expansion until after NATO had established the type of military-to-military relationships that would enable new countries to integrate effectively into the alliance. Several participants in the IWG say that Pentagon representatives made clear that both Secretary of Defense Les Aspin and General Shalikashvili opposed expansion and, in particular, feared diluting the effectiveness of NATO. . . .

In addition to concern about NATO's future military effectiveness, the bureaucracy also feared that expansion would antagonize Russia and bolster nationalists and Communists there. Many State Department debates at this time focused on this fear, and views on expansion there were more divided than those in the Pentagon. In September, Yeltsin had written a letter to Clinton and other NATO heads of state backtracking on positive remarks he had made in Warsaw on Polish membership in NATO and suggesting that if NATO expanded, Russia should be on the same fast track as the Central Europeans. Then, in early October, Yeltsin's troops fired on his opposition in Parliament, and it appeared to many that the political situation in Russia was deteriorating.

During this period a small group at the State Department—including Lynn Davis, the under secretary for arms control and international security affairs; Thomas Donilon, the chief of staff; and Stephen Flanagan, a member of the Policy Planning Staff—advocated a fast-track approach to expansion. This group argued that in January 1994, NATO should lay out criteria, put forward a clear timetable, and perhaps even offer "associate membership" to a first set of countries. At a series of lunches with Secretary Christopher, organized to present him with the pros and cons of expansion, these individuals pressed him to move the process forward as quickly as possible, saying, as one participant recalled, that NATO should "strike while the iron is hot." . . . Flanagan, Donilon, and Davis worried that without the prospect of membership in a key Western institution, Central and Eastern Europe would lose the momentum for reform. NATO and the European Union (EU) were the premier institutions in Europe, and the EU, absorbed in the internal problems associated with the Maastricht Treaty, would clearly postpone its own expansion. These officials wanted to encourage states such as Poland and Hungary to continue on the path of reform—to adopt civilian control of the military, to build a free polity and economy, and to settle border disputes—by providing the carrot of NATO membership if they succeeded.

This pro-expansion group also drew on compelling arguments from two other government officials. Charles Gati, a specialist on Eastern Europe serving on the Policy Planning Staff, had written a memo in September 1993 arguing that the new democracies were fragile, that the ex-Communists were likely to gain power in Poland, and that if NATO helped Poland succeed in carrying out reforms, it would have a huge impact on the rest of the region. Donilon took this memo straight to Christopher, who found the reasoning impressive. When the ex-Communists did win parliamentary elections in Poland weeks later, Gati's words carried even greater weight.

The other argument came from Dennis Ross, the special Middle East coordinator for the Clinton administration, who had been director of policy planning under Secretary of State James A. Baker III. Given his involvement in the German unification process and the development of the NACC, Ross attended two of the Christopher lunches on NATO. During one, he reminded the group that critics had believed that NATO could not successfully bring in a united Germany in 1990, but it did, and without damaging U.S.-Soviet relations. He suggested that NATO involve Russia in the expansion process rather than confront its former enemy. Ross argued that the previous administration's experience with German unification offered good reason to believe that the current administration could overcome problems with Russia.

Inside the State Department's regional bureaus dealing with Europe and with the New Independent States (NIS), however, bureaucrats expressed tremendous opposition to a fast-track approach and in a number of cases to any idea of expansion. Many who worked on NATO issues feared problems of managing the alliance if Clinton pushed ahead with this contentious issue. Those who worked on Russia issues thought expansion would undermine reform efforts there.

In these State Department debates, the most important proponent of a much more cautious and gradualist approach to expansion was Strobe Talbott, then ambassador-at-large for the NIS. Talbott proved important for two reasons: As a longtime friend, he had direct access to Clinton, and as a former journalist, he could write quickly, clearly, and persuasively. Christopher asked Talbott and Nicholas Burns—the senior director for Russian, Ukrainian, and Eurasian Affairs at the NSC—to comment on the fast-track approach. He and Burns argued to both Christopher and Lake that Russia would not understand a quick expansion, which would impair the U.S.-Russian relationship and, given the domestic turmoil in Russia in late September and early October, might push Russia over the edge.

One Saturday in mid-October, when Talbott was out of town, Lynn Davis forcefully argued to Christopher at a NATO discussion lunch that NACC and the PFP were simply not enough. When Talbott returned that afternoon and learned about the thrust of the meeting, he quickly wrote a paper reiterating the importance of a gradual approach to expansion. The next day, he delivered a memo to Christopher stating, "Laying down criteria could be quite provocative, and badly timed with what is going on in Russia." Instead, he suggested, "Take the one new idea that seems to be universally accepted, PFP, and make that the centerpiece of our NATO position." Talbott argued that the administration should not put forward any criteria on NATO membership that would automatically exclude Russia and Ukraine, and that the administration could never manage the relationship if it did not offer Russia the prospect of joining the alliance at a future date. He firmly believed that Clinton should mention neither dates nor names in Brussels.[3]

By Monday morning, October 18, Christopher had decided to support the gradual rather than fast-track approach, which meant that any agreement among leading officials would place the policy emphasis on the PFP. Among Clinton's top foreign policy advisers, Lake sought to push ahead with expansion, Aspin and Shalikashvili sought to delay consideration of expansion and instead supported the PFP, and Christopher fell somewhere in between, open to gradual expansion but concerned about Russia's reaction. At the White House later that day, Clinton endorsed the consensus of his principal foreign policy advisers that, at the January summit, the alliance should formally present the PFP, and he should announce NATO's intention eventually to expand. This decision reflected the consensus that had emerged from the bargaining within agencies and in the IWG, which had easily agreed on the PFP, but which could not agree on issues such as criteria, a timetable, or "associate membership" status. In the end, the IWG agreed on what its principals in turn could accept: to put forward the PFP and to say something general about NATO's eventual expansion.

The consensus emerged because, as with many decisions, opponents and proponents of expansion had different interpretations of what they had decided, and this ambiguity created support for the decision throughout the bureaucracy. Vociferous opponents of NATO expansion believed the administration's principals had decided to promote the PFP while postponing a decision on enlargement. Those in the middle, who could live with expansion but did not want to do anything concrete in 1994, also saw the October decision as consistent with their preferences. Finally, the decision that Clinton should comment on expansion pleased proponents of near-term enlargement, as they believed such a treatment would help to move the process along on a faster track.

The October 18 meeting would be the last of its kind on NATO expansion for another year. Given the meeting's ambiguous outcome—the foreign policy principals had not given the president a timetable to endorse—confusion reigned concerning the policy's direction. For the moment, the decision to develop the PFP was the Clinton administration's NATO outreach policy.

Yet from the moment the participants went their separate ways, observers could tell they interpreted the decision differently. Secretary of State Christopher's entourage, on its way to Budapest to brief the Central Europeans (and then on to Moscow to explain the policy to Yeltsin), said the January summit would send the signal that NATO's door would open at some future date (and apparently even State Department officials on Christopher's plane disagreed about how to present the decision). The senior official conducting the airborne press briefing stated, "We believe that the summit should formally open the door to NATO expansion as an evolutionary process."[4] Meanwhile, Secretary of Defense Aspin and his advisers, attending the NATO defense ministers' meeting in Travamünde, Germany, to gain alliance endorsement of the PFP, emphasized that NATO would not enlarge soon. According to one report, Lake called Aspin in a pique saying the secretary of defense had veered from the script.[5]

PHASE 2: THE PRESIDENT SPEAKS

After mid-October, administration officials knew the president would say something about NATO enlargement on his trip to Europe in January. But no one was sure how much he would say and how specific he would be. After all, the bureaucratic wrangling had produced a decision that the president should emphasize the PFP while delivering a vague statement that NATO could eventually take in new members. The first official statement prior to the summit came from Secretary Christopher at the plenary session of the Conference on Security and Cooperation in Europe (CSCE) in Rome on November 30. Noting that the United States was proposing a Partnership for Peace, he also stated, "At the same time, we propose to open the door to an evolutionary expansion of NATO's membership."[6] Two days later, at the NAC ministerial in Brussels, he said, "The Partnership is an important step in its own right. But it can also be a key step toward NATO membership."[7]

Meanwhile, prominent figures from previous administrations pressured Clinton to be more forthcoming on expansion at the summit. Former secretary of state Henry Kissinger complained in an op-ed piece that the PFP "would dilute what is left of the Atlantic Alliance into a vague multilateralism," and he called for movement to bring Poland, Hungary, and the Czech Republic into some form of "qualified membership." Former national security adviser Zbigniew Brzezinski urged NATO members to sign a formal treaty of alliance with Russia and to lay out a more explicit path to full NATO membership for the leading Central European candidates. Former secretary of state James A. Baker III also made the case for a "clear road map" with "clear benchmarks" for the prospective members.[8]

During this time, Brzezinski had been meeting with Lake to share ideas about his two-track approach to expansion, and he also invited Lake to his home to meet a number of Central and Eastern European leaders. Since the debate at the White House focused more on "whether" than concretely "how," these meetings with Brzezinski helped Lake to clarify his own thinking and emphasized to him the importance of keeping the process moving forward. Significantly, Brzezinski argued that Russia would be more likely to develop as a stable, democratic presence in Europe if the West removed all temptations to reassert imperial control and precluded Russia's ability to intimidate its former satellites.

In late December, Lake's staff members, who were in general opposed to moving expansion onto the near-term agenda, presented him with the draft briefing memoranda for the different stops on the president's upcoming trip to Europe. Several of his staffers say he threw a fit on seeing the initial work, because the memos emphasized the PFP. According to Nicholas Burns, Lake wanted a presidential statement in January that would leave no doubt about the policy's direction.

But high-level opposition to any push toward expansion continued to color the agenda. The Pentagon appeared unanimously to share the view that the policy should be sequential; countries would participate in the PFP for a number of years and then the alliance might start addressing the issue of expansion. General Shalikashvili, at a White House press briefing on January 4, emphasized the value of the PFP as a way of ensuring that the alliance create no new divisions in Europe, and he suggested postponing discussions of membership to a future date. . . .

But, he added, in words that Clinton would make much more significant a week later, "It is useful to remember that we are talking so much less today about whether extension of the alliance [should take place], but so much more about how and when." Pentagon officials, however, had a much different view of what "when" meant than did proponents of expansion at the NSC and State, believing the PFP should operate for several years before the alliance began thinking about expansion.

Prior to the summit, even Clinton still seemed unsure of how far he wanted to go. The strong showing of nationalists and Communists in the December 1993 Russian parliamentary elections had sent shockwaves through the administration. On January 4, Clinton said in an exchange with reporters at the White House,

> I'm not against expanding NATO. I just think that if you look at the consensus of the NATO members at this time, there's not a consensus to expand NATO at this time and we don't want to give the impression that we're creating another dividing line in Europe after we've worked for decades to get rid of the one that existed before.[9]

This was hardly the signal the Central Europeans had hoped to receive.

Just prior to his trip, Clinton sent Polish-born General Shalikashvili, Czech-born U.S. ambassador to the UN Madeleine Albright, and Hungarian-born State Department adviser Charles Gati to Central Europe to explain the administration's policy and to quell criticisms stemming from this region prior to the summit. Albright argued forcefully to the Central

European leaders that the PFP would provide the best vehicle for these countries to gain future NATO membership, and she reiterated that it was not a question of whether, but when.

In Brussels, Clinton said that the PFP "sets in motion a process that leads to the enlargement of NATO." According to Donilon, Lake wanted the president to make a more forceful statement in Prague to give a clear impetus to expansion. Sitting around a table in Prague prior to Clinton's remarks, Lake, Donilon, and presidential speechwriter Robert Boorstin wrote the statement that Clinton agreed to deliver. Echoing what Albright had told the Central Europeans, the president said, "While the Partnership is not NATO membership, neither is it a permanent holding room. It changes the entire NATO dialogue so that now the question is no longer whether NATO will take on new members but when and how."[10]

To proponents such as Lake, this statement was a clear victory, and it laid the basis for moving the process along. He wanted the alliance to address the "when" as soon as possible. For expansion skeptics, to whom "when" meant after the PFP had created a new military environment in Europe, the president's words meant nothing specific and reflected, they believed, the outcome of the October 18 decision; they concluded that although the president had stated that expansion was theoretically possible, the administration would not undertake any actual effort to expand the alliance anytime soon. Their failure to recognize the importance of the president's remarks—at least as Lake and other expansion proponents interpreted them—would lead to their surprise later in the year that the process had been moving forward.

Administration critics would later suggest that Clinton supported expansion purely for political purposes, to woo voters of Polish, Czech, and Hungarian descent. Numerous foreign policy officials in the administration, who deny that domestic political considerations came up in their meetings on expansion, hotly dispute this claim. Lake says that although everyone knew the political context of the NATO enlargement debate, he never had "an explicit discussion" with the president about the domestic political implications of expansion. Domestic politics probably played a more complicated role in this policy decision than a simple attempt to court ethnic votes in key Midwestern and northeastern states. First, for several political reasons, Clinton needed to demonstrate U.S. leadership. His administration's policy in Bosnia was failing miserably, and this failure overshadowed every other foreign policy issue at the time. Second, even if ethnic pressures did not drive the decision, Clinton would have alienated these vocal and powerful domestic constituencies had he decided against expanding NATO; Republicans thus would have gained another issue to use in congressional elections later that year. If domestic politics did not drive the decision, it gave it more resonance for the White House, and both parties certainly used the policy for political purposes: Clinton's speeches in places like Cleveland and Detroit in 1995–1996 provide clear evidence of the perceived value of NATO expansion to those communities, and the Republicans included NATO expansion as a plank in their Contract with America during the 1994 congressional campaign.

The bureaucratic decision-making process had not advanced much between October 1993 and the president's trip to Europe in January 1994. But regardless of where the bureaucratic consensus remained, Clinton had opened the door for expansion with his forceful remarks in Brussels and Prague. This is turn gave Lake the impetus he needed, and because of his proximity and access to the president, for the moment he could move the process along without having to gain the backing of the rest of the bureaucracy.

PHASE 3: FROM RHETORIC TO REALITY

For several months after Clinton's pronouncements in January, neither his advisers nor the bureaucracy paid much attention to NATO expansion, largely because of the crises in Bosnia that winter and because of the attention they paid to getting the PFP up and running. In early spring, the NATO expansion process began moving forward again, at Lake's instigation. In April, Lake held a meeting with his deputy, Samuel R. "Sandy" Berger, and one of his staffers, Daniel Fried, a specialist on Central and Eastern Europe, to discuss how to follow up on the president's January remarks and to prepare for the president's trip to Warsaw that July. Lake asked for an action plan on enlargement, and when Fried reminded him of the bureaucracy's continued strong opposition, Lake replied that the president wanted to move forward and Lake therefore needed an action plan to make it happen.

To write the policy paper, Fried brought in two old colleagues: Burns at NSC and Alexander Vershbow, then in the European bureau of the State Department but soon to become the NSC's senior director for European affairs. . . . Despite his NSC portfolio on Russian affairs, Burns was not opposed to NATO expansion, which pleased Fried; Burns likewise appreciated that Fried accepted a gradual approach and understood that the strategy had to include a place for Russia. Unlike the authors of many policy papers that need approval, or clearance, from key actors at each of the relevant agencies, this troika worked alone, thus sidestepping the need for bureaucratic bargaining. Before the president's Warsaw trip, Lake invited Talbott and State Department Policy Planning Director James Steinberg to the White House to discuss the draft paper with Fried and Burns. Talbott sought assurances that the proposed process would be gradual, consistent with the policy he had pushed the previous October.

Many people believe Talbott opposed enlargement during this time, especially because most of the Russia specialists outside government vehemently opposed expanding NATO. Talbott clearly opposed making any immediate moves and emphasized that the process must be gradual and include rather than isolate Russia. But many of Talbott's colleagues say that once he became deputy secretary of state in February 1994 and more regularly considered the broader European landscape and the needs of the Central and Eastern Europeans, he warmed to expansion. . . . Talbott encouraged Christopher to bring Richard Holbrooke back from his post as ambassador to Germany to be assistant secretary of state for European affairs in summer 1994, both to fix the Bosnia policy and to work on NATO expansion. By the following year, Talbott had become one of the most articulate Clinton administration spokespersons in favor of the NATO expansion policy.

By summer, the NSC and State Department positions had converged. Thinking in more gradual terms than Lake had been pushing earlier in the year, the troika's views now coincided with the consensus that had developed in the State Department. The efforts to begin figuring out a way to develop a timetable for both the expansion track and the NATO-Russian track led to a major push in summer and fall 1994 to get an expansion policy on firmer footing.

In Warsaw in July, Clinton spoke more forcefully on the issue than many in the bureaucracy would have preferred, just as he had done in Brussels and Prague earlier in the year. In an exchange with reporters after his meeting with Lech Walesa, he said, "I have always stated my support for the idea that NATO will expand. . . . And now what we have to do is to get the NATO partners together and to discuss what the next steps should be."[11] By emphasizing the need to meet with U.S. allies, the president gave a green light to those who wanted a concrete plan.

Two months later, addressing a conference in Berlin, Vice President Al Gore proved even more outspoken, saying,

> Everyone realizes that a military alliance, when faced with a fundamental change in the threat for which it was founded, either must define a convincing new rationale or become decrepit. Everyone knows that economic and political organizations tailored for a divided continent must now adapt to new circumstances—including acceptance of new members—or be exposed as mere bastions of privilege.[12]

Holbrooke apparently had major input on this speech and one staffer for the JCS said the vice president's remarks gave the military its first inkling that the administration's NATO policy had changed since January. Senior military representatives objected to the draft text of Gore's remarks, but to no avail.

Despite his inclination toward expanding the alliance, Clinton understood concerns about Russia's reaction. After all, Clinton's foreign policy had centered in part on U.S. assistance for the Yeltsin government's reform program, and he did not want to undercut Yeltsin before the 1996 Russian presidential election. In late September, Yeltsin came to Washington, and Clinton had a chance to tell him face to face that NATO was potentially open to all of Europe's new democracies, including Russia, and that it would not expand in a way that threatened Russia's interests. At a White House luncheon, Clinton told Yeltsin that he had discussed NATO expansion with key allied leaders, and he made sure Yeltsin understood that NATO would not announce the new members until after the Russian and U.S. 1996 presidential elections. At the same time, Clinton wanted to ensure that any advances in the process that might take place in the meantime—during the NATO ministerials—would not surprise the Russian president.

With Holbrooke coming back to the State Department and with Vershbow and Fried both now special assistants to the president at the NSC, expansion proponents had gained more power within the bureaucracy than they had during the previous autumn. Lake successfully circumvented bureaucratic opposition to get Clinton to make forceful statements that expansion would occur. His troika had continued to update its action plan throughout the summer and fall, and by October 1994 its strategy paper proposed the timeline that the alliance eventually followed: a series of studies and consultations designed to lead to a membership invitation to the first group and a NATO-Russian accord in 1997. But concerns about the military dimension of expansion still existed in the Pentagon, without whose efforts to address the nuts and bolts of expanding the military alliance the decision could not have moved from theory to practice.

For their next task, proponents had to convince skeptics within the administration that the president was serious. . . . For NATO expansion, the enforcer would be Holbrooke, the newly installed assistant secretary of state, whom Christopher had brought back to the department at the urging of Talbott, Donilon, and Under Secretary for Political Affairs Peter Tarnoff.

Holbrooke held his first interagency meeting on NATO expansion at the State Department in late September, almost immediately after taking office. He wanted to make clear that he would set up and run the mechanism to expand NATO, because the president wanted it to happen. Holbrooke knew that most Pentagon officials preferred concentrating on making the PFP work rather than moving ahead with expansion, and he wanted to make sure everyone understood that he was taking charge. His opportunity came at this meeting when the senior representative from the Joint Chiefs of Staff (JCS), three-star General Wesley Clark, questioned Holbrooke's plans to move forward on the "when" and "how" questions of expansion. To the Pentagon's way of thinking, no one had yet made a decision that would warrant this action. Holbrooke shocked those in attendance by declaring, "That sounds like insubordination to me. Either you are on the president's program or you are not."[13]

According to participants, Deputy Assistant Secretary of Defense Joseph Kruzel, one of the key figures in developing the PFP program, argued that the issue had been debated in October 1993 and the decision at that time, the last formal meeting on the subject at the highest levels, was *not* to enlarge. Other Pentagon officials in attendance argued that only the "principals" could make this decision, and thus another meeting needed to be held at the highest level. Holbrooke responded that those taking this view had not been listening to what the president had been saying. The skeptics simply could not believe that Holbrooke was resting his whole case on remarks Clinton had made in Brussels, Prague, and Warsaw. Former defense secretary William Perry still refers to Holbrooke as having "presumed" at that point that the administration had decided to enlarge NATO, whereas Clinton had made no formal decision to that effect.

After this dramatic outburst, Holbrooke asked Clark to set up a meeting to brief this interagency group on what they would need to do to implement the policy. Through this request, Holbrooke enabled the JCS to voice their concerns but also forced them to begin acting on the issue. At the Pentagon two weeks later, a team with representatives from both the Office of the Secretary of Defense (OSD) and the JCS presented to the interagency group the full range of military requirements each country would need to meet to join NATO. The JCS briefer pointed, for example, to the 1,200 Atlantic Alliance standardization agreements the former Warsaw Pact armed forces would have to address to become compatible with NATO. Holbrooke, now playing "good cop," responded by saying that this briefing was exactly what the group needed, and he invited them to work with him to make the process a smooth one. This briefing would, in fact, serve as the basis both for the briefing to the NAC later in the fall and for the NATO study conducted the following year.

Because Pentagon officials did not believe the administration had ever made a formal decision, Perry called Clinton and asked for a meeting of the foreign policy team to clarify the president's intentions. At the meeting, Perry presented his arguments for holding back and giving the PFP another year before deciding on enlargement. He wanted time to move forward on the NATO-Russian track and to convince Moscow that NATO did not threaten Russia's interests, before the alliance moved ahead on the expansion track. Instead, the president endorsed the two-track plan that Lake and his staff, as well as the State Department, now pushed—the plan that ultimately led to the May 1997 signing of the NATO-Russian Founding Act and the July 1997 NATO summit in Madrid inviting Poland, Hungary, and the Czech Republic to begin talks on accession to full NATO membership.

THE AMBIGUITY OF THE DECISION

Like so many decision-making processes, the NATO expansion process was not at all clear-cut. The best evidence of its ambiguities comes from asking participants a simple question: "When did you believe that the decision to expand NATO had been made?" Their answers demonstrate that what you see depends on where you stand; attitudes toward the decision affected individuals' views of what was happening. Most supporters, including Lake, cite the period between the October 1993 meeting of the principals and Clinton's trip to Europe in January 1994. The answers of opponents, on the other hand, generally range over the second half of 1994, depending on when they finally realized the president was serious. One State Department official who opposed expansion said that when he objected to language circulating in an interagency memo on the issue in August 1994, a colleague told him it was the same language the president had used in Warsaw the previous month. At that point, he says, he understood that the policy had moved from theory to reality. Others, such as Perry, did not start to believe that expansion was on the table until after the Holbrooke interagency meeting in September 1994. In support of this last interpretation, Brzezinski pointed out at the time that until Clinton *answered* the questions "when" and "how," rather than simply *asking* them, the United States had no decisive plan for Europe.[14]

These interpretations vary so widely because the president and his top advisers did not make a formal decision about a timetable or process for expansion until long after Clinton had started saying NATO would enlarge. The when, who, how, and even why came only over time and not always through a formal decision-making process. In January 1994, when the president first said that he expected the alliance to take in new members, no consensus existed among his top advisers on the difficult questions of when and how. Clinton's advisers could as reasonably believe that his remarks amounted to no more than a vague statement that NATO might someday expand as they could believe that the president wanted to begin moving forward *now*. Whereas proponents of expansion took his statements as a signal to begin planning how to put theory into practice, the president did not make an explicit decision in the presence of his top foreign policy advisers until nearly a year later, and some opponents therefore choose to believe that the course was not set until that meeting.

Readers may find it unsatisfying that I have not uncovered either *the* moment of decision or the president's ulterior motive. Truthfully, however, most policies—even those as significant as this one—develop in a more ambiguous fashion. This process was hardly unique to the Clinton administration. White House meetings often result in participants, as well as those they inform, having conflicting understandings of what the administration has decided. Policy entrepreneurs use presidential statements to push forward an issue that remains highly contentious in the bureaucracy. Each step alone seems trivial. But cumulatively, they can result in momentous policies.

As for motive, Walesa and Havel may well have made a huge impression on a president open to emotional appeals. Still, given that Clinton cared so much about the fate of Russian reform, Walesa's appeal to bring Poland and other Central European nations into the West could hardly have been sufficient. Rather, Clinton's motive was probably more complex, and he probably had only a vague idea of when he himself made the formal commitment to expand NATO. For Clinton, the appeal by the Central Europeans to erase the line drawn for them in 1945, the need to demonstrate U.S. leadership at a time when others questioned that leadership, the domestic political consequences of the choice, and his own Wilsonian orientation toward spreading liberalism combined by the second half of 1994—if not earlier—to produce a presidential preference favoring expansion. . . . Once Clinton spoke out in favor of NATO expansion in January 1994, expansion supporters within the administration had what they needed to begin to turn rhetoric into reality.

DISCUSSION QUESTIONS

1. What prompted President Clinton to consider NATO expansion in the first place?
2. Who within the administration was a strong supporter of expansion?
3. What type of policy did the various bureaucracies favor regarding the expansion of NATO?
4. What exactly was President Clinton's position on NATO expansion?
5. Considering the expansion timetable as it developed, whose advice did President Clinton appear to pay most attention to?
6. How did the changing make-up of the State Department affect the debate on expanding NATO?
7. How does the example of the NATO expansion debates illustrate the bureaucratic politics model and the influence of outside factors on presidential decision-making?

NOTES

1. For information on Secretary Christopher's intervention at the June 1993 NAC meeting, see *U.S. Department of State Dispatch* 4, no. 25:3.

2. Anthony Lake, "From Containment to Enlargement," *Vital Speeches of the Day* 60 (October 15, 1993): 13–19.

3. For quotations from the Talbott memo, see Michael Dobbs, "Wider Alliance Would Increase U.S. Commitments," *Washington Post*, July 5, 1995, A1, 16; Michael R. Gordon, "U.S. Opposes Move to Rapidly Expand NATO Membership," *New York Times*, January 2, 1994, A1, 7.

4. The official is quoted in Elaine Sciolino, "U.S. to Offer Plan on a Role in NATO for Ex-Soviet Bloc," *New York Times*, October 21, 1993, A1, 9.

5. Elaine Sciolino, "3 Players Seek a Director for Foreign Policy Story," *New York Times*, November 8, 1993, A1, 12; Stephen Kinzer, "NATO Favors U.S. Plan for Ties with the East, but Timing Is Vague," *New York Times*, October 22, 1993, A1, 8.

6. *U.S. Department of State Dispatch*, December 13, 1993.

7. *U.S. Department of State Dispatch*, December 13, 1993.

8. See Henry Kissinger, "Not This Partnership," *Washington Post*, November 24, 1993, A17; Zbigniew Brzezinski, "A Bigger—and Safer—Europe," *New York Times*, December 1, 1993, A23; and James A. Baker III, "Expanding to the East: A New NATO," *Los Angeles Times*, December 5, 1993, M2.

9. Remarks by the president in a photo-op with the Netherlands prime minister Ruud Lubbers, January 4, 1994, *Public Papers* (1994): 5–6.

10. On the Brussels statement of January 10, 1994, see *U.S. Department of State Dispatch Supplement*, January 1994, 3–4; for the Prague remarks, see Clinton, *Public Papers*, bk. I (1994), 40.

11. For his exchange with reporters in Warsaw after meeting with Walesa on July 6, 1994, see Clinton, *Public Papers* (1994), 1206.

12. *U.S. Department of State Dispatch*, September 12, 1994, 597–98.

13. Quoted in Dobbs, "Wider Alliance." Confirmed by author interviews with numerous officials who attended the meeting.

14. Zbigniew Brzezinski, "A Plan for Europe," *Foreign Affairs* 74 (January/February 1995): 27–28.

22

Sources of Humanitarian Intervention

Beliefs, Information, and Advocacy in U.S. Decisions on Somalia and Bosnia

Jon Western

On November 21, 1992, General Colin Powell's chief deputy on the Joint Chiefs of Staff, Admiral David Jeremiah, stunned a National Security Council Deputies Committee meeting on Somalia by announcing, "If you think U.S. forces are needed, we can do the job."[1] Four days later, President George H. W. Bush decided U.S. forces were needed. On December 9, 1992, 1,300 marines landed in Mogadishu, and within weeks more than 25,000 U.S. soldiers were on the ground in Somalia.

Prior to the November 21 deputies meeting, virtually no one in or out of the administration expected that President Bush or his top political and military advisers would support a major U.S. humanitarian mission to Somalia.[2] For more than a year, the Bush administration, and General Powell and the Joint Chiefs of Staff in particular, had steadfastly opposed calls for humanitarian military interventions in Somalia, Liberia, Bosnia, and elsewhere.[3] None of these conflicts was relevant to U.S. vital interests.[4] They were simply humanitarian tragedies.

With respect to Somalia, senior Bush administration and military officials had argued repeatedly throughout most of 1992 that the deeply rooted inter-clan conflicts that permeated Somalia would make any military intervention extraordinarily risky. The basic position of the Joint Chiefs of Staff and the senior White House staff was that military force would not be able to protect itself or the distribution of humanitarian relief, because the nature of the conflict made it virtually impossible to distinguish friend from enemy or civilian from combatant. In short, the administration argued, roaming armed bandits fueled by ancient hatreds and intermingled with the civilian population was a recipe for disaster.

Yet after nearly a year of extensive opposition to the use of American military force in Somalia, in November 1992 President Bush, with the firm support of all of his key advisers—including General Powell—decided to launch a massive U.S. military intervention in Somalia. Why did the Joint Chiefs of Staff reverse [their] estimates from that of July 1992, that Somalia was a "bottomless pit," to its November proclamation that "we can do the job"? Nothing in that period changed the political, military, or logistical factors on the ground. The crisis had long before reached a critical humanitarian mass. What explains the sudden change of heart within the Bush administration on Somalia?

This chapter details the factors that led to the decision to intervene in Somalia. It reveals the circuitous path by which the Bush administration adamantly opposed intervention for more than a year and then abruptly shifted its position following the election of Bill Clinton in November 1992. It is a case study on the influence of domestic politics, competing elite beliefs, information advantages, and advocacy strategies on military intervention, with the major chasm coming between "selective engagers" in the Bush administration—those who argued that U.S. military intervention should be reserved for those isolated cases when U.S. vital strategic interests were directly threatened, not strictly humanitarian considerations—and "liberal humanitarianists," or those who supported military intervention to provide humanitarian relief to aggrieved populations and to stop or prevent atrocities perpetrated against civilians. Ultimately, the decision to intervene in Somalia became intertwined with the humanitarian tragedy of Bosnia and the presidential election of 1992.

SELECTIVE ENGAGERS AND NO VITAL INTERESTS

In 1990 and 1991 civil wars erupted in Somalia and in Yugoslavia. While neither war captured much U.S. public or elite attention, by the end of 1992 both conflicts had become the focal point of American foreign policy. But in 1990 and 1991, U.S. policy toward Somalia and the former Yugoslavia, respectively, reflected the prevailing views among President Bush and his core advisers—almost all of whom could be classified as selective engagers—that with the end of the Cold War, both the horn of Africa and the Balkans had dramatically diminished in strategic importance to the United States. For selective engagers, the dissolution of Yugoslavia was of concern to the extent that unleashed ancient ethnic hatreds might create regional instability. The prudent choice in Yugoslavia—despite the profound transitions occurring throughout the rest of Eastern and Central Europe—was to support some form of centralized authority and to press for gradual change. From 1990 until the outbreak of war in Croatia in 1991 and Bosnia in March 1992, the administration devoted its diplomatic energies to strategies to forestall the collapse of the Yugoslav federation. Once violence erupted, the policy shifted from prevention to containment.

In Somalia, U.S. policy was similarly focused. During the Cold War, the United States contributed vast sums to Somali leader Siad Barre in an effort to stabilize the Horn of Africa in the face of the Soviet-backed regime of Mengistu Haile Mariam in Ethiopia. With the erosion of Soviet influence and competition, U.S. contributions to Barre were no longer seen as imperative to U.S. geostrategic interests. Without the financial backing of the United States to prop up Barre's corrupt regime, Somalia quickly disintegrated into inter-ethnic civil conflict. Because the 1991–1992 crisis posed little threat to U.S. political or economic interests and did not constitute a threat to regional or international stability, the Bush administration's position throughout much of 1991 and most of 1992 was that the crisis was an internal Somali problem. The Somali leaders needed to resolve the crisis themselves.

INITIAL INFORMATION AND PROPAGANDA ADVANTAGES

Bosnia

Prior to the war in Bosnia, few Americans or foreign policy elites focused on Bosnia. To the extent that attention was paid to the crisis during the initial months of violence, the widely accepted view was that presented by selective engagers in the Bush administration. The administration criticized the Serb leadership in Belgrade for the violence and worked diplomatically to isolate Slobodan Milosevic's regime, but it nonetheless firmly believed and publicly emphasized the view that the conflict was the inevitable consequence of intractable and primordial hatreds that had been unleashed with the collapse of the tight communist control. On numerous occasions, President Bush and his advisers equated the Bosnian crisis as rooted in ethnic animosities that went back hundreds of years. Based on this analysis of the conflict, the administration argued publicly that the prudent policy was to refrain from involvement in a situation that could only lead to a Vietnam-style quagmire for the United States. Consequently, most Americans came to perceive Bosnia as the tragic but inevitable resurrection of ancient hatreds. The public supported the administration's limited policy to contain the conflict from spreading to areas that were of geostrategic interest to the United States—in particular, Kosovo, Macedonia, Albania, Greece, Turkey, or Bulgaria.

Initially, no one was in a position to challenge critically the administration's paradigmatic framing of the conflict. In the spring of 1992, no clear precedent had been set for post–Cold War humanitarian interventions, and because Yugoslavia had been a relatively advanced economic and political society during the Cold War, very few nongovernmental humanitarian organizations had any presence or experience there. Furthermore, because only a few members of Congress had much interest in or understanding of events in Yugoslavia, most deferred to the administration's resources and expertise on the conflict. As a result, those who might have opposed the administration's analysis—such as a few liberal humanitarianists in Congress who did have some regional interest—lacked a strong organizational and political base on which to mobilize public and political opposition to the Bush administration's policies on Bosnia.

For its part, the U.S. media covering Eastern and Central Europe also had little expertise in the Balkans. Few of the major news organizations had experienced correspondents on the ground. When the war in Croatia broke out in June 1991, journalists scrambled to cover the story. As early as the fall of 1991, American reporters and administration officials began warning that although the violence in Croatia was terrible, conditions in the more ethnically diverse Bosnia would be much worse. Consequently, when violence erupted in Bosnia in March 1992, there was widespread acceptance, at least initially, among journalists that the conflict there was simply a further manifestation of the unchecked nationalist hatreds that had been widely predicted.

In addition, many journalists and editors wanted to ensure "objective" and "balanced" reporting, which meant that stories often identified and reported atrocities as though all sides were equally culpable. All of this produced predictable pressures and influences on the reporting during the first several months of the war in Bosnia, reporting that portrayed the violence as tragic but ultimately endorsed the administration's line that the conflict was caused by age-old ethnic hatreds and was one in which all sides were equally culpable.

Further aiding the Bush administration's policies were the support and informational advantages of Joint Chiefs of Staff chairman General Colin Powell and his senior advisers. Powell and his advisers strongly believed that foreign military intervention in limited conflicts would inevitably degenerate into a Vietnam-type quagmire. The Joint Chiefs stressed the inherent military dilemmas associated with any type of U.S. force deployment in Bosnia. For example, during a discussion in June on whether to use U.S. military aircraft in support of an emergency humanitarian airlift to Sarajevo, senior planners told members of Congress that even such a limited operation would require the presence of more than fifty thousand U.S. ground troops to secure a perimeter of thirty miles around the airport. Brent Scowcroft, who had been national security adviser during these deliberations, acknowledged that the Joint Chiefs "probably inflated the estimates of what it would take to accomplish some of these limited objectives, but once you have the Joint Chiefs making their estimates, it's pretty hard for armchair strategists to challenge them and say they are wrong."[5]

Consequently, throughout the first four months of the conflict in Bosnia the American public largely accepted the administration's view that the conflict was fueled by ancient hatreds about which the United States could do little. Little information emanated from the scene of the conflict to contradict that judgment, and in the face of a proliferation of "objective" reporting from Bosnia, there was very little discernable tendency within American public opinion toward a more forceful U.S. response to the crisis.

Somalia

Meanwhile, the collapse of nearly all state structures in Somalia and intense fighting between rival factions—led respectively by General Mohamed Farah Aideed and Ali Mahdi Mohamed—in the wake of Siad Barre's flight from Mogadishu in January 1991 left much of the country's civilian population under severe threat of malnutrition and starvation. Amid increasing security concerns, the United Nations withdrew its relief operations in mid-1991, leaving only a few nongovernmental organizations (NGOs) to deal with the escalating humanitarian crisis. By January 1992, the International Committee of the Red Cross was estimating that almost half of the country's six million people faced severe nutritional needs, with many liable to die of starvation without some form of immediate assistance.[6] Three hundred thousand had already died of malnutrition; more than three thousand people were starving to death daily.[7]

As with the former Yugoslavia, selective engagers in the Bush administration did not see any tangible U.S. interests at stake in Somalia. The administration deferred to the United Nations for a response to the crisis. But even here, selective engagers were focused on their own perceptions of U.S. interests and remained wary of supporting new military initiatives through the United Nations. During UN Security Council debates in April 1992, the Bush administration opposed initiatives to create an armed UN security force, fearing that new peacekeeping missions would further bloat an already inefficient UN bureaucracy and inevitably necessitate greater U.S. military involvement.

For liberal humanitarianists, Somalia was significant but only one of many regional conflicts that had humanitarian concerns. Wars in Afghanistan, Angola, Chad, Liberia, Mozambique, southern Sudan, Sri Lanka, the former Yugoslavia, and elsewhere were all producing humanitarian challenges that diverted concentrated liberal attention and resources from Somalia. The few NGOs working in Somalia issued reports beginning in the fall of 1991 citing catastrophic conditions, and efforts were made by UN Secretary-General Boutros Boutros-Ghali to mediate a settlement between the warring factions. But neither the UN mediation efforts nor the ad hoc reports from humanitarian organizations attracted attention. No galvanizing force either linked disparate humanitarian organizations or mobilized the press corps. Consequently, even though the famine intensified dramatically in the fall of 1991 and early 1992, Somalia emerged in the public discourse very slowly in 1992, and there was very little discussion on the crisis within the elite foreign policy community.

By June 1992, nearly 4.5 million were on the brink of starvation in Somalia, and nearly a hundred thousand people were dead in Bosnia, with another million displaced from their homes; still there was no concerted pressure on the selective engagers within the Bush administration to alter their policies on either Somalia or Bosnia. The administration strongly believed that even though both crises were tragic, each was rooted in intractable causes and each ultimately fell outside of U.S. interests. Furthermore, military commanders in the Joint Chiefs who opposed U.S. participation in limited wars remained convinced that military options in both Somalia and Bosnia were wholly untenable.

THE EROSION OF INITIAL INFORMATION ADVANTAGES

The Bush administration's position in Somalia and Bosnia, however, began to come under pressure in the summer of 1992. Throughout the summer, both the media and liberal humanitarianists gradually developed and dedicated more resources for information-collection efforts to challenge the administration's framing of the two conflicts.

In Somalia, in late June, the U.S. ambassador to Kenya, Smith Hempstone Jr., traveled to refugee camps on the Somali-Kenyan border for the first time. He reported his trip in a cable titled "A Day in Hell," which presented a vivid report of the humanitarian suffering. The cable resonated with many liberal humanitarianists in the State Department who believed that the Bush administration needed to do more in Somalia, and it was immediately leaked to the press. Meanwhile, liberal humanitarianists in Congress, led by Senators Nancy Kassebaum (R-KS) and Paul Simon (D-IL), conducted fact-finding missions to Somalia in June and July, and reported horrific conditions. They returned and urged their colleagues to support sending an armed UN security mission to Somalia. As other international aid organizations also began to weigh in heavily on the political debate in Washington, Boutros-Ghali again stressed that a million Somali children were at immediate risk and that more than four million people needed food assistance urgently.

All of this political pressure began to find a response at the White House. In late July, President Bush encouraged his staff to examine additional diplomatic efforts to enhance the UN efforts in Somalia. However, if the president was beginning to feel some political pressure to take action, his concern was limited to finding ways in which the United States could assist the United Nations in dealing with the problem. The United States supported a Security Council resolution passed on July 26 authorizing an emergency airlift to provide relief to southern Somalia, but according to Brent Scowcroft, "there was no discussion of using U.S. force for any purpose at this point."[8]

At the staff level, this constraint led to a bureaucratic deadlock. Some liberal humanitarianists sought to put forward military options for provision of relief, whereas selective engagers remained opposed to the use of force, calling Somalia a "bottomless pit."[9] This opposition frustrated the liberal humanitarianists. James Bishop, who was then acting assistant secretary of state for human rights and humanitarian affairs, recalls,

> I went to one interagency meeting and there was this brigadier general from the Joint Staff. We came up with this option to use helicopter gunships to support relief delivery. This general sat there and said we couldn't use helicopters in such a dusty environment. Hell, we had just fought a massive war in the Persian Gulf desert with lots of helicopters. I was evacuated from Mogadishu in January 1991 in a Marine Corps helicopter that operated just fine. But that was their attitude. They didn't want anything to do with it and they were prepared to lie to keep them out of it. At every meeting, no matter the proposal, the Joint Chiefs opposed it.[10]

By early August, according to Herman Cohen, then the assistant secretary of state for African affairs, "We were [being] told to be forward leaning, but the president paid even less attention to us."[11]

BOSNIA: IMPACT OF CAMP DISCLOSURES

Meanwhile, throughout July and early August, liberal humanitarianists greatly intensified their pressure on the Bush administration to intervene in Bosnia. At the time, the administration's control of the public message on Bosnia began to be challenged as independent reports from Bosnia started to contradict its statements. Instead of suggesting that the conflict was the spontaneous actions of neighbor killing neighbor, journalists reported on the activities of small bands of radical Serb nationalists and paramilitaries accused of committing horrific atrocities in highly organized campaigns.

This view of a highly coordinated and systematic campaign of violence was reinforced in early August by the disclosure of Serb-controlled concentration-style camps in Bosnia. The images were haunting and, for many, conclusive proof that the U.S. administration was deliberately distorting the events in Bosnia, especially given the administration's initial attempts to downplay the reports on the camps.

The pressure on the selective engagers in the wake of the camp disclosures in early August was particularly intense. Between August 2 and August 14, forty-eight news stories on Bosnia, totaling 151 minutes and 30 seconds, were broadcast on the three major network evening news programs.[12] The stories challenged Bush's policies and gave significant attention to the views and criticisms of Bush's political rival, Bill Clinton. Several stories contrasted Clinton's visible outrage at the concentration camps with Bush's tempered reaction.[13] On August 9, *ABC World News Tonight* ran a profile distinguishing Clinton's and Bush's approaches to Bosnia, extensively quoting Clinton on the need for strong, decisive U.S. leadership.

Liberal humanitarianists in Congress also escalated pressure on the president. On August 14, the Senate Foreign Relations Committee released a scathing report on ethnic cleansing, presenting the Serb campaign as a deliberate and highly coordinated, politically driven campaign of violence—not the result of spontaneous, bottom-up hatreds.

Amid this escalation in political pressure surrounding the disclosure of the camps in Bosnia, Bush urgently assembled his national security team on August 8 at his vacation home in Kennebunkport, Maine, to discuss the matter. Although there is no evidence that public opinion had shifted toward greater support for direct U.S. involvement in Bosnia, the 1992 Republican Presidential Convention was only two weeks away, and the mobilized political opposition to Bush's handling of the crisis struck a nervous chord among Bush's political advisers. Bush, who had taken tremendous pride in his foreign policy accomplishments—overseeing the fall of the Berlin Wall, the reunification of Germany, the Persian Gulf War, and the dissolution of the Soviet Union—was now being publicly castigated by highly respected foreign policy commentators. This was a particularly sensitive issue among Bush's senior political advisers—James Baker, Dennis Ross, Margaret Tutwiler, and Robert Zoellick—all of whom had moved from the State Department to the White House on August 1 to take charge of Bush's failing reelection bid.

In particular, selective engagers in Bush's political camp feared that liberal humanitarianists and hard-line interventionists in the bureaucracy were altering the public conception of Bosnia and making the administration look callous in the face of an egregious humanitarian crisis. Several liberal humanitarianists and hard-line commentators and members of Congress suggested that intervention could be done without fear of U.S. forces becoming embroiled in a Vietnam-style situation. They focused their attention on Serb aggression and on Milosevic as the primary culprit for the violence. Their prescription was that if the United States removed Milosevic or directed a targeted military strike against him and his radical supporters, the violence in Bosnia would quickly dissipate.

Despite the intensity of the political pressure, selective engagers at the White House and within the military remained convinced that Bosnia would be a quagmire. After meeting his advisers on August 8, Bush reiterated his caution: "We are not going to get bogged down in some guerrilla warfare."[14] He also ordered his team to contest the liberal humanitarian view that U.S. intervention could quickly break the siege of Sarajevo at little cost in American lives. Scowcroft recalls his reaction to the domestic criticism unleashed at the time: "I was very suspicious that people who had never supported the use of force for our national interests were now screaming for us to use force in Yugoslavia. . . . I disagreed with the humanitarianists who deliberately down-played the intractability of the conflict, who demonized Milosevic and saw this simply as a war of aggression. Milosevic was a factor, but to that extent there were also national hatreds there, that couldn't be ignored."[15]

Over the next several days, selective engagers in the Bush camp and within the Joint Chiefs intensified their public campaign to sell their beliefs about the potential dangers associated with direct U.S. involvement in the conflict. On August 11, Lieutenant General Barry McCaffrey, a principal deputy to General Powell, publicly discussed the Joint Chiefs' views with *ABC World News Tonight*, saying emphatically that despite the tragedy, "there is no military solution." Earlier that day, senior military planners told a congressional hearing that between 60,000 and 120,000 ground troops would be needed to break the siege of Sarajevo and ensure uninterrupted relief.[16] Other commanders suggested that a field army of at least 400,000 troops would be needed to implement a cease-fire.

SOMALIA: AIRLIFT IS SUPPORTED

In the midst of the public furor over the camp disclosure in Bosnia, President Bush announced an abrupt shift on his Somalia policy and ordered U.S. Air Force C-130s to assist in providing relief to famine victims in Somalia. The president also reversed his opposition to funding the deployment of five hundred Pakistani peacekeepers to Somalia; in fact, he announced that the Pentagon would provide transportation for the five-hundred-man team and its equipment.

Conventional arguments suggest that the media compelled the president to act in Somalia—that vivid images of starving and emaciated children in Somalia provoked a sense of moral outrage within the American populace. However, among the three major U.S. television networks, Somalia was mentioned in only fifteen news stories in all of 1992 prior to Bush's decision to begin the airlift, and nearly half of these "showed only fleeting glimpses of Somalia's plight" as part of other stories.[17]

The evidence suggests that Bush's policy shift on Somalia in fact came in response to both the increasing pressure to do something in Somalia and also in response to the political backlash on Bosnia that occurred on the eve of the Republican Convention. Scowcroft recalls, "[The Bosnian camp issue] probably did have a significant influence on us. We did not want to portray the administration as wholly flint-hearted realpolitik, and an airlift in Somalia was a lot cheaper [than intervention in Bosnia] to demonstrate that we had a heart."[18]

FURTHER MOBILIZATION OF INTERVENTIONISTS

On Bosnia, the selective engagers in the administration continued their public strategy to downplay the magnitude of the violence and to characterize the conflict as one of ancient blood feuds. Acting secretary of state Lawrence Eagleburger proclaimed, "It is difficult to explain, but this war is not rational. There is no rationality at all about ethnic conflict. It is gut; it is hatred; it's not for any common set of values or purposes; it just goes on. And that kind of warfare is most difficult to bring to a halt."[19] Later in a television interview he argued, "I'm not prepared to accept arguments that there must be something between the kind of involvement of Vietnam and doing nothing, that the *New York Times* and the *Washington Post* keep blabbing about, that there must be some form in the middle. That's again, what got us into Vietnam—do a little bit, and it doesn't work. What do you do next?"[20]

By September, liberal humanitarianists began a concerted effort to identify the likely effect of the upcoming winter on the civilian population in Bosnia. As part of the effort, they detailed estimates of civilian casualties that displaced populations would face in the impending winter months. Andrew Natsios, the assistant administrator for food and humanitarian assistance for the Agency for International Development, warned Eagleburger in a letter that "immediate and massive action must be taken now to avert a tragedy by the onset of the winter season."[21] A week later, a secret Central Intelligence Agency analysis estimate that as many as 250,000 Bosnian Muslims might die from starvation and exposure was leaked to the press even before it was briefed to the National Security Council (NSC).[22] NGOs began working with professional staff members of the Senate Intelligence Committee to increase congressional oversight of the intelligence community's collection and analysis of war crimes and atrocities and to report as to whether Serb actions constituted genocide under the 1948 UN Convention on the Prevention and Punishment of the Crime of Genocide.[23]

As liberal humanitarian and hard-line interventionist voices began to permeate Washington's political debate, serious concern emerged among the Joint Chiefs of Staff that the intense political and public debate over intervention was leading toward direct U.S. involvement in Bosnia.[24] In response, General Powell embarked on an unprecedented public campaign to keep U.S. troops out of Bosnia. On September 27, Powell invited Michael Gordon of the *New York Times* to his office for an extensive interview. Gordon describes Powell as at times angry during the interview and says that he "assailed the proponents of limited military intervention to protect the Bosnians." Powell argued that "as soon as they tell me it is limited, it means they do not care whether you achieve a result or not. As soon as they tell me 'surgical,' I head for the bunker." He further complained about the civilians calling for military action in Bosnia:

> These are the same folks who have stuck us into problems before that we have lived to regret. I have some memories of us being put into situations like that which did not turn out quite the way that the people who put us in thought, i.e., Lebanon, if you want a more recent real experience, where a bunch of Marines were put in there as a symbol, as a sign. Except those poor young folks did not know exactly what their mission was. They did not know really what they were doing there. It was very confusing. Two hundred and forty-one of them died as a result.[25]

Two days later, the *New York Times* published a scathing editorial directed at General Powell, "At Least Slow the Slaughter." It strongly criticized Powell and his reluctance to intervene in Bosnia:

> The war in Bosnia is not a fair fight and it is not war. It is slaughter.
> When Americans spend more than $280 billion a year for defense, surely they ought to be getting more for their money than no-can-do. It is the prerogative of civilian leaders confronting this historic nightmare to ask the military for a range of options more sophisticated than off or on, stay out completely or go in all the way to total victory.
> With that in hand, President Bush could tell General Powell what President Lincoln once told General McClellan: "If you don't want to use the Army, I should like to borrow it for a while."[26]

By all accounts, Powell was livid. In his memoirs, he recalls that he "erupted" in anger. He then dashed off a [furious] rebuttal in which he argued that the conflict is "especially complex" and has "deep ethnic and religious roots that go back a thousand years."[27]

In sum, all of these various pressures put Powell and his advisers on the defensive. The State Department was initiating new policy initiatives that, while stopping short of outright U.S. intervention, were seen by the military command staff as the initial steps to a much greater U.S. involvement. Liberal humanitarianists in Congress were demanding more. In addition, the media was openly questioning Powell's leadership. This was the cumulative pressure on Powell and the Bush administration in early November when Bill Clinton, who had campaigned on an activist policy in Bosnia, won the 1992 presidential election.

Throughout much of September, October, and early November, Somalia again fell off the radar screen. After an initial wave of news broadcasts and printed reports on Somalia following the decision to begin the airlift, the media moved to other international stories. Within the NSC also Somalia quickly disappeared. Those within the NSC who worked on Africa turned their focus toward the negotiations in South Africa leading up to free elections and to the brutal civil wars in Angola and Mozambique—both cases that were deemed more important to overall U.S. geostrategic interests than was Somalia.

This indifference to the situation in Somalia was felt within the bureaucracy and the interagency task force that had been established to monitor the airlift. The U.S. air relief was dropping food into Baidoa, and feeding centers had been established, but those most in need were not able to get to the supplies. On November 6, the Office of Food and Disaster Assistance reported that more than 25 percent of Somali children under the age of five had already died. Despite these conditions, there was very little bureaucratic movement on additional remedies to the crisis.

THE PRESIDENTIAL ELECTION

When on November 8 Bill Clinton won the presidential election, the general belief within the Washington foreign policy elite community was that the new team would shift markedly toward a liberal humanitarian foreign policy agenda.

There was wide speculation that Clinton would take quick action on Bosnia, lifting the arms embargo and possibly using U.S. air power to strike Serb targets. Sensing the power shift, within days of the election liberal humanitarianist staffers at the State Department circulated a new initiative to lift the arms embargo against Bosnia. By November 16, every relevant bureau in the State Department had signed on to the policy proposal. Furthermore, momentum quickly grew for dramatically expanding UN peacekeeping forces in Bosnia and dedicating NATO air assets to support the peacekeepers; the UN Security Council agreed to the measure on November 16.

SOMALIA: PRESSURE BUILDS AGAIN

In early November, dozens of international relief groups and representatives from the UN High Commission on Refugees again urged the international community to step up its efforts to mitigate the famine. InterAction, a coalition of 160 U.S.-based nongovernmental relief organizations, issued public and private appeals to President Bush detailing the extensive problems that relief groups were facing in Somalia without any security from roaming bandits. InterAction requested that the United States increase its support for the UN to provide security for relief operations. Furthermore, the UN secretary-general reiterated his criticism that the Bush administration—with all of its public focus on the Bosnian war in Europe—was ignoring the more acute plight of millions of black Africans in Somalia.

In response to this pressure, a wide range of policy options was discussed at a series of interagency meetings during the first three weeks of November. The question of military intervention was not open for discussion, because of continued and absolute opposition from the military. Instead, the interagency group outlined a series of recommendations short of U.S. military participation and forwarded them to a Deputies Committee meeting of the NSC on November 20.

CLINTON'S FIRST TRIP TO WASHINGTON

On November 19, two weeks after the election, President-elect Bill Clinton arrived in Washington for separate briefings from President Bush and General Powell. Although both meetings were designed to be thorough discussions of U.S. national security priorities (i.e., U.S. relations with Russia and China, and the future of the NATO alliance, including NATO expansion), in both meetings Clinton pressed Bush and Powell extensively about Bosnia. On this subject, the meeting with Powell was especially tense. Even before the meeting, Powell and his colleagues in the Joint Chiefs had been highly concerned that Clinton might propel the United States into Bosnia on an ambiguous, feel-good mission. According to Powell's account, Clinton started their meeting by asking, "Wasn't there some way, he wanted to know, that we could influence the situation [in Bosnia] through air power, something not too punitive?" Powell lamented later, "There it was again, the ever-popular solution from the skies, with a good humanist twist; let's not hurt anybody." Powell says he didn't want to sound too negative on the first meeting and that he told the president-elect that he would have his staff "give the matter more thought."[28]

CUMULATIVE PRESSURE

By now, liberal humanitarianists had mobilized extensive public and internal political pressure on the administration on both Somalia and Bosnia.

At the White House, Scowcroft recalls that the president, coming off of his postelection blues, was personally affected by the reports and by the pressure he was receiving on Somalia from groups like InterAction. Bush began asking his advisers whether anything could be done on Somalia. At the same time, the Joint Chiefs were increasingly anxious that the new president might escalate U.S. military involvement in Bosnia. They were especially embittered—as is strikingly evident in Powell's discussion with Clinton—by liberal humanitarianist claims that intervention in support of humanitarian missions, and in Bosnia in particular, could be done on the cheap.

This cumulative pressure ultimately catapulted a policy reversal by the Joint Chiefs—again, not on Bosnia but on Somalia. The day after Powell's meeting with Clinton, the Deputies Committee met to discuss the situation in Somalia. Three options were put on the table: increasing U.S. financial and material support for the current UN peacekeeping forces in Somalia; coordinating a broader UN effort in which the United States would provide logistical support but no ground troops; and initiating a U.S.-led multinational military intervention to Somalia. According to John Hirsch and former ambassador to Somalia Robert Oakley's account, however, the only consensus at the November 20 meeting was that the third option "was not a serious option."[29] In fact, the option of military intervention was not even raised for discussion.

The next day, however, Admiral Jeremiah returned and, as we have seen, stunned the deputies meeting by announcing that if force was desired in Somalia, the military could do the job. Admiral Jeremiah recalls that by then, the frustration within the Joint Chiefs had reached a critical mass:

> There was a lot of pressure on us to do something. . . . [W]e had [had] weeks of hand wringing and futzing around [by the civilian policymakers] trying to figure out the right thing to do. Nobody wants to send troops . . . [where groups] . . . have been fighting for hundreds of years.
>
> When I said it, I was frustrated because we were taking all of the heat on Somalia and Bosnia. Everyone wanted us to volunteer—to go into Bosnia and to go into Somalia—but nobody was making decisions about what they wanted to do.
>
> During the November 21 deputies meeting, I presented our [the Joint Chiefs of Staff] view that—*if you decide*—this is what it will take to do the job. Were our figures overkill? Probably. But we weren't going to go in with a weak force. We said just give us the resources and let's get on with it already.[30]

Scowcroft recalls that he, too, was startled by the Joint Chiefs' abrupt shift: "I know that the military had long felt that [Somalia would be a quagmire because the combatants would be virtually indistinguishable from the civilians]. I was struck, and I still am, with the alacrity with which Colin Powell changed gears."[31]

THE PRESIDENT'S DECISION

On November 25, after receiving briefings on the famine and the military situation, the president told his advisers that he wanted to deploy U.S. forces to Somalia. The president's decision was directly linked to the cumulative pressures of the public criticism on both Somalia and Bosnia. It was also tied to the fact that the Joint Chiefs were prepared to support the action, and that military commanders now believed they could effectively mitigate the famine. In addition, according to Scowcroft, by this time, Bush had become more sensitive to his presidential legacy, which had become jeopardized by the exhaustive liberal criticism of the administration's apparent callousness to humanitarian crises. Somalia seemed like a good contribution to that legacy.

For their part, the Joint Chiefs' abrupt shift on Somalia also reflected the cumulative pressure and criticism from liberals on them for their reluctance to use force in support of the crisis in Bosnia. Powell's support for intervention in Somalia was explicitly based on the condition that U.S. forces would not be called into a similar effort in Bosnia.

CONCLUSION

The cases of Somalia and Bosnia in 1992 have several idiosyncrasies that make generalizations difficult. But one implication from these cases is that a starting point for future research on why the United States intervenes in some humanitarian crises and not others is to examine competing normative beliefs and the politics of intervention. After Bosnia, Haiti, Kosovo, northern Iraq, Rwanda, Sierra Leone, Somalia, Sudan, and elsewhere, in the past decade American foreign policy elites have expressed differing normative beliefs about when and where the United States should intervene. These competing beliefs appear to rotate around the selective-engager and liberal-humanitarian axis. The cases presented here suggest that these beliefs not only exist but are also significant contributors to our understanding of why the United States intervenes.

This suggests in turn that humanitarian impulses have increasingly become part of the political discourse within American foreign policy and probably cannot be ignored or rejected outright. Indeed, those who seek to establish some universal grand strategy restricting the use of force to only those situations where American vital interests are directly threatened may well find themselves under intense and persistent pressure that will detract attention from other foreign policy initiatives and ultimately could lead to some form of intervention under less than desirable or optimal terms.

In addition to competing beliefs, the intervention decision on Somalia also reveals that advocacy, information, and advocacy resources can also influence American foreign policy outcomes. Initially, President Bush and his advisers faced little opposition to their policies on Somalia and Bosnia. They captured significant information advantages on both Somalia and Bosnia, with little or no liberal humanitarian or media presence on the ground in either; selective engagers effectively portrayed the conflict as one fueled by ancient tribal hatreds about which the United States could do little.

The shifts in the Bush administration's policy on Somalia—first in August 1992 and then again in November 1992—came only in the face of mobilized political opposition. The critical variables behind these policy shifts stemmed from the shift in information and propaganda advantages once competing elites and the media developed and dedicated resources to the conflict areas to challenge the administration's framing of the crisis. Given the vast increases in global telecommunications technologies, future administrations are likely to find it difficult to develop and sustain information advantages.

DISCUSSION QUESTIONS

1. What does Western mean when he classifies people as "selective engagers" and "liberal humanitarianists"?
2. Why did the government initially not want to intervene in either Bosnia or Somalia?
3. Describe the opposition that the liberal humanitarianists faced concerning relief to Somalia.
4. How did the presidential election affect America's intervention decisions?
5. What were some of the major factors that changed the government's position on intervening in Somalia? Why not Bosnia?

NOTES

1. Quoted in John L. Hirsch and Robert B. Oakley, *Somalia and Operation Restore Hope: Reflections on Peacemaking and Peacekeeping* (Washington, DC: U.S. Institute of Peace, 1995), 43.

2. In fact, the option of U.S. military deployment was not even on the agenda for discussion for the November 21 meeting, according to several participants. Author interview with Admiral David Jeremiah, Oakton, Virginia, April 29, 1999; telephone interview with Andrew Natsios, who was then the president's special representative, on Somalia, Boston, Massachusetts, March 29, 1999; interview with

Herman Cohen, who was then assistant secretary of state for African affairs, Arlington, Virginia, March 30, 1999; interview with James Woods, who was then deputy assistant secretary of defense for Africa and international security policy, Arlington, Virginia, March 30, 1999; and interview with Walter Kansteiner, who was the staff member responsible for Africa on the National Security Council, Washington, DC, March 29, 1999.

3. Interviews with Kansteiner, Cohen, Natsios, and with James Bishop, who was then acting assistant secretary of state for human rights and humanitarian affairs, Washington, DC, March 29, 1999.

4. U.S. Department of State *Dispatch* Supplement (DSDS), September 1992, 14; interview with Kansteiner.

5. Interview with Brent Scowcroft, Washington, DC, April 29, 1999.

6. Cited in Walter Clarke, *Somalia: Background Information for Operation Restore Hope, 1992–1993* (Carlisle Barracks, PA: U.S. Army War College, December 1992).

7. Mohamed Sahoun, *Somalia: The Missed Opportunities* (Washington, DC: U.S. Institute of Peace, 1994), 16.

8. Interview with Scowcroft.

9. Quoted from Don Oberdorfer, "The Path to Intervention: A Massive Tragedy We Could Do Something About," *Washington Post*, December 6, 1992, A1.

10. Interview with Bishop.

11. Interview with Cohen.

12. Network Evening News Abstracts, Television News Archives, August 2–14, 1992, Vanderbilt University, http://tvnews.vanderbilt.edu/eveningnews.html.

13. See, for example, *ABC World News Tonight*, August 8, 9, and 10, 1992; *NBC Nightly News*, August 7, 8, and 10, 1992; and *CBS Evening News*, August 8 and 9, 1992, all from Network Evening News Abstracts, Television News Archives, Vanderbilt University, http://tvnews.vanderbilt.edu/eveningnews.html.

14. Quoted in Jim Hoagland, "August Guns: How Sarajevo Will Reshape U.S. Strategy," *Washington Post*, August 9, 1992, C1.

15. Interview with Scowcroft.

16. Quoted in Michael Gordon, "Conflict in the Balkans: 60,000 Needed for Bosnia, a U.S. General Estimates," *New York Times*, August 12, 1992, 8.

17. Warren P. Strobel, *Late-Breaking Foreign Policy: The News Media's Influence on Peace Operations* (Washington, DC: U.S. Institute of Peace, 1997), 131–37.

18. Interview with Scowcroft.

19. Quoted in U.S. Department of State *Dispatch* Supplement (DSDS), September 1992, 14.

20. Quoted in U.S. Department of State *Dispatch* Supplement.

21. Quoted in Michael Gordon, "Winter May Kill 100,000 in Bosnia, the CIA Warns," *New York Times*, September 30, 1992, 13.

22. Quoted in Gordon, "Winter May Kill 100,000."

23. Interview with William Hill, director, Office of East European Analysis, Bureau of Intelligence and Research, U.S. Department of State, Washington, DC, March 22, 1999.

24. Interview with Jeremiah.

25. Quoted in Michael Gordon, "Powell Delivers a Resounding No on Using Limited Force in Bosnia," *New York Times*, September 28, 1999, 1.

26. "At Least Slow the Slaughter," *New York Times*, October 4, 1992, 16.

27. Colin Powell, "Why Generals Get Nervous," *New York Times*, October 8, 1992, 35.

28. Colin Powell, *My American Journey: An Autobiography* (New York: Random House, 1995), 562.

29. Hirsch and Oakley, *Somalia and Operation Restore Hope*, 43.

30. Interview with Jeremiah.

31. Interview with Scowcroft.

23

Last Stand

Seymour M. Hersh

On May 31, [2006,] Secretary of State Condoleezza Rice announced what appeared to be a major change in U.S. foreign policy. The Bush administration, she said, would be willing to join Russia, China, and its European allies in direct talks with Iran about its nuclear program. There was a condition, however: the negotiations would not begin until, as the president put it in a June 19 speech at the U.S. Merchant Marine Academy, "the Iranian regime fully and verifiably suspends its uranium enrichment and reprocessing activities." Iran, which has insisted on its right to enrich uranium, was being asked to concede the main point of the negotiations before they started. The question was whether the administration expected the Iranians to agree, or was laying the diplomatic groundwork for future military action. In his speech, Bush also talked about "freedom for the Iranian people," and he added, "Iran's leaders have a clear choice." There was an unspoken threat: the U.S. Strategic Command, supported by the Air Force, has been drawing up plans, at the president's direction, for a major bombing campaign in Iran.

Inside the Pentagon, senior commanders have increasingly challenged the president's plans, according to active-duty and retired officers and officials. The generals and admirals have told the administration that the bombing campaign will probably not succeed in destroying Iran's nuclear program. They have also warned that an attack could lead to serious economic, political, and military consequences for the United States.

A crucial issue in the military's dissent, the officers said, is the fact that American and European intelligence agencies have not found specific evidence of clandestine activities or hidden facilities; the war planners are not sure what to hit. "The target array in Iran is huge, but it's amorphous," a high-ranking general told me. "The question we face is, When does innocent infrastructure evolve into something nefarious?" The high-ranking general added that the military's experience in Iraq, where intelligence on weapons of mass destruction was deeply flawed, has affected its approach to Iran. "We built this big monster with Iraq, and there was nothing there. This is son of Iraq," he said.

"There is a war about the war going on inside the building," a Pentagon consultant said. "If we go, we have to find something."

In President Bush's June speech, he accused Iran of pursuing a secret weapons program along with its civilian nuclear-research program (which it is allowed, with limits, under the Nuclear Nonproliferation Treaty). The senior officers in the Pentagon do not dispute the president's contention that Iran intends to eventually build a bomb, but they are frustrated by the intelligence gaps. A former senior intelligence official told me that people in the Pentagon were asking, "What's the evidence? We've got a million tentacles out there, overt and covert, and these guys"—the Iranians—"have been working on this for eighteen years, and we have nothing?" . . .

A senior military official told me, "Even if we knew where the Iranian enriched uranium was—and we don't—we don't know where world opinion would stand. The issue is whether it's a clear and present danger. If you're a military planner, you try to weigh options. What is the capability of the Iranian response, and the likelihood of a punitive response—like cutting off oil shipments? What would that cost us?" Secretary of Defense Donald Rumsfeld and his senior aides "really think they can do this on the cheap, and they underestimate the capability of the adversary," he said.

In 1986, Congress authorized the chairman of the Joint Chiefs of Staff to act as the "principal military adviser" to the president. In this case, I was told, the current chairman, Marine General Peter Pace, has gone further in his advice to the White House by addressing the consequences of an attack on Iran. "Here's the military telling the president what he can't do politically"—raising concerns about rising oil prices, for example—the former senior intelligence official said. "The JCS [Joint Chiefs of Staff] chairman going to the president with an economic argument—what's going on here?" (General Pace and the White House declined to comment. The Defense Department responded to a detailed request for comment by saying that the administration was "working diligently" on a diplomatic solution and that it could not comment on classified matters.)

A retired four-star general, who ran a major command, said, "The system is starting to sense the end of the road, and they don't want to be condemned by history. They want to be able to say, 'We stood up.'"

The military leadership is also raising tactical arguments against the proposal for bombing Iran, many of which are related to the consequences for Iraq. According to retired Army Major General William Nash, who was commanding general of the First Armored Division, served in Iraq and Bosnia, and worked for the United Nations in Kosovo, attacking Iran would heighten the risks to American and coalition forces inside Iraq. [*This analysis was done in 2006.—Ed.*] "What if one hundred thousand Iranian volunteers came across the border?" Nash asked. "If we bomb Iran, they cannot retaliate militarily by air—only on the ground or by sea, and only in Iraq or the Gulf. A military planner cannot discount that possibility, and he cannot make an ideological assumption that the Iranians wouldn't do it. We're not talking about victory or defeat—only about what damage Iran could do to our interests." Nash, now a senior fellow at the Council on Foreign Relations, said, "Their first possible response would be to send forces into Iraq. And, since the Iraqi Army has limited capacity, it means that the coalition forces would have to engage them."

The Americans serving as advisers to the Iraqi police and military may be at special risk, Nash added, since an American bombing "would be seen not only as an attack on Shiites but as an attack on all Muslims. Throughout the Middle East, it would likely be seen as another example of American imperialism. It would probably cause the war to spread."

In contrast, some conservatives are arguing that America's position in Iraq would improve if Iran chose to retaliate there, according to a government consultant with close ties to the Pentagon's civilian leaders, because Iranian interference would divide the Shiites into pro- and anti-Iranian camps, and unify the Kurds and the Sunnis. The Iran hawks in the White House and the State Department, including Elliott Abrams and Michael Doran, both of whom [were] National Security Council advisers on the Middle East, also have an answer for those who believe that the bombing of Iran would put American soldiers in Iraq at risk, the consultant said. He described the counterargument this way: "Yes, there will be Americans under attack, but they are under attack now."

Iran's geography would also complicate an air war. The senior military official said that, when it came to air strikes, "this is not Iraq," which is fairly flat, except in the northeast. "Much of Iran is akin to Afghanistan in terms of topography and flight mapping—a pretty tough target," the military official said. Over rugged terrain, planes have to come in closer, and "Iran has a lot of mature air-defense systems and networks," he said. "Global operations are always risky, and if we go down that road we have to be prepared to follow up with ground troops."

The U.S. Navy has a separate set of concerns. Iran has more than seven hundred undeclared dock and port facilities along its Persian Gulf coast. The small ports, known as "invisible piers," were constructed two decades ago by Iran's Revolutionary Guards to accommodate small private boats used for smuggling. (The Guards relied on smuggling to finance their activities and enrich themselves.) The ports, an Iran expert who advises the U.S.

government told me, provide "the infrastructure to enable the Guards to go after American aircraft carriers with suicide water bombers"—small vessels loaded with high explosives. He said that the Iranians have conducted exercises in the Strait of Hormuz, the narrow channel linking the Persian Gulf to the Arabian Sea and then on to the Indian Ocean (the strait is regularly traversed by oil tankers) in which a thousand small Iranian boats simulated attacks on American ships. "That would be the hardest problem we'd face in the water: a thousand small targets weaving in and out among our ships."

America's allies in the Gulf also believe that an attack on Iran would endanger them, and many American military planners agree. "Iran can do a lot of things—all asymmetrical," a Pentagon adviser on counter-insurgency told me. "They have agents all over the Gulf, and the ability to strike at will." In May, according to a well-informed oil-industry expert, the Emir of Qatar made a private visit to Tehran to discuss security in the Gulf after the Iraq war. He sought some words of non-aggression from the Iranian leadership. Instead, the Iranians suggested that Qatar, which is the site of the regional headquarters of the U.S. Central Command, would be its first target in the event of an American attack. Qatar is a leading exporter of gas and currently operates several major offshore oil platforms, all of which would be extremely vulnerable. (Nasser bin Hamad M. al-Khalifa, Qatar's ambassador to Washington, denied that any threats were issued during the Emir's meetings in Tehran. He told me that it was "a very nice visit.")

A retired American diplomat, who has experience in the Gulf, confirmed that the Qatari government is "very scared of what America will do" in Iran, and "scared to death" about what Iran would do in response. Iran's message to the oil-producing Gulf states, the retired diplomat said, has been that it will respond, and "You are on the wrong side of history."

In late April [2006], the military leadership, headed by General Pace, achieved a major victory when the White House dropped its insistence that the plan for a bombing campaign include the possible use of a nuclear device to destroy Iran's uranium-enrichment plant at Natanz, nearly two hundred miles south of Tehran. The huge complex includes large underground facilities built into seventy-five-foot-deep holes in the ground and designed to hold as many as fifty thousand centrifuges. "Bush and Cheney were dead serious about the nuclear planning," the former senior intelligence official told me. "And Pace stood up to them. Then the word came back: 'OK, the nuclear option is politically unacceptable.'" At the time, a number of retired officers, including two army major generals who served in Iraq, Paul Eaton and Charles Swannack Jr., had begun speaking out against the administration's handling of the Iraq war. This period is known to many in the Pentagon as "the April Revolution."

"An event like this doesn't get papered over very quickly," the former official added. "The bad feelings over the nuclear option are still felt. The civilian hierarchy feels extraordinarily betrayed by the brass, and the brass feel they were tricked into it [the nuclear planning] by being asked to provide all options in the planning papers."

Sam Gardiner, a military analyst who taught at the National War College before retiring from the Air Force as a colonel, said that Rumsfeld's second-guessing and micromanagement were a fundamental problem. "Plans are more and more being directed and run by civilians from the Office of the Secretary of Defense," Gardiner said. "It causes a lot of tensions. I'm hearing that the military is increasingly upset about not being taken seriously by Rumsfeld and his staff."

Gardiner went on: "The consequence is that, for Iran and other missions, Rumsfeld will be pushed more and more in the direction of special operations, where he has direct authority and does not have to put up with the objections of the chiefs." Since taking office in 2001, Rumsfeld has been engaged in a running dispute with many senior commanders over his plans to transform the military, and his belief that future wars will be fought, and won, with airpower and Special Forces. That combination worked, at first, in Afghanistan, but the growing stalemate there, and in Iraq, has created a rift, especially inside the army. The senior military official said, "The policymakers are in love with Special Ops—the guys on camels."

The discord over Iran can, in part, be ascribed to Rumsfeld's testy relationship with the generals. They see him as high-handed and unwilling to accept responsibility for what has gone wrong in Iraq. A former Bush administration official described a recent meeting between Rumsfeld and four-star generals and admirals at a military commanders' conference, on a base outside Washington, that, he was told, went badly. The commanders later told General Pace that "they didn't come here to be lectured by the defense secretary. They wanted to tell Rumsfeld what their concerns were." A few of the officers attended a subsequent meeting between Pace and Rumsfeld, and were unhappy, the former official said, when "Pace did not repeat any of their complaints. There was disappointment about Pace." The retired four-star general also described the commanders' conference as "very fractious." He added, "We've got twenty-five hundred dead, people running all over the world doing stupid things, and officers outside the Beltway asking, 'What the hell is going on?'"

Pace's supporters say that he is in a difficult position, given Rumsfeld's penchant for viewing generals who disagree with him as disloyal. "It's a very narrow line between being responsive and effective and being outspoken and ineffective," the former senior intelligence official said.

But Rumsfeld is not alone in the administration where Iran is concerned; he is closely allied with Vice President Dick Cheney, and, the Pentagon consultant said, "the president generally defers to the vice-president on all these issues," such as dealing with the specifics of a bombing campaign if diplomacy fails. "He feels that Cheney has an informational advantage. Cheney is not a renegade. He represents the conventional wisdom in all of this. He appeals to the strategic-bombing lobby in the air force—who think that carpet bombing is the solution to all problems."

Bombing may not work against Natanz, let alone against the rest of Iran's nuclear program. The possibility of using tactical nuclear weapons gained support in the administration because of the belief that it was the only way to insure the destruction of Natanz's buried laboratories. When that option proved to be politically untenable (a nuclear warhead would, among other things, vent fatal radiation for miles), the Air Force came up with a new bombing plan, using advanced guidance systems to deliver a series of large bunker-busters—conventional bombs filled with high explosives—on the same target, in swift succession. The Air Force argued that the impact would generate sufficient concussive force to accomplish what a tactical nuclear warhead would achieve, but without provoking an outcry over what would be the first use of a nuclear weapon in a conflict since Nagasaki.

The new bombing concept provoked controversy among Pentagon planners and outside experts. Robert Pape, a professor at the University of Chicago who has taught at the Air Force's School of Advanced Air and Space Studies, told me, "We always have a few new toys, new gimmicks, and rarely do these new tricks lead to a phenomenal breakthrough. The dilemma is that Natanz is a very large underground area, and even if the roof came down we won't be able to get a good estimate of the bomb damage without people on the ground. We don't even know where it goes underground, and we won't have much confidence in assessing what we've actually done. Absent capturing an Iranian nuclear scientist and documents, it's impossible to set back the program for sure."

One complicating aspect of the multiple-hit tactic, the Pentagon consultant told me, is "the liquefaction problem"—the fact that the soil would lose its consistency owing to the enormous heat generated by the impact of the first bomb. "It will be like bombing water, with its currents and eddies. The bombs would likely be diverted." Intelligence has also shown that for the past two years the Iranians have been shifting their most sensitive nuclear-related materials and production facilities, moving some into urban areas, in anticipation of a bombing raid.

"The air force is hawking it to the other services," the former senior intelligence official said. "They're all excited by it, but they're being terribly criticized for it." The main problem, he said, is that the other services do not believe the tactic will work: "The navy says, 'It's not our plan.' The marines are against it—they know they're going to be the guys on the ground if things go south."

"It's the bomber mentality," the Pentagon consultant said. "The air force is saying, 'We've got it covered, we can hit all the distributed targets.'" The arsenal includes a cluster bomb that can deploy scores of small bomb-lets with individual guidance systems to home in on specific targets. The weapons were deployed in Kosovo and during the early stages of the 2003 invasion of Iraq, and the Air Force is claiming that the same techniques can be used with larger bombs, allowing them to be targeted from twenty-five thousand feet against a multitude of widely dispersed targets. "The chiefs all know that 'shock and awe' is dead on arrival," the Pentagon consultant said. "All except the air force."

"Rumsfeld and Cheney are the pushers on this—they don't want to re-peat the mistake of doing too little," the government consultant with ties to Pentagon civilians told me. "The lesson they took from Iraq is that there should have been more troops on the ground [an impossibility in Iran, because of the overextension of American forces in Iraq] so the air war in Iran will be one of overwhelming force."

Many of the Bush administration's supporters viewed the abrupt change in negotiating policy as a deft move that won public plaudits and obscured the fact that Washington had no other good options. "The United States has done what its international partners have asked it to do," said Patrick Clawson, who is an expert on Iran and the deputy director for research at the Washington Institute for Near East Policy, a conservative think tank. "The ball is now in their court—for both the Iranians and the Europeans." Bush's goal, Clawson said, was to assuage his allies, as well as Russia and China, whose votes, or abstentions, in the United Nations would be needed if the talks broke down and the United States decided to seek Security Council sanctions or a UN resolution that allowed for the use of force against Iran.

"If Iran refuses to restart negotiations, it will also be difficult for Rus-sia and China to reject a UN call for International Atomic Energy Agency [IAEA] inspections," Clawson said. "And the longer we go without accel-erated IAEA access, the more important the issue of Iran's hidden facili-ties will become." The drawback to the new American position, Clawson added, was that "the Iranians might take Bush's agreeing to join the talks as a sign that their hard line has worked."

Clawson acknowledged that intelligence on Iran's nuclear-weapons prog-ress was limited. "There was a time when we had reasonable confidence in what we knew," he said. "We could say, 'There's less time than we think,' or, 'It's going more slowly.' Take your choice. Lack of information is a problem, but we know they've made rapid progress with their centrifuges." (The most recent American intelligence estimate is that Iran could build a warhead sometime between 2010 and 2015.)

Flynt Leverett, a former National Security Council aide for the Bush ad-ministration, told me, "The only reason Bush and Cheney relented about talking to Iran was because they were within weeks of a diplomatic meltdown in the United Nations. Russia and China were going to stiff us"—that is, prevent the passage of a UN resolution. Leverett, a project director at the New America Foundation, added that the White House's proposal, despite offering trade and economic incentives for Iran, has not "resolved any of the fundamental contradictions of U.S. policy." The precondition for the talks, he said—an open-ended halt to all Iranian enrichment activity—"amounts to the president wanting a guarantee that they'll surrender before he talks to them. Iran cannot accept long-term constraints on its fuel-cycle activity as part of a settlement without a security guarantee"—for example, some form of mutual non-aggression pact with the United States.

Leverett told me that, without a change in U.S. policy, the balance of power in the negotiations will shift to Russia. "Russia sees Iran as a beach-head against American interests in the Middle East, and they're playing a very sophisticated game," he said. "Russia is quite comfortable with Iran having nuclear fuel cycles that would be monitored, and they'll support the Iranian position"—in part because it gives them the opportunity to sell billions of dollars' worth of nuclear fuel and materials to Tehran. "They believe they can manage their long- and short-term interests with Iran, and still manage the security interests," Leverett said. China, which, like Russia, has veto power on the Security Council, was motivated in part by its growing need for oil, he said. "They don't want punitive measures, such as sanctions, on energy producers, and they don't want to see the U.S. take a unilateral stance on a state that matters to them." But, he said, "they're happy to let Russia take the lead in this." (China, a major purchaser of Iranian oil, is negotiating a multibillion-dollar deal with Iran for the purchase of liquefied natural gas over a period of twenty-five years.) As for the Bush administration, he added, "unless there's a shift, it's only a question of when its policy falls apart."

It's not clear whether the administration will be able to keep the Europeans in accord with American policy if the talks break down. Morton Abramowitz, a former head of State Department intelligence, who was one of the founders of the International Crisis Group, said, "The world is different than it was three years ago, and while the Europeans want good relations with us, they will not go to war with Iran unless they know that an exhaustive negotiating effort was made by Bush. There's just too much involved, like the price of oil. There will be great pressure put on the Europeans, but I don't think they'll roll over and support a war."

The Europeans, like the generals at the Pentagon, are concerned about the quality of intelligence. A senior European intelligence official said that while "there was every reason to assume" that the Iranians were working on a bomb, there wasn't enough evidence to exclude the possibility that they were bluffing, and hadn't moved beyond a civilian research program. The intelligence official was not optimistic about the current negotiations.

"It's a mess, and I don't see any possibility, at the moment, of solving the problem," he said. "The only thing to do is contain it. The question is, What is the redline? Is it when you master the nuclear fuel cycle? Or is it just about building a bomb?" Every country had a different criterion, he said. One worry he had was that, in addition to its security concerns, the Bush administration was driven by its interest in "democratizing" the region. "The United States is on a mission," he said.

A European diplomat told me that his government would be willing to discuss Iran's security concerns—a dialogue he said Iran offered Washington three years ago. The diplomat added that "no one wants to be faced with the alternative if the negotiations don't succeed: either accept the bomb or bomb them. That's why our goal is to keep the pressure on, and see what Iran's answer will be."

A second European diplomat, speaking of the Iranians, said, "Their tactic is going to be to stall and appear reasonable—to say, 'Yes, but . . .' We know what's going on, and the timeline we're under. The Iranians have repeatedly been in violation of IAEA safeguards and have given us years of cover-up and deception. The international community does not want them to have a bomb, and if we let them continue to enrich, that's throwing in the towel—giving up before we talk." The diplomat went on: "It would be a mistake to predict an inevitable failure of our strategy. Iran is a regime that is primarily concerned with its own survival, and if its existence is threatened it would do whatever it needed to do—including backing down."

The Iranian regime's calculations about its survival also depend on internal political factors. The nuclear program is popular with the Iranian people, including those—the young and the secular—who are most hostile to the religious leadership. Mahmoud Ahmadinejad, the president of Iran, has effectively used the program to rally the nation behind him, and against Washington. Ahmadinejad and the ruling clerics have said that they believe Bush's goal is not to prevent them from building a bomb but to drive them out of office.

Several current and former officials I spoke to expressed doubt that President Bush would settle for a negotiated resolution of the nuclear crisis. A former high-level Pentagon civilian official, who still deals with sensitive issues for the government, said that Bush remains confident in his military decisions. The president and others in the administration often invoke Winston Churchill, both privately and in public, as an example of a politician who, in his own time, was punished in the polls but was rewarded by history for rejecting appeasement. In one speech, Bush said, "Churchill seemed like a Texan to me. He wasn't afraid of public-opinion polls. . . . He charged ahead, and the world is better for it."

The Israelis have insisted for years that Iran has a clandestine program to build a bomb, and will do so as soon as it can. Israeli officials have emphasized that their "redline" is the moment Iran masters the nuclear fuel cycle, acquiring the technical ability to produce weapons-grade uranium. "Iran managed to surprise everyone in terms of the enrichment capability," one diplomat familiar with the Israeli position told me, referring to Iran's announcement, this spring [2006], that it had successfully enriched uranium to the 3.6 percent level needed to fuel a nuclear-power reactor. The Israelis believe that Iran must be stopped as soon as possible, because, once it is able to enrich uranium for fuel, the next step—enriching it to the 90 percent level needed for a nuclear bomb—is merely a mechanical process.

Israeli intelligence, however, has also failed to provide specific evidence about secret sites in Iran, according to current and former military and intelligence officials. In May [2006], Prime Minister Ehud Olmert visited Washington and, addressing a joint session of Congress, said that Iran "stands on the verge of acquiring nuclear weapons" that would pose "an existential threat" to Israel. Olmert noted that Ahmadinejad had questioned the reality of the Holocaust, and he added, "It is not Israel's threat alone. It is a threat to all those committed to stability in the Middle East and to the well-being of the world at large." But at a secret intelligence exchange that took place at the Pentagon during the visit, the Pentagon consultant said, "What the Israelis provided fell way short" of what would be needed to publicly justify preventive action.

The issue of what to do, and when, seems far from resolved inside the Israeli government. Martin Indyk, a former U.S. ambassador to Israel, who is now the director of the Brookings Institution's Saban Center for Middle East Policy, told me, "Israel would like to see diplomacy succeed, but they're worried that in the meantime Iran will cross a threshold of nuclear know-how—and they're worried about an American military attack not working. They assume they'll be struck first in retaliation by Iran." Indyk added, "At the end of the day, the United States can live with Iranian, Pakistani, and Indian nuclear bombs—but for Israel there's no mutual assured destruction. If they have to live with an Iranian bomb, there will be a great deal of anxiety in Israel, and a lot of tension between Israel and Iran, and between Israel and the U.S."

Iran has not, so far, officially answered President Bush's proposal. But its initial response has been dismissive. In a June 22 [2006] interview with the *Guardian*, Ali Larijani, Iran's chief nuclear negotiator, rejected Washington's demand that Iran suspend all uranium enrichment before talks could begin. "If they want to put this prerequisite, why are we negotiating at all?" Larijani said. "We should put aside the sanctions and give up all this talk about regime change." He characterized the American offer as a "sermon," and insisted that Iran was not building a bomb. "We don't want the bomb," he said. Ahmadinejad has said that Iran would make a formal counterproposal by August 22, but in early July Ayatollah Ali Khamenei,

Iran's supreme religious leader, declared, on state radio, "Negotiation with the United States has no benefits for us."

Despite the tough rhetoric, Iran would be reluctant to reject a dialogue with the United States, according to Giandomenico Picco, who, as a representative of the United Nations, helped to negotiate the ceasefire that ended the Iran-Iraq War, in 1988. "If you engage a superpower, you feel you are a superpower," Picco told me. "And now the haggling in the Persian bazaar begins. We are negotiating over a carpet"—the suspected weapons program—"that we're not sure exists, and that we don't want to exist. And if at the end there never was a carpet, it'll be the negotiation of the century."

If the talks do break down, and the administration decides on military action, the generals will, of course, follow their orders; the American military remains loyal to the concept of civilian control. But some officers have been pushing for what they call the "middle way," which the Pentagon consultant described as "a mix of options that require a number of Special Forces teams and air cover to protect them to send into Iran to grab the evidence so the world will know what Iran is doing." He added that, unlike Rumsfeld, he and others who support this approach were under no illusion that it could bring about regime change. The goal, he said, was to resolve the Iranian nuclear crisis.

Mohamed ElBaradei, the director general of the IAEA, said in a speech this spring [2006] that his agency believed there was still time for diplomacy to achieve that goal. "We should have learned some lessons from Iraq," ElBaradei, who won the Nobel Peace Prize last year, said. "We should have learned that we should be very careful about assessing our intelligence. . . . We should have learned that we should try to exhaust every possible diplomatic means to solve the problem before thinking of any other enforcement measures."

He went on: "When you push a country into a corner, you are always giving the driver's seat to the hard-liners. . . . If Iran were to move out of the nonproliferation regime altogether, if Iran were to develop a nuclear weapon program, we clearly will have a much, much more serious problem."

DISCUSSION QUESTIONS

1. What is the military's view of a bombing campaign of Iran over the possibility of developing nuclear weapons?
2. What are some problems for the United States if a bombing campaign is launched? How and against whom would Iran likely retaliate?
3. What was the "April Revolution"? Who won?
4. How is Rumsfeld's role with the military described by Hersh?

5. What group was prompting the bombing strategy against Iran?
6. Why are Russia and China unlikely to cooperate on sanctions or actions against Iran?
7. What are the Europeans' views on dealing with Iran?
8. What is the Israelis' "redline" for taking action again Iran?

24

Obama: The Consequentialist

Ryan Lizza

Barack Obama came to Washington [in 2005], having spent his professional life as a part-time lawyer, part-time law professor, and part-time state legislator in Illinois. As an undergraduate, he took courses in history and international relations, but neither his academic life nor his work in Springfield gave him an especially profound grasp of foreign affairs. As he coasted toward winning a seat in the U.S. Senate in 2004, he began to reach out to a broad range of foreign policy experts—politicians, diplomats, academics, and journalists.

As a student during the Reagan years, Obama gravitated toward conventionally left-leaning positions. At Occidental he demonstrated in favor of divesting from apartheid South Africa. At Columbia, he wrote a forgettable essay in *Sundial*, a campus publication, in favor of the nuclear-freeze movement. As a professor at the University of Chicago, he focused on civil rights law and race. And, as a candidate who emphasized his "story," Obama argued that what he lacked in experience with foreign affairs he made up for with foreign travel: four years in Indonesia as a boy, and trips to Pakistan, India, Kenya, and Europe during and after college. But there was no mistaking the lightness of his resume. Just a year before coming to Washington, State Senator Obama was not immersed in the dangers of nuclear Pakistan or an ascendant China; as a provincial legislator, he was investigating the dangers of a toy known as the Yo-Yo Water Ball. (He tried, unsuccessfully, to have it banned.)

Obama had always read widely, and now he was determined to get a deeper education. He read popular books on foreign affairs by Fareed Zakaria and Thomas Friedman. He met with Anthony Lake, who had left the Nixon administration over Vietnam and went on to work in Democratic administrations, and with Susan Rice, who had served in the Clinton administration and carried with her the guilt of having failed to act to prevent the Rwandan genocide. He also contacted Samantha Power, a thirty-four-year-old journalist and Harvard professor specializing in human rights. In her twenties, Power had reported from the Balkans and witnessed the campaigns of ethnic cleansing there. In 2002, after graduating from Harvard Law School, she wrote *A Problem from Hell*, which surveyed the grim history of six genocides committed in the twentieth century. Propounding a liberal-interventionist view, Power argued that "mass killing" on the scale of Rwanda or Bosnia must be prevented by other nations, including the United States. She wrote that America and its allies rarely have perfect information about when a regime is about to commit genocide; a president, therefore, must have "a bias toward belief" that massacres are imminent. Stopping the execution of thousands of foreigners, she wrote, was, in some cases, worth the cost in dollars, troops, and strained alliances. The book, which was extremely influential, especially on the left, won a Pulitzer Prize in 2003. Critics considered her views radical and dangerously impractical.

After reading *A Problem from Hell*, Obama invited Power to dinner. He said he wanted to talk about foreign policy. The meal lasted four hours. As a fledgling member of the Senate Foreign Relations Committee, and an ambitious politician with his sights set on higher office, Obama agreed to have Power spend a year in his office as a foreign policy fellow.

In his first news conference after winning election to the Senate, the press asked whether he intended to run for president, but he assured reporters, as well as his aides, that he would not even consider it until 2012 or 2016. He knew that he could not have a serious impact on issues like Iraq or the Sudan as a junior committee member, but he was determined to learn the institution and to acquire, as Hillary Clinton had, a reputation not for celebrity but for substance. In foreign affairs, as in so much else, he was determined to break free of the old ideologies and categories. But he would take it step by step.

Obama entered the Senate in 2005, at a moment of passionate foreign policy debate within the Democratic Party. The invasion of Iraq was seen as interventionism executed under false pretenses and with catastrophic consequences. Many on the left argued that liberal interventionists, particularly in Congress and in the press, had given crucial cover to the Bush administration during the run-up to the war. Hillary Clinton, who often sided with the humanitarian hawks in her husband's White House, and who went on to vote for the Iraq war, in 2002, seemed to some to be the embodiment of all that had gone wrong.

One reaction among liberals to the Bush years and to Iraq was to retreat from "idealism" toward "realism," in which the United States would act cautiously and, above all, according to national interests rather than moral imperatives. The debate is rooted in the country's early history. America, John Quincy Adams argued, "does not go abroad in search of monsters to destroy. She is the well-wisher to freedom and independence of all," but the "champion and vindicator only of her own."

In 1966, Adams's words were repeated by George Kennan, perhaps the most articulate realist of the twentieth century, in opposing the Vietnam War. To Kennan and his intellectual followers, foreign policy problems are always more complicated than Americans, in their native idealism, usually allow. The use of force to stop human-rights abuses or to promote democracy, they argue, usually ends poorly. In the fall of 2002, six months before the invasion of Iraq, Kennan said, "Today, if we went into Iraq, as the president would like us to do, you know where you begin. You never know where you are going to end."

As Obama sorted through the arguments, other foreign policy liberals were determined to prevent Iraq from besmirching the whole program of liberal internationalism. Humanitarian intervention—which Power helped advance, though she vigorously opposed the Iraq war—should not be abandoned because of the failures in Baghdad. Nor should American diplomacy turn away from emphasizing the virtues of bringing the world democracy. Anne-Marie Slaughter, a professor of international affairs at Princeton and a Democrat, wrote in the liberal journal *Democracy* that an overreaction to the Bush years might mean that "realists could again rule the day, embracing order and stability over ideology and values."

After little more than a year in the Senate, Obama was bored, and began to take seriously the frequent calls to run for president. To be a candidate, he needed to distinguish himself from his foremost potential opponent, Hillary Clinton, as well as from President Bush. One of the clearest paths to distinction, especially in the primaries, was to emphasize his early opposition, as a state senator, to the Iraq war. He started to move away from the ideas of people like Power and Slaughter. He pointedly noted that George H. W. Bush's management of the end of the Cold War was masterly. The president had sometimes kept quiet about the aspirations of pro-democracy activists in Russia, Ukraine, and elsewhere, in order to maintain the confidence of Mikhail Gorbachev in the Kremlin. It was just the sort of political performance to which Obama aspired.

In making the case against Hillary Clinton, Obama slyly argued that the George W. Bush years were in some ways a continuation of the Bill Clinton years, and that the United States needed to return to the philosophy of an earlier era. The proselytizing about democracy and the haste to bomb other countries in the name of humanitarian aid had "stretched our military to the breaking point and distracted us from the growing threats of a dangerous world," Obama said in a speech in 2006, a few weeks before he announced his presidential candidacy. He spoke of "a strategy no longer driven by ideology and politics but one that is based on a realistic assessment of the sobering facts on the ground and our interests in the region. This kind of realism has been missing since the very conception of this war, and it is what led me to publicly oppose it in 2002."

In 2007, Obama called Zbigniew Brzezinski, President Carter's national security adviser and the reigning realist of the Democratic foreign policy establishment. Obama told him that he had read his recent book, *Second Chance*, in which Brzezinski criticized Presidents Clinton and George W. Bush and their handling of the post–Cold War world. They began to speak and exchange e-mails about policy, and Brzezinski traveled with Obama during a stretch of the campaign. In September 2007, Brzezinski introduced Obama at an event in Clinton, Iowa, where the candidate discussed the failures in Iraq. "I thought he had a really incisive grasp of what the twenty-first century is all about and how America has to relate to it," Brzezinski told me. "He was reacting in a way that I very much shared, and we had a meeting of the minds—namely, that George Bush put the United States on a suicidal course."

As he campaigned in New Hampshire, in 2007, Obama said that he would not leave troops in Iraq even to stop genocide. "Well, look, if that's the criteria by which we are making decisions on the deployment of U.S. forces, then by that argument you would have three hundred thousand troops in the Congo right now, where millions have been slaughtered as a consequence of ethnic strife, which we haven't done," he said. "We would be deploying unilaterally and occupying the Sudan, which we haven't done."

At a campaign event in Pennsylvania, Obama said, "The truth is that my foreign policy is actually a return to the traditional bipartisan realistic policy of George Bush's father, of John F. Kennedy, of, in some ways, Ronald Reagan."

In the end, Barack Obama overcame Hillary Clinton's campaign warnings that he was too callow, too naive about dealing with rogue regimes, and too untested to respond to the "3 A.M." emergencies from all corners of the globe. Obama entered the White House at a moment of radical transition in global politics, and one of his most significant appointments was Clinton as his secretary of state. Although he had made plain in the campaign that he disagreed with some of her foreign policy views, he admired her discipline and believed that, as a member of the cabinet, she wouldn't publicly break with the president. And he would need her. Obama faced economic catastrophe at home and American wars in Iraq and Afghanistan; serious regional threats from Pakistan and Iran; global terrorism; the ascendance of China and India; and a situation that was almost impossible to discuss—a vivid sense of American decline.

Obama: The Consequentialist

American values and interests are woven together, and no president is always either an idealist or a realist. Officials who identify with the same label often disagree with one another. Humanitarian interventionists were divided over the second Iraq war; Cold War realists split over détente with the Soviet Union. The categories describe only broad ideological directions and tendencies. But, as Richard Haass, the president of the Council on Foreign Relations, observed, "The battle between realists and idealists is the fundamental fault line of the American foreign-policy debate."

After the inauguration, the realists began to win that debate within the administration. The two most influential foreign policy advisers in the White House are Thomas Donilon, the national security adviser, and Denis McDonough, a deputy national security adviser. Donilon, who is fifty-five, is a longtime Washington lawyer, lobbyist, and Democratic Party strategist. McDonough started out as a congressional staffer and campaign adviser to Obama, a role that has given him a reputation as a non-ideological political fixer.

The National Security Council (NSC) is a bureaucracy that helps the president streamline decision-making, and Donilon seems to have thought extensively about how that system works. Like the president, he values staff discretion. His rule for hiring at the NSC is to find people who are, in his words, "high value, low maintenance." Obama's NSC adopted the model of the first Bush administration. "It's essentially based on the process that was put in place by General Brent Scowcroft and Bob Gates in the late nineteen-eighties," Donilon told me, speaking of Bush's national security adviser and his deputy, the current secretary of defense. The most important feature, Donilon said, is that the NSC, based at the White House, controls "the sole process through which policy would be developed."

One of Donilon's overriding beliefs, which Obama adopted as his own, was that America needed to rebuild its reputation, extricate itself from the Middle East and Afghanistan, and turn its attention toward Asia and China's unchecked influence in the region. America was "overweighted" in the former and "underweighted" in the latter, Donilon told me. "We've been on a little bit of a Middle East detour over the course of the last ten years," Kurt Campbell, the assistant secretary of state for East Asian and Pacific Affairs, said. "And our future will be dominated utterly and fundamentally by developments in Asia and the Pacific region."

In December 2009, Obama announced that he would draw down U.S. troops from Iraq and Afghanistan by the end of his first term. He also promised, in a speech to the United Nations General Assembly last year, that he was "moving toward a more targeted approach" that "dismantles terrorist networks without deploying large American armies."

"The project of the first two years has been to effectively deal with the legacy issues that we inherited, particularly the Iraq war, the Afghan war, and the war against al Qaeda, while rebalancing our resources and our posture in the world," Benjamin Rhodes, one of Obama's deputy national security advisers, said. "If you were to boil it all down to a bumper sticker, it's 'Wind down these two wars, reestablish American standing and leadership in the world, and focus on a broader set of priorities, from Asia and the global economy to a nuclear-nonproliferation regime.'"

Obama's lengthy bumper-sticker credo did not include a call to promote democracy or protect human rights. Obama aides who focused on these issues were awarded lesser White House positions. Samantha Power became senior director of multilateral affairs at the NSC. Michael McFaul, a Stanford professor who believes that the United States should make democracy promotion the heart of its foreign policy, landed a mid-level position at the White House.

Most of the foreign policy issues that Obama emphasized in his first two years involved stepping away from idealism. In the hope of persuading Iran's regime to abandon its nuclear ambitions, Obama pointedly rejected Bush's "axis of evil" terminology. In a video message to Iranians on March 20, 2009, he respectfully addressed "the people and leaders of the Islamic Republic of Iran." In order to engage China on economic issues, Obama didn't press very hard on human rights. And because any effort to push the Israelis and Palestinians toward a final settlement would benefit from help from Egypt, Jordan, and Saudi Arabia, Obama was not especially outspoken about the sins of Middle Eastern autocrats and kings.

Despite the realist tilt, Obama has argued from the start that he was anti-ideological, that he defied traditional categories and ideologies. In Oslo, in December of 2009, accepting the Nobel Peace Prize, Obama said, "Within America, there has long been a tension between those who describe themselves as realists or idealists—a tension that suggests a stark choice between the narrow pursuit of interests or an endless campaign to impose our values around the world." The speech echoed Obama's 2002 address to an antiwar demonstration in Chicago's Federal Plaza. In Chicago, he had confounded his leftist audience by emphasizing the need to fight some wars, but not "dumb" ones, like the one in Iraq. In Oslo, he surprised a largely left-leaning audience by talking about the martial imperatives of a commander in chief overseeing two wars. Obama's aides often insist that he is an anti-ideological politician interested only in what actually works. He is, one says, a "consequentialist."

Meanwhile, Secretary of State Hillary Clinton turned her department into something of a haven for the ideas that flourished late in the Clinton administration. She picked Anne-Marie Slaughter as her director of policy planning—a job first held by George Kennan in the Truman administration. She also brought in Harold Koh, the State Department's legal adviser and a scholar on issues concerning human rights and democracy. Walking around the mazelike building in Foggy Bottom, you get the sense that if you duck into any office, you will find earnest young women and men discussing globalization, the possibility that Facebook can topple tyrannies, and what is called "soft power"—the ability to bend the world toward your view through attraction, not coercion.

Not long ago, I met with Kris Balderston, the State Department's representative for global partnerships. He started working with Clinton ten years ago, when he guided her through the politics of upstate New York during her Senate race. Now he works on an array of entrepreneurial projects that complement traditional diplomacy. He talked excitedly about working with Vietnamese Americans to build stronger ties to Vietnam and about distributing vaccines in partnership with Coca-Cola. He pointed to a bookcase stocked with devices that looked like a cross between a lantern and a paint bucket. These were advanced cookstoves. "This is a problem that the secretary saw when she was First Lady," Balderston said, explaining how lethal cooking smoke can be. "One half of the world cooks in open fires. Two million people die a year from it—that's more than malaria and tuberculosis combined, and nearly as much as HIV." On a trip to Congo in 2009, Clinton met a woman in a refugee camp who had been raped in the jungle on the outskirts of the camp while gathering wood for her stove. Telling the story at the State Department, Clinton was angrier than Balderston had ever seen her. "We have got to do something about this," she said. Balderston spends much of his time trying to build a market for inexpensive, clean-burning cookstoves in the developing world.

But Clinton's involvement in soft-power initiatives was matched by the kind of hardheadedness about foreign policy she had displayed during her presidential campaign. She has repeatedly aligned herself with the most consistent realist in the Obama administration: Secretary of Defense Robert Gates, who was deputy national security adviser in the first Bush administration and secretary of defense under George W. Bush. Clinton's advisers told me that, during her first two years in Foggy Bottom, Clinton agreed with Gates on every major issue. "Secretary Clinton can push the agenda she pushes because she is tough and people know she is tough," Slaughter said.

> It's very interesting—you've had three women secretaries of state, and she's the first one who can stand up and say publicly, "We are going to empower women and girls around the world. We are going to make development a priority of foreign policy. We are going to engage people as well as governments."
>
> Madeleine Albright believed in the importance of those issues, but she could never have made it the core of her public agenda. She was the first woman secretary of state, which meant that she had to out-tough the tough guys. She did that on the Balkans. Condi Rice helped double foreign aid, but she was first and foremost a Cold Warrior, and she could throw around ICBMs and SLBMs

and MIRVs with the best of them. That was the only way she could make it, not only as a woman in the nineteen-eighties but as an African American woman. You had to be way tougher and way more knowledgeable about weapons than any man.

A former administration official said, "Hillary has to guard her flank. And one of the ways she guards her flank is she rarely deviates from Gates. If she and Gates both weigh in, they are much more likely to get their way."

Obama's first test at managing the clashing ideologies within his administration came during the review of Afghanistan policy in 2009. During the campaign, Obama said that he would add troops in Afghanistan, a war, he argued, that Bush had neglected. But Obama's campaign promise bumped hard against the judgment of several new advisers, including Richard Holbrooke, who tried to convince the president that sending forty thousand more troops to Afghanistan, as the military urged, was counterproductive. It would prevent Obama from rebalancing American foreign policy toward the Pacific, and it would have little impact on al Qaeda, which is based largely in Pakistan. Obama had appointed Holbrooke his special representative for Afghanistan and Pakistan, and Holbrooke, a brash and influential diplomat, found himself in the unusual circumstance of being ignored. He wanted to send far fewer troops and reenergize regional diplomacy, including reconciliation talks with the Taliban. He believed that the lesson of Vietnam was that the diplomats, rather than the generals, needed to be in charge, but he could rarely penetrate the insular world of Obama's White House to make that case to the president. . . .

In the end, Obama made a decision about Afghanistan that was at odds with his own goal of rebalancing toward Asia and the Pacific. "The U.S. has been on a greater Middle East detour largely of its own choosing through a war of choice in Iraq and what became a war of choice in 2009 in Afghanistan," Haass said. "Afghanistan is entirely inconsistent with the focus of time and resources on Asia. If your goal is to reorient or refocus or rebalance U.S. policy, the administration's commitment to so doing is at the moment more rhetorical than actual."

Obama came into office emphasizing bureaucratic efficiency, which he believed would lead to wise rulings. But the Afghanistan decision, like all government work, was driven by politics and ideology. Obama's eagerness to keep his campaign promise, the military's view that reducing troops meant a loss of face, Clinton's decision to align with Gates, and Holbrooke's inability to influence the White House staff all ultimately conspired to push Obama toward the surge.

Obama's other key campaign promise—to engage with the leaders of countries hostile to the United States—sometimes meant deemphasizing democracy and human rights, which had been tainted by Bush's "freedom agenda" in the Middle East. Tyrannical regimes are less likely to make deals with you if you talk persistently about overthrowing them. Obama's speech in Cairo, delivered on June 4, 2009, and devoted to improving America's relationship with the Muslim world, was organized as a list of regional priorities. He discussed the wars in Iraq and Afghanistan, Arab-Israeli peace, and Iran's nuclear ambitions. He then gave a hesitant endorsement of America's commitment to democracy in the region. He began, "I know there has been controversy about the promotion of democracy in recent years, and much of this controversy is connected to the war in Iraq. So let me be clear: no system of government can or should be imposed upon one nation by any other."

A week later, however, a disputed presidential election in Iran triggered large demonstrations there, which were soon labeled the "Green Revolution." For the first five months after his inauguration, Obama had tried to engage with the regime of President Mahmoud Ahmadinejad in an effort to persuade Iran to abandon its nuclear ambitions. Now he faced the choice between keeping his distance and coming to the aid of the nascent pro-democracy movement, which was rallying behind Mir-Hossein Mousavi, who had finished second behind Ahmadinejad. Obama chose to keep his distance, providing only mild rhetorical support. In an interview with CNBC after the protests began, he said that "the difference between Ahmadinejad and Mousavi in terms of their actual policies may not be as great as has been advertised."

During the peak of the protests in Iran, Jared Cohen, a young staffer at the State Department who worked for Slaughter, contacted officials at Twitter and asked the company not to perform a planned upgrade that would have shut down the service temporarily in Iran, where protesters were using it to get information to the international media. The move violated Obama's rule of non-interference.

White House officials "were so mad that somebody had actually 'interfered' in Iranian politics, because they were doing their [utmost] to not interfere," the former administration official said. "Now, to be fair to them, it was also the understanding that if we interfered it could look like the Green movement was Western-backed, but that really wasn't the core of it. The core of it was we were still trying to engage the Iranian government and we did not want to do anything that made us side with the protesters. To the secretary's credit, she realized, I think, before other people, that this is ridiculous, that we had to change our line." The official said that Cohen "almost lost his job over it. If it had been up to the White House, they would have fired him."

Clinton did not betray any disagreement with the president over Iran policy, but in an interview with me she cited Cohen's action with pride: "When it came to the elections, we had a lot of messages from people inside

Iran and their supporters outside of Iran saying, 'For heaven's sakes, don't claim this as part of the democracy agenda. This is indigenous to us. We are struggling against this tyrannical regime. If you are too outspoken in our support, we will lose legitimacy!' Now, that's a tough balancing act. It's easy to stand up if you don't worry about the consequences. Now, we were very clear in saying, 'We are supporting those who are protesting peacefully,' and we put our social-media gurus at work in trying to keep connections going, so that we helped to provide that base for communicating that was necessary for the demonstrations."

One suggestion that came up in interviews with Obama's current and former foreign policy advisers was that the administration's policy debates sometimes broke down along gender lines. The realists who view foreign policy as a great chess game—and who want to focus on China and India—are usually men. The idealists, who talk about democracy and human rights, are often women. (White House officials told me that this critique is outlandish.)

Slaughter, who admired Clinton but felt alienated by people at the White House, resigned in February, and in her farewell speech at the State Department she described a gender divide at the heart of Obama's foreign policy team. She argued that in the twenty-first century, America needed to focus on societies as well as on states. "Unfortunately, the people who focus on those two worlds here in Washington are still often very different groups. The world of states is still the world of high politics, hard power, realpolitik, and, largely, men," she said. "The world of societies is still too often the world of low politics, soft power, human rights, democracy, and development, and, largely, women. One of the best parts of my two years here has been the opportunity to work with so many amazing and talented women—truly extraordinary people. But Washington still has a ways to go before their voices are fully heard and respected."

On August 12, 2010, Obama sent a five-page memorandum called "Political Reform in the Middle East and North Africa" to Vice President Joseph Biden, Clinton, Gates, Donilon, the chairman of the Joint Chiefs of Staff, and the other senior members of his foreign policy team. Though the Iranian regime had effectively crushed the Green Revolution, the country was still experiencing sporadic protests. Egypt would face crucial parliamentary elections in November. The memo began with a stark conclusion about trends in the region.

"Progress toward political reform and openness in the Middle East and North Africa lags behind other regions and has, in some cases, stalled," the president wrote. He noted that even the more liberal countries were cracking down on public gatherings, the press, and political opposition groups. But something was stirring. There was "evidence of growing citizen discontent with the region's regimes," he wrote. It was likely that "if present trends continue," allies there would "opt for repression rather than reform to manage domestic dissent."

Obama's analysis showed a desire to balance interests and ideals. The goals of reform and democracy were couched in the language of U.S. interests rather than the sharp moral language that statesmen often use in public. "Increased repression could threaten the political and economic stability of some of our allies, leave us with fewer capable, credible partners who can support our regional priorities, and further alienate citizens in the region," Obama wrote. "Moreover, our regional and international credibility will be undermined if we are seen or perceived to be backing repressive regimes and ignoring the rights and aspirations of citizens."

Obama instructed his staff to come up with "tailored," "country by country" strategies on political reform. He told his advisers to challenge the traditional idea that stability in the Middle East always served U.S. interests. Obama wanted to weigh the risks of both "continued support for increasingly unpopular and repressive regimes" and a "strong push by the United States for reform."

He also wrote that "the advent of political succession in a number of countries offers a potential opening for political reform in the region." If the United States managed the coming transitions "poorly," it "could have negative implications for U.S. interests, including for our standing among Arab publics."

The review was led by three NSC staffers: Samantha Power; Gayle Smith, who works on development issues; and Dennis Ross, a Middle East expert with a broad portfolio in the White House. Soon, they and officials from other agencies were sitting in the White House, debating the costs and benefits of supporting autocrats. A White House official involved said the group studied "the taboos, all the questions you're not supposed to ask." For example, they tested the assumption that the president could not publicly criticize President Hosni Mubarak because it would jeopardize Egypt's cooperation on issues related to Israel or its assistance in tracking terrorists. Not true, they concluded: the Egyptians pursued peace with Israel and crushed terrorists because it was in their interest to do so, not because the United States asked them to.

They tested the idea that countries with impoverished populations needed to develop economically before they were prepared for open political systems—a common argument that democracy promoters often run up against. Again, they concluded that the conventional wisdom was wrong. "All roads led to political reform," the White House official said.

The group was just finishing its work, on December 17, when Mohamed Bouazizi, a vegetable vender in Tunisia, set himself on fire outside a municipal building to protest the corruption of the country's political system— an act that inspired protests in Tunisia and, eventually, the entire region.

Democracy in the Middle East, one of the most fraught issues of the Bush years, was suddenly the signature conflict of Obama's foreign policy.

On January 25, the first crucial day of the protests in Egypt, and eleven days after the removal of President Zine el-Abidine Ben Al in Tunisia, Secretary Clinton declared her support for free assembly, but added, "Our assessment is that the Egyptian government is stable and is looking for ways to respond to the legitimate needs and interests of the Egyptian people." That evening, Obama delivered his State of the Union address, in which he praised the demonstrators in Tunisia, "where the will of the people proved more powerful than the writ of a dictator," and expressed support for the "democratic aspirations of all people." But he did not mention Egypt. Shady ei-Ghazaly Harb, one of the leaders of the coalition that started the Egyptian revolution, told me that the message the protesters got from the Obama administration on the first day of the revolution was "Go home. We need this regime."

A number of familiar ex-diplomats and politicians, led by Dick Cheney, Henry Kissinger, and Zbigniew Brzezinski, criticized the treatment of Mubarak, and Israel and Saudi Arabia called on the administration to stick with him. But as the protests strengthened, it became clear that Mubarak was doomed. According to a senior administration official, "The question in our mind was, 'How do you manage that?'"

Obama's instinct was to try to have it both ways. He wanted to position the United States on the side of the protesters: it's always a good idea, politically, to support brave young men and women risking their lives for freedom, especially when their opponent is an eighty-two-year-old dictator with Swiss bank accounts. Some of Obama's White House aides regretted having stood idly by while the Iranian regime brutally suppressed the Green Revolution; Egypt offered a second chance. Nonetheless, Obama wanted to assure other autocratic allies that the United States did not hastily abandon its friends, and he feared that the uprising could spin out of control. "Look at all the revolutions in history, especially the ones that are driven from the ground up, and they tend to be very chaotic and hard to find an equilibrium," one senior official said. The French Revolution, for instance, he said, "ended up in chaos, and they ended up with Bonaparte." Obama's ultimate position, it seemed, was to talk like an idealist while acting like a realist.

This wasn't an easy balance to maintain, and the first major problem arose when State Department officials learned that if Mubarak stepped down immediately, the Egyptian constitution would require a presidential election in sixty days, long before any of the moderate parties could get organized. Egyptian officials warned the administration that it could lead to the Muslim Brotherhood's taking over power. . . .

Obama decided not to call for Mubarak to step down. Instead, the United States would encourage a transition led by Mubarak's newly installed vice-president, Omar Suleiman. The strategy was to avoid the constitutional process that the State Department feared would lead to chaos. The senior official told me in the midst of the crisis, "I don't think that because a group of young people get on the street that we are obliged to be for them."

On January 29, the White House made two major decisions: the United States would announce that it supported a transition in Egypt, and Obama would send an emissary to Mubarak to explain that, in the judgment of the United States, he could not survive the protests. The emissary would tell Mubarak that his best option was to try to leave a positive legacy by steering the country toward a real democratic transformation. Frank G. Wisner, the former U.S. ambassador to Egypt, who had long known Mubarak well, would deliver the message. The next day, Clinton appeared on five Sunday morning talk shows to announce that Obama supported an "orderly transition" in Egypt. That afternoon, Wisner boarded a U.S. government plane for Cairo.

On January 31, Wisner met with Mubarak in Cairo. The next day, word leaked out that Mubarak would address the country. That afternoon, Obama's national security advisers met in the Situation Room to discuss two issues: whether Obama should call Mubarak and whether Obama should make a public statement. Obama joined the meeting unexpectedly. As the discussion continued, Mubarak's speech appeared on television, and the president and his aides paused to watch. "I am now careful to conclude my work for Egypt by presenting Egypt to the next government in a constitutional way which will protect Egypt," Mubarak said. "I want to say, in clear terms, that in the next few months that are remaining of my current reign I will work very hard to carry out all the necessary measures to transfer power."

In Tahrir Square, the protesters erupted in rage at the meandering and confusing speech. Obama now seemed to be uncomfortable taking an attitude of cool detachment from the people in the street. He called Mubarak, and tried to find a graceful way for the Egyptian president to exit that would also take care of the constitutional concerns Egyptian officials kept raising. He asked if there was a way to alter the constitution to allow for a stable transition. He asked if there was a way to set up a caretaker government. A White House official summarized Mubarak's response as "Muslim Brotherhood, Muslim Brotherhood, Muslim Brotherhood."

Obama then made a public statement that was more confrontational: "An orderly transition must be meaningful, it must be peaceful, and it must begin now." The urgent message alienated Israel and Saudi Arabia, among other allies. It also startled some people in the State Department. Clinton "walked a very narrow line and managed to do it without making the Egyptians too angry on either side," a senior State Department official said. "After the president gave his statement, the people surrounding Mubarak began to get quite angry."

The inherent contradictions of an administration trying to simultaneously encourage and contain the forces of revolution in Egypt broke into
the open on February 5 when Wisner, who was then in New York, participated via videoconference in an international-affairs conference in Munich.
After outlining the constitutional argument for keeping Mubarak in power,
he said, "I therefore believe that President Mubarak's continued leadership
is critical; it's his opportunity to write his own legacy. He's given sixty years
of his life to the service of his country." According to friends, Wisner, who
had talked with Obama before he went to Cairo, believed that his statement
was consistent with the policy he was told to follow.

Clinton was at the conference in Munich, and, shortly after Wisner made
his remarks, a senior administration official gathered the press corps traveling with her in a small dining room at the Charles Hotel to brief us on
the secretary's meetings. The official hadn't heard Wisner's comments, but
when a reporter read a long excerpt off his BlackBerry the official blanched,
his mouth agape.

"Wisner," the official said, "was not speaking for the U.S. government or
the Obama administration. He was speaking as a private citizen."

The public and private components of the administration's Egypt policy
were at odds, and Wisner had risked blowing everything up. His tenure as
an envoy was over. "They threw me under the bus," a close friend remem-
bers him saying.

Wisner referred dismissively to the "reelection committee" at the White
House, according to the friend. But in this case Obama's political interests—needing to be seen as on the side of the protesters—aligned with the
policy views of the idealists. An Obama adviser declared, "Obama didn't
give the Tahrir Square crowds every last thing they sought from him at the
precise moment they sought it. But he went well beyond what many of
America's allies in the region wished to see."

In March, I traveled to Cairo with Secretary Clinton. One evening, she
was scheduled to meet with Egyptians who had been prominent in the
protests that brought down Mubarak. However, one group, called the Coalition of Youth Revolution, which includes leaders from the activist movements and opposition parties in Egypt, boycotted the meeting. As Clinton
talked with other civil-society members upstairs at the Four Seasons Hotel,
four members of the abstaining coalition agreed to talk with me and three
other journalists in the lobby. I asked why they weren't upstairs with the
secretary of state. "Hillary was against the revolution from the beginning
to the last day, OK?" Mohammed Abbas, of the Muslim Brotherhood, said.
"Obama supported this revolution. She was against." . . .

On March 16, Clinton flew from Cairo to Tunis to continue her tour of
revolutionary North Africa. The route took us over the Mediterranean just
off the coast of Libya. The GPS maps in the cabin of Clinton's plane lit

up with the name "Benghazi," reminding everyone that, on the ground, Muammar Qaddafi's men were marching on that city. Earlier in the day, Qaddafi had gone on the radio to warn the citizens of Benghazi. "It's over. We are coming tonight," he said. "We will find you in your closets."

Protesters had started to gather in Benghazi on February 15. Qaddafi's security forces reacted with violence four days later, firing on a crowd of some twenty thousand demonstrators in Benghazi and killing at least a hundred of them. On February 26, the United Nations passed a resolution that placed an arms embargo and economic sanctions on the Libyan regime and referred Qaddafi to the International Criminal Court. Two days later, the United States, through lobbying led by Clinton and Power, helped remove Libya from its seat on the UN Human Rights Council. By tightening an economic noose around Qaddafi and isolating him diplomatically, Obama and the international community were beginning to use the tools that Power had outlined in *A Problem from Hell.*

The debate then narrowed to whether the United States and others should intervene militarily. The principal option was to set up a no-fly zone to prevent Libyan planes from attacking the protest movement, which had quickly turned into a full-scale rebellion based in the eastern half of the country. The decision about intervention in Libya was an unusually clear choice between interests and values. "Of all the countries in the region there, our real interests in Libya are minimal," Brent Scowcroft told me. For a president whose long-term goal was to extricate the United States from Middle East conflicts, it was an especially vexing debate.

Within the administration, Robert Gates, the defense secretary, was the most strenuous opponent of establishing a no-fly zone, or any other form of military intervention. Like Scowcroft, Gates objected to intervention because he did not think it was in the United States' vital interest. He also pointed out a fact that many people didn't seem to understand: the first step in creating a no-fly zone would be to bomb the Libyan air defenses. Clinton disagreed with him and argued the case for intervention with Obama. It was the first major issue on which she and Gates had different views.

The days leading up to Obama's decision were perplexing to outsiders. American presidents usually lead the response to world crises, but Obama seemed to stay hidden that week. From the outside, it looked as though the French were dragging him into the conflict. On March 14, Clinton arrived in Paris, but she had no firm decision to convey. According to a French official, when Clinton met with President Nicolas Sarkozy she declined to endorse the no-fly zone, which Sarkozy interpreted as American reluctance to do anything. "We started to wonder where, exactly, the administration was going," the official said. . . .

The next evening, Obama held a meeting in the Situation Room. By then, it had become clear that the rebels, who had once seemed on the verge of sweeping Qaddafi out of power, were weak, and poorly armed; they had lost almost all the gains of the previous days. In New York, the Lebanese, the French, and the United Kingdom had prepared a UN resolution to implement a no-fly zone, and the world was waiting to see if Obama would join the effort. The White House meeting opened with an assessment of the situation on the ground in Libya. Qaddafi's forces were on the outskirts of Ajdabiyah, which supplies water and fuel to Benghazi. "The president was told Qaddafi is going to retake Ajdabiyah in twenty-four hours," a White House official who was in the meeting said. "And then the last stop on the train is Benghazi. If he got there, he would complete the military offensive, and that could be the place where he goes house to house and where a massacre could occur."

Obama asked if a no-fly zone would prevent that grim scenario. His intelligence and military advisers said no. Qaddafi was using tanks, not war planes, to crush the rebellion. Obama asked his aides to come up with some more robust military options, and left for dinner. At a second meeting that night, he was presented with the option of pushing for a broader resolution that would allow for the United States to protect the Libyan rebels by bombing government forces. He instructed Susan Rice, the U.S. ambassador to the UN, to pursue that option.

On March 17, I interviewed Clinton in Tunis. She was sitting under a canopy by the hotel pool, eating breakfast. Although she had been noncommittal with the diplomats in France two days earlier, she now made it clear that the Obama administration had made a decision. It was well known that she favored intervention, but she was frank about the difficulty in making such decisions. "I get up every morning and I look around the world," she said. "People are being killed in Cote d'Ivoire, they're being killed in the Eastern Congo, they're being oppressed and abused all over the world by dictators and really unsavory characters. So we could be intervening all over the place. But that is not a—what is the standard? Is the standard, you know, a leader who won't leave office in Ivory Coast and is killing his own people? Gee, that sounds familiar. So part of it is having to make tough choices and wanting to help the international community accept responsibility."

Clinton insisted that the United States had to have regional support before it took action, and emphasized that it was crucial that UN action had been supported by the Arab League. "So now we're going to see whether the Security Council will support the Arab League. Not support the United States—support the Arab League. That is a significant difference. And for those who want to see the United States always acting unilaterally, it's not satisfying. But, for the world we're trying to build, where we have a lot of responsible actors who are willing to step up and lead, it is exactly what we should be doing."

The French and the British were shocked by the quick turn of events. Instead of the president announcing the administration's position from the East Room of the White House, the UN envoy quietly proposed transforming a tepid resolution for a no-fly zone into permission for full-scale military intervention in Libya. Some officials thought it was a trick. Was it possible that the Americans were trying to make the military options appear so bleak that China and Russia would be sure to block action?

Gradually, it became clear that the United States was serious. Clinton spoke with her Russian counterpart, Sergey Lavrov, who had previously told her that Russia would "never never" support even a no-fly zone. The Russians agreed to abstain. Without the cover of the Russians, the Chinese almost never veto Security Council resolutions. The vote, on March 17, was 10–0, with five abstentions. It was the first time in its sixty-six years that the United Nations authorized military action to preempt an "imminent massacre." Tom Malinowski, the Washington director of Human Rights Watch, wrote, "It was, by any objective standard, the most rapid multinational military response to an impending human rights crisis in history."

As the bombs dropped on Libyan tanks, President Obama made a point of continuing his long-scheduled trip to South America. He wanted to show that America has interests in the rest of the world, even as it was drawn into yet another crisis in the Middle East.

[In spring 2011] Obama officials often expressed impatience with questions about theory or about the elusive quest for an Obama doctrine.

One senior administration official reminded me what the former British prime minister Harold Macmillan said when asked what was likely to set the course of his government: "Events, dear boy, events."

Obama has emphasized bureaucratic efficiency over ideology, and approached foreign policy as if it were case law, deciding his response to every threat or crisis on its own merits. "When you start applying blanket policies on the complexities of the current world situation, you're going to get yourself into trouble," he said in a [2011] interview with NBC News.

Obama's reluctance to articulate a grand synthesis has alienated both realists and idealists. "On issues like whether to intervene in Libya there's really not a compromise and consensus," Slaughter said. "You can't be a little bit realist and a little bit democratic when deciding whether or not to stop a massacre."

Brzezinski has also become disillusioned with the president. "I greatly admire his insights and understanding. I don't think he really has a policy that's implementing those insights and understandings. The rhetoric is always terribly imperative and categorical: 'You must do this,' 'He must do that,' 'This is unacceptable.'" Brzezinski added, "He doesn't strategize. He sermonizes."

The one consistent thread running through most of Obama's decisions has been that America must act humbly in the world. Unlike his immediate predecessors, Obama came of age politically during the post–Cold War era, a time when America's unmatched power created widespread resentment. Obama believes that highly visible American leadership can taint a foreign-policy goal just as easily as it can bolster it. In 2007, Obama said, "America must show—through deeds as well as words—that we stand with those who seek a better life. That child looking up at the helicopter must see America and feel hope."

In 2009 and early 2010, Obama was sometimes criticized for not acting at all. He was cautious during Iran's Green Revolution and deferential to his generals during the review of Afghanistan strategy. But his response to the Arab Spring has been bolder. He broke with Mubarak at a point when some of the older establishment advised against it. In Libya, he overruled Gates and his military advisers and pushed our allies to adopt a broad and risky intervention. It is too early to know the consequences of these decisions. . . .

Nonetheless, Obama may be moving toward something resembling a doctrine. One of his advisers described the president's actions in Libya as "leading from behind." That's not a slogan designed for signs at the 2012 Democratic Convention, but it does accurately describe the balance that Obama now seems to be finding. It's a different definition of leadership than America is known for, and it comes from two unspoken beliefs: that the relative power of the United States is declining, as rivals like China rise, and that the United States is reviled in many parts of the world. Pursuing our interests and spreading our ideals thus requires stealth and modesty as well as military strength. "It's so at odds with the John Wayne expectation for what America is in the world," the adviser said. "But it's necessary for shepherding us through this phase."

DISCUSSION QUESTIONS

1. What was Barack Obama's background on foreign policy? Who were the individuals that influenced his foreign policy views as he ran for president?

2. How does Lizza characterize the foreign policy views of Barack Obama as he contemplated running for president?

3. What is the "fundamental fault line of the American foreign-policy debate," and where would you locate Obama's views on that fault line?

4. Drawing on President Obama's foreign policy advisors' views, what were the administration's key aims in foreign policy that were set out?

5. How has President Obama stepped away from his idealism in foreign policy, and how has the State Department sought to perpetuate that idealism?
6. How did President Obama decide among the clashing ideologies among his foreign policy team regarding Afghanistan and Iran? How did his proposal for the Middle East convey his foreign policy approach?
7. How did the "Arab Spring" test the Obama foreign policy approach? Did his approach change during the course of the uprisings?
8. To what extent is there an Obama Doctrine in foreign policy? How is Obama a "consequentialist"? Is this the best way to summarize his foreign policy?

Index

9/11 Commission, 170–71

Aaron, David, 348
Abbas, Mahmoud, 101
Abourezk, James, 73
Abramoff, Jack, 97
Abramowitz, Morton, 424
Acheson, Dean, 59–60, 65, 193, 194, 268, 275
Adams, Gordon, 169–70
Adams, John Quincy, 431
Afghanistan: diplomacy and development, 240, 244, 247–48; Obama administration and, 9, 21, 234, 322–23, 433–34, 436
Afghanistan war, 5, 8, 12, 50, 144, 149, 221, 264, 274; surge strategy, 9, 21, 234, 322
Africa, 82, 225, 246, 247
African American lobby, 26, 81–82
African governments, China and, 23, 48
African Growth and Opportunity Act, 82
Agency for International Development, 408
Ahmadinejad, Mahmoud, 425, 426, 437
Aideed, Mohamed Farah, 403
Air Force, 329, 422–23
al-Awlaki, Anwar, 171
Albright, Madeleine, 119, 163, 390–91, 435
Allen, Richard, 209, 219
Allison, Graham, 321, 322, 325, 364, 379
al Qaeda, 50, 91, 102, 149, 171, 254, 271; OFAC agents assigned to, 288;

as top military priority, 255–56; in underdeveloped nations, 249
American-Arab Anti-Discrimination Committee (ADC), 73
American Hellenic Institute (AHI), 76–77
American Hellenic Institute Public Affairs Committee (AHIPAC), 76
American-Israel Public Affairs Committee (AIPAC), 70–74, 95; as de facto agent for a foreign government, 97; influence with Congress, 97–98; policy conferences, 72; on university campuses, 101. *See also* Israel (Jewish) Lobby
American Revolution, 56, 57
Americans for Peace Now, 98
Amitay, Morris, 97
Anti-Apartheid Act of 1986, 82
Anti-Ballistic Missile Treaty of 1972, 231
anti-globalization movement, 176–77, 309–10
Arab American Institute (AAI), 73
Arab American lobbies, 73, 85, 96
Arab League, 203, 444
Arab Spring protests, 3, 324, 439–46. *See also* Green Revolution
Arab states, 92–93, 420. *See also* Afghanistan; Iran; Iraq; Saudi Arabia
Arafat, Yasser, 101
Aristide, Jean-Bertrand, 197, 271
Armenian Assembly, 67, 78
Armenian genocide resolution, 67–68

449

Thomas, Bill, 312
Thomson, James C., Jr., 323–24
Thurmond, Strom, 57
Tiananmen Square massacre, 49, 51, 218
Tilt-Rotor Technology Coalition, 377
Tocqueville, Alexis de, 10
Tokyo Round negotiations, 306, 307
To Move a Nation (Hilsman), 160
Tower, John, 366
Tower Commission, 216, 219
Trade Act of 1974, 71, 175, 307
Trade Adjustment Assistance (TAA), 315
trade agreements, 225–26
Trade Expansion Act of 1962, 175, 303
trade policy, 174–77; 2007 and after,
    313–16; agricultural, 305; antidumping,
    304, 305; committees, 304, 305, 311–12;
    congressional authority, 301, 304, 306–8;
    constitutional framework, 301–3; Doha
    Round, 305, 313, 316; domestic politics
    and, 176–77; environmental concerns,
    309, 313–14; fast-track procedures, 8,
    176, 230, 231, 306–8, 310; interagency
    coordinating committee structure, 304;
    Kennedy Round, 303, 306; multilateral
    "rounds," 302, 303; non-markups,
    307; Office of the United States Trade
    Representative (USTR), 175–76, 303–5,
    307; opening of American economy, 308–
    9; partisanship, 309–16, *311*; president
    and trade promotion authority, 176,
    230, 231, 314–15; President's Special
    Representative for Trade Negotiations
    (STR), 175, 303; social issues and
    partisanship, 309–13; societal economic
    interests, 305–6; stasis, 316; tariffs, 60,
    175, 286, 302–4; Tokyo Round, 306, 307;
    Uruguay Round/WTO accord, 307
trade promotion authority, 176, 230, 231,
    312–14
TransAfrica (TransAfrica Forum), 81–82
Transforming America's Israel Lobby (Fleshler),
    73–74
transnational linkages, 1–2, 34
Trans-Pacific Partnership (TPP), 2, 315–16
Transportation Security Administration
    (TSA), 288, 289–90, 291
treaties, 7, 57, 182, 228
Treaty of Versailles, 225
TRICARE, 262–63
Truman, Harry S., 16, 59–60, 139, 182, 319;
    unilateral actions, 162, 192, 194–95

Truman administration, 60, 65–66
Tunisia, 439–40
Turkey, 7, 48, 52, 243; Armenian genocide
    resolution and, 67–68, 77–78; arms
    embargo, 76; populist influence on
    policy, 60
Turkish American lobby, 26, 67–68, 77–78,
    85, 86
Turkish Coalition of America (TCA), 77
Turner, Stansfield, 348, 351, 352, 355
Tutwiler, Margaret, 406
two-party system, 13

Ukraine, 80, 388
UN High Commission on Refugees, 410–11
unilateralism, 9, 31, 59, 62, 161–63, 189–
    90; partisan differences, 147, 148, 149–
    50. *See also* president, war initiated by
United Kingdom, 33, 34, 59
United Nations, 8, 48, 147, *147*, 166, 249;
    Iran and, 423–24, 427; Korean War
    and, 194–95; outstanding U.S. dues, 61,
    166, 231; peacekeeping missions, 403,
    407; Somalia and, 403–4; unilateral
    actions by president and, 192–94; UN
    Participation Act of 1945, 193, 194
United Nations Charter, 192–93, 228
United Nations Convention on the
    Prevention and Punishment of the Crime
    of Genocide, 408
United Nations Security Council resolutions,
    20; 1973, 162; Bosnia, 198; Haiti, 197;
    Iraq, 195–96, 200–202; Israel and,
    90; Libya, 202–3; unilateral action by
    president, 189, 190, 192, 194
United States: attraction for immigrants, 37–
    38; becomes major power in 1898, 109;
    as current world leader, 49–50; foreign
    aid budget, 89–90; GDP, 35–36; global
    role of, 4, 21; Great Recession of 2008, 3,
    33, 315; hegemonic decline questioned,
    34–35; national debt, 23, 24, 38–39, 43,
    50, 62, 253, 254; Palestine, complicity
    in crimes against, 102; political gridlock,
    40–41; research and development, 38;
    traditional allies, slippage of, 48
United States Agency for International
    Development (USAID), 167–68, 239–40,
    243–44; Bureau of Policy, Planning, and
    Learning, 247; USAID Forward, 246
United States International Trade
    Commission (USITC), 176, 305

About the Editor and Contributors

EDITOR

James M. McCormick is professor and chair of the department of political science at Iowa State University. He has also held positions at the University of New Mexico, Ohio University, the University of Toledo, and Texas A&M University. He received his PhD from Michigan State University and served as an American Political Science Association Congressional Fellow in 1986–1987. McCormick is the author of *American Foreign Policy and Process* and editor of *A Reader in American Foreign Policy*. He has published numerous articles and chapters on foreign policy and international politics in such journals as *World Politics, American Political Science Review, American Journal of Political Science, International Studies Quarterly, Journal of Politics,* and *Legislative Studies Quarterly.* He was recipient of the Iowa State University Foundation Award for Outstanding Research at Mid-Career in 1990, a Fulbright Senior Award to New Zealand in 1993, the Fulbright-SyCip Distinguished Lecturer Award to the Philippines in 2003, the 2010 Iowa State University International Service Award, and the 2011 Quincy Wright Distinguished Scholar Award by the International Studies Association—Midwest.

CONTRIBUTORS

Gordon Adams is a professor in the U.S. Foreign Policy Program at the School of International Service at American University and a Distinguished Fellow at the Stimson Center.

Adam J. Berinsky is an associate professor of political science at the Massachusetts Institute of Technology.

Hillary Rodham Clinton is the U.S. secretary of state in the Obama administration.

I. M. (Mac) Destler is the Saul I. Stern Professor at the School of Public Policy, University of Maryland, and visiting fellow at the Peterson Institute of International Economics. His *In the Shadow of the Oval Office* (2009, coauthored with Ivo H. Daalder) assesses the roles and performance of presidential national security advisers.

Peter D. Feaver is a professor of political science, director of the Triangle Institute for Security Studies, and director of the Program in American Grand Strategy at Duke University.

Louis Fisher is a scholar in residence with the Constitution Project. He worked from 1970 to 2010 as senior specialist in separation of powers for the Congressional Research Service at the Library of Congress and as a specialist in constitutional law with the Law Library.

Christopher Gelpi is a professor of political science at Duke University.

James M. Goldgeier is a professor of political science and international affairs at George Washington University.

Patrick J. Haney is a professor of political science at Miami University, Ohio.

Seymour M. Hersh is a Washington-based investigator journalist and a regular contributor to the *New Yorker* on military and national security issues.

Robert Jervis is the Adlai E. Stevenson Professor of International Politics at Columbia University.

Christopher M. Jones is a professor of political science and associate vice provost for university honors at Northern Illinois University. He served as president of the Foreign Policy Analysis Section of the International Studies Association from 2008 to 2010.

Matthew Leatherman is a research associate for the Stimson Center's Budgeting for Foreign Affairs and Defense Program.

James M. Lindsay is senior vice president, director of studies, and the Maurice R. Greenberg Chair at the Council on Foreign Relations.

Ryan Lizza is the Washington correspondent for the *New Yorker*.

Walter Russell Mead is the James Clarke Chace Professor of Foreign Affairs and the Humanities at Bard College and editor-at-large of the *American Interest*.

John Mearsheimer is the R. Wendell Harrison Distinguished Service Professor of Political Science at the University of Chicago

Michael Nelson is the Fulmer Professor of Political Science at Rhodes College and a senior fellow at the University of Virginia's Miller Center of Public Affairs.

Miroslav Nincic is a professor of political science at the University of California, Davis.

Joseph S. Nye Jr. is the University Distinguished Service Professor and former dean of the John F. Kennedy School of Government at Harvard University.

Gideon Rachman is chief foreign affairs commentator for the *Financial Times* and author of *Zero-Sum Future: American Power in an Age of Anxiety*.

Philip A. Russo is a professor of political science and director of the Center for Public Management and Regional Affairs at Miami University.

Steve Smith is vice-chancellor and chief executive of the University of Exeter.

The late **James C. Thomson Jr.** was a professor emeritus of journalism, history, and international relations at Boston University.

Stephen Walt is the Robert and Renee Belfer Professor of International Affairs at the Kennedy School of Government at Harvard University.

Jon Western is a Five College associate professor of international relations at Mount Holyoke College and the Five Colleges.